# THE NEW
# ENGLISH BIBLE

## THE NEW TESTAMENT
*Popular Edition*

# THE BIBLE
## A NEW ENGLISH TRANSLATION

*Planned and directed by representatives of*

THE BAPTIST UNION OF GREAT BRITAIN
AND IRELAND

THE CHURCH OF ENGLAND

THE CHURCH OF SCOTLAND

THE CONGREGATIONAL CHURCH IN
ENGLAND AND WALES

THE COUNCIL OF CHURCHES FOR WALES

THE IRISH COUNCIL OF CHURCHES

THE LONDON YEARLY MEETING OF
THE SOCIETY OF FRIENDS

THE METHODIST CHURCH OF
GREAT BRITAIN

THE PRESBYTERIAN CHURCH OF
ENGLAND


THE BRITISH AND FOREIGN BIBLE
SOCIETY

THE NATIONAL BIBLE SOCIETY OF
SCOTLAND

# THE NEW
# ENGLISH BIBLE

## THE NEW TESTAMENT

### SECOND EDITION

OXFORD UNIVERSITY PRESS
CAMBRIDGE UNIVERSITY PRESS
1970

*The* New *English Bible : The New Testament*
*First edition* 1961
*Second edition* 1970

PRINTED IN GREAT BRITAIN
AT THE UNIVERSITY PRESS, OXFORD
BY VIVIAN RIDLER
PRINTER TO THE UNIVERSITY

# PREFACE

## TO THE NEW ENGLISH BIBLE

IN MAY 1946 the General Assembly of the Church of Scotland received an overture from the Presbytery of Stirling and Dunblane, where it had been initiated by the Reverend G. S. Hendry, recommending that a translation of the Bible be made in the language of the present day, inasmuch as the language of the Authorized Version, already archaic when it was made, had now become even more definitely archaic and less generally understood. The General Assembly resolved to make an approach to other Churches, and, as a result, delegates of the Church of England, the Church of Scotland, and the Methodist, Baptist, and Congregational Churches met in conference in October. They recommended that the work should be undertaken; that a completely new translation should be made, rather than a revision, such as had earlier been contemplated by the University Presses of Oxford and Cambridge; and that the translators should be free to employ a contemporary idiom rather than reproduce the traditional 'biblical' English.

In January 1947 a second conference, held like the first in the Central Hall, Westminster, included representatives of the University Presses. At the request of this conference, the Churches named above appointed representatives to form the Joint Committee on the New Translation of the Bible. This Committee met for the first time in July of the same year. By January 1948, when its third meeting was held, invitations to be represented had been sent to the Presbyterian Church of England, the Society of Friends, the Churches in Wales, the Churches in Ireland, the British and Foreign Bible Society, and the National Bible Society of Scotland: these invitations were accepted. At a much later stage the hierarchies of the Roman Catholic Church in England and Scotland accepted an invitation to appoint representatives, and these attended as observers.

The Joint Committee provided for the actual work of translation from the original tongues by appointing three panels, to deal, respectively, with the Old Testament, the Apocrypha, and the New Testament. Their members were

v

scholars drawn from various British universities, whom the Committee believed to be representative of competent biblical scholarship at the present time. Apprehending, however, that sound scholarship does not necessarily carry with it a delicate sense of English style, the Committee appointed a fourth panel, of trusted literary advisers, to whom all the work of the translating panels was to be submitted for scrutiny. It should be said that denominational considerations played no part in the appointment of the panels.

The Joint Committee issued general directions to the panels, in pursuance of the aims which the enterprise had in view. The translating panels adopted the following procedure. An individual was invited to submit a draft translation of a particular book, or group of books. Normally he would be a member of the panel concerned. Very occasionally a draft translation was invited from a scholar outside the panel, who was known to have worked specially on the book in question. The draft was circulated in typescript to members of the panel for their consideration. They then met together and discussed the draft round a table, verse by verse, sentence by sentence. Each member brought his view about the meaning of the original to the judgement of his fellows, and discussion went on until they reached a common mind. There are passages where, in the present state of our knowledge, no one could say with certainty which of two (or even more) possible mean.ings is intended. In such cases, after careful discussion, alternative meanings have been recorded in footnotes, but only where they seemed of sufficient importance. There is probably no member of a panel who has not found himself obliged to give up, perhaps with lingering regret, a cherished view about the meaning of this or that difficult passage, but in the end the panel accepted corporate responsibility for the interpretation set forth in the translation adopted.

The resultant draft was now remitted to the panel of literary advisers. They scrutinized it, once again, verse by verse, sentence by sentence, and took pains to secure, as best they could, the tone and level of language appropriate to the different kinds of writing to be found in the Bible, whether narrative, familiar discourse, argument, law, rhetoric or poetry. The translation thus amended was returned to the translating panel, who examined it to make sure that the meaning intended had not been in any way misunderstood. Passages of peculiar difficulty might on occasion pass repeatedly between the panels. The final form of the version was reached by agreement between the translators concerned and the literary advisers. It was then ready for submission to the Joint Committee.

Since January 1948 the Joint Committee has met regularly twice a year in the Jerusalem Chamber, Westminster Abbey, with four exceptions during 1954–5 when the Langham Room in the precincts of the Abbey was kindly made available. At these meetings the Committee has received reports on the progress of the work from the Conveners of the four panels, and its members have had in their hands typescripts of the books so far translated and revised. They have made such comments and given such advice or decisions as they judged to be necessary, and from time to time they have met members of the panels in conference.

Of the original members of the panels most have happily been able to stay with the work all through, though some have been lost, through death or otherwise, and their places have been filled by fresh appointments.

The Committee has warmly appreciated the courteous hospitality of the Dean of Westminster and of the Trustees of the Central Hall. We owe a great debt to the support and the experienced counsel of the University Presses of Oxford and Cambridge. We recognize gratefully the service rendered to the enterprise by the Reverend Dr. G. S. Hendry and the Reverend Professor J. K. S. Reid, who have successively held the office of Secretary to the Committee. To those who have borne special responsibility, as Chairmen of the Joint Committee, we owe more than could readily be told. Dr. J. W. Hunkin, Bishop of Truro, our first Chairman, brought to the work an exuberant vigour and initiative without which the formidable project might hardly have got off the ground at all. On his lamented death in 1950 he was succeeded by Dr. A. T. P. Williams, then Bishop of Durham and subsequently Bishop of Winchester, who for eighteen years guided our enterprise with judicious wisdom, tact, and benign firmness, but who to our sorrow died when the end of the task was in sight. To both of these we would put on record the gratitude of the Committee and of all engaged in the enterprise.

If we embarked on mentioning the names of those who have served on the various committees and panels, the list would be a long one; and if we mentioned some and not others, the selection would be an invidious one. There are, nevertheless, three names the omission of which would be

# PREFACE

utterly wrong. As Vice-Chairman and Director, Dr. C. H. Dodd has from start to finish given outstanding leadership and guidance to the project, bringing to the work scholarship, sensitivity, and an ever watchful eye. Professor Sir Godfrey Driver, Joint Director since 1965, has also brought to the work a wealth of knowledge and wisdom; to his enthusiasm, tenacity of purpose, and unflagging devotion the whole enterprise is greatly indebted. Professor W. D. McHardy, Deputy Director since 1968, has made an invaluable contribution particularly, but by no means exclusively, in the sphere of the Apocrypha. It is right that the names of these three scholars should always be associated with The New English Bible. Our debt to them is incalculably great.

DONALD EBOR:
*Chairman of the Joint Committee*

# CONTENTS

# CONTENTS

# INTRODUCTION

## TO THE NEW TESTAMENT

THIS TRANSLATION of the New Testament was undertaken with the object of providing English readers, whether familiar with the Bible or not, with a faithful rendering of the best available Greek text into the current speech of our own time, and a rendering which should harvest the gains of recent biblical scholarship.

It is now some three centuries and a half since King James's men put out what we have come to know as the Authorized Version. Two hundred and seventy years later the New Testament was revised. The Revised Version of the New Testament, which appeared in 1881, marked a new departure especially in that it abandoned the so-called Received Text, which had reigned ever since printed editions of the New Testament began, but which the advance of textual criticism had antiquated. The Revisers no longer followed (as their predecessors had done) the text of the majority of manuscripts, which, being for the most part of late date, had been exposed not only to the accidental corruptions of long-continued copying, but also in part to deliberate correction and 'improvement'. Instead, they followed a very small group of manuscripts, the earliest, and in their judgement the best, of those which had survived. During the years which have passed since their time, textual criticism has not stood still. Manuscripts have been discovered of substantially earlier date than any which the Revisers knew. Other important sources of evidence have been either freshly discovered or made more fully available. Meanwhile the methods of textual criticism have themselves been refined and estimates of the value of particular manuscripts have sometimes been reconsidered. The problem of restoring a form of text as near as possible to the vanished autographs now appears less simple than it did to our predecessors. There is not at the present time any critical text which would command the same degree of general acceptance as the Revisers' text did in its day. Nor has the time come, in the judgement of most scholars, to construct such a text, since new material constantly comes to light, and the debate continues. The present translators therefore could do no other than consider variant readings on their merits, and, having weighed the evidence for themselves, select for translation in each passage the reading which to the best of their judgement seemed most likely to represent what the author wrote. Where other readings seemed to deserve serious consideration they have been recorded in footnotes. In assessing the evidence, the translators have taken into account (*a*) ancient manuscripts of the New Testament in Greek, (*b*) manuscripts of early translations into other languages, and (*c*) quotations from the New Testament by early Christian writers. These three sources of evidence are collectively referred to as 'witnesses'. A large number of variants, however, are such as could make no appreciable difference to the meaning so far as it could be represented in translation, and these have been passed over in silence. The translators are well aware that their judgement is at best provisional, but they believe the text they have followed to be an improvement on that underlying the earlier translations. This text can now be read in *The Greek New Testament*, edited by R. V. G. Tasker (Oxford and Cambridge University Presses, 1964).

So much for the text. The next step was the effort to understand the original as accurately as possible, as a preliminary to turning it into English. The Revisers of 1881 believed that a better knowledge of the Greek language made it possible to correct a number of mistranslations in the older version, though in doing so they were somewhat limited by the instruction 'to introduce as few alterations as possible . . . consistently with faithfulness'. Since their time the study of the Greek language has no more stood still than has textual criticism. In particular, our knowledge of the kind of Greek used by most of the New Testament writers has been greatly enriched since 1881 by the discovery of many thousands of papyrus documents in popular or non-literary Greek of about the same period as the New Testament. It would be wrong to suggest that they lead to any far-reaching change in our understanding of the Greek of the New Testament period, but they have often made possible a better appreciation of the finer shades of idiom, which sometimes clarifies the meaning of passages in the New Testament. Its language is indeed in many respects more flexible and easy-going than the Revisers were ready to allow, and invites the translator to use a larger freedom.

Our task, however, differed in an important respect

from that of the Revisers of 1881. They were instructed not only to introduce as few alterations as possible, but also 'to limit, as far as possible, the expression of such alterations to the language of the Authorised and earlier English Versions'. The present translators were subject to no such limitation. In accordance with the original decision of the Joint Committee they were to make the attempt to use consistently the idiom of contemporary English to convey the meaning of the Greek.

The older translators, on the whole, considered that fidelity to the original demanded that they should reproduce, as far as possible, characteristic features of the language in which it was written, such as the syntactical order of words, the structure and division of sentences, and even such irregularities of grammar as were indeed natural enough to authors writing in the easy idiom of popular Hellenistic Greek, but less natural when turned into English. The present translators were enjoined to replace Greek constructions and idioms by those of contemporary English.

This meant a different theory and practice of translation, and one which laid a heavier burden on the translators. Fidelity in translation was not to mean keeping the general framework of the original intact while replacing Greek words by English words more or less equivalent. A word, indeed, in one language is seldom the exact equivalent of a word in a different language. Each word is the centre of a whole cluster of meanings and associations, and in different languages these clusters overlap but do not often coincide. The place of a word in the clause or sentence, or even in a larger unit of thought, will determine what aspect of its total meaning is in the foreground. The translator can hardly hope to convey in another language every shade of meaning that attaches to the word in the original, but if he is free to exploit a wide range of English words covering a similar area of meaning and association he may hope to carry over the meaning of the sentence as a whole. Thus we have not felt obliged (as did the Revisers of 1881) to make an effort to render the same Greek word everywhere by the same English word. We have in this respect returned to the wholesome practice of King James's men, who (as they expressly state in their preface) recognized no such obligation.

We have conceived our task to be that of understanding the original as precisely as we could (using all available aids), and then saying again in our own native idiom what we believed the author to be saying in his. We have found that in practice this frequently compelled us to make decisions where the older method of translation allowed a comfortable ambiguity. In such places we have been aware that we take a risk, but we have thought it our duty to take the risk rather than remain on the fence.

In doing our work, we have constantly striven to follow our instructions and render the Greek, as we understood it, into the English of the present day, that is, into the natural vocabulary, constructions, and rhythms of contemporary speech. We have sought to avoid archaism, jargon, and all that is either stilted or slipshod.

It should be said that our intention has been to offer a translation in the strict sense, and not a paraphrase, and we have not wished to encroach on the field of the commentator. But if the best commentary is a good translation, it is also true that every intelligent translation is in a sense a paraphrase. The line between translation and paraphrase is a fine one. But we have had recourse to deliberate paraphrase with great caution, and only in a few passages where without it we could see no way to attain our aim of making the meaning as clear as it could be made. Taken as a whole, our version claims to be a translation, free, it may be, rather than literal, but a faithful translation nevertheless, so far as we could compass it.

For this edition, the translation of the New Testament has been given a careful revision, in which account has been taken of numerous criticisms and suggestions which have come in from various quarters. It is hoped that the modifications introduced, mostly in minor details and seldom reflecting any substantial change of view about the meaning of a passage, will be found to be in the direction of improvement.

In the course of revision, consideration has been given to passages from the Old Testament quoted in the New. These have now been harmonized with the present version of the Old Testament, where this seemed desirable, and practicable. But the quotations are in Greek, and the Greek is by no means always an exact equivalent of the Hebrew. Where it is not, we have deemed it our duty to render the Greek as it lay before us, and not to attempt to reproduce the underlying Hebrew. On this point there has been consultation between representatives of the Old and the New Testament panels.

# INTRODUCTION

The translators are as conscious as anyone can be of the limitations and imperfections of their work. No one who has not tried it can know how impossible an art translation is. Only those who have meditated long upon the Greek original are aware of the richness and subtlety of meaning that may lie even within the most apparently simple sentence, or know the despair that attends all efforts to bring it out through the medium of a different language. Yet we may hope that we have been able to convey to our readers something at least of what the New Testament has said to us during these years of work, and trust that under the providence of Almighty God this translation may open the truth of the Scriptures to many who have been hindered in their approach to it by barriers of language.

C. H. D.

# MARGINAL NUMBERS

The conventional verse divisions in the New Testament date only from 1551 and have no basis in the manuscripts. Any system of division into numbered verses is foreign to the spirit of this translation, which is intended to convey the meaning in continuous natural English rather than to correspond sentence by sentence with the Greek.

For purposes of reference, and of comparison with other translations, verse numbers are placed in the margin opposite the line in which the first word belonging to the verse in question appears. Sometimes, however, successive verses are combined in a continuous English sentence, so that the precise point where a new verse begins cannot be fixed; occasionally in the interests of clarity the order of successive verses is reversed (e.g. at John 4. 7, 8).

# THE GOSPEL

# THE

# GOSPEL ACCORDING TO

# MATTHEW

## THE COMING OF CHRIST

A TABLE OF THE DESCENT of Jesus Christ, 1
son of David, son of Abraham.

Abraham was the father of Isaac, Isaac of Jacob, 2
Jacob of Judah and his brothers, Judah of Perez and Zarah 3
(their mother was Tamar), Perez of Hezron, Hezron of
Ram, Ram of Amminadab, Amminadab of Nahshon, 4
Nahshon of Salma, Salma of Boaz (his mother was 5
Rahab), Boaz of Obed (his mother was Ruth), Obed of
Jesse; and Jesse was the father of King David. 6

David was the father of Solomon (his mother had been
the wife of Uriah), Solomon of Rehoboam, Rehoboam of 7
Abijah, Abijah of Asa, Asa of Jehoshaphat, Jehoshaphat 8
of Joram, Joram of Azariah, Azariah of Jotham, Jotham 9
of Ahaz, Ahaz of Hezekiah, Hezekiah of Manasseh, Manas- 10
seh of Amon, Amon of Josiah; and Josiah was the father of 11
Jeconiah and his brothers at the time of the deportation to
Babylon.

After the deportation Jeconiah was the father of Shealtiel, 12
Shealtiel of Zerubbabel, Zerubbabel of Abiud, Abiud of 13
Eliakim, Eliakim of Azor, Azor of Zadok, Zadok of Achim, 14
Achim of Eliud, Eliud of Eleazar, Eleazar of Matthan, 15
Matthan of Jacob, Jacob of Joseph, the husband of Mary, 16
who gave birth to[a] Jesus called Messiah.

There were thus fourteen generations in all from Abra- 17
ham to David, fourteen from David until the deportation
to Babylon, and fourteen from the deportation until the
Messiah.

[a] *Some witnesses read* Joseph, to whom was betrothed Mary, a virgin,
who gave birth to. . . .; *one witness has* Joseph, and Joseph, to whom
Mary, a virgin, was betrothed, was the father of . . .

3

18 THIS IS THE STORY of the birth of the Messiah. Mary his
mother was betrothed to Joseph; before their marriage she
19 found that she was with child by the Holy Spirit. Being a
man of principle, and at the same time wanting to save her
from exposure, Joseph desired to have the marriage con-
20 tract set aside quietly. He had resolved on this, when an
angel of the Lord appeared to him in a dream. 'Joseph son
of David,' said the angel, 'do not be afraid to take Mary
home with you as your wife. It is by the Holy Spirit that
21 she has conceived this child. She will bear a son; and you
shall give him the name Jesus (Saviour), for he will save
22 his people from their sins.' All this happened in order to
23 fulfil what the Lord declared through the prophet: 'The
virgin will conceive and bear a son, and he shall be called
24 Emmanuel', a name which means 'God is with us'. Rising
from sleep Joseph did as the angel had directed him; he
25 took Mary home to be his wife, but had no intercourse with
her until her son was born. And he named the child Jesus.

2 JESUS WAS BORN at Bethlehem in Judaea during the
reign of Herod. After his birth astrologers from the east
2 arrived in Jerusalem, asking, 'Where is the child who is
born to be king of the Jews?*a* We observed the rising of his
3 star, and we have come to pay him homage.' King Herod
was greatly perturbed when he heard this; and so was the
4 whole of Jerusalem. He called a meeting of the chief priests
and lawyers of the Jewish people, and put before them the
5 question: 'Where is it that the Messiah is to be born?' 'At
Bethlehem in Judaea', they replied; and they referred him
6 to the prophecy which reads: 'Bethlehem in the land of
Judah, you are far from least in the eyes of*b* the rulers of
Judah; for out of you shall come a leader to be the shepherd of my people Israel.'
7 Herod next called the astrologers to meet him in private,
and ascertained from them the time when the star had
8 appeared. He then sent them on to Bethlehem, and said,
'Go and make a careful inquiry for the child. When you
have found him, report to me, so that I may go myself and
pay him homage.'
9 They set out at the king's bidding; and the star which
they had seen at its rising went ahead of them until it
10 stopped above the place where the child lay. At the sight
11 of the star they were overjoyed. Entering the house, they

---

*a Or* Where is the king of the Jews who has just been born? *b Or*
least among.

4

saw the child with Mary his mother, and bowed to the ground in homage to him; then they opened their treasures and offered him gifts: gold, frankincense, and myrrh. And being warned in a dream not to go back to Herod, they returned home another way. 12

After they had gone, an angel of the Lord appeared to Joseph in a dream, and said to him, 'Rise up, take the child and his mother and escape with them to Egypt, and stay there until I tell you; for Herod is going to search for the child to do away with him.' So Joseph rose from sleep, and taking mother and child by night he went away with them to Egypt, and there he stayed till Herod's death. This was to fulfil what the Lord had declared through the prophet: 'I called my son out of Egypt.' 13 14 15

When Herod saw how the astrologers had tricked him he fell into a passion, and gave orders for the massacre of all children in Bethlehem and its neighbourhood, of the age of two years or less, corresponding with the time he had ascertained from the astrologers. So the words spoken through Jeremiah the prophet were fulfilled: 'A voice was heard in Rama, wailing and loud laments; it was Rachel weeping for her children, and refusing all consolation, because they were no more.' 16 17 18

The time came that Herod died; and an angel of the Lord appeared in a dream to Joseph in Egypt and said to him, 'Rise up, take the child and his mother, and go with them to the land of Israel, for the men who threatened the child's life are dead.' So he rose, took mother and child with him, and came to the land of Israel. Hearing, however, that Archelaus had succeeded his father Herod as king of Judaea, he was afraid to go there. And being warned by a dream, he withdrew to the region of Galilee; there he settled in a town called Nazareth. This was to fulfil the words spoken through the prophets: 'He shall be called a Nazarene.' 19 20 21 22 23

About that time John the Baptist appeared as a preacher in the Judaean wilderness; his theme was: 'Repent; for the kingdom of Heaven is upon you!' It is of him that the prophet Isaiah spoke when he said, 'A voice crying aloud in the wilderness, "Prepare a way for the Lord; clear a straight path for him."' 3 2 3

John's clothing was a rough coat of camel's hair, with a leather belt round his waist, and his food was locusts and wild honey. They flocked to him from Jerusalem, from all 4 5

6 Judaea, and the whole Jordan valley, and were baptized by him in the River Jordan, confessing their sins.

7 When he saw many of the Pharisees and Sadducees coming for baptism he said to them: 'You vipers' brood! Who warned you to escape from the coming retribution?

8 9 Then prove your repentance by the fruit it bears; and do not presume to say to yourselves, "We have Abraham for our father." I tell you that God can make children for

10 Abraham out of these stones here. Already the axe is laid to the roots of the trees; and every tree that fails to pro-

11 duce good fruit is cut down and thrown on the fire. I baptize you with water, for repentance; but the one who comes after me is mightier than I. I am not fit to take off his shoes. He will baptize you with the Holy Spirit and

12 with fire. His shovel is ready in his hand and he will winnow his threshing-floor; the wheat he will gather into his granary, but he will burn the chaff on a fire that can never go out.'

13 Then Jesus arrived at the Jordan from Galilee, and

14 came to John to be baptized by him. John tried to dissuade him. 'Do you come to me?' he said; 'I need rather to

15 be baptized by you.' Jesus replied, 'Let it be so for the present; we do well to conform in this way with all that

16 God requires.' John then allowed him to come. After baptism Jesus came up out of the water at once, and at that moment heaven opened; he saw the Spirit of God

17 descending like a dove to alight upon him; and a voice from heaven was heard saying, 'This is my Son, my Beloved,[a] on whom my favour rests.'

4 JESUS WAS THEN LED AWAY by the Spirit into the wilderness, to be tempted by the devil.

2 For forty days and nights he fasted, and at the end of

3 them he was famished. The tempter approached him and said, 'If you are the Son of God, tell these stones to become

4 bread.' Jesus answered, 'Scripture says, "Man cannot live on bread alone; he lives on every word that God utters."'

5 The devil then took him to the Holy City and set him on

6 the parapet of the temple. 'If you are the Son of God,' he said, 'throw yourself down; for Scripture says, "He will put his angels in charge of you, and they will support you in their arms, for fear you should strike your foot against

7 a stone."' Jesus answered him, 'Scripture says again, "You are not to put the Lord your God to the test."'

[a] Or This is my only Son.

6

Once again, the devil took him to a very high mountain, 8
and showed him all the kingdoms of the world in their
glory. 'All these', he said, 'I will give you, if you will only 9
fall down and do me homage.' But Jesus said, 'Begone, 10
Satan! Scripture says, "You shall do homage to the Lord
your God and worship him alone."'

Then the devil left him; and angels appeared and waited 11
on him.

When he heard that John had been arrested, Jesus with- 12
drew to Galilee; and leaving Nazareth he went and settled 13
at Capernaum on the Sea of Galilee, in the district of
Zebulun and Naphtali. This was to fulfil the passage in 14
the prophet Isaiah which tells of 'the land of Zebulun, the 15
land of Naphtali, the Way of the Sea, the land beyond
Jordan, heathen Galilee', and says:

'The people that lived in darkness saw a great light; 16
  light dawned on the dwellers in the land of death's dark
    shadow.'

From that day Jesus began to proclaim the message: 'Re- 17
pent; for[a] the kingdom of Heaven is upon you.'

JESUS WAS WALKING by the Sea of Galilee when he 18
saw two brothers, Simon called Peter and his brother
Andrew, casting a net into the lake; for they were fishermen. Jesus said to them, 'Come with me, and I will make 19
you fishers of men.' And at once they left their nets and 20
followed him.

He went on, and saw another pair of brothers, James son 21
of Zebedee and his brother John; they were in the boat
with their father Zebedee, overhauling their nets. He called
them, and at once they left the boat and their father, and 22
followed him.

He went round the whole of Galilee, teaching in the syna- 23
gogues, preaching the gospel of the Kingdom, and curing
whatever illness or infirmity there was among the people.
His fame reached the whole of Syria; and sufferers from 24
every kind of illness, racked with pain, possessed by devils,
epileptic, or paralysed, were all brought to him, and he
cured them. Great crowds also followed him, from Galilee 25
and the Ten Towns,[b] from Jerusalem and Judaea, and
from Transjordan.

---

[a] *Some witnesses omit* Repent; for.          [b] *Greek* Decapolis.

7

## THE SERMON ON THE MOUNT

5 WHEN HE SAW the crowds he went up the hill.
There he took his seat, and when his disciples had
2 gathered round him he began to address them. And this is
the teaching he gave:

3 'How blest are those who know their need of God;
the kingdom of Heaven is theirs.

4 How blest are the sorrowful;
they shall find consolation.

5 How blest are those of a gentle spirit;
they shall have the earth for their possession.

6 How blest are those who hunger and thirst to see right
prevail;[a]
they shall be satisfied.

7 How blest are those who show mercy;
mercy shall be shown to them.

8 How blest are those whose hearts are pure;
they shall see God.

9 How blest are the peacemakers;
God shall call them his sons.

10 How blest are those who have suffered persecution for
the cause of right;
the kingdom of Heaven is theirs.

11 'How blest you are, when you suffer insults and persecu-
12 tion and every kind of calumny for my sake. Accept it
with gladness and exultation, for you have a rich reward
in heaven; in the same way they persecuted the prophets
before you.

13 'You are salt to the world. And if salt becomes tasteless,
how is its saltness to be restored? It is now good for
nothing but to be thrown away and trodden underfoot.

14 'You are light for all the world. A town that stands on a
15 hill cannot be hidden. When a lamp is lit, it is not put under
the meal-tub, but on the lamp-stand, where it gives light
16 to everyone in the house. And you, like the lamp, must
shed light among your fellows, so that, when they see the
good you do, they may give praise to your Father in
heaven.

17 DO NOT SUPPOSE that I have come to abolish the Law
and the prophets; I did not come to abolish, but to complete.

[a] Or to do what is right.

I tell you this: so long as heaven and earth endure, not 18
a letter, not a stroke, will disappear from the Law until
all that must happen has happened.[a] If any man therefore 19
sets aside even the least of the Law's demands, and teaches
others to do the same, he will have the lowest place in the
kingdom of Heaven, whereas anyone who keeps the Law,
and teaches others so, will stand high in the kingdom of
Heaven. I tell you, unless you show yourselves far better 20
men than the Pharisees and the doctors of the law, you
can never enter the kingdom of Heaven.

'You have learned that our forefathers were told, "Do not 21
commit murder; anyone who commits murder must be
brought to judgement." But what I tell you is this: Anyone 22
who nurses anger against his brother[b] must be brought to
judgement. If he abuses his brother he must answer for it
to the court; if he sneers at him he will have to answer for
it in the fires of hell.

'If, when you are bringing your gift to the altar, you 23
suddenly remember that your brother has a grievance
against you, leave your gift where it is before the altar. 24
First go and make your peace with your brother, and only
then come back and offer your gift.

'If someone sues you, come to terms with him promptly 25
while you are both on your way to court; otherwise he may
hand you over to the judge, and the judge to the constable,
and you will be put in jail. I tell you, once you are there 26
you will not be let out till you have paid the last farthing.

'You have learned that they were told, "Do not commit 27
adultery." But what I tell you is this: If a man looks on 28
a woman with a lustful eye, he has already committed
adultery with her in his heart.

'If your right eye is your undoing, tear it out and fling 29
it away; it is better for you to lose one part of your body
than for the whole of it to be thrown into hell. And if your 30
right hand is your undoing, cut it off and fling it away; it
is better for you to lose one part of your body than for the
whole of it to go to hell.

'They were told, "A man who divorces his wife must give 31
her a note of dismissal." But what I tell you is this: If a 32
man divorces his wife for any cause other than unchastity
he involves her in adultery; and anyone who marries a
divorced woman commits adultery.

'Again, you have learned that our forefathers were told, 33

---

[a] *Or before all that it stands for is achieved.*    [b] *Some witnesses insert* without good cause.

"Do not break your oath", and, "Oaths sworn to the Lord
34 must be kept." But what I tell you is this: You are not to
35 swear at all—not by heaven, for it is God's throne, nor by
earth, for it is his footstool, nor by Jerusalem, for it is the
36 city of the great King, nor by your own head, because you
37 cannot turn one hair of it white or black. Plain "Yes" or
"No" is all you need to say; anything beyond that comes
from the devil.

38    'You have learned that they were told, "Eye for eye,
39 tooth for tooth." But what I tell you is this: Do not set
yourself against the man who wrongs you. If someone
slaps you on the right cheek, turn and offer him your left.
40 If a man wants to sue you for your shirt, let him have your
41 coat as well. If a man in authority makes you go one mile,
42 go with him two. Give when you are asked to give; and do
not turn your back on a man who wants to borrow.

43    'You have learned that they were told, "Love your
44 neighbour, hate your enemy." But what I tell you is this:
45 Love your enemies[a] and pray for your persecutors;[b] only
so can you be children of your heavenly Father, who makes
his sun rise on good and bad alike, and sends the rain on
46 the honest and the dishonest. If you love only those who
love you, what reward can you expect? Surely the tax-
47 gatherers do as much as that. And if you greet only your
brothers, what is there extraordinary about that? Even
48 the heathen do as much. There must be no limit to your
goodness, as your heavenly Father's goodness knows no
bounds.

6    'BE CAREFUL not to make a show of your religion before
men; if you do, no reward awaits you in your Father's
house in heaven.
2    'Thus, when you do some act of charity, do not announce
it with a flourish of trumpets, as the hypocrites do in synagogue and in the streets to win admiration from men. I tell
3 you this: they have their reward already. No; when you
do some act of charity, do not let your left hand know what
4 your right is doing; your good deed must be secret, and
your Father who sees what is done in secret will reward
you.[c]
5    'Again, when you pray, do not be like the hypocrites;
they love to say their prayers standing up in synagogue

---

[a] *Some witnesses insert* bless those who curse you, do good to those
who hate you.    [b] *Some witnesses insert* and those who treat you
spitefully.    [c] *Some witnesses add* openly.

and at the street-corners, for everyone to see them. I tell
you this: they have their reward already. But when you  6
pray, go into a room by yourself, shut the door, and pray
to your Father who is there in the secret place; and your
Father who sees what is secret will reward you.[a]

'In your prayers do not go babbling on like the heathen,  7
who imagine that the more they say the more likely they
are to be heard. Do not imitate them. Your Father knows  8
what your needs are before you ask him.

'This is how you should pray:                              9

"Our Father in heaven,
  thy name be hallowed;
  thy kingdom come,                                       10
  thy will be done,
  on earth as in heaven.
Give us today our daily bread.[b]                         11
Forgive us the wrong we have done,                        12
  as we have forgiven those who have wronged us.
And do not bring us to the test,                          13
  but save us from the evil one."[c][d]

For if you forgive others the wrongs they have done, your  14
heavenly Father will also forgive you; but if you do not  15
forgive others, then the wrongs you have done will not be
forgiven by your Father.

'So too when you fast, do not look gloomy like the hypo-  16
crites: they make their faces unsightly so that other people
may see that they are fasting. I tell you this: they have
their reward already. But when you fast, anoint your head  17
and wash your face, so that men may not see that you are  18
fasting, but only your Father who is in the secret place;
and your Father who sees what is secret will give you your
reward.

'Do NOT STORE UP for yourselves treasure on earth,  19
where it grows rusty and moth-eaten, and thieves break in
to steal it. Store up treasure in heaven, where there is no  20
moth and no rust to spoil it, no thieves to break in and
steal. For where your treasure is, there will your heart be  21
also.

'The lamp of the body is the eye. If your eyes are sound,  22
you will have light for your whole body; if the eyes are  23

---

[a] *Some witnesses add* openly.        [b] *Or* our bread for the morrow.
[c] *Or* from evil.        [d] *Some witnesses add* For thine is the kingdom
and the power and the glory, for ever. Amen.

bad, your whole body will be in darkness. If then the only light you have is darkness, the darkness is doubly dark.

24 'No servant can be the slave of two masters; for either he will hate the first and love the second, or he will be devoted to the first and think nothing of the second. You cannot serve God and Money.

25 'Therefore I bid you put away anxious thoughts about food and drink to keep you alive, and clothes to cover your body. Surely life is more than food, the body more than 26 clothes. Look at the birds of the air; they do not sow and reap and store in barns, yet your heavenly Father feeds 27 them. You are worth more than the birds! Is there a man of you who by anxious thought can add a foot to his 28 height*ᵃ*? And why be anxious about clothes? Consider how the lilies grow in the fields; they do not work, they do not 29 spin;*ᵇ* and yet, I tell you, even Solomon in all his splendour 30 was not attired like one of these. But if that is how God clothes the grass in the fields, which is there today, and tomorrow is thrown on the stove, will he not all the more 31 clothe you? How little faith you have! No, do not ask anxiously, "What are we to eat? What are we to drink? 32 What shall we wear?" All these are things for the heathen to run after, not for you, because your heavenly Father 33 knows that you need them all. Set your mind on God's kingdom and his justice before everything else, and all the 34 rest will come to you as well. So do not be anxious about tomorrow; tomorrow will look after itself. Each day has troubles enough of its own.

7 1 2 'PASS NO JUDGEMENT, and you will not be judged. For as you judge others, so you will yourselves be judged, and whatever measure you deal out to others will be dealt back 3 to you. Why do you look at the speck of sawdust in your brother's eye, with never a thought for the great plank in 4 your own? Or how can you say to your brother, "Let me take the speck out of your eye", when all the time there is 5 that plank in your own? You hypocrite! First take the plank out of your own eye, and then you will see clearly to take the speck out of your brother's.

6 'Do not give dogs what is holy; do not throw your pearls to the pigs: they will only trample on them, and turn and tear you to pieces.

7 'Ask, and you will receive; seek, and you will find; knock,

---

*ᵃ* Or a day to his life.　　*ᵇ* One *witness reads* Consider the lilies: they neither card nor spin, nor labour.

and the door will be opened. For everyone who asks re- 8
ceives, he who seeks finds, and to him who knocks, the
door will be opened.

'Is there a man among you who will offer his son a stone 9
when he asks for bread, or a snake when he asks for fish? 10
If you, then, bad as you are, know how to give your chil- 11
dren what is good for them, how much more will your
heavenly Father give good things to those who ask him!

'Always treat others as you would like them to treat 12
you: that is the Law and the prophets.

'Enter by the narrow gate. The gate is wide that leads to 13
perdition, there is plenty of room on the road,[a] and many
go that way; but the gate that leads to life is small and the 14
road is narrow,[b] and those who find it are few.

'Beware of false prophets, men who come to you dressed up 15
as sheep while underneath they are savage wolves. You will 16
recognize them by the fruits they bear. Can grapes be picked
from briars, or figs from thistles? In the same way, a good 17
tree always yields good fruit, and a poor tree bad fruit. A 18
good tree cannot bear bad fruit, or a poor tree good fruit. And 19
when a tree does not yield good fruit it is cut down and burnt.
That is why I say you will recognize them by their fruits. 20

'Not everyone who calls me "Lord, Lord" will enter the 21
kingdom of Heaven, but only those who do the will of my
heavenly Father. When that day comes, many will say to 22
me, "Lord, Lord, did we not prophesy in your name, cast
out devils in your name, and in your name perform many
miracles?" Then I will tell them to their face, "I never 23
knew you; out of my sight, you and your wicked ways!"

'What then of the man who hears these words of mine 24
and acts upon them? He is like a man who had the sense to
build his house on rock. The rain came down, the floods 25
rose, the wind blew, and beat upon that house; but it did
not fall, because its foundations were on rock. But what of 26
the man who hears these words of mine and does not act
upon them? He is like a man who was foolish enough to
build his house on sand. The rain came down, the floods 27
rose, the wind blew, and beat upon that house; down it
fell with a great crash.'

When Jesus had finished this discourse the people were 28
astounded at his teaching; unlike their own teachers he 29
taught with a note of authority.

---

[a] *Some witnesses read* The road that leads to perdition is wide with
plenty of room.          [b] *Some witnesses read* but the road that leads
to life is small and narrow.

## TEACHING AND HEALING

8 AFTER HE HAD COME DOWN from the hill he
2 was followed by a great crowd. And now a leper[a] approached him, bowed low, and said, 'Sir, if only you will,
3 you can cleanse me.' Jesus stretched out his hand, touched him, and said, 'Indeed I will; be clean again.' And his
4 leprosy was cured immediately. Then Jesus said to him, 'Be sure you tell nobody; but go and show yourself to the priest, and make the offering laid down by Moses for your cleansing; that will certify the cure.'

5 When he had entered Capernaum a centurion came up
6 to ask his help. 'Sir,' he said, 'a boy of mine lies at home
7 paralysed and racked with pain.' Jesus said, 'I will come
8 and cure him.'[b] But the centurion replied, 'Sir, who am I to have you under my roof? You need only say the word
9 and the boy will be cured. I know, for I am myself under orders, with soldiers under me. I say to one, "Go", and he goes; to another, "Come here", and he comes; and to my
10 servant, "Do this", and he does it.' Jesus heard him with astonishment, and said to the people who were following him, 'I tell you this: nowhere, even in Israel, have I found such faith.

11 'Many, I tell you, will come from east and west to feast with Abraham, Isaac, and Jacob in the kingdom of Heaven.
12 But those who were born to the kingdom will be driven out into the dark, the place of wailing and grinding of teeth.'
13 Then Jesus said to the centurion, 'Go home now; because of your faith, so let it be.' At that moment the boy recovered.

14 Jesus then went to Peter's house and found Peter's
15 mother-in-law in bed with fever. So he took her by the hand; the fever left her, and she got up and waited on him.

16 When evening fell, they brought to him many who were possessed by devils; and he drove the spirits out with a
17 word and healed all who were sick, to fulfil the prophecy of Isaiah: 'He took away our illnesses and lifted our diseases from us.'[c]

18 AT THE SIGHT of the crowds surrounding him Jesus gave
19 word to cross to the other shore. A doctor of the law came

---

[a] *The words* leper, leprosy, *as used in this translation, refer to some disfiguring skin disease which entailed ceremonial defilement. It is different from what is now called leprosy.*     [b] *Or* Am I to come and cure him?     [c] *Or and bore the burden of our diseases.*

up, and said, 'Master, I will follow you wherever you go.'
Jesus replied, 'Foxes have their holes, the birds their  20
roosts; but the Son of Man has nowhere to lay his head.'
Another man, one of his disciples, said to him, 'Lord, let  21
me go and bury my father first.' Jesus replied, 'Follow me,  22
and leave the dead to bury their dead.'

Jesus then got into the boat, and his disciples followed.  23
All at once a great storm arose on the lake, till the waves  24
were breaking right over the boat; but he went on sleeping.
So they came and woke him up, crying: 'Save us, Lord; we  25
are sinking!' 'Why are you such cowards?' he said; 'how  26
little faith you have!' Then he stood up and rebuked the
wind and the sea, and there was a dead calm. The men  27
were astonished at what had happened, and exclaimed,
'What sort of man is this? Even the wind and the sea obey
him.'

When he reached the other side, in the country of the  28
Gadarenes, he was met by two men who came out from the
tombs; they were possessed by devils, and so violent that
no one dared pass that way. 'You son of God,' they shouted,  29
'what do you want with us? Have you come here to torment
us before our time?' In the distance a large herd of pigs was  30
feeding; and the devils begged him: 'If you drive us out,  31
send us into that herd of pigs.' 'Begone!' he said. Then they  32
came out and went into the pigs; the whole herd rushed
over the edge into the lake, and perished in the water.

The men in charge of them took to their heels, and made  33
for the town, where they told the whole story, and what
had happened to the madmen. Thereupon all the town  34
came out to meet Jesus; and when they saw him they
begged him to leave the district and go. So he got into the  9
boat and crossed over, and came to his own town.

And now some men brought him a paralysed man lying  2
on a bed. Seeing their faith Jesus said to the man, 'Take
heart, my son; your sins are forgiven.' At this some of the  3
lawyers said to themselves, 'This is blasphemous talk.'
Jesus knew what they were thinking, and said, 'Why do  4
you harbour these evil thoughts? Is it easier to say, "Your  5
sins are forgiven", or to say, "Stand up and walk"? But to  6
convince you that the Son of Man has the right on earth
to forgive sins'—he turned to the paralysed man—'stand
up, take your bed, and go home.' Thereupon the man got  7
up, and went off home. The people were filled with awe at  8
the sight, and praised God for granting such authority to
men.

⁹ As he passed on from there Jesus saw a man named Matthew at his seat in the custom-house, and said to him, 'Follow me'; and Matthew rose and followed him.

¹⁰ When Jesus was at table in the house, many bad characters—tax-gatherers and others—were seated with him and
¹¹ his disciples. The Pharisees noticed this, and said to his
disciples, 'Why is it that your master eats with tax-
¹² gatherers and sinners?' Jesus heard it and said, 'It is not
¹³ the healthy that need a doctor, but the sick. Go and learn
what that text means, "I require mercy, not sacrifice."
I did not come to invite virtuous people, but sinners.'

¹⁴ Then John's disciples came to him with the question:
'Why do we and the Pharisees fast, but your disciples do
¹⁵ not?' Jesus replied, 'Can you expect the bridegroom's
friends to go mourning while the bridegroom is with them?
The time will come when the bridegroom will be taken
away from them; that will be the time for them to fast.

¹⁶ 'No one sews a patch of unshrunk cloth on to an old
coat; for then the patch tears away from the coat, and
¹⁷ leaves a bigger hole. Neither do you put new wine into old
wine-skins; if you do, the skins burst, and then the wine
runs out and the skins are spoilt. No, you put new wine
into fresh skins; then both are preserved.'

¹⁸ Even as he spoke, there came a president of the synagogue, who bowed low before him and said, 'My daughter
has just died; but come and lay your hand on her, and she
¹⁹ will live.' Jesus rose and went with him, and so did his
disciples.

²⁰ Then a woman who had suffered from haemorrhages for
twelve years came up from behind, and touched the edge
²¹ of his cloak; for she said to herself, 'If I can only touch his
²² cloak, I shall be cured.' But Jesus turned and saw her, and
said, 'Take heart, my daughter; your faith has cured you.'
And from that moment she recovered.

²³ When Jesus arrived at the president's house and saw the
²⁴ flute-players and the general commotion, he said, 'Be off!
The girl is not dead: she is asleep'; and they only laughed
²⁵ at him. But, when everyone had been turned out, he went
into the room and took the girl by the hand, and she got up.
²⁶ This story became the talk of all the country round.

²⁷ As he passed on Jesus was followed by two blind men,
²⁸ who cried out, 'Son of David, have pity on us!' And when
he had gone indoors they came to him. Jesus asked, 'Do
you believe that I have the power to do what you want?'

'Yes, sir', they said. Then he touched their eyes, and said, 29
'As you have believed, so let it be'; and their sight was 30
restored. Jesus said to them sternly, 'See that no one hears
about this.' But as soon as they had gone out they talked 31
about him all over the country-side.

They were on their way out when a man was brought to 32
him, who was dumb and possessed by a devil; the devil 33
was cast out and the patient recovered his speech. Filled
with amazement the onlookers said, 'Nothing like this has
ever been seen in Israel.'[a]

So JESUS WENT ROUND all the towns and villages teach- 35
ing in their synagogues, announcing the good news of the
Kingdom, and curing every kind of ailment and disease.
The sight of the people moved him to pity: they were like 36
sheep without a shepherd, harassed and helpless; and he 37
said to his disciples, 'The crop is heavy, but labourers are
scarce; you must therefore beg the owner to send labourers 38
to harvest his crop.'

Then he called his twelve disciples to him and gave them 10
authority to cast out unclean spirits and to cure every
kind of ailment and disease.

These are the names of the twelve apostles: first Simon, 2
also called Peter, and his brother Andrew; James son of
Zebedee, and his brother John; Philip and Bartholomew, 3
Thomas and Matthew the tax-gatherer, James son of
Alphaeus, Lebbaeus,[b] Simon, a member of the Zealot 4
party, and Judas Iscariot, the man who betrayed him.

These twelve Jesus sent out with the following instruc- 5
tions: 'Do not take the road to gentile lands, and do not
enter any Samaritan town; but go rather to the lost sheep 6
of the house of Israel. And as you go proclaim the message: 7
"The kingdom of Heaven is upon you." Heal the sick, raise 8
the dead, cleanse lepers, cast out devils. You received without cost; give without charge.

'Provide no gold, silver, or copper to fill your purse, no 9 10
pack for the road, no second coat, no shoes, no stick; the
worker earns his keep.

'When you come to any town or village, look for some 11
worthy person in it, and make your home there until you
leave. Wish the house peace as you enter it, so that, if it is 12 13
worthy, your peace may descend on it; if it is not worthy,
your peace can come back to you. If anyone will not 14

---

[a] *Some witnesses add* (34) But the Pharisees said, 'He casts out devils
by the prince of devils.'          [b] *Some witnesses read* Thaddaeus.

receive you or listen to what you say, then as you leave that
15  house or that town shake the dust of it off your feet. I tell
you this: on the day of judgement it will be more bearable
for the land of Sodom and Gomorrah than for that town.

16      'Look, I send you out like sheep among wolves; be wary
as serpents, innocent as doves.

17      'And be on your guard, for men will hand you over to
18  their courts, they will flog you in the synagogues, and you
will be brought before governors and kings, for my sake,
19  to testify before them and the heathen. But when you are
arrested, do not worry about what you are to say; when
20  the time comes, the words you need will be given you; for
it is not you who will be speaking: it will be the Spirit of
your Father speaking in you.

21      'Brother will betray brother to death, and the father his
child; children will turn against their parents and send
22  them to their death. All will hate you for your allegiance
to me; but the man who holds out to the end will be saved.
23  When you are persecuted in one town, take refuge in
another; I tell you this: before you have gone through all
the towns of Israel the Son of Man will have come.

24      'A pupil does not rank above his teacher, or a servant
25  above his master. The pupil should be content to share his
teacher's lot, the servant to share his master's. If the
master has been called Beelzebub, how much more his
household!

26      'So do not be afraid of them. There is nothing covered up
that will not be uncovered, nothing hidden that will not be
27  made known. What I say to you in the dark you must repeat in broad daylight; what you hear whispered you must
28  shout from the house-tops. Do not fear those who kill the
body, but cannot kill the soul. Fear him rather who is able
to destroy both soul and body in hell.

29      'Are not sparrows two a penny? Yet without your
30  Father's leave not one of them can fall to the ground. As
for you, even the hairs of your head have all been counted.
31  So have no fear; you are worth more than any number of
sparrows.

32      'Whoever then will acknowledge me before men, I will
33  acknowledge him before my Father in heaven; and whoever disowns me before men, I will disown him before my
Father in heaven.

34      'You must not think that I have come to bring peace to
the earth; I have not come to bring peace, but a sword.
35  I have come to set a man against his father, a daughter

against her mother, a son's wife against her mother-in-law; and a man will find his enemies under his own roof.   36

'No man is worthy of me who cares more for father or   37
mother than for me; no man is worthy of me who cares
more for son or daughter; no man is worthy of me who   38
does not take up his cross and walk in my footsteps. By   39
gaining his life a man will lose it; by losing his life for my
sake, he will gain it.

'To receive you is to receive me, and to receive me is to   40
receive the One who sent me. Whoever receives a prophet   41
as a prophet will be given a prophet's reward, and whoever
receives a good man because he is a good man will be given
a good man's reward. And if anyone gives so much as a   42
cup of cold water to one of these little ones, because he is
a disciple of mine, I tell you this: that man will assuredly
not go unrewarded.'

When Jesus had finished giving his twelve disciples their   11
instructions, he left that place and went to teach and
preach in the neighbouring towns.

Jοhn, who was in prison, heard what Christ was   2
doing, and sent his own disciples to him with this message:   3
'Are you the one who is to come, or are we to expect some
other?' Jesus answered, 'Go and tell John what you hear   4
and see: the blind recover their sight, the lame walk, the   5
lepers are made clean, the deaf hear, the dead are raised to
life, the poor are hearing the good news—and happy is the   6
man who does not find me a stumbling-block.'

When the messengers were on their way back, Jesus   7
began to speak to the people about John: 'What was the
spectacle that drew you to the wilderness? A reed-bed
swept by the wind? No? Then what did you go out to see?   8
A man dressed in silks and satins? Surely you must look in
palaces for that. But why did you go out? To see a pro-   9
phet? Yes indeed, and far more than a prophet. He is the   10
man of whom Scripture says,

> "Here is my herald, whom I send on ahead of you,
> and he will prepare your way before you."

I tell you this: never has there appeared on earth a mother's   11
son greater than John the Baptist, and yet the least in the
kingdom of Heaven is greater than he.

'Ever since the coming of John the Baptist the kingdom   12
of Heaven has been subjected to violence and violent men[a]

---

<sup>a</sup> *Or* has been forcing its way forward, and men of force . . .

13 are seizing it. For all the prophets and the Law foretold
14 things to come until John appeared, and John is the
15 destined Elijah, if you will but accept it. If you have ears,
then hear.

16 'How can I describe this generation? They are like
children sitting in the market-place and shouting at each
other,

17 "We piped for you and you would not dance."
"We wept and wailed, and you would not mourn."

18 For John came, neither eating nor drinking, and they say,
19 "He is possessed." The Son of Man came eating and drinking, and they say, "Look at him! a glutton and a drinker,
a friend of tax-gatherers and sinners!" And yet God's wisdom is proved right by its results.'

20 THEN HE SPOKE of the towns in which most of his
miracles had been performed, and denounced them for
21 their impenitence. 'Alas for you, Chorazin!' he said; 'alas
for you, Bethsaida! If the miracles that were performed in
you had been performed in Tyre and Sidon, they would
22 have repented long ago in sackcloth and ashes. But it will
be more bearable, I tell you, for Tyre and Sidon on the day
23 of judgement than for you. And as for you, Capernaum,
will you be exalted to the skies? No, brought down to the
depths! For if the miracles had been performed in Sodom
which were performed in you, Sodom would be standing to
24 this day. But it will be more bearable, I tell you, for the
land of Sodom on the day of judgement than for you.'

25 At that time Jesus spoke these words: 'I thank thee,
Father, Lord of heaven and earth, for hiding these things
from the learned and wise, and revealing them to the
26 27 simple. Yes, Father, such*a* was thy choice. Everything is
entrusted to me by my Father; and no one knows the Son
but the Father, and no one knows the Father but the Son
and those to whom the Son may choose to reveal him.

28 'Come to me, all whose work is hard, whose load is
29 heavy; and I will give you relief. Bend your necks to my
yoke, and learn from me, for I am gentle and humble-
30 hearted; and your souls will find relief. For my yoke is
good to bear, my load is light.'

*a Or* Yes, I thank thee, Father, that such . . .

## CONTROVERSY

ONCE ABOUT THAT TIME Jesus went through 12
the cornfields on the Sabbath; and his disciples, feeling hungry, began to pluck some ears of corn and eat them.
The Pharisees noticed this, and said to him, 'Look, your 2
disciples are doing something which is forbidden on the
Sabbath.' He answered, 'Have you not read what David 3
did when he and his men were hungry? He went into the 4
House of God and ate the sacred bread, though neither he
nor his men had a right to eat it, but only the priests. Or 5
have you not read in the Law that on the Sabbath the priests
in the temple break the Sabbath and it is not held against
them? I tell you, there is something greater than the temple 6
here. If you had known what that text means, "I require 7
mercy, not sacrifice", you would not have condemned the
innocent. For the Son of Man is sovereign over the 8
Sabbath.'

He went on to another place, and entered their syna- 9
gogue. A man was there with a withered arm, and they 10
asked Jesus, 'Is it permitted to heal on the Sabbath?'
(They wanted to frame a charge against him.) But he said 11
to them, 'Suppose you had one sheep, which fell into a ditch
on the Sabbath; is there one of you who would not catch
hold of it and lift it out? And surely a man is worth far 12
more than a sheep! It is therefore permitted to do good on
the Sabbath.' Turning to the man he said, 'Stretch out 13
your arm.' He stretched it out, and it was made sound
again like the other. But the Pharisees, on leaving the 14
synagogue, laid a plot to do away with him.

Jesus was aware of it and withdrew. Many followed, and 15
he cured all who were ill; and he gave strict injunctions 16
that they were not to make him known. This was to fulfil 17
Isaiah's prophecy:

'Here is my servant, whom I have chosen, 18
my beloved, on whom my favour rests;
I will put my Spirit upon him,
and he will proclaim judgement among the nations.
He will not strive, he will not shout, 19
nor will his voice be heard in the streets.
He will not snap off the broken reed, 20
nor snuff out the smouldering wick,
until he leads justice on to victory.
In him the nations shall place their hope.' 21

22 THEN THEY BROUGHT HIM a man who was possessed;
he was blind and dumb; and Jesus cured him, restoring
23 both speech and sight. The bystanders were all amazed, and
the word went round: 'Can this be the Son of David?'
24 But when the Pharisees heard it they said, 'It is only by
Beelzebub prince of devils that this man drives the devils
out.'

25 He knew what was in their minds; so he said to them,
'Every kingdom divided against itself goes to ruin; and no
town, no household, that is divided against itself can stand.
26 And if it is Satan who casts out Satan, Satan is divided
27 against himself; how then can his kingdom stand? And if
it is by Beelzebub that I cast out devils, by whom do your
own people drive them out? If this is your argument, they
28 themselves will refute you. But if it is by the Spirit of God
that I drive out the devils, then be sure the kingdom of
God has already come upon you.

29 'Or again, how can anyone break into a strong man's
house and make off with his goods, unless he has first tied
the strong man up before ransacking the house?

30 'He who is not with me is against me, and he who does
not gather with me scatters.

31 'And so I tell you this: no sin, no slander, is beyond forgiveness for men, except slander spoken against the Spirit,
32 and that will not be forgiven. Any man who speaks a word
against the Son of Man will be forgiven; but if anyone
speaks against the Holy Spirit, for him there is no forgiveness, either in this age or in the age to come.

33 'Either make the tree good and its fruit good, or make
the tree bad and its fruit bad; you can tell a tree by its
34 fruit. You vipers' brood! How can your words be good
when you yourselves are evil? For the words that the
mouth utters come from the overflowing of the heart.
35 A good man produces good from the store of good within
himself; and an evil man from evil within produces evil.

36 'I tell you this: there is not a thoughtless word that
comes from men's lips but they will have to account for it
37 on the day of judgement. For out of your own mouth you
will be acquitted; out of your own mouth you will be condemned.'

38 At this some of the doctors of the law and the Pharisees
39 said, 'Master, we should like you to show us a sign.' He
answered: 'It is a wicked, godless generation that asks for
a sign; and the only sign that will be given it is the sign of
40 the prophet Jonah. Jonah was in the sea-monster's belly

for three days and three nights, and in the same way the
Son of Man will be three days and three nights in the
bowels of the earth. At the Judgement, when this genera- 41
tion is on trial, the men of Nineveh will appear against it[a]
and ensure its condemnation, for they repented at the
preaching of Jonah; and what is here is greater than Jonah.
The Queen of the South will appear at the Judgement 42
when this generation is on trial,[b] and ensure its condemnation, for she came from the ends of the earth to hear the
wisdom of Solomon; and what is here is greater than
Solomon.

'When an unclean spirit comes out of a man it wanders 43
over the deserts seeking a resting-place, and finds none.
Then it says, "I will go back to the home I left." So it re- 44
turns and finds the house unoccupied, swept clean, and
tidy. Off it goes and collects seven other spirits more 45
wicked than itself, and they all come in and settle down;
and in the end the man's plight is worse than before. That
is how it will be with this wicked generation.'

He was still speaking to the crowd when his mother and 46
brothers appeared; they stood outside, wanting to speak
to him. Someone said, 'Your mother and your brothers are 47
here outside; they want to speak to you.' Jesus turned to 48
the man who brought the message, and said, 'Who is my
mother? Who are my brothers?'; and pointing to the 49
disciples, he said, 'Here are my mother and my brothers.
Whoever does the will of my heavenly Father is my bro- 50
ther, my sister, my mother.'

THAT SAME DAY Jesus went out and sat by the lake-side, 13
where so many people gathered round him that he had to 2
get into a boat. He sat there, and all the people stood on
the shore. He spoke to them in parables, at some length. 3
He said: 'A sower went out to sow. And as he sowed, 4
some seed fell along the footpath; and the birds came and
ate it up. Some seed fell on rocky ground, where it had 5
little soil, and it sprouted quickly because it had no depth
of earth; but when the sun rose the young corn was 6
scorched, and as it had no root it withered away. Some 7
seed fell among thistles; and the thistles shot up, and
choked the corn. And some of the seed fell into good soil, 8
where it bore fruit, yielding a hundredfold or, it might be,
sixtyfold or thirtyfold. If you have ears, then hear.' 9

[a] *Or* will rise again together with it.    [b] *Or* At the Judgement the
Queen of the South will be raised to life together with this generation.

10   The disciples went up to him and asked, 'Why do you
11   speak to them in parables?' He replied, 'It has been granted
     to you to know the secrets of the kingdom of Heaven; but
12   to those others it has not been granted. For the man who
     has will be given more, till he has enough and to spare; and
13   the man who has not will forfeit even what he has. That is
     why I speak to them in parables; for they look without
14   seeing, and listen without hearing or understanding. There
     is a prophecy of Isaiah which is being fulfilled for them:
     "You may hear and hear, but you will never understand;
15   you may look and look, but you will never see. For this
     people's mind has become gross; their ears are dulled, and
     their eyes are closed. Otherwise, their eyes might see, their
     ears hear, and their mind understand, and then they might
     turn again, and I would heal them."
16   'But happy are your eyes because they see, and your
17   ears because they hear! Many prophets and saints, I tell
     you, desired to see what you now see, yet never saw it; to
     hear what you hear, yet never heard it.
18 19   'You, then, may hear the parable of the sower. When a
     man hears the word that tells of the Kingdom but fails to
     understand it, the evil one comes and carries off what has
     been sown in his heart. There you have the seed sown
20   along the footpath. The seed sown on rocky ground stands
     for the man who, on hearing the word, accepts it at once
21   with joy; but as it strikes no root in him he has no staying-
     power, and when there is trouble or persecution on account
22   of the word he falls away at once. The seed sown among
     thistles represents the man who hears the word, but worldly
     cares and the false glamour of wealth choke it, and it proves
23   barren. But the seed that fell into good soil is the man who
     hears the word and understands it, who accordingly bears
     fruit, and yields a hundredfold or, it may be, sixtyfold or
     thirtyfold.'
24   Here is another parable that he put before them: 'The
     kingdom of Heaven is like this. A man sowed his field with
25   good seed; but while everyone was asleep his enemy came,
26   sowed darnel among the wheat, and made off. When the
     corn sprouted and began to fill out, the darnel could be
27   seen among it. The farmer's men went to their master and
     said, "Sir, was it not good seed that you sowed in your
28   field? Then where has the darnel come from?" "This is an
     enemy's doing", he replied. "Well then," they said, "shall
29   we go and gather the darnel?" "No," he answered; "in
     gathering it you might pull up the wheat at the same time.

Let them both grow together till harvest; and at harvest- 30
time I will tell the reapers, 'Gather the darnel first, and tie
it in bundles for burning; then collect the wheat into my
barn.'"'

And this is another parable that he put before them: 31
'The kingdom of Heaven is like a mustard-seed, which a
man took and sowed in his field. As a seed, mustard is 32
smaller than any other; but when it has grown it is bigger
than any garden-plant; it becomes a tree, big enough for
the birds to come and roost among its branches.'

He told them also this parable: 'The kingdom of Heaven 33
is like yeast, which a woman took and mixed with half a
hundredweight of flour till it was all leavened.'

In all this teaching to the crowds Jesus spoke in parables; 34
in fact he never spoke to them without a parable. This was 35
to fulfil the prophecy of Isaiah:[a]

'I will open my mouth in parables;
  I will utter things kept secret since the world was made.'

He then dismissed the people, and went into the house, 36
where his disciples came to him and said, 'Explain to us
the parable of the darnel in the field.' And this was his 37
answer: 'The sower of the good seed is the Son of Man. The 38
field is the world; the good seed stands for the children of
the Kingdom, the darnel for the children of the evil one.
The enemy who sowed the darnel is the devil. The harvest 39
is the end of time. The reapers are angels. As the darnel, 40
then, is gathered up and burnt, so at the end of time the 41
Son of Man will send out his angels, who will gather
out of his kingdom whatever makes men stumble, and
all whose deeds are evil, and these will be thrown into 42
the blazing furnace, the place of wailing and grinding of
teeth. And then the righteous will shine as brightly as the 43
sun in the kingdom of their Father. If you have ears, then
hear.

'The kingdom of Heaven is like treasure lying buried in 44
a field. The man who found it, buried it again; and for
sheer joy went and sold everything he had, and bought
that field.

'Here is another picture of the kingdom of Heaven. 45
A merchant looking out for fine pearls found one of very 46
special value; so he went and sold everything he had, and
bought it.

---

* *Some witnesses omit* of Isaiah.

47 'Again the kingdom of Heaven is like a net let down into
48 the sea, where fish of every kind were caught in it. When
it was full, it was dragged ashore. Then the men sat down
and collected the good fish into pails and threw the worth-
49 less away. That is how it will be at the end of time. The
angels will go forth, and they will separate the wicked from
50 the good, and throw them into the blazing furnace, the
place of wailing and grinding of teeth.

51 'Have you understood all this?' he asked; and they
52 answered, 'Yes.' He said to them, 'When, therefore, a
teacher of the law has become a learner in the kingdom of
Heaven, he is like a householder who can produce from his
store both the new and the old.'

53 WHEN HE HAD FINISHED these parables Jesus left
54 that place, and came to his home town, where he taught
the people in their synagogue. In amazement they asked,
'Where does he get this wisdom from, and these miraculous
55 powers? Is he not the carpenter's son? Is not his mother
called Mary, his brothers James, Joseph, Simon, and
56 Judas? And are not all his sisters here with us? Where then
57 has he got all this from?' So they fell foul of him, and this
led him to say, 'A prophet will always be held in honour,
58 except in his home town, and in his own family.' And he
did not work many miracles there: such was their want of
faith.

14 It was at that time that reports about Jesus reached the
2 ears of Prince Herod. 'This is John the Baptist,' he said to
his attendants; 'John has been raised to life, and that is
why these miraculous powers are at work in him.'

3 NOW HEROD had arrested John, put him in chains, and
thrown him into prison, on account of Herodias, his brother
4 Philip's wife; for John had told him: 'You have no right to
5 her.' Herod would have liked to put him to death, but he
was afraid of the people, in whose eyes John was a prophet.
6 But at his birthday celebrations the daughter of Herodias
7 danced before the guests, and Herod was so delighted that
he took an oath to give her anything she cared to ask.
8 Prompted by her mother, she said, 'Give me here on a dish
9 the head of John the Baptist.' The king was distressed
when he heard it; but out of regard for his oath and for his
10 guests, he ordered the request to be granted, and had John
11 beheaded in prison. The head was brought in on a dish and
12 given to the girl; and she carried it to her mother. Then

John's disciples came and took away the body, and buried it; and they went and told Jesus.

WHEN HE HEARD what had happened Jesus withdrew 13 privately by boat to a lonely place; but people heard of it, and came after him in crowds by land from the towns. When he came ashore, he saw a great crowd; his heart 14 went out to them, and he cured those of them who were sick. When it grew late the disciples came up to him and 15 said, 'This is a lonely place, and the day has gone; send the people off to the villages to buy themselves food.' He 16 answered, 'There is no need for them to go; give them something to eat yourselves.' 'All we have here', they said, 17 'is five loaves and two fishes.' 'Let me have them', he 18 replied. So he told the people to sit down on the grass; then, 19 taking the five loaves and the two fishes, he looked up to heaven, said the blessing, broke the loaves, and gave them to the disciples; and the disciples gave them to the people. They all ate to their hearts' content; and the scraps left 20 over, which they picked up, were enough to fill twelve great baskets. Some five thousand men shared in this 21 meal, to say nothing of women and children.

Then he made the disciples embark and go on ahead to 22 the other side, while he sent the people away; after doing 23 that, he went up the hill-side to pray alone. It grew late, and he was there by himself. The boat was already some 24 furlongs from the shore,[a] battling with a head-wind and a rough sea. Between three and six in the morning he came 25 to them, walking over the lake. When the disciples saw him 26 walking on the lake they were so shaken that they cried out in terror: 'It is a ghost!' But at once he spoke to them: 27 'Take heart! It is I; do not be afraid.'

Peter called to him: 'Lord, if it is you, tell me to come to 28 you over the water.' 'Come', said Jesus. Peter stepped 29 down from the boat, and walked over the water towards Jesus. But when he saw the strength of the gale he was 30 seized with fear; and beginning to sink, he cried, 'Save me, Lord.' Jesus at once reached out and caught hold of him, 31 and said, 'Why did you hesitate? How little faith you have!' They then climbed into the boat; and the wind 32 dropped. And the men in the boat fell at his feet, exclaim- 33 ing, 'Truly you are the Son of God.'

So they finished the crossing and came to land at Gennes- 34 aret. There Jesus was recognized by the people of the 35

[a] *Some witnesses read* already well out on the water.

place, who sent out word to all the country round. And all
36 who were ill were brought to him, and he was begged to
allow them simply to touch the edge of his cloak. And
everyone who touched it was completely cured.

15 THEN JESUS WAS APPROACHED by a group of Pharisees
2 and lawyers from Jerusalem, with the question: 'Why do
your disciples break the ancient tradition? They do not
3 wash their hands before meals.' He answered them: 'And
what of you? Why do you break God's commandment
4 in the interest of your tradition? For God said, "Honour
your father and mother", and, "The man who curses his
5 father or mother must suffer death." But you say, "If a
man says to his father or mother, 'Anything of mine which
might have been used for your benefit is set apart for God',
6 then he must not honour his father or his mother." You
have made God's law null and void out of respect for your
7 tradition. What hypocrisy! Isaiah was right when he pro-
8 phesied about you: "This people pays me lip-service, but
9 their heart is far from me; their worship of me is in
vain, for they teach as doctrines the commandments of
men."'

10 He called the crowd and said to them, 'Listen to me, and
11 understand this: a man is not defiled by what goes into his
mouth, but by what comes out of it.'

12 Then the disciples came to him and said, 'Do you know
that the Pharisees have taken great offence at what you
13 have been saying?' His answer was: 'Any plant that is not
of my heavenly Father's planting will be rooted up.
14 Leave them alone; they are blind guides,*a* and if one
blind man guides another they will both fall into the
ditch.'

15 16 Then Peter said, 'Tell us what that parable means.' Jesus
17 answered, 'Are you still as dull as the rest? Do you not see
that whatever goes in by the mouth passes into the stomach
18 and so is discharged into the drain? But what comes out
of the mouth has its origins in the heart; and that is what
19 defiles a man. Wicked thoughts, murder, adultery, fornication, theft, perjury, slander—these all proceed from the
20 heart; and these are the things that defile a man; but to
eat without first washing his hands, that cannot defile
him.'

*a Some witnesses insert* of blind men.

## JESUS AND HIS DISCIPLES

JESUS THEN LEFT that place and withdrew to the 21 region of Tyre and Sidon. And a Canaanite woman 22 from those parts came crying out, 'Sir! have pity on me, Son of David; my daughter is tormented by a devil.' But 23 he said not a word in reply. His disciples came and urged him: 'Send her away; see how she comes shouting after us.' Jesus replied, 'I was sent to the lost sheep of the house of 24 Israel, and to them alone.' But the woman came and fell 25 at his feet and cried, 'Help me, sir.' To this Jesus replied, 26 'It is not right to take the children's bread and throw it to the dogs.' 'True, sir,' she answered; 'and yet the dogs eat 27 the scraps that fall from their masters' table.' Hearing this 28 Jesus replied, 'Woman, what faith you have! Be it as you wish!' And from that moment her daughter was restored to health.

After leaving that region Jesus took the road by the Sea 29 of Galilee and went up to the hills. When he was seated there, crowds flocked to him, bringing with them the lame, 30 blind, dumb, and crippled, and many other sufferers; they threw them down at his feet, and he healed them. Great 31 was the amazement of the people when they saw the dumb speaking, the crippled strong, the lame walking, and sight restored to the blind; and they gave praise to the God of Israel.

Jesus called his disciples and said to them, 'I feel sorry 32 for all these people; they have been with me now for three days and have nothing to eat. I do not want to send them away unfed; they might turn faint on the way.' The disci- 33 ples replied, 'Where in this lonely place can we find bread enough to feed such a crowd?' 'How many loaves have 34 you?' Jesus asked. 'Seven,' they replied; 'and there are a few small fishes.' So he ordered the people to sit down on 35 the ground; then he took the seven loaves and the fishes, 36 and after giving thanks to God he broke them and gave to the disciples, and the disciples gave to the people. They 37 all ate to their hearts' content; and the scraps left over, which they picked up, were enough to fill seven baskets. Four thousand men shared in this meal, to say nothing of 38 women and children. He then dismissed the crowds, got 39 into a boat, and went to the neighbourhood of Magadan.

The Pharisees and Sadducees came, and to test him they 16 asked him to show them a sign from heaven. His answer 2

29

4 was:[a] 'It is a wicked generation that asks for a sign; and the only sign that will be given it is the sign of Jonah.' So he went off and left them.

5 In crossing to the other side the disciples had forgotten
6 to take bread with them. So, when Jesus said to them, 'Beware, be on your guard against the leaven of the Phari-
7 sees and Sadducees', they began to say among themselves,
8 'It is because we have brought no bread!' Knowing what was in their minds, Jesus said to them: 'Why do you talk
9 about bringing no bread? Where is your faith? Do you not understand even yet? Do you not remember the five loaves for the five thousand, and how many basketfuls you picked
10 up? Or the seven loaves for the four thousand, and how many
11 basketfuls you picked up? How can you fail to see that I was not speaking about bread? Be on your guard, I said,
12 against the leaven of the Pharisees and Sadducees.' Then they understood: they were to be on their guard, not against baker's leaven, but against the teaching of the Pharisees and Sadducees.

13 WHEN HE CAME to the territory of Caesarea Philippi, Jesus asked his disciples, 'Who do men say that the Son
14 of Man is[b]?' They answered, 'Some say John the Baptist, others Elijah, others Jeremiah, or one of the prophets.'
15 16 'And you,' he asked, 'who do you say I am?' Simon Peter answered: 'You are the Messiah, the Son of the living God.'
17 Then Jesus said: 'Simon son of Jonah, you are favoured indeed! You did not learn that from mortal man; it was
18 revealed to you by my heavenly Father. And I say this to you: You are Peter, the Rock; and on this rock I will build my church, and the powers of death shall never conquer it.[c]
19 I will give you the keys of the kingdom of Heaven; what you forbid on earth shall be forbidden in heaven, and what
20 you allow on earth shall be allowed in heaven.' He then gave his disciples strict orders not to tell anyone that he was the Messiah.

21 From that time Jesus began to make it clear to his disciples that he had to go to Jerusalem, and there to suffer much from the elders, chief priests, and doctors of the law; to be put to death and to be raised again on the

[a] *Some witnesses here insert* 'In the evening you say, "It will be fine weather, for the sky is red"; (3) and in the morning you say, "It will be stormy today; the sky is red and lowering." You know how to interpret the appearance of the sky; can you not interpret the signs of the times?' [b] *Some witnesses read* that I, the Son of Man, am. [c] *Or the gates of death shall never close upon it.*

third day. At this Peter took him by the arm and began 22
to rebuke him: 'Heaven forbid!' he said. 'No, Lord, this
shall never happen to you.' Then Jesus turned and said to 23
Peter, 'Away with you, Satan; you are a stumbling-block
to me. You think as men think, not as God thinks.'

Jesus then said to his disciples, 'If anyone wishes to be 24
a follower of mine, he must leave self behind; he must take
up his cross and come with me. Whoever cares for his own 25
safety is lost; but if a man will let himself be lost for my
sake, he will find his true self. What will a man gain by 26
winning the whole world, at the cost of his true self? Or
what can he give that will buy that self back? For the Son 27
of Man is to come in the glory of his Father with his angels,
and then he will give each man the due reward for what
he has done. I tell you this: there are some of those stand- 28
ing here who will not taste death before they have seen
the Son of Man coming in his kingdom.'

Six days later Jesus took Peter, James, and John the 17
brother of James, and led them up a high mountain where
they were alone; and in their presence he was transfigured; 2
his face shone like the sun, and his clothes became white
as the light. And they saw Moses and Elijah appear, con- 3
versing with him. Then Peter spoke: 'Lord,' he said, 'how 4
good it is that we are here! If you wish it, I will make three
shelters here, one for you, one for Moses, and one for
Elijah.' While he was still speaking, a bright cloud sud- 5
denly overshadowed them, and a voice called from the
cloud: 'This is my Son, my Beloved,ᵃ on whom my favour
rests; listen to him.' At the sound of the voice the disciples 6
fell on their faces in terror. Jesus then came up to them, 7
touched them, and said, 'Stand up; do not be afraid.' And 8
when they raised their eyes they saw no one, but only
Jesus.

On their way down the mountain, Jesus enjoined them 9
not to tell anyone of the vision until the Son of Man had
been raised from the dead. The disciples put a question to 10
him: 'Why then do our teachers say that Elijah must come
first?' He replied, 'Yes, Elijah will come and set everything 11
right. But I tell you that Elijah has already come, and 12
they failed to recognize him, and worked their will upon
him; and in the same way the Son of Man is to suffer at
their hands.' Then the disciples understood that he meant 13
John the Baptist.

ᵃ *Or* This is my only Son.

31

14  When they returned to the crowd, a man came up to
15  Jesus, fell on his knees before him, and said, 'Have pity,
sir, on my son: he is an epileptic and has bad fits, and he
16  keeps falling about, often into the fire, often into water.
I brought him to your disciples, but they could not cure
17  him.' Jesus answered, 'What an unbelieving and perverse
generation! How long shall I be with you? How long must
18  I endure you? Bring him here to me.' Jesus then spoke
sternly to the boy; the devil left him, and from that
moment he was cured.

19  Afterwards the disciples came to Jesus and asked him
20  privately, 'Why could not we cast it out?' He answered,
'Your faith is too small. I tell you this: if you have faith
no bigger even than a mustard-seed, you will say to this
mountain, "Move from here to there!", and it will move;
nothing will prove impossible for you.'[a]

22  THEY WERE GOING about together in Galilee when
Jesus said to them, 'The Son of Man is to be given up into
23  the power of men, and they will kill him; then on the third
day he will be raised again.' And they were filled with grief.

24  On their arrival at Capernaum the collectors of the
temple-tax came up to Peter and asked, 'Does your master
25  not pay temple-tax?' 'He does', said Peter. When he went
indoors Jesus forestalled him by asking, 'What do you
think about this, Simon? From whom do earthly monarchs
collect tax or toll? From their own people, or from aliens?'
26  'From aliens', said Peter. 'Why then,' said Jesus, 'their
27  own people are exempt! But as we do not want to cause
offence, go and cast a line in the lake; take the first fish
that comes to the hook, open its mouth, and you will find
a silver coin; take that and pay it in; it will meet the tax
for us both.'

18   At that time the disciples came to Jesus and asked, 'Who
2  is the greatest in the kingdom of Heaven?' He called a
3  child, set him in front of them, and said, 'I tell you this:
unless you turn round and become like children, you will
4  never enter the kingdom of Heaven. Let a man humble
himself till he is like this child, and he will be the greatest
5  in the kingdom of Heaven. Whoever receives one such
6  child in my name receives me. But if a man is a cause of
stumbling to one of these little ones who have faith in me,
it would be better for him to have a millstone hung round

[a] *Some witnesses add* (21) But there is no means of casting out this sort
but prayer and fasting.

his neck and be drowned in the depths of the sea. Alas for 7
the world that such causes of stumbling arise! Come they
must, but woe betide the man through whom they come!

'If your hand or your foot is your undoing, cut it off and 8
fling it away; it is better for you to enter into life maimed
or lame, than to keep two hands or two feet and be thrown
into the eternal fire. If it is your eye that is your undoing, 9
tear it out and fling it away; it is better to enter into life
with one eye than to keep both eyes and be thrown into
the fires of hell.

'Never despise one of these little ones; I tell you, they 10
have their guardian angels in heaven, who look continually
on the face of my heavenly Father.[a]

'What do you think? Suppose a man has a hundred 12
sheep. If one of them strays, does he not leave the other
ninety-nine on the hillside and go in search of the one that
strayed? And if he should find it, I tell you this: he is more 13
delighted over that sheep than over the ninety-nine that
never strayed. In the same way, it is not your heavenly 14
Father's will that one of these little ones should be
lost.

'If your brother commits a sin,[b] go and take the matter 15
up with him, strictly between yourselves, and if he listens
to you, you have won your brother over. If he will not 16
listen, take one or two others with you, so that all facts
may be duly established on the evidence of two or three
witnesses. If he refuses to listen to them, report the matter 17
to the congregation; and if he will not listen even to the
congregation, you must then treat him as you would a
pagan or a tax-gatherer.

'I tell you this: whatever you forbid on earth shall be 18
forbidden in heaven, and whatever you allow on earth
shall be allowed in heaven.

'Again I tell you this: if two of you agree on earth about 19
any request you have to make, that request will be granted
by my heavenly Father. For where two or three have met 20
together in my name, I am there among them.'

Then Peter came up and asked him, 'Lord, how often am 21
I to forgive my brother if he goes on wronging me? As
many as seven times?' Jesus replied, 'I do not say seven 22
times; I say seventy times seven.[c]

'The kingdom of Heaven, therefore, should be thought 23
of in this way: There was once a king who decided to settle

[a] *Some witnesses add* (11) For the Son of Man came to save the lost.
[b] *Some witnesses insert* against you.      [c] *Or* seventy-seven times.

24 accounts with the men who served him. At the outset there appeared before him a man whose debt ran into millions.[a]
25 Since he had no means of paying, his master ordered him to be sold to meet the debt, with his wife, his children, and
26 everything he had. The man fell prostrate at his master's feet. "Be patient with me," he said, "and I will pay in full";
27 and the master was so moved with pity that he let the
28 man go and remitted the debt. But no sooner had the man gone out than he met a fellow-servant who owed him a few pounds;[b] and catching hold of him he gripped him by the
29 throat and said, "Pay me what you owe." The man fell at his fellow-servant's feet, and begged him, "Be patient with
30 me, and I will pay you"; but he refused, and had him jailed
31 until he should pay the debt. The other servants were deeply distressed when they saw what had happened, and
32 they went to their master and told him the whole story. He accordingly sent for the man. "You scoundrel!" he said to him; "I remitted the whole of your debt when you appealed
33 to me; were you not bound to show your fellow-servant the
34 same pity as I showed you?" And so angry was the master that he condemned the man to torture until he should pay
35 the debt in full. And that is how my heavenly Father will deal with you, unless you each forgive your brother from your hearts.'

19 WHEN JESUS HAD FINISHED this discourse he left Galilee and came into the region of Judaea across Jordan.
2 Great crowds followed him, and he healed them there.
3 Some Pharisees came and tested him by asking, 'Is it lawful for a man to divorce his wife on any and every
4 ground?'[c] He asked in return, 'Have you never read that the Creator made them from the beginning male and
5 female?'; and he added, 'For this reason a man shall leave his father and mother, and be made one with his wife; and
6 the two shall become one flesh. It follows that they are no longer two individuals: they are one flesh. What God has
7 joined together, man must not separate.' 'Why then', they objected, 'did Moses lay it down that a man might divorce
8 his wife by note of dismissal?' He answered, 'It was because your minds were closed that Moses gave you permission to divorce your wives; but it was not like that
9 when all began. I tell you, if a man divorces his wife for

---

[a] *Literally* who owed 10,000 talents.  [b] *Literally* owed him 100 denarii.  [c] *Or* Is there any ground on which it is lawful for a man to divorce his wife?

any cause other than unchastity, and marries another, he
commits adultery.'[a]

The disciples said to him, 'If that is the position with 10
husband and wife, it is better not to marry.' To this he re- 11
plied, 'That is something which not everyone can accept,
but only those for whom God has appointed it. For while 12
some are incapable of marriage because they were born so,
or were made so by men, there are others who have themselves renounced marriage for the sake of the kingdom of
Heaven. Let those accept it who can.'

They brought children for him to lay his hands on them 13
with prayer. The disciples rebuked them, but Jesus said to 14
them, 'Let the children come to me; do not try to stop them;
for the kingdom of Heaven belongs to such as these.' And 15
he laid his hands on the children, and went his way.

And now a man came up and asked him, 'Master, what 16
good must I do to gain eternal life?' 'Good?' said Jesus. 17
'Why do you ask me about that? One alone is good. But
if you wish to enter into life, keep the commandments.'
'Which commandments?' he asked. Jesus answered, 'Do 18
not murder; do not commit adultery; do not steal; do not
give false evidence; honour your father and mother; and 19
love your neighbour as yourself.' The young man answered, 20
'I have kept all these. Where do I still fall short?' Jesus 21
said to him, 'If you wish to go the whole way, go, sell your
possessions, and give to the poor, and then you will have
riches in heaven; and come, follow me.' When the young 22
man heard this, he went away with a heavy heart; for he
was a man of great wealth.

Jesus said to his disciples, 'I tell you this: a rich man 23
will find it hard to enter the kingdom of Heaven. I repeat, 24
it is easier for a camel to pass through the eye of a needle
than for a rich man to enter the kingdom of God.' The 25
disciples were amazed to hear this. 'Then who can be
saved?' they asked. Jesus looked at them, and said, 'For 26
men this is impossible; but everything is possible for God.'

At this Peter said, 'We here have left everything to be- 27
come your followers. What will there be for us?' Jesus re- 28
plied, 'I tell you this: in the world that is to be, when the
Son of Man is seated on his throne in heavenly splendour,
you my followers will have thrones of your own, where you
will sit as judges of the twelve tribes of Israel. And anyone 29
who has left brothers or sisters, father, mother, or children,

[a] *Some witnesses add* And the man who marries a woman so divorced
commits adultery.

land or houses for the sake of my name will be repaid many

30 times over, and gain eternal life. But many who are first will be last, and the last first.

20     'The kingdom of Heaven is like this. There was once a landowner who went out early one morning to hire

2 labourers for his vineyard; and after agreeing to pay them

3 the usual day's wage*a* he sent them off to work. Going out three hours later he saw some more men standing idle in

4 the market-place. "Go and join the others in the vineyard," he said, "and I will pay you a fair wage"; so off they went.

5 At midday he went out again, and at three in the afternoon,

6 and made the same arrangement as before. An hour before sunset he went out and found another group standing there; so he said to them, "Why are you standing about

7 like this all day with nothing to do?" "Because no one has hired us", they replied; so he told them, "Go and join the

8 others in the vineyard." When evening fell, the owner of the vineyard said to his steward, "Call the labourers and give them their pay, beginning with those who came last and

9 ending with the first." Those who had started work an hour before sunset came forward, and were paid the full day's

10 wage.*b* When it was the turn of the men who had come first, they expected something extra, but were paid the

11 same amount as the others. As they took it, they grumbled

12 at their employer: "These late-comers have done only one hour's work, yet you have put them on a level with us, who

13 have sweated the whole day long in the blazing sun!" The owner turned to one of them and said, "My friend, I am not being unfair to you. You agreed on the usual wage for

14 the day,*c* did you not? Take your pay and go home. I

15 choose to pay the last man the same as you. Surely I am free to do what I like with my own money. Why be jealous

16 because I am kind?" Thus will the last be first, and the first last.'

# CHALLENGE TO JERUSALEM

17 JESUS WAS JOURNEYING towards Jerusalem, and on the way he took the Twelve aside, and said to

18 them, 'We are now going to Jerusalem, and the Son of Man will be given up to the chief priests and the doctors

19 of the law; they will condemn him to death and hand him

---

*a Literally* one denarius for the day.      *b Literally* one denarius each.      *c Literally* You agreed on a denarius.

over to the foreign power, to be mocked and flogged and crucified, and on the third day he will be raised to life again.'

The mother of Zebedee's sons then came before him, 20 with her sons. She bowed low and begged a favour. 'What 21 is it you wish?' asked Jesus. 'I want you', she said, 'to give orders that in your kingdom my two sons here may sit next to you, one at your right, and the other at your left.' Jesus turned to the brothers and said, 'You do not under- 22 stand what you are asking. Can you drink the cup that I am to drink?' 'We can', they replied. Then he said to them, 23 'You shall indeed share my cup; but to sit at my right or left is not for me to grant; it is for those to whom it has already been assigned by my Father.'

When the other ten heard this, they were indignant 24 with the two brothers. So Jesus called them to him and 25 said, 'You know that in the world, rulers lord it over their subjects, and their great men make them feel the weight of authority; but it shall not be so with you. Among you, 26 whoever wants to be great must be your servant, and who- 27 ever wants to be first must be the willing slave of all— like the Son of Man; he did not come to be served, but to 28 serve, and to give up his life as a ransom for many.'

As they were leaving Jericho he was followed by a great 29 crowd of people. At the roadside sat two blind men. When 30 they heard it said that Jesus was passing they shouted, 'Have pity on us, Son of David.' The people told them 31 sharply to be quiet. But they shouted all the more, 'Sir, have pity on us; have pity on us, Son of David.' Jesus 32 stopped and called the men. 'What do you want me to do for you?' he asked. 'Sir,' they answered, 'we want our 33 sight.' Jesus was deeply moved, and touched their eyes. 34 At once their sight came back, and they followed him.

THEY WERE NOW nearing Jerusalem; and when they 21 reached Bethphage at the Mount of Olives, Jesus sent two disciples with these instructions: 'Go to the village oppo- 2 site, where you will at once find a donkey tethered with her foal beside her; untie them, and bring them to me. If 3 anyone speaks to you, say, "Our Master needs them"; and he will let you take them at once.'[a] This was to fulfil the 4 prophecy which says, 'Tell the daughter of Zion, "Here is 5 your king, who comes to you in gentleness, riding on an ass, riding on the foal of a beast of burden."'

[a] Or "Our Master needs them and will send them back straight away."

37

6 7 The disciples went and did as Jesus had directed, and brought the donkey and her foal; they laid their cloaks on
8 them and Jesus mounted. Crowds of people carpeted the road with their cloaks, and some cut branches from the
9 trees to spread in his path. Then the crowd that went ahead and the others that came behind raised the shout: 'Hosanna to the Son of David! Blessings on him who comes in the name of the Lord! Hosanna in the heavens!'
10 When he entered Jerusalem the whole city went wild
11 with excitement. 'Who is this?' people asked, and the crowd replied, 'This is the prophet Jesus, from Nazareth in Galilee.'
12 Jesus then went into the temple and drove out all who were buying and selling in the temple precincts; he upset the tables of the money-changers and the seats of the
13 dealers in pigeons; and said to them, 'Scripture says, "My house shall be called a house of prayer"; but you are making it a robbers' cave.'
14 In the temple blind men and cripples came to him, and
15 he healed them. The chief priests and doctors of the law saw the wonderful things he did, and heard the boys in the
16 temple shouting, 'Hosanna to the Son of David!', and they asked him indignantly, 'Do you hear what they are saying?' Jesus answered, 'I do; have you never read that text, "Thou hast made children and babes at the breast sound
17 aloud thy praise"?' Then he left them and went out of the city to Bethany, where he spent the night.
18 19 Next morning on his way to the city he felt hungry; and seeing a fig-tree at the roadside he went up to it, but found nothing on it but leaves. He said to the tree, 'You shall never bear fruit any more!'; and the tree withered away
20 at once. The disciples were amazed at the sight. 'How is it',
21 they asked, 'that the tree has withered so suddenly?' Jesus answered them, 'I tell you this: if only you have faith and have no doubts, you will do what has been done to the fig-tree; and more than that, you need only say to this mountain, "Be lifted from your place and hurled into the sea",
22 and what you say will be done. And whatever you pray for in faith you will receive.'
23 He entered the temple, and the chief priests and elders of the nation came to him with the question: 'By what authority are you acting like this? Who gave you this
24 authority?' Jesus replied, 'I have a question to ask you too; answer it, and I will tell you by what authority I act.
25 The baptism of John: was it from God, or from men?' This

set them arguing among themselves: 'If we say, "from God", he will say, "Then why did you not believe him?" But if we say, "from men", we are afraid of the people, for they all take John for a prophet.' So they answered, 'We do not know.' And Jesus said: 'Then neither will I tell you by what authority I act. 26 27

'But what do you think about this? A man had two sons. He went to the first, and said, "My boy, go and work today in the vineyard." "I will, sir", the boy replied; but he never went. The father came to the second and said the same. "I will not", he replied, but afterwards he changed his mind and went. Which of these two did as his father wished?' 'The second', they said. Then Jesus answered, 'I tell you this: tax-gatherers and prostitutes are entering the kingdom of God ahead of you. For when John came to show you the right way to live, you did not believe him, but the tax-gatherers and prostitutes did; and even when you had seen that, you did not change your minds and believe him. 28 29 30 31 32

'Listen to another parable. There was a landowner who planted a vineyard: he put a wall round it, hewed out a winepress, and built a watch-tower; then he let it out to vine-growers and went abroad. When the vintage season approached, he sent his servants to the tenants to collect the produce due to him. But they took his servants and thrashed one, killed another, and stoned a third. Again, he sent other servants, this time a larger number; and they did the same to them. At last he sent to them his son. "They will respect my son", he said. But when they saw the son the tenants said to one another, "This is the heir; come on, let us kill him, and get his inheritance." And they took him, flung him out of the vineyard, and killed him. When the owner of the vineyard comes, how do you think he will deal with those tenants?' 'He will bring those bad men to a bad end', they answered, 'and hand the vineyard over to other tenants, who will let him have his share of the crop when the season comes.' Then Jesus said to them, 'Have you never read in the scriptures: "The stone which the builders rejected has become the main corner-stone. This is the Lord's doing, and it is wonderful in our eyes"? Therefore, I tell you, the kingdom of God will be taken away from you, and given to a nation that yields the proper fruit.'*a* 33 34 35 36 37 38 39 40 41 42 43

When the chief priests and Pharisees heard his parables, 45

*a Some witnesses add* (44) Any man who falls on this stone will be dashed to pieces; and if it falls on a man he will be crushed by it.

46 they saw that he was referring to them; they wanted to arrest him, but they were afraid of the people, who looked on Jesus as a prophet.

22 1 2 THEN JESUS SPOKE to them again in parables: 'The kingdom of Heaven is like this. There was a king who pre-
3 pared a feast for his son's wedding; but when he sent his servants to summon the guests he had invited, they would
4 not come. He sent others again, telling them to say to the guests, "See now! I have prepared this feast for you. I have had my bullocks and fatted beasts slaughtered; everything
5 is ready; come to the wedding at once." But they took no notice; one went off to his farm, another to his business,
6 and the others seized the servants, attacked them brutally,
7 and killed them. The king was furious; he sent troops to
8 kill those murderers and set their town on fire. Then he said to his servants, "The wedding-feast is ready; but the
9 guests I invited did not deserve the honour. Go out to the main thoroughfares, and invite everyone you can find to
10 the wedding." The servants went out into the streets, and collected all they could find, good and bad alike. So the hall was packed with guests.

11 'When the king came in to see the company at table, he
12 observed one man who was not dressed for a wedding. "My friend," said the king, "how do you come to be here without
13 your wedding clothes?" He had nothing to say. The king then said to his attendants, "Bind him hand and foot; turn him out into the dark, the place of wailing and grinding of
14 teeth." For though many are invited, few are chosen.'

15 THEN THE PHARISEES went away and agreed on a plan
16 to trap him in his own words. Some of their followers were sent to him in company with men of Herod's party. They said, 'Master, you are an honest man, we know; you teach in all honesty the way of life that God requires, truckling to
17 no man, whoever he may be. Give us your ruling on this: are we or are we not permitted to pay taxes to the Roman
18 Emperor?' Jesus was aware of their malicious intention and said to them, 'You hypocrites! Why are you trying to
19 catch me out? Show me the money in which the tax is
20 paid.' They handed him a silver piece. Jesus asked, 'Whose
21 head is this, and whose inscription?' 'Caesar's', they re-plied. He said to them, 'Then pay Caesar what is due to
22 Caesar, and pay God what is due to God.' This answer took them by surprise, and they went away and left him alone.

The same day Sadducees came to him, maintaining that 23
there is no resurrection. Their question was this: 'Master, 24
Moses said, "If a man should die childless, his brother shall
marry the widow and carry on his brother's family." Now 25
we knew of seven brothers. The first married and died, and
as he was without issue his wife was left to his brother.
The same thing happened with the second, and the third, 26
and so on with all seven. Last of all the woman died. At the 27 28
resurrection, then, whose wife will she be, for they had all
married her?' Jesus answered: 'You are mistaken, because 29
you know neither the scriptures nor the power of God.
At the resurrection men and women do not marry; they 30
are like angels in heaven.

'But about the resurrection of the dead, have you never 31
read what God himself said to you: "I am the God of 32
Abraham, the God of Isaac, and the God of Jacob"? He is
not God of the dead but of the living.' The people heard 33
what he said, and were astounded at his teaching.

Hearing that he had silenced the Sadducees, the Pha- 34
risees met together; and one of their number*a* tested him 35
with this question: 'Master, which is the greatest com- 36
mandment in the Law?' He answered, '"Love the Lord 37
your God with all your heart, with all your soul, with all
your mind." That is the greatest commandment. It comes 38
first. The second is like it: "Love your neighbour as your- 39
self." Everything in the Law and the prophets hangs on 40
these two commandments.'

Turning to the assembled Pharisees Jesus asked them, 41
'What is your opinion about the Messiah? Whose son is 42
he?' 'The son of David', they replied. 'How then is it', he 43
asked, 'that David by inspiration calls him "Lord"? For
he says, "The Lord said to my Lord, 'Sit at my right hand 44
until I put your enemies under your feet.'"' If David calls 45
him "Lord", how can he be David's son?' Not a man could 46
say a word in reply; and from that day forward no one
dared ask him another question.

JESUS THEN ADDRESSED the people and his disciples in 23 1 2
these words: 'The doctors of the law and the Pharisees sit
in the chair of Moses; therefore do what they tell you; pay 3
attention to their words. But do not follow their practice;
for they say one thing and do another. They make up 4
heavy packs and pile them on men's shoulders, but will

*a Some witnesses insert a lawyer.*

5 not raise a finger to lift the load themselves. Whatever they do is done for show. They go about with broad phylacteries[a]
6 and with large tassels on their robes; they like to have places of honour at feasts and the chief seats in synagogues,
7 to be greeted respectfully in the street, and to be addressed as "rabbi".

8 'But you must not be called "rabbi"; for you have one
9 Rabbi, and you are all brothers. Do not call any man on earth "father"; for you have one Father, and he is in
10 heaven. Nor must you be called "teacher"; you have one
11 Teacher, the Messiah. The greatest among you must be
12 your servant. For whoever exalts himself will be humbled; and whoever humbles himself will be exalted.

13 'Alas, alas for you, lawyers and Pharisees, hypocrites that you are! You shut the door of the kingdom of Heaven in men's faces; you do not enter yourselves, and when others are entering, you stop them.[b]

15 'Alas for you, lawyers and Pharisees, hypocrites! You travel over sea and land to win one convert; and when you have won him you make him twice as fit for hell as you are yourselves.

16 'Alas for you, blind guides! You say, "If a man swears by the sanctuary, that is nothing; but if he swears by the
17 gold in the sanctuary, he is bound by his oath." Blind fools! Which is the more important, the gold, or the sanctuary
18 which sanctifies the gold? Or you say, "If a man swears by the altar, that is nothing; but if he swears by the offering
19 that lies on the altar, he is bound by his oath." What blindness! Which is the more important, the offering, or
20 the altar which sanctifies it? To swear by the altar, then,
21 is to swear both by the altar and by whatever lies on it; to swear by the sanctuary is to swear both by the sanctuary
22 and by him who dwells there; and to swear by heaven is to swear both by the throne of God and by him who sits upon it.

23 'Alas for you, lawyers and Pharisees, hypocrites! You pay tithes of mint and dill and cummin; but you have overlooked the weightier demands of the Law, justice, mercy, and good faith. It is these you should have prac-
24 tised, without neglecting the others. Blind guides! You strain off a midge, yet gulp down a camel!

---

[a] *See Deuteronomy 6. 8–9 and Exodus 13. 9.*     [b] *Some witnesses add* (14) Alas for you, lawyers and Pharisees, hypocrites! You eat up the property of widows, while you say long prayers for appearance' sake. You will receive the severest sentence.

'Alas for you, lawyers and Pharisees, hypocrites! You 25
clean the outside of cup and dish, which you have filled
inside by robbery and self-indulgence! Blind Pharisee! 26
Clean the inside of the cup first; then the outside will be
clean also.

'Alas for you, lawyers and Pharisees, hypocrites! You 27
are like tombs covered with whitewash; they look well
from outside, but inside they are full of dead men's bones
and all kinds of filth. So it is with you: outside you look 28
like honest men, but inside you are brim-full of hypocrisy
and crime.

'Alas for you, lawyers and Pharisees, hypocrites! You 29
build up the tombs of the prophets and embellish the
monuments of the saints, and you say, "If we had been 30
alive in our fathers' time, we should never have taken part
with them in the murder of the prophets." So you acknow- 31
ledge that you are the sons of the men who killed the prophets. Go on then, finish off what your fathers began![a]   32

'You snakes, you vipers' brood, how can you escape 33
being condemned to hell? I send you therefore prophets, 34
sages, and teachers; some of them you will kill and crucify,
others you will flog in your synagogues and hound from
city to city. And so, on you will fall the guilt of all the 35
innocent blood spilt on the ground, from innocent Abel to
Zechariah son of Berachiah, whom you murdered between
the sanctuary and the altar. Believe me, this generation 36
will bear the guilt of it all.

'O Jerusalem, Jerusalem, the city that murders the 37
prophets and stones the messengers sent to her! How often
have I longed to gather your children, as a hen gathers her
brood under her wings; but you would not let me. Look, 38
look! there is your temple, forsaken by God.[b][c] And I tell 39
you, you shall never see me until the time when you say,
"Blessings on him who comes in the name of the Lord."'

## PROPHECIES AND WARNINGS

JESUS WAS LEAVING the temple when his disciples 24
came and pointed to the temple buildings. He answered, 2
'Yes, look at it all. I tell you this: not one stone will be left
upon another; all will be thrown down.'

---

[a] *Or* You too must come up to your fathers' standards.     [b] *Or*
Look, your home is desolate.     [c] *Some witnesses add* and laid
waste.

3 When he was sitting on the Mount of Olives the disciples came to speak to him privately. 'Tell us,' they said, 'when will this happen? And what will be the signal for your coming and the end of the age?'

4 5 Jesus replied: 'Take care that no one misleads you. For many will come claiming my name and saying, "I am the 6 Messiah"; and many will be misled by them. The time is coming when you will hear the noise of battle near at hand and the news of battles far away; see that you are not alarmed. Such things are bound to happen; but the end is 7 still to come. For nation will make war upon nation, kingdom upon kingdom; there will be famines and earthquakes 8 in many places. With all these things the birth-pangs of the new age begin.

9 'You will then be handed over for punishment and execution; and men of all nations will hate you for your 10 allegiance to me. Many will fall from their faith; they will 11 betray one another and hate one another. Many false 12 prophets will arise, and will mislead many; and as lawless- 13 ness spreads, men's love for one another will grow cold. But 14 the man who holds out to the end will be saved. And this gospel of the Kingdom will be proclaimed throughout the earth as a testimony to all nations; and then the end will come.

15 'So when you see "the abomination of desolation", of which the prophet Daniel spoke, standing in the holy place 16 (let the reader understand), then those who are in Judaea 17 must take to the hills. If a man is on the roof, he must not 18 come down to fetch his goods from the house; if in the 19 field, he must not turn back for his coat. Alas for women with child in those days, and for those who have children at 20 the breast! Pray that it may not be winter when you have 21 to make your escape, or Sabbath. It will be a time of great distress; there has never been such a time from the begin- 22 ning of the world until now, and will never be again. If that time of troubles were not cut short, no living thing could survive; but for the sake of God's chosen it will be cut short.

23 'Then, if anyone says to you, "Look, here is the Messiah", 24 or, "There he is", do not believe it. Impostors will come claiming to be messiahs or prophets, and they will produce great signs and wonders to mislead even God's chosen, if 25 such a thing were possible. See, I have forewarned you. 26 If they tell you, "He is there in the wilderness", do not go out; or if they say, "He is there in the inner room", do not

believe it. Like lightning from the east, flashing as far as  27
the west, will be the coming of the Son of Man.

'Wherever the corpse is, there the vultures will gather.  28

'As soon as the distress of those days has passed, the sun  29
will be darkened, the moon will not give her light, the stars
will fall from the sky, the celestial powers will be shaken.
Then will appear in heaven the sign that heralds the Son of  30
Man. All the peoples of the world will make lamentation,
and they will see the Son of Man coming on the clouds of
heaven with great power and glory. With a trumpet blast  31
he will send out his angels, and they will gather his chosen
from the four winds, from the farthest bounds of heaven
on every side.

'Learn a lesson from the fig-tree. When its tender shoots  32
appear and are breaking into leaf, you know that summer
is near. In the same way, when you see all these things,  33
you may know that the end is near,[a] at the very door. I tell  34
you this: the present generation will live to see it all. Hea-  35
ven and earth will pass away; my words will never pass
away.

'But about that day and hour no one knows, not even  36
the angels in heaven, not even the Son; only the Father.

'As things were in Noah's days, so will they be when the  37
Son of Man comes. In the days before the flood they ate  38
and drank and married, until the day that Noah went into
the ark, and they knew nothing until the flood came and  39
swept them all away. That is how it will be when the Son
of Man comes. Then there will be two men in the field; one  40
will be taken, the other left; two women grinding at the  41
mill; one will be taken, the other left.

'Keep awake, then; for you do not know on what day  42
your Lord is to come. Remember, if the householder had  43
known at what time of night the burglar was coming, he
would have kept awake and not have let his house be
broken into. Hold yourselves ready, therefore, because the  44
Son of Man will come at the time you least expect him.

'Who is the trusty servant, the sensible man charged by  45
his master to manage his household staff and issue their
rations at the proper time? Happy that servant who is  46
found at his task when his master comes! I tell you this: he  47
will be put in charge of all his master's property. But if he  48
is a bad servant and says to himself, "The master is a long
time coming", and begins to bully the other servants and  49
to eat and drink with his drunken friends, then the master  50

[a] Or that he is near.

will arrive on a day that servant does not expect, at a time
51 he does not know, and will cut him in pieces. Thus he will
find his place among the hypocrites, where there is wailing
and grinding of teeth.

25 'When that day comes, the kingdom of Heaven will be
like this. There were ten girls, who took their lamps and
2 went out to meet the bridegroom. Five of them were foolish,
3 and five prudent; when the foolish ones took their lamps,
4 they took no oil with them, but the others took flasks of
5 oil with their lamps. As the bridegroom was late in coming
6 they all dozed off to sleep. But at midnight a cry was
heard: "Here is the bridegroom! Come out to meet him."
7 With that the girls all got up and trimmed their lamps.
8 The foolish said to the prudent, "Our lamps are going out;
9 give us some of your oil." "No," they said; "there will never
be enough for all of us. You had better go to the shop and
10 buy some for yourselves." While they were away the bridegroom arrived; those who were ready went in with him to
11 the wedding; and the door was shut. And then the other
five came back. "Sir, sir," they cried, "open the door for us."
12 13 But he answered, "I declare, I do not know you." Keep
awake then; for you never know the day or the hour.

14 'It is like a man going abroad, who called his servants
15 and put his capital in their hands; to one he gave five bags
of gold, to another two, to another one, each according to
16 his capacity. Then he left the country. The man who had
the five bags went at once and employed them in business,
17 and made a profit of five bags, and the man who had the
18 two bags made two. But the man who had been given one
bag of gold went off and dug a hole in the ground, and hid
19 his master's money. A long time afterwards their master
20 returned, and proceeded to settle accounts with them. The
man who had been given the five bags of gold came and
produced the five he had made: "Master," he said, "you
21 left five bags with me; look, I have made five more." "Well
done, my good and trusty servant!" said the master. "You
have proved trustworthy in a small way; I will now put
you in charge of something big. Come and share your
22 master's delight." The man with the two bags then came
and said, "Master, you left two bags with me; look, I have
23 made two more." "Well done, my good and trusty servant!"
said the master. "You have proved trustworthy in a small
way; I will now put you in charge of something big. Come
24 and share your master's delight." Then the man who had
been given one bag came and said, "Master, I knew you

to be a hard man: you reap where you have not sown, you gather where you have not scattered; so I was afraid, and 25 I went and hid your gold in the ground. Here it is—you have what belongs to you." "You lazy rascal!" said the 26 master. "You knew that I reap where I have not sown, and gather where I have not scattered? Then you ought to 27 have put my money on deposit, and on my return I should have got it back with interest. Take the bag of gold from 28 him, and give it to the one with the ten bags. For the man 29 who has will always be given more, till he has enough and to spare; and the man who has not will forfeit even what he has. Fling the useless servant out into the dark, the place 30 of wailing and grinding of teeth!"

'When the Son of Man comes in his glory and all the 31 angels with him, he will sit in state on his throne, with all 32 the nations gathered before him. He will separate men into two groups, as a shepherd separates the sheep from the goats, and he will place the sheep on his right hand and the 33 goats on his left. Then the king will say to those on his 34 right hand, "You have my Father's blessing; come, enter and possess the kingdom that has been ready for you since the world was made. For when I was hungry, you gave me 35 food; when thirsty, you gave me drink; when I was a stranger you took me into your home, when naked you 36 clothed me; when I was ill you came to my help, when in prison you visited me." Then the righteous will reply, 37 "Lord, when was it that we saw you hungry and fed you, or thirsty and gave you drink, a stranger and took you 38 home, or naked and clothed you? When did we see you ill 39 or in prison, and come to visit you?" And the king will 40 answer, "I tell you this: anything you did for one of my brothers here, however humble, you did for me." Then he 41 will say to those on his left hand, "The curse is upon you; go from my sight to the eternal fire that is ready for the devil and his angels. For when I was hungry you gave me 42 nothing to eat, when thirsty nothing to drink; when I was 43 a stranger you gave me no home, when naked you did not clothe me; when I was ill and in prison you did not come to my help." And they too will reply, "Lord, when was it 44 that we saw you hungry or thirsty or a stranger or naked or ill or in prison, and did nothing for you?" And he will 45 answer, "I tell you this: anything you did not do for one of these, however humble, you did not do for me." And they 46 will go away to eternal punishment, but the righteous will enter eternal life.'

# THE FINAL CONFLICT

26 WHEN JESUS HAD FINISHED this discourse
2  he said to his disciples, 'You know that in two days'
time it will be Passover, and the Son of Man is to be
handed over for crucifixion.'

3    Then the chief priests and the elders of the nation met in
4  the palace of the High Priest, Caiaphas; and there they
conferred together on a scheme to have Jesus arrested by
5  some trick and put to death. 'It must not be during the
festival,' they said, 'or there may be rioting among the
people.'

6  JESUS WAS AT BETHANY in the house of Simon the leper,
7  when a woman came to him with a small bottle of fragrant
oil, very costly; and as he sat at table she began to pour
8  it over his head. The disciples were indignant when they
9  saw it. 'Why this waste?' they said; 'it could have been
10 sold for a good sum and the money given to the poor.' Jesus
was aware of this, and said to them, 'Why must you make
trouble for the woman? It is a fine thing she has done for
11 me. You have the poor among you always; but you will not
12 always have me. When she poured this oil on my body it
13 was her way of preparing me for burial. I tell you this:
wherever in all the world this gospel is proclaimed, what
she has done will be told as her memorial.'

14 THEN ONE OF THE TWELVE, the man called Judas
15 Iscariot, went to the chief priests and said, 'What will you
give me to betray him to you?' They weighed him out[a]
16 thirty silver pieces. From that moment he began to look
out for an opportunity to betray him.

17   On the first day of Unleavened Bread the disciples came
to ask Jesus, 'Where would you like us to prepare for your
18 Passover supper?' He answered, 'Go to a certain man in
the city, and tell him, "The Master says, 'My appointed
time is near; I am to keep Passover with my disciples at
19 your house.'"' The disciples did as Jesus directed them and
prepared for Passover.

20   In the evening he sat down with the twelve disciples;
21 and during supper he said, 'I tell you this: one of you will
22 betray me.' In great distress they exclaimed one after the
23 other, 'Can you mean me, Lord?' He answered, 'One who

* Or agreed to pay him . . .

has dipped his hand into this bowl with me will betray me. The Son of Man is going the way appointed for him in the 24 scriptures; but alas for that man by whom the Son of Man is betrayed! It would be better for that man if he had never been born.' Then Judas spoke, the one who was to betray 25 him: 'Rabbi, can you mean me?' Jesus replied. 'The words are yours.'[a]

During supper Jesus took bread, and having said the 26 blessing he broke it and gave it to the disciples with the words: 'Take this and eat; this is my body.' Then he took 27 a cup, and having offered thanks to God he gave it to them with the words: 'Drink from it, all of you. For this is my 28 blood, the blood of the covenant, shed for many for the forgiveness of sins. I tell you, never again shall I drink 29 from the fruit of the vine until that day when I drink it new with you in the kingdom of my Father.'

After singing the Passover Hymn, they went out to the 30 Mount of Olives. Then Jesus said to them, 'Tonight you 31 will all fall from your faith on my account; for it stands written: "I will strike the shepherd down and the sheep of his flock will be scattered." But after I am raised again, I 32 will go on before you into Galilee.' Peter replied, 'Everyone 33 else may fall away on your account, but I never will.' Jesus said to him, 'I tell you, tonight before the cock crows 34 you will disown me three times.' Peter said, 'Even if I 35 must die with you, I will never disown you.' And all the disciples said the same.

JESUS THEN CAME with his disciples to a place called 36 Gethsemane. He said to them, 'Sit here while I go over there to pray.' He took with him Peter and the two sons 37 of Zebedee. Anguish and dismay came over him, and he 38 said to them, 'My heart is ready to break with grief. Stop here, and stay awake with me.' He went on a little, fell on 39 his face in prayer, and said, 'My Father, if it is possible, let this cup pass me by. Yet not as I will, but as thou wilt.'

He came to the disciples and found them asleep; and he 40 said to Peter, 'What! Could none of you stay awake with me one hour? Stay awake, and pray that you may be 41 spared the test. The spirit is willing, but the flesh is weak.'

He went away a second time, and prayed: 'My Father, 42 if it is not possible for this cup to pass me by without my drinking it, thy will be done.' He came again and found 43 them asleep, for their eyes were heavy. So he left them and 44

[a] *Or It is as you say.*

49

went away again; and he prayed the third time, using the same words as before.

45    Then he came to the disciples and said to them, 'Still sleeping? Still taking your ease? The hour has come! The
46 Son of Man is betrayed to sinful men. Up, let us go forward; the traitor is upon us.'

47    While he was still speaking, Judas, one of the Twelve, appeared; with him was a great crowd armed with swords and cudgels, sent by the chief priests and the elders of the
48 nation. The traitor gave them this sign: 'The one I kiss is
49 your man; seize him'; and stepping forward at once, he
50 said, 'Hail, Rabbi!', and kissed him. Jesus replied, 'Friend, do what you are here to do.'[a] They then came forward, seized Jesus, and held him fast.

51    At that moment one of those with Jesus reached for his sword and drew it, and he struck at the High Priest's
52 servant and cut off his ear. But Jesus said to him, 'Put up
53 your sword. All who take the sword die by the sword. Do you suppose that I cannot appeal to my Father, who would at once send to my aid more than twelve legions of angels?
54 But how then could the scriptures be fulfilled, which say that this must be?'

55    At the same time Jesus spoke to the crowd: 'Do you take me for a bandit, that you have come out with swords and cudgels to arrest me? Day after day I sat teaching in the
56 temple, and you did not lay hands on me. But this has all happened to fulfil what the prophets wrote.'

Then the disciples all deserted him and ran away.

57 JESUS WAS LED OFF under arrest to the house of Cai-aphas the High Priest, where the lawyers and elders were
58 assembled. Peter followed him at a distance till he came to the High Priest's courtyard, and going in he sat down there among the attendants, meaning to see the end of it all.

59    The chief priests and the whole Council tried to find some allegation against Jesus on which a death-sentence could
60 be based; but they failed to find one, though many came
61 forward with false evidence. Finally two men alleged that he had said, 'I can pull down the temple of God, and re-
62 build it in three days.' At this the High Priest rose and said to him, 'Have you no answer to the charge that these wit-
63 nesses bring against you?' But Jesus kept silence. The High Priest then said, 'By the living God I charge you to

        [a] *Or Friend, what are you here for?*

tell us: Are you the Messiah, the Son of God?' Jesus replied, 64
'The words are yours.*ᵃ* But I tell you this: from now on, you will see the Son of Man seated at the right hand of God*ᵇ* and coming on the clouds of heaven.' At these words 65 the High Priest tore his robes and exclaimed, 'Blasphemy! Need we call further witnesses? You have heard the blasphemy. What is your opinion?' 'He is guilty,' they answered; 'he should die.' 66

Then they spat in his face and struck him with their fists; 67 and others said, as they beat him, 'Now, Messiah, if you 68 are a prophet, tell us who hit you.'

Meanwhile Peter was sitting outside in the courtyard 69 when a serving-maid accosted him and said, 'You were there too with Jesus the Galilean.' Peter denied it in face 70 of them all. 'I do not know what you mean', he said. He 71 then went out to the gateway, where another girl, seeing him, said to the people there, 'This fellow was with Jesus of Nazareth.' Once again he denied it, saying with an oath, 72 'I do not know the man.' Shortly afterwards the bystanders 73 came up and said to Peter, 'Surely you are another of them; your accent gives you away!' At this he broke into 74 curses and declared with an oath: 'I do not know the man.' At that moment a cock crew; and Peter remembered how 75 Jesus had said, 'Before the cock crows you will disown me three times.' He went outside, and wept bitterly.

W HEN MORNING CAME, the chief priests and the elders 27 of the nation met in conference to plan the death of Jesus. They then put him in chains and led him away, to hand 2 him over to Pilate, the Roman Governor.

When Judas the traitor saw that Jesus had been con- 3 demned, he was seized with remorse, and returned the thirty silver pieces to the chief priests and elders. 'I have 4 sinned,' he said; 'I have brought an innocent man to his death.' But they said, 'What is that to us? See to that yourself.' So he threw the money down in the temple and 5 left them, and went and hanged himself.

Taking up the money, the chief priests argued: 'This 6 cannot be put into the temple fund; it is blood-money.' So 7 after conferring they used it to buy the Potter's Field, as a burial-place for foreigners. This explains the name 'Blood 8 Acre', by which that field has been known ever since; and 9 in this way fulfilment was given to the prophetic utterance of Jeremiah: 'They took*ᶜ* the thirty silver pieces, the price

*ᵃ Or It is as you say.*          *ᵇ Literally of the Power.*          *ᶜ Or I took.*

set on a man's head (for that was his price among the
10  Israelites), and gave the money for the potter's field, as the
Lord directed me.'

11      Jesus was now brought before the Governor; and as he
stood there the Governor asked him, 'Are you the king of
12  the Jews?' 'The words are yours',[a] said Jesus; and to the
charges laid against him by the chief priests and elders he
13  made no reply. Then Pilate said to him, 'Do you not hear
14  all this evidence that is brought against you?'; but he still
refused to answer one word, to the Governor's great
astonishment.

15      At the festival season it was the Governor's custom to
16  release one prisoner chosen by the people. There was then
in custody a man of some notoriety, called Jesus[b] Bar-
17  Abbas. When they were assembled Pilate said to them,
'Which would you like me to release to you—Jesus[b] Bar-
18  Abbas, or Jesus called Messiah?' For he knew that it was
out of malice that they had brought Jesus before him.

19      While Pilate was sitting in court a message came to him
from his wife: 'Have nothing to do with that innocent
man; I was much troubled on his account in my dreams
last night.'

20      Meanwhile the chief priests and elders had persuaded the
crowd to ask for the release of Bar-Abbas and to have Jesus
21  put to death. So when the Governor asked, 'Which of the
two do you wish me to release to you?', they said, 'Bar-
22  Abbas.' 'Then what am I to do with Jesus called Messiah?'
asked Pilate; and with one voice they answered, 'Crucify
23  him!' 'Why, what harm has he done?' Pilate asked; but
they shouted all the louder, 'Crucify him!'

24      Pilate could see that nothing was being gained, and a
riot was starting; so he took water and washed his hands
in full view of the people, saying, 'My hands are clean of
25  this man's blood; see to that yourselves.' And with one
voice the people cried, 'His blood be on us, and on our
26  children.' He then released Bar-Abbas to them; but he had
Jesus flogged, and handed him over to be crucified.

27  PILATE'S SOLDIERS then took Jesus into the Governor's
headquarters, where they collected the whole company
28  round him. They stripped him and dressed him in a scarlet
29  mantle; and plaiting a crown of thorns they placed it on
his head, with a cane in his right hand. Falling on their

----

*a* Or It is as you say.          *b* *Some witnesses omit* Jesus.

knees before him they jeered at him: 'Hail, King of the
Jews!' They spat on him, and used the cane to beat him 30
about the head. When they had finished their mockery, 31
they took off the mantle and dressed him in his own
clothes.

Then they led him away to be crucified. On their way 32
out they met a man from Cyrene, Simon by name, and
pressed him into service to carry his cross.

So they came to a place called Golgotha (which means 33
'Place of a skull') and there he was offered a draught of 34
wine mixed with gall; but when he had tasted it he would
not drink.

After fastening him to the cross they divided his clothes 35
among them by casting lots, and then sat down there to 36
keep watch. Over his head was placed the inscription giving 37
the charge: 'This is Jesus the king of the Jews.'

Two bandits were crucified with him, one on his right 38
and the other on his left.

The passers-by hurled abuse at him: they wagged their 39
heads and cried, 'You would pull the temple down, would 40
you, and build it in three days? Come down from the cross
and save yourself, if you are indeed the Son of God.' So too 41
the chief priests with the lawyers and elders mocked at him:
'He saved others,' they said, 'but he cannot save himself. 42
King of Israel, indeed! Let him come down now from the
cross, and then we will believe him. Did he trust in God? 43
Let God rescue him, if he wants him—for he said he was
God's Son.' Even the bandits who were crucified with him 44
taunted him in the same way.

From midday a darkness fell over the whole land, which 45
lasted until three in the afternoon; and about three Jesus 46
cried aloud, '*Eli, Eli, lema sabachthani?*', which means, 'My
God, my God, why hast thou forsaken me?' Some of the 47
bystanders, on hearing this, said, 'He is calling Elijah.' One 48
of them ran at once and fetched a sponge, which he soaked
in sour wine, and held it to his lips on the end of a cane.
But the others said, 'Let us see if Elijah will come to save 49
him.'

Jesus again gave a loud cry, and breathed his last. At 50 51
that moment the curtain of the temple was torn in two
from top to bottom. There was an earthquake, the rocks
split and the graves opened, and many of God's saints were 52
raised from sleep; and coming out of their graves after his 53
resurrection they entered the Holy City, where many saw
them. And when the centurion and his men who were 54

keeping watch over Jesus saw the earthquake and all that
was happening, they were filled with awe, and they said,
'Truly this man was a son of God.'[a]

55 A NUMBER OF WOMEN were also present, watching
from a distance; they had followed Jesus from Galilee and
56 waited on him. Among them were Mary of Magdala, Mary
the mother of James and Joseph, and the mother of the
sons of Zebedee.

57     When evening fell, there came a man of Arimathaea,
Joseph by name, who was a man of means, and had him-
58 self become a disciple of Jesus. He approached Pilate, and
asked for the body of Jesus; and Pilate gave orders that
59 he should have it. Joseph took the body, wrapped it in a
60 clean linen sheet, and laid it in his own unused tomb,
which he had cut out of the rock; he then rolled a large
61 stone against the entrance, and went away. Mary of
Magdala was there, and the other Mary, sitting opposite
the grave.

62     Next day, the morning after that Friday, the chief
63 priests and the Pharisees came in a body to Pilate. 'Your
Excellency,' they said, 'we recall how that impostor said
while he was still alive, "I am to be raised again after three
64 days." So will you give orders for the grave to be made
secure until the third day? Otherwise his disciples may
come, steal the body, and then tell the people that he has
been raised from the dead; and the final deception will be
65 worse than the first.' 'You may have your guard,' said
66 Pilate; 'go and make it secure as best you can.' So they
went and made the grave secure; they sealed the stone, and
left the guard in charge.

28 THE SABBATH WAS OVER, and it was about daybreak
on Sunday, when Mary of Magdala and the other Mary
2 came to look at the grave. Suddenly there was a violent
earthquake; an angel of the Lord descended from heaven;
he came to the stone and rolled it away, and sat himself
3 down on it. His face shone like lightning; his garments
4 were white as snow. At the sight of him the guards shook
with fear and lay like the dead.

5     The angel then addressed the women: 'You', he said,
'have nothing to fear. I know you are looking for Jesus
6 who was crucified. He is not here; he has been raised again,
as he said he would be. Come and see the place where he

                    [a] *Or* the Son of God.

was laid, and then go quickly and tell his disciples: "He has 7
been raised from the dead and is going on before you into
Galilee; there you will see him." That is what I had to
tell you.'

They hurried away from the tomb in awe and great joy, 8
and ran to tell the disciples. Suddenly Jesus was there in 9
their path. He gave them his greeting, and they came up
and clasped his feet, falling prostrate before him. Then 10
Jesus said to them, 'Do not be afraid. Go and take word to
my brothers that they are to leave for Galilee. They will
see me there.'

The women had started on their way when some of the 11
guard went into the city and reported to the chief priests
everything that had happened. After meeting with the 12
elders and conferring together, the chief priests offered the
soldiers a substantial bribe and told them to say, 'His 13
disciples came by night and stole the body while we were
asleep.' They added, 'If this should reach the Governor's 14
ears, we will put matters right with him and see that you
do not suffer.' So they took the money and did as they were 15
told. This story became widely known, and is current in
Jewish circles to this day.

The eleven disciples made their way to Galilee, to the 16
mountain where Jesus had told them to meet him. When 17
they saw him, they fell prostrate before him, though some
were doubtful. Jesus then came up and spoke to them. He 18
said: 'Full authority in heaven and on earth has been committed to me. Go forth therefore and make all nations my 19
disciples; baptize men everywhere in the name of the
Father and the Son and the Holy Spirit, and teach them 20
to observe all that I have commanded you. And be
assured, I am with you always, to the end of time.'

# THE
# GOSPEL ACCORDING TO
# MARK

## THE COMING OF CHRIST

1 HERE BEGINS THE GOSPEL of Jesus Christ
the Son of God.[a]

2 In the prophet Isaiah it stands written: 'Here is
my herald whom I send on ahead of you, and he will pre-
3 pare your way. A voice crying aloud in the wilderness,
"Prepare a way for the Lord; clear a straight path for
4 him."' And so it was that John the Baptist appeared in
the wilderness proclaiming a baptism in token of repentance,
5 for the forgiveness of sins; and they flocked to him from
the whole Judaean country-side and the city of Jerusalem,
and were baptized by him in the River Jordan, confessing
their sins.

6 John was dressed in a rough coat of camel's hair, with
a leather belt round his waist, and he fed on locusts and
7 wild honey. His proclamation ran: 'After me comes one
who is mightier than I. I am not fit to unfasten his shoes.
8 I have baptized you with water; he will baptize you with
the Holy Spirit.'

9 It happened at this time that Jesus came from Nazareth
10 in Galilee and was baptized in the Jordan by John. At the
moment when he came up out of the water, he saw the
heavens torn open and the Spirit, like a dove, descending
11 upon him. And a voice spoke from heaven: 'Thou art my
Son, my Beloved;[b] on thee my favour rests.'

12 Thereupon the Spirit sent him away into the wilderness,
13 and there he remained for forty days tempted by Satan.
He was among the wild beasts; and the angels waited on
him.

[a] *Some witnesses omit* the Son of God.     [b] *Or* Thou art my only
Son.

56

# IN GALILEE:
## SUCCESS AND OPPOSITION

AFTER JOHN HAD BEEN ARRESTED, Jesus 14
came into Galilee proclaiming the Gospel of God: 'The 15
time has come; the kingdom of God is upon you; repent,
and believe the Gospel.'

Jesus was walking by the Sea of Galilee when he saw 16
Simon and his brother Andrew on the lake at work with
a casting-net; for they were fishermen. Jesus said to them, 17
'Come with me, and I will make you fishers of men.' And 18
at once they left their nets and followed him.

When he had gone a little further he saw James son of 19
Zebedee and his brother John, who were in the boat overhauling their nets. He called them; and, leaving their 20
father Zebedee in the boat with the hired men, they went
off to follow him.

They came to Capernaum, and on the Sabbath he went 21
to synagogue and began to teach. The people were as- 22
tounded at his teaching, for, unlike the doctors of the law,
he taught with a note of authority. Now there was a man 23
in the synagogue possessed by an unclean spirit. He
shrieked: 'What do you want with us, Jesus of Nazareth? 24
Have you*a* come to destroy us? I know who you are—the
Holy One of God.' Jesus rebuked him: 'Be silent', he said, 25
'and come out of him.' And the unclean spirit threw the 26
man into convulsions and with a loud cry left him. They 27
were all dumbfounded and began to ask one another, 'What
is this? A new kind of teaching! He speaks with authority.
When he gives orders, even the unclean spirits submit.'
The news spread rapidly, and he was soon spoken of all 28
over the district of Galilee.

On leaving the synagogue they went straight to the 29
house of Simon and Andrew; and James and John went
with them. Simon's mother-in-law was ill in bed with fever. 30
They told him about her at once. He came forward, took 31
her by the hand, and helped her to her feet. The fever left
her and she waited upon them.

That evening after sunset they brought to him all who 32
were ill or possessed by devils; and the whole town was 33
there, gathered at the door. He healed many who suffered 34
from various diseases, and drove out many devils. He

*a* Or You have.

57

would not let the devils speak, because they knew who he was.

35 Very early next morning he got up and went out. He went away to a lonely spot and remained there in prayer.
36 37 But Simon and his companions searched him out, found
38 him, and said, 'They are all looking for you.' He answered, 'Let us move on to the country towns in the neighbourhood; I have to proclaim my message there also; that is
39 what I came out to do.' So all through Galilee he went, preaching in the synagogues and casting out the devils.

40 Once he was approached by a leper, who knelt before him begging his help. 'If only you will,' said the man, 'you
41 can cleanse me.' In warm indignation Jesus stretched out his hand,[a] touched him, and said, 'Indeed I will; be clean
42 again.' The leprosy left him immediately, and he was
43 44 clean. Then he dismissed him with this stern warning: 'Be sure you say nothing to anybody. Go and show yourself to the priest, and make the offering laid down by Moses for
45 your cleansing; that will certify the cure.' But the man went out and made the whole story public; he spread it far and wide, until Jesus could no longer show himself in any town, but stayed outside in the open country. Even so, people kept coming to him from all quarters.

2 When after some days he returned to Capernaum, the
2 news went round that he was at home; and such a crowd collected that the space in front of the door was not big enough to hold them. And while he was proclaiming the
3 message to them, a man was brought who was paralysed.
4 Four men were carrying him, but because of the crowd they could not get him near. So they opened up the roof over the place where Jesus was, and when they had broken through the stretcher on which the
5 paralysed man was lying. When Jesus saw their faith, he said to the paralysed man, 'My son, your sins are forgiven.'

6 Now there were some lawyers sitting there and they
7 thought to themselves, 'Why does the fellow talk like that? This is blasphemy! Who but God alone can forgive sins?'
8 Jesus knew in his own mind that this was what they were thinking, and said to them: 'Why do you harbour thoughts
9 like these? Is it easier to say to this paralysed man, "Your sins are forgiven", or to say, "Stand up, take your bed, and
10 walk"? But to convince you that the Son of Man has the

[a] *Some witnesses read* Jesus was sorry for him and stretched out his hand; *one witness has simply* He stretched out his hand.

right on earth to forgive sins'—he turned to the paralysed man—'I say to you, stand up, take your bed, and go home.' 11 And he got up, and at once took his stretcher and went out 12 in full view of them all, so that they were astounded and praised God. 'Never before', they said, 'have we seen the like.'

Once more he went away to the lake-side. All the crowd 13 came to him, and he taught them there. As he went along, 14 he saw Levi son of Alphaeus at his seat in the custom-house, and said to him, 'Follow me'; and Levi rose and followed him.

When Jesus was at table in his house, many bad charac- 15 ters—tax-gatherers and others—were seated with him and his disciples; for there were many who followed him. Some 16 doctors of the law who were Pharisees noticed him eating in this bad company, and said to his disciples, 'He eats with tax-gatherers and sinners!' Jesus heard it and said 17 to them, 'It is not the healthy that need a doctor, but the sick; I did not come to invite virtuous people, but sinners.'

Once, when John's disciples and the Pharisees were 18 keeping a fast, some people came to him and said, 'Why is it that John's disciples and the disciples of the Pharisees are fasting, but yours are not?' Jesus said to them, 'Can 19 you expect the bridegroom's friends to fast while the bridegroom is with them? As long as they have the bride-groom with them, there can be no fasting. But the time 20 will come when the bridegroom will be taken away from them, and on that day they will fast.

'No one sews a patch of unshrunk cloth on to an old 21 coat; if he does, the patch tears away from it, the new from the old, and leaves a bigger hole. No one puts new 22 wine into old wine-skins; if he does, the wine will burst the skins, and then wine and skins are both lost. Fresh skins for new wine!'

One Sabbath he was going through the cornfields; and 23 his disciples, as they went, began to pluck ears of corn. The Pharisees said to him, 'Look, why are they doing what 24 is forbidden on the Sabbath?' He answered, 'Have you 25 never read what David did when he and his men were hungry and had nothing to eat? He went into the House 26 of God, in the time of Abiathar the High Priest, and ate the sacred bread, though no one but a priest is allowed to eat it, and even gave it to his men.'

He also said to them, 'The Sabbath was made for the 27

28 sake of man and not man for the Sabbath: therefore the Son of Man is sovereign even over the Sabbath.'

3 On another occasion when he went to synagogue, there was a man in the congregation who had a withered arm;
2 and they were watching to see whether Jesus would cure him on the Sabbath, so that they could bring a charge
3 against him. He said to the man with the withered arm,
4 'Come and stand out here.' Then he turned to them: 'Is it permitted to do good or to do evil on the Sabbath, to save
5 life or to kill?' They had nothing to say; and, looking round at them with anger and sorrow at their obstinate stupidity, he said to the man, 'Stretch out your arm.' He stretched it
6 out and his arm was restored. But the Pharisees, on leaving the synagogue, began plotting against him with the partisans of Herod to see how they could make away with him.

7 JESUS WENT AWAY to the lake-side with his disciples.
8 Great numbers from Galilee, Judaea and Jerusalem, Idumaea and Transjordan, and the neighbourhood of Tyre and
9 Sidon, heard what he was doing and came to see him. So he told his disciples to have a boat ready for him, to save him
10 from being crushed by the crowd. For he cured so many that sick people of all kinds came crowding in upon him to
11 touch him. The unclean spirits too, when they saw him, would fall at his feet and cry aloud, 'You are the Son of
12 God'; but he insisted that they should not make him known.

13 He then went up into the hill-country and called the
14 men he wanted; and they went and joined him. He appointed twelve as his companions, whom he would send
15 out to proclaim the Gospel, with a commission to drive out
16 devils. So he appointed the Twelve: to Simon he gave the
17 name Peter; then came the sons of Zebedee, James and his brother John, to whom he gave the name Boanerges,
18 Sons of Thunder; then Andrew and Philip and Bartholomew and Matthew and Thomas and James the son of Alphaeus and Thaddaeus and Simon, a member of the
19 Zealot party, and Judas Iscariot, the man who betrayed him.
20 He entered a house; and once more such a crowd col-
21 lected round them that they had no chance to eat. When his family heard of this, they set out to take charge of him; for people were saying that he was out of his mind.[a]

---

[a] Or of him. 'He is out of his mind', they said.

The doctors of the law, too, who had come down from 22
Jerusalem, said, 'He is possessed by Beelzebub', and, 'He
drives out devils by the prince of devils.' So he called them 23
to come forward, and spoke to them in parables: 'How can
Satan drive out Satan? If a kingdom is divided against 24
itself, that kingdom cannot stand; if a household is divided 25
against itself, that house will never stand; and if Satan is 26
in rebellion against himself, he is divided and cannot stand;
and that is the end of him.

'On the other hand, no one can break into a strong man's 27
house and make off with his goods unless he has first tied
the strong man up; then he can ransack the house.

'I tell you this: no sin, no slander, is beyond forgiveness 28
for men; but whoever slanders the Holy Spirit can never 29
be forgiven; he is guilty of eternal sin.' He said this because 30
they had declared that he was possessed by an unclean
spirit.

Then his mother and his brothers arrived, and remaining 31
outside sent in a message asking him to come out to them.
A crowd was sitting round and word was brought to him: 32
'Your mother and your brothers are outside asking for you.'
He replied, 'Who is my mother? Who are my brothers?' 33
And looking round at those who were sitting in the circle 34
about him he said, 'Here are my mother and my brothers.
Whoever does the will of God is my brother, my sister, my 35
mother.'

ON ANOTHER OCCASION he began to teach by the lake- 4
side. The crowd that gathered round him was so large that
he had to get into a boat on the lake, and there he sat, with
the whole crowd on the beach right down to the water's
edge. And he taught them many things by parables. 2

As he taught he said:

'Listen! A sower went out to sow. And it happened that 3 4
as he sowed, some seed fell along the footpath; and the
birds came and ate it up. Some seed fell on rocky ground, 5
where it had little soil, and it sprouted quickly because it
had no depth of earth; but when the sun rose the young 6
corn was scorched, and as it had no root it withered away.
Some seed fell among thistles; and the thistles shot up and 7
choked the corn, and it yielded no crop. And some of the 8
seed fell into good soil, where it came up and grew, and
bore fruit; and the yield was thirtyfold, sixtyfold, even
a hundredfold.' He added, 'If you have ears to hear, then 9
hear.'

10   When he was alone, the Twelve and others who were
11   round him questioned him about the parables. He replied,
'To you the secret of the kingdom of God has been given;
but to those who are outside everything comes by way of
12   parables, so that (as Scripture says) they may look and
look, but see nothing; they may hear and hear, but understand nothing; otherwise they might turn to God and be
forgiven.'

13   So he said, 'You do not understand this parable? How then
14   are you to understand any parable? The sower sows the
15   word. Those along the footpath are people in whom the
word is sown, but no sooner have they heard it than Satan
comes and carries off the word which has been sown in
16   them. It is the same with those who receive the seed on
rocky ground; as soon as they hear the word, they accept
17   it with joy, but it strikes no root in them; they have no
staying-power; then, when there is trouble or persecution
18   on account of the word, they fall away at once. Others
again receive the seed among thistles; they hear the word,
19   but worldly cares and the false glamour of wealth and all
kinds of evil desire come in and choke the word, and it
20   proves barren. And there are those who receive the seed in
good soil; they hear the word and welcome it; and they
bear fruit thirtyfold, sixtyfold, or a hundredfold.'

21   He said to them, 'Do you bring in the lamp to put it
under the meal-tub, or under the bed? Surely it is brought
22   to be set on the lamp-stand. For nothing is hidden unless it
is to be disclosed, and nothing put under cover unless it is
23   to come into the open. If you have ears to hear, then
hear.'

24   He also said, 'Take note of what you hear; the measure
you give is the measure you will receive, with something
25   more besides. For the man who has will be given more, and
the man who has not will forfeit even what he has.'

26   He said, 'The kingdom of God is like this. A man scatters
27   seed on the land; he goes to bed at night and gets up in the
morning, and the seed sprouts and grows—how, he does
28   not know. The ground produces a crop by itself, first the
29   blade, then the ear, then full-grown corn in the ear; but as
soon as the crop is ripe, he plies the sickle, because harvest-
time has come.'

30   He said also, 'How shall we picture the kingdom of God,
31   or by what parable shall we describe it? It is like the
mustard-seed, which is smaller than any seed in the ground
32   at its sowing. But once sown, it springs up and grows taller

than any other plant, and forms branches so large that the
birds can settle in its shade.'

With many such parables he would give them his 33
message, so far as they were able to receive it. He never 34
spoke to them except in parables; but privately to his
disciples he explained everything.

## MIRACLES OF CHRIST

THAT DAY, in the evening, he said to them, 'Let us 35
cross over to the other side of the lake.' So they left 36
the crowd and took him with them in the boat where he
had been sitting; and there were other boats accompanying
him. A heavy squall came on and the waves broke over the 37
boat until it was all but swamped. Now he was in the stern 38
asleep on a cushion; they roused him and said, 'Master, we
are sinking! Do you not care?' He awoke, rebuked the 39
wind, and said to the sea, 'Hush! Be still!' The wind
dropped and there was a dead calm. He said to them, 'Why 40
are you such cowards? Have you no faith even now?' They 41
were awestruck and said to one another, 'Who can this be?
Even the wind and the sea obey him.'

So they came to the other side of the lake, into the 5
country of the Gerasenes. As he stepped ashore, a man 2
possessed by an unclean spirit came up to him from among
the tombs where he had his dwelling. He could no longer 3
be controlled; even chains were useless; he had often been 4
fettered and chained up, but he had snapped his chains
and broken the fetters. No one was strong enough to
master him. And so, unceasingly, night and day, he would 5
cry aloud among the tombs and on the hill-sides and cut
himself with stones. When he saw Jesus in the distance, he 6
ran and flung himself down before him, shouting loudly, 7
'What do you want with me, Jesus, son of the Most High
God? In God's name do not torment me.' (For Jesus was 8
already saying to him, 'Out, unclean spirit, come out of
this man!') Jesus asked him, 'What is your name?' 'My 9
name is Legion,' he said, 'there are so many of us.' And he 10
begged hard that Jesus would not send them out of the
country.

Now there happened to be a large herd of pigs feeding on 11
the hill-side, and the spirits begged him, 'Send us among 12
the pigs and let us go into them.' He gave them leave; 13
and the unclean spirits came out and went into the pigs; and

the herd, of about two thousand, rushed over the edge into the lake and were drowned.

14 The men in charge of them took to their heels and carried the news to the town and country-side; and the people 15 came out to see what had happened. They came to Jesus and saw the madman who had been possessed by the legion of devils, sitting there clothed and in his right mind; and they 16 were afraid. The spectators told them how the madman 17 had been cured and what had happened to the pigs. Then they begged Jesus to leave the district.

18 As he was stepping into the boat, the man who had been 19 possessed begged to go with him. Jesus would not allow it, but said to him, 'Go home to your own folk and tell them 20 what the Lord in his mercy has done for you.' The man went off and spread the news in the Ten Towns*a* of all that Jesus had done for him; and they were all amazed.

21 As soon as Jesus had returned by boat to the other shore, a great crowd once more gathered round him. While he 22 was by the lake-side, the president of one of the synagogues came up, Jairus by name, and, when he saw him, threw 23 himself down at his feet and pleaded with him. 'My little daughter', he said, 'is at death's door. I beg you to come and lay your hands on her to cure her and save her life.' 24 So Jesus went with him, accompanied by a great crowd which pressed upon him.

25 Among them was a woman who had suffered from 26 haemorrhages for twelve years; and in spite of long treatment by many doctors, on which she had spent all she had, there had been no improvement; on the contrary, she had 27 grown worse. She had heard what people were saying about Jesus, so she came up from behind in the crowd and touched 28 his cloak; for she said to herself, 'If I touch even his clothes, 29 I shall be cured.' And there and then the source of her haemorrhages dried up and she knew in herself that she 30 was cured of her trouble. At the same time Jesus, aware that power had gone out of him, turned round in the 31 crowd and asked, 'Who touched my clothes?' His disciples said to him, 'You see the crowd pressing upon you and yet 32 you ask, "Who touched me?"' Meanwhile he was looking 33 round to see who had done it. And the woman, trembling with fear when she grasped what had happened to her, came and fell at his feet and told him the whole truth. 34 He said to her, 'My daughter, your faith has cured you. Go in peace, free for ever from this trouble.'

*a Greek* Decapolis.

While he was still speaking, a message came from the 35
president's house, 'Your daughter is dead; why trouble
the Rabbi further?' But Jesus, overhearing the message as 36
it was delivered, said to the president of the synagogue,
'Do not be afraid; only have faith.' After this he allowed no 37
one to accompany him except Peter and James and James's
brother John. They came to the president's house, where 38
he found a great commotion, with loud crying and wailing.
So he went in and said to them, 'Why this crying and com- 39
motion? The child is not dead: she is asleep'; and they only 40
laughed at him. But after turning all the others out, he
took the child's father and mother and his own companions
and went in where the child was lying. Then, taking hold 41
of her hand, he said to her, '*Talitha cum*', which means,
'Get up, my child.' Immediately the girl got up and walked 42
about—she was twelve years old. At that they were beside
themselves with amazement. He gave them strict orders 43
to let no one hear about it, and told them to give her something to eat.

He left that place and went to his home town accom- 6
panied by his disciples. When the Sabbath came he began 2
to teach in the synagogue; and the large congregation who
heard him were amazed and said, 'Where does he get it
from?', and, 'What wisdom is this that has been given
him?', and, 'How does he work such miracles? Is not this 3
the carpenter, the son of Mary,[a] the brother of James and
Joseph and Judas and Simon? And are not his sisters here
with us?' So they fell foul of him. Jesus said to them, 'A 4
prophet will always be held in honour except in his home
town, and among his kinsmen and family.' He could work 5
no miracle there, except that he put his hands on a few sick
people and healed them; and he was taken aback by their 6
want of faith.

ON ONE OF HIS TEACHING JOURNEYS round the
villages he summoned the Twelve and sent them out in 7
pairs on a mission. He gave them authority over unclean
spirits, and instructed them to take nothing for the journey 8
beyond a stick: no bread, no pack, no money in their belts.
They might wear sandals, but not a second coat. 'When 9 10
you are admitted to a house', he added, 'stay there until
you leave those parts. At any place where they will not 11
receive you or listen to you, shake the dust off your feet
as you leave, as a warning to them.' So they set out and 12

[a] *Some witnesses read* Is not this the son of the carpenter and Mary . . .

13 called publicly for repentance. They drove out many devils, and many sick people they anointed with oil and cured.

14 Now King Herod heard of it, for the fame of Jesus had spread; and people were saying,[a] 'John the Baptist has been raised to life, and that is why these miraculous powers

15 are at work in him.' Others said, 'It is Elijah.' Others again,

16 'He is a prophet like one of the old prophets.' But Herod, when he heard of it, said, 'This is John, whom I beheaded, raised from the dead.'

17 For this same Herod had sent and arrested John and put him in prison on account of his brother Philip's wife,

18 Herodias, whom he had married. John had told Herod, 'You

19 have no right to your brother's wife.' Thus Herodias nursed a grudge against him and would willingly have killed him,

20 but she could not; for Herod went in awe of John, knowing him to be a good and holy man; so he kept him in custody. He liked to listen to him, although the listening left him greatly perplexed.

21 Herodias found her opportunity when Herod on his birthday gave a banquet to his chief officials and com-

22 manders and the leading men of Galilee. Her daughter came in[b] and danced, and so delighted Herod and his guests that the king said to the girl, 'Ask what you like and

23 I will give it you.' And he swore an oath to her: 'Whatever

24 you ask I will give you, up to half my kingdom.' She went out and said to her mother, 'What shall I ask for?' She

25 replied, 'The head of John the Baptist.' The girl hastened back at once to the king with her request: 'I want you to give me here and now, on a dish, the head of John the

26 Baptist.' The king was greatly distressed, but out of regard for his oath and for his guests he could not bring himself to

27 refuse her. So the king sent a soldier of the guard with orders to bring John's head. The soldier went off and beheaded

28 him in the prison, brought the head on a dish, and gave it to the girl; and she gave it to her mother.

29 When John's disciples heard the news, they came and took his body away and laid it in a tomb.

30 The apostles now rejoined Jesus and reported to him all

31 that they had done and taught. He said to them, 'Come with me, by yourselves, to some lonely place where you can rest quietly.' (For they had no leisure even to eat, so

---

[a] *Some witnesses read* and he said . . .     [b] *Or* A festive occasion came when Herod on his birthday gave . . . of Galilee. The daughter of Herodias came in . . .

many were coming and going.) Accordingly, they set off 32
privately by boat for a lonely place. But many saw them 33
leave and recognized them, and came round by land,
hurrying from all the towns towards the place, and arrived
there first. When he came ashore, he saw a great crowd; 34
and his heart went out to them, because they were like
sheep without a shepherd; and he had much to teach them.
As the day wore on, his disciples came up to him and said, 35
'This is a lonely place and it is getting very late; send the 36
people off to the farms and villages round about, to buy
themselves something to eat.' 'Give them something to eat 37
yourselves', he answered. They replied, 'Are we to go and
spend twenty pounds*a* on bread to give them a meal?' 'How 38
many loaves have you?' he asked; 'go and see.' They found
out and told him, 'Five, and two fishes also.' He ordered 39
them to make the people sit down in groups on the green
grass, and they sat down in rows, a hundred rows of fifty 40
each. Then, taking the five loaves and the two fishes, he 41
looked up to heaven, said the blessing, broke the loaves,
and gave them to the disciples to distribute. He also
divided the two fishes among them. They all ate to their 42
hearts' content; and twelve great basketfuls of scraps were 43
picked up, with what was left of the fish. Those who ate 44
the loaves numbered five thousand men.

As soon as it was over he made his disciples embark and 45
cross to Bethsaida ahead of him, while he himself sent the
people away. After taking leave of them, he went up the 46
hill-side to pray. It grew late and the boat was already well 47
out on the water, while he was alone on the land. Some- 48
where between three and six in the morning, seeing them
labouring at the oars against a head-wind, he came towards
them, walking on the lake. He was going to pass them by;
but when they saw him walking on the lake, they thought 49
it was a ghost and cried out; for they all saw him and were 50
terrified. But at once he spoke to them: 'Take heart! It is I;
do not be afraid.' Then he climbed into the boat beside 51
them, and the wind dropped. At this they were completely
dumbfounded, for they had not understood the incident of 52
the loaves; their minds were closed.

So they finished the crossing and came to land at Genne- 53
saret, where they made fast. When they came ashore, he 54
was immediately recognized; and the people scoured that 55
whole country-side and brought the sick on stretchers to
any place where he was reported to be. Wherever he went, 56

*a Literally* 200 *denarii.*

to farmsteads, villages, or towns, they laid out the sick
in the market-places and begged him to let them simply
touch the edge of his cloak; and all who touched him were
cured.

# GROWING TENSION

7   A GROUP OF PHARISEES, with some doctors of
2       the law who had come from Jerusalem, met him and
noticed that some of his disciples were eating their food with
'defiled' hands—in other words, without washing them.
3   (For the Pharisees and the Jews in general never eat without washing the hands,[a] in obedience to an old-established
4   tradition; and on coming from the market-place they
never eat without first washing. And there are many other
points on which they have a traditional rule to maintain,
for example, washing of cups and jugs and copper bowls.)
5   Accordingly, these Pharisees and the lawyers asked him,
'Why do your disciples not conform to the ancient tradi-
6   tion, but eat their food with defiled hands?' He answered,
'Isaiah was right when he prophesied about you hypocrites
in these words: "This people pays me lip-service, but their
7   heart is far from me: their worship of me is in vain, for
8   they teach as doctrines the commandments of men." You
neglect the commandment of God, in order to maintain the
tradition of men.'
9       He also said to them, 'How well you set aside the commandment of God in order to maintain[b] your tradition!
10  Moses said, "Honour your father and your mother", and,
"The man who curses his father or mother must suffer
11  death." But you hold that if a man says to his father or
mother, "Anything of mine which might have been used
for your benefit is Corban"' (meaning, set apart for God),
12  'he is no longer permitted to do anything for his father or
13  mother. Thus by your own tradition, handed down among
you, you make God's word null and void. And many other
things that you do are just like that.'
14      On another occasion he called the people and said to
15  them, 'Listen to me, all of you, and understand this: nothing that goes into a man from outside can defile him; no,
it is the things that come out of him that defile a man.'[c]

---

[a] *Some witnesses insert* with the fist; *others insert* frequently, *or*
thoroughly.        [b] *Some witnesses read* establish.        [c] *Some wit-*
*nesses here add* (16) If you have ears to hear, then hear.

When he had left the people and gone indoors, his dis- 17
ciples questioned him about the parable. He said to them, 18
'Are you as dull as the rest? Do you not see that nothing
that goes from outside into a man can defile him, because 19
it does not enter into his heart but into his stomach, and
so passes out into the drain?' Thus he declared all foods
clean. He went on, 'It is what comes out of a man that 20
defiles him. For from inside, out of a man's heart, come 21
evil thoughts, acts of fornication, of theft, murder, adul- 22
tery, ruthless greed, and malice; fraud, indecency, envy,
slander, arrogance, and folly; these evil things all come 23
from inside, and they defile the man.'

Then he left that place and went away into the territory 24
of Tyre. He found a house to stay in, and he would have
liked to remain unrecognized, but this was impossible. Al- 25
most at once a woman whose young daughter was possessed
by an unclean spirit heard of him, came in, and fell at his
feet. (She was a Gentile, a Phoenician of Syria by national- 26
ity.) She begged him to drive the spirit out of her daughter. He said to her, 'Let the children be satisfied first; it is 27
not fair to take the children's bread and throw it to the
dogs.' 'Sir,' she answered, 'even the dogs under the table 28
eat the children's scraps.' He said to her, 'For saying that, 29
you may go home content; the unclean spirit has gone out
of your daughter.' And when she returned home, she found 30
the child lying in bed; the spirit had left her.

On his return journey from Tyrian territory he went by 31
way of Sidon to the Sea of Galilee through the territory of
the Ten Towns.[a] They brought to him a man who was deaf 32
and had an impediment in his speech, with the request that
he would lay his hand on him. He took the man aside, 33
away from the crowd, put his fingers into his ears, spat,
and touched his tongue. Then, looking up to heaven, he 34
sighed, and said to him, '*Ephphatha*', which means 'Be
opened.' With that his ears were opened, and at the same 35
time the impediment was removed and he spoke plainly.
Jesus forbade them to tell anyone; but the more he forbade 36
them, the more they published it. Their astonishment 37
knew no bounds: 'All that he does, he does well,' they said;
'he even makes the deaf hear and the dumb speak.'

THERE WAS ANOTHER OCCASION about this time when 8
a huge crowd had collected, and, as they had no food, Jesus
called his disciples and said to them, 'I feel sorry for all 2

----

[a] *Greek* Decapolis.

these people; they have been with me now for three days
3 and have nothing to eat. If I send them home unfed, they
will turn faint on the way; some of them have come from
4 a distance.' The disciples answered, 'How can anyone pro-
5 vide all these people with bread in this lonely place?' 'How
many loaves have you?' he asked; and they answered,
6 'Seven.' So he ordered the people to sit down on the
ground; then he took the seven loaves, and, after giving
thanks to God, he broke the bread and gave it to his disciples to distribute; and they served it out to the people.
7 They had also a few small fishes, which he blessed and
8 ordered them to distribute. They all ate to their hearts'
content, and seven baskets were filled with the scraps that
9 were left. The people numbered about four thousand. Then
10 he dismissed them; and, without delay, got into the boat
with his disciples and went to the district of Dalmanu-
tha.*

11     Then the Pharisees came out and engaged him in discussion. To test him they asked him for a sign from heaven.
12 He sighed deeply to himself and said, 'Why does this
generation ask for a sign? I tell you this: no sign shall be
13 given to this generation.' With that he left them, re-
embarked, and went off to the other side of the lake.

14     Now they had forgotten to take bread with them; they
15 had no more than one loaf in the boat. He began to warn
them: 'Beware,' he said, 'be on your guard against the
16 leaven of the Pharisees and the leaven of Herod.' They said
17 among themselves, 'It is because we have no bread.' Knowing what was in their minds, he asked them, 'Why do you
talk about having no bread? Have you no inkling yet? Do
18 you still not understand? Are your minds closed? You have
eyes: can you not see? You have ears: can you not hear?
19 Have you forgotten? When I broke the five loaves among
five thousand, how many basketfuls of scraps did you pick
20 up?' 'Twelve', they said. 'And how many when I broke
the seven loaves among four thousand?' They answered,
21 'Seven.' He said, 'Do you still not understand?'

22     They arrived at Bethsaida. There the people brought a
23 blind man to Jesus and begged him to touch him. He took
the blind man by the hand and led him away out of the
village. Then he spat on his eyes, laid his hands upon him,
24 and asked whether he could see anything. The man's sight
began to come back, and he said, 'I see men; they look like
25 trees, but they are walking about.' Jesus laid his hands on

*a Some witnesses give Magedan; others give Magdala.*

his eyes again; he looked hard, and now he was cured so
that he saw everything clearly. Then Jesus sent him home, 26
saying, 'Do not tell anyone in the village.'[a]

JESUS AND HIS DISCIPLES set out for the villages of 27
Caesarea Philippi. On the way he asked his disciples, 'Who
do men say I am?' They answered, 'Some say John the 28
Baptist, others Elijah, others one of the prophets.' 'And 29
you,' he asked, 'who do you say I am?' Peter replied: 'You
are the Messiah.' Then he gave them strict orders not to tell 30
anyone about him; and he began to teach them that the 31
Son of Man had to undergo great sufferings, and to be rejected by the elders, chief priests, and doctors of the law;
to be put to death, and to rise again three days afterwards.
He spoke about it plainly. At this Peter took him by the 32
arm and began to rebuke him. But Jesus turned round, 33
and, looking at his disciples, rebuked Peter. 'Away with
you, Satan,' he said; 'you think as men think, not as God
thinks.'

Then he called the people to him, as well as his disciples, 34
and said to them, 'Anyone who wishes to be a follower of
mine must leave self behind; he must take up his cross, and
come with me. Whoever cares for his own safety is lost; 35
but if a man will let himself be lost for my sake and for the
Gospel, that man is safe. What does a man gain by winning 36
the whole world at the cost of his true self? What can he 37
give to buy that self back? If anyone is ashamed of me 38
and mine[b] in this wicked and godless age, the Son of Man
will be ashamed of him, when he comes in the glory of his
Father and of the holy angels.'[c]

He also said, 'I tell you this: there are some of those 9
standing here who will not taste death before they have
seen the kingdom of God already come in power.'

Six days later Jesus took Peter, James, and John with 2
him and led them up a high mountain where they were
alone; and in their presence he was transfigured; his clothes 3
became dazzling white, with a whiteness no bleacher on
earth could equal. They saw Elijah appear, and Moses with 4
him, and there they were, conversing with Jesus. Then 5
Peter spoke: 'Rabbi,' he said, 'how good it is that we are
here! Shall we make three shelters, one for you, one for
Moses, and one for Elijah?' (For he did not know what to 6

---

[a] *Some witnesses read* Do not go into the village.          [b] *Some wit-*
*nesses read* me and my words.          [c] *Some witnesses read* Father with
the holy angels.

7 say; they were so terrified.) Then a cloud appeared, casting its shadow over them, and out of the cloud came a voice:
8 'This is my Son, my Beloved;[a] listen to him.' And now suddenly, when they looked around, there was nobody to be seen but Jesus alone with themselves.
9 On their way down the mountain, he enjoined them not to tell anyone what they had seen until the Son of Man had
10 risen from the dead. They seized upon those words, and discussed among themselves what this 'rising from the dead'
11 could mean. And they put a question to him: 'Why do our
12 teachers say that Elijah must come first?' He replied, 'Yes, Elijah does come first to set everything right. Yet how is it[b] that the scriptures say of the Son of Man that he is to endure great sufferings and to be treated with contempt?
13 However, I tell you, Elijah has already come and they have worked their will upon him, as the scriptures say of him.'
14 When they came back to the disciples they saw a large crowd surrounding them and lawyers arguing with them.
15 As soon as they saw Jesus the whole crowd were overcome
16 with awe, and they ran forward to welcome him. He asked
17 them, 'What is this argument about?' A man in the crowd spoke up: 'Master, I brought my son to you. He is possessed
18 by a spirit which makes him speechless. Whenever it attacks him, it dashes him to the ground, and he foams at the mouth, grinds his teeth, and goes rigid. I asked your
19 disciples to cast it out, but they failed.' Jesus answered: 'What an unbelieving and perverse generation! How long shall I be with you? How long must I endure you? Bring
20 him to me.' So they brought the boy to him; and as soon as the spirit saw him it threw the boy into convulsions, and he fell on the ground and rolled about foaming at the
21 mouth. Jesus asked his father, 'How long has he been like
22 this?' 'From childhood,' he replied; 'often it has tried to make an end of him by throwing him into the fire or into water. But if it is at all possible for you, take pity upon us
23 and help us.' 'If it is possible!' said Jesus. 'Everything is
24 possible to one who has faith.' 'I have faith,' cried the
25 boy's father; 'help me where faith falls short.' Jesus saw then that the crowd was closing in upon them, so he rebuked the unclean spirit. 'Deaf and dumb spirit,' he said,
26 'I command you, come out of him and never go back!' After crying aloud and racking him fiercely, it came out; and

[a] Or This is my only Son.      [b] Or Elijah, you say, comes first to set everything right: then how is it . . .

the boy looked like a corpse; in fact, many said, 'He is dead.' But Jesus took his hand and raised him to his feet, 27 and he stood up.

Then Jesus went indoors, and his disciples asked him 28 privately, 'Why could not we cast it out?' He said, 'There 29 is no means of casting out this sort but prayer.'[a]

THEY NOW LEFT that district and made a journey 30 through Galilee. Jesus wished it to be kept secret; for he 31 was teaching his disciples, and telling them, 'The Son of Man is now to be given up into the power of men, and they will kill him, and three days after being killed, he will rise again.' But they did not understand what he said, and 32 were afraid to ask.

So they came to Capernaum; and when he was indoors, 33 he asked them, 'What were you arguing about on the way?' They were silent, because on the way they had been dis- 34 cussing who was the greatest. He sat down, called the 35 Twelve, and said to them, 'If anyone wants to be first, he must make himself last of all and servant of all.' Then he 36 took a child, set him in front of them, and put his arm round him. 'Whoever receives one of these children in my 37 name', he said, 'receives me; and whoever receives me, receives not me but the One who sent me.'

John said to him, 'Master, we saw a man driving out 38 devils in your name, and as he was not one of us, we tried to stop him.' Jesus said, 'Do not stop him; no one who 39 does a work of divine power in my name will be able the next moment to speak evil of me. For he who is not against 40 us is on our side. I tell you this: if anyone gives you a cup of 41 water to drink because you are followers of the Messiah, that man assuredly will not go unrewarded.

'As for the man who is a cause of stumbling to one of 42 these little ones who have faith, it would be better for him to be thrown into the sea with a millstone round his neck. If your hand is your undoing, cut it off; it is better for you 43 to enter into life maimed than to keep both hands and go to hell and the unquenchable fire.[b] And if your foot is your 45 undoing, cut it off; it is better to enter into life a cripple than to keep both your feet and be thrown into hell.[c] And 47 if it is your eye, tear it out; it is better to enter into the

[a] *Some witnesses add* and fasting.      [b] *Some witnesses add* (44) where the devouring worm never dies and the fire is not quenched. [c] *Some witnesses add* (46) where the devouring worm never dies and the fire is not quenched.

kingdom of God with one eye than to keep both eyes and
48  be thrown into hell, where the devouring worm never dies
and the fire is not quenched.
49      'For everyone will be salted with fire.
50      'Salt is a good thing; but if the salt loses its saltness,
what will you season it with?
'Have salt in yourselves; and be[a] at peace with one
another.'

10  On leaving those parts he came into the regions
of Judaea and Transjordan; and when a crowd gathered
round him once again, he followed his usual practice and
2  taught them. The question was put to him:[b] 'Is it lawful
3  for a man to divorce his wife?' This was to test him. He
4  asked in return, 'What did Moses command you?' They
answered, 'Moses permitted a man to divorce his wife by
5  note of dismissal.' Jesus said to them, 'It was because your
6  minds were closed that he made this rule for you; but in
the beginning, at the creation, God made them male and
7  female. For this reason a man shall leave his father and
8  mother, and be made one with his wife;[c] and the two shall
become one flesh. It follows that they are no longer two
9  individuals: they are one flesh. What God has joined together, man must not separate.'
10      When they were indoors again the disciples questioned
11  him about this matter; he said to them, 'Whoever divorces
his wife and marries another commits adultery against
12  her: so too, if she divorces her husband and marries
another, she commits adultery.'
13      They brought children for him to touch. The disciples
14  rebuked them, but when Jesus saw this he was indignant,
and said to them, 'Let the children come to me; do not try
to stop them; for the kingdom of God belongs to such as
15  these. I tell you, whoever does not accept the kingdom of
16  God like a child will never enter it.' And he put his arms
round them, laid his hands upon them, and blessed them.
17      As he was starting out on a journey, a stranger ran up,
and, kneeling before him, asked, 'Good Master, what must
18  I do to win eternal life?' Jesus said to him, 'Why do you
19  call me good? No one is good except God alone. You know
the commandments: "Do not murder; do not commit

[a] *Or* Have the salt of fellowship and be . . .; *or* You have the salt of
fellowship between you; then be . . .   [b] *Some witnesses read* The
Pharisees came forward and asked him the question . . .   [c] *Some
witnesses omit* and be made . . . wife.

adultery; do not steal; do not give false evidence; do not defraud; honour your father and mother."' 'But, Master,' 20 he replied, 'I have kept all these since I was a boy.' Jesus 21 looked straight at him; his heart warmed to him, and he said, 'One thing you lack: go, sell everything you have, and give to the poor, and you will have riches in heaven; and come, follow me.' At these words his face fell and he 22 went away with a heavy heart; for he was a man of great wealth.

Jesus looked round at his disciples and said to them, 23 'How hard it will be for the wealthy to enter the kingdom of God!' They were amazed that he should say this, but 24 Jesus insisted, 'Children, how hard it is$^a$ to enter the king-dom of God! It is easier for a camel to pass through the eye 25 of a needle than for a rich man to enter the kingdom of God.' They were more astonished than ever, and said to 26 one another, 'Then who can be saved?' Jesus looked at 27 them and said, 'For men it is impossible, but not for God; everything is possible for God.'

At this Peter spoke. 'We here', he said, 'have left every- 28 thing to become your followers.' Jesus said, 'I tell you this: 29 there is no one who has given up home, brothers or sisters, mother, father or children, or land, for my sake and for the Gospel, who will not receive in this age a hundred times as 30 much—houses, brothers and sisters, mothers and children, and land—and persecutions besides; and in the age to come eternal life. But many who are first will be last and the 31 last first.'

## CHALLENGE TO JERUSALEM

THEY WERE ON THE ROAD, going up to Jeru- 32 salem, Jesus leading the way; and the disciples were filled with awe, while those who followed behind were afraid. He took the Twelve aside and began to tell them what was to happen to him. 'We are now going to Jerusalem,' he 33 said; 'and the Son of Man will be given up to the chief priests and the doctors of the law; they will condemn him to death and hand him over to the foreign power. He will 34 be mocked and spat upon, flogged and killed; and three days afterwards, he will rise again.'

James and John, the sons of Zebedee, approached him 35 and said, 'Master, we should like you to do us a favour.'

---

$^a$ *Some witnesses insert* for those who trust in riches.

36 37 'What is it you want me to do?' he asked. They answered, 'Grant us the right to sit in state with you, one at your
38 right and the other at your left.' Jesus said to them, 'You do not understand what you are asking. Can you drink the cup that I drink, or be baptized with the baptism I am
39 baptized with?' 'We can', they answered. Jesus said, 'The cup that I drink you shall drink, and the baptism I am
40 baptized with shall be your baptism; but to sit at my right or left is not for me to grant; it is for those to whom it has already been assigned.'[a]

41 When the other ten heard this, they were indignant with
42 James and John. Jesus called them to him and said, 'You know that in the world the recognized rulers lord it over their subjects, and their great men make them feel the
43 weight of authority. That is not the way with you; among
44 you, whoever wants to be great must be your servant, and whoever wants to be first must be the willing slave of all.
45 For even the Son of Man did not come to be served but to serve, and to give up his life as a ransom for many.'

46 They came to Jericho; and as he was leaving the town, with his disciples and a large crowd, Bartimaeus son of
47 Timaeus, a blind beggar, was seated at the roadside. Hearing that it was Jesus of Nazareth, he began to shout, 'Son
48 of David, Jesus, have pity on me!' Many of the people told him to hold his tongue; but he shouted all the more, 'Son
49 of David, have pity on me.' Jesus stopped and said, 'Call him'; so they called the blind man and said, 'Take heart;
50 stand up; he is calling you.' At that he threw off his cloak,
51 sprang up, and came to Jesus. Jesus said to him, 'What do you want me to do for you?' 'Master,' the blind man
52 answered, 'I want my sight back.' Jesus said to him, 'Go; your faith has cured you.' And at once he recovered his sight and followed him on the road.

11 THEY WERE NOW APPROACHING Jerusalem, and when they reached Bethphage and Bethany, at the Mount
2 of Olives, he sent two of his disciples with these instructions: 'Go to the village opposite, and, just as you enter, you will find tethered there a colt which no one has yet
3 ridden. Untie it and bring it here. If anyone asks, "Why are you doing that?", say, "Our Master[b] needs it, and will
4 send it back here without delay."' So they went off, and found the colt tethered at a door outside in the street. They

*a Some witnesses add* by my Father.    *b Or* Its owner.

were untying it when some of the bystanders asked, 'What 5
are you doing, untying that colt?' They answered as Jesus 6
had told them, and were then allowed to take it. So they 7
brought the colt to Jesus and spread their cloaks on it, and
he mounted. And people carpeted the road with their 8
cloaks, while others spread brushwood which they had cut
in the fields; and those who went ahead and the others 9
who came behind shouted, 'Hosanna! Blessings on him
who comes in the name of the Lord! Blessings on the 10
coming kingdom of our father David! Hosanna in the
heavens!'

He entered Jerusalem and went into the temple, where 11
he looked at the whole scene; but, as it was now late, he
went out to Bethany with the Twelve.

On the following day, after they had left Bethany, he 12
felt hungry, and, noticing in the distance a fig-tree in leaf, 13
he went to see if he could find anything on it. But when
he came there he found nothing but leaves; for it was
not the season for figs. He said to the tree, 'May no one 14
ever again eat fruit from you!' And his disciples were
listening.

So they came to Jerusalem, and he went into the temple 15
and began driving out those who bought and sold in the
temple. He upset the tables of the money-changers and the
seats of the dealers in pigeons; and he would not allow 16
anyone to use the temple court as a thoroughfare for carrying goods. Then he began to teach them, and said, 'Does 17
not Scripture say, "My house shall be called a house of
prayer for all the nations"? But you have made it a robbers'
cave.' The chief priests and the doctors of the law heard of 18
this and sought some means of making away with him; for
they were afraid of him, because the whole crowd was
spellbound by his teaching. And when evening came he 19
went out of the city.

Early next morning, as they passed by, they saw that 20
the fig-tree had withered from the roots up; and Peter, 21
recalling what had happened, said to him, 'Rabbi, look,
the fig-tree which you cursed has withered.' Jesus an- 22
swered them, 'Have faith in God. I tell you this: if anyone 23
says to this mountain, "Be lifted from your place and
hurled into the sea", and has no inward doubts, but believes that what he says is happening, it will be done
for him. I tell you, then, whatever you ask for in 24
prayer, believe that you have received it and it will be
yours.

25   'And when you stand praying, if you have a grievance against anyone, forgive him, so that your Father in heaven may forgive you the wrongs you have done.'[a]

27   THEY CAME ONCE MORE to Jerusalem. And as he was walking in the temple court the chief priests, lawyers, and
28 elders came to him and said, 'By what authority are you acting like this? Who gave you authority to act in this
29 way?' Jesus said to them, 'I have a question to ask you too; and if you give me an answer, I will tell you by what
30 authority I act. The baptism of John: was it from God, or
31 from men? Answer me.' This set them arguing among themselves: 'What shall we say? If we say, "from God",
32 he will say, "Then why did you not believe him?" Shall we say, "from men"?'—but they were afraid of the people, for all held that John was in fact a prophet.
33 So they answered, 'We do not know.' And Jesus said to them, 'Then neither will I tell you by what authority I act.'

12   He went on to speak to them in parables: 'A man planted a vineyard and put a wall round it, hewed out a winepress, and built a watch-tower; then he let it out to vine-growers
2 and went abroad. When the season came, he sent a servant to the tenants to collect from them his share of the produce.
3 But they took him, thrashed him, and sent him away
4 empty-handed. Again, he sent them another servant, whom they beat about the head and treated outrageously.
5 So he sent another, and that one they killed; and many more besides, of whom they beat some, and killed others.
6 He had now only one left to send, his own dear son.[b] In the
7 end he sent him. "They will respect my son", he said. But the tenants said to one another, "This is the heir; come on,
8 let us kill him, and the property will be ours." So they seized him and killed him, and flung his body out of the
9 vineyard. What will the owner of the vineyard do? He will come and put the tenants to death and give the vineyard to others.

10   'Can it be that you have never read this text: "The stone which the builders rejected has become the main corner-
11 stone. This is the Lord's doing, and it is wonderful in our eyes"?'
12   Then they began to look for a way to arrest him, for

---

[a] *Some witnesses add* (26) But if you do not forgive others, then the wrongs you have done will not be forgiven by your Father in heaven.
[b] *Or his only son.*

they saw that the parable was aimed at them; but they were afraid of the people, so they left him alone and went away.

A NUMBER OF PHARISEES and men of Herod's party 13 were sent to trap him with a question. They came and 14 said, 'Master, you are an honest man, we know, and truckle to no one, whoever he may be; you teach in all honesty the way of life that God requires. Are we or are we not permitted to pay taxes to the Roman Emperor? Shall we pay 15 or not?' He saw how crafty their question was, and said, 'Why are you trying to catch me out? Fetch me a silver piece, and let me look at it.' They brought one, and he said 16 to them, 'Whose head is this, and whose inscription?' 'Caesar's', they replied. Then Jesus said, 'Pay Caesar what 17 is due to Caesar, and pay God what is due to God.' And they heard him with astonishment.

Next Sadducees came to him. (It is they who say that 18 there is no resurrection.) Their question was this: 'Master, 19 Moses laid it down for us that if there are brothers, and one dies leaving a wife but no child, then the next should marry the widow and carry on his brother's family. Now 20 there were seven brothers. The first took a wife and died without issue. Then the second married her, and he too 21 died without issue. So did the third. Eventually the seven 22 of them died, all without issue. Finally the woman died. At 23 the resurrection, when they come back to life, whose wife will she be, since all seven had married her?' Jesus said to 24 them, 'You are mistaken, and surely this is the reason: you do not know either the scriptures or the power of God. When they rise from the dead, men and women do not 25 marry; they are like angels in heaven.

'But about the resurrection of the dead, have you never 26 read in the Book of Moses, in the story of the burning bush, how God spoke to him and said, "I am the God of Abraham, the God of Isaac, and the God of Jacob"? God is not 27 God of the dead but of the living. You are greatly mistaken.'

Then one of the lawyers, who had been listening to these 28 discussions and had noted how well he answered, came forward and asked him, 'Which commandment is first of all?' Jesus answered, 'The first is, "Hear, O Israel: the 29 Lord our God is the only Lord; love the Lord your God 30 with all your heart, with all your soul, with all your mind, and with all your strength." The second is this: "Love your 31

neighbour as yourself." There is no other commandment
32 greater than these.' The lawyer said to him, 'Well said,
Master. You are right in saying that God is one and beside
33 him there is no other. And to love him with all your heart,
all your understanding, and all your strength, and to love
your neighbour as yourself—that is far more than any
34 burnt offerings or sacrifices.' When Jesus saw how sensibly
he answered, he said to him, 'You are not far from the
kingdom of God.'

After that nobody ventured to put any more questions
35 to him; and Jesus went on to say, as he taught in the
temple, 'How can the teachers of the law maintain that
36 the Messiah is "Son of David"? David himself said, when
inspired by the Holy Spirit, "The Lord said to my Lord,
'Sit at my right hand until I put your enemies under your
37 feet.'" David himself calls him "Lord"; how can he also be
David's son?'

38     There was a great crowd and they listened eagerly.*a* He
said as he taught them, 'Beware of the doctors of the law,
who love to walk up and down in long robes, receiving
39 respectful greetings in the street; and to have the chief
40 seats in synagogues, and places of honour at feasts. These
are the men who eat up the property of widows, while they
say long prayers for appearance' sake, and they will receive
the severest sentence.'*b*

41     Once he was standing opposite the temple treasury,
watching as people dropped their money into the chest.
42 Many rich people were giving large sums. Presently there
came a poor widow who dropped in two tiny coins, to-
43 gether worth a farthing. He called his disciples to him.
'I tell you this,' he said: 'this poor widow has given more
44 than any of the others; for those others who have given
had more than enough, but she, with less than enough,
has given all that she had to live on.'

13 As he was leaving the temple, one of his disciples
exclaimed, 'Look, Master, what huge stones! What fine
2 buildings!' Jesus said to him, 'You see these great buildings? Not one stone will be left upon another; all will be
thrown down.'

3     When he was sitting on the Mount of Olives facing the
temple he was questioned privately by Peter, James, John,

*a Or* The mass of the people listened eagerly.      *b Or* As for those
who eat up the property of widows, while they say long prayers for
appearance' sake, they will have an even sterner judgement to face.

and Andrew. 'Tell us,' they said, 'when will this happen? 4
What will be the sign when the fulfilment of all this is at
hand?'

Jesus began: 'Take care that no one misleads you. Many 5 6
will come claiming my name, and saying, "I am he"; and
many will be misled by them.

'When you hear the noise of battle near at hand and the 7
news of battles far away, do not be alarmed. Such things
are bound to happen; but the end is still to come. For 8
nation will make war upon nation, kingdom upon kingdom; there will be earthquakes in many places; there will
be famines. With these things the birth-pangs of the new
age begin.

'As for you, be on your guard. You will be handed over 9
to the courts. You will be flogged in synagogues. You will
be summoned to appear before governors and kings on my
account to testify in their presence. But before the end the 10
Gospel must be proclaimed to all nations. So when you are 11
arrested and taken away, do not worry beforehand about
what you will say, but when the time comes say whatever
is given you to say; for it is not you who will be speaking,
but the Holy Spirit. Brother will betray brother to death, 12
and the father his child; children will turn against their
parents and send them to their death. All will hate you for 13
your allegiance to me; but the man who holds out to the
end will be saved.

'But when you see "the abomination of desolation" 14
usurping a place which is not his (let the reader understand), then those who are in Judaea must take to the hills.
If a man is on the roof, he must not come down into the 15
house to fetch anything out; if in the field, he must not 16
turn back for his coat. Alas for women with child in those 17
days, and for those who have children at the breast! Pray 18
that it may not come in winter. For those days will bring 19
distress such as never has been until now since the beginning of the world which God created—and will never be
again. If the Lord had not cut short that time of troubles, 20
no living thing could survive. However, for the sake of his
own, whom he has chosen, he has cut short the time.

'Then, if anyone says to you, "Look, here is the Messiah", 21
or, "Look, there he is", do not believe it. Impostors will 22
come claiming to be messiahs or prophets, and they will
produce signs and wonders to mislead God's chosen, if such
a thing were possible. But you be on your guard; I have 23
forewarned you of it all.

24 'But in those days, after that distress, the sun will be
25 darkened, the moon will not give her light; the stars will
come falling from the sky, the celestial powers will be
26 shaken. Then they will see the Son of Man coming in the
27 clouds with great power and glory, and he will send out
the angels and gather his chosen from the four winds, from
the farthest bounds of earth to the farthest bounds of
heaven.

28 'Learn a lesson from the fig-tree. When its tender shoots
appear and are breaking into leaf, you know that summer
29 is near. In the same way, when you see all this happening,
you may know that the end is near,[a] at the very door.
30 I tell you this: the present generation will live to see it all.
31 Heaven and earth will pass away; my words will never
pass away.

32 'But about that day or that hour no one knows, not even
the angels in heaven, not even the Son; only the Father.

33 'Be alert, be wakeful.[b] You do not know when the
34 moment comes. It is like a man away from home: he has
left his house and put his servants in charge, each with his
own work to do, and he has ordered the door-keeper to
35 stay awake. Keep awake, then, for you do not know when
the master of the house is coming. Evening or midnight,
36 cock-crow or early dawn—if he comes suddenly, he must
37 not find you asleep. And what I say to you, I say to everyone: Keep awake.'

## THE FINAL CONFLICT

14 NOW THE FESTIVAL of Passover and Unleavened
Bread was only two days off; and the chief priests
and the doctors of the law were trying to devise some
2 cunning plan to seize him and put him to death. 'It must
not be during the festival,' they said, 'or we should have
rioting among the people.'

3 Jesus was at Bethany, in the house of Simon the leper.
As he sat at table, a woman came in carrying a small bottle
of very costly perfume, pure oil of nard. She broke it open
4 and poured the oil over his head. Some of those present
5 said to one another angrily, 'Why this waste? The perfume
might have been sold for thirty pounds[c] and the money

---

[a] *Or* that he is near.          [b] *Some witnesses add* and pray.
[c] *Literally* 300 denarii; *some witnesses read* more than 300 denarii.

given to the poor'; and they turned upon her with fury.
But Jesus said, 'Let her alone. Why must you make 6
trouble for her? It is a fine thing she has done for me. You 7
have the poor among you always, and you can help them
whenever you like; but you will not always have me.
She has done what lay in her power; she is beforehand 8
with anointing my body for burial. I tell you this: wherever 9
in all the world the Gospel is proclaimed, what she has done
will be told as her memorial.'

Then Judas Iscariot, one of the Twelve, went to the chief 10
priests to betray him to them. When they heard what he 11
had come for, they were greatly pleased, and promised
him money; and he began to look for a good opportunity
to betray him.

Now on the first day of Unleavened Bread, when 12
the Passover lambs were being slaughtered, his disciples
said to him, 'Where would you like us to go and prepare
for your Passover supper?' So he sent out two of his 13
disciples with these instructions: 'Go into the city, and
a man will meet you carrying a jar of water. Follow him,
and when he enters a house give this message to the house- 14
holder: "The Master says, 'Where is the room reserved for
me to eat the Passover with my disciples?'" He will show 15
you a large room upstairs, set out in readiness. Make the
preparations for us there.' Then the disciples went off, and 16
when they came into the city they found everything just
as he had told them. So they prepared for Passover.

In the evening he came to the house with the Twelve. 17
As they sat at supper Jesus said, 'I tell you this: one of you 18
will betray me—one who is eating with me.' At this they 19
were dismayed; and one by one they said to him, 'Not I,
surely?' 'It is one of the Twelve', he said, 'who is dipping 20
into the same bowl with me. The Son of Man is going the 21
way appointed for him in the scriptures; but alas for that
man by whom the Son of Man is betrayed! It would be
better for that man if he had never been born.'

During supper he took bread, and having said the bless- 22
ing he broke it and gave it to them, with the words: 'Take
this; this is my body.' Then he took a cup, and having 23
offered thanks to God he gave it to them; and they all
drank from it. And he said, 'This is my blood, the blood of 24
the covenant, shed for many. I tell you this: never again 25
shall I drink from the fruit of the vine until that day when
I drink it new in the kingdom of God.'

26   After singing the Passover Hymn, they went out to the
27   Mount of Olives. And Jesus said, 'You will all fall from your
     faith; for it stands written: "I will strike the shepherd down
28   and the sheep will be scattered." Nevertheless, after I am
29   raised again I will go on before you into Galilee.' Peter
     answered, 'Everyone else may fall away, but I will not.'
30   Jesus said, 'I tell you this: today, this very night, before
     the cock crows twice, you yourself will disown me three
31   times.' But he insisted and repeated: 'Even if I must die
     with you, I will never disown you.' And they all said the
     same.

32   WHEN THEY REACHED a place called Gethsemane, he
33   said to his disciples, 'Sit here while I pray.' And he took
     Peter and James and John with him. Horror and dismay
34   came over him, and he said to them, 'My heart is ready
35   to break with grief; stop here, and stay awake.' Then he
     went forward a little, threw himself on the ground, and
     prayed that, if it were possible, this hour might pass him
36   by. 'Abba, Father,' he said, 'all things are possible to thee;
     take this cup away from me. Yet not what I will, but what
     thou wilt.'
37   He came back and found them asleep; and he said to
     Peter, 'Asleep, Simon? Were you not able to stay awake for
38   one hour? Stay awake, all of you; and pray that you may
     be spared the test. The spirit is willing, but the flesh is
39 40 weak.' Once more he went away and prayed.[a] On his re-
     turn he found them asleep again, for their eyes were heavy;
     and they did not know how to answer him.
41   The third time he came and said to them, 'Still sleeping?
     Still taking your ease? Enough![b] The hour has come. The
42   Son of Man is betrayed to sinful men. Up, let us go for-
     ward! My betrayer is upon us.'
43   Suddenly, while he was still speaking, Judas, one of the
     Twelve, appeared, and with him was a crowd armed with
     swords and cudgels, sent by the chief priests, lawyers, and
44   elders. Now the traitor had agreed with them upon a
     signal: 'The one I kiss is your man; seize him and get him
45   safely away.' When he reached the spot, he stepped for-
     ward at once and said to Jesus, 'Rabbi', and kissed him.
46   Then they seized him and held him fast.
47   One of the party[c] drew his sword, and struck at the High

---

*a Some witnesses add* using the same words.        *b The Greek is*
*obscure; a possible meaning is* 'The money has been paid', 'The account
is settled.'        *c Or of the bystanders.*

Priest's servant, cutting off his ear. Then Jesus spoke: 'Do 48
you take me for a bandit, that you have come out with
swords and cudgels to arrest me? Day after day I was 49
within your reach as I taught in the temple, and you did
not lay hands on me. But let the scriptures be fulfilled.'
Then the disciples all deserted him and ran away. 50

Among those following was a young man with nothing 51
on but a linen cloth. They tried to seize him; but he slipped 52
out of the linen cloth and ran away naked.

THEN THEY LED Jesus away to the High Priest's house, 53
where the chief priests, elders, and doctors of the law were
all assembling. Peter followed him at a distance right 54
into the High Priest's courtyard; and there he remained,
sitting among the attendants, warming himself at the
fire.

The chief priests and the whole Council tried to find 55
some evidence against Jesus to warrant a death-sentence,
but failed to find any. Many gave false evidence against 56
him, but their statements did not tally. Some stood up and 57
gave false evidence against him to this effect: 'We heard 58
him say, "I will pull down this temple, made with human
hands, and in three days I will build another, not made
with hands."' But even on this point their evidence did 59
not agree.

Then the High Priest stood up in his place and ques- 60
tioned Jesus: 'Have you no answer to the charges that
these witnesses bring against you?' But he kept silence; 61
he made no reply.

Again the High Priest questioned him: 'Are you the
Messiah, the Son of the Blessed One?' Jesus said, 'I am; 62
and you will see the Son of Man seated at the right hand of
God[a] and coming with the clouds of heaven.' Then the 63
High Priest tore his robes and said, 'Need we call further
witnesses? You have heard the blasphemy. What is your 64
opinion?' Their judgement was unanimous: that he was
guilty and should be put to death.

Some began to spit on him, blindfolded him, and struck 65
him with their fists, crying out, 'Prophesy!'[b] And the High
Priest's men set upon him with blows.

Meanwhile Peter was still below in the courtyard. One 66
of the High Priest's serving-maids came by and saw him 67
there warming himself. She looked into his face and said,

[a] *Literally of the Power.*          [b] *Some witnesses add Who hit you?*
*as in Matthew and Luke.*

'You were there too, with this man from Nazareth, this
68 Jesus.' But he denied it: 'I know nothing,' he said; 'I do
not understand what you mean.' Then he went outside into
69 the porch;[a] and the maid saw him there again and began
70 to say to the bystanders, 'He is one of them'; and again
he denied it.

Again, a little later, the bystanders said to Peter, 'Surely
71 you are one of them. You must be; you are a Galilean.' At
this he broke out into curses, and with an oath he said, 'I
72 do not know this man you speak of.' Then the cock crew
a second time; and Peter remembered how Jesus had said
to him, 'Before the cock crows twice you will disown me
three times.' And he burst into tears.

15 As soon as morning came, the chief priests, having
made their plan with the elders and lawyers in full council,
put Jesus in chains; then they led him away and handed
2 him over to Pilate. Pilate asked him, 'Are you the king
3 of the Jews?' He replied, 'The words are yours.'[b] And the
4 chief priests brought many charges against him. Pilate
questioned him again: 'Have you nothing to say in your
defence? You see how many charges they are bringing
5 against you.' But, to Pilate's astonishment, Jesus made no
further reply.

6 At the festival season the Governor used to release one
7 prisoner at the people's request. As it happened, the man
known as Barabbas was then in custody with the rebels
8 who had committed murder in the rising. When the crowd
9 appeared[c] asking for the usual favour, Pilate replied, 'Do
10 you wish me to release for you the king of the Jews?' For
he knew it was out of malice that they had brought Jesus
11 before him. But the chief priests incited the crowd to ask
12 him to release Barabbas rather than Jesus. Pilate spoke
to them again: 'Then what shall I do with the man you call
13 king of the Jews?' They shouted back, 'Crucify him!'
14 'Why, what harm has he done?' Pilate asked; but they
15 shouted all the louder, 'Crucify him!' So Pilate, in his
desire to satisfy the mob, released Barabbas to them;
and he had Jesus flogged and handed him over to be
crucified.

16 Then the soldiers took him inside the courtyard (the
Governor's headquarters[d]) and called together the whole
17 company. They dressed him in purple, and plaiting a

---

[a] *Some witnesses insert* and a cock crew.      [b] *Or* It is as you say.
[c] *Some witnesses read* shouted.      [d] *Greek* praetorium.

crown of thorns, placed it on his head. Then they began to    18
salute him with, 'Hail, King of the Jews!' They beat him    19
about the head with a cane and spat upon him, and then
knelt and paid mock homage to him. When they had    20
finished their mockery, they stripped him of the purple
and dressed him in his own clothes.

THEN THEY TOOK HIM OUT to crucify him. A man    21
called Simon, from Cyrene, the father of Alexander and
Rufus, was passing by on his way in from the country, and
they pressed him into service to carry his cross.

They brought him to the place called Golgotha, which    22
means 'Place of a skull'. He was offered drugged wine, but    23
he would not take it. Then they fastened him to the cross.    24
They divided his clothes among them, casting lots to
decide what each should have.

The hour of the crucifixion was nine in the morning, and    25 26
the inscription giving the charge against him read, 'The
king of the Jews.' Two bandits were crucified with him,    27
one on his right and the other on his left.[a]

The passers-by hurled abuse at him: 'Aha!' they cried,    29
wagging their heads, 'you would pull the temple down,
would you, and build it in three days? Come down from    30
the cross and save yourself!' So too the chief priests and    31
lawyers jested with one another: 'He saved others,' they
said, 'but he cannot save himself. Let the Messiah, the    32
king of Israel, come down now from the cross. If we see
that, we shall believe.' Even those who were crucified
with him taunted him.

At midday a darkness fell over the whole land, which    33
lasted till three in the afternoon; and at three Jesus cried    34
aloud, '*Eli, Eli, lema sabachthani?*', which means, 'My God,
my God, why hast thou forsaken me?'[b] Some of the by-    35
standers, on hearing this, said, 'Hark, he is calling Elijah.'
A man ran and soaked a sponge in sour wine and held it to    36
his lips on the end of a cane. 'Let us see', he said, 'if Elijah
will come to take him down.' Then Jesus gave a loud cry    37
and died. And the curtain of the temple was torn in two    38
from top to bottom. And when the centurion who was    39
standing opposite him saw how he died,[c] he said, 'Truly
this man was a son of God.'[d]

[a] *Some witnesses add* (28) Thus that text of Scripture came true which
says, 'He was reckoned among criminals.'        [b] *Some witnesses read*
My God, my God, why hast thou shamed me?        [c] *Some witnesses
read* saw that he died with a cry.        [d] *Or* the Son of God.

40 A NUMBER OF WOMEN were also present, watching from a distance. Among them were Mary of Magdala, Mary the mother of James the younger and of Joseph, and
41 Salome, who had all followed him and waited on him when he was in Galilee, and there were several others who had come up to Jerusalem with him.

42 By this time evening had come; and as it was Prepara-
43 tion-day (that is, the day before the Sabbath), Joseph of Arimathaea, a respected member of the Council, a man who looked forward to the kingdom of God, bravely went
44 in to Pilate and asked for the body of Jesus. Pilate was surprised to hear that he was already dead; so he sent for the centurion and asked him whether it was long since he
45 died. And when he heard the centurion's report, he gave
46 Joseph leave to take the dead body. So Joseph bought a linen sheet, took him down from the cross, and wrapped him in the sheet. Then he laid him in a tomb cut out of the
47 rock, and rolled a stone against the entrance. And Mary of Magdala and Mary the mother of Joseph were watching and saw where he was laid.

16 When the Sabbath was over, Mary of Magdala, Mary the mother of James, and Salome bought[a] aromatic oils in-
2 tending to go and anoint him; and very early on the Sunday morning, just after sunrise, they came to the tomb.
3 They were wondering among themselves who would roll away the stone for them from the entrance to the tomb,
4 when they looked up and saw that the stone, huge as it
5 was, had been rolled back already. They went into the tomb, where they saw a youth sitting on the right-hand side, wearing a white robe; and they were dumbfounded.
6 But he said to them, 'Fear nothing; you are looking for Jesus of Nazareth, who was crucified. He has been raised again; he is not here; look, there is the place where they
7 laid him. But go and give this message to his disciples and Peter: "He is going on before you into Galilee; there
8 you will see him, as he told you."' Then they went out and ran away from the tomb, beside themselves with terror. They said nothing to anybody, for they were afraid.[b]

And they delivered all these instructions briefly to Peter and his companions. Afterwards Jesus himself sent out by

[a] *Some witnesses omit* When the Sabbath . . . Salome, *reading* And they went and bought . . .      [b] *At this point some of the most ancient witnesses bring the book to a close.*

them from east to west the sacred and imperishable message of eternal salvation.[a]

When he had risen from the dead early on Sunday morning he appeared first to Mary of Magdala, from whom he had formerly cast out seven devils. She went and carried the news to his mourning and sorrowful followers, but when they were told that he was alive and that she had seen him they did not believe it. 9 10 11

Later he appeared in a different guise to two of them as they were walking, on their way into the country. These also went and took the news to the others, but again no one believed them. 12 13

Afterwards while the Eleven were at table he appeared to them and reproached them for their incredulity and dullness, because they had not believed those who had seen him after he was raised from the dead. Then he said to them: 'Go forth to every part of the world, and proclaim the Good News to the whole creation. Those who believe it and receive baptism will find salvation; those who do not believe will be condemned. Faith will bring with it these miracles: believers will cast out devils in my name and speak in strange tongues; if they handle snakes or drink any deadly poison, they will come to no harm; and the sick on whom they lay their hands will recover.' 14 15 16 17 18

So after talking with them the Lord Jesus was taken up into heaven, and he took his seat at the right hand of God; but they went out to make their proclamation everywhere, and the Lord worked with them and confirmed their words by the miracles that followed.[b] 19 20

---

[a] *Some witnesses add this paragraph, which in one of them is the conclusion of the book.* [b] *Some witnesses give verses 9–20 either instead of, or in addition to, the paragraph* And they delivered ... eternal salvation *(here printed before verse 9), and so bring the book to a close. Others insert further additional matter.*

# THE
# GOSPEL ACCORDING TO
# LUKE

1 THE AUTHOR TO THEOPHILUS: Many
   writers have undertaken to draw up an account of
2 the events that have happened among us, following
the traditions handed down to us by the original eyewit-
3 nesses and servants of the Gospel. And so I in my turn,
your Excellency, as one who has gone over the whole
course of these events in detail, have decided to write a
4 connected narrative for you, so as to give you authentic
knowledge about the matters of which you have been
informed.

## THE COMING OF CHRIST

5 IN THE DAYS of Herod king of Judaea there was a
   priest named Zechariah, of the division of the priesthood
called after Abijah. His wife also was of priestly descent;
6 her name was Elizabeth. Both of them were upright and
devout, blamelessly observing all the commandments and
7 ordinances of the Lord. But they had no children, for
Elizabeth was barren, and both were well on in years.
8 Once, when it was the turn of his division and he was
9 there to take part in divine service, it fell to his lot, by
priestly custom, to enter the sanctuary of the Lord and
10 offer the incense; and the whole congregation was at prayer
11 outside. It was the hour of the incense-offering. There appeared to him an angel of the Lord, standing on the right
12 of the altar of incense. At this sight, Zechariah was startled,
13 and fear overcame him. But the angel said to him, 'Do not
be afraid, Zechariah; your prayer has been heard: your wife
Elizabeth will bear you a son, and you shall name him
14 John. Your heart will thrill with joy and many will be
15 glad that he was born; for he will be great in the eyes of

the Lord. He shall never touch wine or strong drink. From
his very birth he will be filled with the Holy Spirit; and 16
he will bring back many Israelites to the Lord their God.
He will go before him as forerunner,[a] possessed by the 17
spirit and power of Elijah, to reconcile father and child,
to convert the rebellious to the ways of the righteous, to
prepare a people that shall be fit for the Lord.'

Zechariah said to the angel, 'How can I be sure of this? 18
I am an old man and my wife is well on in years.'

The angel replied, 'I am Gabriel; I stand in attendance 19
upon God, and I have been sent to speak to you and bring
you this good news. But now listen: you will lose your 20
power of speech, and remain silent until the day when these
things happen to you, because you have not believed me,
though at their proper time my words will be proved true.'

Meanwhile the people were waiting for Zechariah, sur- 21
prised that he was staying so long inside. When he did 22
come out he could not speak to them, and they realized
that he had had a vision in the sanctuary. He stood there
making signs to them, and remained dumb.

When his period of duty was completed Zechariah re- 23
turned home. After this his wife Elizabeth conceived, and 24
for five months she lived in seclusion, thinking, 'This is the 25
Lord's doing; now at last he has deigned to take away my
reproach among men.'

In the sixth month the angel Gabriel was sent from God 26
to a town in Galilee called Nazareth, with a message for 27
a girl betrothed to a man named Joseph, a descendant of
David; the girl's name was Mary. The angel went in and 28
said to her, 'Greetings, most favoured one! The Lord is
with you.' But she was deeply troubled by what he said 29
and wondered what this greeting might mean. Then the 30
angel said to her, 'Do not be afraid, Mary, for God has
been gracious to you; you shall conceive and bear a son, 31
and you shall give him the name Jesus. He will be great; 32
he will bear the title "Son of the Most High"; the Lord God
will give him the throne of his ancestor David, and he will 33
be king over Israel[b] for ever; his reign shall never end.'
'How can this be?' said Mary; 'I am still a virgin.' The 34 35
angel answered, 'The Holy Spirit will come upon you, and
the power of the Most High will overshadow you; and for
that reason the holy child to be born will be called "Son of
God".[c] Moreover your kinswoman Elizabeth has herself 36

---

[a] *Or* In his sight he will go forth.          [b] *Literally* the house of Jacob.
[c] *Or* the child to be born will be called holy, "Son of God".

conceived a son in her old age; and she who is reputed barren
37 is now in her sixth month, for God's promises can never
38 fail.'[a] 'Here am I,' said Mary; 'I am the Lord's servant; as
you have spoken, so be it.' Then the angel left her.

39    About this time Mary set out and went straight to a
40 town in the uplands of Judah. She went into Zechariah's
41 house and greeted Elizabeth. And when Elizabeth heard
Mary's greeting, the baby stirred in her womb. Then Eliza-
42 beth was filled with the Holy Spirit and cried aloud, 'God's
blessing is on you above all women, and his blessing is on
43 the fruit of your womb. Who am I, that the mother of my
44 Lord should visit me? I tell you, when your greeting
sounded in my ears, the baby in my womb leapt for joy.
45 How happy is she who has had faith that the Lord's
promise would be fulfilled!'

46    And Mary[b] said:

'Tell out, my soul, the greatness of the Lord,
47    rejoice, rejoice, my spirit, in God my saviour;
48    so tenderly has he looked upon his servant,
           humble as she is.
    For, from this day forth,
    all generations will count me blessed,
49    so wonderfully has he dealt with me,
           the Lord, the Mighty One.

    His name is Holy;
50    his mercy sure from generation to generation
           toward those who fear him;
51    the deeds his own right arm has done
           disclose his might:
    the arrogant of heart and mind he has put to rout,
52    he has brought down monarchs from their thrones,
           but the humble have been lifted high.
53    The hungry he has satisfied with good things,
           the rich sent empty away.

54    He has ranged himself at the side of Israel his servant;
55           firm in his promise to our forefathers,
    he has not forgotten to show mercy to Abraham
           and his children's children, for ever.'

56    Mary stayed with her about three months and then
returned home.

---

[a] *Some witnesses read* for with God nothing will prove impossible.
[b] *So the majority of witnesses; some read* Elizabeth; *the original may
have had no name.*

NOW THE TIME CAME for Elizabeth's child to be born, 57
and she gave birth to a son. When her neighbours and 58
relatives heard what great favour the Lord had shown
her, they were as delighted as she was. Then on the eighth 59
day they came to circumcise the child; and they were
going to name him Zechariah after his father. But his 60
mother spoke up and said, 'No! he is to be called John.'
'But', they said, 'there is nobody in your family who has 61
that name.' They inquired of his father by signs what he 62
would like him to be called. He asked for a writing-tablet 63
and to the astonishment of all wrote down, 'His name is
John.' Immediately his lips and tongue were freed and he 64
began to speak, praising God. All the neighbours were 65
struck with awe, and everywhere in the uplands of Judaea
the whole story became common talk. All who heard it 66
were deeply impressed and said, 'What will this child become?' For indeed the hand of the Lord was upon him.[a]

And Zechariah his father was filled with the Holy Spirit 67
and uttered this prophecy:

'Praise to the God of Israel! 68
For he has turned to his people, saved them and set them
free,
and has raised up a deliverer of victorious power 69
from the house of his servant David.

So he promised: age after age he proclaimed 70
by the lips of his holy prophets,
that he would deliver us from our enemies, 71
out of the hands of all who hate us;
that he would deal mercifully with our fathers, 72
calling to mind his solemn covenant.

Such was the oath he swore to our father Abraham, 73
to rescue us from enemy hands, 74
and grant us, free from fear, to worship him
with a holy worship, with uprightness of heart, 75
in his presence, our whole life long.

And you, my child, you shall be called Prophet of the 76
Highest,
for you will be the Lord's forerunner, to prepare his way
and lead his people to salvation through knowledge 77
of him,
by the forgiveness of their sins:

[a] *Some witnesses read* 'What will this child become, for indeed the hand
of the Lord is upon him?'

78     for in the tender compassion of our God
         the morning sun from heaven will rise[a] upon us,
79   to shine on those who live in darkness, under the cloud
         of death,
         and to guide our feet into the way of peace.'

80     As the child grew up he became strong in spirit; he lived
out in the wilds until the day when he appeared publicly
before Israel.

2   IN THOSE DAYS a decree was issued by the Emperor
Augustus for a registration to be made throughout the
2  Roman world. This was the first registration of its kind;
3  it took place when Quirinius[b] was governor of Syria. For
this purpose everyone made his way to his own town;
4  and so Joseph went up to Judaea from the town of Naz-
5  areth in Galilee, to register at the city of David, called
Bethlehem, because he was of the house of David by
descent; and with him went Mary who was betrothed to
6  him. She was expecting a child, and while they were there
7  the time came for her baby to be born, and she gave birth
to a son, her first-born. She wrapped him in his swaddling
clothes, and laid him in a manger, because there was no
room for them to lodge in the house.
8     Now in this same district there were shepherds out in the
fields, keeping watch through the night over their flock,
9  when suddenly there stood before them an angel of the
Lord, and the splendour of the Lord shone round them.
10  They were terror-stricken, but the angel said, 'Do not be
afraid; I have good news for you: there is great joy coming
11  to the whole people. Today in the city of David a deliverer
12  has been born to you—the Messiah, the Lord.[c] And this is
your sign: you will find a baby lying wrapped in his
13  swaddling clothes, in a manger.' All at once there was with
the angel a great company of the heavenly host, singing the
praises of God:

14          'Glory to God in highest heaven,
         and on earth his peace for men on whom his favour
            rests.'[d]

15     After the angels had left them and gone into heaven the
shepherds said to one another, 'Come, we must go straight

---

[a] *Some witnesses read* has risen.      [b] *Or* This was the first registration carried out while Quirinius . . .      [c] *Some witnesses read* to
you—the Lord's Messiah.      [d] *Some witnesses read* and on earth
his peace, his favour towards men.

to Bethlehem and see this thing that has happened, which
the Lord has made known to us.' So they went with all 16
speed and found their way to Mary and Joseph; and the
baby was lying in the manger. When they saw him, they 17
recounted what they had been told about this child; and 18
all who heard were astonished at what the shepherds said.
But Mary treasured up all these things and pondered over 19
them. Meanwhile the shepherds returned glorifying and 20
praising God for what they had heard and seen; it had all
happened as they had been told.

Eight days later the time came to circumcise him, and 21
he was given the name Jesus, the name given by the angel
before he was conceived.

Then, after their purification had been completed in 22
accordance with the Law of Moses, they brought him up
to Jerusalem to present him to the Lord (as prescribed in 23
the law of the Lord: 'Every first-born male shall be deemed
to belong to the Lord'), and also to make the offering as 24
stated in the law: 'A pair of turtle doves or two young
pigeons.'

There was at that time in Jerusalem a man called Simeon. 25
This man was upright and devout, one who watched and
waited for the restoration of Israel, and the Holy Spirit
was upon him. It had been disclosed to him by the Holy 26
Spirit that he would not see death until he had seen the
Lord's Messiah. Guided by the Spirit he came into the 27
temple; and when the parents brought in the child Jesus to
do for him what was customary under the Law, he took 28
him in his arms, praised God, and said:

'This day, Master, thou givest thy servant his discharge 29
        in peace;
     now thy promise is fulfilled.
For I have seen with my own eyes 30
the deliverance which thou hast made ready in full view 31
        of all the nations:
a light that will be a revelation to the heathen, 32
     and glory to thy people Israel.'

The child's father and mother were full of wonder at 33
what was being said about him. Simeon blessed them and 34
said to Mary his mother, 'This child is destined to be a sign
which men reject; and you too shall be pierced to the 35
heart. Many in Israel will stand or fall*a* because of him,
and thus the secret thoughts of many will be laid bare.'

        *a* Or Many in Israel will fall and rise again . . .

95

36   There was also a prophetess, Anna the daughter of
     Phanuel, of the tribe of Asher. She was a very old woman,
     who had lived seven years with her husband after she was
37   first married, and then alone as a widow to the age of
     eighty-four.[a] She never left the temple, but worshipped
38   day and night, fasting and praying. Coming up at that
     very moment, she returned thanks to God; and she talked
     about the child to all who were looking for the liberation
     of Jerusalem.
39      When they had done everything prescribed in the law
     of the Lord, they returned to Galilee to their own town of
40   Nazareth. The child grew big and strong and full of wis-
     dom; and God's favour was upon him.
41      Now it was the practice of his parents to go to Jerusalem
42   every year for the Passover festival; and when he was
43   twelve, they made the pilgrimage as usual. When the
     festive season was over and they started for home, the boy
     Jesus stayed behind in Jerusalem. His parents did not
44   know of this; but thinking that he was with the party they
     journeyed on for a whole day, and only then did they begin
45   looking for him among their friends and relations. As they
     could not find him they returned to Jerusalem to look for
46   him; and after three days they found him sitting in the
     temple surrounded by the teachers, listening to them and
47   putting questions; and all who heard him were amazed at
48   his intelligence and the answers he gave. His parents were
     astonished to see him there, and his mother said to him,
     'My son, why have you treated us like this? Your father
     and I have been searching for you in great anxiety.'
49   'What made you search?' he said. 'Did you not know that
50   I was bound to be in my Father's house?' But they did not
51   understand what he meant. Then he went back with them
     to Nazareth, and continued to be under their authority;
52   his mother treasured up all these things in her heart. As
     Jesus grew up he advanced in wisdom and in favour with
     God and men.

3 IN THE FIFTEENTH YEAR of the Emperor Tiberius,
     when Pontius Pilate was governor of Judaea, when Herod
     was prince of Galilee, his brother Philip prince of Ituraea
2    and Trachonitis, and Lysanias prince of Abilene, during
     the high-priesthood of Annas and Caiaphas, the word of
3    God came to John son of Zechariah in the wilderness. And
     he went all over the Jordan valley proclaiming a baptism

     [a] *Or* widow for another eighty-four years.

in token of repentance for the forgiveness of sins, as it is  4
written in the book of the prophecies of Isaiah:

> 'A voice crying aloud in the wilderness,
> "Prepare a way for the Lord;
> clear a straight path for him.
> Every ravine shall be filled in,                                  5
> and every mountain and hill levelled;
> the corners shall be straightened,
> and the rugged ways made smooth;
> and all mankind shall see God's deliverance."'                    6

Crowds of people came out to be baptized by him, and  7
he said to them: 'You vipers' brood! Who warned you to
escape from the coming retribution? Then prove your re-  8
pentance by the fruit it bears; and do not begin saying to
yourselves, "We have Abraham for our father." I tell you
that God can make children for Abraham out of these
stones here. Already the axe is laid to the roots of the  9
trees; and every tree that fails to produce good fruit is cut
down and thrown on the fire.'

The people asked him, 'Then what are we to do?' He re-  10 11
plied, 'The man with two shirts must share with him who
has none, and anyone who has food must do the same.'
Among those who came to be baptized were tax-gatherers,  12
and they said to him, 'Master, what are we to do?' He told  13
them, 'Exact no more than the assessment.' Soldiers on  14
service also asked him, 'And what of us?' To them he said,
'No bullying; no blackmail; make do with your pay!'

The people were on the tiptoe of expectation, all wonder-  15
ing about John, whether perhaps he was the Messiah, but  16
he spoke out and said to them all: 'I baptize you with
water; but there is one to come who is mightier than I.
I am not fit to unfasten his shoes. He will baptize you with
the Holy Spirit and with fire. His shovel is ready in his  17
hand, to winnow his threshing-floor and gather the wheat
into his granary; but he will burn the chaff on a fire that
can never go out.'

In this and many other ways he made his appeal to the  18
people and announced the good news. But Prince Herod,  19
when he was rebuked by him over the affair of his brother's
wife Herodias and for his other misdeeds, crowned them  20
all by shutting John up in prison.

DURING A GENERAL BAPTISM of the people, when  21
Jesus too had been baptized and was praying, heaven

22 opened and the Holy Spirit descended on him in bodily form like a dove; and there came a voice from heaven, 'Thou art my Son, my Beloved;*a* on thee my favour rests.'*b*

23 When Jesus began his work he was about thirty years
24 old, the son, as people thought, of Joseph, son of Heli, son of Matthat, son of Levi, son of Melchi, son of Jannai, son
25 of Joseph, son of Mattathiah, son of Amos, son of Nahum,
26 son of Esli, son of Naggai, son of Maath, son of Mattathiah,
27 son of Semein, son of Josech, son of Joda, son of Johanan, son of Rhesa, son of Zerubbabel, son of Shealtiel,
28 son of Neri, son of Melchi, son of Addi, son of Cosam, son
29 of Elmadam, son of Er, son of Joshua, son of Eliezer, son of
30 Jorim, son of Matthat, son of Levi, son of Symeon, son of
31 Judah, son of Joseph, son of Jonam, son of Eliakim, son of Melea, son of Menna, son of Mattatha, son of Nathan,
32 son of David, son of Jesse, son of Obed, son of Boaz,
33 son of Salmon, son of Nahshon, son of Amminadab,*c* son
34 of Arni,*d* son of Hezron, son of Perez, son of Judah, son of Jacob, son of Isaac, son of Abraham, son of Terah, son of
35 Nahor, son of Serug, son of Reu, son of Peleg, son of Eber,
36 son of Shelah, son of Cainan, son of Arpachshad, son of
37 Shem, son of Noah, son of Lamech, son of Methuselah, son of Enoch, son of Jared, son of Mahalaleel, son of Cainan,
38 son of Enosh, son of Seth, son of Adam, son of God.

4 Full of the Holy Spirit, Jesus returned from the Jordan,
2 and for forty days was led by the Spirit up and down the wilderness and tempted by the devil.

All that time he had nothing to eat, and at the end of it
3 he was famished. The devil said to him, 'If you are the Son
4 of God, tell this stone to become bread.' Jesus answered, 'Scripture says, "Man cannot live on bread alone."'

5 Next the devil led him up and showed him in a flash all
6 the kingdoms of the world. 'All this dominion will I give to you,' he said, 'and the glory that goes with it; for it has been put in my hands and I can give it to anyone I choose.
7 You have only to do homage to me and it shall all be yours.'
8 Jesus answered him, 'Scripture says, "You shall do homage to the Lord your God and worship him alone."'

9 The devil took him to Jerusalem and set him on the parapet of the temple. 'If you are the Son of God,' he said,
10 'throw yourself down; for Scripture says, "He will give

---

*a Or* Thou art my only Son.       *b Some witnesses read* My Son art thou; this day I have begotten thee.       *c Some witnesses add* son of Admin.       *d Some witnesses read* Aram; *Ruth 4. 19 and 1 Chronicles 2. 9 have* Ram.

his angels orders to take care of you", and again, "They  11
will support you in their arms for fear you should strike
your foot against a stone." ' Jesus answered him, 'It has  12
been said, "You are not to put the Lord your God to the
test." '

So, having come to the end of all his temptations, the  13
devil departed, biding his time.


## IN GALILEE:
## SUCCESS AND OPPOSITION

THEN JESUS, armed with the power of the Spirit,  14
returned to Galilee; and reports about him spread
through the whole country-side. He taught in their syna-  15
gogues and all men sang his praises.

So he came to Nazareth, where he had been brought up,  16
and went to synagogue on the Sabbath day as he regularly
did. He stood up to read the lesson and was handed the  17
scroll of the prophet Isaiah. He opened the scroll and found
the passage which says,

'The spirit of the Lord is upon me because he has anointed  18
    me;
he has sent me to announce good news to the poor,
to proclaim release for prisoners and recovery of sight
    for the blind;
to let the broken victims go free,
to proclaim the year of the Lord's favour.'  19

He rolled up the scroll, gave it back to the attendant, and  20
sat down; and all eyes in the synagogue were fixed on him.

He began to speak: 'Today', he said, 'in your very hear-  21
ing this text has come true.'[a] There was a general stir of  22
admiration; they were surprised that words of such grace
should fall from his lips. 'Is not this Joseph's son?' they
asked. Then Jesus said, 'No doubt you will quote the pro-  23
verb to me, "Physician, heal yourself!", and say, "We have
heard of all your doings at Capernaum; do the same here
in your own home town." I tell you this,' he went on: 'no  24
prophet is recognized in his own country. There were many  25
widows in Israel, you may be sure, in Elijah's time, when
for three years and six months the skies never opened, and

[a] *Or* 'Today', he said, 'this text which you have just heard has come
true.'

26 famine lay hard over the whole country; yet it was to none of those that Elijah was sent, but to a widow at Sarepta in
27 the territory of Sidon. Again, in the time of the prophet Elisha there were many lepers in Israel, and not one of
28 them was healed, but only Naaman, the Syrian.' At these
29 words the whole congregation were infuriated. They leapt up, threw him out of the town, and took him to the brow of the hill on which it was built, meaning to hurl him over
30 the edge. But he walked straight through them all, and went away.

31 Coming down to Capernaum, a town in Galilee, he taught
32 the people on the Sabbath, and they were astounded at his
33 teaching, for what he said had the note of authority. Now there was a man in the synagogue possessed by a devil, an
34 unclean spirit. He shrieked at the top of his voice, 'What do you want with us, Jesus of Nazareth? Have you[a] come to destroy us? I know who you are—the Holy One of God.'
35 Jesus rebuked him: 'Be silent', he said, 'and come out of him.' Then the devil, after throwing the man down in front of the people, left him without doing him any in-
36 jury. Amazement fell on them all and they said to one another: 'What is there in this man's words? He gives orders to the unclean spirits with authority and power,
37 and out they go.' So the news spread, and he was the talk of the whole district.

38 On leaving the synagogue he went to Simon's house. Simon's mother-in-law was in the grip of a high fever; and
39 they asked him to help her. He came and stood over her and rebuked the fever. It left her, and she got up at once and waited on them.

40 At sunset all who had friends suffering from one disease or another brought them to him; and he laid his hands on
41 them one by one and cured them. Devils also came out of many of them, shouting, 'You are the Son of God.' But he rebuked them and forbade them to speak, because they knew that he was the Messiah.

42 When day broke he went out and made his way to a lonely spot. But the people went in search of him, and when they came to where he was they pressed him not to leave them.
43 But he said, 'I must give the good news of the kingdom of God to the other towns also, for that is what I was sent
44 to do.' So he proclaimed the Gospel in the synagogues of Judaea.[b]

[a] *Or* You have.      ` *Or* the Jewish synagogues; *some witnesses* read the synagogues of Galilee.

One day as he stood by the Lake of Gennesaret, and the 5
people crowded upon him to listen to the word of God, he 2
noticed two boats lying at the water's edge; the fishermen
had come ashore and were washing their nets. He got into 3
one of the boats, which belonged to Simon, and asked him
to put out a little way from the shore; then he went on
teaching the crowds from his seat in the boat. When he had 4
finished speaking, he said to Simon, 'Put out into deep
water and let down your nets for a catch.' Simon answered, 5
'Master, we were hard at work all night and caught nothing
at all; but if you say so, I will let down the nets.' They did 6
so and made a big haul of fish; and their nets began to
split. So they signalled to their partners in the other boat 7
to come and help them. This they did, and loaded both
boats to the point of sinking. When Simon saw what had 8
happened he fell at Jesus's knees and said, 'Go, Lord, leave
me, sinner that I am!' For he and all his companions were 9
amazed at the catch they had made; so too were his part- 10
ners James and John, Zebedee's sons. 'Do not be afraid,'
said Jesus to Simon; 'from now on you will be catching
men.' As soon as they had brought the boats to land, they 11
left everything and followed him.

He was once in a certain town where there happened to 12
be a man covered with leprosy; seeing Jesus, he bowed to
the ground and begged his help. 'Sir,' he said, 'if only you
will, you can cleanse me.' Jesus stretched out his hand, 13
touched him, and said, 'Indeed I will; be clean again.' The
leprosy left him immediately. Jesus then ordered him not 14
to tell anybody. 'But go,' he said, 'show yourself to the
priest, and make the offering laid down by Moses for
your cleansing; that will certify the cure.' But the talk 15
about him spread all the more; great crowds gathered
to hear him and to be cured of their ailments. And 16
from time to time he would withdraw to lonely places for
prayer.

One day he was teaching, and Pharisees and teachers of 17
the law were sitting round. People had come from every
village of Galilee and from Judaea and Jerusalem,*a* and the
power of the Lord was with him to heal the sick. Some 18
men appeared carrying a paralysed man on a bed. They
tried to bring him in and set him down in front of Jesus, but 19
finding no way to do so because of the crowd, they went

---

*a Some witnesses read* and Pharisees and teachers of the law, who had
come from every village of Galilee and from Judaea and Jerusalem,
were sitting round.

up on to the roof and let him down through the tiling, bed and all, into the middle of the company in front of Jesus.

20 When Jesus saw their faith, he said, 'Man, your sins are forgiven you.'

21 The lawyers and the Pharisees began saying to themselves, 'Who is this fellow with his blasphemous talk?

22 Who but God alone can forgive sins?' But Jesus knew what they were thinking and answered them: 'Why do you

23 harbour thoughts like these? Is it easier to say, "Your sins

24 are forgiven you", or to say, "Stand up and walk"? But to convince you that the Son of Man has the right on earth to forgive sins'—he turned to the paralysed man—'I say to

25 you, stand up, take your bed, and go home.' And at once he rose to his feet before their eyes, took up the bed he had

26 been lying on, and went home praising God. They were all lost in amazement and praised God; filled with awe they said, 'You would never believe the things we have seen today.'

27 Later, when he went out, he saw a tax-gatherer, Levi by name, at his seat in the custom-house, and said to him,

28 'Follow me'; and he rose to his feet, left everything behind, and followed him.

29 Afterwards Levi held a big reception in his house for Jesus; among the guests was a large party of tax-gatherers

30 and others. The Pharisees and the lawyers of their sect complained to his disciples: 'Why do you eat and drink',

31 they said, 'with tax-gatherers and sinners?' Jesus answered them: 'It is not the healthy that need a doctor, but

32 the sick; I have not come to invite virtuous people, but to call sinners to repentance.'

33 Then they said to him, 'John's disciples are much given to fasting and the practice of prayer, and so are the

34 disciples of the Pharisees; but yours eat and drink.' Jesus replied, 'Can you make the bridegroom's friends fast while

35 the bridegroom is with them? But a time will come: the bridegroom will be taken away from them, and that will be the time for them to fast.'

36 He told them this parable also: 'No one tears a piece from a new cloak to patch an old one; if he does, he will have made a hole in the new cloak, and the patch from the

37 new will not match the old. Nor does anyone put new wine into old wine-skins; if he does, the new wine will burst the

38 skins, the wine will be wasted, and the skins ruined. Fresh

39 skins for new wine! And no one after drinking old wine wants new; for he says, "The old wine is good."'

One Sabbath he was going through the cornfields, and 6
his disciples were plucking the ears of corn, rubbing them
in their hands, and eating them. Some of the Pharisees 2
said, 'Why are you doing what is forbidden on the Sabbath?' Jesus answered, 'So you have not read what David 3
did when he and his men were hungry? He went into the 4
House of God and took the sacred bread to eat and gave it
to his men, though priests alone are allowed to eat it, and
no one else.' He also said, 'The Son of Man is sovereign even 5
over the Sabbath.'

On another Sabbath he had gone to synagogue and was 6
teaching. There happened to be a man in the congregation
whose right arm was withered; and the lawyers and the 7
Pharisees were on the watch to see whether Jesus would
cure him on the Sabbath, so that they could find a charge
to bring against him. But he knew what was in their minds 8
and said to the man with the withered arm, 'Get up and
stand out here.' So he got up and stood there. Then Jesus 9
said to them, 'I put the question to you: is it permitted to do
good or to do evil on the Sabbath, to save life or to destroy
it?' He looked round at them all and then said to the man, 10
'Stretch out your arm.' He did so, and his arm was restored.
But they were beside themselves with anger, and began to 11
discuss among themselves what they could do to Jesus.

During this time he went out one day into the hills to 12
pray, and spent the night in prayer to God. When day 13
broke he called his disciples to him, and from among them
he chose twelve and named them Apostles: Simon, to 14
whom he gave the name of Peter, and Andrew his brother,
James and John, Philip and Bartholomew, Matthew and 15
Thomas, James son of Alphaeus, and Simon who was
called the Zealot, Judas son of James, and Judas Iscariot 16
who turned traitor.

He came down the hill with them and took his stand on 17
level ground. There was a large concourse of his disciples
and great numbers of people from Jerusalem and Judaea
and from the seaboard of Tyre and Sidon, who had come to
listen to him, and to be cured of their diseases. Those who 18
were troubled with unclean spirits were cured; and every- 19
one in the crowd was trying to touch him, because power
went out from him and cured them all.

THEN TURNING TO HIS DISCIPLES he began to speak: 20
'How blest are you who are in need; the kingdom of God
is yours.

21    'How blest are you who now go hungry; your hunger shall be satisfied.

'How blest are you who weep now; you shall laugh.

22    'How blest you are when men hate you, when they out-law you and insult you, and ban your very name as in-
23    famous, because of the Son of Man. On that day be glad and dance for joy; for assuredly you have a rich reward in heaven; in just the same way did their fathers treat the prophets.

24    'But alas for you who are rich; you have had your time of happiness.

25    'Alas for you who are well-fed now; you shall go hungry.

'Alas for you who laugh now; you shall mourn and weep.

26    'Alas for you when all speak well of you; just so did their fathers treat the false prophets.

27    'But to you who hear me I say:

'Love your enemies; do good to those who hate you;
28    bless those who curse you; pray for those who treat you
29    spitefully. When a man hits you on the cheek, offer him the other cheek too; when a man takes your coat, let him
30    have your shirt as well. Give to everyone who asks you; when a man takes what is yours, do not demand it back.
31    Treat others as you would like them to treat you.

32    'If you love only those who love you, what credit is that
33    to you? Even sinners love those who love them. Again, if you do good only to those who do good to you, what credit
34    is that to you? Even sinners do as much. And if you lend only where you expect to be repaid, what credit is that to you? Even sinners lend to each other to be repaid in
35    full. But you must love your enemies and do good; and lend without expecting any return;[a] and you will have a rich reward: you will be sons of the Most High, because he
36    himself is kind to the ungrateful and wicked. Be com-passionate as your Father is compassionate.

37    'Pass no judgement, and you will not be judged; do not condemn, and you will not be condemned; acquit, and you
38    will be acquitted; give, and gifts will be given you. Good measure, pressed down, shaken together, and running over, will be poured into your lap; for whatever measure you deal out to others will be dealt to you in return.'

39    He also offered them a parable: 'Can one blind man be guide to another? Will they not both fall into the ditch?

[a] *Or* without ever giving up hope; *some witnesses read* without giving up hope of anyone.

A pupil is not superior to his teacher; but everyone, when 40
his training is complete, will reach his teacher's level.

'Why do you look at the speck of sawdust in your 41
brother's eye, with never a thought for the great plank in
your own? How can you say to your brother, "My dear 42
brother, let me take the speck out of your eye", when you
are blind to the plank in your own? You hypocrite! First
take the plank out of your own eye, and then you will see
clearly to take the speck out of your brother's.

'There is no such thing as a good tree producing worth- 43
less fruit, nor yet a worthless tree producing good fruit.
For each tree is known by its own fruit: you do not gather 44
figs from thistles, and you do not pick grapes from
brambles. A good man produces good from the store of 45
good within himself; and an evil man from evil within
produces evil. For the words that the mouth utters come
from the overflowing of the heart.

'Why do you keep calling me "Lord, Lord"—and never 46
do what I tell you? Everyone who comes to me and hears 47
what I say, and acts upon it—I will show you what he is
like. He is like a man who, in building his house, dug deep 48
and laid the foundations on rock. When the flood came, the
river burst upon that house, but could not shift it, because
it had been soundly built. But he who hears and does not 49
act is like a man who built his house on the soil without
foundations. As soon as the river burst upon it, the house
collapsed, and fell with a great crash.'

WHEN HE HAD FINISHED addressing the people, he 7
went to Capernaum. A centurion there had a servant 2
whom he valued highly; this servant was ill and near to
death. Hearing about Jesus, he sent some Jewish elders 3
with the request that he would come and save his servant's
life. They approached Jesus and pressed their petition 4
earnestly: 'He deserves this favour from you,' they said,
'for he is a friend of our nation and it is he who built us our 5
synagogue.' Jesus went with them; but when he was not 6
far from the house, the centurion sent friends with this
message: 'Do not trouble further, sir; it is not for me to
have you under my roof, and that is why I did not presume 7
to approach you in person. But say the word and my
servant will be cured. I know, for in my position I am my- 8
self under orders, with soldiers under me. I say to one,
"Go", and he goes; to another, "Come here", and he comes;
and to my servant, "Do this", and he does it.' When Jesus 9

heard this, he admired the man, and, turning to the crowd that was following him, he said, 'I tell you, nowhere, even

10 in Israel, have I found faith like this.' And the messengers returned to the house and found the servant in good health.

11 Afterwards[a] Jesus went to a town called Nain, accom-
12 panied by his disciples and a large crowd. As he approached the gate of the town he met a funeral. The dead man was the only son of his widowed mother; and many of the
13 townspeople were there with her. When the Lord saw her his heart went out to her, and he said, 'Weep no more.'
14 With that he stepped forward and laid his hand on the bier; and the bearers halted. Then he spoke: 'Young man,
15 rise up!' The dead man sat up and began to speak; and
16 Jesus gave him back to his mother. Deep awe fell upon them all, and they praised God. 'A great prophet has arisen among us', they said, and again, 'God has shown his care
17 for his people.' The story of what he had done ran through all parts of Judaea and the whole neighbourhood.

18 19 John too was informed of all this by his disciples. Summoning two of their number he sent them to the Lord with this message: 'Are you the one who is to come, or are we
20 to expect some other?' The messengers made their way to Jesus and said, 'John the Baptist has sent us to you: he asks, "Are you the one who is to come, or are we to expect
21 some other?"' There and then he cured many sufferers from diseases, plagues, and evil spirits; and on many blind
22 people he bestowed sight. Then he gave them his answer: 'Go', he said, 'and tell John what you have seen and heard: how the blind recover their sight, the lame walk, the lepers are made clean, the deaf hear, the dead are raised to life,
23 the poor are hearing the good news—and happy is the man who does not find me a stumbling-block.'
24 After John's messengers had left, Jesus began to speak about him to the crowds: 'What was the spectacle that drew you to the wilderness? A reed-bed swept by the wind?
25 No? Then what did you go out to see? A man dressed in silks and satins? Surely you must look in palaces for grand
26 clothes and luxury. But what did you go out to see? A prophet? Yes indeed, and far more than a prophet.
27 He is the man of whom Scripture says,

"Here is my herald, whom I send on ahead of you,
    and he will prepare your way before you."

*a Some witnesses read* On the next day.

I tell you, there is not a mother's son greater than John, 28
and yet the least in the kingdom of God is greater than he.'

When they heard him, all the people, including the 29
tax-gatherers, praised God, for they had accepted John's
baptism; but the Pharisees and lawyers, who refused his 30
baptism, had rejected[a] God's purpose for their themselves.

'How can I describe the people of this generation? What 31
are they like? They are like children sitting in the market- 32
place and shouting at each other,

"We piped for you and you would not dance."
"We wept and wailed, and you would not mourn."

For John the Baptist came neither eating bread nor drink- 33
ing wine, and you say, "He is possessed." The Son of Man 34
came eating and drinking, and you say, "Look at him!
a glutton and a drinker, a friend of tax-gatherers and
sinners!" And yet God's wisdom is proved right by all who 35
are her children.'

One of the Pharisees invited him to eat with him; he 36
went to the Pharisee's house and took his place at table.
A woman who was living an immoral life in the town had 37
learned that Jesus was at table in the Pharisee's house and
had brought oil of myrrh in a small flask. She took her 38
place behind him, by his feet, weeping. His feet were
wetted with her tears and she wiped them with her hair,
kissing them and anointing them with the myrrh. When 39
his host the Pharisee saw this he said to himself, 'If this
fellow were a real prophet, he would know who this woman
is that touches him, and what sort of woman she is, a
sinner.' Jesus took him up and said, 'Simon, I have some- 40
thing to say to you.' 'Speak on, Master', said he. 'Two men 41
were in debt to a money-lender: one owed him five hundred
silver pieces, the other fifty. As neither had anything to 42
pay with he let them both off. Now, which will love him
most?' Simon replied, 'I should think the one that was let 43
off most.' 'You are right', said Jesus. Then turning to the 44
woman, he said to Simon, 'You see this woman? I came to
your house: you provided no water for my feet; but this
woman has made my feet wet with her tears and wiped
them with her hair. You gave me no kiss; but she has been 45
kissing my feet ever since I came in. You did not anoint 46

[a] *Or '. . . greater than he. And all the people, including the tax-
gatherers, when they heard him, accepted John's baptism and acknowledged the righteous dealing of God; but the Pharisees and lawyers,
by refusing his baptism, rejected . . .'*

my head with oil; but she has anointed my feet with myrrh.
47 And so, I tell you, her great love proves that her many sins
have been forgiven; where little has been forgiven, little
48 love is shown.' Then he said to her, 'Your sins are forgiven.'
49 The other guests began to ask themselves, 'Who is this,
50 that he can forgive sins?' But he said to the woman, 'Your
faith has saved you; go in peace.'

8 AFTER THIS he went journeying from town to town and
village to village, proclaiming the good news of the king-
2 dom of God. With him were the Twelve and a number of
women who had been set free from evil spirits and in-
firmities: Mary, known as Mary of Magdala, from whom
3 seven devils had come out, Joanna, the wife of Chuza a
steward of Herod's, Susanna, and many others. These
women provided for them out of their own resources.
4 People were now gathering in large numbers, and as they
made their way to him from one town after another, he said
5 in a parable: 'A sower went out to sow his seed. And as he
sowed, some seed fell along the footpath, where it was
6 trampled on, and the birds ate it up. Some seed fell on
rock and, after coming up, withered for lack of moisture.
7 Some seed fell in among thistles, and the thistles grew up
8 with it and choked it. And some of the seed fell into
good soil, and grew, and yielded a hundredfold.' As he
said this he called out, 'If you have ears to hear, then
hear.'
9 10 His disciples asked him what this parable meant, and he
said, 'It has been granted to you to know the secrets of the
kingdom of God; but the others have only parables, so
that they may look but see nothing, hear but understand
nothing.
11 'This is what the parable means. The seed is the word of
12 God. Those along the footpath are the men who hear it,
and then the devil comes and carries off the word from
13 their hearts for fear they should believe and be saved. The
seed sown on rock stands for those who receive the word
with joy when they hear it, but have no root; they are
believers for a while, but in the time of testing they desert.
14 That which fell among thistles represents those who hear,
but their further growth is choked by cares and wealth
and the pleasures of life, and they bring nothing to
15 maturity. But the seed in good soil represents those who
bring a good and honest heart to the hearing of the word,
hold it fast, and by their perseverance yield a harvest.

'Nobody lights a lamp and then covers it with a basin 16
or puts it under the bed. On the contrary, he puts it on a
lamp-stand so that those who come in may see the light.
For there is nothing hidden that will not become public, 17
nothing under cover that will not be made known and
brought into the open.

'Take care, then, how you listen; for the man who has 18
will be given more, and the man who has not will forfeit
even what he thinks he has.'

His mother and his brothers arrived but could not get to 19
him for the crowd. He was told, 'Your mother and brothers 20
are standing outside, and they want to see you.' He replied, 21
'My mother and my brothers—they are those who hear the
word of God and act upon it.'

One day he got into a boat with his disciples and said 22
to them, 'Let us cross over to the other side of the lake.'
So they put out; and as they sailed along he went to sleep. 23
Then a heavy squall struck the lake; they began to ship
water and were in grave danger. They went to him, and 24
roused him, crying, 'Master, Master, we are sinking!' He
awoke, and rebuked the wind and the turbulent waters.
The storm subsided and all was calm. 'Where is your 25
faith?' he asked. In fear and astonishment they said to one
another, 'Who can this be? He gives his orders to wind and
waves, and they obey him.'

So they landed in the country of the Gergesenes,[a] which 26
is opposite Galilee. As he stepped ashore he was met by a 27
man from the town who was possessed by devils. For a
long time he had neither worn clothes nor lived in a house,
but stayed among the tombs. When he saw Jesus he cried 28
out, and fell at his feet shouting. 'What do you want with
me, Jesus, son of the Most High God? I implore you, do not
torment me.'

For Jesus was already ordering the unclean spirit to 29
come out of the man. Many a time it had seized him, and
then, for safety's sake, they would secure him with chains
and fetters; but each time he broke loose, and with the
devil in charge made off to the solitary places.

Jesus asked him, 'What is your name?' 'Legion', he re- 30
plied. This was because so many devils had taken possession of him. And they begged him not to banish them to 31
the Abyss.

There happened to be a large herd of pigs nearby, feed- 32
ing on the hill; and the spirits begged him to let them go

[a] *Some witnesses read* Gerasenes; *others read* Gadarenes.

33 into these pigs. He gave them leave; the devils came out of the man and went into the pigs, and the herd rushed over the edge into the lake and were drowned.

34 The men in charge of them saw what had happened, and, taking to their heels, they carried the news to the town and 35 country-side; and the people came out to see for themselves. When they came to Jesus, and found the man from whom the devils had gone out sitting at his feet clothed and 36 in his right mind, they were afraid. The spectators told 37 them how the madman had been cured. Then the whole population of the Gergesene*a* district asked him to go, for they were in the grip of a great fear. So he got into the 38 boat and returned. The man from whom the devils had gone out begged leave to go with him; but Jesus sent him 39 away: 'Go back home,' he said, 'and tell them everything that God has done for you.' The man went all over the town spreading the news of what Jesus had done for him.

40 When Jesus returned, the people welcomed him, for they 41 were all expecting him. Then a man appeared—Jairus was his name and he was president of the synagogue. Throwing himself down at Jesus's feet he begged him to come to his 42 house, because he had an only daughter, about twelve years old, who was dying. And while Jesus was on his way he could hardly breathe for the crowds.

43 Among them was a woman who had suffered from haemorrhages for twelve years; and*b* nobody had been able to 44 cure her. She came up from behind and touched the edge 45 of*c* his cloak, and at once her haemorrhage stopped. Jesus said, 'Who was it that touched me?' All disclaimed it, and Peter and his companions said, 'Master, the crowds are 46 hemming you in and pressing upon you!' But Jesus said, 'Someone did touch me, for I felt that power had gone out 47 from me.' Then the woman, seeing that she was detected, came trembling and fell at his feet. Before all the people she explained why she had touched him and how she had 48 been instantly cured. He said to her, 'My daughter, your faith has cured you. Go in peace.'

49 While he was still speaking, a man came from the president's house with the message, 'Your daughter is dead; 50 trouble the Rabbi no further.' But Jesus heard, and interposed. 'Do not be afraid,' he said; 'only show faith and she 51 will be well again.' On arrival at the house he allowed no

---

*a Some witnesses read* Gerasene; *others read* Gadarene.  *b Some witnesses add* though she had spent all she had on doctors.  *c Some witnesses omit* the edge of.

one to go in with him except Peter, John, and James, and
the child's father and mother. And all were weeping and 52
lamenting for her. He said, 'Weep no more; she is not dead:
she is asleep'; and they only laughed at him, well knowing 53
that she was dead. But Jesus took hold of her hand and 54
called her: 'Get up, my child.' Her spirit returned, she stood 55
up immediately, and he told them to give her something to
eat. Her parents were astounded; but he forbade them to 56
tell anyone what had happened.

HE NOW CALLED the Twelve together and gave them 9
power and authority to overcome all the devils and to cure
diseases, and sent them to proclaim the kingdom of God 2
and to heal. 'Take nothing for the journey,' he told them, 3
'neither stick nor pack, neither bread nor money; nor are
you each to have a second coat. When you are admitted to 4
a house, stay there, and go on from there. As for those who 5
will not receive you, when you leave their town shake the
dust off your feet as a warning to them.' So they set out 6
and travelled from village to village, and everywhere they
told the good news and healed the sick.

Now Prince Herod heard of all that was happening, and 7
did not know what to make of it; for some were saying
that John had been raised from the dead, others that Elijah 8
had appeared, others again that one of the old prophets
had come back to life. Herod said, 'As for John, I beheaded 9
him myself; but who is this I hear such talk about?' And
he was anxious to see him.

On their return the apostles told Jesus all they had done; 10
and he took them with him and withdrew privately to a
town called Bethsaida. But the crowds found out and 11
followed him. He welcomed them, and spoke to them about
the kingdom of God, and cured those who were in need of
healing. When evening was drawing on, the Twelve came 12
up to him and said, 'Send these people away; then they
can go into the villages and farms round about to find food
and lodging; for we are in a lonely place here.' 'Give them 13
something to eat yourselves', he replied. But they said, 'All
we have is five loaves and two fishes, nothing more—unless
perhaps we ourselves are to go and buy provisions for all this
company.' (There were about five thousand men.) He said to 14
his disciples, 'Make them sit down in groups of fifty or so.'
They did so and got them all seated. Then, taking the five 15 16
loaves and the two fishes, he looked up to heaven, said the
blessing over them, broke them, and gave them to the

17 disciples to distribute to the people. They all ate to their hearts' content; and when the scraps they left were picked up, they filled twelve great baskets.

18 One day when he was praying alone in the presence of his disciples, he asked them, 'Who do the people say I am?'
19 They answered, 'Some say John the Baptist, others Elijah, others that one of the old prophets has come back to life.'
20 'And you,' he said, 'who do you say I am?' Peter answered,
21 'God's Messiah.' Then he gave them strict orders not to
22 tell this to anyone. And he said, 'The Son of Man has to undergo great sufferings, and to be rejected by the elders, chief priests, and doctors of the law, to be put to death and to be raised again on the third day.'

23 And to all he said, 'If anyone wishes to be a follower of mine, he must leave self behind; day after day he must
24 take up his cross, and come with me. Whoever cares for his own safety is lost; but if a man will let himself be lost for
25 my sake, that man is safe. What will a man gain by winning
26 the whole world, at the cost of his true self? For whoever is ashamed of me and mine,[a] the Son of Man will be ashamed of him, when he comes in his glory and the glory
27 of the Father and the holy angels. And I tell you this: there are some of those standing here who will not taste death before they have seen the kingdom of God.'

28 About eight days after this conversation he took Peter, John, and James with him and went up into the hills to
29 pray. And while he was praying the appearance of his face
30 changed and his clothes became dazzling white. Suddenly there were two men talking with him; these were Moses
31 and Elijah, who appeared in glory and spoke of his depar-
32 ture, the destiny he was to fulfil in Jerusalem. Meanwhile Peter and his companions had been in a deep sleep; but when they awoke, they saw his glory and the two men
33 who stood beside him. And as these were moving away from Jesus, Peter said to him, 'Master, how good it is that we are here! Shall we make three shelters, one for you, one for Moses, and one for Elijah?'; but he spoke without
34 knowing what he was saying. The words were still on his lips, when there came a cloud which cast a shadow over
35 them; they were afraid as they entered the cloud, and from it came a voice: 'This is my Son, my Chosen; listen to him.'
36 When the voice had spoken, Jesus was seen to be alone. The disciples kept silence and at that time told nobody anything of what they had seen.

a *Some witnesses read* me and my words.

Next day when they came down from the hills he was 37
met by a large crowd. All at once there was a shout from 38
a man in the crowd: 'Master, look at my son, I implore
you, my only child. From time to time a spirit seizes him, 39
gives a sudden scream, and throws him into convulsions
with foaming at the mouth, and it keeps on mauling him
and will hardly let him go. I asked your disciples to cast 40
it out, but they could not.' Jesus answered, 'What an 41
unbelieving and perverse generation! How long shall I be
with you and endure you all? Bring your son here.' But 42
before the boy could reach him the devil dashed him to the
ground and threw him into convulsions. Jesus rebuked the
unclean spirit, cured the boy, and gave him back to his
father. And they were all struck with awe at the majesty 43
of God.

Amid the general wonder and admiration at all he was
doing, Jesus said to his disciples. 'What I now say is for 44
you: ponder my words. The Son of Man is to be given up
into the power of men.' But they did not understand this 45
saying; it had been hidden from them, so that they should
not*a* grasp its meaning, and they were afraid to ask him
about it.

A dispute arose among them: which of them was the 46
greatest? Jesus knew what was passing in their minds, so 47
he took a child by the hand and stood him at his side, and 48
said, 'Whoever receives this child in my name receives me;
and whoever receives me receives the One who sent me.
For the least among you all—he is the greatest.'

'Master,' said John, 'we saw a man driving out devils in 49
your name, but as he is not one of us we tried to stop him.'
Jesus said to him, 'Do not stop him, for he who is not 50
against you is on your side.'

# JOURNEYS AND ENCOUNTERS

A S THE TIME APPROACHED when he was to be 51
taken up to heaven, he set his face resolutely towards
Jerusalem, and sent messengers ahead. They set out and 52
went into a Samaritan village to make arrangements for
him; but the villagers would not have him because he was 53
making for Jerusalem. When the disciples James and John 54
saw this they said, 'Lord, may we call down fire from

* Or *it was so obscure to them that they could not . . .*

113

55 heaven to burn them up[a]?' But he turned and rebuked
56 them,[b] and they went on to another village.

57      As they were going along the road a man said to him,
58 'I will follow you wherever you go.' Jesus answered, 'Foxes
have their holes, the birds their roosts; but the Son of
59 Man has nowhere to lay his head.' To another he said,
'Follow me', but the man replied, 'Let me go and bury my
60 father first.' Jesus said, 'Leave the dead to bury their dead;
you must go and announce the kingdom of God.'

61      Yet another said, 'I will follow you, sir; but let me first
62 say good-bye to my people at home.' To him Jesus said,
'No one who sets his hand to the plough and then keeps
looking back[c] is fit for the kingdom of God.'

10      After this the Lord appointed a further seventy-two[d] and
sent them on ahead in pairs to every town and place he was
2 going to visit himself. He said to them: 'The crop is heavy,
but labourers are scarce; you must therefore beg the
3 owner to send labourers to harvest his crop. Be on your way.
4 And look, I am sending you like lambs among wolves. Carry
no purse or pack, and travel barefoot. Exchange no greet-
5 ings on the road. When you go into a house, let your first
6 words be, "Peace to this house." If there is a man of peace
there, your peace will rest upon him; if not, it will return
7 and rest upon you. Stay in that one house, sharing their
food and drink; for the worker earns his pay. Do not move
8 from house to house. When you come into a town and they
9 make you welcome, eat the food provided for you; heal the
sick there, and say, "The kingdom of God has come close
10 to you." When you enter a town and they do not make you
11 welcome, go out into its streets and say, "The very dust of
your town that clings to our feet we wipe off to your shame.
Only take note of this: the kingdom of God has come close."
12 I tell you, it will be more bearable for Sodom on the great
Day than for that town.

13      'Alas for you, Chorazin! Alas for you, Bethsaida! If the
miracles that were performed in you had been performed
in Tyre and Sidon, they would have repented long ago,
14 sitting in sackcloth and ashes. But it will be more bearable
15 for Tyre and Sidon at the Judgement than for you. And as
for you, Capernaum, will you be exalted to the skies? No,
brought down to the depths!

[a] *Some witnesses add* as Elijah did.          [b] *Some witnesses insert*
'You do not know', he said, 'to what spirit you belong; (56) for the
Son of Man did not come to destroy men's lives but to save them.'
[c] *Some witnesses read* No one who looks back as he sets hand to the
plough . . .          [d] *Some witnesses read* seventy.

'Whoever listens to you listens to me; whoever rejects 16
you rejects me. And whoever rejects me rejects the One
who sent me.'

The seventy-two[a] came back jubilant. 'In your name, 17
Lord,' they said, 'even the devils submit to us.' He replied, 18
'I watched how Satan fell, like lightning, out of the sky.
And now you see that I have given you the power to tread 19
underfoot snakes and scorpions and all the forces of the
enemy, and nothing will ever harm you.[b] Nevertheless, 20
what you should rejoice over is not that the spirits submit
to you, but that your names are enrolled in heaven.'

At that moment Jesus exulted in the Holy[c] Spirit and 21
said, 'I thank thee, Father, Lord of heaven and earth, for
hiding these things from the learned and wise, and revealing them to the simple. Yes, Father, such[d] was thy
choice.' Then turning to his disciples he said,[e] 'Everything 22
is entrusted to me by my Father; and no one knows who
the Son is but the Father, or who the Father is but the
Son, and those to whom the Son may choose to reveal
him.'

Turning to his disciples in private he said, 'Happy the 23
eyes that see what you are seeing! I tell you, many pro- 24
phets and kings wished to see what you now see, yet never
saw it; to hear what you hear, yet never heard it.'

On one occasion a lawyer came forward to put this 25
test question to him: 'Master, what must I do to inherit
eternal life?' Jesus said, 'What is written in the Law? 26
What is your reading of it?' He replied, 'Love the Lord 27
your God with all your heart, with all your soul, with all
your strength, and with all your mind; and your neighbour as yourself.' 'That is the right answer,' said Jesus; 'do 28
that and you will live.'

But he wanted to vindicate himself, so he said to Jesus, 29
'And who is my neighbour?' Jesus replied, 'A man was on 30
his way from Jerusalem down to Jericho when he fell in
with robbers, who stripped him, beat him, and went off
leaving him half dead. It so happened that a priest was 31
going down by the same road; but when he saw him, he
went past on the other side. So too a Levite came to the 32
place, and when he saw him went past on the other side.

[a] *Some witnesses read* seventy.          [b] *Or* and he will have no way at
all to harm you.          [c] *Some witnesses omit* Holy.          [d] *Or* Yes,
I thank thee, Father, that such . . .          [e] *Some witnesses omit*
Then . . . he said.

33 But a Samaritan who was making the journey came upon
34 him, and when he saw him was moved to pity. He went up
and bandaged his wounds, bathing them with oil and wine.
Then he lifted him on to his own beast, brought him to an
35 inn, and looked after him there. Next day he produced
two silver pieces and gave them to the innkeeper, and said,
"Look after him; and if you spend any more, I will repay
36 you on my way back." Which of these three do you think
was neighbour to the man who fell into the hands of the
37 robbers?' He answered, 'The one who showed him kindness.' Jesus said, 'Go and do as he did.'

38    While they were on their way Jesus came to a village
where a woman named Martha made him welcome in her
39 home. She had a sister, Mary, who seated herself at the
40 Lord's feet and stayed there listening to his words. Now
Martha was distracted by her many tasks, so she came to
him and said, 'Lord, do you not care that my sister has
left me to get on with the work by myself? Tell her to come
41 and lend a hand.' But the Lord answered, 'Martha, Martha,
42 you are fretting and fussing about so many things; but one
thing is necessary.*a* The part that Mary has chosen is best;
and it shall not be taken away from her.'

11    Once, in a certain place, Jesus was at prayer. When he
ceased, one of his disciples said, 'Lord, teach us to pray, as
2 John taught his disciples.' He answered, 'When you pray,
say,

> "Father,*b* thy name be hallowed;
> thy kingdom come.*c*
3    Give us each day our daily bread.*d*
4    And forgive us our sins,
> for we too forgive all who have done us wrong.
> And do not bring us to the test."*e*

5    Then he said to them, 'Suppose one of you has a friend
who comes to him in the middle of the night and says, "My
6 friend, lend me three loaves, for a friend of mine on a
journey has turned up at my house, and I have nothing to
7 offer him"; and he replies from inside, "Do not bother me.
The door is shut for the night; my children and I have

---

*a Some witnesses read* but few things are necessary, *or rather,* one
alone; *others omit* you are fretting . . . necessary.          *b Some witnesses read* Our Father in heaven.          *c One witness reads* thy kingdom come upon us; *some others have* thy Holy Spirit come upon us
and cleanse us; *some insert* thy will be done, on earth as in heaven.
*d Or* our bread for the morrow.          *e Some witnesses add* but save
us from the evil one (*or* from evil).

gone to bed; and I cannot get up and give you what you want." I tell you that even if he will not provide for him 8 out of friendship, the very shamelessness of the request will make him get up and give him all he needs. And so I say 9 to you, ask, and you will receive; seek, and you will find; knock, and the door will be opened. For everyone who 10 asks receives, he who seeks finds, and to him who knocks, the door will be opened.

'Is there a father among you who will offer his son[a] a 11 snake when he asks for fish, or a scorpion when he asks for 12 an egg? If you, then, bad as you are, know how to give 13 your children what is good for them, how much more will the heavenly Father give the Holy Spirit[b] to those who ask him!'

HE WAS DRIVING OUT a devil which was dumb; and 14 when the devil had come out, the dumb man began to speak. The people were astonished, but some of them said, 15 'It is by Beelzebub prince of devils that he drives the devils out.' Others, by way of a test, demanded of him a sign 16 from heaven. But he knew what was in their minds, and 17 said, 'Every kingdom divided against itself goes to ruin, and a divided household falls. Equally if Satan is divided 18 against himself, how can his kingdom stand?—since, as you would have it, I drive out the devils by Beelzebub. If 19 it is by Beelzebub that I cast out devils, by whom do your own people drive them out? If this is your argument, they themselves will refute you. But if it is by the finger of God 20 that I drive out the devils, then be sure the kingdom of God has already come upon you.

'When a strong man fully armed is on guard over his 21 castle his possessions are safe. But when someone stronger 22 comes upon him and overpowers him, he carries off the arms and armour on which the man had relied and divides the plunder.

'He who is not with me is against me, and he who does 23 not gather with me scatters.[c]

'When an unclean spirit comes out of a man it wanders 24 over the deserts seeking a resting-place; and if it finds none, it says, "I will go back to the home I left." So it returns 25 and finds the house[d] swept clean, and tidy. Off it goes and 26 collects seven other spirits more wicked than itself, and

---

[a] *Some witnesses insert* a stone when he asks for bread, or . . .
[b] *Some witnesses read* a good gift; *some others read* good things.
[c] *Some witnesses add* me.      [d] *Some witnesses insert* unoccupied.

they all come in and settle down; and in the end the man's plight is worse than before.'

27 While he was speaking thus, a woman in the crowd called out, 'Happy the womb that carried you and the breasts that 28 suckled you!' He rejoined, 'No, happy are those who hear the word of God and keep it.'

29 With the crowds swarming round him he went on to say: 'This is a wicked generation. It demands a sign, and the 30 only sign that will be given it is the sign of Jonah. For just as Jonah was a sign to the Ninevites, so will the Son of 31 Man be to this generation. At the Judgement, when the men of this generation are on trial, the Queen of the South will appear against[a] them and ensure their condemnation, for she came from the ends of the earth to hear the wisdom 32 of Solomon; and what is here is greater than Solomon. The men of Nineveh will appear at the Judgement when this generation is on trial, and ensure[b] its condemnation, for they repented at the preaching of Jonah; and what is here is greater than Jonah.

33 'No one lights a lamp and puts it in a cellar,[c] but rather on the lamp-stand so that those who enter may see the 34 light. The lamp of your body is the eye. When your eyes are sound, you have light for your whole body; but when 35 the eyes are bad, you are in darkness. See to it then that 36 the light you have is not darkness. If you have light for your whole body with no trace of darkness, it will all be as bright as when a lamp flashes its rays upon you.'

37 WHEN HE HAD FINISHED SPEAKING, a Pharisee 38 invited him to a meal. He came in and sat down. The Pharisee noticed with surprise that he had not begun by 39 washing before the meal. But the Lord said to him, 'You Pharisees! You clean the outside of cup and plate; but inside you there is nothing but greed and wickedness. 40 You fools! Did not he who made the outside make the 41 inside too? But let what is in the cup[d] be given in charity, and all is clean.

42 'Alas for you Pharisees! You pay tithes of mint and rue and every garden-herb, but have no care for justice and the love of God. It is these you should have practised, without neglecting the others.[e]

---

[a] *Or* will be raised to life together with . . .     [b] *Or* At the Judgement the men of Nineveh will rise again together with this generation and will ensure . . .     [c] *Some witnesses insert* or under the meal-tub.
[d] *Or* what you can afford.     [e] *Some witnesses omit* It is . . . others.

'Alas for you Pharisees! You love the seats of honour in **43** synagogues, and salutations in the market-places.

'Alas, alas, you are like unmarked graves over which **44** men may walk without knowing it.'

In reply to this one of the lawyers said, 'Master, when **45** you say things like this you are insulting us too.' Jesus **46** rejoined: 'Yes, you lawyers, it is no better with you! For you load men with intolerable burdens, and will not put a single finger to the load.

'Alas, you build the tombs of the prophets whom your **47** fathers murdered, and so testify that you approve of the **48** deeds your fathers did; they committed the murders and you provide the tombs.

'This is why the Wisdom of God said, "I will send them **49** prophets and messengers; and some of these they will persecute and kill"; so that this generation will have to **50** answer for the blood of all the prophets shed since the foundation of the world; from the blood of Abel to the **51** blood of Zechariah who perished between the altar and the sanctuary. I tell you, this generation will have to answer for it all.

'Alas for you lawyers! You have taken away the key of **52** knowledge. You did not go in yourselves, and those who were on their way in, you stopped.'

After he had left the house, the lawyers and Pharisees **53** began to assail him fiercely and to ply him with a host of questions, laying snares to catch him with his own words. **54**

MEANWHILE, WHEN A CROWD of many thousands had **12** gathered, packed so close that they were treading on one another, he began to speak first to his disciples: 'Beware of the leaven of the Pharisees; I mean their hypocrisy. There is nothing covered up that will not be uncovered, **2** nothing hidden that will not be made known. You may **3** take it, then, that everything you have said in the dark will be heard in broad daylight, and what you have whispered behind closed doors will be shouted from the house-tops.

'To you who are my friends I say: Do not fear those who **4** kill the body and after that have nothing more they can do. I will warn you whom to fear: fear him who, after he **5** has killed, has authority to cast into hell. Believe me, he is the one to fear.

'Are not sparrows five for twopence? And yet not one **6** of them is overlooked by God. More than that, even the **7** hairs of your head have all been counted. Have no fear; you are worth more than any number of sparrows.

8 'I tell you this: everyone who acknowledges me before men, the Son of Man will acknowledge before the angels of
9 God; but he who disowns me before men will be disowned before the angels of God.

10 'Anyone who speaks a word against the Son of Man will receive forgiveness; but for him who slanders the Holy Spirit there will be no forgiveness.

11 'When you are brought before synagogues and state authorities, do not begin worrying about how you will
12 conduct your defence or what you will say. For when the time comes the Holy Spirit will instruct you what to say.'

13 A man in the crowd said to him, 'Master, tell my brother
14 to divide the family property with me.' He replied, 'My good man, who set me over you to judge or arbitrate?'[a]
15 Then he said to the people, 'Beware! Be on your guard against greed of every kind, for even when a man has more
16 than enough, his wealth does not give him life.' And he told them this parable: 'There was a rich man whose land
17 yielded heavy crops. He debated with himself: "What am
18 I to do? I have not the space to store my produce. This is what I will do," said he: "I will pull down my storehouses and build them bigger. I will collect in them all my corn
19 and other goods, and then say to myself, 'Man, you have plenty of good things laid by, enough for many years: take
20 life easy, eat, drink, and enjoy yourself.'" But God said to him, "You fool, this very night you must surrender your life; you have made your money—who will get it now?"
21 That is how it is with the man who amasses wealth for himself and remains a pauper in the sight of God.[b]

22 'Therefore', he said to his disciples, 'I bid you put away anxious thoughts about food to keep you alive and clothes
23 to cover your body. Life is more than food, the body more
24 than clothes. Think of the ravens: they neither sow nor reap; they have no storehouse or barn; yet God feeds them.
25 You are worth far more than the birds! Is there a man among you who by anxious thought can add a foot to his
26 height[c]? If, then, you cannot do even a very little thing, why are you anxious about the rest?

27 'Think of the lilies: they neither spin nor weave;[d] yet I

---

[a] *Some witnesses omit* or arbitrate.     [b] *Some witnesses omit* That ... God; *others add at the end* When he said this he cried out, 'If you have ears to hear, then hear.'     [c] *Or* a day to his life.
[d] *Some witnesses read* they grow, they do not toil or spin.

tell you, even Solomon in all his splendour was not attired
like one of these. But if that is how God clothes the grass, 28
which is growing in the field today, and tomorrow is
thrown on the stove, how much more will he clothe you!
How little faith you have! And so you are not to set your 29
mind on food and drink; you are not to worry. For all these 30
are things for the heathen to run after; but you have a
Father who knows that you need them. No, set your mind 31
upon his kingdom, and all the rest will come to you as
well.

'Have no fear, little flock; for your Father has chosen 32
to give you the Kingdom. Sell your possessions and give in 33
charity. Provide for yourselves purses that do not wear
out, and never-failing treasure in heaven, where no thief
can get near it, no moth destroy it. For where your treasure 34
is, there will your heart be also.

'Be ready for action, with belts fastened and lamps 35
alight. Be like men who wait for their master's return from 36
a wedding-party, ready to let him in the moment he
arrives and knocks. Happy are those servants whom the 37
master finds on the alert when he comes. I tell you this: he
will fasten his belt, seat them at table, and come and wait
on them. Even if it is the middle of the night or before 38
dawn when he comes, happy they if he finds them alert.
And remember, if the householder had known what time 39
the burglar was coming he would not have let his house be
broken into. Hold yourselves ready, then, because the Son 40
of Man will come at the time you least expect him.'

Peter said, 'Lord, do you intend this parable specially 41
for us or is it for everyone?' The Lord said, 'Well, who is 42
the trusty and sensible man whom his master will appoint
as his steward, to manage his servants and issue their
rations at the proper time? Happy that servant who is 43
found at his task when his master comes! I tell you this: 44
he will be put in charge of all his master's property. But if 45
that servant says to himself, "The master is a long time
coming", and begins to bully the menservants and maids,
and eat and drink and get drunk; then the master will 46
arrive on a day that servant does not expect, at a time he
does not know, and will cut him in pieces. Thus he will
find his place among the faithless.

'The servant who knew his master's wishes, yet made no 47
attempt to carry them out, will be flogged severely. But one 48
who did not know them and earned a beating will be
flogged less severely. Where a man has been given much,

much will be expected of him; and the more a man has had entrusted to him the more he will be required to repay.

49 'I have come to set fire to the earth, and how I wish it
50 were already kindled! I have a baptism to undergo, and
51 what constraint I am under until the ordeal is over! Do you suppose I came to establish peace on earth? No indeed,
52 I have come to bring division. For from now on, five members of a family will be divided, three against two
53 and two against three; father against son and son against father, mother against daughter and daughter against mother, mother against son's wife and son's wife against her mother-in-law.'

54 He also said to the people, 'When you see cloud banking up in the west, you say at once, "It is going to rain", and
55 rain it does. And when the wind is from the south, you say,
56 "There will be a heat-wave", and there is. What hypocrites you are! You know how to interpret the appearance of earth and sky; how is it you cannot interpret this fateful hour?

57 'And why can you not judge for yourselves what is the
58 right course? When you are going with your opponent to court, make an effort to settle with him while you are still on the way; otherwise he may drag you before the judge, and the judge hand you over to the constable, and the
59 constable put you in jail. I tell you, you will not come out till you have paid the last farthing.'

13 At that very time there were some people present who told him about the Galileans whose blood Pilate had
2 mixed with their sacrifices. He answered them: 'Do you imagine that, because these Galileans suffered this fate, they must have been greater sinners than anyone else in
3 Galilee? I tell you they were not; but unless you repent,
4 you will all of you come to the same end. Or the eighteen people who were killed when the tower fell on them at Siloam—do you imagine they were more guilty than all
5 the other people living in Jerusalem? I tell you they were not; but unless you repent, you will all of you come to the same end.'

6 He told them this parable: 'A man had a fig-tree growing in his vineyard; and he came looking for fruit on it, but
7 found none. So he said to the vine-dresser, "Look here! For the last three years I have come looking for fruit on this fig-tree without finding any. Cut it down. Why should it
8 go on using up the soil?" But he replied, "Leave it, sir, this

one year while I dig round it and manure it. And if it bears 9
next season, well and good; if not, you shall have it down."'

One Sabbath he was teaching in a synagogue, and there 10 11
was a woman there possessed by a spirit that had crippled
her for eighteen years. She was bent double and quite
unable to stand up straight. When Jesus saw her he called 12
her and said, 'You are rid of your trouble.' Then he laid 13
his hands on her, and at once she straightened up and
began to praise God. But the president of the synagogue, 14
indignant with Jesus for healing on the Sabbath, intervened and said to the congregation, 'There are six working-
days: come and be cured on one of them, and not on the
Sabbath.' The Lord gave him his answer: 'What hypo- 15
crites you are!' he said. 'Is there a single one of you who
does not loose his ox or his donkey from the manger
and take it out to water on the Sabbath? And here is this 16
woman, a daughter of Abraham, who has been kept
prisoner by Satan for eighteen long years: was it wrong for
her to be freed from her bonds on the Sabbath?' At these 17
words all his opponents were covered with confusion, while
the mass of the people were delighted at all the wonderful
things he was doing.

'What is the kingdom of God like?' he continued. 'What 18
shall I compare it with? It is like a mustard-seed which 19
a man took and sowed in his garden; and it grew to be a
tree and the birds came to roost among its branches.'

Again he said, 'The kingdom of God, what shall I com- 20
pare it with? It is like yeast which a woman took and 21
mixed with half a hundredweight of flour till it was all
leavened.'

HE CONTINUED HIS JOURNEY through towns and 22
villages, teaching as he made his way towards Jerusalem.
Someone asked him, 'Sir, are only a few to be saved?' His 23
answer was: 'Struggle to get in through the narrow door; 24
for I tell you that many will try to enter and not be able.

'When once the master of the house has got up and 25
locked the door, you may stand outside and knock, and
say, "Sir, let us in!", but he will only answer, "I do not
know where you come from." Then you will begin to say, 26
"We sat at table with you and you taught in our streets."
But he will repeat, "I tell you, I do not know where you 27
come from. Out of my sight, all of you, you and your
wicked ways!" There will be wailing and grinding of teeth 28
there, when you see Abraham, Isaac, and Jacob, and all

the prophets, in the kingdom of God, and yourselves
29 thrown out. From east and west people will come, from
30 north and south, for the feast in the kingdom of God. Yes,
and some who are now last will be first, and some who are
first will be last.'

31    At that time a number of Pharisees came to him and
said, 'You should leave this place and go on your way;
32 Herod is out to kill you.' He replied, 'Go and tell that fox,
"Listen: today and tomorrow I shall be casting out devils
and working cures; on the third day I reach my goal."
33 However, I must be on my way today and tomorrow and
the next day, because it is unthinkable for a prophet to
meet his death anywhere but in Jerusalem.

34    'O Jerusalem, Jerusalem, the city that murders the prophets and stones the messengers sent to her! How often
have I longed to gather your children, as a hen gathers her
35 brood under her wings; but you would not let me. Look,
look! there is your temple, forsaken by God. And I tell you,
you shall never see me until the time comes when you say,
"Blessings on him who comes in the name of the Lord!"'

14 ONE SABBATH he went to have a meal in the house of
a leading Pharisee; and they were watching him closely.
2 There, in front of him, was a man suffering from dropsy.
3 Jesus asked the lawyers and the Pharisees: 'Is it permitted
4 to cure people on the Sabbath or not?' They said nothing.
5 So he took the man, cured him, and sent him away. Then
he turned to them and said, 'If one of you has a donkey[a]
or an ox and it falls into a well, will he hesitate to haul it
6 up on the Sabbath day?' To this they could find no reply.

7    When he noticed how the guests were trying to secure
8 the places of honour, he spoke to them in a parable: 'When
you are asked by someone to a wedding-feast, do not sit
down in the place of honour. It may be that some person
9 more distinguished than yourself has been invited; and the
host will come and say to you, "Give this man your seat."
Then you will look foolish as you begin to take the lowest
10 place. No, when you receive an invitation, go and sit down
in the lowest place, so that when your host comes he will
say, "Come up higher, my friend." Then all your fellow-
11 guests will see the respect in which you are held. For
everyone who exalts himself will be humbled; and whoever
humbles himself will be exalted.'

*a Some witnesses read* son.

Then he said to his host, 'When you are having a party 12 for lunch or supper, do not invite your friends, your brothers or other relations, or your rich neighbours; they will only ask you back again and so you will be repaid. But when you give a party, ask the poor, the crippled, the 13 lame, and the blind; and so find happiness. For they have 14 no means of repaying you; but you will be repaid on the day when good men rise from the dead.'

One of the company, after hearing all this, said to him, 15 'Happy the man who shall sit at the feast in the kingdom of God!' Jesus answered, 'A man was giving a big dinner 16 party and had sent out many invitations. At dinner-time 17 he sent his servant with a message for his guests, "Please come, everything is now ready." They began one and all 18 to excuse themselves. The first said, "I have bought a piece of land, and I must go and look over it; please accept my apologies." The second said, "I have bought five yoke of 19 oxen, and I am on my way to try them out; please accept my apologies." The next said, "I have just got married and 20 for that reason I cannot come." When the servant came 21 back he reported this to his master. The master of the house was angry and said to him, "Go out quickly into the streets and alleys of the town, and bring me in the poor, the crippled, the blind, and the lame." The servant said, 22 "Sir, your orders have been carried out and there is still room." The master replied, "Go out on to the highways and 23 along the hedgerows and make them come in; I want my house to be full. I tell you that not one of those who were 24 invited shall taste my banquet."'

Once when great crowds were accompanying him, he 25 turned to them and said: 'If anyone comes to me and does 26 not hate his father and mother, wife and children, brothers and sisters, even his own life, he cannot be a disciple of mine. No one who does not carry his cross and come with 27 me can be a disciple of mine. Would any of you think of 28 building a tower without first sitting down and calculating the cost, to see whether he could afford to finish it? Other- 29 wise, if he has laid its foundation and then is not able to complete it, all the onlookers will laugh at him. "There is 30 the man", they will say, "who started to build and could not finish." Or what king will march to battle against an- 31 other king, without first sitting down to consider whether with ten thousand men he can face an enemy coming to meet him with twenty thousand? If he cannot, then, long 32 before the enemy approaches, he sends envoys, and asks

33 for terms. So also none of you can be a disciple of mine without parting with all his possessions.

34 'Salt is a good thing; but if salt itself becomes tasteless,
35 what will you use to season it? It is useless either on the land or on the dung-heap: it can only be thrown away. If you have ears to hear, then hear.'

15 ANOTHER TIME, the tax-gatherers and other bad
2 characters were all crowding in to listen to him; and the Pharisees and the doctors of the law began grumbling among themselves: 'This fellow', they said, 'welcomes
3 sinners and eats with them.' He answered them with this
4 parable: 'If one of you has a hundred sheep and loses one of them, does he not leave the ninety-nine in the open pasture and go after the missing one until he has found it?
5 6 How delighted he is then! He lifts it on to his shoulders, and home he goes to call his friends and neighbours together. "Rejoice with me!" he cries. "I have found my lost sheep."
7 In the same way, I tell you, there will be greater joy in heaven over one sinner who repents than over ninety-nine righteous people who do not need to repent.

8 'Or again, if a woman has ten silver pieces and loses one of them, does she not light the lamp, sweep out the house,
9 and look in every corner till she has found it? And when she has, she calls her friends and neighbours together, and says, "Rejoice with me! I have found the piece that I lost."
10 In the same way, I tell you, there is joy among the angels of God over one sinner who repents.'

11 Again he said: 'There was once a man who had two sons;
12 and the younger said to his father, "Father, give me my share of the property." So he divided his estate between
13 them. A few days later the younger son turned the whole of his share into cash and left home for a distant country,
14 where he squandered it in reckless living. He had spent it all, when a severe famine fell upon that country and he
15 began to feel the pinch. So he went and attached himself to one of the local landowners, who sent him on to his farm
16 to mind the pigs. He would have been glad to fill his belly with[a] the pods that the pigs were eating; and no one gave
17 him anything. Then he came to his senses and said, "How many of my father's paid servants have more food than
18 they can eat, and here am I, starving to death! I will set off and go to my father, and say to him, 'Father, I have sinned,
19 against God and against you; I am no longer fit to be called

[a] *Some witnesses read* to have his fill of . . .

your son; treat me as one of your paid servants.'" So he 20
set out for his father's house. But while he was still a long
way off his father saw him, and his heart went out to him.
He ran to meet him, flung his arms round him, and kissed
him. The son said, "Father, I have sinned, against God and 21
against you; I am no longer fit to be called your son."[a]
But the father said to his servants, "Quick! fetch a robe, 22
my best one, and put it on him; put a ring on his finger
and shoes on his feet. Bring the fatted calf and kill it, and 23
let us have a feast to celebrate the day. For this son of mine 24
was dead and has come back to life; he was lost and is
found." And the festivities began.

'Now the elder son was out on the farm; and on his way 25
back, as he approached the house, he heard music and
dancing. He called one of the servants and asked what it 26
meant. The servant told him, "Your brother has come 27
home, and your father has killed the fatted calf because he
has him back safe and sound." But he was angry and re- 28
fused to go in. His father came out and pleaded with him; but 29
he retorted, "You know how I have slaved for you all these
years; I never once disobeyed your orders; and you never
gave me so much as a kid, for a feast with my friends. But 30
now that this son of yours turns up, after running through
your money with his women, you kill the fatted calf for
him." "My boy," said the father, "you are always with me, 31
and everything I have is yours. How could we help cele- 32
brating this happy day? Your brother here was dead and
has come back to life, was lost and is found."'

He said to his disciples, 'There was a rich man who had 16
a steward, and he received complaints that this man was
squandering the property. So he sent for him, and said, 2
"What is this that I hear? Produce your accounts, for you
cannot be manager here any longer." The steward said to 3
himself, "What am I to do now that my employer is dis-
missing me? I am not strong enough to dig, and too proud
to beg. I know what I must do, to make sure that, when I 4
have to leave, there will be people to give me house and
home." He summoned his master's debtors one by one. To 5
the first he said, "How much do you owe my master?"
He replied, "A thousand gallons of olive oil." He said, 6
"Here is your account. Sit down and make it five hundred;
and be quick about it." Then he said to another, "And you, 7
how much do you owe?" He said, "A thousand bushels of
wheat", and was told, "Take your account and make it

[a] *Some witnesses add* treat me as one of your paid servants.

8 eight hundred." And the master applauded the dishonest steward for acting so astutely. For the worldly are more astute than the other-worldly in dealing with their own kind.

9 'So I say to you, use your worldly wealth to win friends for yourselves, so that when money is a thing of the past you may be received into an eternal home.

10 'The man who can be trusted in little things can be trusted also in great; and the man who is dishonest in little 11 things is dishonest also in great things. If, then, you have not proved trustworthy with the wealth of this world, who 12 will trust you with the wealth that is real? And if you have proved untrustworthy with what belongs to another, who will give you what is your own?

13 'No servant can be the slave of two masters; for either he will hate the first and love the second, or he will be devoted to the first and think nothing of the second. You cannot serve God and Money.'

14 The Pharisees, who loved money, heard all this and 15 scoffed at him. He said to them, 'You are the people who impress your fellow-men with your righteousness; but God sees through you; for what sets itself up to be admired by men is detestable in the sight of God.

16 'Until John, it was the Law and the prophets: since then, there is the good news of the kingdom of God, and everyone forces his way in.

17 'It is easier for heaven and earth to come to an end than for one dot or stroke of the Law to lose its force.

18 'A man who divorces his wife and marries another commits adultery; and anyone who marries a woman divorced from her husband commits adultery.

19 'There was once a rich man, who dressed in purple and the finest linen, and feasted in great magnificence every 20 day. At his gate, covered with sores, lay a poor man named 21 Lazarus, who would have been glad to satisfy his hunger with the scraps from the rich man's table. Even the dogs used to 22 come and lick his sores. One day the poor man died and was carried away by the angels to be with Abraham. The rich 23 man also died and was buried, and in Hades, where he was in torment, he looked up; and there, far away, was Abra-24 ham with Lazarus close beside him. "Abraham, my father," he called out, "take pity on me! Send Lazarus to dip the tip of his finger in water, to cool my tongue, for I am in 25 agony in this fire." But Abraham said, "Remember, my child, that all the good things fell to you while you were

alive, and all the bad to Lazarus; now he has his consola- tion here and it is you who are in agony. But that is not 26 all: there is a great chasm fixed between us; no one from our side who wants to reach you can cross it, and none may pass from your side to us." "Then, father," he replied, "will 27 you send him to my father's house, where I have five 28 brothers, to warn them, so that they too may not come to this place of torment?" But Abraham said, "They have 29 Moses and the prophets; let them listen to them." "No, 30 father Abraham," he replied, "but if someone from the dead visits them, they will repent." Abraham answered, 31 "If they do not listen to Moses and the prophets they will pay no heed even if someone should rise from the dead."'

HE SAID TO HIS DISCIPLES, 'Causes of stumbling are 17 bound to arise; but woe betide the man through whom they come. It would be better for him to be thrown into 2 the sea with a millstone round his neck than to cause one of these little ones to stumble. Keep watch on your- 3 selves.

'If your brother wrongs you, reprove him; and if he repents, forgive him. Even if he wrongs you seven times 4 in a day and comes back to you seven times saying, "I am sorry", you are to forgive him.'

The apostles said to the Lord, 'Increase our faith'; and 5 6 the Lord replied, 'If you had [faith no bigger even than a mustard-seed, you could say to this mulberry-tree, "Be rooted up and replanted in the sea"; and it would at once obey you.

'Suppose one of you has a servant ploughing or minding 7 sheep. When he comes back from the fields, will the master say, "Come along at once and sit down"? Will he not 8 rather say, "Prepare my supper, fasten your belt, and then wait on me while I have my meal; you can have yours afterwards"? Is he grateful to the servant for carrying out 9 his orders? So with you: when you have carried out all 10 your orders, you should say, "We are servants and deserve no credit; we have only done our duty."'

In the course of his journey to Jerusalem he was travel- 11 ling through the borderlands of Samaria and Galilee. As he 12 was entering a village he was met by ten men with leprosy. They stood some way off and called out to him, 'Jesus, 13 Master, take pity on us.' When he saw them he said, 'Go 14 and show yourselves to the priests'; and while they were on their way, they were made clean. One of them, finding 15

16 himself cured, turned back praising God aloud. He threw
   himself down at Jesus's feet and thanked him. And he was
17 a Samaritan. At this Jesus said: 'Were not all ten cleansed?
18 The other nine, where are they? Could none be found to
   come back and give praise to God except this foreigner?'
19 And he said to the man, 'Stand up and go on your way;
   your faith has cured you.'

20 THE PHARISEES ASKED HIM, 'When will the kingdom
   of God come?' He said, 'You cannot tell by observation
21 when the kingdom of God comes. There will be no saying,
   "Look, here it is!" or "there it is!"; for in fact the kingdom
   of God is among you.'[a]

22    He said to the disciples, 'The time will come when you
   will long to see one of the days of the Son of Man, but you
23 will not see it. They will say to you, "Look! There!" and
24 "Look! Here!" Do not go running off in pursuit. For like
   the lightning-flash that lights up the earth from end to end,
25 will the Son of Man be when his day comes. But first he
   must endure much suffering and be repudiated by this
   generation.

26    'As things were in Noah's days, so will they be in the
27 days of the Son of Man. They ate and drank and married,
   until the day that Noah went into the ark and the flood
28 came and made an end of them all. As things were in Lot's
   days, also: they ate and drank; they bought and sold;
29 they planted and built; but the day that Lot went out
   from Sodom, it rained fire and sulphur from the sky and
30 made an end of them all—it will be like that on the day
   when the Son of Man is revealed.

31    'On that day the man who is on the roof and his belongings in the house must not come down to pick them
32 up; he, too, who is in the fields must not go back. Re-
33 member Lot's wife. Whoever seeks to save his life will
   lose it; and whoever loses it will save it, and live.

34    'I tell you, on that night there will be two men in one
35 bed: one will be taken, the other left. There will be two
   women together grinding corn: one will be taken, the
37 other left.'[b] When they heard this they asked, 'Where,
   Lord?' He said, 'Where the corpse is, there the vultures
   will gather.'

   [a] Or for in fact the kingdom of God is within you, or for in fact the
   kingdom of God is within your grasp, or for suddenly the kingdom of
   God will be among you.       [b] Some witnesses add (36) two men in
   the fields: one will be taken, the other left.

He spoke to them in a parable to show that they 18
should keep on praying and never lose heart: 'There was 2
once a judge who cared nothing for God or man, and in the 3
same town there was a widow who constantly came before
him demanding justice against her opponent. For a long 4
time he refused; but in the end he said to himself, "True,
I care nothing for God or man; but this widow is so great 5
a nuisance that I will see her righted before she wears me
out with her persistence."' The Lord said, 'You hear what 6
the unjust judge says; and will not God vindicate his 7
chosen, who cry out to him day and night, while he listens
patiently to them[a]? I tell you, he will vindicate them soon 8
enough. But when the Son of Man comes, will he find faith
on earth?'

And here is another parable that he told. It was aimed 9
at those who were sure of their own goodness and looked
down on everyone else. 'Two men went up to the temple 10
to pray, one a Pharisee and the other a tax-gatherer. The 11
Pharisee stood up and prayed thus:[b] "I thank thee, O God,
that I am not like the rest of men, greedy, dishonest,
adulterous; or, for that matter, like this tax-gatherer. I 12
fast twice a week; I pay tithes on all that I get." But the 13
other kept his distance and would not even raise his eyes
to heaven, but beat upon his breast, saying, "O God, have
mercy on me, sinner that I am." It was this man, I tell 14
you, and not the other, who went home acquitted of his
sins. For everyone who exalts himself will be humbled;
and whoever humbles himself will be exalted.'

They even brought babies for him to touch. When the 15
disciples saw them they rebuked them, but Jesus called for 16
the children and said, 'Let the little ones come to me; do
not try to stop them; for the kingdom of God belongs to
such as these. I tell you that whoever does not accept the 17
kingdom of God like a child will never enter it.'

A man of the ruling class put this question to him: 'Good 18
Master, what must I do to win eternal life?' Jesus said to 19
him, 'Why do you call me good? No one is good except
God alone. You know the commandments: "Do not com- 20
mit adultery; do not murder; do not steal; do not give
false evidence; honour your father and mother."' The man 21
answered, 'I have kept all these since I was a boy.' On 22
hearing this Jesus said, 'There is still one thing lacking:

---

[a] *Or* delays to help them.     [b] *Some witnesses read* stood up by
himself and prayed thus; *others read* stood up and prayed thus
privately.

sell everything you have and distribute to the poor, and
23 you will have riches in heaven; and come, follow me.' At
these words his heart sank; for he was a very rich man.
24 When Jesus saw it he said, 'How hard it is for the wealthy
25 to enter the kingdom of God! It is easier for a camel to go
through the eye of a needle than for a rich man to enter the
26 kingdom of God.' Those who heard asked, 'Then who can
27 be saved?' He answered, 'What is impossible for men is
possible for God.'

28 Peter said, 'We here have left our belongings to become
29 your followers.' Jesus said, 'I tell you this: there is no one
who has given up home, or wife, brothers, parents, or chil-
30 dren, for the sake of the kingdom of God, who will not be
repaid many times over in this age, and in the age to come
have eternal life.'

## CHALLENGE TO JERUSALEM

31 HE TOOK THE TWELVE ASIDE and said, 'We
are now going up to Jerusalem; and all that was written
32 by the prophets will come true for the Son of Man. He will
be handed over to the foreign power. He will be mocked,
33 maltreated, and spat upon. They will flog him and kill
34 him. And on the third day he will rise again.' But they
understood nothing of all this; they did not grasp what
he was talking about; its meaning was concealed from
them.

35 As he approached Jericho a blind man sat at the road-
36 side begging. Hearing a crowd going past, he asked what
37 was happening. They told him, 'Jesus of Nazareth is
38 passing by.' Then he shouted out, 'Jesus, Son of David,
39 have pity on me.' The people in front told him to hold his
tongue; but he called out all the more, 'Son of David, have
40 pity on me.' Jesus stopped and ordered the man to be
41 brought to him. When he came up he asked him, 'What do
you want me to do for you?' 'Sir, I want my sight back',
42 he answered. Jesus said to him, 'Have back your sight;
43 your faith has cured you.' He recovered his sight instantly;
and he followed Jesus, praising God. And all the people
gave praise to God for what they had seen.

19 Entering Jericho he made his way through the city.
2 There was a man there named Zacchaeus; he was super-
3 intendent of taxes and very rich. He was eager to see
what Jesus looked like; but, being a little man, he could

not see him for the crowd. So he ran on ahead and climbed ⁴
a sycomore-tree in order to see him, for he was to pass that
way. When Jesus came to the place, he looked up and said, ⁵
'Zacchaeus, be quick and come down; I must come and
stay with you today.' He climbed down as fast as he could ⁶
and welcomed him gladly. At this there was a general ⁷
murmur of disapproval. 'He has gone in', they said, 'to be
the guest of a sinner.' But Zacchaeus stood there and said ⁸
to the Lord, 'Here and now, sir, I give half my possessions
to charity; and if I have cheated anyone, I am ready to
repay him four times over.' Jesus said to him, 'Salvation ⁹
has come to this house today!—for this man too is a son
of Abraham, and the Son of Man has come to seek and ¹⁰
save what is lost.'

While they were listening to this, he went on to tell them ¹¹
a parable, because he was now close to Jerusalem and they
thought the reign of God might dawn at any moment.
He said, 'A man of noble birth went on a long journey ¹²
abroad, to be appointed king and then return. But first ¹³
he called ten of his servants and gave them a pound each,
saying, "Trade with this while I am away." His fellow- ¹⁴
citizens hated him, and they sent a delegation on his heels
to say, "We do not want this man as our king." However, ¹⁵
back he came as king, and sent for the servants to whom
he had given the money, to see what profit each had made.
The first came and said, "Your pound, sir, has made ten ¹⁶
more." "Well done," he replied; "you are a good servant. ¹⁷
You have shown yourself trustworthy in a very small
matter, and you shall have charge of ten cities." The second ¹⁸
came and said, "Your pound, sir, has made five more";
and he also was told, "You too, take charge of five cities." ¹⁹
The third came and said, "Here is your pound, sir; I kept ²⁰
it put away in a handkerchief. I was afraid of you, because ²¹
you are a hard man: you draw out what you never put in
and reap what you did not sow." "You rascal!" he replied; ²²
"I will judge you by your own words. You knew, did you,
that I am a hard man, that I draw out what I never put in,
and reap what I did not sow? Then why did you not put ²³
my money on deposit, and I could have claimed it with
interest when I came back?" Turning to his attendants he ²⁴
said, "Take the pound from him and give it to the man with
ten." "But, sir," they replied, "he has ten already." "I tell ²⁵ ²⁶
you," he went on, "the man who has will always be given
more; but the man who has not will forfeit even what he
has. But as for those enemies of mine who did not want me ²⁷

for their king, bring them here and slaughter them in my presence." '

28 WITH THAT JESUS WENT FORWARD and began the
29 ascent to Jerusalem. As he approached Bethphage and Bethany at the hill called Olivet, he sent two of the
30 disciples with these instructions: 'Go to the village opposite; as you enter it you will find tethered there a colt which no one has yet ridden. Untie it and bring it here.
31 If anyone asks why you are untying it, say, "Our Master
32 needs it." ' The two went on their errand and found it as
33 he had told them; and while they were untying the colt,
34 its owners asked, 'Why are you untying that colt?' They
35 answered, 'Our Master needs it.' So they brought the colt to Jesus.

Then they threw their cloaks on the colt, for Jesus to
36 mount, and they carpeted the road with them as he went
37 on his way. And now, as he approached the descent from the Mount of Olives, the whole company of his disciples in their joy began to sing aloud the praises of God for all the great things they had seen:

38      'Blessings on him who comes as king in the name
           of the Lord!
        Peace in heaven, glory in highest heaven!'

39      Some Pharisees who were in the crowd said to him,
40 'Master, reprimand your disciples.' He answered, 'I tell you, if my disciples keep silence the stones will shout aloud.'
41 42     When he came in sight of the city, he wept over it and said, 'If only you had known, on this great day, the way that leads to peace! But no; it is hidden from your sight.
43 For a time will come upon you, when your enemies will set up siege-works against you; they will encircle you and
44 hem you in at every point; they will bring you to the ground, you and your children within your walls, and not leave you one stone standing on another, because you did not recognize God's moment when it came.'
45      Then he went into the temple and began driving out the
46 traders, with these words: 'Scripture says, "My house shall be a house of prayer"; but you have made it a robbers' cave.'
47      Day by day he taught in the temple. And the chief priests and lawyers were bent on making an end of him,
48 with the support of the leading citizens, but found they were helpless, because the people all hung upon his words.

ONE DAY, as he was teaching the people in the temple 20
and telling them the good news, the priests and lawyers,
and the elders with them, came upon him and accosted him. 2
'Tell us', they said, 'by what authority you are acting like
this; who gave you this authority?' He answered them, 'I 3
have a question to ask you too: tell me, was the baptism 4
of John from God or from men?' This set them arguing 5
among themselves: 'If we say, "from God", he will say,
"Why did you not believe him?" And if we say, "from 6
men", the people will all stone us, for they are convinced
that John was a prophet.' So they replied that they could 7
not tell. And Jesus said to them, 'Then neither will I tell 8
you by what authority I act.'

He went on to tell the people this parable: 'A man 9
planted a vineyard, let it out to vine-growers, and went
abroad for a long time. When the season came, he sent a 10
servant to the tenants to collect from them his share of the
produce; but the tenants thrashed him and sent him away
empty-handed. He tried again and sent a second servant; 11
but he also was thrashed, outrageously treated, and sent
away empty-handed. He tried once more with a third; this 12
one too they wounded and flung out. Then the owner of 13
the vineyard said, "What am I to do? I will send my own
dear son;[a] perhaps they will respect him." But when the 14
tenants saw him they talked it over together. "This is the
heir," they said; "let us kill him so that the property may
come to us." So they flung him out of the vineyard and 15
killed him. What then will the owner of the vineyard do to
them? He will come and put these tenants to death and let 16
the vineyard to others.'

When they heard this, they said, 'God forbid!' But he 17
looked straight at them and said, 'Then what does this
text of Scripture mean: "The stone which the builders
rejected has become the main corner-stone"? Any man 18
who falls on that stone will be dashed to pieces; and if it
falls on a man he will be crushed by it.'

The lawyers and chief priests wanted to lay hands on 19
him there and then, for they saw that this parable was
aimed at them; but they were afraid of the people. So they 20
watched their opportunity and sent secret agents in the
guise of honest men, to seize upon some word of his as a
pretext for handing him over to the authority and jurisdiction of the Governor. They put a question to him: 21
'Master,' they said, 'we know that what you speak and

[a] *Or my only son.*

teach is sound; you pay deference to no one, but teach in
22  all honesty the way of life that God requires. Are we or are
we not permitted to pay taxes to the Roman Emperor?'
23 24  He saw through their trick and said, 'Show me a silver
piece. Whose head does it bear, and whose inscription?'
25  'Caesar's', they replied. 'Very well then,' he said, 'pay
Caesar what is due to Caesar, and pay God what is due to
26  God.' Thus their attempt to catch him out in public failed,
and, astonished by his reply, they fell silent.

27     Then some Sadducees came forward. They are the people
who deny that there is a resurrection. Their question was
28  this: 'Master, Moses laid it down for us that if there are
brothers, and one dies leaving a wife but no child, then the
next should marry the widow and carry on his brother's
29  family. Now, there were seven brothers: the first took a
30 31  wife and died childless; then the second married her, then
the third. In this way the seven of them died leaving no
32 33  children. Afterwards the woman also died. At the resurrection whose wife is she to be, since all seven had married
34  her?' Jesus said to them, 'The men and women of this
35  world marry; but those who have been judged worthy of
a place in the other world and of the resurrection from the
36  dead, do not marry, for they are not subject to death any
longer. They are like angels; they are sons of God, because
37  they share in the resurrection. That the dead are raised to
life again is shown by Moses himself in the story of the burning bush, when he calls the Lord, "the God of Abraham,
38  Isaac, and Jacob". God is not God of the dead but of the
living; for him all are*a* alive.'

39     At this some of the lawyers said, 'Well spoken, Master.'
40  For there was no further question that they ventured to
put to him.

41     He said to them, 'How can they say that the Messiah is
42  son of David? For David himself says in the Book of
Psalms: "The Lord said to my Lord, 'Sit at my right
43 44  hand until I make your enemies your footstool.'" Thus
David calls him "Lord"; how then can he be David's
son?'

45     In the hearing of all the people Jesus said to his disciples:
46  'Beware of the doctors of the law who love to walk up and
down in long robes, and have a great liking for respectful
greetings in the street, the chief seats in our synagogues,
47  and places of honour at feasts. These are the men who
eat up the property of widows, while they say long prayers

---

*a* Or they are all.

for appearance' sake; and they will receive the severest sentence.'

He looked up and saw the rich people dropping their 21 gifts into the chest of the temple treasury; and he noticed 2 a poor widow putting in two tiny coins. 'I tell you this,' he 3 said: 'this poor widow has given more than any of them; for those others who have given had more than enough, 4 but she, with less than enough, has given all she had to live on.'

SOME PEOPLE WERE TALKING about the temple and 5 the fine stones and votive offerings with which it was adorned. He said, 'These things which you are gazing at— 6 the time will come when not one stone of them will be left upon another; all will be thrown down.' 'Master,' they asked, 7 'when will it all come about? What will be the sign when it is due to happen?'

He said, 'Take care that you are not misled. For many 8 will come claiming my name and saying, "I am he", and, "The Day is upon us." Do not follow them. And when you 9 hear of wars and insurrections, do not fall into a panic. These things are bound to happen first; but the end does not follow immediately.' Then he added, 'Nation will make 10 war upon nation, kingdom upon kingdom; there will be 11 great earthquakes, and famines and plagues in many places; in the sky terrors and great portents.

'But before all this happens they will set upon you and 12 persecute you. You will be brought before synagogues and put in prison; you will be haled before kings and governors for your allegiance to me. This will be your opportunity to 13 testify; so make up your minds not to prepare your defence 14 beforehand, because I myself will give you power of 15 utterance and a wisdom which no opponent will be able to resist or refute. Even your parents and brothers, your rela- 16 tions and friends, will betray you. Some of you will be put to death; and all will hate you for your allegiance to me. 17 But not a hair of your head shall be lost. By standing firm 18 19 you will win true life for yourselves.

'But when you see Jerusalem encircled by armies, then 20 you may be sure that her destruction is near. Then those 21 who are in Judaea must take to the hills; those who are in the city itself must leave it, and those who are out in the country must not enter; because this is the time of retribu- 22 tion, when all that stands written is to be fulfilled. Alas for 23 women who are with child in those days, or have children

at the breast! For there will be great distress in the land
24 and a terrible judgement upon this people. They will fall
at the sword's point; they will be carried captive into
all countries; and Jerusalem will be trampled down by
foreigners until their day has run its course.

25 'Portents will appear in sun, moon, and stars. On earth
nations will stand helpless, not knowing which way to turn
26 from the roar and surge of the sea; men will faint with
terror at the thought of all that is coming upon the world;
27 for the celestial powers will be shaken. And then they will
see the Son of Man coming on a cloud with great power and
28 glory. When all this begins to happen, stand upright and
hold your heads high, because your liberation is near.'

29 He told them this parable: 'Look at the fig-tree, or any
30 other tree. As soon as it buds, you can see for yourselves
31 that summer is near. In the same way, when you see all
this happening, you may know that the kingdom of God
is near.

32 'I tell you this: the present generation will live to see it
33 all. Heaven and earth will pass away; my words will never
pass away.

34 'Keep a watch on yourselves; do not let your minds be
dulled by dissipation and drunkenness and worldly cares
35 so that the great Day closes upon you suddenly like a trap;
for that day will come on all men, wherever they are, the
36 whole world over. Be on the alert, praying at all times
for strength to pass safely through all these imminent
troubles and to stand in the presence of the Son of Man.'

37 His days were given to teaching in the temple; and then
he would leave the city and spend the night on the hill
38 called Olivet. And in the early morning the people flocked
to listen to him in the temple.[a]


# THE FINAL CONFLICT

22 NOW THE FESTIVAL of Unleavened Bread,
2 known as Passover, was approaching, and the chief
priests and the doctors of the law were trying to devise
some means of doing away with him; for they were afraid
of the people.

3 Then Satan entered into Judas Iscariot, who was one
4 of the Twelve; and Judas went to the chief priests and

---

[a] *Some witnesses here insert the passage printed on p. 190.*

officers of the temple police to discuss ways and means of
putting Jesus into their power. They were greatly pleased 5
and undertook to pay him a sum of money. He agreed, and 6
began to look out for an opportunity to betray him to
them without collecting a crowd.

Then came the day of Unleavened Bread, on which the 7
Passover victim had to be slaughtered, and Jesus sent 8
Peter and John with these instructions: 'Go and prepare
for our Passover supper.' 'Where would you like us to 9
make the preparations?' they asked. He replied, 'As soon 10
as you set foot in the city a man will meet you carrying
a jar of water. Follow him into the house that he enters
and give this message to the householder: "The Master 11
says, 'Where is the room in which I may eat the Passover
with my disciples?'" He will show you a large room up- 12
stairs all set out: make the preparations there.' They 13
went and found everything as he had said. So they prepared for Passover.

When the time came he took his place at table, and the 14
apostles with him; and he said to them, 'How I have 15
longed[a] to eat this Passover with you before my death!
For I tell you, never again shall I[b] eat it until the time 16
when it finds its fulfilment in the kingdom of God.'

Then he took a cup, and after giving thanks he said, 17
'Take this and share it among yourselves; for I tell you, 18
from this moment I shall drink from the fruit of the vine
no more until the time when the kingdom of God comes.'
And he took bread, gave thanks, and broke it; and he gave 19
it to them, with the words: 'This is my body.'[c]

'But mark this—my betrayer is here, his hand with mine 21
on the table. For the Son of Man is going his appointed 22
way; but alas for that man by whom he is betrayed!' At 23
this they began to ask among themselves which of them
it could possibly be who was to do this thing.

Then a jealous dispute broke out: who among them 24
should rank highest? But he said, 'In the world, kings lord 25
it over their subjects; and those in authority are called
their country's "Benefactors". Not so with you: on the 26
contrary, the highest among you must bear himself like
the youngest, the chief of you like a servant. For who is 27

[a] Or said to them, 'I longed . . .'          [b] *Some witnesses read* For I
tell you, I shall not . . .          [c] *Some witnesses add, in whole or in part,
and with various arrangements, the following:* 'which is given for you;
do this as a memorial of me.' (20) In the same way he took the cup
after supper, and said, 'This cup, poured out for you, is the new
covenant sealed by my blood.'

greater—the one who sits at table or the servant who waits
on him? Surely the one who sits at table. Yet here am I
among you like a servant.

28 'You are the men who have stood firmly by me in my
29 times of trial; and now I vest in you the kingship which
30 my Father vested in me; you shall eat and drink at my
table in my kingdom and sit[a] on thrones as judges of the
twelve tribes of Israel.

31 'Simon, Simon, take heed: Satan has been given leave
32 to sift all of you like wheat; but for you I have prayed that
your faith may not fail; and when you have come to your-
33 self, you must lend strength to your brothers.' 'Lord,' he
replied, 'I am ready to go with you to prison and death.'
34 Jesus said, 'I tell you, Peter, the cock will not crow tonight
until you have three times over denied that you know
me.'

35 He said to them, 'When I sent you out barefoot without
purse or pack, were you ever short of anything?' 'No',
36 they answered. 'It is different now,' he said; 'whoever has
a purse had better take it with him, and his pack too; and
37 if he has no sword, let him sell his cloak to buy one. For
Scripture says, "And he was counted among the outlaws",
and these words, I tell you, must find fulfilment in me;
38 indeed, all that is written of me is being fulfilled.' 'Look,
Lord,' they said, 'we have two swords here.' 'Enough,
enough!' he replied.

39 THEN HE WENT OUT and made his way as usual to the
40 Mount of Olives, accompanied by the disciples. When he
reached the place he said to them, 'Pray that you may be
41 spared the hour of testing.' He himself withdrew from
them about a stone's throw, knelt down, and began to
42 pray: 'Father, if it be thy will, take this cup away from
me. Yet not my will but thine be done.'
43 And now there appeared to him an angel from heaven
44 bringing him strength, and in anguish of spirit he prayed
the more urgently; and his sweat was like clots of blood
falling to the ground.[b]
45 When he rose from prayer and came to the disciples he
46 found them asleep, worn out by grief. 'Why are you sleeping?' he said. 'Rise and pray that you may be spared the
test.'

---

[a] *Or* trial; and as my Father gave me the right to reign, so I give you
the right to eat and to drink ... and to sit ...     [b] *Some witnesses
omit* And now ... ground.

WHILE HE WAS STILL SPEAKING a crowd appeared 47
with the man called Judas, one of the Twelve, at their
head. He came up to Jesus to kiss him; but Jesus said, 48
'Judas, would you betray the Son of Man with a kiss?'
When his followers saw what was coming, they said, 49
'Lord, shall we use our swords?' And one of them struck 50
at the High Priest's servant, cutting off his right ear. But 51
Jesus answered, 'Let them have their way.' Then he
touched the man's ear and healed him.*a*

Turning to the chief priests, the officers of the temple 52
police, and the elders, who had come to seize him, he said,
'Do you take me for a bandit, that you have come out
with swords and cudgels to arrest me? Day after day, 53
when I was in the temple with you, you kept your hands
off me. But this is your moment—the hour when darkness reigns.'

Then they arrested him and led him away. They brought 54
him to the High Priest's house, and Peter followed at a
distance. They lit a fire in the middle of the courtyard and 55
sat round it, and Peter sat among them. A serving-maid 56
who saw him sitting in the firelight stared at him and said,
'This man was with him too.' But he denied it: 'Woman,' 57
he said, 'I do not know him.' A little later someone else 58
noticed him and said, 'You also are one of them.' But
Peter said to him, 'No, I am not.' About an hour passed 59
and another spoke more strongly still: 'Of course this
fellow was with him. He must have been; he is a Galilean.'
But Peter said, 'Man, I do not know what you are talking 60
about.' At that moment, while he was still speaking, a
cock crew; and the Lord turned and looked at Peter. And 61
Peter remembered the Lord's words, 'Tonight before the
cock crows you will disown me three times.'*b*

The men who were guarding Jesus mocked at him. They 63
beat him, they blindfolded him, and they kept asking him, 64
'Now, prophet, who hit you? Tell us that.' And so they 65
went on heaping insults upon him.

WHEN DAY BROKE, the elders of the nation, chief priests, 66
and doctors of the law assembled, and he was brought
before their Council. 'Tell us,' they said, 'are you the 67
Messiah?' 'If I tell you,' he replied, 'you will not believe
me; and if I ask questions, you will not answer. But from 68 69

---

*a* Or 'Let me do as much as this', and touching the man's ear, he
healed him.       *b* *Some witnesses add* (62) He went outside, and
wept bitterly, *as in Matthew 26. 75.*

141

now on, the Son of Man will be seated at the right hand of
70 Almighty God.'[a] 'You are the Son of God, then?' they all
71 said, and he replied, 'It is you who say I am.'[b] They said,
'Need we call further witnesses? We have heard it ourselves from his own lips.'

23    With that the whole assembly rose, and they brought
2 him before Pilate. They opened the case against him by
saying, 'We found this man subverting our nation, oppos-
ing the payment of taxes to Caesar, and claiming to be
3 Messiah, a king.'[c] Pilate asked him, 'Are you the king of
4 the Jews?' He replied, 'The words are yours.'[d] Pilate then
said to the chief priests and the crowd, 'I find no case for
5 this man to answer.' But they insisted: 'His teaching is
causing disaffection among the people all through Judaea.
It started from Galilee and has spread as far as this city.'
6    When Pilate heard this, he asked if the man was a
7 Galilean, and on learning that he belonged to Herod's jurisdiction he remitted the case to him, for Herod was also in
8 Jerusalem at that time. When Herod saw Jesus he was
greatly pleased; having heard about him, he had long been
wanting to see him, and had been hoping to see some
9 miracle performed by him. He questioned him at some
10 length without getting any reply; but the chief priests
and lawyers appeared and pressed the case against him
11 vigorously. Then Herod and his troops treated him with
contempt and ridicule, and sent him back to Pilate dressed
12 in a gorgeous robe. That same day Herod and Pilate
became friends; till then there had been a standing feud
between them.
13    Pilate now called together the chief priests, councillors,
14 and people, and said to them, 'You brought this man before
me on a charge of subversion. But, as you see, I have myself examined him in your presence and found nothing in
15 him to support your charges. No more did Herod, for he
has referred him back to us. Clearly he has done nothing to
16 deserve death. I therefore propose to let him off with a
18 flogging.' But[e] there was a general outcry, 'Away with
19 him! Give us Barabbas.' (This man had been put in prison
for a rising that had taken place in the city, and for
20 murder.) Pilate addressed them again, in his desire to
21 release Jesus, but they shouted back, 'Crucify him, crucify

---

[a] *Literally* of the Power of God.        [b] *Or* You are right, for I am.
[c] *Or* to be an anointed king.        [d] *Or* It is as you say.        [e] *Some
witnesses read* (17) At festival time he was obliged to release one person for them; (18) and now . . .

him!' For the third time he spoke to them: 'Why, what 22
wrong has he done? I have not found him guilty of any
capital offence. I will therefore let him off with a flogging.'
But they insisted on their demand, shouting that Jesus 23
should be crucified. Their shouts prevailed and Pilate 24
decided that they should have their way. He released the 25
man they asked for, the man who had been put in prison
for insurrection and murder, and gave Jesus up to their
will.

As THEY LED HIM AWAY to execution they seized upon 26
a man called Simon, from Cyrene, on his way in from the
country, put the cross on his back, and made him walk
behind Jesus carrying it.

Great numbers of people followed, many women among 27
them, who mourned and lamented over him. Jesus turned 28
to them and said, 'Daughters of Jerusalem, do not weep
for me; no, weep for yourselves and your children. For the 29
days are surely coming when they will say, "Happy are the
barren, the wombs that never bore a child, the breasts that
never fed one." Then they will start saying to the mount- 30
ains, "Fall on us", and to the hills, "Cover us." For if these 31
things are done when the wood is green, what will happen
when it is dry?'

There were two others with him, criminals who were 32
being led away to execution; and when they reached the 33
place called The Skull, they crucified him there, and the
criminals with him, one on his right and the other on his
left. Jesus said, 'Father, forgive them; they do not know 34
what they are doing.'[a]

They divided his clothes among them by casting lots.
The people stood looking on, and their rulers jeered at 35
him: 'He saved others: now let him save himself, if this is
God's Messiah, his Chosen.' The soldiers joined in the 36
mockery and came forward offering him their sour wine.
'If you are the king of the Jews,' they said, 'save yourself.' 37
There was an inscription above his head which ran: 'This 38
is the king of the Jews.'

One of the criminals who hung there with him taunted 39
him: 'Are not you the Messiah? Save yourself, and us.' But 40
the other rebuked him: 'Have you no fear of God? You are
under the same sentence as he. For us it is plain justice; 41
we are paying the price for our misdeeds; but this man has
done nothing wrong.' And he said, 'Jesus, remember me 42

[a] *Some witnesses omit* Jesus said, 'Father . . . doing.'

43 when you come to your throne.'[a] He answered, 'I tell you this: today you shall be with me in Paradise.'

44 By now it was about midday and a darkness fell over the
45 whole land, which lasted until three in the afternoon; the sun's light failed. And the curtain of the temple was torn
46 in two. Then Jesus gave a loud cry and said, 'Father, into thy hands I commit my spirit'; and with these words he
47 died. The centurion saw it all, and gave praise to God. 'Beyond all doubt', he said, 'this man was innocent.'
48 The crowd who had assembled for the spectacle, when they saw what had happened, went home beating their breasts.

49 His friends had all been standing at a distance; the women who had accompanied him from Galilee stood with them and watched it all.

50 Now there was a man called Joseph, a member of the
51 Council, a good, upright man, who had dissented from their policy and the action they had taken. He came from the Judaean town of Arimathaea, and he was one who
52 looked forward to the kingdom of God. This man now
53 approached Pilate and asked for the body of Jesus. Taking it down from the cross, he wrapped it in a linen sheet, and laid it in a tomb cut out of the rock, in which no one had
54 been laid before. It was Friday, and the Sabbath was about to begin.

55 The women who had accompanied him from Galilee followed; they took note of the tomb and observed how his
56 body was laid. Then they went home and prepared spices and perfumes; and on the Sabbath they rested in obedience
24 to the commandment. But on the Sunday morning very early they came to the tomb bringing the spices they had
2 prepared. Finding that the stone had been rolled away
3 from the tomb, they went inside; but the body was not to
4 be found. While they stood utterly at a loss, all of a sudden
5 two men in dazzling garments were at their side. They were terrified, and stood with eyes cast down, but the men said,
6 'Why search among the dead for one who lives?[b] Remem-
7 ber what he told you while he was still in Galilee, about the Son of Man: how he must be given up into the power of sinful men and be crucified, and must rise again on the
8 9 third day.' Then they recalled his words and, returning from the tomb, they reported all this to the Eleven and all the others.

[a] *Some witnesses read* come in royal power.    [b] *Some witnesses insert* He is not here: he has been raised.

The women were Mary of Magdala, Joanna, and Mary 10
the mother<sup>a</sup> of James, and they, with the other women,
told the apostles. But the story appeared to them to be 11
nonsense, and they would not believe them.<sup>b</sup>

THAT SAME DAY two of them were on their way to a 13
village called Emmaus, which lay about seven miles from
Jerusalem, and they were talking together about all these 14
happenings. As they talked and discussed it with one 15
another, Jesus himself came up and walked along with
them; but something kept them from seeing who it was. 16
He asked them, 'What is it you are debating as you walk?' 17
They halted, their faces full of gloom, and one, called 18
Cleopas, answered, 'Are you the only person staying in
Jerusalem not to know<sup>c</sup> what has happened there in the
last few days?' 'What do you mean?' he said. 'All this about 19
Jesus of Nazareth,' they replied, 'a prophet powerful in
speech and action before God and the whole people; how 20
our chief priests and rulers handed him over to be sentenced
to death, and crucified him. But we had been hoping that 21
he was the man to liberate Israel. What is more, this is the
third day since it happened, and now some women of our 22
company have astounded us: they went early to the tomb,
but failed to find his body, and returned with a story that 23
they had seen a vision of angels who told them he was
alive. So some of our people went to the tomb and found 24
things just as the women had said; but him they did not
see.'

'How dull you are!' he answered. 'How slow to believe 25
all that the prophets said! Was the Messiah not bound to 26
suffer thus before entering upon his glory?' Then he began 27
with Moses and all the prophets, and explained to them
the passages which referred to himself in every part of
the scriptures.

By this time they had reached the village to which they 28
were going, and he made as if to continue his journey,
but they pressed him: 'Stay with us, for evening draws on, 29
and the day is almost over.' So he went in to stay with
them. And when he had sat down with them at table, he 30
took bread and said the blessing; he broke the bread, and

---

<sup>a</sup> Or wife, or daughter.          <sup>b</sup> Some witnesses add (12) Peter, how-
ever, got up and ran to the tomb, and, peering in, saw the wrappings
and nothing more; and he went home amazed at what had happened.
<sup>c</sup> Or Have you been staying by yourself in Jerusalem, that you do
not know . . .

31 offered it to them. Then their eyes were opened, and they
32 recognized him; and he vanished from their sight. They
said to one another, 'Did we not feel our hearts on fire as
he talked with us on the road and explained the scriptures
to us?'

33 Without a moment's delay they set out and returned to
Jerusalem. There they found that the Eleven and the rest
34 of the company had assembled, and were saying, 'It is
35 true: the Lord has risen; he has appeared to Simon.' Then
they gave their account of the events of their journey and
told how he had been recognized by them at the breaking
of the bread.

36 As they were talking about all this, there he was, stand-
37 ing among them.[a] Startled and terrified, they thought they
38 were seeing a ghost. But he said, 'Why are you so per-
39 turbed? Why do questionings arise in your minds? Look
at my hands and feet. It is I myself. Touch me and see; no
41 ghost has flesh and bones as you can see that I have.'[b] They
were still unconvinced, still wondering, for it seemed too
good to be true. So he asked them, 'Have you anything
42 here to eat?' They offered him a piece of fish they had
43 cooked, which he took and ate before their eyes.

44 And he said to them, 'This is what I meant by saying,
while I was still with you, that everything written about
me in the Law of Moses and in the prophets and psalms
45 was bound to be fulfilled.' Then he opened their minds to
46 understand the scriptures. 'This', he said, 'is what is
written: that the Messiah is to suffer death and to rise
47 from the dead on the third day, and that in his name
repentance bringing the forgiveness of sins is to be pro-
48 claimed to all nations. Begin from Jerusalem; it is you
49 who are the witnesses to it all. And mark this: I am sending
upon you my Father's promised gift; so stay here in this
city until you are armed with the power from above.'

50 Then he led them out as far as Bethany, and blessed
51 them with uplifted hands; and in the act of blessing he
52 parted from them.[c] And they[d] returned to Jerusalem with
53 great joy, and spent all their time in the temple praising
God.

[a] *Some witnesses insert* And he said to them, 'Peace be with you!'
[b] *Some witnesses insert* (40) After saying this he showed them his hands
and feet.    [c] *Some witnesses add* and was carried up into heaven.
[d] *Some witnesses insert* worshipped him and . . .

# THE
# GOSPEL ACCORDING TO
# JOHN

## THE COMING OF CHRIST

**W**HEN ALL THINGS BEGAN, the Word al- 1
ready was.[a] The Word dwelt with God, and what
God was, the Word was. The Word, then, was 2
with God at the beginning, and through him all things came 3
to be; no single thing was created without him. All that
came to be was alive with his life,[b] and that life was the 4
light of men. The light shines on in the dark, and the dark- 5
ness has never mastered it.

There appeared a man named John, sent from God; he 6 7
came as a witness to testify to the light, that all might
become believers through him. He was not himself the 8
light; he came to bear witness to the light. The real light 9
which enlightens every man was even then coming into the
world.[c]

He was in the world;[d] but the world, though it owed its 10
being to him, did not recognize him. He entered his own 11
realm, and his own would not receive him. But to all who 12
did receive him, to those who have yielded him their
allegiance, he gave the right to become children of God,
not born of any human stock, or by the fleshly desire of 13
a human father, but the offspring of God himself. So the 14
Word became flesh; he came to dwell among us, and we
saw his glory, such glory as befits the Father's only Son,
full of grace and truth.

Here is John's testimony to him: he cried aloud, 'This 15
is the man I meant when I said, "He comes after me, but
takes rank before me"; for before I was born, he already
was.'

---

[a] *Or* The Word was at the creation.   [b] *Or* no single created thing
came into being without him. There was life in him . . .
[c] *Or* The light was in being, light absolute, enlightening every man
born into the world.   [d] *Or* The Word, then, was in the world.

147

16 Out of his full store we have all received grace upon
17 grace; for while the Law was given through Moses, grace
18 and truth came through Jesus Christ. No one has ever
seen God; but God's only Son, he who is nearest to the
Father's heart, he has made him known.[a]

19 THIS IS THE TESTIMONY which John gave when the
Jews of Jerusalem sent a deputation of priests and Levites
20 to ask him who he was. He confessed without reserve and
21 avowed, 'I am not the Messiah.' 'What then? Are you
Elijah?' 'No', he replied. 'Are you the prophet we await?'
22 He answered 'No.' 'Then who are you?' they asked. 'We
must give an answer to those who sent us. What account
23 do you give of yourself?' He answered in the words of the
prophet Isaiah: 'I am a voice crying aloud in the wilderness, "Make the Lord's highway straight."'
24 25 Some Pharisees who were in the deputation asked him,
'If you are not the Messiah, nor Elijah, nor the prophet,
26 why then are you baptizing?' 'I baptize in water,' John
replied, 'but among you, though you do not know him,
27 stands the one who is to come after me. I am not good
28 enough to unfasten his shoes.' This took place at Bethany
beyond Jordan, where John was baptizing.
29 The next day he saw Jesus coming towards him. 'Look,'
he said, 'there is the Lamb of God; it is he who takes away
30 the sin of the world. This is he of whom I spoke when I
said, "After me a man is coming who takes rank before
31 me"; for before I was born, he already was. I myself did
not know who he was; but the very reason why I came,
baptizing in water, was that he might be revealed to
Israel.'
32 John testified further: 'I saw the Spirit coming down
33 from heaven like a dove and resting upon him. I did not
know him, but he who sent me to baptize in water had
told me, "When you see the Spirit coming down upon someone and resting upon him, you will know that this is he
34 who is to baptize in Holy Spirit." I saw it myself, and I
have borne witness. This is God's Chosen One.'[b]
35 The next day again John was standing with two of his
36 disciples when Jesus passed by. John looked towards him
37 and said, 'There is the Lamb of God.' The two disciples

[a] *Some witnesses read* but the only one, the one nearest to the Father's
heart, has made him known; *others read* but the only one, himself God,
the nearest to the Father's heart, has made him known.
[b] *Some witnesses read* This is the Son of God.

heard him say this, and followed Jesus. When he turned 38
and saw them following him, he asked, 'What are you
looking for?' They said, 'Rabbi' (which means a teacher),
'where are you staying?' 'Come and see', he replied. So 39
they went and saw where he was staying, and spent the
rest of the day with him. It was then about four in the
afternoon.

One of the two who followed Jesus after hearing what 40
John said was Andrew, Simon Peter's brother. The first 41
thing he did was to find*a* his brother Simon. He said to
him, 'We have found the Messiah' (which is the Hebrew
for 'Christ'). He brought Simon to Jesus, who looked at 42
him and said, 'You are Simon son of John. You shall be
called Cephas' (that is, Peter, the Rock).

The next day Jesus decided to leave for Galilee. He met 43
Philip, who, like Andrew and Peter, came from Bethsaida, 44
and said to him, 'Follow me.' Philip went to find Nathanael, 45
and told him, 'We have met the man spoken of by Moses
in the Law, and by the prophets: it is Jesus son of Joseph,
from Nazareth.' 'Nazareth!' Nathanael exclaimed; 'can 46
anything good come from Nazareth?' Philip said, 'Come
and see.' When Jesus saw Nathanael coming, he said, 47
'Here is an Israelite worthy of the name; there is nothing
false in him.' Nathanael asked him, 'How do you come to 48
know me?' Jesus replied, 'I saw you under the fig-tree
before Philip spoke to you.' 'Rabbi,' said Nathanael, 'you 49
are the Son of God; you are king of Israel.' Jesus answered, 50
'Is this the ground of your faith, that I told you I saw you
under the fig-tree? You shall see greater things than that.'
Then he added, 'In truth, in very truth I tell you all, you 51
shall see heaven wide open, and God's angels ascending
and descending upon the Son of Man.'

## CHRIST THE GIVER OF LIFE

ON THE THIRD DAY there was a wedding at Cana- 2
in-Galilee. The mother of Jesus was there, and Jesus 2
and his disciples were guests also. The wine gave out, so 3
Jesus's mother said to him, 'They have no wine left.' He 4
answered, 'Your concern, mother, is not mine. My hour
has not yet come.' His mother said to the servants, 'Do 5
whatever he tells you.' There were six stone water-jars 6

---

*a Some witnesses read* In the morning he found . . .

standing near, of the kind used for Jewish rites of purifica-
7 tion; each held from twenty to thirty gallons. Jesus said
to the servants, 'Fill the jars with water', and they filled
8 them to the brim. 'Now draw some off', he ordered, 'and
9 take it to the steward of the feast'; and they did so. The
steward tasted the water now turned into wine, not knowing its source; though the servants who had drawn the
10 water knew. He hailed the bridegroom and said, 'Everyone
serves the best wine first, and waits until the guests have
drunk freely before serving the poorer sort; but you have
kept the best wine till now.'
11      This deed at Cana-in-Galilee is the first of the signs by
which Jesus revealed his glory and led his disciples to
believe in him.

12 AFTER THIS he went down to Capernaum in company
with his mother, his brothers, and his disciples, but they
13 did not stay there long. As it was near the time of the
14 Jewish Passover, Jesus went up to Jerusalem. There he
found in the temple the dealers in cattle, sheep, and pigeons,
15 and the money-changers seated at their tables. Jesus
made a whip of cords and drove them out of the temple,
sheep, cattle, and all. He upset the tables of the money-
16 changers, scattering their coins. Then he turned on the
dealers in pigeons: 'Take them out,' he said; 'you must not
17 turn my Father's house into a market.' His disciples recalled the words of Scripture, 'Zeal for thy house will
18 destroy me.' The Jews challenged Jesus: 'What sign', they
19 asked, 'can you show as authority for your action?' 'Destroy this temple,' Jesus replied, 'and in three days I will
20 raise it again.' They said, 'It has taken forty-six years to
build this temple. Are you going to raise it again in three
21 days?' But the temple he was speaking of was his body.
22 After his resurrection his disciples recalled what he had
said, and they believed the Scripture and the words that
Jesus had spoken.

23 WHILE HE WAS in Jerusalem for Passover many gave
their allegiance to him when they saw the signs that he
24 performed. But Jesus for his part would not trust himself
25 to them. He knew men so well, all of them, that he needed
no evidence from others about a man, for he himself
could tell what was in a man.

3 THERE WAS ONE of the Pharisees named Nicodemus,
2 a member of the Jewish Council, who came to Jesus by

night. 'Rabbi,' he said, 'we know that you are a teacher sent by God; no one could perform these signs of yours unless God were with him.' Jesus answered, 'In truth, 3 in very truth I tell you, unless a man has been born over again he cannot see the kingdom of God.' 'But how is it 4 possible', said Nicodemus, 'for a man to be born when he is old? Can he enter his mother's womb a second time and be born?' Jesus answered, 'In truth I tell you, no one can 5 enter the kingdom of God without being born from water and spirit. Flesh can give birth only to flesh; it is spirit that 6 gives birth to spirit. You ought not to be astonished, 7 then, when I tell you that you must be born over again. The 8 wind[a] blows where it wills; you hear the sound of it, but you do not know where it comes from, or where it is going. So with everyone who is born from spirit[a].'

Nicodemus replied, 'How is this possible?' 'What!' said 9 10 Jesus. 'Is this famous teacher of Israel ignorant of such things? In very truth I tell you, we speak of what we know, 11 and testify to what we have seen, and yet you all reject our testimony. If you disbelieve me when I talk to you 12 about things on earth, how are you to believe if I should talk about the things of heaven?

'No one ever went up into heaven except the one who 13 came down from heaven, the Son of Man whose home is in heaven.[b] This Son of Man must be lifted up as the 14 serpent was lifted up by Moses in the wilderness, so that 15 everyone who has faith in him may in him possess eternal life.

'God loved the world so much that he gave his only Son, 16 that everyone who has faith in him may not die but have eternal life. It was not to judge the world that God sent 17 his Son into the world, but that through him the world might be saved.

'The man who puts his faith in him does not come under 18 judgement; but the unbeliever has already been judged in that he has not given his allegiance to God's only Son. Here 19 lies the test: the light has come into the world, but men preferred darkness to light because their deeds were evil. Bad men all hate the light and avoid it, for fear their 20 practices should be shown up. The honest man comes to 21 the light so that it may be clearly seen that God is in all he does.'

---

[a] wind *and* spirit *are translations of the same Greek word, which has both meanings.*      [b] *Some witnesses omit* whose home is in heaven.

22 AFTER THIS, Jesus went into Judaea with his disciples,
23 stayed there with them, and baptized. John too was baptizing at Aenon, near to Salim, because water was plentiful
in that region; and people were constantly coming for
24 baptism. This was before John's imprisonment.

25 Some of John's disciples had fallen into a dispute with
26 Jews about purification; so they came to him and said,
'Rabbi, there was a man with you on the other side of the
Jordan, to whom you bore your witness. Here he is, bap-
27 tizing, and crowds are flocking to him.' John's answer was:
28 'A man can have only what God gives him. You yourselves
can testify that I said, "I am not the Messiah; I have been
29 sent as his forerunner." It is the bridegroom to whom the
bride belongs. The bridegroom's friend, who stands by and
listens to him, is overjoyed at hearing the bridegroom's
30 voice. This joy, this perfect joy, is now mine. As he grows
greater, I must grow less.'

31 He who comes from above is above all others; he who is
from the earth belongs to the earth and uses earthly
32 speech. He who comes from heaven[a] bears witness to what
33 he has seen and heard, yet no one accepts his witness. To
34 accept his witness is to attest that God speaks the truth; for
he whom God sent utters the words of God, so measureless
35 is God's gift of the Spirit. The Father loves the Son and
36 has entrusted him with all authority. He who puts his
faith in the Son has hold of eternal life, but he who disobeys the Son shall not see that life; God's wrath rests
upon him.

4 A REPORT NOW REACHED the Pharisees: 'Jesus is
2 winning and baptizing more disciples than John'; although, in fact, it was only the disciples who were baptiz-
3 ing and not Jesus himself. When Jesus learned this, he left
4 Judaea and set out once more for Galilee. He had to pass
5 through Samaria, and on his way came to a Samaritan
town called Sychar, near the plot of ground which Jacob
6 gave to his son Joseph and the spring called Jacob's well.
It was about noon, and Jesus, tired after his journey, sat
down by the well.

8 The disciples had gone away to the town to buy food.
7 Meanwhile a Samaritan woman came to draw water. Jesus
9 said to her, 'Give me a drink.' The Samaritan woman said,
'What! You, a Jew, ask a drink of me, a Samaritan
woman?' (Jews and Samaritans, it should be noted, do not

---

[a] *Some witnesses insert* is above all and . . .

use vessels in common.[a]) Jesus answered her, 'If only you 10
knew what God gives, and who it is that is asking you for
a drink, you would have asked him and he would have
given you living water.' 'Sir,' the woman said, 'you have 11
no bucket and this well is deep. How can you give me
"living water"? Are you a greater man than Jacob our 12
ancestor, who gave us the well, and drank from it himself,
he and his sons, and his cattle too?' Jesus said, 'Everyone 13
who drinks this water will be thirsty again, but whoever 14
drinks the water that I shall give him will never suffer
thirst any more. The water that I shall give him will be an
inner spring always welling up for eternal life.' 'Sir,' said 15
the woman, 'give me that water, and then I shall not be
thirsty, nor have to come all this way to draw.'

Jesus replied, 'Go home, call your husband and come 16
back.' She answered, 'I have no husband.' 'You are right', 17
said Jesus, 'in saying that you have no husband, for, 18
although you have had five husbands, the man with whom
you are now living is not your husband; you told me the
truth there.' 'Sir,' she replied, 'I can see that you are a 19
prophet. Our fathers worshipped on this mountain, but 20
you Jews say that the temple where God should be worshipped is in Jerusalem.' 'Believe me,' said Jesus, 'the time 21
is coming when you will worship the Father neither on this
mountain, nor in Jerusalem. You Samaritans worship 22
without knowing what you worship, while we worship
what we know. It is from the Jews that salvation comes.
But the time approaches, indeed it is already here, when 23
those who are real worshippers will worship the Father in
spirit and in truth. Such are the worshippers whom the
Father wants. God is spirit, and those who worship him 24
must worship in spirit and in truth.' The woman answered, 25
'I know that Messiah' (that is Christ) 'is coming. When he
comes he will tell us everything.' Jesus said, 'I am he, 26
I who am speaking to you now.'

At that moment his disciples returned, and were aston- 27
ished to find him talking with a woman; but none of them
said, 'What do you want?' or, 'Why are you talking with
her?' The woman put down her water-jar and went away 28
to the town, where she said to the people, 'Come and see 29
a man who has told me everything I ever did. Could this
be the Messiah?' They came out of the town and made 30
their way towards him.

[a] Or Jews, it should be noted, are not on familiar terms with Samaritans; *some witnesses omit these words.*

31     Meanwhile the disciples were urging him, 'Rabbi, have
32 something to eat.' But he said, 'I have food to eat of which
33 you know nothing.' At this the disciples said to one an-
34 other, 'Can someone have brought him food?' But Jesus
said, 'It is meat and drink for me to do the will of him
who sent me until I have finished his work.

35     'Do you not say, "Four months more and then comes
harvest"? But look, I tell you, look round on the fields;
36 they are already white, ripe for harvest. The reaper is
drawing his pay and gathering a crop for eternal life, so
37 that sower and reaper may rejoice together. That is how
the saying comes true: "One sows, and another reaps."
38 I sent you to reap a crop for which you have not toiled.
Others toiled and you have come in for the harvest of
their toil.'

39     Many Samaritans of that town came to believe in him
because of the woman's testimony: 'He told me everything
40 I ever did.' So when these Samaritans had come to him
they pressed him to stay with them; and he stayed there
41 two days. Many more became believers because of what
42 they heard from his own lips. They told the woman, 'It is
no longer because of what you said that we believe, for we
have heard him ourselves; and we know that this is in
truth the Saviour of the world.'

43     WHEN THE TWO DAYS were over he set out for Galilee;
44 for Jesus himself declared that a prophet is without honour
45 in his own country. On his arrival in Galilee the Galileans
gave him a welcome, because they had seen all that he did
at the festival in Jerusalem; they had been at the festival
themselves.

46     Once again he visited Cana-in-Galilee, where he had
turned the water into wine. An officer in the royal service
47 was there, whose son was lying ill at Capernaum. When he
heard that Jesus had come from Judaea into Galilee, he
came to him and begged him to go down and cure his son,
48 who was at the point of death. Jesus said to him, 'Will
none of you ever believe without seeing signs and portents?'
49 The officer pleaded with him, 'Sir, come down before my
50 boy dies.' Then Jesus said, 'Return home; your son will
live.' The man believed what Jesus said and started for
51 home. When he was on his way down his servants met him
52 with the news, 'Your boy is going to live.' So he asked them
what time it was when he began to recover. They said,
53 'Yesterday at one in the afternoon the fever left him.' The

father noted that this was the exact time when Jesus had
said to him, 'Your son will live', and he and all his household became believers.

This was now the second sign which Jesus performed 54
after coming down from Judaea into Galilee.

LATER ON Jesus went up to Jerusalem for one of the 5
Jewish festivals.<sup>a</sup> Now at the Sheep-Pool in Jerusalem 2
there is a place with five colonnades. Its name in the
language of the Jews is Bethesda. In these colonnades 3
there lay a crowd of sick people, blind, lame, and paralysed.<sup>b</sup> Among them was a man who had been crippled for 5
thirty-eight years. When Jesus saw him lying there and 6
was aware that he had been ill a long time, he asked him,
'Do you want to recover?' 'Sir,' he replied, 'I have no one 7
to put me in the pool when the water is disturbed, but
while I am moving, someone else is in the pool before me.'
Jesus answered, 'Rise to your feet, take up your bed and 8
walk.' The man recovered instantly, took up his stretcher, 9
and began to walk.

That day was a Sabbath. So the Jews said to the man 10
who had been cured, 'It is the Sabbath. You are not allowed
to carry your bed on the Sabbath.' He answered, 'The man 11
who cured me said, "Take up your bed and walk."' They 12
asked him, 'Who is the man who told you to take up your
bed and walk?' But the cripple who had been cured did 13
not know; for the place was crowded and Jesus had slipped
away. A little later Jesus found him in the temple and 14
said to him, 'Now that you are well again, leave your sinful
ways, or you may suffer something worse.' The man went 15
away and told the Jews that it was Jesus who had cured
him.

It was works of this kind done on the Sabbath that 16
stirred the Jews to persecute Jesus. He defended himself 17
by saying, 'My Father has never yet ceased his work, and
I am working too.' This made the Jews still more deter- 18
mined to kill him, because he was not only breaking the
Sabbath, but, by calling God his own Father, he claimed
equality with God.

To this charge Jesus replied, 'In truth, in very truth I 19

---

<sup>a</sup> *Some witnesses read* for the Jewish festival.     <sup>b</sup> *Some witnesses
add* waiting for the disturbance of the water; *some further insert* (4)
for from time to time an angel came down into the pool and stirred
up the water. The first to plunge in after this disturbance recovered
from whatever disease had afflicted him.

tell you, the Son can do nothing by himself; he does only
what he sees the Father doing: what the Father does, the
20 Son does. For the Father loves the Son and shows him all
his works, and will show greater yet, to fill you with
21 wonder. As the Father raises the dead and gives them life,
22 so the Son gives life to men, as he determines. And again,
the Father does not judge anyone, but has given full
23 jurisdiction to the Son; it is his will that all should pay the
same honour to the Son as to the Father. To deny honour
to the Son is to deny it to the Father who sent him.
24    'In very truth, anyone who gives heed to what I say and
puts his trust in him who sent me has hold of eternal life,
and does not come up for judgement, but has already
25 passed from death to life. In truth, in very truth I tell you,
a time is coming, indeed it is already here, when the dead
shall hear the voice of the Son of God, and all who hear
26 shall come to life. For as the Father has life-giving power
in himself, so has the Son, by the Father's gift.
27    'As Son of Man, he has also been given the right to pass
28 judgement. Do not wonder at this, because the time is
coming when all who are in the grave shall hear his voice
29 and come out: those who have done right will rise to life;
those who have done wrong will rise to hear their doom.
30 I cannot act by myself; I judge as I am bidden, and my
sentence is just, because my aim is not my own will, but
the will of him who sent me.
31    'If I testify on my own behalf, that testimony does not
32 hold good. There is another who bears witness for me, and
33 I know that his testimony holds. Your messengers have
34 been to John; you have his testimony to the truth. Not
that I rely on human testimony, but I remind you of it for
35 your own salvation. John was a lamp, burning brightly,
36 and for a time you were ready to exult in his light. But I
rely on a testimony higher than John's. There is enough
to testify that the Father has sent me, in the works my
Father gave me to do and to finish—the very works I have
37 in hand. This testimony to me was given by the Father who
sent me, although you never heard his voice, or saw his
38 form. But his word has found no home in you, for you do
39 not believe the one whom he sent. You study the scriptures
diligently, supposing that in having them you have eternal
40 life; yet, although their testimony points to me, you refuse
to come to me for that life.
41 42    'I do not look to men for honour. But with you it is
different, as I know well, for you have no love for God in

you. I have come accredited by my Father, and you have　43
no welcome for me; if another comes self-accredited you
will welcome him. How can you have faith so long as you　44
receive honour from one another, and care nothing for the
honour that comes from him who alone is God? Do not　45
imagine that I shall be your accuser at the Father's tribunal. Your accuser is Moses, the very Moses on whom you
have set your hope. If you believed Moses you would　46
believe what I tell you, for it was about me that he wrote.
But if you do not believe what he wrote, how are you to　47
believe what I say?'

SOME TIME LATER Jesus withdrew to the farther shore　6
of the Sea of Galilee (or Tiberias), and a large crowd of　2
people followed who had seen the signs he performed in
healing the sick. Then Jesus went up the hill-side and sat　3
down with his disciples. It was near the time of Passover,　4
the great Jewish festival. Raising his eyes and seeing a　5
large crowd coming towards him, Jesus said to Philip,
'Where are we to buy bread to feed these people?' This he　6
said to test him; Jesus himself knew what he meant to do.
Philip replied, 'Twenty pounds*a* would not buy enough　7
bread for every one of them to have a little.' One of his　8
disciples, Andrew, the brother of Simon Peter, said to him,
'There is a boy here who has five barley loaves and two　9
fishes; but what is that among so many?' Jesus said, 'Make　10
the people sit down.' There was plenty of grass there, so
the men sat down, about five thousand of them. Then Jesus　11
took the loaves, gave thanks, and distributed them to the
people as they sat there. He did the same with the fishes,
and they had as much as they wanted. When everyone　12
had had enough, he said to his disciples, 'Collect the pieces
left over, so that nothing may be lost.' This they did, and　13
filled twelve baskets with the pieces left uneaten of the
five barley loaves.

　　When the people saw the sign Jesus had performed, the　14
word went round, 'Surely this must be the prophet that
was to come into the world.' Jesus, aware that they meant　15
to come and seize him to proclaim him king, withdrew
again to the hills by himself.

　　At nightfall his disciples went down to the sea, got into　16 17
their boat, and pushed off to cross the water to Capernaum.
Darkness had already fallen, and Jesus had not yet joined
them. By now a strong wind was blowing and the sea grew　18

　　　　　　　　*a* *Literally* 200 denarii.

19 rough. When they had rowed about three or four miles they saw Jesus walking on the sea and approaching the
20 boat. They were terrified, but he called out, 'It is I; do not
21 be afraid.' Then they were ready to take him aboard, and immediately the boat reached the land they were making for.

22 NEXT MORNING the crowd was standing on the opposite shore. They had seen only one boat there, and Jesus, they knew, had not embarked with his disciples, who had
23 gone away without him. Boats from Tiberias, however, came ashore[a] near the place where the people had eaten
24 the bread over which the Lord gave thanks.[b] When the people saw that neither Jesus nor his disciples were any
25 longer there, they themselves went aboard these boats and made for Capernaum in search of Jesus. They found him
26 on the other side. 'Rabbi,' they said, 'when did you come here?' Jesus replied, 'In very truth I know that you have not come looking for me because you saw signs, but because
27 you ate the bread and your hunger was satisfied. You must work, not for this perishable food, but for the food that lasts, the food of eternal life.

'This food the Son of Man will give you, for he it is upon whom God the Father has set the seal of his authority.'
28 'Then what must we do', they asked him, 'if we are to work
29 as God would have us work?' Jesus replied, 'This is the work that God requires: believe in the one whom he has sent.'
30 They said, 'What sign can you give us to see, so that we
31 may believe you? What is the work you do? Our ancestors had manna to eat in the desert; as Scripture says, "He gave
32 them bread from heaven to eat." ' Jesus answered, 'I tell you this: the truth is, not that Moses gave you the bread from heaven, but that my Father gives you the real bread
33 from heaven. The bread that God gives comes down[c] from
34 heaven and brings life to the world.' They said to him,
35 'Sir, give us this bread now and always.' Jesus said to them, 'I am the bread of life. Whoever comes to me shall never be hungry, and whoever believes in me shall never
36 be thirsty. But you, as I said, do not believe although
37 you have seen.[d] All that the Father gives me will come to me, and the man who comes to me I will never turn away.
38 I have come down from heaven, not to do my own will,

---

[a] *Some witnesses read* Other boats from Tiberias came ashore . . .
[b] *Some witnesses omit* over which . . . thanks.          [c] *Or* is he who comes down . . .          [d] *Some witnesses add* me.

158

but the will of him who sent me. It is his will that I should 39
not lose even one of all that he has given me, but raise
them all up on the last day. For it is my Father's will that 40
everyone who looks upon the Son and puts his faith in
him shall possess eternal life; and I will raise him up on
the last day.'

At this the Jews began to murmur disapprovingly be- 41
cause he said, 'I am the bread which came down from
heaven.' They said, 'Surely this is Jesus son of Joseph; we 42
know his father and mother. How can he now say, "I have
come down from heaven"?' Jesus answered, 'Stop mur- 43
muring among yourselves. No man can come to me unless 44
he is drawn by the Father who sent me; and I will raise
him up on the last day. It is written in the prophets: "And 45
they shall all be taught by God." Everyone who has listened
to the Father and learned from him comes to me.

'I do not mean that anyone has seen the Father. He who 46
has come from God has seen the Father, and he alone. In 47
truth, in very truth I tell you, the believer possesses eternal
life. I am the bread of life. Your forefathers ate the manna 48 49
in the desert and they are dead. I am speaking of the bread 50
that comes down from heaven, which a man may eat, and
never die. I am that living bread which has come down 51
from heaven; if anyone eats this bread he shall live for
ever. Moreover, the bread which I will give is my own
flesh; I give it for the life of the world.'

This led to a fierce dispute among the Jews. 'How can 52
this man give us his flesh to eat?' they said. Jesus replied, 53
'In truth, in very truth I tell you, unless you eat the flesh
of the Son of Man and drink his blood you can have no
life in you. Whoever eats my flesh and drinks my blood 54
possesses eternal life, and I will raise him up on the last
day. My flesh is real food; my blood is real drink. Whoever 55 56
eats my flesh and drinks my blood dwells continually in
me and I dwell in him. As the living Father sent me, and 57
I live because of the Father, so he who eats me shall live
because of me. This is the bread which came down from 58
heaven; and it is not like the bread which our fathers ate:
they are dead, but whoever eats this bread shall live for
ever.'

THIS WAS SPOKEN in synagogue when Jesus was teach- 59
ing in Capernaum. Many of his disciples on hearing it 60
exclaimed, 'This is more than we can stomach! Why listen
to such talk?' Jesus was aware that his disciples were 61

murmuring about it and asked them, 'Does this shock
62 you? What if you see the Son of Man ascending to the
63 place where he was before? The spirit alone gives life; the
flesh is of no avail; the words which I have spoken to you
64 are both spirit and life. And yet there are some of you who
have no faith.' For Jesus knew all along who were without
65 faith and who was to betray him. So he said, 'This is why
I told you that no one can come to me unless it has been
granted to him by the Father.'

66    From that time on, many of his disciples withdrew and
67 no longer went about with him. So Jesus asked the Twelve,
68 'Do you also want to leave me?' Simon Peter answered
him, 'Lord, to whom shall we go? Your words are words of
69 eternal life. We have faith, and we know that you are the
70 Holy One of God.' Jesus answered, 'Have I not chosen you,
71 all twelve? Yet one of you is a devil.' He meant Judas, son
of Simon Iscariot. He it was who would betray him, and
he was one of the Twelve.

# THE GREAT CONTROVERSY

7   AFTERWARDS JESUS went about in Galilee. He
    wished to avoid Judaea because the Jews were looking
2 for a chance to kill him. As the Jewish Feast of Tabernacles
3 was close at hand, his brothers said to him, 'You should
leave this district and go into Judaea, so that your disciples
4 there may see the great things you are doing. Surely no one
can hope to be in the public eye if he works in seclusion. If
you really are doing such things as these, show yourself to
5 6 the world.' For even his brothers had no faith in him. Jesus
said to them, 'The right time for me has not yet come, but
7 any time is right for you. The world cannot hate you; but
8 it hates me for exposing the wickedness of its ways. Go to
the festival yourselves. I am not<sup>a</sup> going up to this festival
9 because the right time for me has not yet come.' With this
answer he stayed behind in Galilee.

10    Later, when his brothers had gone to the festival, he
11 went up himself, not publicly, but almost in secret. The
Jews were looking for him at the festival and asking,
12 'Where is he?', and there was much whispering about him
in the crowds. 'He is a good man', said some. 'No,' said
13 others, 'he is leading the people astray.' However, no one
talked about him openly, for fear of the Jews.

---

<sup>a</sup> *Some witnesses read* not yet.

W HEN THE FESTIVAL was already half over, Jesus went  14
up to the temple and began to teach. The Jews were  15
astonished: 'How is it', they said, 'that this untrained man
has such learning?' Jesus replied, 'The teaching that I  16
give is not my own; it is the teaching of him who sent me.
Whoever has the will to do the will of God shall know  17
whether my teaching comes from him or is merely my own.
Anyone whose teaching is merely his own, aims at honour  18
for himself. But if a man aims at the honour of him who
sent him he is sincere, and there is nothing false in him.

'Did not Moses give you the Law? Yet you all break it.  19
Why are you trying to kill me?' The crowd answered, 'You  20
are possessed! Who wants to kill you?' Jesus replied, 'Once  21
only have I done work on the Sabbath, and you are all taken
aback. But consider: Moses gave you the law of circum-  22
cision (not that it originated with Moses but with the
patriarchs) and you circumcise on the Sabbath. Well then,  23
if a child is circumcised on the Sabbath to avoid breaking
the Law of Moses, why are you indignant with me for
giving health on the Sabbath to the whole of a man's body?
Do not judge superficially, but be just in your judgements.'  24

At this some of the people of Jerusalem began to say, 'Is  25
not this the man they want to put to death? And here he  26
is, speaking openly, and they have not a word to say to him.
Can it be that our rulers have actually decided that this is
the Messiah? And yet we know where this man comes from,  27
but when the Messiah appears no one is to know where he
comes from.' Thereupon Jesus cried aloud as he taught in  28
the temple, 'No doubt you know me; no doubt you know
where I come from.*a* Yet I have not come of my own
accord. I was sent by the One who truly is, and him you
do not know. I know him because I come from him and he  29
it is who sent me.' At this they tried to seize him, but no  30
one laid a hand on him because his appointed hour had
not yet come. Yet among the people many believed in  31
him. 'When the Messiah comes,' they said, 'is it likely that
he will perform more signs than this man?'

The Pharisees overheard these mutterings of the people  32
about him, so the chief priests and the Pharisees sent
temple police to arrest him. Then Jesus said, 'For a little  33
longer I shall be with you; then I am going away to him
who sent me. You will look for me, but you will not find  34
me. Where I am, you cannot come.' So the Jews said to  35
one another, 'Where does he intend to go, that we should

   *a* Or Do you know me? And do you know where I come from?

not be able to find him? Will he go to the Dispersion
36 among the Greeks, and teach the Greeks? What did he
mean by saying, "You will look for me, but you will not
find me. Where I am, you cannot come"?'ᵃ

37 ON THE LAST and greatest day of the festival Jesus
stood and cried aloud, 'If anyone is thirsty let him come
38 to me; whoever believes in me, let him drink.' As Scripture
says, 'Streams of living water shall flow out from within
39 him.'ᵇ He was speaking of the Spirit which believers in him
would receive later; for the Spirit had not yet been given,
because Jesus had not yet been glorified.

40      On hearing this some of the people said, 'This must
41 certainly be the expected prophet.' Others said, 'This is
the Messiah.' Others again, 'Surely the Messiah is not to
42 come from Galilee? Does not Scripture say that the Messiah
is to be of the family of David, from David's village of
43 Bethlehem?' Thus he caused a split among the people.
44 Some were for seizing him, but no one laid hands on him.
45      The temple police came back to the chief priests and
Pharisees, who asked, 'Why have you not brought him?'
46 'No man', they answered, 'ever spoke as this man speaks.'
47 48 The Pharisees retorted, 'Have you too been misled? Is
there a single one of our rulers who has believed in him, or
49 of the Pharisees? As for this rabble, which cares nothing
50 for the Law, a curse is on them.' Then one of their number,
Nicodemus (the man who had once visited Jesus), inter-
51 vened. 'Does our law', he asked them, 'permit us to pass
judgement on a man unless we have first given him a
52 hearing and learned the facts?' 'Are you a Galilean too?'
they retorted. 'Study the scriptures and you will find that
prophets do not come from Galilee.'ᶜ

8 12 ONCE AGAIN JESUS addressed the people: 'I am the
light of the world. No follower of mine shall wander in the
13 dark; he shall have the light of life.' The Pharisees said
to him, 'You are witness in your own cause; your testi-
14 mony is not valid.' Jesus replied, 'My testimony is valid,
even though I do bear witness about myself; because I
know where I come from, and where I am going. You do

---

ᵃ *Some witnesses here insert the passage printed on p. 190.*
ᵇ *Or* 'If any man is thirsty let him come to me and drink. He who
believes in me, as Scripture says, streams of living water shall flow
out from within him.'          ᶜ *Some witnesses here insert the passage
7. 53—8. 11, which is printed on p. 190.*

not know either where I come from or where I am going.
You judge by worldly standards. I pass judgement on no 15
man, but if I do judge, my judgement is valid because it is 16
not I alone who judge, but I and he who sent me. In your 17
own law it is written that the testimony of two witnesses
is valid. Here am I, a witness in my own cause, and my 18
other witness is the Father who sent me.' They asked, 19
'Where is your father?' Jesus replied, 'You know neither
me nor my Father; if you knew me you would know my
Father as well.'

These words were spoken by Jesus in the treasury as he 20
taught in the temple. Yet no one arrested him, because his
hour had not yet come.

Again he said to them, 'I am going away. You will look 21
for me, but you will die in your sin; where I am going you
cannot come.' The Jews then said, 'Perhaps he will kill 22
himself: is that what he means when he says, "Where I am
going you cannot come"?' So Jesus continued, 'You belong 23
to this world below, I to the world above. Your home is in
this world, mine is not. That is why I told you that you 24
would die in your sins. If you do not believe that I am
what I am, you will die in your sins.' They asked him, 25
'Who are you?' Jesus answered, 'Why should I speak to
you at all?ª I have much to say about you—and in judge- 26
ment. But he who sent me speaks the truth, and what I
heard from him I report to the world.'

They did not understand that he was speaking to them 27
about the Father. So Jesus said to them, 'When you have 28
lifted up the Son of Man you will know that I am what I
am. I do nothing on my own authority, but in all that I
say, I have been taught by my Father. He who sent me is 29
present with me, and has not left me alone; for I always
do what is acceptable to him.' As he said this, many put 30
their faith in him.

Turning to the Jews who had believed him, Jesus said, 31
'If you dwell within the revelation I have brought, you are
indeed my disciples; you shall know the truth, and the 32
truth will set you free.' They replied, 'We are Abraham's 33
descendants; we have never been in slavery to any man.
What do you mean by saying, "You will become free
men"?' 'In very truth I tell you', said Jesus, 'that everyone 34
who commits sin is a slave. The slave has no permanent 35
standing in the household, but the son belongs to it for
ever. If then the Son sets you free, you will indeed be free. 36

ª *Or* What I have told you all along.

37 'I know that you are descended from Abraham, but you are bent on killing me because my teaching makes no
38 headway with you. I am revealing in words what I saw in my Father's presence; and you are revealing in action
39 what you learned from your father.' They retorted, 'Abraham is our father.' 'If you were Abraham's children',
40 Jesus replied, 'you would do as Abraham did.ᵃ As it is, you are bent on killing me, a man who told you the truth, as I heard it from God. That is not how Abraham acted.
41 You are doing your own father's work.'

They said, 'We are not base-born; God is our father, and
42 God alone.' Jesus said, 'If God were your father, you would love me, for God is the source of my being, and from him I come. I have not come of my own accord; he sent
43 me. Why do you not understand my language? It is because my revelation is beyond your grasp.

44 'Your father is the devil and you choose to carry out your father's desires. He was a murderer from the beginning, and is not rooted in the truth; there is no truth in him. When he tells a lie he is speaking his own language,
45 for he is a liar and the father of lies. But I speak the truth
46 and therefore you do not believe me. Which of you can prove me in the wrong?ᵇ If what I say is true, why do you
47 not believe me? He who has God for his father listens to the words of God. You are not God's children; that is why you do not listen.'

48 The Jews answered, 'Are we not right in saying that you
49 are a Samaritan, and that you are possessed?' 'I am not possessed,' said Jesus; 'I am honouring my Father, but
50 you dishonour me. I do not care about my own glory;
51 there is one who does care, and he is judge. In very truth I tell you, if anyone obeys my teaching he shall never know what it is to die.'

52 The Jews said, 'Now we are certain that you are possessed. Abraham is dead; the prophets are dead; and yet you say, "If anyone obeys my teaching he shall not know
53 what it is to die." Are you greater than our father Abraham, who is dead? The prophets are dead too. What do you claim to be?'

54 Jesus replied, 'If I glorify myself, that glory of mine is worthless. It is the Father who glorifies me, he of whom
55 you say, "He is our God", though you do not know him. But I know him; if I said that I did not know him I

ᵃ *Some witnesses read* 'If you are Abraham's children', Jesus replied, 'do as Abraham did.'      ᵇ *Or* Which of you convicts me of sin?

should be a liar like you. But in truth I know him and
obey his word.

'Your father Abraham was overjoyed to see my day; he 56
saw it and was glad.' The Jews protested, 'You are not yet 57
fifty years old. How can you have seen Abraham?'[a] Jesus 58
said, 'In very truth I tell you, before Abraham was born,
I am.'

They picked up stones to throw at him, but Jesus was 59
not to be seen; and he left the temple.[b]

As HE WENT on his way Jesus saw a man blind from 9
his birth. His disciples put the question, 'Rabbi, who 2
sinned, this man or his parents? Why was he born blind?'
'It is not that this man or his parents sinned,' Jesus an- 3
swered; 'he was born blind so that God's power might be
displayed in curing him. While daylight lasts we[c] must 4
carry on the work of him who sent me; night comes, when
no one can work. While I am in the world I am the light 5
of the world.'

With these words he spat on the ground and made a 6
paste with the spittle; he spread it on the man's eyes, and 7
said to him, 'Go and wash in the pool of Siloam.' (The
name means 'sent'.) The man went away and washed, and
when he returned he could see.

His neighbours and those who were accustomed to see 8
him begging said, 'Is not this the man who used to sit and
beg?' Others said, 'Yes, this is the man.' Others again said, 9
'No, but it is someone like him.' The man himself said,
'I am the man.' They asked him, 'How were your eyes 10
opened?' He replied, 'The man called Jesus made a paste 11
and smeared my eyes with it, and told me to go to Siloam
and wash. I went and washed, and gained my sight.' 'Where 12
is he?' they asked. He answered, 'I do not know.'

THE MAN who had been blind was brought before the 13
Pharisees. As it was a Sabbath day when Jesus made the 14
paste and opened his eyes, the Pharisees now asked him by 15
what means he had gained his sight. The man told them,
'He spread a paste on my eyes; then I washed, and now I
can see.' Some of the Pharisees said, 'This fellow is no man 16
of God; he does not keep the Sabbath.' Others said, 'How

---

[a] *Some witnesses read* How can Abraham have seen you?
[b] *Or the division may be made after the words* was not to be seen; *the
paragraph following would then begin* Then Jesus left the temple, *and
as he went . . .*    [c] *Some witnesses read* I.

could such signs come from a sinful man?' So they took
17 different sides. Then they continued to question him:
'What have you to say about him? It was your eyes he
opened.' He answered, 'He is a prophet.'

18     The Jews would not believe that the man had been blind
and had gained his sight, until they had summoned his
19 parents and questioned them: 'Is this man your son? Do
you say that he was born blind? How is it that he can see
20 now?' The parents replied, 'We know that he is our son,
21 and that he was born blind. But how it is that he can now
see, or who opened his eyes, we do not know. Ask him; he
22 is of age; he will speak for himself.' His parents gave this
answer because they were afraid of the Jews; for the
Jewish authorities had already agreed that anyone who
acknowledged Jesus as Messiah should be banned from the
23 synagogue. That is why the parents said, 'He is of age;
ask him.'

24     So for the second time they summoned the man who had
been blind, and said, 'Speak the truth before God. We
25 know that this fellow is a sinner.' 'Whether or not he is a
sinner, I do not know', the man replied. 'All I know is this:
26 once I was blind, now I can see.' 'What did he do to you?'
27 they asked. 'How did he open your eyes?' 'I have told you
already,' he retorted, 'but you took no notice. Why do you
want to hear it again? Do you also want to become his
28 disciples?' Then they became abusive. 'You are that man's
29 disciple,' they said, 'but we are disciples of Moses. We
know that God spoke to Moses, but as for this fellow, we
do not know where he comes from.'

30     The man replied, 'What an extraordinary thing! Here
is a man who has opened my eyes, yet you do not know
31 where he comes from! It is common knowledge that God
does not listen to sinners; he listens to anyone who is
32 devout and obeys his will. To open the eyes of a man born
33 blind—it is unheard of since time began. If that man had
34 not come from God he could have done nothing.' 'Who are
you to give us lessons,' they retorted, 'born and bred in sin
as you are?' Then they expelled him from the synagogue.

35     Jesus heard that they had expelled him. When he found
36 him he asked, 'Have you faith in the Son of Man*a*?' The
man answered, 'Tell me who he is, sir, that I should put
37 my faith in him.' 'You have seen him,' said Jesus; 'indeed,
38 it is he who is speaking to you.' 'Lord, I believe', he said,
and bowed before him.

*a Some witnesses read* Son of God.

Jesus said, 'It is for judgement that I have come into this world—to give sight to the sightless and to make blind those who see.' Some Pharisees in his company asked, 'Do you mean that we are blind?' 'If you were blind,' said Jesus, 'you would not be guilty, but because you say "We see", your guilt remains. 39 40 41

'IN TRUTH I tell you, in very truth, the man who does not enter the sheepfold by the door, but climbs in some other way, is nothing but a thief or a robber. The man who enters by the door is the shepherd in charge of the sheep. The door-keeper admits him, and the sheep hear his voice; he calls his own sheep by name, and leads them out. When he has brought them all out, he goes ahead and the sheep follow, because they know his voice. They will not follow a stranger; they will run away from him, because they do not recognize the voice of strangers.' 10 2 3 4 5

This was a parable that Jesus told them, but they did not understand what he meant by it. 6

So Jesus spoke again: 'In truth, in very truth I tell you, I am the door of the sheepfold. The sheep paid no heed to any who came before me, for these were all thieves and robbers. I am the door; anyone who comes into the fold through me shall be safe. He shall go in and out and shall find pasturage. 7 8 9

'The thief comes only to steal, to kill, to destroy; I have come that men may have life, and may have it in all its fullness. I am the good shepherd; the good shepherd lays down his life for the sheep. The hireling, when he sees the wolf coming, abandons the sheep and runs away, because he is no shepherd and the sheep are not his. Then the wolf harries the flock and scatters the sheep. The man runs away because he is a hireling and cares nothing for the sheep. 10 11 12 13

'I am the good shepherd; I know my own sheep and my sheep know me—as the Father knows me and I know the Father—and I lay down my life for the sheep. But there are other sheep of mine, not belonging to this fold, whom I must bring in; and they too will listen to my voice. There will then be one flock, one shepherd. The Father loves me because I lay down my life, to receive it back again. No one has robbed me of it; I am laying it down of my own free will. I have the right to lay it down, and I have the right to receive it back again; this charge I have received from my Father.' 14 15 16 17 18

19   These words once again caused a split among the Jews.
20   Many of them said, 'He is possessed, he is raving. Why
21   listen to him?' Others said, 'No one possessed by an evil
spirit could speak like this. Could an evil spirit open blind
men's eyes?'

22   IT WAS WINTER, and the festival of the Dedication was
23   being held in Jerusalem. Jesus was walking in the temple
24   precincts, in Solomon's Portico. The Jews gathered round
him and asked: 'How long must you keep us in suspense?
25   If you are the Messiah say so plainly.' 'I have told you,'
said Jesus, 'but you do not believe. My deeds done in my
26   Father's name are my credentials, but because you are not
27   sheep of my flock you do not believe. My own sheep listen
28   to my voice; I know them and they follow me. I give them
eternal life and they shall never perish; no one shall snatch
29   them from my care. My Father who has given them to me
is greater than all, and no one can snatch them*a* out of the
30   Father's care. My Father and I are one.'
31 32   Once again the Jews picked up stones to stone him. At
this Jesus said to them, 'I have set before you many good
deeds, done by my Father's power; for which of these
33   would you stone me?' The Jews replied, 'We are not going
to stone you for any good deed, but for your blasphemy.
34   You, a mere man, claim to be a god.'*b* Jesus answered, 'Is
it not written in your own Law, "I said: You are gods"?
35   Those are called gods to whom the word of God was de-
36   livered—and Scripture cannot be set aside. Then why
do you charge me with blasphemy because I, consecrated
and sent into the world by the Father, said, "I am God's
son"?
37   'If I am not acting as my Father would, do not believe
38   me. But if I am, accept the evidence of my deeds, even if
you do not believe me, so that you may recognize and
know that the Father is in me, and I in the Father.'
39   This provoked them to one more attempt to seize him.
But he escaped from their clutches.

---

*a* *Some witnesses read* My Father is greater than all, and that which he
has given me no one can snatch . . . ; *others read* That which my Father
has given me is greater than all, and no one can snatch it . . .
*b Or* claim to be God.

## VICTORY OVER DEATH

JESUS WITHDREW AGAIN across the Jordan, 40
to the place where John had been baptizing earlier.
There he stayed, while crowds came to him. They said, 41
'John gave us no miraculous sign, but all that he said
about this man was true.' Many came to believe in him 42
there.

There was a man named Lazarus who had fallen ill. His 11
home was at Bethany, the village of Mary and her sister
Martha. (This Mary, whose brother Lazarus had fallen ill, 2
was the woman who anointed the Lord with ointment and
wiped his feet with her hair.) The sisters sent a message to 3
him: 'Sir, you should know that your friend lies ill.' When 4
Jesus heard this he said, 'This illness will not end in death;
it has come for the glory of God, to bring glory to the Son
of God.' And therefore, though he loved Martha and her 5
sister and Lazarus, after hearing of his illness Jesus waited 6
for two days in the place where he was.

After this, he said to his disciples, 'Let us go back to 7
Judaea.' 'Rabbi,' his disciples said, 'it is not long since the 8
Jews there were wanting to stone you. Are you going there
again?' Jesus replied, 'Are there not twelve hours of day- 9
light? Anyone can walk in day-time without stumbling,
because he sees the light of this world. But if he walks after 10
nightfall he stumbles, because the light fails him.'

After saying this he added, 'Our friend Lazarus has fallen 11
asleep, but I shall go and wake him.' The disciples said, 12
'Master, if he has fallen asleep he will recover.' Jesus, how- 13
ever, had been speaking of his death, but they thought
that he meant natural sleep. Then Jesus spoke out plainly: 14
'Lazarus is dead. I am glad not to have been there; it will 15
be for your good and for the good of your faith. But let us
go to him.' Thomas, called 'the Twin', said to his fellow- 16
disciples, 'Let us also go, that we may die with him.'

ON HIS ARRIVAL Jesus found that Lazarus had already 17
been four days in the tomb. Bethany was just under two 18
miles from Jerusalem, and many of the people had come 19
from the city to Martha and Mary to condole with them
on their brother's death. As soon as she heard that Jesus 20
was on his way, Martha went to meet him, while Mary
stayed at home.

21   Martha said to Jesus, 'If you had been here, sir, my
22   brother would not have died. Even now I know that
23   whatever you ask of God, God will grant you.' Jesus said,
24   'Your brother will rise again.' 'I know that he will rise
     again', said Martha, 'at the resurrection on the last day.'
25   Jesus said, 'I am the resurrection and I am life.ᵃ If a man
     has faith in me, even though he die, he shall come to life;
26   and no one who is alive and has faith shall ever die. Do
27   you believe this?' 'Lord, I do,' she answered; 'I now believe
     that you are the Messiah, the Son of God who was to come
     into the world.'

28   With these words she went to call her sister Mary, and
     taking her aside, she said, 'The Master is here; he is asking
29   for you.' When Mary heard this she rose up quickly and
30   went to him. Jesus had not yet reached the village, but was
31   still at the place where Martha had met him. The Jews who
     were in the house condoling with Mary, when they saw
     her start up and leave the house, went after her, for they
     supposed that she was going to the tomb to weep there.
32   So Mary came to the place where Jesus was. As soon as
     she caught sight of him she fell at his feet and said, 'O sir,
     if you had only been here my brother would not have died.'
33   When Jesus saw her weeping and the Jews her companions
34   weeping, he sighed heavily and was deeply moved. 'Where
     have you laid him?' he asked. They replied, 'Come and see,
35 36 sir.' Jesus wept. The Jews said, 'How dearly he must have
  37 loved him!' But some of them said, 'Could not this man,
     who opened the blind man's eyes, have done something to
     keep Lazarus from dying?'

38   Jesus again sighed deeply; then he went over to the
39   tomb. It was a cave, with a stone placed against it. Jesus
     said, 'Take away the stone.' Martha, the dead man's sister,
     said to him, 'Sir, by now there will be a stench; he has been
40   there four days.' Jesus said, 'Did I not tell you that if you
41   have faith you will see the glory of God?' So they removed
     the stone.

     Then Jesus looked upwards and said, 'Father, I thank
42   thee; thou hast heard me. I knew already that thou always
     hearest me, but I spoke for the sake of the people standing
     round, that they might believe that thou didst send me.'
43   Then he raised his voice in a great cry: 'Lazarus, come
44   forth.' The dead man came out, his hands and feet swathed
     in linen bands, his face wrapped in a cloth. Jesus said,
     'Loose him; let him go.'

ᵃ *Some witnesses omit* and I am life.

Now many of the Jews who had come to visit Mary and 45
had seen what Jesus did, put their faith in him. But some 46
of them went off to the Pharisees and reported what he
had done.

Thereupon the chief priests and the Pharisees convened 47
a meeting of the Council. 'What action are we taking?'
they said. 'This man is performing many signs. If we leave 48
him alone like this the whole populace will believe in him.
Then the Romans will come and sweep away our temple
and our nation.' But one of them, Caiaphas, who was High 49
Priest that year, said, 'You know nothing whatever; you 50
do not use your judgement; it is more to your interest that
one man should die for the people, than that the whole
nation should be destroyed.' He did not say this of his own 51
accord, but as the High Priest in office that year, he was
prophesying that Jesus would die for the nation—would 52
die not for the nation alone but to gather together the
scattered children of God. So from that day on they 53
plotted his death.

Accordingly Jesus no longer went about publicly in 54
Judaea, but left that region for the country bordering on
the desert, and came to a town called Ephraim, where he
stayed with his disciples.

The jewish passover was now at hand, and many 55
people went up from the country to Jerusalem to purify
themselves before the festival. They looked out for Jesus, 56
and as they stood in the temple they asked one another,
'What do you think? Perhaps he is not coming to the
festival.' Now the chief priests and the Pharisees had given 57
orders that anyone who knew where he was should give
information, so that they might arrest him.

Six days before the Passover festival Jesus came to 12
Bethany, where Lazarus lived whom he had raised from
the dead. There a supper was given in his honour, at which 2
Martha served, and Lazarus sat among the guests with
Jesus. Then Mary brought a pound of very costly perfume, 3
pure oil of nard, and anointed the feet of Jesus and wiped
them with her hair, till the house was filled with the fragrance. At this, Judas Iscariot, a disciple of his—the one 4
who was to betray him—said, 'Why was this perfume 5
not sold for thirty pounds[a] and given to the poor?' He said 6
this, not out of any care for the poor, but because he was

        [a] *Literally* for 300 denarii.

a thief; he used to pilfer the money put into the common
7 purse, which was in his charge. 'Leave her alone', said
Jesus. 'Let her keep it till the day when she prepares for
8 my burial; for you have the poor among you always, but
you will not always have me.'[a]

9　　A great number of the Jews heard that he was there, and
came not only to see Jesus but also Lazarus whom he had
10 raised from the dead. The chief priests then resolved to do
11 away with Lazarus as well, since on his account many
Jews were going over to Jesus and putting their faith in
him.

12 THE NEXT DAY the great body of pilgrims who had
come to the festival, hearing that Jesus was on the way to
13 Jerusalem, took palm branches and went out to meet him,
shouting, 'Hosanna! Blessings on him who comes in the
14 name of the Lord! God bless the king of Israel!' Jesus
found a donkey and mounted it, in accordance with the
15 text of Scripture: 'Fear no more, daughter of Zion; see,
your king is coming, mounted on an ass's colt.'
16　　At the time his disciples did not understand this, but
after Jesus had been glorified they remembered that this
had been written about him, and that this had happened
17 to him. The people who were present when he called
Lazarus out of the tomb and raised him from the dead told
18 what they had seen and heard. That is why the crowd
went to meet him; they had heard of this sign that he had
19 performed. The Pharisees said to one another, 'You see
you are doing no good at all; why, all the world has gone
after him!'

20 AMONG THOSE who went up to worship at the festival
21 were some Greeks. They came to Philip, who was from
Bethsaida in Galilee, and said to him, 'Sir, we should like
22 to see Jesus.' So Philip went and told Andrew, and the two
23 of them went to tell Jesus. Then Jesus replied: 'The hour
24 has come for the Son of Man to be glorified. In truth, in
very truth I tell you, a grain of wheat remains a solitary
grain unless it falls into the ground and dies; but if it dies,
25 it bears a rich harvest. The man who loves himself is lost,
but he who hates himself in this world will be kept safe
26 for eternal life. If anyone serves me, he must follow me;
where I am, my servant will be. Whoever serves me will
be honoured by my Father.

[a] *Some witnesses omit* for you have . . . have me.

'Now my soul is in turmoil, and what am I to say? 27
Father, save me from this hour.*a* No, it was for this that
I came to this hour. Father, glorify thy name.' A voice 28
sounded from heaven: 'I have glorified it, and I will glorify
it again.' The crowd standing by said it was thunder, while 29
others said, 'An angel has spoken to him.' Jesus replied, 30
'This voice spoke for your sake, not mine. Now is the hour 31
of judgement for this world; now shall the Prince of this
world be driven out. And I shall draw all men to myself, 32
when I am lifted up from the earth.' This he said to indi- 33
cate the kind of death he was to die.

The people answered, 'Our Law teaches us that the 34
Messiah continues for ever. What do you mean by saying
that the Son of Man must be lifted up? What Son of Man
is this?' Jesus answered them: 'The light is among you 35
still, but not for long. Go on your way while you have the
light, so that darkness may not overtake you. He who
journeys in the dark does not know where he is going.
While you have the light, trust to the light, so that you 36
may become men of light.' After these words Jesus went
away from them into hiding.

IN SPITE OF the many signs which Jesus had performed 37
in their presence they would not believe in him, for the 38
prophet Isaiah's utterance had to be fulfilled: 'Lord, who
has believed what we reported, and to whom has the Lord's
power been revealed?' So it was that they could not be- 39
lieve, for there is another saying of Isaiah's: 'He has 40
blinded their eyes and dulled their minds, lest they should
see with their eyes, and perceive with their minds, and
turn to me to heal them.' Isaiah said this because*b* he saw 41
his glory and spoke about him.

For all that, even among those in authority a number 42
believed in him, but would not acknowledge him on account of the Pharisees, for fear of being banned from the
synagogue. For they valued their reputation with men 43
rather than the honour which comes from God.

So JESUS CRIED ALOUD: 'When a man believes in me, 44
he believes in him who sent me rather than in me; seeing 45
me, he sees him who sent me. I have come into the world 46
as light, so that no one who has faith in me should remain
in darkness. But if anyone hears my words and pays no 47

---

*a* Or . . . turmoil. Shall I say, "Father, save me from this hour"?
*b* Some witnesses read when.

regard to them, I am not his judge; I have not come to
48 judge the world, but to save the world. There is a judge for
the man who rejects me and does not accept my words; the
49 word that I spoke will be his judge on the last day. I do
not speak on my own authority, but the Father who sent
me has himself commanded me what to say and how to
50 speak. I know that his commands are eternal life. What
the Father has said to me, therefore—that is what I speak.'

## FAREWELL DISCOURSES

13 IT WAS BEFORE the Passover festival. Jesus knew
that his hour had come and he must leave this world and
go to the Father. He had always loved his own who were in
the world, and now he was to show the full extent of his
love.
2     The devil had already put it into the mind of Judas son
3 of Simon Iscariot to betray him. During supper, Jesus,
well aware that the Father had entrusted everything to
him, and that he had come from God and was going back
4 to God, rose from table, laid aside his garments, and taking
5 a towel, tied it round him. Then he poured water into a
basin, and began to wash his disciples' feet and to wipe
them with the towel.
6     When it was Simon Peter's turn, Peter said to him, 'You,
7 Lord, washing my feet?' Jesus replied, 'You do not under-
8 stand now what I am doing, but one day you will.' Peter
said, 'I will never let you wash my feet.' 'If I do not wash
you,' Jesus replied, 'you are not in fellowship with me.'
9 'Then, Lord,' said Simon Peter, 'not my feet only; wash
my hands and head as well!'
10     Jesus said, 'A man who has bathed needs no further
washing;[a] he is altogether clean; and you are clean, though
11 not every one of you.' He added the words 'not every one
of you' because he knew who was going to betray him.
12     After washing their feet and taking his garments again,
he sat down. 'Do you understand what I have done for
13 you?' he asked. 'You call me "Master" and "Lord", and
14 rightly so, for that is what I am. Then if I, your Lord and
Master, have washed your feet, you also ought to wash one
15 another's feet. I have set you an example: you are to do
16 as I have done for you. In very truth I tell you, a servant
is not greater than his master, nor a messenger than the

---

[a] *Some witnesses read* needs only to wash his feet.

one who sent him. If you know this, happy are you if you act upon it. [17]

'I am not speaking about all of you; I know whom I have chosen. But there is a text of Scripture to be fulfilled: "He who eats bread with me has turned against me."[a] I tell you this now, before the event, so that when it happens you may believe that I am what I am. In very truth I tell you, he who receives any messenger of mine receives me; receiving me, he receives the One who sent me.' [18] [19] [20]

After saying this, Jesus exclaimed in deep agitation of spirit, 'In truth, in very truth I tell you, one of you is going to betray me.' The disciples looked at one another in bewilderment: whom could he be speaking of? One of them, the disciple he loved, was reclining close beside Jesus. So Simon Peter nodded to him and said, 'Ask who it is he means.' That disciple, as he reclined, leaned back close to Jesus and asked, 'Lord, who is it?' Jesus replied, 'It is the man to whom I give this piece of bread when I have dipped it in the dish.' Then, after dipping it in the dish, he took it out and gave it to Judas son of Simon Iscariot. As soon as Judas had received it Satan entered him. Jesus said to him, 'Do quickly what you have to do.' No one at the table understood what he meant by this. Some supposed that, as Judas was in charge of the common purse, Jesus was telling him to buy what was needed for the festival, or to make some gift to the poor. As soon as Judas had received the bread he went out. It was night. [21] [22] [23] [24] [25] [26] [27] [28] [29] [30]

WHEN HE HAD GONE OUT Jesus said, 'Now the Son of Man is glorified, and in him God is glorified. If God is glorified in him,[b] God will also glorify him in himself; and he will glorify him now. My children, for a little longer I am with you; then you will look for me, and, as I told the Jews, I tell you now, where I am going you cannot come. I give you a new commandment: love one another; as I have loved you, so you are to love one another. If there is this love among you, then all will know that you are my disciples.' [31] [32] [33] [34] [35]

Simon Peter said to him, 'Lord, where are you going?' Jesus replied, 'Where I am going you cannot follow me now, but one day you will.' Peter said, 'Lord, why cannot I follow you now? I will lay down my life for you.' Jesus answered, 'Will you indeed lay down your life for me? I [36] [37] [38]

[a] *Literally* has lifted his heel against me.     [b] *Some witnesses omit* If God . . . in him.

tell you in very truth, before the cock crows you will have
denied me three times.

14    'Set your troubled hearts at rest. Trust in God always;
2    trust also in me. There are many dwelling-places in my
Father's house; if it were not so I should have told you;
for I am going there on purpose to prepare a place for you.[a]
3    And if I go and prepare a place for you, I shall come again
and receive you to myself, so that where I am you may be
4 5   also; and my way there is known to you.'[b] Thomas said,
'Lord, we do not know where you are going, so how can we
6    know the way?' Jesus replied,'I am the way; I am the truth
and I am life; no one comes to the Father except by me.
7    'If you knew me you would know my Father too.[c] From
8    now on you do know him; you have seen him.' Philip said
to him, 'Lord, show us the Father and we ask no more.'
9    Jesus answered, 'Have I been all this time with you, Philip,
and you still do not know me? Anyone who has seen me has
seen the Father. Then how can you say, "Show us the
10   Father"? Do you not believe that I am in the Father, and
the Father in me? I am not myself the source of the words I
speak to you: it is the Father who dwells in me doing his
11   own work. Believe me when I say that I am in the Father
and the Father in me; or else accept the evidence of the
12   deeds themselves. In truth, in very truth I tell you, he who
has faith in me will do what I am doing; and he will do
13   greater things still because I am going to the Father. Indeed
anything you ask in my name I will do, so that the Father
14   may be glorified in the Son. If you ask[d] anything in my
name I will do it.
15 16   'If you love me you will obey my commands; and I will
ask the Father, and he will give you another to be your
17   Advocate, who will be with you for ever—the Spirit of
truth. The world cannot receive him, because the world
neither sees nor knows him; but you know him, because
18   he dwells with you and is[e] in you. I will not leave you
19   bereft; I am coming back to you. In a little while the world
will see me no longer, but you will see me; because I live,
20   you too will live; then you will know that I am in my
21   Father, and you in me and I in you. The man who has
received my commands and obeys them—he it is who

[a] *Or if it were not so, should I have told you that I am going to prepare a place for you?*    [b] *Some witnesses read also. You know where
I am going and you know the way.*       [c] *Some witnesses read If you
know me you will know my Father too.*    [d] *Some witnesses insert me.*
[e] *Some witnesses read shall be.*

loves me; and he who loves me will be loved by my Father; and I will love him and disclose myself to him.'

Judas asked him—the other Judas, not Iscariot—'Lord, 22 what can have happened, that you mean to disclose yourself to us alone and not to the world?' Jesus replied, 'Anyone 23 who loves me will heed what I say; then my Father will love him, and we will come to him and make our dwelling with him; but he who does not love me does not heed what 24 I say. And the word you hear is not mine: it is the word of the Father who sent me. I have told you all this while I 25 am still here with you; but your Advocate, the Holy Spirit 26 whom the Father will send in my name, will teach you everything, and will call to mind all that I have told you.

'Peace is my parting gift to you, my own peace, such as 27 the world cannot give. Set your troubled hearts at rest, and banish your fears. You heard me say, "I am going away, 28 and coming back to you." If you loved me you would have been glad to hear that I was going to the Father; for the Father is greater than I. I have told you now, beforehand, 29 so that when it happens you may have faith.

'I shall not talk much longer with you, for the Prince of 30 this world approaches. He has no rights over me; but the 31 world must be shown that I love the Father, and do exactly as he commands; so up, let us go forward!*a*

'I AM THE REAL VINE, and my Father is the gardener. 15 Every barren branch of mine he cuts away; and every 2 fruiting branch he cleans, to make it more fruitful still. You have already been cleansed by the word that I spoke 3 to you. Dwell in me, as I in you. No branch can bear fruit 4 by itself, but only if it remains united with the vine; no more can you bear fruit, unless you remain united with me.

'I am the vine, and you the branches. He who dwells in 5 me, as I dwell in him, bears much fruit; for apart from me you can do nothing. He who does not dwell in me is thrown 6 away like a withered branch. The withered branches are heaped together, thrown on the fire, and burnt.

'If you dwell in me, and my words dwell in you, ask 7 what you will, and you shall have it. This is my Father's 8 glory, that you may bear fruit in plenty and so be my disciples.*b* As the Father has loved me, so I have loved you. 9

*a* Or for the Prince of this world is coming, though he has nothing in common with me. But he is coming so that the world may recognize that I love the Father, and do exactly as he commands. Up, and let us go forward to meet him!    *b* Some witnesses read that you may bear fruit in plenty. Thus you will be my disciples.

10 Dwell in my love. If you heed my commands, you will dwell in my love, as I have heeded my Father's commands and dwell in his love.

11 'I have spoken thus to you, so that my joy may be in
12 you, and your joy complete.[a] This is my commandment:
13 love one another, as I have loved you. There is no greater love than this, that a man should lay down his life for his
14 friends. You are my friends, if you do what I command
15 you. I call you servants no longer; a servant does not know what his master is about. I have called you friends, because I have disclosed to you everything that I heard from my
16 Father. You did not choose me: I chose you. I appointed you to go on and bear fruit, fruit that shall last; so that the
17 Father may give you all that you ask in my name. This is my commandment to you: love one another.

18 'If the world hates you, it hated me first, as you know
19 well.[b] If you belonged to the world, the world would love its own; but because you do not belong to the world, because I have chosen you out of the world, for that
20 reason the world hates you. Remember what I said: "A servant is not greater than his master." As they persecuted me, they will persecute you; they will follow your teaching
21 as little as they have followed mine. It is on my account that they will treat you thus, because they do not know the One who sent me.

22 'If I had not come and spoken to them, they would not be guilty of sin; but now they have no excuse for their sin:
23 24 he who hates me, hates my Father. If I had not worked among them and accomplished what no other man has done, they would not be guilty of sin; but now they have
25 both seen and hated both me and my Father.[c] However, this text in their Law had to come true:[d] "They hated me without reason."

26 'But when your Advocate has come, whom I will send you from the Father—the Spirit of truth that issues from
27 the Father—he will bear witness to me. And you also are my witnesses, because you have been with me from the first.

16 'I have told you all this to guard you against the break-
2 down of your faith. They will ban you from the synagogue; indeed, the time is coming when anyone who kills you will

---

[a] *Or* so that I may have joy in you and your joy may be complete.
[b] *Or* bear in mind that it hated me first.    [c] *Or* but now they have indeed seen my work and yet have hated both me and my Father.
[d] *Or* let this text in their Law come true.

suppose that he is performing a religious duty. They will 3
do these things because they do not know either the Father
or me. I have told you all this so that when the time comes 4
for it to happen you may remember my warning. I did not
tell you this at first, because then I was with you; but now 5
I am going away to him who sent me. None of you asks me
"Where are you going?" Yet you are plunged into grief 6
because of what I have told you. Nevertheless I tell you 7
the truth: it is for your good that I am leaving you. If I
do not go, your Advocate will not come, whereas if I go,
I will send him to you. When he comes, he will confute the 8
world, and show where wrong and right and judgement lie.
He will convict them of wrong, by their refusal to believe 9
in me; he will convince them that right is on my side, by 10
showing that I go to the Father when I pass from your
sight; and he will convince them of divine judgement, by 11
showing that the Prince of this world stands condemned.

'There is still much that I could say to you, but the 12
burden would be too great for you now. However, when 13
he comes who is the Spirit of truth, he will guide you into
all the truth; for he will not speak on his own authority,
but will tell only what he hears; and he will make known
to you the things that are coming. He will glorify me, for 14
everything that he makes known to you he will draw from
what is mine. All that the Father has is mine, and that is 15
why I said, "Everything that he makes known to you he
will draw from what is mine."

'A LITTLE WHILE, and you see me no more; again a 16
little while, and you will see me.' Some of his disciples said 17
to one another, 'What does he mean by this: "A little
while, and you will not see me, and again a little while, and
you will see me", and by this: "Because I am going to my
Father"?' So they asked, 'What is this "little while" that 18
he speaks of? We do not know what he means.'

Jesus knew that they were wanting to question him, and 19
said, 'Are you discussing what I said: "A little while, and
you will not see me, and again a little while, and you will
see me"? In very truth I tell you, you will weep and mourn, 20
but the world will be glad. But though you will be plunged
in grief, your grief will be turned to joy. A woman in 21
labour is in pain because her time has come; but when the
child is born she forgets the anguish in her joy that a man
has been born into the world. So it is with you: for the 22
moment you are sad at heart; but I shall see you again,

and then you will be joyful, and no one shall rob you of
23 your joy. When that day comes you will ask nothing of me.
In very truth I tell you, if you ask the Father for any-
24 thing in my name, he will give it you.[a] So far you have
asked nothing in my name. Ask and you will receive, that
your joy may be complete.
25 'Till now I have been using figures of speech; a time is
coming when I shall no longer use figures, but tell you of
26 the Father in plain words. When that day comes you will
make your request in my name, and I do not say that I
27 shall pray to the Father for you, for the Father loves you
himself, because you have loved me and believed that I
28 came from God. I came from the Father and have come
into the world. Now I am leaving the world again and
29 going to the Father.' His disciples said, 'Why, this is plain
30 speaking; this is no figure of speech. We are certain now
that you know everything, and do not need to be questioned;
because of this we believe that you have come from God.'
31 32 Jesus answered, 'Do you now believe? Look,[b] the hour
is coming, has indeed already come, when you are all to be
scattered, each to his home, leaving me alone. Yet I am
33 not alone, because the Father is with me. I have told you
all this so that in me you may find peace. In the world you
will have trouble. But courage! The victory is mine; I have
conquered the world.'

17 AFTER THESE WORDS Jesus looked up to heaven and
said:
'Father, the hour has come. Glorify thy Son, that the
2 Son may glorify thee. For thou hast made him sovereign
over all mankind, to give eternal life to all whom thou hast
3 given him. This is eternal life: to know thee who alone art
truly God, and Jesus Christ whom thou hast sent.
4 'I have glorified thee on earth by completing the work
5 which thou gavest me to do; and now, Father, glorify me
in thy own presence with the glory which I had with thee
before the world began.
6 'I have made thy name known to the men whom thou
didst give me out of the world. They were thine, thou
gavest them to me, and they have obeyed thy command.
7 Now they know that all thy gifts have come to me from
8 thee; for I have taught them all that I learned from thee,

---

[a] *Some witnesses read* if you ask the Father for anything, he will give
it you in my name.     [b] *Or* At the moment you believe; but
look . . .

and they have received it: they know with certainty that
I came from thee; they have had faith to believe that thou
didst send me.

'I pray for them; I am not praying for the world but for 9
those whom thou hast given me, because they belong to
thee. All that is mine is thine, and what is thine is mine; 10
and through them has my glory shone.

'I am to stay no longer in the world, but they are still in 11
the world, and I am on my way to thee. Holy Father, protect by the power of thy name those whom thou hast given
me,*a* that they may be one, as we are one. When I was 12
with them, I protected by the power of thy name those
whom thou hast given me,*b* and kept them safe. Not one
of them is lost except the man who must be lost, for Scripture has to be fulfilled.

'And now I am coming to thee; but while I am still in 13
the world I speak these words, so that they may have my
joy within them in full measure. I have delivered thy word 14
to them, and the world hates them because they are strangers in the world, as I am. I pray thee, not to take them 15
out of the world, but to keep them from the evil one.
They are strangers in the world, as I am. Consecrate them 16 17
by the truth;*c* thy word is truth. As thou hast sent me into 18
the world, I have sent them into the world, and for their 19
sake I now consecrate myself, that they too may be consecrated by the truth.*c*

'But it is not for these alone that I pray, but for those 20
also who through their words put their faith in me; may 21
they all be one: as thou, Father, art in me, and I in thee,
so also may they be in us, that the world may believe that
thou didst send me. The glory which thou gavest me I have 22
given to them, that they may be one, as we are one; I in 23
them and thou in me, may they be perfectly one. Then the
world will learn that thou didst send me, that thou didst
love them as thou didst me.

'Father, I desire that these men, who are thy gift to me, 24
may be with me where I am, so that they may look upon
my glory, which thou hast given me because thou didst
love me before the world began. O righteous Father, 25
although the world does not know thee, I know thee,

---

*a Or* keep in loyalty to thee those whom thou hast given me; *some
witnesses read* protect them by the power of thy name which thou hast
given me.      *b Or* kept in loyalty to thee those whom thou hast given
me; *some witnesses read* protected them by the power of thy name
which thou hast given me.      *c Or* in truth.

26 and these men know that thou didst send me. I made thy name known to them, and will make it known, so that the love thou hadst for me may be in them, and I may be in them.'

## THE FINAL CONFLICT

18 AFTER THESE WORDS, Jesus went out with his disciples, and crossed the Kedron ravine. There was a
2 garden there, and he and his disciples went into it. The place was known to Judas, his betrayer, because Jesus
3 had often met there with his disciples. So Judas took a detachment of soldiers, and police provided by the chief priests and the Pharisees, equipped with lanterns, torches,
4 and weapons, and made his way to the garden. Jesus, knowing all that was coming upon him, went out to them
5 and asked, 'Who is it you want?' 'Jesus of Nazareth', they answered. Jesus said, 'I am he.' And there stood Judas the
6 traitor with them. When he said, 'I am he', they drew
7 back and fell to the ground. Again Jesus asked, 'Who is it
8 you want?' 'Jesus of Nazareth', they answered. Then Jesus said, 'I have told you that I am he. If I am the man you
9 want, let these others go.' (This was to make good his words, 'I have not lost one of those whom thou gavest
10 me.') Thereupon Simon Peter drew the sword he was wearing and struck at the High Priest's servant, cutting off his
11 right ear. (The servant's name was Malchus.) Jesus said to Peter, 'Sheathe your sword. This is the cup the Father has given me; shall I not drink it?'

12 THE TROOPS with their commander, and the Jewish
13 police, now arrested Jesus and secured him. They took him first to Annas.[a] Annas was father-in-law of Caiaphas, the
14 High Priest for that year[a]—the same Caiaphas who had advised the Jews that it would be to their interest if one
15 man died for the whole people. Jesus was followed by Simon Peter and another disciple. This disciple, who was acquainted with the High Priest, went with Jesus into the
16 High Priest's courtyard, but Peter halted at the door outside. So the other disciple, the High Priest's acquaintance, went out again and spoke to the woman at the door, and
17 brought Peter in. The maid on duty at the door said to Peter, 'Are you another of this man's disciples?' 'I am not',

[a] *See note on verse 24.*

he said. The servants and the police had made a charcoal 18
fire, because it was cold, and were standing round it warming themselves. And Peter too was standing with them,
sharing the warmth.

The High Priest questioned Jesus about his disciples and 19
about what he taught. Jesus replied, 'I have spoken openly 20
to all the world; I have always taught in synagogue and in
the temple, where all Jews congregate; I have said nothing
in secret. Why question me? Ask my hearers what I told 21
them; they know what I said.' When he said this, one of 22
the police who was standing next to him struck him on the
face, exclaiming, 'Is that the way to answer the High
Priest?' Jesus replied, 'If I spoke amiss, state it in evi- 23
dence; if I spoke well, why strike me?'

So Annas sent him bound to Caiaphas the High Priest.*a* 24

Meanwhile Simon Peter stood warming himself. The 25
others asked, 'Are you another of his disciples?' But he
denied it: 'I am not', he said. One of the High Priest's 26
servants, a relation of the man whose ear Peter had cut
off, insisted, 'Did I not see you with him in the garden?'
Peter denied again; and just then a cock crew. 27

From caiaphas Jesus was led into the Governor's head- 28
quarters. It was now early morning, and the Jews themselves stayed outside the headquarters to avoid defilement,
so that they could eat the Passover meal.*b* So Pilate went 29
out to them and asked, 'What charge do you bring against
this man?' 'If he were not a criminal,' they replied, 'we 30
should not have brought him before you.' Pilate said, 31
'Take him away and try him by your own law.' The Jews
answered, 'We are not allowed to put any man to death.'
Thus they ensured the fulfilment of the words by which 32
Jesus had indicated the manner of his death.

Pilate then went back into his headquarters and sum- 33
moned Jesus. 'Are you the king of the Jews?' he asked.*c*
Jesus said, 'Is that your own idea, or have others suggested 34
it to you?' 'What! am I a Jew?' said Pilate. 'Your own 35
nation and their chief priests have brought you before me.
What have you done?' Jesus replied, 'My kingdom does 36
not belong to this world. If it did, my followers would be
fighting to save me from arrest by the Jews. My kingly
authority comes from elsewhere.' 'You are a king, then?' 37

---

*a Some witnesses give this verse after first to Annas in verse 13; others at
the end of verse 13.      b Or could share in the offerings of the Passover season.      c Or 'You are king of the Jews, I take it', he said.*

said Pilate. Jesus answered, '"King" is your word. My task
is to bear witness to the truth. For this was I born; for
this I came into the world, and all who are not deaf to
38 truth listen to my voice.' Pilate said, 'What is truth?', and
with those words went out again to the Jews. 'For my part,'
39 he said, 'I find no case against him. But you have a custom
that I release one prisoner for you at Passover. Would you
40 like me to release the king of the Jews?' Again the clamour
rose: 'Not him; we want Barabbas!' (Barabbas was a
bandit.)

19 1 2  Pilate now took Jesus and had him flogged; and the
soldiers plaited a crown of thorns and placed it on his head,
3 and robed him in a purple cloak. Then time after time they
came up to him, crying, 'Hail, King of the Jews!', and
struck him on the face.

4   Once more Pilate came out and said to the Jews, 'Here
he is; I am bringing him out to let you know that I find no
5 case against him'; and Jesus came out, wearing the crown
of thorns and the purple cloak. 'Behold the Man!' said
6 Pilate. The chief priests and their henchmen saw him and
shouted, 'Crucify! crucify!' 'Take him and crucify him
yourselves,' said Pilate; 'for my part I find no case against
7 him.' The Jews answered, 'We have a law; and by that
law he ought to die, because he has claimed to be Son of
God.'

8   When Pilate heard that, he was more afraid than ever,
9 and going back into his headquarters he asked Jesus,
'Where have you come from?' But Jesus gave him no
10 answer. 'Do you refuse to speak to me?' said Pilate.
'Surely you know that I have authority to release you, and
11 I have authority to crucify you?' 'You would have no
authority at all over me', Jesus replied, 'if it had not been
granted you from above; and therefore the deeper guilt
lies with the man who handed me over to you.'

12   From that moment Pilate tried hard to release him; but
the Jews kept shouting, 'If you let this man go, you are no
friend to Caesar; any man who claims to be a king is defy-
13 ing Caesar.' When Pilate heard what they were saying, he
brought Jesus out and took his seat on the tribunal at the
place known as 'The Pavement' ('Gabbatha' in the lan-
14 guage of the Jews). It was the eve of Passover,*a* about
15 noon. Pilate said to the Jews, 'Here is your king.' They
shouted, 'Away with him! Away with him! Crucify him!'
'Crucify your king?' said Pilate. 'We have no king but

*a Or It was Friday in Passover.*

Caesar', the Jews replied. Then at last, to satisfy them, 16 he handed Jesus over to be crucified.

JESUS WAS NOW TAKEN in charge and, carrying his 17 own cross, went out to the Place of the Skull, as it is called (or, in the Jews' language, 'Golgotha'), where they 18 crucified him, and with him two others, one on the right, one on the left, and Jesus between them.

And Pilate wrote an inscription to be fastened to the 19 cross; it read, 'Jesus of Nazareth King of the Jews.' This 20 inscription was read by many Jews, because the place where Jesus was crucified was not far from the city, and the inscription was in Hebrew, Latin, and Greek. Then the 21 Jewish chief priests said to Pilate, 'You should not write "King of the Jews"; write, "He claimed to be king of the Jews."' Pilate replied, 'What I have written, I have 22 written.'

The soldiers, having crucified Jesus, took possession of 23 his clothes, and divided them into four parts, one for each soldier, leaving out the tunic. The tunic was seamless, woven in one piece throughout; so they said to one another, 24 'We must not tear this; let us toss for it'; and thus the text of Scripture came true: 'They shared my garments among them, and cast lots for my clothing.'

That is what the soldiers did. But meanwhile near the 25 cross where Jesus hung stood his mother, with her sister, Mary wife of Clopas, and Mary of Magdala. Jesus saw his 26 mother, with the disciple whom he loved standing beside her. He said to her, 'Mother, there is your son'; and to the 27 disciple, 'There is your mother'; and from that moment the disciple took her into his home.

After that, Jesus, aware that all had now come to its 28 appointed end, said in fulfilment of Scripture, 'I thirst.' A jar stood there full of sour wine; so they soaked a sponge 29 with the wine, fixed it on a javelin,$^a$ and held it up to his lips. Having received the wine, he said, 'It is accomplished!' 30 He bowed his head and gave up his spirit.$^b$

Because it was the eve of Passover,$^c$ the Jews were 31 anxious that the bodies should not remain on the cross for the coming Sabbath, since that Sabbath was a day of great solemnity; so they requested Pilate to have the legs broken and the bodies taken down. The soldiers accord- 32 ingly came to the first of his fellow-victims and to the

$^a$ *So one witness; the others read* on marjoram.     $^b$ *Or* breathed out his life.     $^c$ *Or* Because it was Friday in Passover . . .

33 second, and broke their legs; but when they came to Jesus,
they found that he was already dead, so they did not break
34 his legs. But one of the soldiers stabbed his side with a
35 lance, and at once there was a flow of blood and water. This
is vouched for by an eyewitness, whose evidence is to be
trusted. He knows that he speaks the truth, so that you
36 too may believe; for this happened in fulfilment of the
37 text of Scripture: 'No bone of his shall be broken.' And
another text says, 'They shall look on him whom they
pierced.'

38 AFTER THAT, PILATE was approached by Joseph of
Arimathaea, a disciple of Jesus, but a secret disciple for
fear of the Jews, who*a* asked to be allowed to remove the
body of Jesus. Pilate gave the permission; so Joseph came
39 and took the body away. He was joined by Nicodemus (the
man who had first visited Jesus by night), who brought
with him a mixture of myrrh and aloes, more than half a
40 hundredweight. They took the body of Jesus and wrapped it,
with the spices, in strips of linen cloth according to Jewish
41 burial-customs. Now at the place where he had been crucified there was a garden, and in the garden a new tomb, not
42 yet used for burial. There, because the tomb was near at
hand and it was the eve of the Jewish Sabbath, they laid
Jesus.

20 EARLY ON THE SUNDAY MORNING, while it was still
dark, Mary of Magdala came to the tomb. She saw that
2 the stone had been moved away from the entrance, and
ran to Simon Peter and the other disciple, the one whom
Jesus loved. 'They have taken the Lord out of his tomb,'
she cried, 'and we do not know where they have laid him.'
3 So Peter and the other set out and made their way to the
4 tomb. They were running side by side, but the other
5 disciple outran Peter and reached the tomb first. He peered
in and saw the linen wrappings lying there, but did not
6 enter. Then Simon Peter came up, following him, and he
7 went into the tomb. He saw the linen wrappings lying, and
the napkin which had been over his head, not lying with
the wrappings but rolled together in a place by itself.
8 Then the disciple who had reached the tomb first went in
9 too, and he saw and believed; until then they had not
understood the scriptures, which showed that he must rise
from the dead.

*a* Or of Arimathaea. He was a disciple of Jesus, but had gone into
hiding for fear of the Jews. He now . . .

So the disciples went home again; but Mary stood at the  10 11
tomb outside, weeping. As she wept, she peered into the
tomb; and she saw two angels in white sitting there, one  12
at the head, and one at the feet, where the body of Jesus
had lain. They said to her, 'Why are you weeping?' She  13
answered, 'They have taken my Lord away, and I do not
know where they have laid him.' With these words she  14
turned round and saw Jesus standing there, but did not
recognize him. Jesus said to her, 'Why are you weeping?  15
Who is it you are looking for?' Thinking it was the
gardener, she said, 'If it is you, sir, who removed him, tell
me where you have laid him, and I will take him away.'
Jesus said, 'Mary!' She turned to him and said, 'Rabbuni!'  16
(which is Hebrew for 'My Master'). Jesus said, 'Do not cling  17
to me,*a* for I have not yet ascended to the Father. But
go to my brothers, and tell them that I am now ascending*b*
to my Father and your Father, my God and your God.'
Mary of Magdala went to the disciples with her news: 'I  18
have seen the Lord!' she said, and gave them his message.

Late that Sunday evening, when the disciples were to-  19
gether behind locked doors, for fear of the Jews, Jesus came
and stood among them. 'Peace be with you!' he said,
and then showed them his hands and his side. So when the  20
disciples saw the Lord, they were filled with joy. Jesus  21
repeated, 'Peace be with you!', and said, 'As the Father
sent me, so I send you.' Then he breathed on them, saying,  22
'Receive the Holy Spirit! If you forgive any man's sins,  23
they stand forgiven; if you pronounce them unforgiven,
unforgiven they remain.'

One of the Twelve, Thomas, that is 'the Twin', was not  24
with the rest when Jesus came. So the disciples told him,  25
'We have seen the Lord.' He said, 'Unless I see the mark
of the nails on his hands, unless I put my finger into the
place where the nails were, and my hand into his side,
I will not believe it.'

A week later his disciples were again in the room, and  26
Thomas was with them. Although the doors were locked,
Jesus came and stood among them, saying, 'Peace be with
you!' Then he said to Thomas, 'Reach your finger here;  27
see my hands. Reach your hand here and put it into my
side. Be unbelieving no longer, but believe.' Thomas said,  28
'My Lord and my God!' Jesus said, 'Because you have  29
seen me you have found faith. Happy are they who never
saw me and yet have found faith.'

*a* Or Touch me no more.        *b* Or I am going to ascend . . .

30     There were indeed many other signs that Jesus performed in the presence of his disciples, which are not re-
31  corded in this book. Those here written have been recorded
in order that you may hold the faith[a] that Jesus is the
Christ, the Son of God, and that through this faith you
may possess life by his name.

21  SOME TIME LATER, Jesus showed himself to his disciples
2  once again, by the Sea of Tiberias; and in this way. Simon
Peter and Thomas 'the Twin' were together with Nathanael
of Cana-in-Galilee. The sons of Zebedee and two other
3  disciples were also there. Simon Peter said, 'I am going out
fishing.' 'We will go with you', said the others. So they
started and got into the boat. But that night they caught
nothing.

4     Morning came, and there stood Jesus on the beach, but
5  the disciples did not know that it was Jesus. He called out
to them, 'Friends, have you caught anything?' They
6  answered 'No.' He said, 'Shoot the net to starboard, and
you will make a catch.' They did so, and found they could
not haul the net aboard, there were so many fish in it.
7  Then the disciple whom Jesus loved said to Peter, 'It is
the Lord!' When Simon Peter heard that, he wrapped his
coat about him (for he had stripped) and plunged into the
8  sea. The rest of them came on in the boat, towing the net
full of fish; for they were not far from land, only about
a hundred yards.

9     When they came ashore, they saw a charcoal fire there,
10  with fish laid on it, and some bread. Jesus said, 'Bring
11  some of your catch.' Simon Peter went aboard and dragged
the net to land, full of big fish, a hundred and fifty-three of
them; and yet, many as they were, the net was not torn.
12  Jesus said, 'Come and have breakfast.' None of the disciples dared to ask 'Who are you?' They knew it was the
13  Lord. Jesus now came up, took the bread, and gave it to
them, and the fish in the same way.

14     This makes the third time that Jesus appeared to his
disciples after his resurrection from the dead.

15     After breakfast, Jesus said to Simon Peter, 'Simon son
of John, do you love me more than all else[b]?' 'Yes, Lord,'
he answered, 'you know that I love you.'[c] 'Then feed my
16  lambs', he said. A second time he asked, 'Simon son of
John, do you love me?' 'Yes, Lord, you know I love you.'[c]

[a] *Some witnesses read* that you may come to believe . . .
[b] *Or* more than they do.     [c] *Or* that I am your friend.

'Then tend my sheep.' A third time he said, 'Simon son of  17
John, do you love me[a]?' Peter was hurt that he asked him
a third time, 'Do you love me?'[b] 'Lord,' he said, 'you know
everything; you know I love you.'[c] Jesus said, 'Feed my
sheep.

'And further, I tell you this in very truth: when you  18
were young you fastened your belt about you and walked
where you chose; but when you are old you will stretch
out your arms, and a stranger will bind you fast, and carry
you where you have no wish to go.' He said this to indicate  19
the manner of death by which Peter was to glorify God.
Then he added, 'Follow me.'

Peter looked round, and saw the disciple whom Jesus  20
loved following—the one who at supper had leaned back
close to him to ask the question, 'Lord, who is it that will
betray you?' When he caught sight of him, Peter asked,  21
'Lord, what will happen to him?' Jesus said, 'If it should  22
be my will that he wait until I come, what is it to you?
Follow me.'

That saying of Jesus became current in the brother-  23
hood, and was taken to mean that that disciple would not
die. But in fact Jesus did not say that he would not die;
he only said, 'If it should be my will that he wait until I
come, what is it to you?'

It is this same disciple who attests what has here been  24
written. It is in fact he who wrote it, and we know that
his testimony is true.[d]

There is much else that Jesus did. If it were all to be  25
recorded in detail, I suppose the whole world could not
hold the books that would be written.

[a] Or are you my friend.          [b] Or that at the third asking he
should have said, 'Are you my friend?'          [c] Or that I am your
friend.          [d] *Some witnesses here insert the passage printed on p. 190.*

## AN INCIDENT IN THE TEMPLE*

53 1 * AND THEY WENT each to his home, and Jesus to
2 the Mount of Olives. At daybreak he appeared again
in the temple, and all the people gathered round him. He
3 had taken his seat and was engaged in teaching them when
the doctors of the law and the Pharisees brought in a
woman caught committing adultery. Making her stand
4 out in the middle they said to him, 'Master, this woman
5 was caught in the very act of adultery. In the Law Moses
has laid down that such women are to be stoned. What do
6 you say about it?' They put the question as a test, hoping
to frame a charge against him. Jesus bent down and wrote
7 with his finger on the ground. When they continued to
press their question he sat up straight and said, 'That one
8 of you who is faultless shall throw the first stone.' Then
9 once again he bent down and wrote on the ground. When
they heard what he said, one by one they went away,[a] the
eldest first; and Jesus was left alone, with the woman still
10 standing there. Jesus again sat up and[b] said to the woman,
11 'Where are they? Has no one condemned you?' She answered, 'No one, sir.' Jesus said, 'Nor do I condemn you.
You may go; do not sin again.'

* *This passage, which in the most widely received editions of the New Testament is printed in the text of John, 7. 53—8. 11, has no fixed place in our witnesses. Some of them do not contain it at all. Some place it after Luke 21. 38, others after John 7. 36, or 7. 52, or 21. 24.*

[a] *Some witnesses insert* convicted by their conscience.    [b] *Some witnesses insert* seeing no one but the woman.

# ACTS OF THE
# APOSTLES

# ACTS OF THE APOSTLES

## THE BEGINNINGS OF THE CHURCH

IN THE FIRST PART of my work, Theophilus, I 1
wrote of all that Jesus did and taught from the beginning until the day when, after giving instructions 2
through the Holy Spirit to the apostles whom he had
chosen, he was taken up to heaven. He showed himself to 3
these men after his death, and gave ample proof that he
was alive: over a period of forty days he appeared to them
and taught them about the kingdom of God. While he was 4
in their company he told them not to leave Jerusalem. 'You
must wait', he said, 'for the promise made by my Father,
about which you have heard me speak: John, as you 5
know, baptized with water, but you will be baptized with
the Holy Spirit, and within the next few days.'

So, when they were all together, they asked him, 'Lord, 6
is this the time when you are to establish once again the
sovereignty of Israel?' He answered, 'It is not for you to 7
know about dates or times, which the Father has set within
his own control. But you will receive power when the Holy 8
Spirit comes upon you; and you will bear witness for me
in Jerusalem, and all over Judaea and Samaria, and away
to the ends of the earth.'

When he had said this, as they watched, he was lifted 9
up, and a cloud removed him from their sight. As he was 10
going, and as they were gazing intently into the sky, all at
once there stood beside them two men in white who said, 11
'Men of Galilee, why stand there looking up into the sky?
This Jesus, who has been taken away from you up to
heaven, will come in the same way as you have seen him go.'

Then they returned to Jerusalem from the hill called 12
Olivet, which is near Jerusalem, no farther than a Sabbath
day's journey. Entering the city they went to the room 13
upstairs where they were lodging: Peter and John and
James and Andrew, Philip and Thomas, Bartholomew and

Matthew, James son of Alphaeus and Simon the Zealot,
14 and Judas son of James. All these were constantly at
prayer together, and with them a group of women, including Mary the mother of Jesus, and his brothers.

15   It was during this time that Peter stood up before the
assembled brotherhood, about one hundred and twenty
16 in all, and said: 'My friends, the prophecy in Scripture was
bound to come true, which the Holy Spirit, through the
mouth of David, uttered about Judas who acted as guide
17 to those who arrested Jesus. For he was one of our number
18 and had his place in this ministry.' (This Judas, be it
noted, after buying a plot of land with the price of his
villainy, fell forward on the ground, and burst open, so
19 that his entrails poured out. This became known to everyone in Jerusalem, and they named the property in their
20 own language Akeldama, which means 'Blood Acre'.) 'The
text I have in mind', Peter continued, 'is in the Book of
Psalms: "Let his homestead fall desolate; let there be none
to inhabit it"; and again, "Let another take over his
21 charge." Therefore one of those who bore us company all
the while we had the Lord Jesus with us, coming and going,
22 from John's ministry of baptism until the day when he was
taken up from us—one of those must now join us as a witness to his resurrection.'

23   Two names were put forward: Joseph, who was known
as Barsabbas, and bore the added name of Justus; and
24 Matthias. Then they prayed and said, 'Thou, Lord, who
knowest the hearts of all men, declare which of these two
25 thou hast chosen to receive this office of ministry and apostleship which Judas abandoned to go where he belonged.'
26 They drew lots and the lot fell on Matthias, who was then
assigned a place among the twelve apostles.[a]

2  W HILE THE DAY of Pentecost was running its course they
2 were all together in one place, when suddenly there came
from the sky a noise like that of a strong driving wind,
3 which filled the whole house where they were sitting. And
there appeared to them tongues like flames of fire, dis-
4 persed among them and resting on each one. And they
were all filled with the Holy Spirit and began to talk in
other tongues, as the Spirit gave them power of utterance.
5   Now there were living in Jerusalem devout Jews[b] drawn
6 from every nation under heaven; and at this sound the

---

[a] *Some witnesses read* was then appointed a colleague of the eleven
apostles.      [b] *Some witnesses read* devout men.

crowd gathered, all bewildered because each one heard his own language spoken. They were amazed and in their 7 astonishment exclaimed, 'Why, they are all Galileans, are they not, these men who are speaking? How is it then that 8 we hear them, each of us in his own native language? Par- 9 thians, Medes, Elamites; inhabitants of Mesopotamia, of Judaea and Cappadocia, of Pontus and Asia, of Phrygia 10 and Pamphylia, of Egypt and the districts of Libya around Cyrene; visitors from Rome, both Jews and proselytes, Cretans and Arabs, we hear them telling in our own tongues 11 the great things God has done.' And they were all amazed 12 and perplexed, saying to one another, 'What can this mean?' Others said contemptuously, 'They have been 13 drinking!'

But Peter stood up with the Eleven, raised his voice, and 14 addressed them: 'Fellow Jews, and all you who live in Jerusalem, mark this and give me a hearing. These men 15 are not drunk, as you imagine; for it is only nine in the morning. No, this is what the prophet spoke of: "God says, 16 17 'This will happen in the last days: I will pour out upon everyone a portion of my spirit; and your sons and daughters shall prophesy; your young men shall see visions, and your old men shall dream dreams. Yes, I will endue even 18 my slaves, both men and women, with a portion of my spirit, and they shall prophesy. And I will show portents 19 in the sky above, and signs on the earth below—blood and fire and drifting smoke. The sun shall be turned to 20 darkness, and the moon to blood, before that great, resplendent day, the day of the Lord, shall come. And then, 21 everyone who invokes the name of the Lord shall be saved.'"

'Men of Israel, listen to me: I speak of Jesus of Nazareth, 22 a man singled out by God and made known to you through miracles, portents, and signs, which God worked among you through him, as you well know. When he had 23 been given up to you, by the deliberate will and plan of God, you used heathen men to crucify and kill him. But 24 God raised him to life again, setting him free from the pangs of death, because it could not be that death should keep him in its grip.

'For David says of him:                                          25

"I foresaw that the presence of the Lord would be with me always,
for he is at my right hand so that I may not be shaken;

26    therefore my heart was glad and my tongue spoke my
        joy;
        moreover, my flesh shall dwell in hope,
27    for thou wilt not abandon my soul to death,
        nor let thy loyal servant suffer corruption.
28    Thou hast shown me the ways of life,
        thou wilt fill me with gladness by thy presence."

29    'Let me tell you plainly, my friends, that the patriarch
David died and was buried, and his tomb is here to this
30    very day. It is clear therefore that he spoke as a prophet,
who knew that God had sworn to him that one of his own
31    direct descendants should sit on his throne; and when he
said he was not abandoned to death, and his flesh never
suffered corruption, he spoke with foreknowledge of the
32    resurrection of the Messiah. The Jesus we speak of has
33    been raised by God, as we can all bear witness. Exalted
thus with[a] God's right hand, he received the Holy Spirit
from the Father, as was promised, and all that you now
34    see and hear flows from him. For it was not David who
went up to heaven; his own words are: "The Lord said to
35    my Lord, 'Sit at my right hand until I make your enemies
36    your footstool.'" Let all Israel then accept as certain that
God has made this Jesus, whom you crucified, both Lord
and Messiah.'

37    When they heard this they were cut to the heart, and
said to Peter and the apostles,[b] 'Friends, what are we to
38    do?' 'Repent,' said Peter, 'repent and be baptized, every one
of you, in the name of Jesus the Messiah for the forgiveness
of your sins; and you will receive the gift of the Holy Spirit.
39    For the promise is to you, and to your children, and to all
who are far away, everyone whom the Lord our God may
call.'

40    In these and many other words he pressed his case and
pleaded with them: 'Save yourselves', he said, 'from this
41    crooked age.' Then those who accepted his word were
baptized, and some three thousand were added to their
number that day.

42    They met constantly to hear the apostles teach, and to
43    share the common life, to break bread, and to pray. A sense
of awe was everywhere, and many marvels and signs were
44    brought about through the apostles. All whose faith had
45    drawn them together held everything in common:[c] they

---

[a] *Or* at.    [b] *Some witnesses read* the rest of the apostles.    [c] *Or*
All who had become believers held everything together in common.

would sell their property and possessions and make a general distribution as the need of each required. With one mind 46 they kept up their daily attendance at the temple, and, breaking bread in private houses, shared their meals with unaffected joy, as they praised God and enjoyed the favour 47 of the whole people. And day by day the Lord added to their number those whom he was saving.

ONE DAY at three in the afternoon, the hour of prayer, 3 Peter and John were on their way up to the temple. Now 2 a man who had been a cripple from birth used to be carried there and laid every day by the gate of the temple called 'Beautiful Gate', to beg from people as they went in. When 3 he' saw Peter and John on their way into the temple he asked for charity. But Peter fixed his eyes on him, as John 4 did also, and said, 'Look at us.' Expecting a gift from them, 5 the man was all attention. And Peter said, 'I have no silver 6 or gold; but what I have I give you: in the name of Jesus Christ of Nazareth, walk.' Then he grasped him by the 7 right hand and pulled him up; and at once his feet and ankles grew strong; he sprang up, stood on his feet, and 8 started to walk. He entered the temple with them, leaping and praising God as he went. Everyone saw him walking 9 and praising God, and when they recognized him as the 10 man who used to sit begging at Beautiful Gate, they were filled with wonder and amazement at what had happened to him.

And as he was clutching Peter and John all the people 11 came running in astonishment towards them in Solomon's Portico, as it is called. Peter saw them coming and met 12 them with these words: 'Men of Israel, why be surprised at this? Why stare at us as if we had made this man walk by some power or godliness of our own? The God of Abra- 13 ham, Isaac, and Jacob, the God of our fathers, has given the highest honour to his servant Jesus, whom you com- mitted for trial and repudiated in Pilate's court—re- 14 pudiated the one who was holy and righteous when Pilate had decided to release him. You begged as a favour the release of a murderer, and killed him who has led the way 15 to life. But God raised him from the dead; of that we are witnesses. And the name of Jesus, by awakening faith, has 16 strengthened this man, whom you see and know, and this faith has made him completely well, as you can all see for yourselves.

'And now, my friends, I know quite well that you acted 17

18 in ignorance, and so did your rulers; but this is how God fulfilled what he had foretold in the utterances of all the
19 prophets: that his Messiah should suffer. Repent then and turn to God, so that your sins may be wiped out. Then the
20 Lord may grant you a time of recovery and send you the
21 Messiah he has already appointed, that is, Jesus. He must be received into heaven until the time of universal restoration comes, of which God spoke by his holy prophets.[a]
22 Moses said, "The Lord God will raise up a prophet for you from among yourselves as he raised me;[b] you shall listen
23 to everything he says to you, and anyone who refuses to
24 listen to that prophet must be extirpated from Israel." And so said all the prophets, from Samuel onwards; with one voice they all predicted this present time.
25 'You are the heirs of the prophets; you are within the covenant which God made with your fathers, when he said to Abraham, "And in your offspring all the families on
26 earth shall find blessing." When God raised up his Servant, he sent him to you first, to bring you blessing by turning every one of you from your wicked ways.'

4 They were still addressing the people when the chief[c] priests came upon them, together with the Controller of
2 the Temple and the Sadducees, exasperated at their teaching the people and proclaiming the resurrection from the
3 dead—the resurrection of Jesus. They were arrested and put in prison for the night, as it was already evening.
4 But many of those who had heard the message became believers. The number of men now reached about five thousand.

5 Next day the Jewish rulers, elders, and doctors of the
6 law met in Jerusalem. There were present Annas the High Priest, Caiaphas, Jonathan,[d] Alexander, and all who were
7 of the high-priestly family. They brought the apostles before the court and began the examination. 'By what power', they asked, 'or by what name have such men as you done
8 this?' Then Peter, filled with the Holy Spirit, answered,
9 'Rulers of the people and elders, if the question put to us today is about help given to a sick man, and we are asked
10 by what means he was cured, here is the answer, for all of you and for all the people of Israel: it was by the name of Jesus Christ of Nazareth, whom you crucified, whom God raised from the dead; it is by his name[e] that this man

---

[a] *Some witnesses add* from the beginning of the world.    [b] *Or like* me.    [c] *Some witnesses omit* chief.    [d] *Some witnesses read* John.
[e] *Some witnesses insert* and no other.

stands here before you fit and well. This Jesus is the stone 11
rejected by the builders which has become the keystone—
and you are the builders. There is no salvation in anyone 12
else at all,[a] for there is no other name under heaven granted
to men, by which we may receive salvation.'

Now as they observed the boldness of Peter and John, 13
and noted that they were untrained laymen, they began
to wonder, then recognized them as former companions
of Jesus. And when they saw the man who had been cured 14
standing with them, they had nothing to say in reply. So 15
they ordered them to leave the court, and then discussed
the matter among themselves. 'What are we to do with 16
these men?' they said; 'for it is common knowledge in
Jerusalem that a notable miracle has come about through
them; and we cannot deny it. But to stop this from spread- 17
ing further among the people, we had better caution them
never again to speak to anyone in this name.' They then 18
called them in and ordered them to refrain from all public
speaking and teaching in the name of Jesus.

But Peter and John said to them in reply: 'Is it right in 19
God's eyes for us to obey you rather than God? Judge for
yourselves. We cannot possibly give up speaking of things 20
we have seen and heard.'

The court repeated the caution and discharged them. 21
They could not see how they were to punish them, because
the people were all giving glory to God for what had happened. The man upon whom this miracle of healing had 22
been performed was over forty years old.

As soon as they were discharged they went back to their 23
friends and told them everything that the chief priests and
elders had said. When they heard it, they raised their 24
voices as one man and called upon God:

'Sovereign Lord, maker of heaven and earth and sea and
of everything in them, who by the Holy Spirit,[b] through 25
the mouth of David thy servant, didst say,

"Why did the Gentiles rage and the peoples lay their
plots in vain?
The kings of the earth took their stand and the rulers 26
made common cause
against the Lord and against his Messiah."

They did indeed make common cause in this very city 27
against thy holy servant Jesus whom thou didst anoint as

---

[a] *Some witnesses omit* There is no . . . at all.     [b] *Some witnesses
omit* by the Holy Spirit.

Messiah. Herod and Pontius Pilate conspired with the
28 Gentiles and peoples of Israel to do all the things which,
under thy hand and by thy decree, were foreordained.
29 And now, O Lord, mark their threats, and enable thy
30 servants to speak thy word with all boldness. Stretch out
thy hand to heal and cause signs and wonders to be done
through the name of thy holy servant Jesus.'
31    When they had ended their prayer, the building where
they were assembled rocked, and all were filled with the
Holy Spirit and spoke the word of God with boldness.

32 THE WHOLE BODY of believers was united in heart and
soul. Not a man of them claimed any of his possessions as
33 his own, but everything was held in common, while the
apostles bore witness with great power to the resurrection
34 of the Lord Jesus. They were all held in high esteem; for
they had never a needy person among them, because all
who had property in land or houses sold it, brought the
35 proceeds of the sale, and laid the money at the feet of the
apostles; it was then distributed to any who stood in need.
36    For instance, Joseph, surnamed by the apostles Barnabas (which means 'Son of Exhortation'), a Levite, by birth
37 a Cypriot, owned an estate, which he sold; he brought the
money, and laid it at the apostles' feet.

5    But there was another man, called Ananias, with his
2 wife Sapphira, who sold a property. With the full knowledge of his wife he kept back part of the purchase-money,
3 and part he brought and laid at the apostles' feet. But
Peter said, 'Ananias, how was it that Satan so possessed
your mind that you lied to the Holy Spirit, and kept back
4 part of the price of the land? While it remained, did it not
remain yours? When it was turned into money, was it not
still at your own disposal? What made you think of doing
5 this thing? You have lied not to men but to God.' When
Ananias heard these words he dropped dead; and all the
6 others who heard were awestruck. The younger men rose
and covered his body, then carried him out and buried him.
7    About three hours passed, and then his wife came in,
8 unaware of what had happened. Peter turned to her and
said, 'Tell me, were you paid such and such a price for the
9 land?' 'Yes,' she said, 'that was the price.' Then Peter
said, 'Why did you both conspire to put the Spirit of the
Lord to the test? Hark! there at the door are the footsteps
of those who buried your husband; and they will carry you
10 away.' And suddenly she dropped dead at his feet. When

the young men came in, they found her dead; and they
carried her out and buried her beside her husband. And 11
a great awe fell upon the whole church, and upon all who
heard of these events; and many remarkable and wonder- 12
ful things took place among the people at the hands of the
apostles.

THEY USED TO MEET by common consent in Solomon's
Portico, no one from outside their number venturing to 13
join with them. But people in general spoke highly of
them,[a] and more than that, numbers of men and women 14
were added to their ranks as believers in the Lord.[b] In the 15
end the sick were actually carried out into the streets and
laid there on beds and stretchers, so that even the shadow
of Peter might fall on one or another as he passed by; and 16
the people from the towns round Jerusalem flocked in,
bringing those who were ill or harassed by unclean spirits,
and all of them were cured.

Then the High Priest and his colleagues, the Sadducean 17
party as it then was, were goaded into action by jealousy.
They proceeded to arrest the apostles, and put them in 18
official custody. But an angel of the Lord opened the prison 19
doors during the night, brought them out, and said, 'Go, 20
take your place in the temple and speak to the people, and
tell them about this new life and all it means.' Accordingly 21
they entered the temple at daybreak and went on with
their teaching.

When the High Priest arrived with his colleagues they
summoned the 'Sanhedrin', that is, the full senate of the
Israelite nation, and sent to the jail to fetch the prisoners.
But the police who went to the prison failed to find them 22
there, so they returned and reported, 'We found the jail 23
securely locked at every point, with the warders at their
posts by the doors, but when we opened them we found no
one inside.' When they heard this, the Controller of the 24
Temple and the chief priests were wondering what could
have become of them,[c] and then a man arrived with the 25
report, 'Look! the men you put in prison are there in the
temple teaching the people.' At that the Controller went 26
off with the police and fetched them, but without using
force for fear of being stoned by the people.

[a] *Or . . .* Portico. Although others did not venture to join them, the
common people spoke highly of them.       [b] *Or* and an ever-increasing
number of believers, both men and women, were added to the Lord.
[c] *Or* wondering about them, what this could possibly mean.

27 So they brought them and stood them before the Coun-
28 cil; and the High Priest began his examination. 'We expressly ordered you', he said, 'to desist from teaching in
that name; and what has happened? You have filled
Jerusalem with your teaching, and you are trying to make
29 us responsible for that man's death.' Peter replied for himself and the apostles: 'We must obey God rather than men.
30 The God of our fathers raised up Jesus whom you had done
31 to death[a] by hanging him on a gibbet. He it is whom God
has exalted with his own right hand[b] as leader and saviour,
32 to grant Israel repentance and forgiveness of sins. And we
are witnesses to all this, and so is the Holy Spirit given by
God to those who are obedient to him.'

33 This touched them on the raw, and they wanted to put
34 them to death. But a member of the Council rose to his
feet, a Pharisee called Gamaliel, a teacher of the law held
in high regard by all the people. He moved that the men
35 be put outside for a while. Then he said, 'Men of Israel, be
36 cautious in deciding what to do with these men. Some time
ago Theudas came forward, claiming to be somebody, and
a number of men, about four hundred, joined him. But he
was killed and his whole following was broken up and dis-
37 appeared. After him came Judas the Galilean at the time
of the census; he induced some people to revolt under his
leadership, but he too perished and his whole following was
38 scattered. And so now: keep clear of these men, I tell you;
leave them alone. For if this idea of theirs or its execution
39 is of human origin, it will collapse; but if it is from God,
you will never be able to put them down, and you risk
finding yourselves at war with God.'

40 They took his advice. They sent for the apostles and had
them flogged; then they ordered them to give up speaking
41 in the name of Jesus, and discharged them. So the apostles
went out from the Council rejoicing that they had been
found worthy to suffer indignity for the sake of the Name.
42 And every day they went steadily on with their teaching
in the temple and in private houses, telling the good news
of Jesus the Messiah.[c]

---

[a] *Or . . . Jesus, and you did him to death . . .*      [b] *Or at his right
hand.*      [c] *Or the good news that the Messiah was Jesus.*

## THE CHURCH MOVES OUTWARDS

DURING THIS PERIOD, when disciples were **6** growing in number, there was disagreement between those of them who spoke Greek[a] and those who spoke the language of the Jews.[b] The former party complained that their widows were being overlooked in the daily distribution. So the Twelve called the whole body of disciples **2** together and said, 'It would be a grave mistake for us to neglect the word of God in order to wait at table. There- **3** fore, friends, look out seven men of good reputation from your number, men full of the Spirit and of wisdom, and we will appoint them to deal with these matters, while we **4** devote ourselves to prayer and to the ministry of the Word.' This proposal proved acceptable to the whole body. They **5** elected Stephen, a man full of faith and of the Holy Spirit, Philip, Prochorus, Nicanor, Timon, Parmenas, and Nicolas of Antioch, a former convert to Judaism. These they pre- **6** sented to the apostles, who prayed and laid their hands on them.

The word of God now spread more and more widely; the **7** number of disciples in Jerusalem went on increasing rapidly, and very many of the priests adhered to the Faith.

Stephen, who was full of grace and power, began to work **8** great miracles and signs among the people. But some **9** members of the synagogue called the Synagogue of Freedmen, comprising Cyrenians and Alexandrians and people from Cilicia and Asia, came forward and argued with Stephen, but could not hold their own against the inspired **10** wisdom with which he spoke. They then put up men who **11** alleged that they had heard him make blasphemous statements against Moses and against God. They stirred up the **12** people and the elders and doctors of the law, set upon him and seized him, and brought him before the Council. They produced false witnesses who said, 'This man is for **13** ever saying things against this holy place and against the Law. For we have heard him say that Jesus of Nazareth **14** will destroy this place and alter the customs handed down to us by Moses.' And all who were sitting in the Council **15** fixed their eyes on him, and his face appeared to them like the face of an angel.

Then the High Priest asked, 'Is this so?' And he said, **7 1 2** 'My brothers, fathers of this nation, listen to me. The

[a] *Literally* the Hellenists.     [b] *Literally* the Hebrews.

203

God of glory appeared to Abraham our ancestor while he

3 was in Mesopotamia, before he had settled in Harran, and said: "Leave your country and your kinsfolk and come

4 away to a land that I will show you." Thereupon he left the land of the Chaldaeans and settled in Harran. From there, after his father's death, God led him to migrate to this land

5 where you now live. He gave him nothing in it to call his own, not one yard; but promised to give it in possession to him and his descendants after him, though he was then

6 childless. God spoke in these terms: "Abraham's descendants shall live as aliens in a foreign land, held in slavery

7 and oppression for four hundred years. And I will pass judgement", said God, "on the nation whose slaves they are; and after that they shall come out free, and worship

8 me in this place." He then gave him the covenant of circumcision, and so, after Isaac was born, he circumcised him on the eighth day; and Isaac begot Jacob, and Jacob the twelve patriarchs.

9 'The patriarchs out of jealousy sold Joseph into slavery

10 in Egypt, but God was with him and rescued him from all his troubles. He also gave him a presence and powers of mind which so commended him to Pharaoh king of Egypt, that he appointed him chief administrator for Egypt and the whole of the royal household.

11 'But famine struck all Egypt and Canaan, and caused great hardship; and our ancestors could find nothing to

12 eat. But Jacob heard that there was food in Egypt and

13 sent our fathers there. This was their first visit. On the second visit Joseph was recognized by his brothers, and

14 his family connections were disclosed to Pharaoh. So Joseph sent an invitation to his father Jacob and all his

15 relatives, seventy-five persons altogether; and Jacob went down into Egypt. There he ended his days, as also our

16 forefathers did. Their remains were later removed to Shechem and buried in the tomb which Abraham had bought and paid for from the clan of Emmor at Shechem.

17 'Now as the time approached for God to fulfil the promise he had made to Abraham, our nation in Egypt grew

18 and increased in numbers. At length another king, who

19 knew nothing of Joseph, ascended the throne of Egypt. He made a crafty attack on our race, and cruelly forced our ancestors to expose their children so that they should not

20 survive. At this time Moses was born. He was a fine child and pleasing to God. For three months he was nursed in

21 his father's house, and when he was exposed, Pharaoh's

daughter herself adopted him and brought him up as her
own son. So Moses was trained in all the wisdom of the    22
Egyptians, a powerful speaker and a man of action.

'He was approaching the age of forty, when it occurred    23
to him to look into the conditions of his fellow-countrymen
the Israelites. He saw one of them being ill-treated, so he    24
went to his aid, and avenged the victim by striking down
the Egyptian. He thought his fellow-countrymen would    25
understand that God was offering them deliverance through
him, but they did not understand. The next day he came    26
upon two of them fighting, and tried to bring them to make
up their quarrel. "My men," he said, "you are brothers;
why are you ill-treating one another?" But the man who    27
was at fault pushed him away. "Who set you up as a ruler
and judge over us?" he said. "Are you going to kill me as    28
you killed the Egyptian yesterday?" At this Moses fled the    29
country and settled in Midianite territory. There two sons
were born to him.

'After forty years had passed, an angel appeared to him    30
in the flame of a burning bush in the desert near Mount
Sinai. Moses was amazed at the sight. But as he approached    31
to look closely, the voice of the Lord was heard: "I am the    32
God of your fathers, the God of Abraham, Isaac, and
Jacob." Moses was terrified and dared not look. Then the    33
Lord said to him, "Take off your shoes; the place where
you are standing is holy ground. I have indeed seen how    34
my people are oppressed in Egypt and have heard their
groans; and I have come down to rescue them. Up, then;
let me send you to Egypt."

'This Moses, whom they had rejected with the words,    35
"Who made you ruler and judge?"—this very man was
commissioned as ruler and liberator by God himself,
speaking through the angel who appeared to him in the
bush. It was Moses who led them out, working miracles    36
and signs in Egypt, at the Red Sea, and for forty years in
the desert. It was he again who said to the Israelites, "God    37
will raise up a prophet for you from among yourselves as
ae raised me."[a] He it was who, when they were assembled    38
there in the desert, conversed with the angel who spoke to
aim on Mount Sinai, and with our forefathers; he received
the living utterances of God, to pass on to us.

'But our forefathers would not accept his leadership.    39
They thrust him aside. They wished themselves back in
Egypt, and said to Aaron, "Make us gods to go before us.    40

*ᵃ Or like me.*

As for that Moses, who brought us out of Egypt, we do not
41 know what has become of him." That was when they made
the bull-calf, and offered sacrifice to the idol, and held a
42 feast in honour of the thing their hands had made. But
God turned away from them and gave them over to the
worship of the host of heaven, as it stands written in the
book of the prophets: "Did you bring me victims and offerings those forty years in the desert, you house of Israel?
43 No, you carried aloft the shrine of Moloch and the star of
the god Rephan, the images which you had made for your
adoration. I will banish you beyond Babylon."

44 'Our forefathers had the Tent of the Testimony in the
desert, as God commanded when he told Moses to make it
45 after the pattern which he had seen. Our fathers of the
next generation, with Joshua, brought it with them when
they dispossessed the nations whom God drove out before
46 them, and there it was until the time of David. David
found favour with God and asked to be allowed to provide
47 a dwelling-place for the God of Jacob;[a] but it was Solomon
48 who built him a house. However, the Most High does not
49 live in houses made by men: as the prophet says, "Heaven
is my throne and earth my footstool. What kind of house
will you build for me, says the Lord; where is my resting-
50 place? Are not all these things of my own making?"

51 'How stubborn you are, heathen still at heart and deaf
to the truth! You always fight against the Holy Spirit.
52 Like fathers, like sons. Was there ever a prophet whom your
fathers did not persecute? They killed those who foretold
the coming of the Righteous One; and now you have
53 betrayed him and murdered him, you who received the
Law as God's angels gave it to you, and yet have not
kept it.'

54 This touched them on the raw and they ground their
55 teeth with fury. But Stephen, filled with the Holy Spirit,
and gazing intently up to heaven, saw the glory of God,
56 and Jesus standing at God's right hand. 'Look,' he said,
'there is a rift in the sky; I can see the Son of Man standing
57 at God's right hand!' At this they gave a great shout and
58 stopped their ears. Then they made one rush at him and,
flinging him out of the city, set about stoning him. The
witnesses laid their coats at the feet of a young man named
59 Saul. So they stoned Stephen, and as they did so, he called
60 out, 'Lord Jesus, receive my spirit.' Then he fell on his
knees and cried aloud, 'Lord, do not hold this sin against

a *Some witnesses read* for the house of Jacob.

them', and with that he died. And Saul was among those 8
who approved of his murder.

THIS WAS THE BEGINNING of a time of violent persecution for the church in Jerusalem; and all except the
apostles were scattered over the country districts of Judaea
and Samaria. Stephen was given burial by certain devout 2
men, who made a great lamentation for him. Saul, mean- 3
while, was harrying the church; he entered house after
house, seizing men and women, and sending them to
prison.

As for those who had been scattered, they went through 4
the country preaching the Word. Philip came down to a 5
city in Samaria and began proclaiming the Messiah to
them. The crowds, to a man, listened eagerly to what Philip 6
said, when they heard him and saw the miracles that he
performed. For in many cases of possession the unclean 7
spirits came out with a loud cry; and many paralysed and
crippled folk were cured; and there was great joy in that 8
city.

A man named Simon had been in the city for some time, 9
and had swept the Samaritans off their feet with his
magical arts, claiming to be someone great. All of them, 10
high and low, listened eagerly to him. 'This man', they
said, 'is that power of God which is called "The Great
Power".' They listened because they had for so long been 11
carried away by his magic. But when they came to believe 12
Philip with his good news about the kingdom of God and
the name of Jesus Christ, they were baptized, men and
women alike. Even Simon himself believed, and was bap- 13
tized, and thereupon was constantly in Philip's company.
He was carried away when he saw the powerful signs and
miracles that were taking place.

The apostles in Jerusalem now heard that Samaria had 14
accepted the word of God. They sent off Peter and John,
who went down there and prayed for the converts, asking 15
that they might receive the Holy Spirit. For until then the 16
Spirit had not come upon any of them. They had been
baptized into the name of the Lord Jesus, that and nothing
more. So Peter and John laid their hands on them and 17
they received the Holy Spirit.

When Simon saw that the Spirit was bestowed through 18
the laying on of the apostles' hands, he offered them
money and said, 'Give me the same power too, so that 19
when I lay my hands on anyone, he will receive the Holy

20 Spirit.' Peter replied, 'Your money go with you to damna-
21 tion, because you thought God's gift was for sale! You
have no part nor lot in this, for you are dishonest with God.
22 Repent of this wickedness and pray the Lord to forgive
23 you for imagining such a thing. I can see that you are
doomed to taste the bitter fruit and wear the fetters of
24 sin.'[a] Simon answered, 'Pray to the Lord for me yourselves
and ask that none of the things you have spoken of may
fall upon me.'

25 So, after giving their testimony and speaking the word
of the Lord, they took the road back to Jerusalem, bringing the good news to many Samaritan villages on the way.
26 Then the angel of the Lord said to Philip, 'Start out and
go south to the road that leads down from Jerusalem to
27 Gaza.' (This is the desert road.) So he set out and was on
his way when he caught sight of an Ethiopian. This man
was a eunuch, a high official of the Kandake, or Queen,
of Ethiopia, in charge of all her treasure. He had been
28 to Jerusalem on a pilgrimage and was now on his way
home, sitting in his carriage and reading aloud the
29 prophet Isaiah. The Spirit said to Philip, 'Go and join
30 the carriage.' When Philip ran up he heard him reading
the prophet Isaiah and said, 'Do you understand what you
31 are reading?' He said, 'How can I understand unless
someone will give me the clue?' So he asked Philip to get
in and sit beside him.
32 The passage he was reading was this: 'He was led like
a sheep to be slaughtered; and like a lamb that is dumb
33 before the shearer, he does not open his mouth. He has
been humiliated and has no redress. Who will be able to
speak of his posterity? For he is cut off from the world of
living men.'
34 'Now', said the eunuch to Philip, 'tell me, please, who
it is that the prophet is speaking about here: himself or
35 someone else?' Then Philip began. Starting from this
36 passage, he told him the good news of Jesus. As they were
going along the road, they came to some water. 'Look,'
said the eunuch, 'here is water: what is there to prevent
38 my being baptized?';[b] and he ordered the carriage to stop.
Then they both went down into the water, Philip and the
39 eunuch; and he baptized him. When they came up out of

---

[a] *Literally* you are for gall of bitterness and a fetter of unrighteousness.
[b] *Some witnesses insert* (37) Philip said, 'If you whole-heartedly believe,
it is permitted.' He replied, 'I believe that Jesus Christ is the Son of
God.'

the water the Spirit snatched Philip away, and the eunuch
saw no more of him, but went happily on his way. Philip 40
appeared at Azotus, and toured the country, preaching in
all the towns till he reached Caesarea.

MEANWHILE SAUL was still breathing murderous 9
threats against the disciples of the Lord. He went to the
High Priest and applied for letters to the synagogues at 2
Damascus authorizing him to arrest anyone he found, men
or women, who followed the new way, and bring them to
Jerusalem. While he was still on the road and nearing 3
Damascus, suddenly a light flashed from the sky all
around him. He fell to the ground and heard a voice say- 4
ing, 'Saul, Saul, why do you persecute me?' 'Tell me, 5
Lord,' he said, 'who you are.' The voice answered, 'I am
Jesus, whom you are persecuting. But get up and go into 6
the city, and you will be told what you have to do.'
Meanwhile the men who were travelling with him stood 7
speechless; they heard the voice but could see no one. Saul 8
got up from the ground, but when he opened his eyes he
could not see; so they led him by the hand and brought
him into Damascus. He was blind for three days, and took 9
no food or drink.

There was a disciple in Damascus named Ananias. He 10
had a vision in which he heard the voice of the Lord:
'Ananias!' 'Here I am, Lord', he answered. The Lord said 11
to him, 'Go at once to Straight Street, to the house of
Judas, and ask for a man from Tarsus named Saul. You
will find him at prayer; he has had a vision of a man named 12
Ananias coming in and laying his hands on him to restore
his sight.' Ananias answered, 'Lord, I have often heard 13
about this man and all the harm he has done to thy people
in Jerusalem. And he is here with authority from the chief 14
priests to arrest all who invoke thy name.' But the Lord 15
said to him, 'You must go, for this man is my chosen
instrument to bring my name before the nations and their
kings, and before the people of Israel. I myself will show 16
him all that he must go through for my name's sake.'

So Ananias went. He entered the house, laid his hands on 17
him and said, 'Saul, my brother, the Lord Jesus, who appeared to you on your way here, has sent me to you so that
you may recover your sight, and be filled with the Holy
Spirit.' And immediately it seemed that scales fell from his 18
eyes, and he regained his sight. Thereupon he was baptized,
and afterwards he took food and his strength returned. 19

He stayed some time with the disciples in Damascus.
20 Soon he was proclaiming Jesus publicly in the synagogues:
21 'This', he said, 'is the Son of God.' All who heard were
astounded. 'Is not this the man', they said, 'who was in
Jerusalem trying to destroy those who invoke this name?
Did he not come here for the sole purpose of arresting them
22 and taking them to the chief priests?' But Saul grew more
and more forceful, and silenced the Jews of Damascus
with his cogent proofs that Jesus was the Messiah.

23 As the days mounted up, the Jews hatched a plot against
24 his life; but their plans became known to Saul. They kept
watch on the city gates day and night so that they might
25 murder him; but his converts took him one night and let
him down by the wall, lowering him in a basket.

26 When he reached Jerusalem he tried to join the body
of disciples there; but they were all afraid of him, because
27 they did not believe that he was really a convert. Barnabas, however, took him by the hand and introduced him
to the apostles. He described to them how Saul had seen
the Lord on his journey, and heard his voice, and how he
had spoken out boldly in the name of Jesus at Damascus.
28 Saul now stayed with them, moving about freely in Jeru-
29 salem. He spoke out boldly and openly in the name of the
Lord, talking and debating with the Greek-speaking Jews.[a]
30 But they planned to murder him, and when the brethren
learned of this they escorted him to Caesarea and saw him
off to Tarsus.

31 MEANWHILE THE CHURCH, throughout Judaea,
Galilee, and Samaria, was left in peace to build up its
strength. In the fear of the Lord, upheld by the Holy
Spirit, it held on its way and grew in numbers.

32 Peter was making a general tour, in the course of which
33 he went down to visit God's people at Lydda. There he
found a man named Aeneas who had been bed-ridden with
34 paralysis for eight years. Peter said to him, 'Aeneas, Jesus
Christ cures you; get up and make your bed', and imme-
35 diately he stood up. All who lived in Lydda and Sharon
saw him; and they turned to the Lord.

36 In Joppa there was a disciple named Tabitha (in Greek,
Dorcas, meaning a gazelle), who filled her days with acts
37 of kindness and charity. At that time she fell ill and died;
38 and they washed her body and laid it in a room upstairs. As
Lydda was near Joppa, the disciples, who had heard that

*a Literally the Hellenists.*

Peter was there, sent two men to him with the urgent request, 'Please come over to us without delay.' Peter there- **39**
upon went off with them. When he arrived they took him
upstairs to the room, where all the widows came and stood
round him in tears, showing him the shirts and coats that
Dorcas used to make while she was with them. Peter sent **40**
them all outside, and knelt down and prayed. Then, turning towards the body, he said, 'Get up, Tabitha.' She
opened her eyes, saw Peter, and sat up. He gave her his **41**
hand and helped her to her feet. Then he called the members of the congregation and the widows and showed her
to them alive. The news spread all over Joppa, and many **42**
came to believe in the Lord. Peter stayed on in Joppa for **43**
some time with one Simon, a tanner.

At Caesarea there was a man named Cornelius, a cen- **10**
turion in the Italian Cohort, as it was called. He was a **2**
religious man, and he and his whole family joined in the
worship of God. He gave generously to help the Jewish
people, and was regular in his prayers to God. One day **3**
about three in the afternoon he had a vision in which he
clearly saw an angel of God, who came into his room and
said, 'Cornelius!' He stared at him in terror. 'What is it, **4**
my lord?' he asked. The angel said, 'Your prayers and acts
of charity have gone up to heaven to speak for you before
God. And now send to Joppa for a man named Simon, also **5**
called Peter: he is lodging with another Simon, a tanner, **6**
whose house is by the sea.' So when the angel who was **7**
speaking to him had gone, he summoned two of his servants and a military orderly who was a religious man, told **8**
them the whole story, and sent them to Joppa.

Next day, while they were still on their way and ap- **9**
proaching the city, about noon Peter went up on the roof
to pray. He grew hungry and wanted something to eat. **10**
While they were getting it ready, he fell into a trance.
He saw a rift in the sky, and a thing coming down that **11**
looked like a great sheet of sail-cloth. It was slung by the
four corners, and was being lowered to the ground. In it **12**
he saw creatures of every kind, whatever walks or crawls
or flies. Then there was a voice which said to him, 'Up, **13**
Peter, kill and eat.' But Peter said, 'No, Lord, no: I have **14**
never eaten anything profane or unclean.' The voice came **15**
again a second time: 'It is not for you to call profane what
God counts clean.' This happened three times; and then **16**
the thing was taken up again into the sky.

While Peter was still puzzling over the meaning of the **17**

vision he had seen, the messengers of Cornelius had been
asking the way to Simon's house, and now arrived at the
18  entrance. They called out and asked if Simon Peter was
19  lodging there. But Peter was thinking over the vision,
when the Spirit said to him, 'Some*ᵃ* men are here looking
20  for you; make haste and go downstairs. You may go with
them without any misgiving, for it was I who sent them.'
21  Peter came down to the men and said, 'You are looking
22  for me? Here I am. What brings you here?' 'We are from
the centurion Cornelius,' they replied, 'a good and religious
man, acknowledged as such by the whole Jewish nation.
He was directed by a holy angel to send for you to his
23  house and to listen to what you have to say.' So Peter
asked them in and gave them a night's lodging. Next day
he set out with them, accompanied by some members of
the congregation at Joppa.

24  The day after that, he arrived at Caesarea. Cornelius
was expecting them and had called together his relatives
25  and close friends. When Peter arrived, Cornelius came to
meet him, and bowed to the ground in deep reverence.
26  But Peter raised him to his feet and said, 'Stand up; I am
27  a man like anyone else.' Still talking with him he went in
28  and found a large gathering. He said to them, 'I need not
tell you that a Jew is forbidden by his religion to visit or
associate with a man of another race; yet God has shown
me clearly that I must not call any man profane or un-
29  clean. That is why I came here without demur when you
sent for me. May I ask what was your reason for sending?'
30  Cornelius said, 'Four days ago, just about this time, I
was in the house here saying the afternoon prayers, when
31  suddenly a man in shining robes stood before me. He said:
"Cornelius, your prayer has been heard and your acts of
32  charity remembered before God. Send to Joppa, then, to
Simon Peter, and ask him to come. He is lodging in the
33  house of Simon the tanner, by the sea." So I sent to you
there and then; it was kind of you to come. And now we
are all met here before God, to hear all that the Lord has
ordered you to say.'

34  Peter began: 'I now see how true it is that God has no
35  favourites, but that in every nation the man who is god-
36  fearing and does what is right is acceptable to him. He sent
his word to the Israelites and gave the good news of peace
37  through Jesus Christ, who is Lord of all. I need not tell
you what happened lately all over the land of the Jews,

*ᵃ One witness reads* Two; *others read* Three.

starting from Galilee after the baptism proclaimed by John. You know about Jesus of Nazareth, how God anointed 38 him with the Holy Spirit and with power. He went about doing good and healing all who were oppressed by the devil, for God was with him. And we can bear witness to 39 all that he did in the Jewish country-side and in Jerusalem. He was put to death by hanging on a gibbet; but God 40 raised him to life on the third day, and allowed him to appear, not to the whole people, but to witnesses whom 41 God had chosen in advance—to us, who ate and drank with him after he rose from the dead. He commanded us 42 to proclaim him to the people, and affirm that he is the one who has been designated by God as judge of the living and the dead. It is to him that all the prophets testify, 43 declaring that everyone who trusts in him receives forgiveness of sins through his name.'

Peter was still speaking when the Holy Spirit came upon 44 all who were listening to the message. The believers who 45 had come with Peter, men of Jewish birth, were astonished that the gift of the Holy Spirit should have been poured out even on Gentiles. For they could hear them speaking 46 in tongues of ecstasy and acclaiming the greatness of God. Then Peter spoke: 'Is anyone prepared to withhold the 47 water for baptism from these persons, who have received the Holy Spirit just as we did ourselves?' Then he ordered 48 them to be baptized in the name of Jesus Christ. After that they asked him to stay on with them for a time.

News came to the apostles and the members of the 11 church in Judaea that Gentiles too had accepted the word of God; and when Peter came up to Jerusalem those who 2 were of Jewish birth raised the question with him. 'You 3 have been visiting men who are uncircumcised,' they said, 'and sitting at table with them!' Peter began by laying 4 before them the facts as they had happened.

'I was in the city of Joppa', he said, 'at prayer; and 5 while in a trance I had a vision: a thing was coming down that looked like a great sheet of sail-cloth, slung by the four corners and lowered from the sky till it reached me. I 6 looked intently to make out what was in it and I saw four-footed creatures of the earth, wild beasts, and things that crawl or fly. Then I heard a voice saying to me, "Up, Peter, 7 kill and eat." But I said, "No, Lord, no: nothing profane 8 or unclean has ever entered my mouth." A voice from 9 heaven answered a second time, "It is not for you to call profane what God counts clean." This happened three 10 times, and then they were all drawn up again into the sky.

11 At that moment three men, who had been sent to me from
12 Caesarea, arrived at the house where I was*a* staying; and
the Spirit told me to go with them.*b* My six companions
13 here came with me and we went into the man's house. He
told us how he had seen an angel standing in his house who
14 said, "Send to Joppa for Simon also called Peter. He will
speak words that will bring salvation to you and all your
15 household." Hardly had I begun speaking, when the Holy
Spirit came upon them, just as upon us at the beginning.
16 Then I recalled what the Lord had said: "John baptized
with water, but you will be baptized with the Holy Spirit."
17 God gave them no less a gift than he gave us when we put
our trust in the Lord Jesus Christ; then how could I
possibly stand in God's way?'

18 When they heard this their doubts were silenced. They
gave praise to God and said, 'This means that God has
granted life-giving repentance to the Gentiles also.'

19 MEANWHILE THOSE who had been scattered after
the persecution that arose over Stephen made their way
to Phoenicia, Cyprus, and Antioch, bringing the message
20 to Jews only and to no others. But there were some
natives of Cyprus and Cyrene among them, and these,
when they arrived at Antioch, began to speak to Gentiles
as well, telling them the good news of the Lord Jesus.
21 The power of the Lord was with them, and a great many
became believers, and turned to the Lord.

22 The news reached the ears of the church in Jerusalem;
23 and they sent Barnabas to Antioch. When he arrived and
saw the divine grace at work, he rejoiced, and encouraged
24 them all to hold fast to the Lord with resolute hearts; for
he was a good man, full of the Holy Spirit and of faith. And
large numbers were won over to the Lord.

25 26 He then went off to Tarsus to look for Saul; and when
he had found him, he brought him to Antioch. For a whole
year the two of them lived in fellowship with the congregation there, and gave instruction to large numbers.
It was in Antioch that the disciples first got the name of
Christians.

27 During this period some prophets came down from Jeru-
28 salem to Antioch. One of them, Agabus by name, was

---

*a Some witnesses read* we were.    *b Some witnesses add* making
no distinctions; *others add* without any misgiving, *as in 10. 20.*

inspired to stand up and predict a severe and world-wide
famine, which in fact occurred in the reign of Claudius.
So the disciples agreed to make a contribution, each accord- 29
ing to his means, for the relief of their fellow-Christians in
Judaea. This they did, and sent it off to the elders, in the 30
charge of Barnabas and Saul.

It was about this time that King Herod attacked 12
certain members of the church. He beheaded James, the 2
brother of John, and then, when he saw that the Jews 3
approved, proceeded to arrest Peter also. This happened
during the festival of Unleavened Bread. Having secured 4
him, he put him in prison under a military guard, four
squads of four men each, meaning to produce him in public
after Passover. So Peter was kept in prison under con- 5
stant watch, while the church kept praying fervently for
him to God.

On the very night before Herod had planned to bring 6
him forward, Peter was asleep between two soldiers, secured by two chains, while outside the doors sentries kept
guard over the prison. All at once an angel of the Lord 7
stood there, and the cell was ablaze with light. He tapped
Peter on the shoulder and woke him. 'Quick! Get up', he
said, and the chains fell away from his wrists. The angel 8
then said to him, 'Do up your belt and put your sandals on.'
He did so. 'Now wrap your cloak round you and follow
me.' He followed him out, with no idea that the angel's 9
intervention was real: he thought it was just a vision. But 10
they passed the first guard-post, then the second, and
reached the iron gate leading out into the city, which
opened for them of its own accord. And so they came out
and walked the length of one street; and the angel left him.

Then Peter came to himself. 'Now I know it is true,' he 11
said; 'the Lord has sent his angel and rescued me from
Herod's clutches and from all that the Jewish people were
expecting.' When he realized how things stood, he made 12
for the house of Mary, the mother of John Mark, where a
large company was at prayer. He knocked at the outer 13
door and a maid called Rhoda came to answer it. She 14
recognized Peter's voice and was so overjoyed that instead
of opening the door she ran in and announced that Peter
was standing outside. 'You are crazy', they told her; but 15
she insisted that it was so. Then they said, 'It must be his
guardian angel.'

Meanwhile Peter went on knocking, and when they 16

opened the door and saw him, they were astounded.
17 With a movement of the hand he signed to them to keep
quiet, and told them how the Lord had brought him out
of prison. 'Report this to James and the members of the
church', he said. Then he left the house and went off
elsewhere.

18     When morning came, there was consternation among the
19 soldiers: what could have become of Peter? Herod made
close search, but failed to find him, so he interrogated the
guards and ordered their execution.

     Afterwards he left Judaea to reside for a time at Cae-
20 sarea. He had for some time been furiously angry with the
people of Tyre and Sidon, who now by common agreement
presented themselves at his court. There they won over
Blastus the royal chamberlain, and sued for peace, because
their country drew its supplies from the king's territory.
21 So, on an appointed day, attired in his royal robes and
22 seated on the rostrum, Herod harangued them; and the
populace shouted back, 'It is a god speaking, not a man!'
23 Instantly an angel of the Lord struck him down, because
he had usurped the honour due to God; he was eaten up
with worms and died.

24     Meanwhile the word of God continued to grow and
spread.

25     Barnabas and Saul, their task fulfilled, returned from
Jerusalem,*a* taking John Mark with them.

## THE CHURCH BREAKS BARRIERS

13  THERE WERE AT ANTIOCH, in the congregation there, certain prophets and teachers: Barnabas,
Simeon called Niger, Lucius of Cyrene, Manaen, who had
2 been at the court of Prince Herod, and Saul. While they
were keeping a fast and offering worship to the Lord, the
Holy Spirit said, 'Set Barnabas and Saul apart for me, to do
3 the work to which I have called them.' Then, after further
fasting and prayer, they laid their hands on them and let
them go.

4     So these two, sent out on their mission by the Holy
Spirit, came down to Seleucia, and from there sailed to
5 Cyprus. Arriving at Salamis, they declared the word of
God in the Jewish synagogues. They had John with them

---

*a Some witnesses read* their task fulfilled, returned to Jerusalem; *or,
as it might be rendered,* their task at Jerusalem fulfilled, returned.

as their assistant. They went through the whole island as 6
far as Paphos, and there they came upon a sorcerer, a Jew
who posed as a prophet, Bar-Jesus by name. He was in the 7
retinue of the Governor, Sergius Paulus, an intelligent man,
who had sent for Barnabas and Saul and wanted to hear
the word of God. This Elymas the sorcerer (so his name 8
may be translated) opposed them, trying to turn the
Governor away from the Faith. But Saul, also known as 9
Paul, filled with the Holy Spirit, fixed his eyes on him and 10
said, 'You swindler, you rascal, son of the devil and
enemy of all goodness, will you never stop falsifying the
straight ways of the Lord? Look now, the hand of the 11
Lord strikes: you shall be blind, and for a time you shall
not see the sunlight.' Instantly mist and darkness came
over him and he groped about for someone to lead him by
the hand. When the Governor saw what had happened he 12
became a believer, deeply impressed by what he learned
about the Lord.

Leaving Paphos, Paul and his companions went by sea 13
to Perga in Pamphylia; John, however, left them and returned to Jerusalem. From Perga they continued their 14
journey as far as Pisidian Antioch. On the Sabbath they
went to synagogue and took their seats; and after the 15
readings from the Law and the prophets, the officials of
the synagogue sent this message to them: 'Friends, if you
have anything to say to the people by way of exhortation,
let us hear it.' Paul rose, made a gesture with his hand, and 16
began:

'Men of Israel and you who worship our God, listen to
me! The God of this people of Israel chose our fathers. 17
When they were still living as aliens in Egypt he made
them into a nation and brought them out of that country
with arm outstretched. For some forty years he bore with 18
their conduct*a* in the desert. Then in the Canaanite country 19
he overthrew seven nations, whose lands he gave them to
be their heritage for some four hundred and fifty years, 20
and afterwards appointed judges for them until the time
of the prophet Samuel.

'Then they asked for a king and God gave them Saul the 21
son of Kish, a man of the tribe of Benjamin, who reigned
for forty years. Then he removed him and set up David as 22
their king, giving him his approval in these words: "I have
found David son of Jesse to be a man after my own heart,
who will carry out all my purposes." This is the man from 23

*a Some witnesses read* he sustained them.

whose posterity God, as he promised, has brought Israel
24 a saviour, Jesus. John made ready for his coming by proclaiming baptism as a token of repentance to the whole
25 people of Israel. And when John was nearing the end of
his course, he said, "I am not what you think I am. No,
after me comes one whose shoes I am not fit to unfasten."
26 'My brothers, you who come of the stock of Abraham,
and others among you who revere our God, we are the
people to whom the message of this salvation has been sent.
27 The people of Jerusalem and their rulers did not recognize
him, or understand the words of the prophets which are
read Sabbath by Sabbath; indeed they fulfilled them by
28 condemning him. Though they failed to find grounds for
the sentence of death, they asked Pilate to have him exe-
29 cuted. And when they had carried out all that the scriptures said about him, they took him down from the gibbet
30 and laid him in a tomb. But God raised him from the dead;
31 and there was a period of many days during which he
appeared to those who had come up with him from Galilee
to Jerusalem.
32 'They are now his witnesses before our nation; and we
are here to give you the good news that God, who made the
33 promise to the fathers, has fulfilled it for the children[a] by
raising Jesus from the dead, as indeed it stands written,
in the second[b] Psalm: "You are my son; this day I have
34 begotten you." Again, that he raised him from the dead,
never again to revert to corruption, he declares in these
words: "I will give you the blessings promised to David,
35 holy and sure." This is borne out by another passage:
"Thou wilt not let thy loyal servant suffer corruption."
36 As for David, when he had served the purpose of God in
his own generation, he died, and was gathered to his
37 fathers, and suffered corruption; but the one whom God
38 raised up did not suffer corruption; and you must understand, my brothers, that it is through him that forgiveness
39 of sins is now being proclaimed to you. It is through him
that everyone who has faith is acquitted of everything
for which there was no acquittal under the Law of Moses.
40 Beware, then, lest you bring down upon yourselves the
41 doom proclaimed by the prophets: "See this, you scoffers,
wonder, and begone; for I am doing a deed in your days,
a deed which you will never believe when you are told
of it." '

[a] *Some witnesses read* our children; *others read* us their children.
[b] *Some witnesses read* first.

As they were leaving the synagogue they were asked 42
to come again and speak on these subjects next Sabbath;
and after the congregation had dispersed, many Jews and 43
gentile worshippers went along with Paul and Barnabas,
who spoke to them and urged them to hold fast to the
grace of God.

On the following Sabbath almost the whole city gathered 44
to hear the word of God. When the Jews saw the crowds, 45
they were filled with jealous resentment, and contra-
dicted what Paul said, with violent abuse. But Paul and 46
Barnabas were outspoken in their reply. 'It was necessary',
they said, 'that the word of God should be declared to you
first. But since you reject it and thus condemn yourselves
as unworthy of eternal life, we now turn to the Gentiles.
For these are our instructions from the Lord: "I have 47
appointed you to be a light for the Gentiles, and a means
of salvation to earth's farthest bounds."' When the Gen- 48
tiles heard this, they were overjoyed and thankfully ac-
claimed the word of the Lord, and those who were marked
out for eternal life became believers. So the word of the 49
Lord spread far and wide through the region. But the Jews 50
stirred up feeling among the women of standing who were
worshippers, and among the leading men of the city; a
persecution was started against Paul and Barnabas, and
they were expelled from the district. So they shook the 51
dust off their feet in protest against them and went to
Iconium. And the converts were filled with joy and with 52
the Holy Spirit.

At Iconium similarly they went*a* into the Jewish syna- 14
gogue and spoke to such purpose that a large body both
of Jews and Gentiles became believers. But the uncon- 2
verted Jews stirred up the Gentiles and poisoned their
minds against the Christians. For some time Paul and 3
Barnabas stayed on and spoke boldly and openly in
reliance on the Lord; and he confirmed the message of his
grace by causing signs and miracles to be worked at their
hands. The mass of the townspeople were divided, some 4
siding with the Jews, others with the apostles. But when 5
a move was made by Gentiles and Jews together, with the
connivance of the city authorities, to maltreat them and
stone them, they got wind of it and made their escape to 6
the Lycaonian cities of Lystra and Derbe and the surrounding country, where they continued to spread the 7
good news.

*a* Or *At Iconium they went together . . .*

8   At Lystra sat a crippled man, lame from birth, who had
9 never walked in his life. This man listened while Paul was
speaking. Paul fixed his eyes on him and saw that he had
10 the faith to be cured, so he said to him in a loud voice,
'Stand up straight on your feet'; and he sprang up and
11 started to walk. When the crowds saw what Paul had done,
they shouted, in their native Lycaonian, 'The gods have
12 come down to us in human form.' And they called Barnabas Jupiter, and Paul they called Mercury, because he was
13 the spokesman. And the priest of Jupiter, whose temple
was just outside the city, brought oxen and garlands to
the gates, and he and all the people were about to offer
sacrifice.

14   But when the apostles Barnabas and Paul heard of it,
they tore their clothes and rushed into the crowd shouting,
15 'Men, what is this that you are doing? We are only human
beings, no less mortal than you. The good news we bring
tells you to turn from these follies to the living God, who
16 made heaven and earth and sea and everything in them. In
17 past ages he allowed all nations to go their own way; and
yet he has not left you without some clue to his nature, in
the kindness he shows: he sends you rain from heaven and
crops in their seasons, and gives you food and good cheer
in plenty.'

18   With these words they barely managed to prevent the
crowd from offering sacrifice to them.

19   Then Jews from Antioch and Iconium came on the
scene and won over the crowds. They stoned Paul, and
20 dragged him out of the city, thinking him dead. The converts formed a ring round him, and he got to his feet and
went into the city. Next day he left with Barnabas for
Derbe.

21   After bringing the good news to that town, where they
gained many converts, they returned to Lystra, then to
22 Iconium, and then to Antioch, heartening the converts and
encouraging them to be true to their religion. They warned
them that to enter the kingdom of God we must pass
23 through many hardships. They also appointed elders for
them in each congregation, and with prayer and fasting
committed them to the Lord in whom they had put their
faith.

24   Then they passed through Pisidia and came into Pam-
25 phylia. When they had given the message at Perga, they
26 went down to Attalia, and from there set sail for Antioch,
where they had originally been commended to the grace of

God for the task which they had now completed. When 27
they arrived and had called the congregation together, they
reported all that God had done through them, and how he
had thrown open the gates of faith to the Gentiles. And 28
they stayed for some time with the disciples there.

Now CERTAIN PERSONS who had come down from 15
Judaea began to teach the brotherhood that those who
were not circumcised in accordance with Mosaic practice
could not be saved. That brought them into fierce dis- 2
sension and controversy with Paul and Barnabas. And so
it was arranged that these two and some others from
Antioch should go up to Jerusalem to see the apostles and
elders about this question.

They were sent on their way by the congregation, and 3
travelled through Phoenicia and Samaria, telling the full
story of the conversion of the Gentiles. The news caused
great rejoicing among all the Christians there.

When they reached Jerusalem they were welcomed by 4
the church and the apostles and elders, and reported all
that God had done through them. Then some of the 5
Pharisaic party who had become believers came forward
and said, 'They must be circumcised and told to keep the
Law of Moses.'

The apostles and elders held a meeting to look into this 6
matter; and, after a long debate, Peter rose and addressed 7
them. 'My friends,' he said, 'in the early days, as you yourselves know, God made his choice among you and ordained
that from my lips the Gentiles should hear and believe the
message of the Gospel. And God, who can read men's 8
minds, showed his approval of them by giving the Holy
Spirit to them, as he did to us. He made no difference be- 9
tween them and us; for he purified their hearts by faith.
Then why do you now provoke God by laying on the 10
shoulders of these converts a yoke which neither we nor
our fathers were able to bear? No, we believe that it is by 11
the grace of the Lord Jesus that we are saved, and so
are they.'

At that the whole company fell silent and listened to 12
Barnabas and Paul as they told of all the signs and miracles
that God had worked among the Gentiles through them.

When they had finished speaking, James summed up: 13
'My friends,' he said, 'listen to me. Simeon has told how it 14
first happened that God took notice of the Gentiles, to
choose from among them a people to bear his name; and 15

this agrees with the words of the prophets, as Scripture has it:

16 "Thereafter I will return and rebuild the fallen house of David;

even from its ruins I will rebuild it, and set it up again,

17 that they may seek the Lord—all the rest of mankind, and the Gentiles, whom I have claimed for my own. Thus says the Lord, whose work it is,

18 made known long ago."

19 'My judgement therefore is that we should impose no irksome restrictions on those of the Gentiles who are turn-

20 ing to God, but instruct them by letter to abstain from things polluted by contact with idols, from fornication, from anything that has been strangled, and from blood.[a]

21 Moses, after all, has never lacked spokesmen in every town for generations past; he is read in the synagogues Sabbath by Sabbath.'

22 Then the apostles and elders, with the agreement of the whole church, resolved to choose representatives and send them to Antioch with Paul and Barnabas. They chose two leading men in the community, Judas Barsabbas and Silas,

23 and gave them this letter to deliver:

'We, the apostles and elders, send greetings as brothers to our brothers of gentile origin in Antioch, Syria, and

24 Cilicia. Forasmuch as we have heard that some of our number, without any instructions from us, have[b] disturbed

25 you with their talk and unsettled your minds, we have re-solved unanimously to send to you our chosen representa-

26 tives with our well-beloved Barnabas and Paul, who have devoted themselves to the cause of our Lord Jesus Christ.

27 We are therefore sending Judas and Silas, who will them-

28 selves confirm this by word of mouth. It is the decision of the Holy Spirit, and our decision, to lay no further burden

29 upon you beyond these essentials: you are to abstain from meat that has been offered to idols, from blood, from any-thing that has been strangled,[c] and from fornication.[d] If you keep yourselves free from these things you will be doing right. Farewell.'

[a] *Some witnesses omit* from fornication; *others omit* from anything that has been strangled; *some add* (*after* blood) and to refrain from doing to others what they would not like done to themselves.     [b] *Some witnesses read* have gone out and . . .     [c] *Some witnesses omit* from anything that has been strangled.     [d] *Some witnesses omit* and from fornication; *and some add* and refrain from doing to others what you would not like done to yourselves.

So they were sent off on their journey and travelled 30
down to Antioch, where they called the congregation together, and delivered the letter. When it was read, they 31
all rejoiced at the encouragement it brought. Judas and 32
Silas, who were prophets themselves, said much to encourage and strengthen the members, and, after spending 33
some time there, were dismissed with the good wishes of
the brethren, to return to those who had sent them.*a* But 35
Paul and Barnabas stayed on at Antioch, and there, along
with many others, they taught and preached the word of
the Lord.

## PAUL LEADS THE ADVANCE

AFTER A WHILE Paul said to Barnabas, 'Ought 36
we not to go back now to see how our brothers are
faring in the various towns where we proclaimed the word
of the Lord?' Barnabas wanted to take John Mark with 37
them; but Paul judged that the man who had deserted 38
them in Pamphylia and had not gone on to share in their
work was not the man to take with them now. The dispute 39
was so sharp that they parted company. Barnabas took
Mark with him and sailed for Cyprus, while Paul chose 40
Silas. He started on his journey, commended by the
brothers to the grace of the Lord, and travelled through 41
Syria and Cilicia bringing new strength to the congregations.

He went on to Derbe and to Lystra, and there he found 16
a disciple named Timothy, the son of a Jewish Christian
mother and a Gentile father. He was well spoken of by the 2
Christians at Lystra and Iconium, and Paul wanted to 3
have him in his company when he left the place. So he took
him and circumcised him, out of consideration for the
Jews who lived in those parts; for they all knew that his
father was a Gentile. As they made their way from town 4
to town they handed on the decisions taken by the
apostles and elders in Jerusalem and enjoined their observance. And so, day by day, the congregations grew 5
stronger in faith and increased in numbers.

They travelled through the Phrygian and Galatian 6
region,*b* because they were prevented by the Holy Spirit
from delivering the message in the province of Asia; and 7
when they approached the Mysian border they tried to

---

*a* *Some witnesses add* (34) But Silas decided to remain there.
*b* Or *through Phrygia and the Galatian region.*

enter Bithynia; but the Spirit of Jesus would not allow
8 them, so they skirted*a* Mysia and reached the coast at
9 Troas. During the night a vision came to Paul: a Macedonian stood there appealing to him and saying, 'Come
10 across to Macedonia and help us.' After he had seen this
vision we at once set about getting a passage to Macedonia,
concluding that God had called us to bring them the good
news.

11      So we sailed from Troas and made a straight run to
12 Samothrace, the next day to Neapolis, and from there to
Philippi, a city of the first rank in that district of Macedonia, and a Roman colony. Here we stayed for some days,
13 and on the Sabbath day we went outside the city gate by
the river-side, where we thought there would be a place of
prayer,*b* and sat down and talked to the women who had
14 gathered there. One of them named Lydia, a dealer in
purple fabric from the city of Thyatira, who was a worshipper of God, was listening, and the Lord opened her
15 heart to respond to what Paul said. She was baptized, and
her household with her, and then she said to us, 'If you
have judged me to be a believer in the Lord, I beg you to
come and stay in my house.' And she insisted on our going.

16      Once, when we were on our way to the place of prayer,
we met a slave-girl who was possessed by an oracular
spirit and brought large profits to her owners by telling
17 fortunes. She followed Paul and the rest of us, shouting,
'These men are servants of the Supreme God, and are de-
18 claring to you a way of salvation.' She did this day after
day, until Paul could bear it no longer. Rounding on the
spirit he said, 'I command you in the name of Jesus Christ
to come out of her', and it went out there and then.

19      When the girl's owners saw that their hope of gain had
gone, they seized Paul and Silas and dragged them to the
20 city authorities in the main square; and bringing them
before the magistrates, they said, 'These men are causing
21 a disturbance in our city; they are Jews; they are advocating customs which it is illegal for us Romans to adopt and
22 follow.' The mob joined in the attack; and the magistrates
tore off the prisoners' clothes and ordered them to be
23 flogged. After giving them a severe beating they flung them
into prison and ordered the jailer to keep them under close
24 guard. In view of these orders, he put them in the inner
prison and secured their feet in the stocks.

---

*a* Possibly traversed.          *b* Some *witnesses read* where there was a
recognized place of prayer.

About midnight Paul and Silas, at their prayers, were 25
singing praises to God, and the other prisoners were listening, when suddenly there was such a violent earthquake 26
that the foundations of the jail were shaken; all the doors
burst open and all the prisoners found their fetters un-
fastened. The jailer woke up to see the prison doors wide 27
open, and assuming that the prisoners had escaped, drew
his sword intending to kill himself. But Paul shouted, 'Do 28
yourself no harm; we are all here.' The jailer called for lights, 29
rushed in and threw himself down before Paul and Silas,
trembling with fear. He then escorted them out and said, 30
'Masters, what must I do to be saved?' They said, 'Put 31
your trust in the Lord Jesus, and you will be saved, you
and your household.' Then they spoke the word of the 32
Lord[a] to him and to everyone in his house. At that late 33
hour of the night he took them and washed their wounds;
and immediately afterwards he and his whole family were
baptized. He brought them into his house, set out a meal, 34
and rejoiced with his whole household in his new-found
faith in God.

When daylight came the magistrates sent their officers 35
with instructions to release the men. The jailer reported 36
the message to Paul: 'The magistrates have sent word that
you are to be released. So now you may go free, and blessings on your journey.'[b] But Paul said to the officers: 'They 37
gave us a public flogging, though we are Roman citizens
and have not been found guilty; they threw us into prison,
and are they now to smuggle us out privately? No indeed!
Let them come in person and escort us out.' The officers 38
reported his words. The magistrates were alarmed to hear
that they were Roman citizens, and came and apologized to 39
them. Then they escorted them out and requested them
to go away from the city. On leaving the prison, they went 40
to Lydia's house, where they met their fellow-Christians,
and spoke words of encouragement to them; then they
departed.

THEY NOW TRAVELLED by way of Amphipolis and 17
Apollonia and came to Thessalonica, where there was a
Jewish synagogue. Following his usual practice Paul went 2
to their meetings; and for the next three Sabbaths he
argued with them, quoting texts of Scripture which he 3
expounded and applied to show that the Messiah had to

[a] *Some witnesses read* of God.          [b] *Some witnesses read . . .* free
and take your journey.

suffer and rise from the dead. 'And this Jesus,' he said,
4 'whom I am proclaiming to you, is the Messiah.' Some of
them were convinced and joined Paul and Silas; so did a
great number of godfearing Gentiles and a good many
influential women.[a]
5   But the Jews in their jealousy recruited some low fellows
from the dregs of the populace, roused the rabble, and had
the city in an uproar. They mobbed Jason's house, with
the intention of bringing Paul and Silas before the town
6 assembly. Failing to find them, they dragged Jason himself and some members of the congregation before the
magistrates, shouting, 'The men who have made trouble
7 all over the world have now come here; and Jason has
harboured them. They all flout the Emperor's laws, and
8 assert that there is a rival king, Jesus.' These words caused
a great commotion in the mob, which affected the magis-
9 trates also. They bound over Jason and the others, and
let them go.
10   As soon as darkness fell, the members of the congregation sent Paul and Silas off to Beroea. On arrival, they
11 made their way to the synagogue. The Jews here were more
civil than those at Thessalonica: they received the message
with great eagerness, studying the scriptures every day
12 to see whether it was as they said. Many of them therefore
became believers, and so did a fair number of Gentiles,
13 women of standing as well as men. But when the Thes-
salonian Jews learned that the word of God had now been
proclaimed by Paul in Beroea, they came on there to stir
14 up trouble and rouse the rabble. Thereupon the members
of the congregation sent Paul off at once to go down to the
15 coast, while Silas and Timothy both stayed behind. Paul's
escort brought him as far as Athens, and came away with
instructions for Silas and Timothy to rejoin him with all speed.
16   Now while Paul was waiting for them at Athens he was
17 exasperated to see how the city was full of idols. So he
argued in the synagogue with the Jews and gentile worshippers, and also in the city square every day with casual
18 passers-by. And some of the Epicurean and Stoic philo-
sophers joined issue with him. Some said, 'What can this
charlatan be trying to say?'; others, 'He would appear to
be a propagandist for foreign deities'—this because he was
19 preaching about Jesus and Resurrection. So they took him
and brought him before the Court of Areopagus[b] and said,

[a] *Some witnesses read* a good many wives of leading men.      [b] *Or* brought him to Mars' Hill.

'May we know what this new doctrine is that you pro-
pound? You are introducing ideas that sound strange to 20
us, and we should like to know what they mean.' (Now 21
the Athenians in general and the foreigners there had no
time for anything but talking or hearing about the latest
novelty.)

Then Paul stood up before the Court of Areopagus[a] and 22
said: 'Men of Athens, I see that in everything that concerns religion you are uncommonly scrupulous. For as I 23
was going round looking at the objects of your worship,
I noticed among other things an altar bearing the inscription "To an Unknown God". What you worship but do not
know—this is what I now proclaim.

'The God who created the world and everything in it, 24
and who is Lord of heaven and earth, does not live in
shrines made by men. It is not because he lacks anything 25
that he accepts service at men's hands, for he is himself
the universal giver of life and breath and all else. He cre- 26
ated every race of men of one stock, to inhabit the whole
earth's surface. He fixed the epochs of their history[b] and
the limits of their territory. They were to seek God, and, 27
it might be, touch and find him; though indeed he is not
far from each one of us, for in him we live and move, in 28
him we exist; as some of your own poets[c] have said, "We
are also his offspring." As God's offspring, then, we ought 29
not to suppose that the deity is like an image in gold or
silver or stone, shaped by human craftsmanship and
design. As for the times of ignorance, God has overlooked 30
them; but now he commands mankind, all men everywhere, to repent, because he has fixed the day on which he 31
will have the world judged, and justly judged, by a man
of his choosing; of this he has given assurance to all by
raising him from the dead.'

When they heard about the raising of the dead, some 32
scoffed; and others said, 'We will hear you on this subject
some other time.' And so Paul left the assembly. However, 33 34
some men joined him and became believers, including
Dionysius, a member of the Court of Areopagus; also a
woman named Damaris, and others besides.

After this he left Athens and went to Corinth. There he 18 1 2
fell in with a Jew named Aquila, a native of Pontus, and
his wife Priscilla; he had recently arrived from Italy because Claudius had issued an edict that all Jews should

---

[a] *Or* in the middle of Mars' Hill.                    [b] *Or* fixed the ordered
seasons . . .       [c] *Some witnesses read* some among you.

3 leave Rome. Paul approached them and, because he was
of the same trade, he made his home with them, and they
4 carried on business together; they were tent-makers. He
also held discussions in the synagogue Sabbath by Sabbath,
trying to convince both Jews and Gentiles.

5 Then Silas and Timothy came down from Macedonia,
and Paul devoted himself entirely to preaching, affirming
6 before the Jews that the Messiah was Jesus. But when
they opposed him and resorted to abuse, he shook out the
skirts of his cloak and said to them, 'Your blood be on your
own heads! My conscience is clear; now I shall go to the
7 Gentiles.' With that he left, and went to the house of a
worshipper of God named Titius Justus, who lived next
8 door to the synagogue. Crispus, who held office in the
synagogue, now became a believer in the Lord, with all his
household; and a number of Corinthians listened and be-
9 lieved, and were baptized. One night in a vision the Lord
said to Paul, 'Have no fear: go on with your preaching and
10 do not be silenced, for I am with you and no one shall
attempt to do you harm;[a] and there are many in this city
11 who are my people.' So he settled down for eighteen
months, teaching the word of God among them.

12 But when Gallio was proconsul of Achaia, the Jews set
13 upon Paul in a body and brought him into court. 'This
man', they said, 'is inducing people to worship God in ways
14 that are against the law.' Paul was just about to speak
when Gallio said to them, 'If it had been a question of
crime or grave misdemeanour, I should, of course, have
15 given you Jews a patient hearing, but if it is some bicker-
ing about words and names and your Jewish law, you may
see to it yourselves; I have no mind to be a judge of these
16 17 matters.' And he had them ejected from the court. Then
there was a general attack on Sosthenes, who held office
in the synagogue, and they gave him a beating in full view
of the bench. But all this left Gallio quite unconcerned.

18 Paul stayed on for some time, and then took leave of the
brotherhood and set sail for Syria, accompanied by Priscilla
and Aquila. At Cenchreae he had his hair cut off, because
19 he was under a vow. When they reached Ephesus he
parted from them and went himself into the synagogue,
20 where he held a discussion with the Jews. He was asked
21 to stay longer, but declined and set out from Ephesus,
saying, as he took leave of them, 'I shall come back to you
22 if it is God's will.' On landing at Caesarea, he went up and

[a] Or and you will not be harmed by anyone's attacks.

paid his respects to the church, and then went down to
Antioch. After spending some time there, he set out again 23
and made a journey through the Galatian country and on
through Phrygia, bringing new strength to all the converts.

Now there arrived at Ephesus a Jew named Apollos, 24
an Alexandrian by birth, an eloquent man,[a] powerful in
his use of the scriptures. He had been instructed in the 25
way of the Lord and was full of spiritual fervour; and in
his discourses he taught accurately the facts about Jesus,[b]
though he knew only John's baptism. He now began to 26
speak boldly in the synagogue, where Priscilla and Aquila
heard him; they took him in hand and expounded the new
way[c] to him in greater detail. Finding that he wished to 27
go across to Achaia, the brotherhood gave him their support, and wrote to the congregation there to make him
welcome. From the time of his arrival, he was very helpful
to those who had by God's grace become believers; for 28
he strenuously confuted the Jews, demonstrating publicly
from the scriptures that the Messiah is Jesus.

While Apollos was at Corinth, Paul travelled through 19
the inland regions till he came to Ephesus. There he found
a number of converts, to whom he said, 'Did you receive 2
the Holy Spirit when you became believers?' 'No,' they
replied, 'we have not even heard that there is a Holy
Spirit.' He said, 'Then what baptism were you given?' 3
'John's baptism', they answered. Paul then said, 'The 4
baptism that John gave was a baptism in token of repentance, and he told the people to put their trust in one
who was to come after him, that is, in Jesus.' On hearing 5
this they were baptized into the name of the Lord Jesus;
and when Paul had laid his hands on them, the Holy Spirit 6
came upon them and they spoke in tongues of ecstasy and
prophesied. Altogether they were about a dozen men. 7

During the next three months he attended the syna- 8
gogue and, using argument and persuasion, spoke boldly
and freely about the kingdom of God. But when some 9
proved obdurate and would not believe, speaking evil of
the new way before the whole congregation, he left them,
withdrew his converts, and continued to hold discussions
daily in the lecture-hall of Tyrannus. This went on for 10
two years, with the result that the whole population of
the province of Asia, both Jews and Gentiles, heard the

[a] Or a learned man.  [b] *Some witnesses read* about the Lord.
[c] *Some witnesses read* the way of God.

11 word of the Lord. And through Paul God worked singular
12 miracles: when handkerchiefs and scarves which had been
in contact with his skin were carried to the sick, they were
rid of their diseases and the evil spirits came out of them.
13     But some strolling Jewish exorcists tried their hand at
using the name of the Lord Jesus on those possessed by
evil spirits; they would say, 'I adjure you by Jesus whom
14 Paul proclaims.' There were seven sons of Sceva, a Jewish
15 chief priest, who were using this method, when the evil
spirit answered back and said, 'Jesus I acknowledge, and
16 I know about Paul, but who are you?' And the man with
the evil spirit flew at them, overpowered them all, and
handled them with such violence that they ran out of the
17 house stripped and battered. This became known to everybody in Ephesus, whether Jew or Gentile; they were all
awestruck, and the name of the Lord Jesus gained in
18 honour. Moreover many of those who had become believers came and openly confessed that they had been using
19 magical spells. And a good many of those who formerly
practised magic collected their books and burnt them
publicly. The total value was reckoned up and it came to
20 fifty thousand pieces of silver. In such ways the word of
the Lord showed its power, spreading more and more
widely and effectively.
21     When things had reached this stage, Paul made up his
mind[a] to visit Macedonia and Achaia and then go on to
Jerusalem; and he said, 'After I have been there, I must
22 see Rome also.' So he sent two of his assistants, Timothy
and Erastus, to Macedonia, while he himself stayed some
time longer in the province of Asia.
23     Now about that time, the Christian movement gave rise
24 to a serious disturbance. There was a man named Demetrius, a silversmith who made silver shrines of Diana and
provided a great deal of employment for the craftsmen.
25 He called a meeting of these men and the workers in allied
trades, and addressed them. 'Men,' he said, 'you know that
26 our high standard of living depends on this industry. And
you see and hear how this fellow Paul with his propaganda
has perverted crowds of people, not only at Ephesus but
also in practically the whole of the province of Asia. He is
telling them that gods made by human hands are not gods
27 at all. There is danger for us here; it is not only that our
line of business will be discredited, but also that the
sanctuary of the great goddess Diana will cease to command

[a] *Or Paul, led by the Spirit, resolved . . .*

respect; and then it will not be long before she who is worshipped by all Asia and the civilized world is brought down
from her divine pre-eminence.'

When they heard this they were roused to fury and 28
shouted, 'Great is Diana of the Ephesians!' The whole city 29
was in confusion; they seized Paul's travelling-companions,
the Macedonians Gaius and Aristarchus, and made a con-
certed rush with them into the theatre. Paul wanted 30
to appear before the assembly but the other Christians
would not let him. Even some of the dignitaries of the pro- 31
vince, who were friendly towards him, sent and urged him
not to venture into the theatre. Meanwhile some were 32
shouting one thing, some another; for the assembly was
in confusion and most of them did not know what they
had all come for. But some of the crowd explained the 33
trouble to Alexander, whom the Jews had pushed to the
front, and he, motioning for silence, attempted to make a
defence before the assembly. But when they recognized that 34
he was a Jew, a single cry arose from them all: for about
two hours they kept on shouting, 'Great is Diana of the
Ephesians!'

The town clerk, however, quieted the crowd. 'Men of 35
Ephesus,' he said, 'all the world knows that our city of
Ephesus is temple-warden of the great Diana and of that
symbol of her which fell from heaven. Since these facts are 36
beyond dispute, your proper course is to keep quiet and do
nothing rash. These men whom you have brought here as 37
culprits have committed no sacrilege and uttered no blasphemy against our goddess. If therefore Demetrius and his 38
craftsmen have a case against anyone, assizes are held and
there are such people as proconsuls; let the parties bring
their charges and countercharges. If, on the other hand, you 39
have some further question to raise, it will be dealt with
in the statutory assembly. We certainly run the risk of 40
being charged with riot for this day's work. There is no
justification for it, and if the issue is raised we shall be
unable to give any explanation of this uproar.' With that 41
he dismissed the assembly.

WHEN THE DISTURBANCE had ceased, Paul sent for 20
the disciples and, after encouraging them, said good-bye
and set out on his journey to Macedonia. He travelled 2
through those parts of the country, often speaking words
of encouragement to the Christians there, and so came into
Greece. When he had spent three months there and was on 3

the point of embarking for Syria, a plot was laid against
him by the Jews, so he decided to return by way of Mace-
4 donia. He was accompanied by Sopater son of Pyrrhus,
from Beroea, the Thessalonians Aristarchus and Secundus,
Gaius the Doberian[a] and Timothy, and the Asians Tychicus
5 and Trophimus. These went ahead and waited for us at
6 Troas; we ourselves set sail from Philippi after the Passover season,[b] and in five days reached them at Troas,
where we spent a week.

7     On the Saturday night, in our assembly for the breaking
of bread, Paul, who was to leave next day, addressed them,
8 and went on speaking until midnight. Now there were
many lamps in the upper room where we were assembled;
9 and a youth named Eutychus, who was sitting on the
window-ledge, grew more and more sleepy as Paul went
on talking. At last he was completely overcome by sleep,
fell from the third storey to the ground, and was picked up
10 for dead. Paul went down, threw himself upon him, seizing
him in his arms, and said to them, 'Stop this commotion;
11 there is still life in him.' He then went upstairs, broke
bread and ate, and after much conversation, which lasted
12 until dawn, he departed. And they took the boy away
alive and were immensely comforted.

13     We went ahead to the ship and sailed for Assos, where
we were to take Paul aboard. He had made this arrange-
14 ment, as he was going to travel by road. When he met us
at Assos, we took him aboard and went on to Mitylene.
15 Next day we sailed from there and arrived opposite Chios,
and on the second day we made Samos. On the following
16 day[c] we reached Miletus. For Paul had decided to pass by
Ephesus and so avoid having to spend time in the province
of Asia; he was eager to be in Jerusalem, if he possibly
17 could, on the day of Pentecost. He did, however, send from
Miletus to Ephesus and summon the elders of the con-
18 gregation; and when they joined him, he spoke as follows:
    'You know how, from the day that I first set foot in the
province of Asia, for the whole time that I was with you,
19 I served the Lord in all humility amid the sorrows and
trials that came upon me through the machinations of the
20 Jews. You know that I kept back nothing that was for
your good: I delivered the message to you; I taught you,
21 in public and in your homes; with Jews and Gentiles alike

---

[a] *Some witnesses read* the Derbaean.          [b] *Literally* after the days
of Unleavened Bread.          [c] *Some witnesses read* . . . Samos, and,
after stopping at Trogyllium, on the following day . . .

I insisted on repentance before God and trust in our Lord
Jesus. And now, as you see, I am on my way to Jerusalem, 22
under the constraint of the Spirit.[a] Of what will befall me
there I know nothing, except that in city after city the 23
Holy Spirit assures me that imprisonment and hardships
await me. For myself, I set no store by life; I only want 24
to finish the race, and complete the task which the Lord
Jesus assigned to me, of bearing my testimony to the
gospel of God's grace.

'One word more: I have gone about among you pro- 25
claiming the Kingdom, but now I know that none of you
will see my face again. That being so, I here and now 26
declare that no man's fate can be laid at my door; for I 27
have kept back nothing; I have disclosed to you the whole
purpose of God. Keep watch over yourselves and over all 28
the flock of which the Holy Spirit has given you charge, as
shepherds of the church of the Lord,[b] which he won for
himself by his own blood.[c] I know that when I am gone, 29
savage wolves will come in among you and will not spare the
flock. Even from your own body there will be men coming 30
forward who will distort the truth to induce the disciples
to break away and follow them. So be on the alert; re- 31
member how for three years, night and day, I never ceased
to counsel each of you, and how I wept over you.

'And now I commend you to God and to his gracious 32
word, which has power to build you up and give you your
heritage among all who are dedicated to him. I have not 33
wanted anyone's money or clothes for myself; you all 34
know that these hands of mine earned enough for the
needs of myself and my companions. I showed you that it 35
is our duty to help the weak in this way, by hard work, and
that we should keep in mind the words of the Lord Jesus,
who himself said, "Happiness lies more in giving than in
receiving."'

As he finished speaking, he knelt down with them all 36
and prayed. Then there were loud cries of sorrow from 37
them all, as they folded Paul in their arms and kissed him.
What distressed them most was his saying that they would 38
never see his face again. So they escorted him to his ship.

When we had parted from them and set sail, we made 21
a straight run and came to Cos; next day to Rhodes, and
thence to Patara.[d] There we found a ship bound for 2

---

[a] Or under an inner compulsion.     [b] Some witnesses read of God.
[c] Or, according to some witnesses, by the blood of his Own.
[d] Some witnesses add and Myra.

3 Phoenicia, so we went aboard and sailed in her. We came in sight of Cyprus, and leaving it to port, we continued our voyage to Syria, and put in at Tyre, for there the ship was
4 to unload her cargo. We went and found the disciples and stayed there a week; and they, warned by the Spirit,
5 urged Paul to abandon his visit to Jerusalem. But when our time ashore was ended, we left and continued our journey; and they and their wives and children all escorted us out of the city. We knelt down on the beach and prayed,
6 then bade each other good-bye; we went aboard, and they returned home.

7 We made the passage from Tyre and reached Ptolemais, where we greeted the brotherhood and spent one day with
8 them. Next day we left and came to Caesarea. We went to the home of Philip the evangelist, who was one of the
9 Seven, and stayed with him. He had four unmarried
10 daughters, who possessed the gift of prophecy. When we had been there several days, a prophet named Agabus
11 arrived from Judaea. He came to us, took Paul's belt, bound his own feet and hands with it, and said, 'These are the words of the Holy Spirit: Thus will the Jews in Jerusalem bind the man to whom this belt belongs, and hand
12 him over to the Gentiles.' When we heard this, we and the local people begged and implored Paul to abandon his visit
13 to Jerusalem. Then Paul gave his answer: 'Why all these tears? Why are you trying to weaken my resolution? For my part I am ready not merely to be bound but even to
14 die at Jerusalem for the name of the Lord Jesus.' So, as he would not be persuaded, we gave up and said, 'The Lord's will be done.'

15 At the end of our stay we packed our baggage and took
16 the road up to Jerusalem. Some of the disciples from Caesarea came along with us, bringing a certain Mnason of Cyprus, a Christian from the early days, with whom
17 we were to lodge. So we reached Jerusalem, where the brotherhood welcomed us gladly.

18 Next day Paul paid a visit to James; we were with him,
19 and all the elders attended. He greeted them, and then described in detail all that God had done among the
20 Gentiles through his ministry. When they heard this, they gave praise to God. Then they said to Paul: 'You see, brother, how many thousands of converts we have among
21 the Jews, all of them staunch upholders of the Law. Now they have been given certain information about you: it is said that you teach all the Jews in the gentile world to turn

their backs on Moses, telling them to give up circumcis-
ing their children and following our way of life. What is 22
the position, then? They are sure to hear that you have
arrived. You must therefore do as we tell you. We have 23
four men here who are under a vow; take them with you 24
and go through the ritual of purification with them, paying
their expenses, after which they may shave their heads.
Then everyone will know that there is nothing in the
stories they were told about you, but that you are a practising Jew and keep the Law yourself. As for the gentile 25
converts, we sent them our decision that they must abstain
from meat that has been offered to idols, from blood, from
anything that has been strangled,[a] and from fornication.' So 26
Paul took the four men, and next day, after going through
the ritual of purification with them, he went into the
temple to give notice of the date when the period of purification would end and the offering be made for each one
of them.

## FROM JERUSALEM TO ROME

B UT JUST BEFORE the seven days were up, the 27
Jews from the province of Asia saw him in the temple.
They stirred up the whole crowd, and seized him, shouting, 28
'Men of Israel, help, help! This is the fellow who spreads
his doctrine all over the world, attacking our people, our
law, and this sanctuary. On top of all this he has brought
Gentiles into the temple and profaned this holy place.' For 29
they had previously seen Trophimus the Ephesian with
him in the city, and assumed that Paul had brought him
into the temple.

The whole city was in a turmoil, and people came running 30
from all directions. They seized Paul and dragged him out
of the temple; and at once the doors were shut. While they 31
were clamouring for his death, a report reached the officer
commanding the cohort, that all Jerusalem was in an uproar. He immediately took a force of soldiers with their 32
centurions and came down on the rioters at the double.
As soon as they saw the commandant and his troops, they
stopped beating Paul. The commandant stepped forward, 33
arrested him, and ordered him to be shackled with two
chains; he then asked who the man was and what he had
been doing. Some in the crowd shouted one thing, some 34

---

[a] *Some witnesses omit* from anything that has been strangled.

another. As he could not get at the truth because of the
35 hubbub, he ordered him to be taken into barracks. When
Paul reached the steps, he had to be carried by the soldiers
36 because of the violence of the mob. For the whole crowd
were at their heels yelling, 'Kill him!'
37      Just before Paul was taken into the barracks he said to
the commandant, 'May I have a word with you?' The
38 commandant said, 'So you speak Greek, do you? Then you
are not the Egyptian who started a revolt some time ago
and led a force of four thousand terrorists out into the
39 wilds?' Paul replied, 'I am a Jew, a Tarsian from Cilicia,
a citizen of no mean city. I ask your permission to speak
40 to the people.' When permission had been given, Paul
stood on the steps and with a gesture called for the
attention of the people. As soon as quiet was restored, he
addressed them in the Jewish language:
22      'Brothers and fathers, give me a hearing while I make
2 my defence before you.' When they heard him speaking
to them in their own language, they listened the more
3 quietly. 'I am a true-born Jew,' he said, 'a native of
Tarsus in Cilicia. I was brought up in this city, and as a
pupil of Gamaliel I was thoroughly trained in every point
of our ancestral law. I have always been ardent in God's
4 service, as you all are today. And so I began to persecute
this movement to the death, arresting its followers, men
5 and women alike, and putting them in chains. For this I
have as witnesses the High Priest and the whole Council
of Elders. I was given letters from them to our fellow-Jews
at Damascus, and had started out to bring the Christians
6 there to Jerusalem as prisoners for punishment; and this
is what happened. I was on the road and nearing Damascus,
when suddenly about midday a great light flashed from the
7 sky all around me, and I fell to the ground. Then I heard
a voice saying to me, "Saul, Saul, why do you persecute
8 me?" I answered, "Tell me, Lord, who you are." "I am
Jesus of Nazareth," he said, "whom you are persecuting."
9 My companions saw the light, but did not hear the voice
10 that spoke to me. "What shall I do, Lord?" I said, and
the Lord replied, "Get up and continue your journey to
Damascus; there you will be told of all the tasks that are
11 laid upon you." As I had been blinded by the brilliance of
that light, my companions led me by the hand, and so I
came to Damascus.
12      'There, a man called Ananias, a devout observer of the
13 Law and well spoken of by all the Jews of that place, came

and stood beside me and said, "Saul, my brother, recover your sight." Instantly I recovered my sight and saw him. He went on: "The God of our fathers appointed you to know his will and to see the Righteous One and to hear his very voice, because you are to be his witness before the world, and testify to what you have seen and heard. And now why delay? Be baptized at once, with invocation of his name, and wash away your sins."

'After my return to Jerusalem, I was praying in the temple when I fell into a trance and saw him there, speaking to me. "Make haste", he said, "and leave Jerusalem without delay, for they will not accept your testimony about me." "Lord," I said, "they know that I imprisoned those who believe in thee, and flogged them in every synagogue; and when the blood of Stephen thy witness was shed I stood by, approving, and I looked after the clothes of those who killed him." But he said to me, "Go, for I am sending you far away to the Gentiles."'

Up to this point they had given him a hearing; but now they began shouting, 'Down with him! A scoundrel like that is better dead!' And as they were yelling and waving their cloaks and flinging dust in the air, the commandant ordered him to be brought into the barracks and gave instructions to examine him by flogging, and find out what reason there was for such an outcry against him. But when they tied him up for the lash,[a] Paul said to the centurion who was standing there, 'Can you legally flog a man who is a Roman citizen, and moreover has not been found guilty?' When the centurion heard this, he went and reported it to the commandant. 'What do you mean to do?' he said. 'This man is a Roman citizen.' The commandant came to Paul. 'Tell me, are you a Roman citizen?' he asked. 'Yes', said he. The commandant rejoined, 'It cost me a large sum to acquire this citizenship.' Paul said, 'But it was mine by birth.' Then those who were about to examine him withdrew hastily, and the commandant himself was alarmed when he realized that Paul was a Roman citizen and that he had put him in irons.

THE FOLLOWING DAY, wishing to be quite sure what charge the Jews were bringing against Paul, he released him and ordered the chief priests and the entire Council to assemble. He then took Paul down and stood him before them.

---

[a] *Or* tied him up with thongs.

23     Paul fixed his eyes on the Council and said, 'My brothers, I have lived all my life, and still live today, with a per-
2 fectly clear conscience before God.' At this the High Priest Ananias ordered his attendants to strike him on the mouth.
3 Paul retorted, 'God will strike you, you whitewashed wall! You sit there to judge me in accordance with the Law; and then in defiance of the Law you order me to be struck!'
4 The attendants said, 'Would you insult God's High Priest?'
5 'My brothers,' said Paul, 'I had no idea that he was High Priest; Scripture, I know, says: "You must not abuse the ruler of your people."'
6     Now Paul was well aware that one section of them were Sadducees and the other Pharisees, so he called out in the Council, 'My brothers, I am a Pharisee, a Pharisee born and bred; and the true issue in this trial is our hope of the
7 resurrection of the dead.' At these words the Pharisees and Sadducees fell out among themselves, and the assembly
8 was divided. (The Sadducees deny that there is any resurrection, or angel, or spirit, but the Pharisees accept them.)
9 So a great uproar broke out; and some of the doctors of the law belonging to the Pharisaic party openly took sides and declared, 'We can find no fault with this man; perhaps
10 an angel or spirit has spoken to him.' The dissension was mounting, and the commandant was afraid that Paul would be torn in pieces, so he ordered the troops to go down, pull him out of the crowd, and bring him into the barracks.
11     The following night the Lord appeared to him and said, 'Keep up your courage; you have affirmed the truth about me in Jerusalem, and you must do the same in Rome.'
12     When day broke, the Jews banded together and took
13 an oath not to eat or drink until they had killed Paul. There
14 were more than forty in this conspiracy. They came to the chief priests and elders and said, 'We have bound ourselves by a solemn oath not to taste food until we have killed
15 Paul. It is now for you, acting with the Council, to apply to the commandant to bring him down to you, on the pretext of a closer investigation of his case; and we have arranged to do away with him before he arrives.'
16     But the son of Paul's sister heard of the ambush; he went to the barracks, obtained entry, and reported it to
17 Paul. Paul called one of the centurions and said, 'Take this young man to the commandant; he has something to re-
18 port.' The centurion took him and brought him to the commandant. 'The prisoner Paul', he said, 'sent for me and

asked me to bring this young man to you; he has something to tell you.' The commandant took him by the arm, 19
drew him aside, and asked him, 'What is it you have to
report?' He said, 'The Jews have made a plan among them- 20
selves and will request you to bring Paul down to the
Council tomorrow, on the pretext of obtaining more precise information about him. Do not listen to them; for a 21
party more than forty strong are lying in wait for him. They
have sworn not to eat or drink until they have done away
with him; they are now ready, and wait only for your consent.' So the commandant dismissed the young man, with 22
orders not to let anyone know that he had given him this
information.

Then he called a couple of his centurions and issued 23
these orders: 'Get ready two hundred infantry to proceed to Caesarea, together with seventy cavalrymen and
two hundred light-armed troops;[a] parade three hours after
sunset. Provide also mounts for Paul so that he may ride 24
through under safe escort to Felix the Governor.' And he 25
wrote a letter to this effect:

'Claudius Lysias to His Excellency the Governor Felix. 26
Your Excellency: This man was seized by the Jews and 27
was on the point of being murdered when I intervened
with the troops and removed him, because I discovered
that he was a Roman citizen. As I wished to ascertain the 28
charge on which they were accusing him, I took him down
to their Council. I found that the accusation had to do with 29
controversial matters in their law, but there was no charge
against him meriting death or imprisonment. However, I 30
have now been informed of an attempt to be made on the
man's life, so I am sending him to you at once, and have
also instructed his accusers to state their case against him
before you.'[b]

Acting on their orders, the infantry took Paul and 31
brought him by night to Antipatris. Next day they re- 32
turned to their barracks, leaving the cavalry to escort
him the rest of the way. The cavalry entered Caesarea, 33
delivered the letter to the Governor, and handed Paul over
to him. He read the letter, asked him what province he 34
was from, and learned that he was from Cilicia. 'I will hear 35
your case', he said, 'when your accusers arrive.' He then
ordered him to be held in custody at his headquarters in
Herod's palace.

[a] *Or* two hundred spearmen (*the meaning of the Greek word is uncertain*).
[b] *Some witnesses read* '. . . before you. Farewell.'

24 FIVE DAYS LATER the High Priest Ananias came down,
accompanied by some of the elders and an advocate named
Tertullus, and they laid an information against Paul before
2 the Governor. When the prisoner was called, Tertullus
opened the case.

'Your Excellency,' he said, 'we owe it to you that we
enjoy unbroken peace. It is due to your provident care
that, in all kinds of ways and in all sorts of places, im-
provements are being made for the good of this province.
3 4 We welcome this, sir, most gratefully. And now, not to
take up too much of your time, I crave your indulgence
5 for a brief statement of our case. We have found this man
to be a perfect pest, a fomenter of discord among the Jews
all over the world, a ringleader of the sect of the Nazarenes.
6 He even made an attempt to profane the temple; and then
8 we arrested him.[a] If you will examine him yourself you
can ascertain from him the truth of all the charges we
9 bring.' The Jews supported the attack, alleging that the
facts were as he stated.

10    Then the Governor motioned to Paul to speak, and he
began his reply: 'Knowing as I do that for many years you
have administered justice in this province, I make my
11 defence with confidence. You can ascertain the facts for
yourself. It is not more than twelve days since I went up
12 to Jerusalem on a pilgrimage. They did not find me arguing with anyone, or collecting a crowd, either in the temple
13 or in the synagogues or up and down the city; and they
14 cannot make good the charges they bring against me. But
this much I will admit: I am a follower of the new way
(the "sect" they speak of), and it is in that manner that I
worship the God of our fathers; for I believe all that is
15 written in the Law and the prophets, and in reliance on
God I hold the hope, which my accusers too accept, that
there is to be a resurrection of good and wicked alike.
16 Accordingly I, no less than they, train myself to keep at
all times a clear conscience before God and man.

17    'After an absence of several years I came to bring
18 charitable gifts to my nation and to offer sacrifices. They
found me in the temple ritually purified and engaged in
this service. I had no crowd with me, and there was no
disturbance. But some Jews from the province of Asia
19 were there, and if they had any charge against me it is

---

[a] *Some witnesses insert* It was our intention to try him under our law;
(7) but Lysias the commandant intervened and took him by force out
of our hands, (8) ordering his accusers to come before you.

240

they who ought to have been in court to state it. Failing 20
that, it is for these persons here present to say what crime
they discovered when I was brought before the Council,
apart from this one open assertion which I made as I stood 21
there: "The true issue in my trial before you today is the
resurrection of the dead."'

Then Felix, who happened to be well informed about the 22
Christian movement, adjourned the hearing. 'When Lysias
the commanding officer comes down', he said, 'I will go
into your case.' He gave orders to the centurion to keep 23
Paul under open arrest and not to prevent any of his
friends from making themselves useful to him.

Some days later Felix came with his wife Drusilla, who 24
was a Jewess, and sending for Paul he let him talk to him
about faith in Christ Jesus. But when the discourse turned 25
to questions of morals, self-control, and the coming judgement, Felix became alarmed and exclaimed, 'That will do
for the present; when I find it convenient I will send for
you again.' At the same time he had hopes of a bribe from 26
Paul; and for this reason he sent for him very often and
talked with him. When two years had passed, Felix was 27
succceded by Porcius Festus. Wishing to curry favour with
the Jews, Felix left Paul in custody.

THREE DAYS AFTER taking up his appointment Festus 25
went up from Caesarea to Jerusalem, where the chief priests 2
and the Jewish leaders brought before him the case against
Paul. They asked Festus to favour them against him, and 3
pressed for him to be brought up to Jerusalem, for they
were planning an ambush to kill him on the way. Festus, 4
however, replied, 'Paul is in safe custody at Caesarea, and
I shall be leaving Jerusalem shortly myself; so let your 5
leading men come down with me, and if there is anything
wrong, let them prosecute him.'

After spending eight or ten days at most in Jerusalem, 6
he went down to Caesarea, and next day he took his seat
in court and ordered Paul to be brought up. When he 7
appeared, the Jews who had come down from Jerusalem
stood round bringing many grave charges, which they
were unable to prove. Paul's plea was: 'I have committed 8
no offence, either against the Jewish law, or against the
temple, or against the Emperor.' Festus, anxious to ingra- 9
tiate himself with the Jews, turned to Paul and asked,
'Are you willing to go up to Jerusalem and stand trial on
these charges before me there?' But Paul said, 'I am now 10

standing before the Emperor's tribunal, and that is where
I must be tried. Against the Jews I have committed no
11 offence, as you very well know. If I am guilty of any
capital crime, I do not ask to escape the death penalty;
but if there is no substance in the charges which these men
bring against me, it is not open to anyone to hand me over
12 as a sop to them. I appeal to Caesar!' Then Festus, after
conferring with his advisers, replied, 'You have appealed
to Caesar: to Caesar you shall go.'

13   After an interval of some days King Agrippa and
Bernice arrived at Caesarea on a courtesy visit to Festus.
14 They spent several days there, and during this time Festus
laid Paul's case before the king. 'We have a man', he said,
15 'left in custody by Felix; and when I was in Jerusalem the
chief priests and elders of the Jews laid an information
16 against him, demanding his condemnation. I answered
them, "It is not Roman practice to hand over any accused
man before he is confronted with his accusers and given an
17 opportunity of answering the charge." So when they had
come here with me I lost no time; the very next day I took
my seat in court and ordered the man to be brought up.
18 But when his accusers rose to speak, they brought none
19 of the charges I was expecting; they merely had certain
points of disagreement with him about their peculiar
religion, and about someone called Jesus, a dead man
20 whom Paul alleged to be alive. Finding myself out of my
depth in such discussions, I asked if he was willing to go to
21 Jerusalem and stand his trial there on these issues. But
Paul appealed to be remanded in custody for His Imperial
Majesty's decision, and I ordered him to be detained until
22 I could send him to the Emperor.' Agrippa said to Festus,
'I should rather like to hear the man myself.' 'Tomorrow',
he answered, 'you shall hear him.'

23   So next day Agrippa and Bernice came in full state
and entered the audience-chamber accompanied by high-
ranking officers and prominent citizens; and on the orders
24 of Festus Paul was brought up. Then Festus said, 'King
Agrippa, and all you gentlemen here present with us, you
see this man: the whole body of the Jews approached me
both in Jerusalem and here, loudly insisting that he had no
25 right to remain alive. But it was clear to me that he had
committed no capital crime, and when he himself appealed
26 to His Imperial Majesty, I decided to send him. But I have
nothing definite about him to put in writing for our Sovereign. Accordingly I have brought him up before you all

and particularly before you, King Agrippa, so that as a result of this preliminary inquiry I may have something to report. There is no sense, it seems to me, in sending on 27 a prisoner without indicating the charges against him.'

Agrippa said to Paul, 'You have our permission to speak 26 for yourself.' Then Paul stretched out his hand and began his defence:

'I consider myself fortunate, King Agrippa, that it is 2 before you that I am to make my defence today upon all the charges brought against me by the Jews, particularly 3 as you are expert in all Jewish matters, both our customs and our disputes. And therefore I beg you to give me a patient hearing.

'My life from my youth up, the life I led from the be- 4 ginning among my people and in Jerusalem, is familiar to all Jews. Indeed they have known me long enough and could 5 testify, if they only would, that I belonged to the strictest group in our religion: I lived as a Pharisee. And it is for 6 a hope kindled by God's promise to our forefathers that I stand in the dock today. Our twelve tribes hope to see 7 the fulfilment of that promise, worshipping with intense devotion day and night; and for this very hope I am impeached, and impeached by Jews, Your Majesty. Why is it 8 considered incredible among you that God should raise dead men to life?

'I myself once thought it my duty to work actively 9 against the name of Jesus of Nazareth; and I did so in 10 Jerusalem. It was I who imprisoned many of God's people by authority obtained from the chief priests; and when they were condemned to death, my vote was cast against them. In all the synagogues I tried by repeated punishment to 11 make them renounce their faith; indeed my fury rose to such a pitch that I extended my persecution to foreign cities.

'On one such occasion I was travelling to Damascus with 12 authority and commission from the chief priests; and as I 13 was on my way, Your Majesty, in the middle of the day I saw a light from the sky, more brilliant than the sun, shining all around me and my travelling-companions. We all fell to the ground, and then I heard a voice saying 14 to me in the Jewish language, "Saul, Saul, why do you persecute me? It is hard for you, this kicking against the goad." I said, "Tell me, Lord, who you are"; and the Lord 15 replied, "I am Jesus, whom you are persecuting. But now, 16 rise to your feet and stand upright. I have appeared to you for a purpose: to appoint you my servant and witness, to

testify both to what you have seen and to what you shall
17 yet see of me. I will rescue you from this people and from
18 the Gentiles to whom I am sending you. I send you to open
their eyes and turn them from darkness to light, from the
dominion of Satan to God, so that, by trust in me, they
may obtain forgiveness of sins, and a place with those whom
God has made his own."

19     'And so, King Agrippa, I did not disobey the heavenly
20 vision. I turned first to the inhabitants of Damascus, and
then to Jerusalem and all the country of Judaea, and to the
Gentiles, and sounded the call to repent and turn to God,
21 and to prove their repentance by deeds. That is why the
Jews seized me in the temple and tried to do away with me.
22 But I had God's help, and so to this very day I stand and
testify to great and small alike. I assert nothing beyond
23 what was foretold by the prophets and by Moses: that the
Messiah must suffer, and that he, the first to rise from
the dead, would announce the dawn to Israel and to
the Gentiles.'

24     While Paul was thus making his defence, Festus shouted
at the top of his voice, 'Paul, you are raving; too much
25 study is driving you mad.' 'I am not mad, Your Excellency,'
26 said Paul; 'what I am saying is sober truth. The king is
well versed in these matters, and to him I can speak freely.
I do not believe that he can be unaware of any of these
27 facts, for this has been no hole-and-corner business. King
Agrippa, do you believe the prophets? I know you do.'
28 Agrippa said to Paul, 'You think it will not take much to
29 win me over and make a Christian of me.' 'Much or little,'
said Paul, 'I wish to God that not only you, but all those
also who are listening to me today, might become what I
am, apart from these chains.'

30     With that the king rose, and with him the Governor,
31 Bernice, and the rest of the company, and after they had
withdrawn they talked it over. 'This man', they said, 'is
doing nothing that deserves death or imprisonment.'
32 Agrippa said to Festus, 'The fellow could have been discharged, if he had not appealed to the Emperor.'

27 WHEN IT WAS DECIDED that we should sail for Italy,
Paul and some other prisoners were handed over to a
2 centurion named Julius, of the Augustan Cohort. We embarked in a ship of Adramyttium, bound for ports in the
province of Asia, and put out to sea. In our party was
3 Aristarchus, a Macedonian from Thessalonica. Next day

we landed at Sidon; and Julius very considerately allowed
Paul to go to his friends to be cared for. Leaving Sidon we 4
sailed under the lee of Cyprus because of the head-winds,
then across the open sea off the coast of Cilicia and Pam- 5
phylia, and so reached Myra in Lycia.

There the centurion found an Alexandrian vessel bound 6
for Italy and put us aboard. For a good many days we 7
made little headway, and we were hard put to it to reach
Cnidus. Then, as the wind continued against us, off Salmone
we began to sail under the lee of Crete, and, hugging the 8
coast, struggled on to a place called Fair Havens, not far
from the town of Lasea.

By now much time had been lost, the Fast was already 9
over, and it was risky to go on with the voyage. Paul
therefore gave them this advice: 'I can see, gentlemen,' he 10
said, 'that this voyage will be disastrous: it will mean
grave loss, loss not only of ship and cargo but also of life.'
But the centurion paid more attention to the captain and 11
to the owner of the ship than to what Paul said; and as the 12
harbour was unsuitable for wintering, the majority were in
favour of putting out to sea, hoping, if they could get so
far, to winter at Phoenix, a Cretan harbour exposed south-
west and north-west. So when a southerly breeze sprang 13
up, they thought that their purpose was as good as
achieved, and, weighing anchor, they sailed along the
coast of Crete hugging the land. But before very long a 14
fierce wind, the 'North-easter' as they call it, tore down
from the landward side. It caught the ship and, as it was 15
impossible to keep head to wind, we had to give way and
run before it. We ran under the lee of a small island called 16
Cauda, and with a struggle managed to get the ship's boat
under control. When they had hoisted it aboard, they made 17
use of tackle and undergirded the ship. Then, because they
were afraid of running on to the shallows of Syrtis, they
lowered the mainsail and let her drive. Next day, as we 18
were making very heavy weather, they began to lighten
the ship; and on the third day they jettisoned the ship's 19
gear with their own hands. For days on end there was no 20
sign of either sun or stars, a great storm was raging, and
our last hopes of coming through alive began to fade.

When they had gone for a long time without food, Paul 21
stood up among them and said, 'You should have taken
my advice, gentlemen, not to sail from Crete; then you
would have avoided this damage and loss. But now I urge 22
you not to lose heart; not a single life will be lost, only the

23 ship. For last night there stood by me an angel of the God
24 whose I am and whom I worship. "Do not be afraid, Paul,"
he said; "it is ordained that you shall appear before the
Emperor; and, be assured, God has granted you the lives
25 of all who are sailing with you." So keep up your courage:
I trust in God that it will turn out as I have been told;
26 though we have to be cast ashore on some island.'

27 The fourteenth night came and we were still drifting in
the Sea of Adria. In the middle of the night the sailors felt
28 that land was getting nearer. They sounded and found
twenty fathoms. Sounding again after a short interval
29 they found fifteen fathoms; and fearing that we might be
cast ashore on a rugged coast they dropped four anchors
30 from the stern and prayed for daylight to come. The sailors
tried to abandon ship; they had already lowered the ship's
boat, pretending they were going to lay out anchors from
31 the bows, when Paul said to the centurion and the soldiers,
'Unless these men stay on board you can none of you come
32 off safely.' So the soldiers cut the ropes of the boat and let
her drop away.

33 Shortly before daybreak Paul urged them all to take
some food. 'For the last fourteen days', he said, 'you have
lived in suspense and gone hungry; you have eaten nothing
34 whatever. So I beg you to have something to eat; your
lives depend on it. Remember, not a hair of your heads will
35 be lost.' With these words, he took bread, gave thanks to
36 God in front of them all, broke it, and began eating. Then
they all plucked up courage, and took food themselves.
37 There were on board two hundred and seventy-six of us
38 in all. When they had eaten as much as they wanted they
lightened the ship by dumping the corn in the sea.

39 When day broke they could not recognize the land, but
they noticed a bay with a sandy beach, on which they
40 planned, if possible, to run the ship ashore. So they slipped
the anchors and let them go; at the same time they
loosened the lashings of the steering-paddles, set the fore-
41 sail to the wind, and let her drive to the beach. But they
found themselves caught between cross-currents and ran
the ship aground, so that the bow stuck fast and remained
immovable, while the stern was being pounded to pieces
42 by the breakers. The soldiers thought they had better kill
the prisoners for fear that any should swim away and
43 escape; but the centurion wanted to bring Paul safely
through and prevented them from carrying out their plan.
He gave orders that those who could swim should jump

overboard first and get to land; the rest were to follow, 44
some on planks, some on parts of the ship. And thus it was
that all came safely to land.

Once we had made our way to safety we identified the 28
island as Malta. The rough islanders treated us with un- 2
common kindness: because it was cold and had started to
rain, they lit a bonfire and made us all welcome. Paul had 3
got together an armful of sticks and put them on the fire,
when a viper, driven out by the heat, fastened on his hand.
The islanders, seeing the snake hanging on to his hand, 4
said to one another, 'The man must be a murderer; he may
have escaped from the sea, but divine justice has not let
him live.' Paul, however, shook off the snake into the fire 5
and was none the worse. They still expected that any 6
moment he would swell up or drop down dead, but after
waiting a long time without seeing anything extraordinary
happen to him, they changed their minds and now said,
'He is a god.'

In the neighbourhood of that place there were lands be- 7
longing to the chief magistrate of the island, whose name
was Publius. He took us in and entertained us hospitably
for three days. It so happened that this man's father was in 8
bed suffering from recurrent bouts of fever and dysentery.
Paul visited him and, after prayer, laid his hands upon him
and healed him; whereupon the other sick people on the 9
island came also and were cured. They honoured us with 10
many marks of respect, and when we were leaving they
put on board provision for our needs.

Three months had passed when we set sail in a ship 11
which had wintered in the island; she was the *Castor and
Pollux* of Alexandria. We put in at Syracuse and spent 12
three days there; then we sailed round and arrived at 13
Rhegium. After one day a south wind sprang up and we
reached Puteoli in two days. There we found fellow- 14
Christians and were invited to stay a week with them. And
so to Rome. The Christians there had had news of us and 15
came out to meet us as far as Appii Forum and Tres
Tabernae, and when Paul saw them, he gave thanks to
God and took courage.

WHEN WE ENTERED ROME Paul was allowed to lodge 16
by himself with a soldier in charge of him. Three days later 17
he called together the local Jewish leaders; and when they
were assembled, he said to them: 'My brothers, I, who
never did anything against our people or the customs of

our forefathers, am here as a prisoner; I was handed over
18 to the Romans at Jerusalem. They examined me and would
have liked to release me because there was no capital
19 charge against me; but the Jews objected, and I had no
option but to appeal to the Emperor; not that I had any
20 accusation to bring against my own people. That is why
I have asked to see you and talk to you, because it is for
the sake of the hope of Israel that I am in chains, as you
21 see.' They replied, 'We have had no communication from
Judaea, nor has any countryman of ours arrived with any
22 report or gossip to your discredit. We should like to hear
from you what your views are; all we know about this sect
is that no one has a good word to say for it.'

23    So they fixed a day, and came in large numbers as his
guests. He dealt at length with the whole matter; he
spoke urgently of the kingdom of God and sought to convince them about Jesus by appealing to the Law of Moses
24 and the prophets. This went on from dawn to dusk. Some
were won over by his arguments; others remained sceptical.
25 Without reaching any agreement among themselves they
began to disperse, but not before Paul had said one thing
more: 'How well the Holy Spirit spoke to your fathers
26 through the prophet Isaiah when he said, "Go to this
people and say: You may hear and hear, but you will never
understand; you may look and look, but you will never
27 see. For this people's mind has become gross; their ears
are dulled, and their eyes are closed. Otherwise, their eyes
might see, their ears hear, and their mind understand, and
28 then they might turn again, and I would heal them." Therefore take notice that this salvation of God has been sent
to the Gentiles; the Gentiles will listen.'[a]

30    He stayed there two full years at his own expense, with
31 a welcome for all who came to him, proclaiming the kingdom of God and teaching the facts about the Lord Jesus
Christ quite openly and without hindrance.

[a] *Some witnesses add* (29) After he had spoken, the Jews went away,
arguing vigorously among themselves.

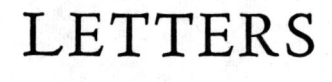

# LETTERS

LETTERS

# THE
# LETTER OF PAUL
# TO THE
# ROMANS

## THE GOSPEL ACCORDING TO PAUL

FROM PAUL, SERVANT of Christ Jesus, apostle 1
by God's call, set apart for the service of the Gospel.
This gospel God announced beforehand in sacred 2
scriptures through his prophets. It is about his Son: on the 3
human level he was born of David's stock, but on the level 4
of the spirit—the Holy Spirit—he was declared Son of
God by a mighty act in that he rose from the dead:[a] it is
about Jesus Christ our Lord. Through him I received the 5
privilege of a commission in his name to lead to faith and
obedience men in all nations, yourselves among them, you 6
who have heard the call and belong to Jesus Christ.

I send greetings to all of you in Rome whom God loves 7
and has called to be his dedicated people. Grace and peace
to you from God our Father and the Lord Jesus Christ.

Let me begin by thanking my God, through Jesus Christ, 8
for you all, because all over the world they are telling the
story of your faith. God is my witness, the God to whom I 9
offer the humble service of my spirit by preaching the
gospel of his Son: God knows how continually I make
mention of you in my prayers, and am always asking that 10
by his will I may, somehow or other, succeed at long last
in coming to visit you. For I long to see you; I want to 11
bring you some spiritual gift to make you strong; or rather, 12
I want to be among you to be myself encouraged by your
faith as well as you by mine.

[a] Or declared Son of God with full powers from the time when he rose
from the dead.

13 But I should like you to know,[a] my brothers, that I have
often planned to come, though so far without success, in
the hope of achieving something among you, as I have in
14 other parts of the world. I am under obligation to Greek
15 and non-Greek, to learned and simple; hence my eagerness
to declare the Gospel to you in Rome as well as to others.
16 For I am not ashamed of the Gospel. It is the saving power
of God for everyone who has faith—the Jew first, but the
17 Greek also—because here is revealed God's way of righting
wrong, a way that starts from faith and ends in faith;[b] as
Scripture says, 'he shall gain life who is justified through
faith'.

18 For we see divine retribution revealed from heaven and
falling upon all the godless wickedness of men. In their
19 wickedness they are stifling the truth. For all that may be
known of God by men lies plain before their eyes; indeed
20 God himself has disclosed it to them. His invisible attri-
butes, that is to say his everlasting power and deity, have
been visible, ever since the world began, to the eye of
reason, in the things he has made. There is therefore no
21 possible defence for their conduct; knowing God, they have
refused to honour him as God, or to render him thanks.
Hence all their thinking has ended in futility, and their
22 misguided minds are plunged in darkness. They boast of
their wisdom, but they have made fools of themselves,
23 exchanging the splendour of immortal God for an image
shaped like mortal man, even for images like birds, beasts,
and creeping things.

24 For this reason God has given them up to the vileness of
their own desires, and the consequent degradation of their
25 bodies, because they have bartered away the true God for
a false one,[c] and have offered reverence and worship to
created things instead of to the Creator, who is blessed
for ever; amen.

26 In consequence, I say, God has given them up to shameful passions. Their women have exchanged natural inter-
27 course for unnatural, and their men in turn, giving up
natural relations with women, burn with lust for one another; males behave indecently with males, and are paid
in their own persons the fitting wage of such perversion.

28 Thus, because they have not seen fit to acknowledge

---

[a] *Some witnesses read* I believe you know.  [b] *Or* . . . wrong. It is
based on faith and addressed to faith.  [c] *Or* the truth of God for
the lie.

God, he has given them up to their own depraved reason. This leads them to break all rules of conduct. They are 29 filled with every kind of injustice, mischief, rapacity, and malice; they are one mass of envy, murder, rivalry, treachery, and malevolence; whisperers and scandal- 30 mongers, hateful to God, insolent, arrogant, and boastful; they invent new kinds of mischief, they show no loyalty to parents, no conscience, no fidelity to their plighted word; 31 they are without natural affection and without pity. They 32 know well enough the just decree of God, that those who behave like this deserve to die, and yet they do it; not only so, they actually applaud such practices.

You therefore have no defence—you who sit in judge- 2 ment, whoever you may be—for in judging your fellow-man you condemn yourself, since you, the judge, are equally guilty. It is admitted that God's judgement is 2 rightly passed upon all who commit such crimes as these; and do you imagine—you who pass judgement on the 3 guilty while committing the same crimes yourself—do you imagine that you, any more than they, will escape the judgement of God? Or do you think lightly of his wealth of 4 kindness, of tolerance, and of patience, without recognizing that God's kindness is meant to lead you to a change of heart? In the rigid obstinacy of your heart you are laying 5 up for yourself a store of retribution for the day of retribu- tion, when God's just judgement will be revealed, and he 6 will pay every man for what he has done. To those who 7 pursue glory, honour, and immortality by steady per- sistence in well-doing, he will give eternal life; but for 8 those who are governed by selfish ambition, who refuse obedience to the truth and take the wrong for their guide, there will be the fury of retribution. There will be trouble 9 and distress for every human being who is an evil-doer, for the Jew first and for the Greek also; and for every well- 10 doer there will be glory, honour, and peace, for the Jew first and also for the Greek.

For God has no favourites: those who have sinned out- 11 12 side the pale of the Law of Moses will perish outside its pale, and all who have sinned under that law will be judged by the law. It is not by hearing the law, but by 13 doing it, that men will be justified before God. When 14 Gentiles who do not possess the law carry out its precepts by the light of nature, then, although they have no law, they are their own law, for they display the effect of the 15 law inscribed on their hearts. Their conscience is called as

witness, and their own thoughts argue the case on either
16 side, against them or even for them, on the day when God
judges the secrets of human hearts through Christ Jesus.
So my gospel declares.

17 But as for you—you may bear the name of Jew; you
18 rely upon the law and are proud of your God; you know
his will; instructed by the law, you know right from
19 wrong; you are confident that you are the one to guide
20 the blind, to enlighten the benighted, to train the stupid,
and to teach the immature, because in the law you see the
21 very shape of knowledge and truth. You, then, who teach
your fellow-man, do you fail to teach yourself? You pro-
22 claim, 'Do not steal'; but are you yourself a thief? You
say, 'Do not commit adultery'; but are you an adulterer?
You abominate false gods; but do you rob their shrines?
23 While you take pride in the law, you dishonour God by
24 breaking it. For, as Scripture says, 'Because of you the
name of God is dishonoured among the Gentiles.'

25 Circumcision has value, provided you keep the law; but
if you break the law, then your circumcision is as if it had
26 never been. Equally, if an uncircumcised man keeps the
27 precepts of the law, will he not count as circumcised? He
may be uncircumcised in his natural state, but by fulfilling the law he will pass judgement on you who break it,
28 for all your written code and your circumcision. The true
Jew is not he who is such in externals, neither is the true
29 circumcision the external mark in the flesh. The true Jew
is he who is such inwardly, and the true circumcision is of
the heart, directed not by written precepts but by the
Spirit; such a man receives his commendation not from
men but from God.

3 Then what advantage has the Jew? What is the value
2 of circumcision? Great, in every way. In the first place, the
3 Jews were entrusted with the oracles of God. What if some
of them were unfaithful? Will their faithlessness cancel
4 the faithfulness of God? Certainly not! God must be true
though every man living were a liar; for we read in Scripture, 'When thou speakest thou shalt be vindicated, and
win the verdict when thou art on trial.'

5 Another question: if our injustice serves to bring out
God's justice, what are we to say? Is it unjust of God
(I speak of him in human terms) to bring retribution upon
6 us? Certainly not! If God were unjust, how could he
judge the world?

7 Again, if the truth of God brings him all the greater

honour because of my falsehood, why should I any longer
be condemned as a sinner? Why not indeed 'do evil that   **8**
good may come', as some libellously report me as saying?
To condemn such men as these is surely no injustice.

What then? Are we Jews any better off?[a] No, not at   **9**
all![b] For we have already drawn up the accusation that
Jews and Greeks alike are all under the power of sin. This   **10**
has scriptural warrant:

'There is no just man, not one;
    no one who understands, no one who seeks God.   **11**
    All have swerved aside, all alike have become debased;   **12**
there is no one to show kindness; no, not one.

Their throat is an open grave,   **13**
    they use their tongues for treachery,
    adders' venom is on their lips,
    and their mouth is full of bitter curses.   **14**

Their feet hasten to shed blood,   **15**
    ruin and misery lie along their paths,   **16**
    they are strangers to the high-road of peace,   **17**
    and reverence for God does not enter their thoughts.'   **18**

Now all the words of the law are addressed, as we know,   **19**
to those who are within the pale of the law, so that no one
may have anything to say in self-defence, but the whole
world may be exposed to the judgement of God. For (again   **20**
from Scripture) 'no human being can be justified in the
sight of God' for having kept the law: law brings only the
consciousness of sin.

But now, quite independently of law, God's justice has   **21**
been brought to light. The Law and the prophets both
bear witness to it: it is God's way of righting wrong,   **22**
effective through faith in Christ for all who have such
faith—all, without distinction. For all alike have sinned,   **23**
and are deprived of the divine splendour, and all are   **24**
justified by God's free grace alone, through his act of
liberation in the person of Christ Jesus. For God designed   **25**
him to be the means of expiating sin by his sacrificial
death, effective through faith. God meant by this to
demonstrate his justice, because in his forbearance he had
overlooked the sins of the past—to demonstrate his justice   **26**
now in the present, showing that he is himself just and
also justifies any man who puts his faith in Jesus.

*a Or Are we Jews any worse off?*     *b Or Not in all respects.*

27  What room then is left for human pride? It is excluded. And on what principle? The keeping of the law would not
28  exclude it, but faith does. For our argument is that a man is justified by faith quite apart from success in keeping the law.

29  Do you suppose God is the God of the Jews alone? Is he not the God of Gentiles also? Certainly, of Gentiles also,
30  if it be true that God is one. And he will therefore justify both the circumcised in virtue of their faith, and the un-
31  circumcised through their faith. Does this mean that we are using faith to undermine law? By no means: we are placing law itself on a firmer footing.

4  WHAT, THEN, are we to say about Abraham, our an-
2  cestor in the natural line? If Abraham was justified by anything he had done, then he has a ground for pride. But
3  he has no such ground before God; for what does Scripture say? 'Abraham put his faith in God, and that faith was
4  counted to him as righteousness.' Now if a man does a piece of work, his wages are not 'counted' as a favour; they
5  are paid as debt. But if without any work to his credit he simply puts his faith in him who acquits the guilty, then
6  his faith is indeed 'counted as righteousness'. In the same sense David speaks of the happiness of the man whom God 'counts' as just, apart from any specific acts of justice:
7  'Happy are they', he says, 'whose lawless deeds are for-
8  given, whose sins are buried away; happy is the man whose
9  sins the Lord does not count against him.' Is this happiness confined to the circumcised, or is it for the uncircumcised also? Consider: we say, 'Abraham's faith was counted as
10  righteousness'; in what circumstances was it so counted? Was he circumcised at the time, or not? He was not yet
11  circumcised, but uncircumcised; and he later received the symbolic rite of circumcision as the hall-mark of the righteousness which faith had given him when he was still uncircumcised. Consequently, he is the father of all who have faith when uncircumcised, so that righteousness is
12  'counted' to them; and at the same time he is the father of such of the circumcised as do not rely upon their circumcision alone, but also walk in the footprints of the faith which our father Abraham had while he was yet uncircumcised.

13  For it was not through law that Abraham, or his pos-
terity, was given the promise that the world should be his inheritance, but through the righteousness that came from
14  faith. For if those who hold by the law, and they alone, are

heirs, then faith is empty and the promise goes for nothing, because law can bring only retribution; but where there is 15 no law there can be no breach of law. The promise was 16 made on the ground of faith, in order that it might be a matter of sheer grace, and that it might be valid for all Abraham's posterity, not only for those who hold by the law, but for those also who have the faith of Abraham. For he is the father of us all, as Scripture says: 'I have 17 appointed you to be father of many nations.' This promise, then, was valid before God, the God in whom he put his faith, the God who makes the dead live and summons things that are not yet in existence as if they already were. When hope seemed hopeless, his faith was such that he 18 became 'father of many nations', in agreement with the words which had been spoken to him: 'Thus shall your descendants be.' Without any weakening of faith he con- 19 templated his own body, as good as dead (for he was about a hundred years old), and the deadness of Sarah's womb, and never doubted God's promise in unbelief, but, strong 20 in faith, gave honour to God, in the firm conviction of his 21 power to do what he had promised. And that is why 22 Abraham's faith was 'counted to him as righteousness'.

Those words were written, not for Abraham's sake alone, 23 but for our sake too: it is to be 'counted' in the same way 24 to us who have faith in the God who raised Jesus our Lord from the dead; for he was given up to death for our mis- 25 deeds, and raised to life to justify us.[a]

THEREFORE, NOW THAT we have been justified through 5 faith, let us continue at peace[b] with God through our Lord Jesus Christ, through whom we have been allowed to enter 2 the sphere of God's grace, where we now stand. Let us exult[c] in the hope of the divine splendour that is to be ours. More than this: let us even exult[d] in our present sufferings, 3 because we know that suffering trains us to endure, and 4 endurance brings proof that we have stood the test, and this proof is the ground of hope. Such a hope is no mockery, 5 because God's love has flooded our inmost heart through the Holy Spirit he has given us.

For at the very time when we were still powerless, then 6 Christ died for the wicked. Even for a just man one of us 7 would hardly die, though perhaps for a good man one might actually brave death; but Christ died for us while 8

[a] *Or* raised to life because we were now justified.   [b] *Some witnesses read* we are at peace.   [c] *Or* We exult.   [d] *Or* we even exult.

we were yet sinners, and that is God's own proof of his
9 love towards us. And so, since we have now been justified
by Christ's sacrificial death, we shall all the more certainly
10 be saved through him from final retribution. For if, when
we were God's enemies, we were reconciled to him through
the death of his Son, how much more, now that we are
11 reconciled, shall we be saved by his life! But that is not all:
we also exult in God through our Lord Jesus, through
whom we have now been granted reconciliation.

12   Mark what follows. It was through one man that sin
entered the world, and through sin death, and thus death
pervaded the whole human race, inasmuch as all men have
13 sinned. For sin was already in the world before there was
law, though in the absence of law no reckoning is kept of
14 sin. But death held sway from Adam to Moses, even over
those who had not sinned as Adam did, by disobeying a
direct command—and Adam foreshadows the Man who
was to come.

15   But God's act of grace is out of all proportion to Adam's
wrongdoing. For if the wrongdoing of that one man
brought death upon so many, its effect is vastly exceeded
by the grace of God and the gift that came to so many by
16 the grace of the one man, Jesus Christ. And again, the
gift of God is not to be compared in its effect with that one
man's sin; for the judicial action, following upon the one
offence, issued in a verdict of condemnation, but the act of
grace, following upon so many misdeeds, issued in a ver-
17 dict of acquittal. For if by the wrongdoing of that one
man death established its reign, through a single sinner,
much more shall those who receive in far greater measure
God's grace, and his gift of righteousness, live and reign
through the one man, Jesus Christ.

18   It follows, then, that as the issue of one misdeed was
condemnation for all men, so the issue of one just act is
19 acquittal and life for all men. For as through the disobedience of the one man the many were made sinners, so
through the obedience of the one man the many will be
made righteous.

20   Law intruded into this process to multiply law-breaking.
But where sin was thus multiplied, grace immeasurably
21 exceeded it, in order that, as sin established its reign by
way of death, so God's grace might establish its reign in
righteousness, and issue in eternal life through Jesus Christ
our Lord.

6   What are we to say, then? Shall we persist in sin, so that

there may be all the more grace? No, no! We died to sin: 2
how can we live in it any longer? Have you forgotten that 3
when we were baptized into union with Christ Jesus we
were baptized into his death? By baptism we were buried 4
with him, and lay dead, in order that, as Christ was raised
from the dead in the splendour of the Father, so also we
might set our feet upon the new path of life.

For if we have become incorporate with him in a death 5
like his, we shall also be one with him in a resurrection like
his. We know that the man we once were has been cruci- 6
fied with Christ, for the destruction of the sinful self, so
that we may no longer be the slaves of sin, since a dead 7
man is no longer answerable for his sin. But if we thus died 8
with Christ, we believe that we shall also come to life with
him. We know that Christ, once raised from the dead, is 9
never to die again: he is no longer under the dominion of
death. For in dying as he died, he died to sin, once for all, 10
and in living as he lives, he lives to God. In the same way 11
you must regard yourselves as dead to sin and alive to
God, in union with Christ Jesus.

So sin must no longer reign in your mortal body, exact- 12
ing obedience to the body's desires. You must no longer 13
put its several parts at sin's disposal, as implements for
doing wrong. No: put yourselves at the disposal of God,
as dead men raised to life; yield your bodies to him as
implements for doing right; for sin shall no longer be your 14
master, because you are no longer under law, but under the
grace of God.

What then? Are we to sin, because we are not under law 15
but under grace? Of course not. You know well enough 16
that if you put yourselves at the disposal of a master, to
obey him, you are slaves of the master whom you obey;
and this is true whether you serve sin, with death as its
result; or obedience, with righteousness as its result. But 17
God be thanked, you, who once were slaves of sin, have
yielded whole-hearted obedience to the pattern of teaching
to which you were made subject,[a] and, emancipated from 18
sin, have become slaves of righteousness (to use words that 19
suit your human weakness)—I mean, as you once yielded
your bodies to the service of impurity and lawlessness,
making for moral anarchy, so now you must yield them to
the service of righteousness, making for a holy life.

When you were slaves of sin, you were free from the 20
control of righteousness; and what was the gain? Nothing 21

---

[a] *Or* which was handed on to you.

but what now makes you ashamed, for the end of that is
22 death. But now, freed from the commands of sin, and
bound to the service of God, your gains are such as make
23 for holiness, and the end is eternal life. For sin pays a wage,
and the wage is death, but God gives freely, and his gift is
eternal life, in union with Christ Jesus our Lord.

7    You cannot be unaware, my friends—I am speaking to
those who have some knowledge of law—that a person is
2 subject to the law so long as he is alive, and no longer. For
example, a married woman is by law bound to her husband
while he lives; but if her husband dies, she is discharged
3 from the obligations of the marriage-law. If, therefore, in
her husband's lifetime she consorts with another man, she
will incur the charge of adultery; but if her husband dies
she is free of the law, and she does not commit adultery by
4 consorting with another man. So you, my friends, have
died to the law by becoming identified with the body of
Christ, and accordingly you have found another husband
in him who rose from the dead, so that we may bear fruit
5 for God. While we lived on the level of our lower nature,
the sinful passions evoked by the law worked in our bodies,
6 to bear fruit for death. But now, having died to that which
held us bound, we are discharged from the law, to serve
God in a new way, the way of the spirit, in contrast to the
old way, the way of a written code.

7    What follows? Is the law identical with sin? Of course
not. But except through law I should never have become
acquainted with sin. For example, I should never have
known what it was to covet, if the law had not said, 'Thou
8 shalt not covet.' Through that commandment sin found its
opportunity, and produced in me all kinds of wrong desires.
9 In the absence of law, sin is a dead thing. There was a time
when, in the absence of law, I was fully alive; but when the
10 commandment came, sin sprang to life and I died. The
commandment which should have led to life proved in my
11 experience to lead to death, because sin found its opportunity in the commandment, seduced me, and through the
commandment killed me.

12    Therefore the law is in itself holy, and the commandment
13 is holy and just and good. Are we to say then that this
good thing was the death of me? By no means. It was sin
that killed me, and thereby sin exposed its true character:
it used a good thing to bring about my death, and so,
through the commandment, sin became more sinful than
ever.

We know that the law is spiritual; but I am not: I am 14
unspiritual, the purchased slave of sin. I do not even 15
acknowledge my own actions as mine, for what I do is not
what I want to do, but what I detest. But if what I do 16
is against my will, it means that I agree with the law and
hold it to be admirable. But as things are, it is no longer I 17
who perform the action, but sin that lodges in me. For I 18
know that nothing good lodges in me—in my unspiritual
nature, I mean—for though the will to do good is there, the
deed is not. The good which I want to do, I fail to do; but 19
what I do is the wrong which is against my will; and if what 20
I do is against my will, clearly it is no longer I who am
the agent, but sin that has its lodging in me.

I discover this principle, then: that when I want to do 21
the right, only the wrong is within my reach. In my inmost 22
self I delight in the law of God, but I perceive that there is 23
in my bodily members a different law, fighting against the
law that my reason approves and making me a prisoner
under the law[a] that is in my members, the law of sin.
Miserable creature that I am, who is there to rescue me out 24
of this body doomed to death[b]? God alone, through Jesus 25
Christ our Lord! Thanks be to God! In a word then, I myself, subject to God's law as a rational being, am yet,[c]
in my unspiritual nature, a slave to the law of sin.

The conclusion of the matter is this: there is no con- 8
demnation for those who are united with Christ Jesus,
because in Christ Jesus the life-giving law of the Spirit has 2
set you free from the law of sin and death. What the law 3
could never do, because our lower nature robbed it of all
potency, God has done: by sending his own Son in a form
like that of our own sinful nature, and as a sacrifice for
sin,[d] he has passed judgement against sin within that very
nature, so that the commandment of the law may find 4
fulfilment in us, whose conduct, no longer under the control of our lower nature, is directed by the Spirit.

Those who live on the level of our lower nature have their 5
outlook formed by it, and that spells death; but those who 6
live on the level of the spirit have the spiritual outlook,
and that is life and peace. For the outlook of the lower 7
nature is enmity with God; it is not subject to the law of
God; indeed it cannot be: those who live on such a level 8
cannot possibly please God.

[a] *Or by means of the law.*     [b] *Or out of the body doomed to this
death.*     [c] *Or Thus, left to myself, while subject . . . rational being,
I am yet . . .*     [d] *Or and to deal with sin.*

9 But that is not how you live. You are on the spiritual level, if only God's Spirit dwells within you; and if a man
10 does not possess the Spirit of Christ, he is no Christian. But if Christ is dwelling within you, then although the body is a dead thing because you sinned, yet the spirit is life itself
11 because you have been justified.[a] Moreover, if the Spirit of him who raised Jesus from the dead dwells within you, then the God who raised Christ Jesus from the dead will also give new life to your mortal bodies through his indwelling Spirit.

12 It follows, my friends, that our lower nature has no
13 claim upon us; we are not obliged to live on that level. If you do so, you must die. But if by the Spirit you put to death all the base pursuits of the body, then you will live.

14 For all who are moved by the Spirit of God are sons
15 of God. The Spirit you have received is not a spirit of slavery leading you back into a life of fear, but a Spirit
16 that makes us sons, enabling us to cry 'Abba! Father!' In that cry the Spirit of God joins with our spirit in testifying
17 that we are God's children; and if children, then heirs. We are God's heirs and Christ's fellow-heirs, if we share his sufferings now in order to share his splendour hereafter.

18 For I reckon that the sufferings we now endure bear no comparison with the splendour, as yet unrevealed, which
19 is in store for us. For the created universe waits with eager
20 expectation for God's sons to be revealed. It was made the victim of frustration, not by its own choice, but because
21 of him who made it so;[b] yet always there was hope, because[c] the universe itself is to be freed from the shackles of mortality and enter upon the liberty and splendour of
22 the children of God. Up to the present, we know, the whole created universe groans in all its parts as if in the pangs of
23 childbirth. Not only so, but even we, to whom the Spirit is given as firstfruits of the harvest to come, are groaning inwardly while we wait for God to make us his sons and[d]
24 set our whole body free. For we have been saved, though only in hope. Now to see is no longer to hope: why should
25 a man endure and wait[e] for what he already sees? But if we hope for something we do not yet see, then, in waiting for it, we show our endurance.

[a] *Or* so that you may live rightly.   [b] *Or* because God subjected it.
[c] *Or* with the hope that . . .   [d] *Some witnesses omit* make us his sons and.   [e] *Some witnesses read* why should a man hope . . .

In the same way the Spirit comes to the aid of our weak- 26
ness. We do not even know how we ought to pray,[a] but
through our inarticulate groans the Spirit himself is plead-
ing for us, and God who searches our inmost being knows 27
what the Spirit means, because he pleads for God's people
in God's own way; and in everything, as we know, he co- 28
operates for good with those who love God[b] and are called
according to his purpose. For God knew his own before 29
ever they were, and also ordained that they should be
shaped to the likeness of his Son, that he might be the
eldest among a large family of brothers; and it is these, so 30
fore-ordained, whom he has also called. And those whom
he called he has justified, and to those whom he justified
he has also given his splendour.

With all this in mind, what are we to say? If God is on 31
our side, who is against us? He did not spare his own Son, 32
but gave him up for us all; and with this gift how can he
fail to lavish upon us all he has to give? Who will be the 33
accuser of God's chosen ones? It is God who pronounces
acquittal; then who can condemn? It is Christ—Christ 34
who died, and, more than that, was raised from the dead—
who is at God's right hand, and indeed pleads our cause.[c]
Then what can separate us from the love of Christ? Can 35
affliction or hardship? Can persecution, hunger, nakedness,
peril, or the sword? 'We are being done to death for thy 36
sake all day long,' as Scripture says; 'we have been treated
like sheep for slaughter'—and yet, in spite of all, over- 37
whelming victory is ours through him who loved us. For 38
I am convinced that there is nothing in death or life, in the
realm of spirits or superhuman powers, in the world as it
is or the world as it shall be, in the forces of the universe,
in heights or depths—nothing in all creation that can 39
separate us from the love of God in Christ Jesus our
Lord.

[a] *Or* what it is right to pray for.  [b] *Or* and, as we know, all things
work together for good for those who love God; *some witnesses read*
and we know God himself co-operates for good with those who love
God.  [c] *Or* Who will be the accuser of God's chosen ones? Will
it be God himself? No, he it is who pronounces acquittal. Who will be
the judge to condemn? Will it be Christ—he who died, and, more than
that, . . . right hand? No, he it is who pleads our cause.

## THE PURPOSE OF GOD IN HISTORY

9 I AM SPEAKING the truth as a Christian, and my
own conscience, enlightened by the Holy Spirit, assures
2 me it is no lie: in my heart there is great grief and unceasing
3 sorrow. For I could even pray to be outcast from Christ
myself for the sake of my brothers, my natural kinsfolk.
4 They are Israelites: they were made God's sons; theirs
is the splendour of the divine presence, theirs the covenants,
5 the law, the temple worship, and the promises. Theirs
are the patriarchs, and from them, in natural descent, sprang
the Messiah.[a] May God, supreme above all, be blessed for
ever![b] Amen.

6 It is impossible that the word of God should have proved
7 false. For not all descendants of Israel are truly Israel, nor,
because they are Abraham's offspring, are they all his true
children;[c] but, in the words of Scripture, 'Through the line
8 of Isaac your descendants shall be traced.'[d] That is to say,
it is not those born in the course of nature who are children
of God; it is the children born through God's promise who
9 are reckoned as Abraham's descendants. For the promise
runs: 'At the time fixed I will come, and Sarah shall have
a son.'

10 But that is not all, for Rebekah's children had one and
11 the same father, our ancestor Isaac; and yet, in order that
God's selective purpose might stand, based not upon men's
12 deeds but upon the call of God, she was told, even before
they were born, when they had as yet done nothing, good
13 or ill, 'The elder shall be servant to the younger'; and that
accords with the text of Scripture, 'Jacob I loved and
Esau I hated.'

14 What shall we say to that? Is God to be charged with
15 injustice? By no means. For he says to Moses, 'Where I
show mercy, I will show mercy, and where I pity, I will
16 pity.' Thus it does not depend on man's will or effort, but
17 on God's mercy. For Scripture says to Pharaoh, 'I have
raised you up for this very purpose, to exhibit my power in
my dealings with you, and to spread my fame over all the
18 world.' Thus he not only shows mercy as he chooses, but
also makes men stubborn as he chooses.

---

[a] Greek Christ.       [b] Or sprang the Messiah, supreme above all, God
blessed for ever; or sprang the Messiah, who is supreme above all.
Blessed be God for ever!       [c] Or all children of God.       [d] Or
God's call shall be for your descendants in the line of Isaac.

You will say, 'Then why does God blame a man? For who 19
can resist his will?' Who are you, sir, to answer God back? 20
Can the pot speak to the potter and say, 'Why did you
make me like this?'? Surely the potter can do what he likes 21
with the clay. Is he not free to make out of the same lump
two vessels, one to be treasured, the other for common use?

But what if God, desiring to exhibit[a] his retribution 22
at work and to make his power known, tolerated very
patiently those vessels which were objects of retribution
due for destruction, and did so in order to make known the 23
full wealth of his splendour upon vessels which were objects
of mercy, and which from the first had been prepared for
this splendour?

Such vessels are we, whom he has called from among 24
Gentiles as well as Jews, as it says in the Book of Hosea: 25
'Those who were not my people I will call My People, and
the unloved nation I will call My Beloved. For in the very 26
place where they were told "you are no people of mine",
they shall be called Sons of the living God.' But Isaiah 27
makes this proclamation about Israel: 'Though the Israelites be countless as the sands of the sea, only a remnant
shall be saved; for the Lord's sentence on the land will be 28
summary and final'; as also he said previously, 'If the 29
Lord of Hosts had not left us the mere germ of a nation,
we should have become like Sodom, and no better than
Gomorrah.'

Then what are we to say? That Gentiles, who made 30
no effort after righteousness, nevertheless achieved it, a
righteousness based on faith; whereas Israel made great 31
efforts after a law of righteousness, but never attained to
it. Why was this? Because their efforts were not based on 32
faith, but (as they supposed) on deeds. They fell over the
'stone' mentioned in Scripture: 'Here I lay in Zion a stone 33
to trip over, a rock to stumble against; but he who has
faith in him will not be put to shame.'

BROTHERS, MY DEEPEST DESIRE and my prayer to 10
God is for their salvation. To their zeal for God I can 2
testify; but it is an ill-informed zeal. For they ignore God's 3
way of righteousness, and try to set up their own, and
therefore they have not submitted themselves to God's
righteousness. For Christ ends the law and brings righteous- 4
ness for everyone who has faith.[b]

[a] *Or* although he had the will to exhibit . . .      [b] *Or* Christ is the
end of the law as a way to righteousness for everyone who has faith.

5  Of legal righteousness Moses writes, 'The man who does
6  this shall gain life by it.' But the righteousness that comes
by faith says, 'Do not say to yourself, "Who can go up to
7  heaven?"' (that is to bring Christ down), 'or, "Who can go
down to the abyss?"' (to bring Christ up from the dead).
8  But what does it say? 'The word is near you: it is upon
your lips and in your heart.' This means the word of faith
9  which we proclaim. If on your lips is the confession, 'Jesus
is Lord', and in your heart the faith that God raised him
10  from the dead, then you will find salvation. For the faith
that leads to righteousness is in the heart, and the confession that leads to salvation is upon the lips.
11  Scripture says, 'Everyone who has faith in him will
12  be saved from shame'—everyone: there is no distinction
between Jew and Greek, because the same Lord is Lord of
all, and is rich enough for the need of all who invoke him.
13  For everyone, as it says again—'everyone who invokes the
14  name of the Lord will be saved'. How could they invoke
one in whom they had no faith? And how could they have
faith in one they had never heard of? And how hear without
15  someone to spread the news? And how could anyone spread
the news without a commission to do so? And that is what
Scripture affirms: 'How welcome are the feet of the
messengers of good news!'
16  But not all have responded to the good news. For Isaiah
17  says, 'Lord, who has believed our message?' We conclude
that faith is awakened by the message, and the message
that awakens it comes through the word of Christ.
18  But, I ask, can it be that they never heard it? Of course
they did: 'Their voice has sounded all over the earth, and
19  their words to the bounds of the inhabited world.' But, I
ask again, can it be that Israel failed to recognize the
message? In reply, I first cite Moses, who says, 'I will use
a nation that is no nation to stir your envy, and a foolish
20  nation to rouse your anger.' But Isaiah is still more daring:
'I was found', he says, 'by those who were not looking for
me; I was clearly shown to those who never asked about
21  me'; while to Israel he says, 'All day long I have stretched
out my hands to an unruly and defiant people.'

11  I ASK THEN, has God rejected his people? I cannot believe it! I am an Israelite myself, of the stock of Abraham,
2  of the tribe of Benjamin. No! God has not rejected the
people which he acknowledged of old as his own. You
know (do you not?) what Scripture says in the story of

Elijah—how Elijah pleads with God against Israel: 'Lord, 3
they have killed thy prophets, they have torn down thine
altars, and I alone am left, and they are seeking my life.'
But what does the divine voice say to him? 'I have left 4
myself seven thousand men who have not knelt to Baal.'
In just the same way at the present time a 'remnant' has 5
come into being, selected by the grace of God. But if it is by 6
grace, then it does not rest on deeds done, or grace would
cease to be grace.

What follows? What Israel sought, Israel has not 7
achieved, but the selected few have achieved it. The rest
were made blind to the truth, exactly as it stands written: 8
'God brought upon them a numbness of spirit; he gave
them blind eyes and deaf ears, and so it is still.' Similarly 9
David says:

'May their table be a snare and a trap,
    both stumbling-block and retribution!
May their eyes become so dim that they lose their sight! 10
Bow down their backs unceasingly!'

I now ask, did their failure mean complete downfall? 11
Far from it! Because they offended, salvation has come to
the Gentiles, to stir Israel to emulation. But if their offence 12
means the enrichment of the world, and if their falling-
off means the enrichment of the Gentiles, how much more
their coming to full strength!

But I have something to say to you Gentiles. I am a 13
missionary to the Gentiles, and as such I give all honour
to that ministry when I try to stir emulation in the men 14
of my own race, and so to save some of them. For if their 15
rejection has meant the reconciliation of the world, what
will their acceptance mean? Nothing less than life from
the dead! If the first portion of dough is consecrated, so 16
is the whole lump. If the root is consecrated, so are the
branches. But if some of the branches have been lopped 17
off, and you, a wild olive, have been grafted in among them,
and have come to share the same root and sap as the olive,
do not make yourself superior to the branches. If you do so, 18
remember that it is not you who sustain the root: the
root sustains you.

You will say, 'Branches were lopped off so that I might 19
be grafted in.' Very well: they were lopped off for lack of 20
faith, and by faith you hold your place. Put away your
pride, and be on your guard; for if God did not spare the 21
native branches, no more will he spare you. Observe the 22

kindness and the severity of God—severity to those who
fell away, divine kindness to you, if only you remain within
23 its scope; otherwise you too will be cut off, whereas they,
if they do not continue faithless, will be grafted in; for it is
24 in God's power to graft them in again. For if you were cut
from your native wild olive and against all nature grafted into the cultivated olive, how much more readily will they, the
natural olive-branches, be grafted into their native stock!

25    For there is a deep truth here, my brothers, of which I
want you to take account, so that you may not be com-
placent about your own discernment: this partial blindness has come upon Israel only until the Gentiles have
26 been admitted in full strength; when that has happened,
the whole of Israel will be saved, in agreement with the
text of Scripture:

'From Zion shall come the Deliverer;
he shall remove wickedness from Jacob.
27    And this is the covenant I will grant them,
when I take away their sins.'

28 In the spreading of the Gospel they are treated as God's
enemies for your sake; but God's choice stands, and they
29 are his friends for the sake of the patriarchs. For the gracious
30 gifts of God and his calling are irrevocable. Just as formerly
you were disobedient to God, but now have received
31 mercy in the time of their disobedience, so now, when you
receive mercy, they have proved disobedient, but only in
32 order that they too may receive mercy. For in making all
mankind prisoners to disobedience, God's purpose was to
show mercy to all mankind.

33    O depth of wealth, wisdom, and knowledge in God! How
unsearchable his judgements, how untraceable his ways!
34 Who knows the mind of the Lord? Who has been his
35 counsellor? Who has ever made a gift to him, to receive
36 a gift in return? Source, Guide, and Goal of all that is—to
him be glory for ever! Amen.


# CHRISTIAN BEHAVIOUR

12 THEREFORE, MY BROTHERS, I implore you
by God's mercy to offer your very selves to him: a
living sacrifice, dedicated and fit for his acceptance, the
2 worship offered by mind and heart.[a] Adapt yourselves no

[a] Or . . . acceptance, for such is the worship which you, as rational
creatures, should offer.

longer to the pattern of this present world, but let your minds be remade and your whole nature thus transformed. Then you will be able to discern the will of God, and to know what is good, acceptable, and perfect.

In virtue of the gift that God in his grace has given me 3 I say to everyone among you: do not be conceited or think too highly of yourself; but think your way to a sober estimate based on the measure of faith that God has dealt to each of you. For just as in a single human body there 4 are many limbs and organs, all with different functions, so all of us, united with Christ, form one body, serving in- 5 dividually as limbs and organs to one another.

The gifts we possess differ as they are allotted to us by 6 God's grace, and must be exercised accordingly: the gift of inspired utterance, for example, in proportion to a man's faith; or the gift of administration, in administration. A 7 teacher should employ his gift in teaching, and one who 8 has the gift of stirring speech should use it to stir his hearers. If you give to charity, give with all your heart; if you are a leader, exert yourself to lead; if you are helping others in distress, do it cheerfully.

Love in all sincerity, loathing evil and clinging to the 9 good. Let love for our brotherhood breed warmth of 10 mutual affection. Give pride of place to one another in esteem.

With unflagging energy, in ardour of spirit, serve the 11 Lord.[a]

Let hope keep you joyful; in trouble stand firm; persist 12 in prayer.

Contribute to the needs of God's people, and practise 13 hospitality.

Call down blessings on your persecutors—blessings, not 14 curses.

With the joyful be joyful, and mourn with the mourners. 15

Care as much about each other as about yourselves. Do 16 not be haughty, but go about with humble folk. Do not keep thinking how wise you are.

Never pay back evil for evil. Let your aims be such as 17 all men count honourable. If possible, so far as it lies with 18 you, live at peace with all men. My dear friends, do not 19 seek revenge, but leave a place for divine retribution; for there is a text which reads, 'Justice is mine, says the Lord, I will repay.' But there is another text: 'If your enemy is 20 hungry, feed him; if he is thirsty, give him a drink; by

[a] *Some witnesses read* meet the demands of the hour.

21 doing this you will heap live coals on his head.' Do not let
evil conquer you, but use good to defeat evil.

13     Every person must submit to the supreme authorities.
There is no authority but by act of God, and the existing
2 authorities are instituted by him; consequently anyone
who rebels against authority is resisting a divine institution, and those who so resist have themselves to thank for
3 the punishment they will receive. For government, a terror
to crime, has no terrors for good behaviour. You wish to
have no fear of the authorities? Then continue to do right
4 and you will have their approval, for they are God's agents
working for your good. But if you are doing wrong, then
you will have cause to fear them; it is not for nothing that
they hold the power of the sword, for they are God's agents
5 of punishment, for retribution on the offender. That is why
you are obliged to submit. It is an obligation imposed not
6 merely by fear of retribution but by conscience. That is
also why you pay taxes. The authorities are in God's
service and to these duties they devote their energies.
7     Discharge your obligations to all men; pay tax and toll,
reverence and respect, to those to whom they are due.
8 Leave no claim outstanding against you, except that of
mutual love. He who loves his neighbour has satisfied
9 every claim of the law. For the commandments, 'Thou
shalt not commit adultery, thou shalt not kill, thou shalt
not steal, thou shalt not covet', and any other commandment there may be, are all summed up in the one rule, 'Love
10 your neighbour as yourself.' Love cannot wrong a neighbour; therefore the whole law is summed up in love.*ᵃ*
11     In all this, remember how critical the moment is. It is time
for you to wake out of sleep, for deliverance is nearer to us
12 now than it was when first we believed. It is far on in the
night; day is near. Let us therefore throw off the deeds of
13 darkness and put on our armour as soldiers of the light. Let
us behave with decency as befits the day: no revelling
or drunkenness, no debauchery or vice, no quarrels or
14 jealousies! Let Christ Jesus himself be the armour that
you wear; give no more thought to satisfying the bodily
appetites.

14 IF A MAN IS WEAK in his faith you must accept him
2 without attempting to settle doubtful points. For instance,
one man will have faith enough to eat all kinds of food,
3 while a weaker man eats only vegetables. The man who

          *ᵃ Or the whole law is fulfilled by love.*

eats must not hold in contempt the man who does not, and
he who does not eat must not pass judgement on the one
who does; for God has accepted him. Who are you to pass 4
judgement on someone else's servant? Whether he stands
or falls is his own Master's business; and stand he will,
because his Master has power to enable him to stand.

Again, this man regards one day more highly than an- 5
other, while that man regards all days alike. On such a
point everyone should have reached conviction in his own
mind. He who respects the day has the Lord in mind in 6
doing so, and he who eats meat has the Lord in mind when
he eats, since he gives thanks to God; and he who abstains
has the Lord in mind no less, since he too gives thanks
to God.

For no one of us lives, and equally no one of us dies, for 7
himself alone. If we live, we live for the Lord; and if we 8
die, we die for the Lord. Whether therefore we live or die,
we belong to the Lord. This is why Christ died and came 9
to life again, to establish his lordship over dead and living.
You, sir, why do you pass judgement on your brother? 10
And you, sir, why do you hold your brother in contempt?
We shall all stand before God's tribunal. For Scripture 11
says, 'As I live, says the Lord, to me every knee shall bow
and every tongue acknowledge God.' So, you see, each of 12
us will have to answer for himself.

Let us therefore cease judging one another, but rather 13
make this simple judgement: that no obstacle or stumbling-
block be placed in a brother's way. I am absolutely con- 14
vinced, as a Christian,*a* that nothing is impure in itself;
only, if a man considers a particular thing impure, then
to him it is impure. If your brother is outraged by what 15
you eat, then your conduct is no longer guided by love.
Do not by your eating bring disaster to a man for whom
Christ died! What for you is a good thing must not become 16
an occasion for slanderous talk; for the kingdom of God is 17
not eating and drinking, but justice, peace, and joy, inspired by the Holy Spirit. He who thus shows himself a 18
servant of Christ is acceptable to God and approved by
men.

Let us then pursue the things that make for peace and 19
build up the common life. Do not ruin the work of God for 20
the sake of food. Everything is pure in itself, but anything
is bad for the man who by his eating causes another to fall.
It is a fine thing to abstain from eating meat or drinking 21

*a* *Or* on the authority of the Lord Jesus.

wine, or doing anything which causes your brother's down-
22 fall. If you have a clear conviction, apply it to yourself in
the sight of God. Happy is the man who can make his
23 decision with a clear conscience![a] But a man who has
doubts is guilty if he eats, because his action does not arise
from his conviction, and anything which does not arise
15 from conviction is sin.[b] Those of us who have a robust
conscience must accept as our own burden the tender
2 scruples of weaker men, and not consider ourselves. Each
of us must consider his neighbour and think what is for his
3 good and will build up the common life. For Christ too did
not consider himself, but might have said, in the words of
Scripture, 'The reproaches of those who reproached thee
4 fell upon me.' For all the ancient scriptures were written
for our own instruction, in order that through the encouragement they give us we may maintain our hope with
5 fortitude. And may God, the source of all fortitude and
all encouragement, grant that you may agree with one
6 another after the manner of Christ Jesus, so that with one
mind and one voice you may praise the God and Father of
our Lord Jesus Christ.
7   In a word, accept one another as Christ accepted us, to
8 the glory of God. I mean that Christ became a servant of
the Jewish people to maintain the truth of God by making
9 good his promises to the patriarchs, and at the same time
to give the Gentiles cause to glorify God for his mercy. As
Scripture says, 'Therefore I will praise thee among the
10 Gentiles and sing hymns to thy name'; and again, 'Gentiles,
11 make merry together with his own people'; and yet again,
'All Gentiles, praise the Lord; let all peoples praise him.'
12 Once again, Isaiah says, 'There shall be the Scion of Jesse,
the one raised up to govern the Gentiles; on him the Gentiles
13 shall set their hope.' And may the God of hope fill you with
all joy and peace by your faith in him, until, by the power
of the Holy Spirit, you overflow with hope.

14 MY FRIENDS, I have no doubt in my own mind that you
yourselves are quite full of goodness and equipped with
knowledge of every kind, well able to give advice to one
15 another; nevertheless I have written to refresh your
memory, and written somewhat boldly at times, in virtue of
16 the gift I have from God. His grace has made me a minister
of Christ Jesus to the Gentiles; my priestly service is the

[a] Or who does not bring judgement upon himself by what he approves!
[b] See p. 275, note d.

preaching of the gospel of God, and it falls to me to offer the Gentiles to him as[a] an acceptable sacrifice, consecrated by the Holy Spirit.

Thus in the fellowship of Christ Jesus I have ground for pride in the service of God. I will venture to speak of those things alone in which I have been Christ's instrument to bring the Gentiles into his allegiance, by word and deed, by the force of miraculous signs and by the power of the Holy Spirit. As a result I have completed the preaching of the gospel of Christ from Jerusalem as far round as Illyricum. It is my ambition to bring the Gospel to places where the very name of Christ has not been heard, for I do not want to build on another man's foundation; but, as Scripture says,

'They who had no news of him shall see,
    and they who never heard of him shall understand.'

That is why I have been prevented all this time from coming to you. But now I have no further scope in these parts, and I have been longing for many years to visit you on my way to Spain; for I hope to see you as I travel through, and to be sent there with your support after having enjoyed your company for a while. But at the moment I am on my way to Jerusalem, on an errand to God's people there. For Macedonia and Achaia have resolved to raise a common fund for the benefit of the poor among God's people at Jerusalem. They have resolved to do so, and indeed they are under an obligation to them. For if the Jewish Christians shared their spiritual treasures with the Gentiles, the Gentiles have a clear duty to contribute to their material needs. So when I have finished this business and delivered the proceeds under my own seal, I shall set out for Spain by way of your city, and I am sure that when I arrive I shall come to you with a full measure of the blessing of Christ.

I implore you by our Lord Jesus Christ and by the love that the Spirit inspires, be my allies in the fight; pray to God for me that I may be saved from unbelievers in Judaea and that my errand to Jerusalem may find acceptance with God's people, so that by his will I may come to you in a happy frame of mind and enjoy a time of rest with you. The God of peace be with you all. Amen.[b]

---

[a] Or ... of God, so that the worship which the Gentiles offer may be ...
[b] See p. 275, note d.

**16** I COMMEND TO YOU PHOEBE, a fellow-Christian who
2 holds office in the congregation at Cenchreae. Give her, in
the fellowship of the Lord, a welcome worthy of God's
people, and stand by her in any business in which she may
need your help, for she has herself been a good friend to
many, including myself.

3 Give my greetings to Prisca and Aquila, my fellow-
4 workers in Christ Jesus. They risked their necks to save my
life, and not I alone but all the gentile congregations are
5 grateful to them. Greet also the congregation at their house.
Give my greetings to my dear friend Epaenetus, the
6 first convert to Christ in Asia, and to Mary, who toiled
7 hard for you. Greet Andronicus and Junias[a] my fellow-
countrymen and comrades in captivity. They are eminent
among the apostles, and they were Christians before I was.

8 Greetings to Ampliatus, my dear friend in the fellowship
9 of the Lord, to Urban my comrade in Christ, and to my
10 dear Stachys. My greetings to Apelles, well proved in
11 Christ's service, to the household of Aristobulus, and my
countryman Herodion, and to those of the household of
12 Narcissus who are in the Lord's fellowship. Greet Tryphae-
na and Tryphosa, who toil in the Lord's service, and dear
13 Persis who has toiled in his service so long. Give my
greetings to Rufus, an outstanding follower of the Lord,
14 and to his mother, whom I call mother too. Greet Asyn-
critus, Phlegon, Hermes, Patrobas, Hermas, and all friends
15 in their company. Greet Philologus and Julia,[b] Nereus and
his sister, and Olympas, and all God's people associated
with them.

16 Greet one another with the kiss of peace. All Christ's
congregations send you their greetings.

17 I implore you, my friends, keep your eye on those who
stir up quarrels and lead others astray, contrary to the
18 teaching you received. Avoid them, for such people are
servants not of Christ our Lord but of their own appetites,
and they seduce the minds of innocent people with smooth
19 and specious words. The fame of your obedience has
spread everywhere. This makes me happy about you; yet
I should wish you to be experts in goodness but simpletons
20 in evil; and the God of peace will soon crush Satan beneath
your feet. The grace of our Lord Jesus be with you![c]

[a] *Or* Junia; *some witnesses read* Julia, *or* Julias.   [b] *Or* Julias;
*some witnesses read* Junia, *or* Junias.   [c] *The words* The grace . . .
with you *are omitted at this point in some witnesses; in some, these or
similar words are given as verse 24, and in some others after verse 27 (see
note on verse 23).*

Greetings to you from my colleague Timothy, and 21
from Lucius, Jason, and Sosipater my fellow-countrymen.
(I Tertius, who took this letter down, add my Christian 22
greetings.) Greetings also from Gaius, my host and host 23
of the whole congregation, and from Erastus, treasurer of
this city, and our brother Quartus.[a]

To HIM who has power to make your standing sure, ac- 25
cording to the Gospel I brought you and the proclamation
of Jesus Christ, according to the revelation of that divine
secret kept in silence for long ages but now disclosed, and 26
through prophetic scriptures by eternal God's command
made known to all nations, to bring them to faith and
obedience—to God who alone is wise, through Jesus 27
Christ,[b] be glory for endless ages! Amen.[c, d]

[a] *Some witnesses add* (24) The grace of our Lord Jesus Christ be with
you all! Amen.    [b] *Some witnesses insert* to whom.    [c] *Here
some witnesses add* The grace of our Lord Jesus Christ be with you!
[d] *Some witnesses place verses 25–27 at the end of chapter 14, one other
places them at the end of chapter 15, and others omit them altogether.*

# THE
# FIRST LETTER OF PAUL
# TO THE
# CORINTHIANS

## UNITY AND ORDER IN THE CHURCH

1 FROM PAUL, APOSTLE of Jesus Christ at God's
call and by God's will, together with our colleague
2 Sosthenes, to the congregation of God's people at
Corinth, dedicated to him in Christ Jesus, claimed by him
as his own, along with all men everywhere who invoke the
name of our Lord Jesus Christ—their Lord as well as ours.
3 Grace and peace to you from God our Father and the
Lord Jesus Christ.

4 I am always thanking God for you. I thank him for his
5 grace given to you in Christ Jesus. I thank him for all the
enrichment that has come to you in Christ. You possess
6 full knowledge and you can give full expression to it, because in you the evidence for the truth of Christ has found
7 confirmation. There is indeed no single gift you lack, while
you wait expectantly for our Lord Jesus Christ to reveal
8 himself. He will keep you firm to the end, without re-
9 proach on the Day of our Lord Jesus. It is God himself who
called you to share in the life of his Son Jesus Christ our
Lord; and God keeps faith.

10 I appeal to you, my brothers, in the name of our Lord
Jesus Christ: agree among yourselves, and avoid divisions;
11 be firmly joined in unity of mind and thought. I have been
told, my brothers, by Chloe's people that there are quarrels
12 among you. What I mean is this: each of you is saying, 'I
am Paul's man', or 'I am for Apollos'; 'I follow Cephas', or
13 'I am Christ's.' Surely Christ has not been divided among
you! Was it Paul who was crucified for you? Was it in the
14 name of Paul that you were baptized? Thank God, I never
15 baptized one of you—except Crispus and Gaius. So no one

can say you were baptized in my name.—Yes, I did baptize 16 the household of Stephanas; I cannot think of anyone else. Christ did not send me to baptize, but to proclaim the 17 Gospel; and to do it without relying on the language of worldly wisdom, so that the fact of Christ on his cross might have its full weight.

This doctrine of the cross is sheer folly to those on their 18 way to ruin, but to us who are on the way to salvation it is the power of God. Scripture says, 'I will destroy the wis- 19 dom of the wise, and bring to nothing the cleverness of the clever.' Where is your wise man now, your man of learning, 20 or your subtle debater—limited, all of them, to this passing age? God has made the wisdom of this world look foolish. As God in his wisdom ordained, the world failed to find him 21 by its wisdom, and he chose to save those who have faith by the folly of the Gospel. Jews call for miracles, Greeks 22 look for wisdom; but we proclaim Christ—yes, Christ 23 nailed to the cross; and though this is a stumbling-block to Jews and folly to Greeks, yet to those who have heard 24 his call, Jews and Greeks alike, he is the power of God and the wisdom of God.

Divine folly is wiser than the wisdom of man, and divine 25 weakness stronger than man's strength. My brothers, think 26 what sort of people you are, whom God has called. Few of you are men of wisdom, by any human standard; few are powerful or highly born. Yet, to shame the wise, God has 27 chosen what the world counts folly, and to shame what is strong, God has chosen what the world counts weakness. He has chosen things low and contemptible, mere nothings, 28 to overthrow the existing order. And so there is no place for 29 human pride in the presence of God. You are in Christ Jesus 30 by God's act, for God has made him our wisdom; he is our righteousness; in him we are consecrated and set free. And 31 so (in the words of Scripture), 'If a man must boast, let him boast of the Lord.'

As for me, brothers, when I came to you, I declared the 2 attested truth of God*a* without display of fine words or wisdom. I resolved that while I was with you I would 2 think of nothing but Jesus Christ—Christ nailed to the cross. I came before you weak, nervous, and shaking with 3 fear. The word I spoke, the gospel I proclaimed, did not 4 sway you with subtle arguments; it carried conviction by spiritual power, so that your faith might be built not upon 5 human wisdom but upon the power of God.

*a Some witnesses read* I declared God's secret purpose . . .

6  And yet I do speak words of wisdom to those who are ripe for it, not a wisdom belonging to this passing age, nor to any of its governing powers, which are declining to their

7  end; I speak God's hidden wisdom, his secret purpose framed from the very beginning to bring us to our full

8  glory. The powers that rule the world have never known it; if they had, they would not have crucified the Lord of

9  glory. But, in the words of Scripture, 'Things beyond our seeing, things beyond our hearing, things beyond our imagining, all prepared by God for those who love him',

10  these it is that God has revealed to us through the Spirit. For the Spirit explores everything, even the depths of

11  God's own nature. Among men, who knows what a man is but the man's own spirit within him? In the same way,

12  only the Spirit of God knows what God is. This is the Spirit that we have received from God, and not the spirit of the world, so that we may know all that God of his own grace

13  has given us; and, because we are interpreting spiritual truths to those who have the Spirit, we speak of these gifts of God in words found for us not by our human wisdom

14  but by the Spirit. A man who is unspiritual refuses what belongs to the Spirit of God; it is folly to him; he cannot grasp it, because it needs to be judged in the light of the

15  Spirit. A man gifted with the Spirit can judge the worth of everything, but is not himself subject to judgement by

16  his fellow-men. For (in the words of Scripture) 'who knows the mind of the Lord? Who can advise him?' We, however, possess the mind of Christ.

3  FOR MY PART, my brothers, I could not speak to you as I should speak to people who have the Spirit. I had to deal with you on the merely natural plane, as infants in Christ.

2  And so I gave you milk to drink, instead of solid food, for which you were not yet ready. Indeed, you are still not

3  ready for it, for you are still on the merely natural plane. Can you not see that while there is jealousy and strife among you, you are living on the purely human level of

4  your lower nature? When one says, 'I am Paul's man', and another, 'I am for Apollos', are you not all too human?

5  After all, what is Apollos? What is Paul? We are simply God's agents in bringing you to the faith. Each of us per-

6  formed the task which the Lord allotted to him: I planted the seed, and Apollos watered it; but God made it grow.

7  Thus it is not the gardeners with their planting and water-

8  ing who count, but God, who makes it grow. Whether they

plant or water, they work as a team,[a] though each will get
his own pay for his own labour. We are God's fellow- 9
workers;[b] and you are God's garden.

Or again, you are God's building. I am like a skilled 10
master-builder who by God's grace laid the foundation,
and someone else is putting up the building. Let each take
care how he builds. There can be no other foundation be- 11
yond that which is already laid; I mean Jesus Christ himself. If anyone builds on that foundation with gold, silver, 12
and fine stone, or with wood, hay, and straw, the work that 13
each man does will at last be brought to light; the day of
judgement will expose it. For that day dawns in fire, and
the fire will test the worth of each man's work. If a man's 14
building stands, he will be rewarded; if it burns, he will 15
have to bear the loss; and yet he will escape with his life, as
one might from a fire. Surely you know that you are God's 16
temple, where the Spirit of God dwells. Anyone who 17
destroys God's temple will himself be destroyed[c] by God,
because the temple of God is holy; and that temple you are.

Make no mistake about this: if there is anyone among 18
you who fancies himself wise—wise, I mean, by the
standards of this passing age—he must become a fool to gain
true wisdom. For the wisdom of this world is folly in God's 19
sight. Scripture says, 'He traps the wise in their own
cunning', and again, 'The Lord knows that the arguments 20
of the wise are futile.' So never make mere men a cause 21
for pride. For though everything belongs to you—Paul, 22
Apollos, and Cephas, the world, life, and death, the present
and the future, all of them belong to you—yet you belong 23
to Christ, and Christ to God.

We must be regarded as Christ's subordinates and as 4
stewards of the secrets of God. Well then, stewards are 2
expected to show themselves trustworthy. For my part, 3
if I am called to account by you or by any human court of
judgement, it does not matter to me in the least. Why, I
do not even pass judgement on myself, for I have nothing 4
on my conscience; but that does not mean I stand acquitted. My judge is the Lord. So pass no premature 5
judgement; wait until the Lord comes. For he will bring
to light what darkness hides, and disclose men's inward
motives; then will be the time for each to receive from
God such praise as he deserves.

---

[a] *Or* Whether they plant or water, it is all the same.    [b] *Or* We
are fellow-workers in God's service.    [c] *Some witnesses read* is
himself destroyed.

6     Into this general picture, my friends, I have brought Apollos and myself on your account, so that you may take our case as an example, and learn to 'keep within the rules', as they say, and may not be inflated with pride as you 7 patronize one and flout the other. Who makes you, my friend, so important? What do you possess that was not given you? If then you really received it all as a gift, why take the credit to yourself?

8     All of you, no doubt, have everything you could desire. You have come into your fortune already. You have come into your kingdom—and left us out. How I wish you had indeed won your kingdom; then you might share it with 9 us! For it seems to me God has made us apostles the most abject of mankind. We are like men condemned to death in the arena, a spectacle to the whole universe—angels as 10 well as men. We are fools for Christ's sake, while you are such sensible Christians. We are weak; you are so powerful. 11 We are in disgrace; you are honoured. To this day we go hungry and thirsty and in rags; we are roughly handled; we 12 wander from place to place; we wear ourselves out working with our own hands. They curse us, and we bless; they 13 persecute us, and we submit to it; they slander us, and we humbly make our appeal. We are treated as the scum of the earth, the dregs of humanity, to this very day.

14     I am not writing thus to shame you, but to bring you to 15 reason; for you are my dear children. You may have ten thousand tutors in Christ, but you have only one father. For in Christ Jesus you are my offspring, and mine alone, 16 through the preaching of the Gospel. I appeal to you there- 17 fore to follow my example. That is the very reason why I have sent Timothy, who is a dear son to me and a most trustworthy Christian; he will remind you of the way of life in Christ which I follow, and which I teach everywhere 18 in all our congregations. There are certain persons who are filled with self-importance because they think I am not 19 coming to Corinth. I shall come very soon, if the Lord will; and then I shall take the measure of these self-important people, not by what they say, but by what power is in 20 them. The kingdom of God is not a matter of talk, but of 21 power. Choose, then: am I to come to you with a rod in my hand, or in love and a gentle spirit?

5 I ACTUALLY HEAR REPORTS of sexual immorality among you, immorality such as even pagans do not 2 tolerate: the union of a man with his father's wife. And

you can still be proud of yourselves! You ought to have gone into mourning; a man who has done such a deed should have been rooted out of your company. For my 3 part, though I am absent in body, I am present in spirit, and my judgement upon the man who did this thing is already given, as if I were indeed present: you all being 4 assembled in the name of our Lord Jesus, and I with you in spirit, with the power of our Lord Jesus over us, this 5 man is to be consigned to Satan for the destruction of the body, so that his spirit may be saved on the Day of the Lord.

Your self-satisfaction ill becomes you. Have you never 6 heard the saying, 'A little leaven leavens all the dough'? The old leaven of corruption is working among you. Purge 7 it out, and then you will be bread of a new baking. As Christians you are unleavened Passover bread; for indeed our Passover has begun; the sacrifice is offered—Christ himself. So we who observe the festival must not use the 8 old leaven, the leaven of corruption and wickedness, but only the unleavened bread which is sincerity and truth.

In my letter I wrote that you must have nothing to do 9 with loose livers. I was not, of course, referring to pagans 10 who lead loose lives or are grabbers and swindlers or idolaters. To avoid them you would have to get out of the world altogether. I now write that you must have nothing 11 to do with any so-called Christian who leads a loose life, or is grasping, or idolatrous, a slanderer, a drunkard, or a swindler. You should not even eat with any such person. What business of mine is it to judge outsiders? God 12 13 is their judge. You are judges within the fellowship. Root out the evil-doer from your community.

IF ONE OF YOUR NUMBER has a dispute with another, 6 has he the face to take it to pagan law-courts instead of to the community of God's people? It is God's people who 2 are to judge the world; surely you know that. And if the world is to come before you for judgement, are you in- competent to deal with these trifling cases? Are you not 3 aware that we are to judge angels? How much more, mere matters of business! If therefore you have such business 4 disputes, how can you entrust jurisdiction to outsiders, men who count for nothing in our community? I write this 5 to shame you. Can it be that there is not a single wise man among you able to give a decision in a brother-Christian's cause? Must brother go to law with brother—and before 6

7 unbelievers? Indeed, you already fall below your standard in going to law with one another at all. Why not rather
8 suffer injury? Why not rather let yourself be robbed? So far from this, you actually injure and rob—injure and rob
9 your brothers! Surely you know that the unjust will never come into possession of the kingdom of God. Make no mistake: no fornicator or idolater, none who are guilty
10 either of adultery or of homosexual perversion, no thieves or grabbers or drunkards or slanderers or swindlers, will
11 possess the kingdom of God. Such were some of you. But you have been through the purifying waters; you have been dedicated to God and justified through the name of the Lord Jesus and the Spirit of our God.
12 'I am free to do anything', you say. Yes, but not everything is for my good. No doubt I am free to do anything, but I for one will not let anything make free with me.
13 'Food is for the belly and the belly for food', you say. True; and one day God will put an end to both. But it is not true that the body is for lust; it is for the Lord—and
14 the Lord for the body. God not only raised our Lord from
15 the dead; he will also raise us by his power. Do you not know that your bodies are limbs and organs of Christ? Shall I then take from Christ his bodily parts and make
16 them over to a harlot? Never! You surely know that anyone who links himself with a harlot becomes physically one with her (for Scripture says, 'The pair shall become one
17 flesh'); but he who links himself with Christ is one with
18 him, spiritually. Shun fornication. Every other sin that a man can commit is outside the body; but the fornicator
19 sins against his own body. Do you not know that your body is a shrine of the indwelling Holy Spirit, and the Spirit is God's gift to you? You do not belong to your-
20 selves; you were bought at a price. Then honour God in your body.

## THE CHRISTIAN IN A PAGAN
## SOCIETY

7 AND NOW for the matters you wrote about.
It is a good thing for a man to have nothing to do
2 with women;[a] but because there is so much immorality, let each man have his own wife and each woman her own
3 husband. The husband must give the wife what is due to

[a] *Or* You say, 'It is a good thing . . . women'; . . .

her, and the wife equally must give the husband his due. The wife cannot claim her body as her own; it is her husband's. Equally, the husband cannot claim his body as his own; it is his wife's. Do not deny yourselves to one another, except when you agree upon a temporary abstinence in order to devote yourselves to prayer; afterwards you may come together again; otherwise, for lack of self-control, you may be tempted by Satan.

All this I say by way of concession, not command. I should like you all to be as I am myself; but everyone has the gift God has granted him, one this gift and another that.

To the unmarried and to widows I say this: it is a good thing if they stay as I am myself; but if they cannot control themselves, they should marry. Better be married than burn with vain desire.

To the married I give this ruling, which is not mine but the Lord's: a wife must not separate herself from her husband; if she does, she must either remain unmarried or be reconciled to her husband; and the husband must not divorce his wife.

To the rest I say this, as my own word, not as the Lord's: if a Christian has a heathen wife, and she is willing to live with him, he must not divorce her; and a woman who has a heathen husband willing to live with her must not divorce her husband. For the heathen husband now belongs to God through his Christian wife, and the heathen wife through her Christian husband. Otherwise your children would not belong to God, whereas in fact they do. If on the other hand the heathen partner wishes for a separation, let him have it. In such cases the Christian husband or wife is under no compulsion; but God's call is a call to live in peace. Think of it: as a wife you may be your husband's salvation; as a husband you may be your wife's salvation.

However that may be, each one must order his life according to the gift the Lord has granted him and his condition when God called him. That is what I teach in all our congregations. Was a man called with the marks of circumcision on him? Let him not remove them. Was he uncircumcised when he was called? Let him not be circumcised. Circumcision or uncircumcision is neither here nor there; what matters is to keep God's commands. Every man should remain in the condition in which he was called. Were you a slave when you were called? Do not let

that trouble you; but if a chance of liberty should come,
22 take it.[a] For the man who as a slave received the call to
be a Christian is the Lord's freedman, and, equally, the
free man who received the call is a slave in the service of
23 Christ. You were bought at a price; do not become slaves
24 of men. Thus each one, my friends, is to remain before
God in the condition in which he received his call.

25   On the question of celibacy, I have no instructions from
the Lord, but I give my judgement as one who by God's
mercy is fit to be trusted.

26   It is my opinion, then, that in a time of stress like the
present this is the best way for a man to live—it is best for
27 a man to be as he is. Are you bound in marriage? Do not
seek a dissolution. Has your marriage been dissolved? Do
28 not seek a wife. If, however, you do marry, there is nothing
wrong in it; and if a virgin marries, she has done no wrong.
But those who marry will have pain and grief in this bodily
life, and my aim is to spare you.

29   What I mean, my friends, is this. The time we live in
will not last long. While it lasts, married men should be as
30 if they had no wives; mourners should be as if they had
nothing to grieve them, the joyful as if they did not rejoice; buyers must not count on keeping what they buy,
31 nor those who use the world's wealth on using it to the full.
For the whole frame of this world is passing away.

32   I want you to be free from anxious care. The unmarried
man cares for the Lord's business; his aim is to please the
33 Lord. But the married man cares for worldly things; his
34 aim is to please his wife; and he has a divided mind. The
unmarried or celibate woman cares[b] for the Lord's business; her aim is to be dedicated to him in body as in spirit;
but the married woman cares for worldly things; her aim
is to please her husband.

35   In saying this I have no wish to keep you on a tight rein.
I am thinking simply of your own good, of what is seemly,
and of your freedom to wait upon the Lord without dis-
traction.

36   But if a man has a partner in celibacy[c] and feels that he
is not behaving properly towards her, if, that is, his instincts are too strong for him,[d] and something must be
done, he may do as he pleases; there is nothing wrong in it;

[a] *Or* but even if a chance of liberty should come, choose rather to
make good use of your servitude.       [b] *Some witnesses read* . . . his
wife. And there is a difference between the wife and the virgin. The
unmarried woman cares . . .       [c] *Or* a virgin daughter (*or* ward).
[d] *Or* if she is ripe for marriage.

let them marry.[a] But if a man is steadfast in his purpose, 37
being under no compulsion, and has complete control of
his own choice; and if he has decided in his own mind to
preserve his partner[b] in her virginity, he will do well. Thus, 38
he who marries his partner[c] does well, and he who does not
will do better.

A wife is bound to her husband as long as he lives. But 39
if the husband die, she is free to marry whom she will,
provided the marriage is within the Lord's fellowship. But 40
she is better off as she is; that is my opinion, and I believe
that I too have the Spirit of God.

Now ABOUT FOOD consecrated to heathen deities.   8
Of course we all 'have knowledge', as you say. This
'knowledge' breeds conceit; it is love that builds. If anyone 2
fancies that he knows, he knows nothing yet, in the true
sense of knowing. But if a man loves,[d] he is acknowledged 3
by God.[e]

Well then, about eating this consecrated food: of course, 4
as you say, 'a false god has no existence in the real world.
There is no god but one.' For indeed, if there be so-called 5
gods, whether in heaven or on earth—as indeed there are
many 'gods' and many 'lords'—yet for us there is one God, 6
the Father, from whom all being comes, towards whom we
move; and there is one Lord, Jesus Christ, through whom
all things came to be, and we through him.

But not everyone knows this. There are some who have 7
been so accustomed to idolatry[f] that even now they eat
this food with a sense of its heathen consecration, and
their conscience, being weak, is polluted by the eating. Cer- 8
tainly food will not bring us into God's presence: if we do
not eat, we are none the worse, and if we eat, we are none
the better. But be careful that this liberty of yours does 9
not become a pitfall for the weak. If a weak character sees 10
you sitting down to a meal in a heathen temple—you, who
'have knowledge'—will not his conscience be emboldened
to eat food consecrated to the heathen deity? This 'know- 11
ledge' of yours is utter disaster to the weak, the brother for
whom Christ died. In thus sinning against your brothers 12
and wounding their conscience,[g] you sin against Christ.

---

[a] *Or let the girl and her lover marry.*      [b] *Or his daughter.*
[c] *Or gives his daughter in marriage.*      [d] *Some witnesses read* loves
God.      [e] *Or he is recognized.*      [f] *Some witnesses read* in whom
the consciousness of the false god is so persistent . . .      [g] *Some
witnesses insert* weak as it is.

13 And therefore, if food be the downfall of my brother, I will never eat meat any more, for I will not be the cause of my brother's downfall.

9 Am i not a free man? Am I not an apostle? Did I not see Jesus our Lord? Are not you my own handiwork,
2 in the Lord? If others do not accept me as an apostle, you at least are bound to do so, for you are yourselves the very seal of my apostolate, in the Lord.
3 4    To those who put me in the dock this is my answer: Have
5 I no right to eat and drink? Have I no right to take a Christian wife about with me, like the rest of the apostles
6 and the Lord's brothers, and Cephas? Or are Barnabas and
7 I alone bound to work for our living? Did you ever hear of a man serving in the army at his own expense? or planting a vineyard without eating the fruit of it? or tending a
8 flock without using its milk? Do not suppose I rely on
9 these human analogies, for the law says the same; in the Law of Moses we read, 'You shall not muzzle a threshing
10 ox.' Do you suppose God's concern is with oxen? Or is the reference clearly to ourselves? Of course it refers to us, in the sense that the ploughman should plough and the thresher thresh in the hope of getting some of the produce.
11 If we have sown a spiritual crop for you, is it too much to
12 expect from you a material harvest? If you allow others these rights, have not we a stronger claim?
    But I have availed myself of no such right. On the contrary, I put up with all that comes my way rather than
13 offer any hindrance to the gospel of Christ. You know (do you not?) that those who perform the temple service eat the temple offerings, and those who wait upon the altar
14 claim their share of the sacrifice. In the same way the Lord gave instructions that those who preach the Gospel
15 should earn their living by the Gospel. But I have never taken advantage of any such right, nor do I intend to claim it in this letter. I had rather die! No one shall make
16 my boast an empty boast. Even if I preach the Gospel, I can claim no credit for it; I cannot help myself; it would be
17 misery to me not to preach. If I did it of my own choice, I should be earning my pay; but since I do it apart from
18 my own choice, I am simply discharging a trust.[a] Then what is my pay? The satisfaction of preaching the Gospel

[a] *Or* If I do it willingly I am earning my pay; if I did it unwillingly I should still have a trust laid upon me.

without expense to anyone; in other words, of waiving the rights which my preaching gives me.

I am a free man and own no master; but I have made 19 myself every man's servant, to win over as many as possible. To Jews I became like a Jew, to win Jews; as 20 they are subject to the Law of Moses, I put myself under that law to win them, although I am not myself subject to it. To win Gentiles, who are outside the Law, I made my- 21 self like one of them, although I am not in truth outside God's law, being under the law of Christ. To the weak I 22 became weak, to win the weak. Indeed, I have become everything in turn to men of every sort, so that in one way or another I may save some. All this I do for the sake of 23 the Gospel, to bear my part in proclaiming it.

You know (do you not?) that at the sports all the runners 24 run the race, though only one wins the prize. Like them, run to win! But every athlete goes into strict training. 25 They do it to win a fading wreath; we, a wreath that never fades. For my part, I run with a clear goal before me; I am 26 like a boxer who does not beat the air; I bruise my own 27 body and make it know its master, for fear that after preaching to others I should find myself rejected.

You should understand, my brothers, that our ancestors 10 were all under the pillar of cloud, and all of them passed through the Red Sea; and so they all received baptism 2 into the fellowship of Moses in cloud and sea. They all ate 3 the same supernatural food, and all drank the same super- 4 natural drink; I mean, they all drank from the supernatural rock that accompanied their travels—and that rock was Christ. And yet, most of them were not accepted 5 by God, for the desert was strewn with their corpses.

These events happened as symbols to warn us not to set 6 our desires on evil things, as they did. Do not be idolaters, 7 like some of them; as Scripture has it, 'the people sat down to feast and rose up to revel'. Let us not commit 8 fornication, as some of them did—and twenty-three thousand died in one day. Let us not put the power of the 9 Lord*a* to the test, as some of them did—and were destroyed by serpents. Do not grumble against God, as some of them 10 did—and were destroyed by the Destroyer.

All these things that happened to them were symbolic, 11 and were recorded for our benefit as a warning. For upon us the fulfilment of the ages has come. If you feel sure that 12 you are standing firm, beware! You may fall. So far you 13

*a Some witnesses read* of Christ.

have faced no trial beyond what man can bear. God keeps
faith, and he will not allow you to be tested above your
powers, but when the test comes he will at the same time
provide a way out, by enabling you to sustain it.

14 15  SO THEN, DEAR FRIENDS, shun idolatry. I speak to you
as men of sense. Form your own judgement on what I say.
16 When we bless 'the cup of blessing', is it not a means of
sharing in the blood of Christ? When we break the bread,
17 is it not a means of sharing in the body of Christ? Because
there is one loaf, we, many as we are, are one body;*a* for it
is one loaf of which we all partake.
18    Look at the Jewish people. Are not those who partake
19 in the sacrificial meal sharers in the altar? What do I imply
by this? that an idol is anything but an idol? or food
20 offered to it anything more than food? No; but the
sacrifices the heathen offer are offered (in the words of
Scripture) 'to demons and to that which is not God'; and
21 I will not have you become partners with demons. You
cannot drink the cup of the Lord and the cup of demons.
You cannot partake of the Lord's table and the table of
22 demons. Can we defy the Lord? Are we stronger than
he?
23    'We are free to do anything', you say. Yes, but is everything good for us? 'We are free to do anything', but does
24 everything help the building of the community? Each of
you must regard, not his own interests, but the other
man's.
25    You may eat anything sold in the meat-market without
26 raising questions of conscience; for the earth is the Lord's
and everything in it.
27    If an unbeliever invites you to a meal and you care to go,
eat whatever is put before you, without raising questions
28 of conscience. But if somebody says to you, 'This food has
been offered in sacrifice', then, out of consideration for him,
29 and for conscience' sake, do not eat it—not your conscience,
I mean, but the other man's.
    'What?' you say, 'is my freedom to be called in question
30 by another man's conscience? If I partake with thankful-
ness, why am I blamed for eating food over which I have
31 said grace?' Well, whether you eat or drink, or whatever
32 you are doing, do all for the honour of God: give no offence
33 to Jews, or Greeks, or to the church of God. For my part

*a* Or For we, many as we are, are one loaf, one body.

I always try to meet everyone half-way, regarding not my own good but the good of the many, so that they may be saved. Follow my example as I follow Christ's. 11

I commend you for always keeping me in mind, and 2 maintaining the tradition I handed on to you. But I wish 3 you to understand that, while every man has Christ for his Head, woman's head is man,[a] as Christ's Head is God. A man who keeps his head covered when he prays or pro- 4 phesies brings shame on his head; a woman, on the con- 5 trary, brings shame on her head if she prays or prophesies bare-headed; it is as bad as if her head were shaved. If a 6 woman is not to wear a veil she might as well have her hair cut off; but if it is a disgrace for her to be cropped and shaved, then she should wear a veil. A man has no need 7 to cover his head, because man is the image of God, and the mirror of his glory, whereas woman reflects the glory of man.[b] For man did not originally spring from woman, 8 but woman was made out of man; and man was not created 9 for woman's sake, but woman for the sake of man; and 10 therefore it is woman's duty to have a sign of authority[c] on her head, out of regard for the angels.[d] And yet, in 11 Christ's fellowship woman is as essential to man as man to woman. If woman was made out of man, it is through 12 woman that man now comes to be; and God is the source of all.

Judge for yourselves: is it fitting for a woman to pray to 13 God bare-headed? Does not Nature herself teach you that 14 while flowing locks disgrace a man, they are a woman's 15 glory? For her locks were given for covering.

However, if you insist on arguing, let me tell you, there 16 is no such custom among us, or in any of the congregations of God's people.

In giving you these injunctions I must mention a prac- 17 tice which I cannot commend: your meetings tend to do more harm than good. To begin with, I am told that when 18 you meet as a congregation you fall into sharply divided groups; and I believe there is some truth in it (for dissen- 19 sions are necessary if only to show which of your members are sound). The result is that when you meet as a congrega- 20 tion, it is impossible for you to eat the Lord's Supper,

---

[a] *Or* a woman's head is her husband.   [b] *Or* a woman reflects her husband's glory.   [c] *Some witnesses read* to have a veil.   [d] *Or* and therefore a woman should keep her dignity on her head, for fear of the angels.

21 because each of you is in such a hurry to eat his own, and
22 while one goes hungry another has too much to drink. Have
you no homes of your own to eat and drink in? Or are you
so contemptuous of the church of God that you shame its
poorer members? What am I to say? Can I commend you?
On this point, certainly not!

23      For the tradition which I handed on to you came to me
from the Lord himself: that the Lord Jesus, on the night
24 of his arrest, took bread and, after giving thanks to God,
broke it and said: 'This is my body, which is for you; do
25 this as a memorial of me.' In the same way, he took the
cup after supper, and said: 'This cup is the new covenant
sealed by my blood. Whenever you drink it, do this as a
26 memorial of me.' For every time you eat this bread and
drink the cup, you proclaim the death of the Lord, until
he comes.

27      It follows that anyone who eats the bread or drinks the
cup of the Lord unworthily will be guilty of desecrating
28 the body and blood of the Lord. A man must test himself
before eating his share of the bread and drinking from the
29 cup. For he who eats and drinks eats and drinks judgement
30 on himself if he does not discern the Body. That is why
many of you are feeble and sick, and a number have died.
31 But if we examined ourselves, we should not thus fall
32 under judgement. When, however, we do fall under the
Lord's judgement, he is disciplining us, to save us from
being condemned with the rest of the world.

33      Therefore, my brothers, when you meet for a meal, wait
34 for one another. If you are hungry, eat at home, so that in
meeting together you may not fall under judgement. The
other matters I will arrange when I come.


## SPIRITUAL GIFTS

12   ABOUT GIFTS OF THE SPIRIT, there are some
things of which I do not wish you to remain ignorant.
2      You know how, in the days when you were still pagan,
you were swept off to those dumb heathen gods, however
3 you happened to be led.[a] For this reason I must impress
upon you that no one who says 'A curse on Jesus!' can be
speaking under the influence of the Spirit of God. And no

[a] Or . . . pagan, you would be seized by some power which drove you
to those dumb heathen gods.

one can say 'Jesus is Lord!' except under the influence of the Holy Spirit.

There are varieties of gifts, but the same Spirit. There 4 5 are varieties of service, but the same Lord. There are many 6 forms of work, but all of them, in all men, are the work of the same God. In each of us the Spirit is manifested in one 7 particular way, for some useful purpose. One man, through 8 the Spirit, has the gift of wise speech, while another, by the power of the same Spirit, can put the deepest knowledge into words. Another, by the same Spirit, is granted 9 faith; another, by the one Spirit, gifts of healing, and 10 another miraculous powers; another has the gift of prophecy, and another ability to distinguish true spirits from false; yet another has the gift of ecstatic utterance of different kinds, and another the ability to interpret it. But all these gifts are the work of one and the same 11 Spirit, distributing them separately to each individual at will.

For Christ is like a single body with its many limbs and 12 organs, which, many as they are, together make up one body. For indeed we were all brought into one body by 13 baptism, in the one Spirit, whether we are Jews or Greeks, whether slaves or free men, and that one Holy Spirit was poured out for all of us to drink.

A body is not one single organ, but many. Suppose the 14 15 foot should say, 'Because I am not a hand, I do not belong to the body', it does belong to the body none the less. Suppose the ear were to say, 'Because I am not an eye, I do 16 not belong to the body', it does still belong to the body. If 17 the body were all eye, how could it hear? If the body were all ear, how could it smell? But, in fact, God appointed 18 each limb and organ to its own place in the body, as he chose. If the whole were one single organ, there would not 19 be a body at all; in fact, however, there are many different 20 organs, but one body. The eye cannot say to the hand, 'I 21 do not need you'; nor the head to the feet, 'I do not need you.' Quite the contrary: those organs of the body which 22 seem to be more frail than others are indispensable, and 23 those parts of the body which we regard as less honourable are treated with special honour. To our unseemly parts is given a more than ordinary seemliness, whereas our 24 seemly parts need no adorning. But God has combined the various parts of the body, giving special honour to the humbler parts, so that there might be no sense of division 25 in the body, but that all its organs might feel the same

26 concern for one another. If one organ suffers, they all suffer together. If one flourishes, they all rejoice together.
27 Now you are Christ's body, and each of you a limb or
28 organ of it. Within our community God has appointed, in the first place apostles, in the second place prophets, thirdly teachers; then miracle-workers, then those who have gifts of healing, or ability to help others or power to guide them, or the gift of ecstatic utterance of various
29 kinds. Are all apostles? all prophets? all teachers? Do all
30 work miracles? Have all gifts of healing? Do all speak in
31 tongues of ecstasy? Can all interpret them? The higher gifts are those you should aim at.

And now I will show you the best way of all.

13 I may speak in tongues of men or of angels, but if I am without love, I am a sounding gong or a clanging cymbal.
2 I may have the gift of prophecy, and know every hidden truth; I may have faith strong enough to move mountains;
3 but if I have no love, I am nothing. I may dole out all I possess, or even give my body to be burnt,[a] but if I have no love, I am none the better.

4 Love is patient; love is kind and envies no one. Love is
5 never boastful, nor conceited, nor rude; never selfish, not
6 quick to take offence. Love keeps no score of wrongs; does not gloat over other men's sins, but delights in the truth.
7 There is nothing love cannot face; there is no limit to its faith, its hope, and its endurance.

8 Love will never come to an end. Are there prophets? their work will be over. Are there tongues of ecstasy? they
9 will cease. Is there knowledge? it will vanish away; for our
10 knowledge and our prophecy alike are partial, and the
11 partial vanishes when wholeness comes. When I was a child, my speech, my outlook, and my thoughts were all childish. When I grew up, I had finished with childish
12 things. Now we see only puzzling reflections in a mirror, but then we shall see face to face. My knowledge now is partial; then it will be whole, like God's knowledge of me.
13 In a word, there are three things that last for ever: faith, hope, and love; but the greatest of them all is love.

14 Put love first; but there are other gifts of the Spirit at
2 which you should aim also, and above all prophecy. When a man is using the language of ecstasy he is talking with God, not with men, for no man understands him; he is no
3 doubt inspired, but he speaks mysteries. On the other hand, when a man prophesies, he is talking to men, and his

[a] *Some witnesses read* even seek glory by self-sacrifice.

words have power to build; they stimulate and they encourage. The language of ecstasy is good for the speaker 4 himself, but it is prophecy that builds up a Christian community. I should be pleased for you all to use the tongues 5 of ecstasy, but better pleased for you to prophesy. The prophet is worth more than the man of ecstatic speech—unless indeed he can explain its meaning, and so help to build up the community. Suppose, my friends, that when 6 I come to you I use ecstatic language: what good shall I do you, unless what I say contains something by way of revelation, or enlightenment, or prophecy, or instruction?

Even with inanimate things that produce sounds—a 7 flute, say, or a lyre—unless their notes mark definite intervals, how can you tell what tune is being played? Or again, 8 if the trumpet-call is not clear, who will prepare for battle? In the same way if your ecstatic utterance yields no precise 9 meaning, how can anyone tell what you are saying? You will be talking into the air. How many different kinds of 10 sound there are, or may be, in the world! Nothing is altogether soundless. Well then, if I do not know the meaning 11 of the sound the speaker makes, his words will be gibberish to me, and mine to him. You are, I know, eager for gifts of 12 the Spirit; then aspire above all to excel in those which build up the church.

I say, then, that the man who falls into ecstatic utter- 13 ance should pray for the ability to interpret. If I use such 14 language in my prayer, the Spirit in me prays, but my intellect lies fallow. What then? I will pray as I am in- 15 spired to pray, but I will also pray intelligently. I will sing hymns as I am inspired to sing, but I will sing intelligently too. Suppose you are praising God in the language of 16 inspiration: how will the plain man who is present be able to say 'Amen' to your thanksgiving, when he does not know what you are saying? Your prayer of thanksgiving 17 may be all that could be desired, but it is no help to the other man. Thank God, I am more gifted in ecstatic utter- 18 ance than any of you,[a] but in the congregation I would 19 rather speak five intelligible words, for the benefit of others as well as myself, than thousands of words in the language of ecstasy.

Do not be childish, my friends. Be as innocent of evil as 20 babes, but at least be grown-up in your thinking. We read 21 in the Law: 'I will speak to this nation through men of

[a] *Or* . . . man. I say the thanksgiving; I use ecstatic speech more than any of you.

strange tongues, and by the lips of foreigners; and even so
22 they will not heed me, says the Lord.' Clearly then these
'strange tongues' are not intended as a sign for believers,
but for unbelievers, whereas prophecy is designed not for
23 unbelievers but for those who hold the faith. So if the
whole congregation is assembled and all are using the
'strange tongues' of ecstasy, and some uninstructed persons
or unbelievers should enter, will they not think you are
24 mad? But if all are uttering prophecies, the visitor, when
he enters, hears from everyone something that searches
25 his conscience and brings conviction, and the secrets of
his heart are laid bare. So he will fall down and worship
God, crying, 'God is certainly among you!'

26 To sum up, my friends: when you meet for worship, each
of you contributes a hymn, some instruction, a revelation,
an ecstatic utterance, or the interpretation of such an
utterance. All of these must aim at one thing: to build up
27 the church. If it is a matter of ecstatic utterance, only two
should speak, or at most three, one at a time, and someone
28 must interpret. If there is no interpreter, the speaker had
better not address the meeting at all, but speak to himself
29 and to God. Of the prophets, two or three may speak,
while the rest exercise their judgement upon what is said.
30 If someone else, sitting in his place, receives a revelation,
31 let the first speaker stop. You can all prophesy, one at a
time, so that the whole congregation may receive instruc-
32 tion and encouragement. It is for prophets to control pro-
33 phetic inspiration, for the God who inspires them is not
a God of disorder but of peace.

34 As in all congregations of God's people, women[a] should
not address the meeting. They have no licence to speak, but
35 should keep their place as the law directs. If there is something they want to know, they can ask their own husbands
at home. It is a shocking thing that a woman should address the congregation.

36 Did the word of God originate with you? Or are you the
37 only people to whom it came? If anyone claims to be inspired or a prophet, let him recognize that what I write
38 has the Lord's authority. If he does not acknowledge this,
God does not acknowledge him.[b]

39 In short, my friends, be eager to prophesy; do not forbid
40 ecstatic utterance; but let all be done decently and in order.

---

[a] *Or* of peace, as in all communities of God's people. Women . . .
[b] *Some witnesses read* If he refuses to recognize this, let him refuse!

## LIFE AFTER DEATH

AND NOW, MY BROTHERS, I must remind you 15 of the gospel that I preached to you; the gospel which you received, on which you have taken your stand, and 2 which is now bringing you salvation. Do you still hold fast the Gospel as I preached it to you? If not, your conversion was in vain.[a]

First and foremost, I handed on to you the facts which 3 had been imparted to me: that Christ died for our sins, in accordance with the scriptures; that he was buried; that he 4 was raised to life on the third day, according to the scriptures; and that he appeared to Cephas, and afterwards to 5 the Twelve. Then he appeared to over five hundred of our 6 brothers at once, most of whom are still alive, though some have died. Then he appeared to James, and afterwards to 7 all the apostles.

In the end he appeared even to me. It was like an ab- 8 normal birth; I had persecuted the church of God and am 9 therefore inferior to all other apostles—indeed not fit to be called an apostle. However, by God's grace I am what 10 I am, nor has his grace been given to me in vain; on the contrary, in my labours I have outdone them all—not I, indeed, but the grace of God working with me. But what 11 matter, I or they? This is what we all proclaim, and this is what you believed.

Now if this is what we proclaim, that Christ was raised 12 from the dead, how can some of you say there is no resurrection of the dead? If there be no resurrection, then Christ 13 was not raised; and if Christ was not raised, then our 14 gospel is null and void, and so is your faith; and we turn 15 out to be lying witnesses for God, because we bore witness that he raised Christ to life, whereas, if the dead are not raised, he did not raise him. For if the dead are not raised, 16 it follows that Christ was not raised; and if Christ was not 17 raised, your faith has nothing in it and you are still in your old state of sin. It follows also that those who have died 18 within Christ's fellowship are utterly lost. If it is for this 19 life only that Christ has given us hope,[b] we of all men are most to be pitied.

But the truth is, Christ was raised to life—the firstfruits 20

[a] *Or* Do you remember the terms in which I preached the Gospel to you?—for I assume you did not accept it thoughtlessly.    [b] *Or* If it is only an uncertain hope that our life in Christ has given us . . .

21 of the harvest of the dead. For since it was a man who
brought death into the world, a man also brought resurrec-
22 tion of the dead. As in Adam all men die, so in Christ all
23 will be brought to life; but each in his own proper place:
Christ the firstfruits, and afterwards, at his coming, those
24 who belong to Christ. Then comes the end, when he delivers up the kingdom to God the Father, after abolishing
25 every kind of domination, authority, and power. For he is
destined to reign until God has put all enemies under his
26 27 feet; and the last enemy to be abolished is death.[a] Scripture says, 'He has put all things in subjection under his
feet.' But in saying 'all things', it clearly means to exclude
28 God who subordinates them; and when all things are thus
subject to him, then the Son himself will also be made subordinate to God who made all things subject to him, and
thus God will be all in all.

29    Again, there are those who receive baptism on behalf of
the dead. Why should they do this? If the dead are not
raised to life at all, what do they mean by being baptized
on their behalf?

30    And we ourselves—why do we face these dangers hour
31 by hour? Every day I die: I swear it by my pride in you,
my brothers—for in Christ Jesus our Lord I am proud of
32 you. If, as the saying is, I 'fought wild beasts' at Ephesus,
what have I gained by it?[b] If the dead are never raised to
life, 'let us eat and drink, for tomorrow we die'.

33    Make no mistake: 'Bad company is the ruin of a good
34 character.' Come back to a sober and upright life and leave
your sinful ways. There are some who know nothing of
God; to your shame I say it.

35    But, you may ask, how are the dead raised? In what kind
36 of body? How foolish! The seed you sow does not come to
37 life unless it has first died; and what you sow is not the
body that shall be, but a naked grain, perhaps of wheat, or
38 of some other kind; and God clothes it with the body of his
39 choice, each seed with its own particular body. All flesh is
not the same flesh: there is flesh of men, flesh of beasts,
40 of birds, and of fishes—all different. There are heavenly
bodies and earthly bodies; and the splendour of the heavenly bodies is one thing, the splendour of the earthly,
41 another. The sun has a splendour of its own, the moon

[a] *Or* Then at the end, when . . . power (for he . . . feet), the last enemy,
death, will be abolished.    [b] *Or* If, as men do, I had fought wild
beasts at Ephesus, what good would it be to me? *or* If I had been in
no better case than one fighting beasts in the arena at Ephesus, what
good would it be to me?

another splendour, and the stars another, for star differs from star in brightness. So it is with the resurrection of the 42 dead. What is sown in the earth as a perishable thing is raised imperishable. Sown in humiliation, it is raised in 43 glory; sown in weakness, it is raised in power; sown as an 44 animal body, it is raised as a spiritual body.

If there is such a thing as an animal body, there is also a spiritual body. It is in this sense that Scripture says, 45 'The first man, Adam, became an animate being', whereas the last Adam has become a life-giving spirit. Observe, the 46 spiritual does not come first; the animal body comes first, and then the spiritual. The first man was made 'of the dust 47 of the earth': the second man is from heaven. The man 48 made of dust is the pattern of all men of dust, and the heavenly man is the pattern of all the heavenly. As we 49 have worn the likeness of the man made of dust, so we shall wear the likeness of the heavenly man.

What I mean, my brothers, is this: flesh and blood can 50 never possess the kingdom of God, and the perishable cannot possess immortality. Listen! I will unfold a mystery: 51 we shall not all die, but we shall all be changed in a flash, 52 in the twinkling of an eye, at the last trumpet-call. For the trumpet will sound, and the dead will rise immortal, and we shall be changed. This perishable being must be 53 clothed with the imperishable, and what is mortal must be clothed with immortality. And when[a] our mortality has 54 been clothed with immortality, then the saying of Scripture will come true: 'Death is swallowed up; victory is won!' 'O Death, where is your victory? O Death, where is 55 your sting?' The sting of death is sin, and sin gains its 56 power from the law; but, God be praised, he gives us the 57 victory through our Lord Jesus Christ.

Therefore, my beloved brothers, stand firm and immov- 58 able, and work for the Lord always, work without limit, since you know that in the Lord your labour cannot be lost.

## CHRISTIAN GIVING

AND NOW about the collection in aid of God's people: 16 you should follow my directions to our congregations in Galatia. Every Sunday each of you is to put aside and 2 keep by him a sum in proportion to his gains, so that there

[a] *Some witnesses insert* our perishable nature has been clothed with the imperishable, and . . .

3 may be no collecting when I come. When I arrive, I will give letters of introduction to persons approved by you,

4 and send them to carry your gift to Jerusalem. If it should seem worth while for me to go as well, they shall go with me.

5 I shall come to Corinth after passing through Macedo-

6 nia—for I am travelling by way of Macedonia—and I may stay with you, perhaps even for the whole winter, and

7 then you can help me on my way wherever I go next. I do not want this to be a flying visit; I hope to spend some

8 time with you, if the Lord permits. But I shall remain at

9 Ephesus until Whitsuntide, for a great opportunity has opened for effective work, and there is much opposition.

10 If Timothy comes, see that you put him at his ease; for it is the Lord's work that he is engaged upon, as I am my-

11 self; so no one must slight him. Send him happily on his way to join me, since I am waiting for him with our friends.

12 As for our friend Apollos, I urged him strongly to go to Corinth with the others, but he was quite determined not to go[a] at present; he will go when opportunity offers.

13 Be alert; stand firm in the faith; be valiant and strong.

14 Let all you do be done in love.

15 I have a request to make of you, my brothers. You know that the Stephanas family were the first converts in Achaia,

16 and have laid themselves out to serve God's people. I wish you to give their due position to such persons, and indeed

17 to everyone who labours hard at our common task. It is a great pleasure to me that Stephanas, Fortunatus, and Achaicus have arrived, because they have done what you

18 had no chance to do; they have relieved my mind—and no doubt yours too. Such men deserve recognition.

19 Greetings from the congregations in Asia. Many greetings in the Lord from Aquila and Prisca and the congrega-

20 tion at their house. Greetings from all the brothers. Greet one another with the kiss of peace.

21 This greeting is in my own hand—P A U L.

22 If anyone does not love the Lord, let him be outcast. *Marana tha*—Come, O Lord!

23 The grace of the Lord Jesus Christ be with you.

24 My love to you all in Christ Jesus. Amen.

[a] *Or but it was by no means the will of God that he should go . . .*

# THE
# SECOND LETTER OF PAUL
# TO THE
# CORINTHIANS

## PERSONAL RELIGION AND
## THE MINISTRY

FROM PAUL, APOSTLE of Christ Jesus by God's 1
will, and our colleague Timothy, to the congregation
of God's people at Corinth, together with all who are
dedicated to him throughout the whole of Achaia.

Grace and peace to you from God our Father and the 2
Lord Jesus Christ.

Praise be to the God and Father of our Lord Jesus 3
Christ, the all-merciful Father, the God whose consolation
never fails us! He comforts us in all our troubles, so that 4
we in turn may be able to comfort others in any trouble
of theirs and to share with them the consolation we ourselves receive from God. As Christ's cup of suffering over- 5
flows, and we suffer with him, so also through Christ our
consolation overflows. If distress be our lot, it is the price 6
we pay for your consolation, for your salvation; if our lot
be consolation, it is to help us to bring you comfort, and
strength to face with fortitude the same sufferings we now
endure. And our hope for you is firmly grounded;[a] for we 7
know that if you have part in the suffering, you have part
also in the divine consolation.

In saying this, we should like you to know, dear friends, 8
how serious was the trouble that came upon us in the
province of Asia. The burden of it was far too heavy for us
to bear, so heavy that we even despaired of life. Indeed, we 9

---

[a] *Some witnesses give these clauses* If distress . . . firmly grounded *in different sequence.*

299

felt in our hearts that we had received a death-sentence. This was meant to teach us not to place reliance on ourselves,
10 but on God who raises the dead. From such mortal peril God delivered us; and he will deliver us again,[a] he on whom our hope is fixed. Yes, he will continue to deliver
11 us, if you will co-operate by praying for us. Then, with so many people praying for our deliverance, there will be many to give thanks on our behalf for the gracious favour God has shown towards us.

12 There is one thing we are proud of: our conscience assures us that in our dealings with our fellow-men, and above all in our dealings with you, our conduct has been governed by a devout and godly sincerity,[b] by the grace
13 of God and not by worldly wisdom. There is nothing in our letters to you but what you can read for yourselves, and
14 understand too. Partial as your present knowledge of us is, you will I hope come to understand fully that you have as much reason to be proud of us, as we of you, on the Day of our Lord Jesus.

15 It was because I felt so confident about all this that I had intended to come first of all to you[c] and give you the
16 benefit of a double visit: I meant to visit you on my way to Macedonia, and after leaving Macedonia, to return to you, and you would then send me on my way to Judaea.
17 That was my intention; did I lightly change my mind?[d] Or do I, when I frame my plans, frame them as a worldly man might, so that it should rest with me to say 'yes' and
18 'yes', or 'no' and 'no'? As God is true, the language in which we address you is not an ambiguous blend of Yes
19 and No. The Son of God, Christ Jesus, proclaimed among you by us (by Silvanus and Timothy, I mean, as well as myself), was never a blend of Yes and No. With him it
20 was, and is, Yes. He is the Yes pronounced upon God's promises, every one of them. That is why, when we give glory to God, it is through Christ Jesus that we say 'Amen'.
21 And if you and we belong to Christ, guaranteed as his and
22 anointed, it is all God's doing; it is God also who has set his seal upon us, and as a pledge of what is to come has given the Spirit to dwell in our hearts.
23 I appeal to God to witness what I am going to say; I stake my life upon it: it was out of consideration for you

---

[a] *Some witnesses read* and he still delivers us.   [b] *Some witnesses read* by sincere and godly singleness of mind.   [c] *Or* had originally intended to come to you . . .   [d] *Or* In forming this intention, did I act irresponsibly?

that I did not after all come to Corinth. Do not think we 24
are dictating the terms of your faith; your hold on the
faith is secure enough. We are working with you for your
own happiness. So I made up my mind that my next 2
visit to you must not be another painful one. If I cause 2
pain to you, who is left to cheer me up, except you, whom
I have offended? This is precisely the point I made in my 3
letter: I did not want, I said, to come and be made miserable by the very people who ought to have made me happy;
and I had sufficient confidence in you all to know that for
me to be happy is for all of you to be happy. That letter I 4
sent you came out of great distress and anxiety; how many
tears I shed as I wrote it! But I never meant to cause you
pain; I wanted you rather to know the love, the more than
ordinary love, that I have for you.

Any injury that has been done, has not been done to me; 5
to some extent, not to labour the point, it has been done
to you all. The penalty on which the general meeting has 6
agreed has met the offence well enough. Something very 7
different is called for now: you must forgive the offender
and put heart into him; the man's sorrow must not be
made so severe as to overwhelm him. I urge you therefore 8
to assure him of your love for him by a formal act. I wrote, 9
I may say, to see how you stood the test, whether you
fully accepted my authority. But anyone who has your 10
forgiveness has mine too; and when I speak of forgiving
(so far as there is anything for me to forgive), I mean that
as the representative of Christ I have forgiven him for
your sake.[a] For Satan must not be allowed to get the 11
better of us; we know his wiles all too well.

Then when I came to Troas, where I was to preach the 12
gospel of Christ, and where an opening awaited me for the
Lord's work, I still found no relief of mind, for my col- 13
league Titus was not there to meet me; so I took leave of
the people there and went off to Macedonia. But thanks 14
be to God, who continually leads us about, captives in
Christ's triumphal procession, and everywhere uses us to
reveal and spread abroad the fragrance of the knowledge
of himself! We are indeed the incense offered by Christ to 15
God, both for those who are on the way to salvation, and
for those who are on the way to perdition: to the latter it 16
is a deadly fume that kills, to the former a vital fragrance
that brings life. Who is equal to such a calling? At least we 17

[a] *Or* that I have forgiven him for your sake, in the presence of
Christ.

do not go hawking the word of God about, as so many do; when we declare the word we do it in sincerity, as from God and in God's sight, as members of Christ.

3 ARE WE BEGINNING all over again to produce our credentials? Do we, like some people, need letters of intro-
2 duction to you, or from you? No, you are all the letter we need, a letter written on our heart; any man can see it for
3 what it is and read it for himself. And as for you, it is plain that you are a letter that has come from Christ, given to us to deliver: a letter written not with ink but with the Spirit of the living God, written not on stone tablets but on the pages of the human heart.
4 It is in full reliance upon God, through Christ, that we
5 make such claims. There is no question of our being quali-fied in ourselves: we cannot claim anything as our own.
6 The qualification we have comes from God; it is he who has qualified us to dispense his new covenant—a covenant expressed not in a written document, but in a spiritual bond; for the written law condemns to death, but the Spirit gives life.
7 The law, then, engraved letter by letter upon stone, dispensed death, and yet it was inaugurated with divine splendour. That splendour, though it was soon to fade, made the face of Moses so bright that the Israelites could not gaze
8 steadily at him. But if so, must not even greater splendour
9 rest upon the divine dispensation of the Spirit? If splendour accompanied the dispensation under which we are con-demned, how much richer in splendour must that one be
10 under which we are acquitted! Indeed, the splendour that once was is now no splendour at all; it is outshone by a
11 splendour greater still. For if that which was soon to fade had its moment of splendour, how much greater is the splendour of that which endures!
12 13 With such a hope as this we speak out boldly; it is not for us to do as Moses did: he put a veil over his face to keep the Israelites from gazing on that fading splendour until it
14 was gone. But in any case their minds had been made insensitive, for that same veil is there to this very day when the lesson is read from the old covenant; and it is never lifted, because only in Christ is the old covenant
15 abrogated.[a] But to this very day, every time the Law of
16 Moses is read, a veil lies over the minds of the hearers. How-ever, as Scripture says of Moses, 'whenever he turns to the

    [a] *Or* in Christ is it abolished.

Lord the veil is removed'.<sup>a</sup> Now the Lord of whom this 17
passage speaks is the Spirit; and where the Spirit of the
Lord is, there is liberty. And because for us there is no veil 18
over the face, we all reflect as in a mirror the splendour of
the Lord; thus we are transfigured into his likeness, from
splendour to splendour; such is the influence of the Lord
who is Spirit.

SEEING THEN THAT WE have been entrusted with this **4**
commission, which we owe entirely to God's mercy, we
never lose heart. We have renounced the deeds that men 2
hide for very shame; we neither practise cunning nor distort the word of God; only by declaring the truth openly
do we recommend ourselves, and then it is to the common
conscience of our fellow-men and in the sight of God. And 3
if indeed our gospel be found veiled, the only people who
find it so are those on the way to perdition. Their un- 4
believing minds are so blinded by the god of this passing
age, that the gospel of the glory of Christ, who is the very
image of God, cannot dawn upon them and bring them
light. It is not ourselves that we proclaim; we proclaim 5
Christ Jesus as Lord, and ourselves as your servants, for
Jesus' sake. For the same God who said, 'Out of darkness 6
let light shine', has caused his light to shine within us, to
give the light of revelation—the revelation of the glory of
God in the face of Jesus Christ.

We are no better than pots of earthenware to contain 7
this treasure, and this proves that such transcendent power
does not come from us, but is God's alone. Hard-pressed 8
on every side, we are never hemmed in; bewildered, we are
never at our wits' end; hunted, we are never abandoned 9
to our fate; struck down, we are not left to die. Wherever 10
we go we carry death with us in our body, the death that
Jesus died, that in this body also life may reveal itself, the
life that Jesus lives. For continually, while still alive, we 11
are being surrendered into the hands of death, for Jesus'
sake, so that the life of Jesus also may be revealed in this
mortal body of ours. Thus death is at work in us, and life 12
in you.

But Scripture says, 'I believed, and therefore I spoke 13
out', and we too, in the same spirit of faith, believe and
therefore speak out; for we know that he who raised the 14
Lord Jesus to life will with Jesus raise us too, and bring us
to his presence, and you with us. Indeed, it is for your sake 15

<sup>a</sup> *Or* as Scripture says, when one turns to the Lord the veil is removed.

that all things are ordered, so that, as the abounding grace of God is shared by more and more, the greater may be the chorus of thanksgiving that ascends to the glory of God.

16 No wonder we do not lose heart! Though our outward humanity is in decay, yet day by day we are inwardly
17 renewed. Our troubles are slight and short-lived; and their
18 outcome an eternal glory which outweighs them far. Meanwhile our eyes are fixed, not on the things that are seen, but on the things that are unseen: for what is seen passes
5 away; what is unseen is eternal. For we know that if the earthly frame that houses us today should be demolished, we possess a building which God has provided—a house
2 not made by human hands, eternal, and in heaven. In this present body we do indeed groan; we yearn to have our
3 heavenly habitation put on over this one—in the hope that, being thus clothed, we shall not find ourselves naked.
4 We groan indeed, we who are enclosed within this earthly frame; we are oppressed because we do not want to have the old body stripped off. Rather our desire is to have the new body put on over it, so that our mortal part may be
5 absorbed into life immortal. God himself has shaped us for this very end; and as a pledge of it he has given us the Spirit.

6 Therefore we never cease to be confident. We know that so long as we are at home in the body we are exiles from
7 8 the Lord; faith is our guide, we do not see him.[a] We are confident, I repeat, and would rather leave our home in the
9 body and go to live with the Lord. We therefore make it our ambition, wherever we are, here or there, to be accept-
10 able to him. For we must all have our lives laid open before the tribunal of Christ, where each must receive what is due to him for his conduct in the body, good or bad.

11 WITH THIS FEAR of the Lord before our eyes we address our appeal to men. To God our lives lie open, as I hope
12 they also lie open to you in your heart of hearts. This is not another attempt to recommend ourselves to you: we are rather giving you a chance to show yourselves proud of us; then you will have something to say to those whose
13 pride is all in outward show and not in inward worth. It may be we are beside ourselves, but it is for God; if we are
14 in our right mind, it is for you. For the love of Christ leaves us no choice, when once we have reached the conclusion that one man died for all and therefore all mankind

[a] *Or faith is our guide and not the things we see.*

304

has died. His purpose in dying for all was that men, while 15 still in life, should cease to live for themselves, and should live for him who for their sake died and was raised to life. With us therefore worldly standards have ceased to count 16 in our estimate of any man; even if once they counted in our understanding of Christ, they do so now no longer. When anyone is united to Christ, there is a new world;[a] 17 the old order has gone, and a new order has already begun.[b]

From first to last this has been the work of God. He has 18 reconciled us men to himself through Christ, and he has enlisted us in this service of reconciliation. What I mean 19 is, that God was in Christ reconciling the world to himself,[c] no longer holding men's misdeeds against them, and that he has entrusted us with the message of reconciliation. We come therefore as Christ's ambassadors. It is as if God 20 were appealing to you through us: in Christ's name, we implore you, be reconciled to God! Christ was innocent of 21 sin, and yet for our sake God made him one with the sinfulness of men,[d] so that in him we might be made one with the goodness of God himself. Sharing in God's work, we 6 urge this appeal upon you: you have received the grace of God; do not let it go for nothing. God's own words are: 2

'In the hour of my favour I gave heed to you;
on the day of deliverance I came to your aid.'

The hour of favour has now come; now, I say, has the day of deliverance dawned.

In order that our service may not be brought into dis- 3 credit, we avoid giving offence in anything. As God's 4 servants, we try to recommend ourselves in all circumstances by our steadfast endurance: in distress, hardships, and dire straits; flogged, imprisoned, mobbed; overworked, 5 sleepless, starving. We recommend ourselves by the inno- 6 cence of our behaviour, our grasp of truth, our patience and kindliness; by gifts of the Holy Spirit, by sincere love, by declaring the truth, by the power of God. We wield the 7 weapons of righteousness in right hand and left. Honour 8 and dishonour, praise and blame, are alike our lot: we are the impostors who speak the truth, the unknown men 9 whom all men know; dying we still live on; disciplined by

---

[a] *Or* a new act of creation.    [b] *Or* When anyone is united to Christ he is a new creature: his old life is over; a new life has already begun.
[c] *Or* God was reconciling the world to himself by Christ.    [d] *Or* and yet God made him a sin-offering for us.

10 suffering, we are not done to death; in our sorrows we have always cause for joy; poor ourselves, we bring wealth to many; penniless, we own the world.

11 Men of Corinth, we have spoken very frankly to you; 12 we have opened our heart wide to you all. On our part there is no constraint; any constraint there may be is in 13 yourselves. In fair exchange then (may a father speak so to his children?) open wide your hearts to us.

## PROBLEMS OF CHURCH LIFE AND DISCIPLINE

14 DO NOT UNITE yourselves with unbelievers; they are no fit mates for you. What has righteousness to do 15 with wickedness? Can light consort with darkness? Can Christ agree with Belial, or a believer join hands with an 16 unbeliever? Can there be a compact between the temple of God and the idols of the heathen? And the temple of the living God is what we are. God's own words are: 'I will live and move about among them; I will be their God, and 17 they shall be my people.' And therefore, 'come away and leave them, separate yourselves, says the Lord; touch 18 nothing unclean. Then I will accept you, says the Lord, the Ruler of all being; I will be a father to you, and you 7 shall be my sons and daughters.' Such are the promises that have been made to us, dear friends. Let us therefore cleanse ourselves from all that can defile flesh or spirit, and in the fear of God complete our consecration.

2 DO MAKE A PLACE for us in your hearts! We have wronged no one, ruined no one, taken advantage of no one. 3 I do not want to blame you. Why, as I have told you before, the place you have in our heart is such that, come 4 death, come life, we meet it together. I am perfectly frank with you. I have great pride in you. In all our many troubles my cup is full of consolation, and overflows with joy.

5 Even when we reached Macedonia there was still no relief for this poor body of ours; instead, there was trouble at every turn, quarrels all round us, forebodings in our 6 heart. But God, who brings comfort to the downcast, has 7 comforted us by the arrival of Titus, and not merely by his arrival, but by his being so greatly comforted about

you. He has told us how you long for me, how sorry you are, and how eager to take my side; and that has made me happier still.

Even if I did wound you by the letter I sent, I do not now regret it. I may have been sorry for it when I saw that the letter had caused you pain, even if only for a time; but now I am happy, not that your feelings were wounded but that the wound led to a change of heart. You bore the smart as God would have you bear it, and so you are no losers by what we did. For the wound which is borne in God's way brings a change of heart too salutary to regret; but the hurt which is borne in the world's way brings death. You bore your hurt in God's way, and see what its results have been! It made you take the matter seriously and vindicate yourselves. How angered you were, how apprehensive! How your longing for me awoke, yes, and your devotion and your eagerness to see justice done! At every point you have cleared yourselves of blame in this trouble. And so, although I did send you that letter, it was not the offender or his victim that most concerned me. My aim in writing was to help to make plain to you, in the sight of God, how truly you are devoted to us. That is why we have been so encouraged.

But besides being encouraged ourselves we have also been delighted beyond everything by seeing how happy Titus is: you have all helped to set his mind completely at rest. Anything I may have said to him to show my pride in you has been justified. Every word we ever addressed to you bore the mark of truth; and the same holds of the proud boast we made in the presence of Titus: that also has proved true. His heart warms all the more to you as he recalls how ready you all were to do what he asked, meeting him as you did in fear and trembling. How happy I am now to have complete confidence in you!

WE MUST TELL YOU, friends, about the grace of gene- 8 rosity which God has imparted to*ᵃ* our congregations in Macedonia. The troubles they have been through have tried them hard, yet in all this they have been so exuberantly happy that from the depths of their poverty they have shown themselves lavishly open-handed. Going to the limit of their resources, as I can testify, and even beyond that limit, they begged us most insistently, and on their own initiative, to be allowed to share in this generous

ᵃ *Or* how gracious God has been to . . .

5 service to their fellow-Christians. And their giving surpassed our expectations; for they gave their very selves, offering them in the first instance to the Lord, but also,
6 under God, to us. The upshot is that we have asked Titus, who began it all, to visit you and bring this work of
7 generosity also to completion. You are so rich in everything—in faith, speech, knowledge, and zeal of every kind, as well as in the loving regard you have for us*a*—surely you should show yourselves equally lavish in this generous
8 service! This is not meant as an order; by telling you how
9 keen others are I am putting your love to the test. For you know how generous our Lord Jesus Christ has been: he was rich, yet for your sake he became poor, so that through his poverty you might become rich.

10 Here is my considered opinion on the matter. What I ask you to do is in your own interests. You made a good beginning last year both in the work you did and in your
11 willingness to undertake it. Now I want you to go on and finish it: be as eager to complete the scheme as you were
12 to adopt it, and give according to your means. Provided there is an eager desire to give, God accepts what a man
13 has; he does not ask for what he has not. There is no question of relieving others at the cost of hardship to
14 yourselves; it is a question of equality. At the moment your surplus meets their need, but one day your need may
15 be met from their surplus. The aim is equality; as Scripture has it, 'The man who got much had no more than enough, and the man who got little did not go short.'

16 I thank God that he has made Titus as keen on your
17 behalf as we are! For Titus not only welcomed our request; he is so eager that by his own desire he is now leaving to
18 come to you. With him we are sending one of our company whose reputation is high among our congregations every-
19 where for his services to the Gospel. Moreover they have duly appointed him to travel with us and help in this beneficent work, by which we do honour to the Lord him-
20 self and show our own eagerness to serve. We want to guard against any criticism of our handling of this generous
21 gift; for our aims are entirely honourable, not only in the Lord's eyes, but also in the eyes of men.

22 With these men we are sending another of our company whose enthusiasm we have had many opportunities of testing, and who is now all the more earnest because of the

---

*a* *Some witnesses read* the love we have for you, *or* the love which we have kindled in your hearts.

great confidence he has in you. If there is any question 23
about Titus, he is my partner and my associate in dealings
with you; as for the others, they are delegates of our congregations, an honour to Christ.*a* Then give them clear 24
expression of your love and justify our pride in you; justify
it to them, and through them to the congregations.

About the provision of aid for God's people, it is super- 9
fluous for me to write to you. I know how eager you are to 2
help; I speak of it with pride to the Macedonians: I tell
them that Achaia had everything ready last year; and
most of them have been fired by your zeal. My purpose in 3
sending these friends is to ensure that what we have said
about you in this matter should not prove to be an empty
boast. By that I mean, I want you to be prepared, as I told
them you were; for if I bring with me men from Macedo- 4
nia and they find you are not prepared, what a disgrace
it will be to us, let alone to you, after all the confidence we
have shown! I have accordingly thought it necessary to ask 5
these friends to go on ahead to Corinth, to see that your
promised bounty is in order before I come; it will then be
awaiting me as a bounty indeed, and not as an extor-
tion.

Remember: sparse sowing, sparse reaping; sow bounti- 6
fully, and you will reap bountifully. Each person should 7
give as he has decided for himself; there should be no re-
luctance, no sense of compulsion; God loves a cheerful
giver. And it is in God's power to provide you richly with 8
every good gift; thus you will have ample means in yourselves to meet each and every situation, with enough and
to spare for every good cause. Scripture says of such a man: 9
'He has lavished his gifts on the needy, his benevolence
stands fast for ever.' Now he who provides seed for sowing 10
and bread for food will provide the seed for you to sow; he
will multiply it and swell the harvest of your benevolence,
and you will always be rich enough to be generous. 11
Through our action such generosity will issue in thanksgiving to God, for as a piece of willing service this is not 12
only a contribution towards the needs of God's people;
more than that, it overflows in a flood of thanksgiving to
God. For through the proof which this affords, many will 13
give honour to God when they see how humbly you obey
him and how faithfully you confess the gospel of Christ;
and will thank him for your liberal contribution to their
need and to the general good. And as they join in prayer 14

*a* Or they are . . . congregations; they reflect Christ.

on your behalf, their hearts will go out to you because of the richness of the grace which God has imparted to you.

15 Thanks be to God for his gift beyond words!

# TRIALS OF A CHRISTIAN MISSIONARY

10 BUT I, PAUL, appeal to you by the gentleness and magnanimity of Christ—I, so feeble (you say) when I
2 am face to face with you, so brave when I am away. Spare me, I beg you, the necessity of such bravery when I come, for I reckon I could put on as bold a face as you please
3 against those who charge us with moral weakness. Weak men we may be, but it is not as such that we fight our
4 battles. The weapons we wield are not merely human,[a]
5 but divinely potent to demolish strongholds; we demolish sophistries and all that rears its proud head against the knowledge of God; we compel every human thought to
6 surrender in obedience to Christ; and we are prepared to punish all rebellion when once you have put yourselves in our hands.

7 Look facts in the face.[b] Someone is convinced, is he, that he belongs to Christ? Let him think again, and reflect
8 that we belong to Christ as much as he does. Indeed, if I am somewhat over-boastful about our authority—an authority given by the Lord to build you up, not pull you
9 down—I shall make my boast good. So you must not think
10 of me as one who scares you by the letters he writes. 'His letters', so it is said, 'are weighty and powerful; but when he appears he has no presence, and as a speaker he is
11 beneath contempt.' People who talk in that way should reckon with this: when I come, my actions will show the same man as my letters showed in my absence.

12 We should not dare to class ourselves or compare ourselves with any of those who put forward their own claims. What fools they are to measure themselves by themselves, to find in themselves their own standard of comparison![c]
13 With us there will be no attempt to boast beyond our

---

[a] *Or* charge us with worldly standards. We live, no doubt, in the world; but it is not on that level that we fight our battles. The weapons we wield are not those of the world . . .    [b] *Or* You are looking only at what catches the eye.    [c] *Some witnesses read* On the contrary we measure ourselves by ourselves, by our own standard of comparison.

proper sphere; and our sphere is determined by the limit
God laid down for us, which permitted us to come as far
as Corinth. We are not overstretching our commission, as 14
we should be if it did not extend to you, for we were the
first to reach Corinth in preaching the gospel of Christ. And 15
we do not boast of work done where others have laboured,
work beyond our proper sphere. Our hope is rather that,
as your faith grows, we may attain a position among you
greater than ever before, but still within the limits of our
sphere. Then we can carry the Gospel to lands that lie 16
beyond you, never priding ourselves on work already done
in another man's sphere. If a man must boast, let him 17
boast of the Lord. Not the man who recommends himself, 18
but the man whom the Lord recommends—he and he
alone is to be accepted.

I wish you would bear with me in a little of my folly; 11
please do bear with me. I am jealous for you, with a divine 2
jealousy; for I betrothed you to Christ, thinking to present
you as a chaste virgin to her true and only husband. But as 3
the serpent in his cunning seduced Eve, I am afraid that
your thoughts may be corrupted and you may lose your*a*
single-hearted devotion to Christ. For if someone comes 4
who proclaims another Jesus, not the Jesus whom we proclaimed, or if you then receive a spirit different from the
Spirit already given to you, or a gospel different from the
gospel you have already accepted, you manage to put up
with that well enough. Have I in any way come short 5
of those superlative apostles? I think not. I may be no 6
speaker, but knowledge I have; at all times we have made
known to you the full truth.

Or was this my offence, that I made no charge for preach- 7
ing the gospel of God, lowering myself to help in raising you?
It is true that I took toll of other congregations, accepting*b* 8
support from them to serve you. Then, while I was with 9
you, if I ran short I sponged on no one; anything I needed
was fully met by our friends who came from Macedonia;
I made it a rule, as I always shall, never to be a burden to
you. As surely as the truth of Christ is in me, I will pre- 10
serve my pride in this matter throughout Achaia, and
nothing shall stop me. Why? Is it that I do not love you? 11
God knows I do.

And I shall go on doing as I am doing now, to cut the 12
ground from under those who would seize any chance to

---

*a Some witnesses insert* purity and . . .       *b Or Did I take toll of
other congregations by accepting . . . ?*

put their vaunted apostleship on the same level as ours.
13 Such men are sham-apostles, crooked in all their practices,
14 masquerading as apostles of Christ. There is nothing surprising about that; Satan himself masquerades as an
15 angel of light. It is therefore a simple thing for his agents to masquerade as agents of good. But they will meet the end their deeds deserve.

16 I repeat: let no one take me for a fool; but if you must, then give me the privilege of a fool, and let me have my
17 little boast like others. I am not speaking here as a
18 Christian, but like a fool, if it comes to bragging. So many people brag of their earthly distinctions that I shall do so
19 too. How gladly you bear with fools, being yourselves so
20 wise! If a man tyrannizes over you, exploits you, gets you in his clutches, puts on airs, and hits you in the face, you
21 put up with it. And we, you say, have been weak! I admit the reproach.

But if there is to be bravado (and here I speak as a fool),
22 I can indulge in it too. Are they Hebrews? So am I. Is-
23 raelites? So am I. Abraham's descendants? So am I. Are they servants of Christ? I am mad to speak like this, but I can outdo them. More overworked than they, scourged more severely, more often imprisoned, many a time face
24 to face with death. Five times the Jews have given me the
25 thirty-nine strokes; three times I have been beaten with rods; once I was stoned; three times I have been shipwrecked, and for twenty-four hours I was adrift on the
26 open sea. I have been constantly on the road; I have met dangers from rivers, dangers from robbers, dangers from my fellow-countrymen, dangers from foreigners, dangers in towns, dangers in the country, dangers at sea, dangers
27 from false friends. I have toiled and drudged, I have often gone without sleep; hungry and thirsty, I have often gone fasting; and I have suffered from cold and exposure.

28 Apart from these external things,[a] there is the responsibility that weighs on me every day, my anxious concern
29 for all our congregations. If anyone is weak, do I not share his weakness? If anyone is made to stumble, does my heart
30 not blaze with indignation? If boasting there must be, I
31 will boast of the things that show up my weakness. The God and Father of the Lord Jesus (blessed be his name
32 for ever!) knows that what I say is true. When I was in Damascus, the commissioner of King Aretas kept the city
33 under observation so as to have me arrested; and I was

[a] Or Apart from things which I omit.

let down in a basket, through a window in the wall, and so escaped his clutches.

I AM OBLIGED TO BOAST. It does no good; but I shall 12 go on to tell of visions and revelations granted by the Lord. I know a Christian man who fourteen years ago 2 (whether in the body or out of it, I do not know—God knows) was caught up as far as the third heaven. And I 3 know that this same man (whether in the body or out of it, I do not know—God knows) was caught up into paradise, 4 and heard words so secret that human lips may not repeat them. About such a man as that I am ready to boast; but 5 I will not boast on my own account, except of my weaknesses. If I should choose to boast, it would not be the 6 boast of a fool, for I should be speaking the truth. But I refrain, because I should not like anyone to form an estimate of me which goes beyond the evidence of his own eyes and ears. And so, to keep me from being unduly 7 elated by the magnificence of such revelations, I was given[a] a sharp physical pain[b] which came as Satan's messenger to bruise me; this was to save me from being unduly elated. Three times I begged the Lord to rid me of it, but his 8 9 answer was: 'My grace is all you need; power comes to its full strength in weakness.' I shall therefore prefer to find my joy and pride in the very things that are my weakness; and then the power of Christ will come and rest upon me. Hence I am well content, for Christ's sake, with weakness, 10 contempt, persecution, hardship, and frustration; for when I am weak, then I am strong.

I AM BEING VERY FOOLISH, but it was you who drove 11 me to it; my credentials should have come from you. In no respect did I fall short of these superlative apostles, even if I am a nobody. The marks of a true apostle were there, 12 in the work I did among you, which called for such constant fortitude, and was attended by signs, marvels, and miracles. Is there anything in which you were treated 13 worse than the other congregations—except this, that I never sponged upon you? How unfair of me! I crave forgiveness.

---

[a] *Some witnesses read* . . . *ears, and because of the magnificence of the revelations themselves. Therefore to keep me from being unduly elated I was given* . . .    [b] *Or a painful wound to my pride (literally a stake, or thorn, for the flesh).*

14 Here am I preparing to pay you a third visit; and I am not going to sponge upon you. It is you I want, not your money; parents should make provision for their children, 15 not children for their parents. As for me, I will gladly spend what I have for you—yes, and spend myself to the limit. If I love you overmuch, am I to be loved the less? 16 But, granted that I did not prove a burden to you, still I was unscrupulous enough, you say, to use a trick to catch 17 you. Who, of the men I have sent to you, was used by me 18 to defraud you? I begged Titus to visit you, and I sent our friend with him. Did Titus defraud you? Have we not both been guided by the same Spirit, and followed the same course?

19 Perhaps you think that all this time we have been addressing our defence to you. No; we are speaking in God's sight, and as Christian men. Our whole aim, my own dear 20 people, is to build you up. I fear that when I come I may perhaps find you different from what I wish you to be, and that you may find me also different from what you wish. I fear I may find quarrelling and jealousy, angry tempers and personal rivalries, backbiting and gossip, 21 arrogance and general disorder. I am afraid that, when I come again, my God may humiliate me in your presence, that I may have tears to shed over many of those who have sinned in the past and have not repented of their unclean lives, their fornication and sensuality.

13 This will be my third visit to you; and all facts must be 2 established by the evidence of two or three witnesses. To those who have sinned in the past, and to everyone else, I repeat the warning I gave before; I gave it in person on my second visit, and I give it now in absence. It is that when 3 I come this time, I will show no leniency. Then you will have the proof you seek of the Christ who speaks through me, the Christ who, far from being weak with you, makes 4 his power felt among you. True, he died on the cross in weakness, but he lives by the power of God; and we who share his weakness shall by the power of God live with him in your service.

5 Examine yourselves: are you living the life of faith? Put yourselves to the test. Surely you recognize that Jesus Christ is among you?—unless of course you prove unequal 6 to the test. I hope you will come to see that we are not 7 unequal to it. Our prayer to God is that you may do no wrong; we are not concerned to be vindicated ourselves; we want you to do what is right, even if we should seem to

be discredited. For we have no power to act against the 8
truth, but only for it. We are well content to be weak at 9
any time if only you are strong. Indeed, my whole prayer
is that all may be put right with you. My purpose in 10
writing this letter before I come, is to spare myself, when
I come, any sharp exercise of authority—authority which
the Lord gave me for building up and not for pulling down.

And now, my friends, farewell. Mend your ways; take 11
our appeal to heart; agree with one another; live in peace;
and the God of love and peace will be with you. Greet one 12
another with the kiss of peace. All God's people send you 13
greetings.

The grace of the Lord Jesus Christ, and the love of God, 14
and fellowship in the Holy Spirit, be with you all.

# THE
# LETTER OF PAUL
# TO THE
# GALATIANS

## FAITH AND FREEDOM

FROM PAUL, AN APOSTLE, not by human appointment or human commission, but by commission from Jesus Christ and from God the Father who raised
2 him from the dead. I and the group of friends now with me send greetings to the Christian congregations of Galatia.

3 Grace and peace to you from God the Father and our
4 Lord Jesus Christ,[a] who sacrificed himself for our sins, to rescue us out of this present age of wickedness, as our God
5 and Father willed; to whom be glory for ever and ever. Amen.

6 I am astonished to find you turning so quickly away from him who called you by grace,[b] and following a differ-
7 ent gospel. Not that it is in fact another gospel; only there are persons who unsettle your minds by trying to
8 distort the gospel of Christ. But if anyone, if we ourselves or an angel from heaven, should preach a gospel at variance with the gospel we preached to you, he shall be held out-
9 cast. I now repeat what I have said before: if anyone preaches a gospel at variance with the gospel which you received, let him be outcast!

10 Does my language now sound as if I were canvassing for men's support? Whose support do I want but God's alone? Do you think I am currying favour with men? If I still sought men's favour, I should be no servant of Christ.

11 I must make it clear to you, my friends, that the gospel
12 you heard me preach is no human invention. I did not take

[a] *Some witnesses read* God our Father and the Lord Jesus Christ.
[b] *Some witnesses read* from Christ who called you by grace, *or* from him who called you by grace of Christ.

316

it over from any man; no man taught it me; I received it through a revelation of Jesus Christ.

You have heard what my manner of life was when I was 13 still a practising Jew: how savagely I persecuted the church of God, and tried to destroy it; and how in the 14 practice of our national religion I was outstripping many of my Jewish contemporaries in my boundless devotion to the traditions of my ancestors. But then in his good 15 pleasure God, who had set me apart from birth and called me through his grace, chose to reveal his Son to me and 16 through me, in order that I might proclaim him among the Gentiles. When that happened, without consulting any human being, without going up to Jerusalem to see those 17 who were apostles before me, I went off at once to Arabia, and afterwards returned to Damascus.

Three years later I did go up to Jerusalem to get to know 18 Cephas. I stayed with him for a fortnight, without seeing 19 any other of the apostles, except*ᵃ* James the Lord's brother. What I write is plain truth; before God I am not lying.    20

Next I went to the regions of Syria and Cilicia, and 21 22 remained unknown by sight*ᵇ* to Christ's congregations in Judaea. They only heard it said, 'Our former persecutor is 23 preaching the good news of the faith which once he tried to destroy'; and they praised God for me.    24

Next, fourteen years later, I went again*ᶜ* to Jerusalem 2 with Barnabas, taking Titus with us. I went up because it 2 had been revealed by God that I should do so. I laid before them—but at a private interview with the men of repute— the gospel which I am accustomed to preach to the Gentiles, to make sure that the race I had run, and was running, should not be run in vain. Yet even my companion 3 Titus, Greek though he is, was not compelled to be circumcised. That course was urged only as a concession to certain*ᵈ* 4 sham-Christians, interlopers who had stolen in to spy upon the liberty we enjoy in the fellowship of Christ Jesus. These men wanted to bring us into bondage, but not for 5 one moment did I yield to their dictation; I was determined that the full truth of the Gospel should be maintained for you.*ᵉ*

---

*ᵃ Or but only.*     *ᵇ Or unknown personally.*     *ᶜ Some witnesses omit again.*     *ᵈ Or The question was later raised because of certain . . .*
*ᵉ Or, following the reading of some witnesses, Yet even . . . is, was under no absolute compulsion to be circumcised, but for the sake of certain . . . of Christ Jesus, with the intention of bringing us into bondage, I yielded to their demand for the moment, to ensure that gospel truth should not be prevented from reaching you.*

6    But as for the men of high reputation (not that their
importance matters to me: God does not recognize these
personal distinctions)—these men of repute, I say, did not
7  prolong the consultation,[a] but on the contrary acknowledged that I had been entrusted with the Gospel for
Gentiles as surely as Peter had been entrusted with the
8  Gospel for Jews. For God whose action made Peter an
apostle to the Jews, also made me an apostle to the
Gentiles.

9    Recognizing, then, the favour thus bestowed upon me,
those reputed pillars of our society, James, Cephas, and
John, accepted Barnabas and myself as partners, and
shook hands upon it, agreeing that we should go to the
10  Gentiles while they went to the Jews. All they asked was
that we should keep their poor in mind, which was the
very thing I made[b] it my business to do.

11    But when Cephas came to Antioch, I opposed him to his
12  face, because he was clearly in the wrong. For until certain
persons[c] came from James he was taking his meals with
gentile Christians; but when they[d] came he drew back and
began to hold aloof, because he was afraid of the advocates
13  of circumcision. The other Jewish Christians showed the
same lack of principle; even Barnabas was carried away
14  and played false like the rest. But when I saw that their
conduct did not square with[e] the truth of the Gospel, I
said to Cephas, before the whole congregation, 'If you, a
Jew born and bred, live like a Gentile, and not like a Jew,
how can you insist that Gentiles must live like Jews?'

15    We ourselves are Jews by birth, not Gentiles and sinners.
16  But we know that no man is ever justified by doing what
the law demands, but only through faith in Christ Jesus;
so we too have put our faith in Jesus Christ, in order that
we might be justified through this faith, and not through
deeds dictated by law; for by such deeds, Scripture says,
no mortal man shall be justified.

17    If now, in seeking to be justified in Christ, we ourselves
no less than the Gentiles turn out to be sinners against the
law,[f] does that mean that Christ is an abettor of sin? No,
18  never! No, if I start building up again a system which I
have pulled down, then it is that I show myself up as a
19  transgressor of the law. For through the law I died to law—

[a] *Or* gave me no further instructions.      [b] *Or* had made, *or* have
made.        [c] *Some witnesses read* a certain person.      [d] *Some
witnesses read* he.      [e] *Or* I saw that they were not making progress
towards . . .      [f] *Or* no less than the Gentiles have accepted the
position of sinners against the law.

to live for God. I have been crucified with Christ: the life 20
I now live is not my life, but the life which Christ lives in
me; and my present bodily life is lived by faith in the Son
of God, who loved me and gave himself up for me. I will 21
not nullify the grace of God; if righteousness comes by law,
then Christ died for nothing.

You stupid galatians! You must have been be- 3
witched—you before whose eyes Jesus Christ was openly
displayed upon his cross! Answer me one question: did you 2
receive the Spirit by keeping the law or by believing the
gospel message[a]? Can it be that you are so stupid? You 3
started with the spiritual; do you now look to the material
to make you perfect? Have all your great experiences been 4
in vain—if vain indeed they should be? I ask then: when 5
God gives you the Spirit and works miracles among you,
why is this? Is it because you keep the law, or is it because
you have faith in the gospel message? Look at Abraham: he 6
put his faith in God, and that faith was counted to him as
righteousness.

You may take it, then, that it is the men of faith who are 7
Abraham's sons. And Scripture, foreseeing that God would 8
justify the Gentiles through faith, declared the Gospel to
Abraham beforehand: 'In you all nations shall find blessing.' Thus it is the men of faith who share the blessing 9
with faithful Abraham.

On the other hand those who rely on obedience to the 10
law are under a curse; for Scripture says, 'A curse is on all
who do not persevere in doing everything that is written
in the Book of the Law.' It is evident that no one is ever 11
justified before God in terms of law; because we read, 'he
shall gain life who is justified through faith'. Now law is 12
not at all a matter of having faith: we read, 'he who does
this shall gain life by what he does'.

Christ bought us freedom from the curse of the law by 13
becoming for our sake an accursed thing; for Scripture
says, 'A curse is on everyone who is hanged on a gibbet.'
And the purpose of it all was that the blessing of Abraham 14
should in Jesus Christ be extended to the Gentiles, so that
we might receive the promised Spirit through faith.

My brothers, let me give you an illustration. Even in 15
ordinary life, when a man's will and testament has been
duly executed, no one else can set it aside or add a codicil.
Now the promises were pronounced to Abraham and to 16

[a] *Or* or by the message of faith, *or* or by hearing and believing.

his 'issue'. It does not say 'issues' in the plural, but in the singular, 'and to your issue'; and the 'issue' intended is
17 Christ. What I am saying is this: a testament, or covenant, had already been validated by God; it cannot be invalidated, and its promises rendered ineffective, by a law made
18 four hundred and thirty years later. If the inheritance is by legal right, then it is not by promise; but it was by promise that God bestowed it as a free gift on Abraham.

19     Then what of the law? It was added to make wrong-doing a legal offence.[a] It was a temporary measure pending the arrival of the 'issue' to whom the promise was made. It was promulgated through angels, and there was an
20 intermediary; but an intermediary is not needed for one party acting alone, and God is one.

21     Does the law, then, contradict the promises? No, never! If a law had been given which had power to bestow life, then indeed righteousness would have come from keeping
22 the law. But Scripture has declared the whole world to be prisoners in subjection to sin, so that faith in Jesus Christ may be the ground on which the promised blessing is given, and given to those who have such faith.

23     Before this faith came, we were close prisoners in the
24 custody of law, pending the revelation of faith. Thus the law was a kind of tutor in charge of us until Christ should
25 come,[b] when we should be justified through faith; and now that faith has come, the tutor's charge is at an end.

26     For through faith you are all sons of God in union with
27 Christ Jesus. Baptized into union with him, you have all
28 put on Christ as a garment. There is no such thing as Jew and Greek, slave and freeman, male and female; for you
29 are all one person in Christ Jesus. But if you thus belong to Christ, you are the 'issue' of Abraham, and so heirs by promise.

4     This is what I mean: so long as the heir is a minor, he is no better off than a slave, even though the whole estate is
2 his; he is under guardians and trustees until the date fixed
3 by his father. And so it was with us. During our minority
4 we were slaves to the elemental spirits of the universe,[c] but when the term was completed, God sent his own Son, born
5 of a woman, born under the law, to purchase freedom for the subjects of the law, in order that we might attain the status of sons.

---

[a] *Or* added because of offences.      [b] *Or* a kind of tutor to conduct us to Christ.      [c] *Or* the elements of the natural world, *or* elementary ideas belonging to this world.

To prove that you are sons, God has sent into our hearts 6 the Spirit of his Son, crying 'Abba! Father!' You are there- 7 fore no longer a slave but a son, and if a son, then also by God's own act an heir.

Formerly, when you did not acknowledge God, you were 8 the slaves of beings which in their nature are no gods.*ᵃ* But now that you do acknowledge God—or rather, now 9 that he has acknowledged you—how can you turn back to the mean and beggarly spirits of the elements?*ᵇ* Why do you propose to enter their service all over again? You keep 10 special days and months and seasons and years. You make 11 me fear that all the pains I spent on you may prove to be labour lost.

P UT YOURSELVES in my place, my brothers, I beg you, 12 for I have put myself in yours. It is not that you did me any wrong. As you know, it was bodily illness that ori- 13 ginally*ᶜ* led to my bringing you the Gospel, and you resisted 14 any temptation to show scorn or disgust at the state of my poor body;*ᵈ* you welcomed me as if I were an angel of God, as you might have welcomed Christ Jesus himself. Have 15 you forgotten how happy you thought yourselves in having me with you? I can say this for you: you would have torn out your very eyes, and given them to me, had that been possible! And have I now made myself your enemy by 16 being frank with you?

The persons I have referred to are envious of you, but 17 not with an honest envy:*ᵉ* what they really want is to bar the door to you so that you may come to envy*ᶠ* them. It is 18 always a fine thing to deserve an honest envy*ᵍ*—always, and not only when I am present with you, dear children. 19 For my children you are, and I am in travail with you over again until you take the shape of Christ. I wish I could be 20 with you now; then I could modify my tone;*ʰ* as it is, I am at my wits' end about you.

T ELL ME NOW, you who are so anxious to be under law, 21 will you not listen to what the Law says? It is written 22 there that Abraham had two sons, one by his slave and the other by his free-born wife. The slave-woman's son was 23

---

*ᵃ Or* were slaves to 'gods' which in reality do not exist.          *ᵇ See note on 4. 3.*          *ᶜ Or* formerly, *or* on the first of my two visits. *ᵈ Or* you showed neither scorn nor disgust at the trial my poor body was enduring.          *ᵉ Or* paying court to you, but not with honest intentions.          *ᶠ Or* pay court to.          *ᵍ Or* to be honourably wooed. *ʰ Or* now, and could exchange words with you.

321

born in the course of nature, the free woman's through
24 God's promise. This is an allegory. The two women stand
for two covenants. The one bearing children into slavery
is the covenant that comes from Mount Sinai: that is Hagar.
25 Sinai is a mountain in Arabia and it represents the Jerusalem of today, for she and her children are in slavery.
26 But the heavenly Jerusalem is the free woman; she is our
27 mother. For Scripture says, 'Rejoice, O barren woman
who never bore child; break into a shout of joy, you who
never knew a mother's pangs; for the deserted wife shall
have more children than she who lives with the husband.'
28 And you, my brothers, like Isaac, are children of God's
29 promise. But just as in those days the natural-born son
30 persecuted the spiritual son, so it is today. But what does
Scripture say? 'Drive out the slave-woman and her son,
for the son of the slave shall not share the inheritance with
31 the free woman's son.' You see, then, my brothers, we are
no slave-woman's children; our mother is the free woman.
5 Christ set us free, to be free men.[a] Stand firm, then, and
refuse to be tied to the yoke of slavery again.
2 Mark my words: I, Paul, say to you that if you receive
3 circumcision Christ will do you no good at all. Once again,
you can take it from me that every man who receives
circumcision is under obligation to keep the entire law.
4 When you seek to be justified by way of law, your relation
with Christ is completely severed: you have fallen out of
5 the domain of God's grace. For to us, our hope of attaining
that righteousness which we eagerly await is the work of
6 the Spirit through faith. If we are in union with Christ
Jesus circumcision makes no difference at all, nor does the
want of it; the only thing that counts is faith active in
love.[b]
7 You were running well; who was it hindered you from
8 following the truth? Whatever persuasion he used, it did
9 not come from God who is calling you; 'a little leaven',
10 remember, 'leavens all the dough'. United with you in the
Lord, I am confident that you will not take the wrong
view; but the man who is unsettling your minds, whoever
11 he may be, must bear God's judgement. And I, my friends,
if I am still advocating circumcision, why is it I am still
persecuted? In that case, my preaching of the cross is a
12 stumbling-block no more. As for these agitators, they had
better go the whole way and make eunuchs of themselves!

[a] *Or* What Christ has done is to set us free.    [b] *Or* inspired by love.

You, MY FRIENDS, were called to be free men; only do 13
not turn your freedom into licence for your lower nature,
but be servants to one another in love. For the whole law 14
can be summed up in a single commandment: 'Love your
neighbour as yourself.' But if you go on fighting one an- 15
other, tooth and nail, all you can expect is mutual destruction.

I mean this: if you are guided by the Spirit you will not 16
fulfil the desires of your lower nature. That nature sets its 17
desires against the Spirit, while the Spirit fights against it.
They are in conflict with one another so that what you will
to do you cannot do. But if you are led by the Spirit, you 18
are not under law.

Anyone can see the kind of behaviour that belongs to 19
the lower nature: fornication, impurity, and indecency;
idolatry and sorcery; quarrels, a contentious temper, 20
envy, fits of rage, selfish ambitions, dissensions, party
intrigues, and jealousies; drinking bouts, orgies, and the 21
like. I warn you, as I warned you before, that those who
behave in such ways will never inherit the kingdom of God.

But the harvest of the Spirit is love, joy, peace, patience, 22
kindness, goodness, fidelity, gentleness, and self-control. 23
There is no law dealing with such things as these. And 24
those who belong to Christ Jesus have crucified the lower
nature with its passions and desires. If the Spirit is the 25
source of our life, let the Spirit also direct our course.

We must not be conceited, challenging one another to 26
rivalry, jealous of one another. If a man should do some- 6
thing wrong, my brothers, on a sudden impulse,[a] you who
are endowed with the Spirit must set him right again very
gently. Look to yourself, each one of you: you may be
tempted too. Help one another to carry these heavy loads, 2
and in this way you will fulfil the law of Christ.

For if a man imagines himself to be somebody, when 3
he is nothing, he is deluding himself. Each man should 4
examine his own conduct for himself; then he can measure
his achievement by comparing himself with himself and
not with anyone else. For everyone has his own proper 5
burden to bear.

When anyone is under instruction in the faith, he should 6
give his teacher a share of all good things he has.

Make no mistake about this: God is not to be fooled; a 7
man reaps what he sows. If he sows seed in the field of his 8
lower nature, he will reap from it a harvest of corruption,

[a] *Or* If a man is caught doing something wrong, my brothers, . . .

but if he sows in the field of the Spirit, the Spirit will bring
9 him a harvest of eternal life. So let us never tire of doing
good, for if we do not slacken our efforts we shall in due
10 time reap our harvest. Therefore, as opportunity offers,
let us work for the good of all, especially members of the
household of the faith.

11 You see these big letters? I am now writing to you in my
12 own hand. It is all those who want to make a fair outward
and bodily show who are trying to force circumcision upon
you; their sole object is to escape persecution for the cross
13 of Christ. For even those who do receive circumcision are
not thoroughgoing observers of the law; they only want
you to be circumcised in order to boast of your having
14 submitted to that outward rite. But God forbid that I
should boast of anything but the cross of our Lord Jesus
Christ, through which*a* the world is crucified to me and I
15 to the world! Circumcision is nothing; uncircumcision is
16 nothing; the only thing that counts is new creation! Whoever they are who take this principle for their guide, peace
and mercy be upon them, and upon the whole Israel of
God!
17 In future let no one make trouble for me, for I bear the
marks of Jesus branded on my body.
18 The grace of our Lord Jesus Christ be with your spirit,
my brothers. Amen.

*a* Or whom.

# THE
# LETTER OF PAUL
# TO THE
# EPHESIANS

## THE GLORY OF CHRIST
## IN THE CHURCH

FROM PAUL, APOSTLE of Christ Jesus, com- 1
missioned by the will of God, to God's people at
Ephesus,[a] believers incorporate in Christ Jesus.

Grace to you and peace from God our Father and the 2
Lord Jesus Christ.

Praise be to the God and Father of our Lord Jesus 3
Christ, who has bestowed on us in Christ every spiritual
blessing in the heavenly realms. In Christ he chose us 4
before the world was founded, to be dedicated, to be
without blemish in his sight, to be full of love; and he[b] 5
destined us—such was his will and pleasure—to be ac- 6
cepted as his sons through Jesus Christ, in order that the
glory of his gracious gift, so graciously bestowed on us in
his Beloved, might redound to his praise. For in Christ our 7
release is secured and our sins are forgiven through the
shedding of his blood. Therein lies the richness of God's free
grace lavished upon us, imparting full wisdom and insight. 8
He has made known to us his hidden purpose—such was 9
his will and pleasure determined beforehand in Christ—
to be put into effect when the time was ripe: namely, that 10
the universe, all in heaven and on earth, might be brought
into a unity in Christ.

In Christ indeed we have been given our share in the 11
heritage, as was decreed in his design whose purpose is
everywhere at work. For it was his will that we, who were 12
the first to set our hope on Christ,[c] should cause his glory

---

[a] *Some witnesses omit* at Ephesus.   [b] *Or . . .* sight. In his love
he . . .   [c] *Or* who already enjoyed the hope of Christ, *or* whose
expectation and hope are in Christ.

13 to be praised. And you too, when you had heard the message
of the truth, the good news of your salvation, and had
believed it, became incorporate in Christ and received the
14 seal of the promised Holy Spirit; and that Spirit is the
pledge that we shall enter upon our heritage, when God
has redeemed what is his own, to his praise and glory.

15 Because of all this, now that I have heard of the faith
you have in the Lord Jesus and of the love you bear to-
16 wards all God's people, I never cease to give thanks for
17 you when I mention you in my prayers. I pray that the
God of our Lord Jesus Christ, the all-glorious Father, may
give you the spiritual powers of wisdom and vision, by
18 which there comes the knowledge of him. I pray that your
inward eyes may be illumined, so that you may know what
is the hope to which he calls you, what the wealth and
glory of the share he offers you among his people in their
19 heritage, and how vast the resources of his power open to
us who trust in him. They are measured by his strength
20 and the might which he exerted in Christ when he raised
him from the dead, when he enthroned him at his right
21 hand in the heavenly realms, far above all government
and authority, all power and dominion, and any title of
sovereignty that can be named, not only in this age but in
22 the age to come. He put everything in subjection beneath
his feet, and appointed him as supreme head to the church,
23 which is his body and as such holds within it the fullness
of him who himself receives the entire fullness of God.[a]

2 TIME WAS when you were dead in your sins and wicked-
2 ness, when you followed the evil ways of this present age,
when you obeyed the commander of the spiritual powers
of the air, the spirit now at work among God's rebel sub-
3 jects. We too were once of their number: we all lived our
lives in sensuality, and obeyed the promptings of our own
instincts and notions. In our natural condition we, like the
4 rest, lay under the dreadful judgement of God. But God,
5 rich in mercy, for the great love he bore us, brought us to
life with Christ even when we were dead in our sins; it is
6 by his grace you are saved. And in union with Christ Jesus
he raised us up and enthroned us with him in the heavenly
7 realms, so that he might display in the ages to come how

[a] *Or* as supreme head to the church, which is his body and as such
holds within it the fullness of him who fills the universe in all its parts;
*or* as supreme head to the church which is his body, and to be all that
he himself is who fills the universe in all its parts.

immense are the resources of his grace, and how great his kindness to us in Christ Jesus. For it is by his grace you 8 are saved, through trusting him; it is not your own doing. It is God's gift, not a reward for work done. There is no- 9 thing for anyone to boast of. For we are God's handiwork, 10 created in Christ Jesus to devote ourselves to the good deeds for which God has designed us.

Remember then your former condition: you, Gentiles as 11 you are outwardly,*ª* you, 'the uncircumcised' so called by those who are called 'the circumcised' (but only with reference to an outward rite)—you were at that time 12 separate from Christ, strangers to the community of Israel, outside God's covenants and the promise that goes with them. Your world was a world without hope and without God. But now in union with Christ Jesus you who once 13 were far off have been brought near through the shedding of Christ's blood. For he is himself our peace. Gentiles and 14 Jews, he has made the two one, and in his own body of flesh and blood has broken down the enmity which stood like a dividing wall between them; for he annulled the law 15 with its rules and regulations, so as to create out of the two a single new humanity in himself, thereby making peace. This was his purpose, to reconcile the two in a single body 16 to God through the cross, on which he killed the enmity.*ᵇ*

So he came and proclaimed the good news: peace to you 17 who were far off, and peace to those who were near by; for through him we both alike have access to the Father 18 in the one Spirit. Thus you are no longer aliens in a foreign 19 land, but fellow-citizens with God's people, members of God's household. You are built upon the foundation laid 20 by the apostles and prophets, and Christ Jesus himself is the foundation-stone.*ᶜ* In him the whole building*ᵈ* is 21 bonded together and grows into a holy temple in the Lord. In him you too are being built with all the rest into a 22 spiritual dwelling for God.

WITH THIS IN MIND I make my prayer, I, Paul, who 3 in the cause of you Gentiles am now the prisoner of Christ Jesus—for surely you have heard how God has assigned the 2 gift of his grace to me for your benefit. It was by a revela- 3 tion that his secret was made known to me. I have already

---

*ª* Or by birth.   *ᵇ* Or . . . cross. Thus in his own person he put the enmity to death.   *ᶜ* Or built upon the foundation of the apostles and prophets, and Christ Jesus himself is the keystone.   *ᵈ* Or every structure.

4 written a brief account of this, and by reading it you may
5 perceive that I understand the secret of Christ. In former
generations this was not disclosed to the human race; but
now it has been revealed by inspiration to his dedicated
6 apostles and prophets, that through the Gospel the Gentiles
are joint heirs with the Jews, part of the same body,
7 sharers together in the promise made in Christ Jesus. Such
is the gospel of which I was made a minister, by God's gift,
bestowed unmerited on me in the working of his power.
8 To me, who am less than the least of all God's people, he
has granted of his grace the privilege of proclaiming to the
Gentiles the good news of the unfathomable riches of
9 Christ, and of bringing to light how this hidden purpose
was to be put into effect. It was hidden for long ages in
10 God the creator of the universe, in order that now, through
the church, the wisdom of God in all its varied forms might
be made known to the rulers and authorities in the realms
11 of heaven. This is in accord with his age-long purpose,
12 which he achieved in Christ Jesus our Lord. In him we
have access to God with freedom, in the confidence born
13 of trust in him. I beg you, then, not to lose heart over my
sufferings for you; indeed, they are your glory.
14    With this in mind, then, I kneel in prayer to the Father,
15 from whom every family[a] in heaven and on earth takes its
16 name, that out of the treasures of his glory he may grant
you strength and power through his Spirit in your inner
17 being, that through faith Christ may dwell in your hearts
18 in love. With deep roots and firm foundations, may you be
strong to grasp, with all God's people, what is the breadth
19 and length and height and depth of the love of Christ, and
to know it, though it is beyond knowledge. So may you
attain to fullness of being, the fullness of God himself.[b]
20    Now to him who is able to do immeasurably more than
all we can ask or conceive, by the power which is at work
21 among us, to him be glory in the church and in Christ Jesus
from generation to generation evermore! Amen.

4 I ENTREAT YOU, THEN—I, a prisoner for the Lord's
2 sake: as God has called you, live up to your calling. Be
humble always and gentle, and patient too. Be forbearing
3 with one another and charitable. Spare no effort to make
fast with bonds of peace the unity which the Spirit gives.
4 There is one body and one Spirit, as there is also one hope
5 held out in God's call to you; one Lord, one faith, one

    [a] Or his whole family.        [b] Or the fullness which God requires.

baptism; one God and Father of all, who is over all and 6
through all and in all.

But each of us has been given his gift, his due portion of 7
Christ's bounty. Therefore Scripture says: 8

> 'He ascended into the heights
> with captives in his train;
> he gave gifts to men.'

Now, the word 'ascended' implies that he also descended 9
to the lowest level, down to the very earth.[a] He who de- 10
scended is no other than he who ascended far above all
heavens, so that he might fill the universe. And these were 11
his gifts: some to be apostles, some prophets, some
evangelists, some pastors and teachers, to equip God's 12
people for work in his service, to the building up of the
body of Christ. So shall we all at last attain to the unity 13
inherent in our faith and our knowledge of the Son of God
—to mature manhood, measured by nothing less than the
full stature of Christ. We are no longer to be children, 14
tossed by the waves and whirled about by every fresh gust
of teaching, dupes of crafty rogues and their deceitful
schemes. No, let us speak the truth in love; so shall we 15
fully grow up into Christ. He is the head, and on him the 16
whole body depends. Bonded and knit together by every
constituent joint, the whole frame grows through the due
activity of each part, and builds itself up in love.

This then is my word to you, and I urge it upon you in 17
the Lord's name. Give up living like pagans with their
good-for-nothing notions. Their wits are beclouded, they 18
are strangers to the life that is in God, because ignorance
prevails among them and their minds have grown hard as
stone. Dead to all feeling, they have abandoned them- 19
selves to vice, and stop at nothing to satisfy their foul
desires. But that is not how you learned Christ. For were 20 21
you not told of him, were you not as Christians taught the
truth as it is in Jesus?—that, leaving your former way of 22
life, you must lay aside that old human nature which,
deluded by its lusts, is sinking towards death. You must 23
be made new in mind and spirit, and put on the new nature 24
of God's creating, which shows itself in the just and devout
life called for by the truth.

Then throw off falsehood; speak the truth to each other, 25
for all of us are the parts of one body.

If you are angry, do not let anger lead you into sin; do 26

_____
[a] *Or* descended to the regions beneath the earth.

27 not let sunset find you still nursing it; leave no loop-hole for the devil.

28 The thief must give up stealing, and instead work hard and honestly with his own hands, so that he may have something to share with the needy.

29 No bad language must pass your lips, but only what is good and helpful to the occasion, so that it brings a blessing
30 to those who hear it. And do not grieve the Holy Spirit of God, for that Spirit is the seal with which you were marked
31 for the day of our final liberation. Have done with spite and passion, all angry shouting and cursing, and bad feeling of every kind.

32 Be generous to one another, tender-hearted, forgiving one another as God in Christ forgave you.

5 In a word, as God's dear children, try to be like him,
2 and live in love as Christ loved you, and gave himself up on your behalf as an offering and sacrifice whose fragrance is pleasing to God.

3 Fornication and indecency of any kind, or ruthless greed, must not be so much as mentioned among you, as
4 befits the people of God. No coarse, stupid, or flippant talk; these things are out of place; you should rather be
5 thanking God. For be very sure of this: no one given to fornication or indecency, or the greed which makes an idol of gain, has any share in the kingdom of Christ and of God.

6 Let no one deceive you with shallow arguments; it is for all these things that God's dreadful judgement is com-
7 ing upon his rebel subjects. Have no part or lot with them.
8 For though you were once all darkness, now as Christians you are light. Live like men who are at home in daylight,
9 for where light is, there all goodness springs up, all justice
10 and truth. Try to find out what would please the Lord;
11 take no part in the barren deeds of darkness, but show them
12 up for what they are. The things they do in secret it would
13 be shameful even to mention. But everything, when once the light has shown it up, is illumined, and everything thus
14 illumined is all light. And so the hymn says:

> 'Awake, sleeper,
> rise from the dead,
> and Christ will shine upon you.'

15 Be most careful then how you conduct yourselves: like
16 sensible men, not like simpletons. Use the present oppor-
17 tunity to the full, for these are evil days. So do not be fools,

but try to understand what the will of the Lord is. Do not 18
give way to drunkenness and the dissipation that goes
with it, but let the Holy Spirit fill you: speak to one an- 19
other in psalms, hymns, and[a] songs; sing and make music
in your hearts to the Lord; and in the name of our Lord 20
Jesus Christ give thanks every day for everything to our
God and Father.

Be subject to one another out of reverence for Christ. 21

Wives, be subject to your husbands as to the Lord; for 22 23
the man is the head of the woman, just as Christ also is the
head of the church. Christ is, indeed, the Saviour of the
body; but just as the church is subject to Christ, so must 24
women be to their husbands in everything.

Husbands, love your wives, as Christ also loved the 25
church and gave himself up for it, to consecrate it, cleansing 26
it by water and word, so that he might present the church 27
to himself all glorious, with no stain or wrinkle or anything
of the sort, but holy and without blemish. In the same 28
way men also are bound to love their wives, as they love
their own bodies. In loving his wife a man loves himself.
For no one ever hated his own body: on the contrary, he 29
provides and cares for it; and that is how Christ treats the
church, because it is his body, of which we are living parts. 30
Thus it is that (in the words of Scripture) 'a man shall 31
leave his father and mother and shall be joined to his wife,
and the two shall become one flesh'. It is a great truth that 32
is hidden here. I for my part refer it to Christ and to the
church, but it applies also individually: each of you must 33
love his wife as his very self; and the woman must see to it
that she pays her husband all respect.

Children, obey your parents, for it is right that you 6
should. 'Honour your father and mother' is the first com- 2
mandment with a promise attached, in the words: 'that it 3
may be well with you and that you may live long in the
land'.

You fathers, again, must not goad your children to re- 4
sentment, but give them the instruction, and the correction, which belong to a Christian upbringing.

Slaves, obey your earthly masters with fear and trem- 5
bling, single-mindedly, as serving Christ. Do not offer 6
merely the outward show of service, to curry favour with
men, but, as slaves of Christ, do whole-heartedly the will
of God. Give the cheerful service of those who serve the 7
Lord, not men. For you know that whatever good each 8

[a] *Some witnesses insert* spiritual, *as in Colossians 3. 16.*

man may do, slave or free, will be repaid him by the Lord.

9 You masters, also, must do the same by them. Give up using threats; remember you both have the same Master in heaven, and he has no favourites.

10 Finally then, find your strength in the Lord, in his
11 mighty power. Put on all the armour which God provides, so that you may be able to stand firm against the devices
12 of the devil. For our fight is not against human foes, but against cosmic powers, against the authorities and potentates of this dark world, against the superhuman
13 forces of evil in the heavens. Therefore, take up God's armour; then you will be able to stand your ground when things are at their worst, to complete every task and still
14 to stand. Stand firm, I say. Fasten on the belt of truth;
15 for coat of mail put on integrity; let the shoes on your feet
16 be the gospel of peace, to give you firm footing; and, with all these, take up the great shield of faith, with which you will be able to quench all the flaming arrows of the evil one.
17 Take salvation for helmet; for sword, take that which the
18 Spirit gives you—the words that come from God. Give yourselves wholly to prayer and entreaty; pray on every occasion in the power of the Spirit. To this end keep watch and persevere, always interceding for all God's people; and
19 pray for me, that I may be granted the right words when I open my mouth, and may boldly and freely make
20 known his hidden purpose, for which I am an ambassador —in chains. Pray that I may speak of it boldly, as it is my duty to speak.

21 You will want to know about my affairs, and how I am; Tychicus will give you all the news. He is our dear brother
22 and trustworthy helper in the Lord's work. I am sending him to you on purpose to let you know all about us, and to put fresh heart into you.

23 Peace to the brotherhood and love, with faith, from
24 God the Father and the Lord Jesus Christ. God's grace be with all who love our Lord Jesus Christ, grace and immortality.[a]

    [a] *Or* who love . . . Christ with love imperishable.

# THE
# LETTER OF PAUL
# TO THE
# PHILIPPIANS

## THE APOSTLE AND HIS FRIENDS

FROM PAUL AND TIMOTHY, servants of Christ 1
Jesus, to all those of God's people, incorporate in
Christ Jesus, who live at Philippi, including their
bishops and deacons.

Grace to you and peace from God our Father and the 2
Lord Jesus Christ.

I thank my God whenever I think of you; and when I 3 4
pray for you all, my prayers are always joyful, because of 5
the part you have taken in the work of the Gospel from
the first day until now. Of one thing I am certain: the One 6
who started the good work in you will bring it to completion by the Day of Christ Jesus. It is indeed only right that 7
I should feel like this about you all, because you hold me
in such affection, and because, when I lie in prison or
appear in the dock to vouch for the truth of the Gospel,
you all share in the privilege that is mine.[a] God knows 8
how I long for you all, with the deep yearning of Christ
Jesus himself. And this is my prayer, that your love may 9
grow ever richer and richer in knowledge and insight of
every kind, and may thus bring you the gift of true dis- 10
crimination.[b] Then on the Day of Christ you will be flawless
and without blame, reaping the full harvest of righteous- 11
ness that comes through Jesus Christ, to the glory and praise
of God.

Friends, I want you to understand that the work of the 12
Gospel has been helped on, rather than hindered, by this
business of mine. My imprisonment in Christ's cause has 13

[a] Or I am justified in taking this view about you all, because I hold
you in closest union, as those who, when I lie . . . of the Gospel, all
share in the privilege that is mine.       [b] Or may teach you by
experience what things are most worth while.

become common knowledge to all at headquarters[a] here,
14 and indeed among the public at large; and it has given
confidence to most of our fellow-Christians to speak the
word of God fearlessly and with extraordinary courage.

15    Some, indeed, proclaim Christ in a jealous and quarrel-
16 some spirit; others proclaim him in true goodwill, and
these are moved by love for me; they know that it is to
17 defend the Gospel that I am where I am. But the others,
moved by personal rivalry, present Christ from mixed
motives, meaning to stir up fresh trouble for me as I lie in
18 prison.[b] What does it matter? One way or another, in pretence or sincerity, Christ is set forth, and for that I rejoice.

19    Yes, and rejoice I will, knowing well that the issue of it all
will be my deliverance, because you are praying for me
and the Spirit of Jesus Christ is given me for support.[c]
20 For, as I passionately hope, I shall have no cause to be
ashamed, but shall speak so boldly that now as always the
greatness of Christ will shine out clearly in my person,
21 whether through my life or through my death. For to me
22 life is Christ, and death gain; but what if my living on in
the body may serve some good purpose? Which then am
23 I to choose? I cannot tell. I am torn two ways: what I
should like is to depart and be with Christ; that is better
24 by far; but for your sake there is greater need for me to
25 stay on in the body. This indeed I know for certain: I shall
stay, and stand by you all to help you forward and to add
26 joy to your faith, so that when I am with you again, your
pride in me may be unbounded in Christ Jesus.

27    Only, let your conduct be worthy of the gospel of Christ,
so that whether I come and see you for myself or hear about
you from a distance, I may know that you are standing
firm, one in spirit, one in mind, contending as one man for
28 the gospel faith, meeting your opponents without so much
as a tremor. This is a sure sign to them that their doom is
sealed, but a sign of your salvation, and one afforded by
29 God himself; for you have been granted the privilege not
only of believing in Christ but also of suffering for him.
30 You and I are engaged in the same contest; you saw me
in it once, and, as you hear, I am in it still.

2    IF THEN our common life in Christ yields anything to
stir the heart, any loving consolation, any sharing of the

---

[a] *Or* to all the imperial guard, *or* to all at the Residency (*Greek* Praetorium).    [b] *Or* meaning to make use of my imprisonment to stir
up fresh trouble.    [c] *Or* supplies me with all I need.

Spirit, any warmth of affection or compassion, fill up my **2**
cup of happiness by thinking and feeling alike, with the
same love for one another, the same turn of mind, and a
common care for unity. There must be no room for rivalry **3**
and personal vanity among you, but you must humbly
reckon others better than yourselves. Look to each other's **4**
interest and not merely to your own.

Let your bearing towards one another arise out of your **5**
life in Christ Jesus.[a] For the divine nature was his from the **6**
first; yet he did not think to snatch at equality with God,[b]
but made himself nothing, assuming the nature of a slave. **7**
Bearing the human likeness, revealed in human shape, he **8**
humbled himself, and in obedience accepted even death—
death on a cross. Therefore God raised him to the heights **9**
and bestowed on him the name above all names, that at the **10**
name of Jesus every knee should bow—in heaven, on earth,
and in the depths—and every tongue confess, 'Jesus Christ **11**
is Lord', to the glory of God the Father.

So you too, my friends, must be obedient, as always; **12**
even more, now that I am away, than when I was with
you. You must work out your own salvation in fear and
trembling; for it is God who works in you, inspiring both **13**
the will and the deed, for his own chosen purpose.

Do all you have to do without complaint or wrangling. **14**
Show yourselves guileless and above reproach, faultless **15**
children of God in a warped and crooked generation, in
which you shine[c] like stars in a dark world[d] and proffer **16**
the word of life.[e] Thus you will be my pride on the Day of
Christ, proof that I did not run my race in vain, or work
in vain. But if my life-blood is to crown that sacrifice **17**
which is the offering up of your faith, I am glad of it, and
I share my gladness with you all. Rejoice, you no less than **18**
I, and let us share our joy.

I HOPE (under the Lord Jesus) to send Timothy to you **19**
soon; it will cheer me to hear news of you. There is no one **20**
else here who sees things as I do, and takes[f] a genuine
interest in your concerns; they are all bent on their own **21**
ends, not on the cause of Christ Jesus. But Timothy's **22**
record is known to you: you know that he has been at my
side in the service of the Gospel like a son working under

[a] *Or* Have that bearing towards one another which was also found in
Christ Jesus.       [b] *Or* yet he did not prize his equality with God.
[c] *Or* . . . generation. Shine out among them . . .       [d] *Or* in the
firmament.       [e] *Or* as the very principle of its life.       [f] *Or* no
one else here like him, who takes . . .

23 his father. Timothy, then, I hope to send as soon as ever
24 I can see how things are going with me; and I am confident, under the Lord, that I shall myself be coming before long.
25     I feel also I must send our brother Epaphroditus, my
fellow-worker and comrade, whom you commissioned to
26 minister to my needs. He has been missing all of you
sadly, and has been distressed that you heard he was ill.
27 (He was indeed dangerously ill, but God was merciful to
him, and merciful no less to me, to spare me sorrow upon
28 sorrow.) For this reason I am all the more eager to send
him, to give you the happiness of seeing him again, and to
29 relieve my sorrow. Welcome him then in the fellowship of
the Lord with whole-hearted delight. You should honour
30 men like him; in Christ's cause he came near to death,
risking his life to render me the service you could not give.
3     And now, friends, farewell; I wish you joy in the Lord.

To REPEAT what I have written to you before is no
2 trouble to me, and it is a safeguard for you. Beware of
those dogs and their malpractices. Beware of those who
3 insist on mutilation—'circumcision' I will not call it; we
are the circumcised, we whose worship is spiritual,[a] whose
pride is in Christ Jesus, and who put no confidence in any-
4 thing external. Not that I am without grounds myself even
for confidence of that kind. If anyone thinks to base his
claims on externals, I could make a stronger case for my-
5 self: circumcised on my eighth day, Israelite by race, of
the tribe of Benjamin, a Hebrew born and bred;[b] in my
6 attitude to the law, a Pharisee; in pious zeal, a persecutor
7 of the church; in legal rectitude, faultless. But all such
8 assets I have written off because of Christ. I would say
more: I count everything sheer loss, because all is far out-
weighed by the gain of knowing Christ Jesus my Lord, for
whose sake I did in fact lose everything. I count it so
9 much garbage,[c] for the sake of gaining Christ and finding
myself incorporate in him, with no righteousness of my
own, no legal rectitude, but the righteousness which comes[d]
10 from faith in Christ, given by God in response to faith. All
I care for is to know Christ, to experience the power of his

---

[a] *Some witnesses read* who worship God in the spirit; *others read* who
worship by the Spirit of God.        [b] *Or* a Hebrew-speaking Jew of
a Hebrew-speaking family.        [c] *Or* dung.        [d] *Or* and in him
finding that, though I have no righteousness of my own, no legal
rectitude, I have the righteousness which comes . . .

resurrection, and to share his sufferings, in growing con-
formity with his death, if only I may finally arrive at the 11
resurrection from the dead.

It is not to be thought that I have already achieved all 12
this. I have not yet reached perfection, but I press on,
hoping to take hold of that for which Christ once took hold
of me. My friends, I do not reckon myself to have got hold 13
of it yet. All I can say is this: forgetting what is behind
me, and reaching out for that which lies ahead, I press 14
towards the goal to win the prize which is God's call to the
life above, in Christ Jesus.

Let us then keep to this way of thinking, those of us who 15
are mature. If there is any point on which you think dif-
ferently, this also God will make plain to you. Only let our 16
conduct be consistent with the level we have already
reached.

Agree together, my friends, to follow my example. You 17
have us for a model; watch those whose way of life conforms to it. For, as I have often told you, and now tell you 18
with tears in my eyes, there are many whose way of life
makes them enemies of the cross of Christ. They are 19
heading for destruction, appetite is their god, and they
glory in their shame. Their minds are set on earthly things.
We, by contrast, are citizens of heaven, and from heaven 20
we expect our deliverer to come, the Lord Jesus Christ.
He will transfigure the body belonging to our humble 21
state, and give it a form like that of his own resplendent
body, by the very power which enables him to make all
things subject to himself. Therefore, my friends, beloved 4
friends whom I long for, my joy, my crown, stand thus firm
in the Lord, my beloved!

I beg Euodia, and I beg Syntyche, to agree together 2
in the Lord's fellowship. Yes, and you too, my loyal com- 3
rade, I ask you to help these women, who shared my
struggles in the cause of the Gospel, with Clement and
my other fellow-workers, whose[a] names are in the roll of
the living.

Farewell; I wish you all joy in the Lord. I will say it 4
again; all joy be yours.

Let your magnanimity be manifest to all. 5

The Lord is near; have no anxiety, but in everything 6
make your requests known to God in prayer and petition
with thanksgiving. Then the peace of God, which is beyond 7

[a] *Some witnesses read* my fellow-workers, and the others whose . . .

our utmost understanding,[a] will keep guard over your hearts and your thoughts, in Christ Jesus.

8 And now, my friends, all that is true, all that is noble, all that is just and pure, all that is lovable and gracious,[b] whatever is excellent and admirable—fill all your thoughts with these things.

9 The lessons I taught you, the tradition I have passed on, all that you heard me say or saw me do, put into practice; and the God of peace will be with you.

10 IT IS A GREAT JOY to me, in the Lord, that after so long your care for me has now blossomed afresh. You did care about me before for that matter; it was opportunity that

11 you lacked. Not that I am alluding to want, for I have learned to find resources in myself whatever my circum-

12 stances. I know what it is to be brought low, and I know what it is to have plenty. I have been very thoroughly initiated into the human lot with all its ups and downs—

13 fullness and hunger, plenty and want. I have strength for

14 anything through him who gives me power. But it was kind of you to share the burden of my troubles.

15 As you know yourselves, Philippians, in the early days of my mission, when I set out from Macedonia, you alone of all our congregations were my partners in payments and

16 receipts; for even at Thessalonica you contributed to my

17 needs, not once but twice over. Do not think I set my heart upon the gift; all I care for is the profit accruing to

18 you. However, here I give you my receipt for everything— for more than everything; I am paid in full, now that I have received from Epaphroditus what you sent. It is a fragrant

19 offering, an acceptable sacrifice, pleasing to God. And my God will supply all your wants out of the magnificence of

20 his riches in Christ Jesus. To our God and Father be glory for endless ages! Amen.

21 Give my greetings, in the fellowship of Christ Jesus, to each one of God's people. The brothers who are now with

22 me send their greetings to you, and so do all God's people here, particularly those who belong to the imperial estab- lishment.

23 The grace of our Lord Jesus Christ be with your spirit.

[a] *Or* of far more worth than human reasoning.
[b] *Or* of good repute.

# THE
# LETTER OF PAUL
# TO THE
# COLOSSIANS

## THE CENTRE OF CHRISTIAN BELIEF

FROM PAUL, APOSTLE of Christ Jesus com- 1
missioned by the will of God, and our colleague
Timothy, to God's people at Colossae, brothers in 2
the faith, incorporate in Christ.

Grace to you and peace from God our Father.

In all our prayers to God, the Father of our Lord Jesus 3
Christ, we thank him for you, because we have heard of the 4
faith you hold in Christ Jesus, and the love you bear towards all God's people. Both spring from the hope stored 5
up for you in heaven—that hope of which you learned
when the message of the true Gospel first came to you. In 6
the same way it is coming to men the whole world over;
everywhere it is growing and bearing fruit as it does among
you, and has done since the day when you heard of the
graciousness of God and recognized it for what in truth it
is. You were taught this by Epaphras, our dear fellow- 7
servant, a trusted worker for Christ on our[a] behalf, and 8
it is he who has brought us the news of your God-given
love.[b]

For this reason, ever since the day we heard of it, we 9
have not ceased to pray for you. We ask God that you may
receive from him all wisdom and spiritual understanding
for full insight into his will, so that your manner of life may 10
be worthy of the Lord and entirely pleasing to him. We
pray that you may bear fruit in active goodness of every
kind, and grow in the knowledge of God. May he strengthen 11

---

[a] Some witnesses read your.    [b] Or your love within the fellowship of the Spirit.

you, in his glorious might, with ample power to meet what-
12 ever comes with fortitude, patience, and joy; and to give
thanks[a] to the Father who has made you fit to share the
heritage of God's people in the realm of light.

13  He rescued us from the domain of darkness and brought
14 us away into the kingdom of his dear Son, in whom our
15 release is secured and our sins forgiven. He is the image
of the invisible God; his is the primacy over[b] all created
16 things. In him everything in heaven and on earth was
created, not only things visible but also the invisible orders
of thrones, sovereignties, authorities, and powers: the
whole universe has been created through him and for him.
17 And he exists before everything, and all things are held
18 together in him. He is, moreover, the head of the body, the
church. He is its origin, the first to return from the dead,
19 to be in all things alone supreme. For in him the complete
20 being of God, by God's own choice, came to dwell. Through
him God chose to reconcile the whole universe to himself, making peace through the shedding of his blood upon
the cross—to reconcile all things, whether on earth or in
heaven, through him alone.

21  Formerly you were yourselves estranged from God; you
were his enemies in heart and mind, and your deeds were
22 evil. But now by Christ's death in his body of flesh and
blood God has reconciled you to himself, so that he may
present you before himself as dedicated men, without
23 blemish and innocent in his sight. Only you must continue
in your faith, firm on your foundations, never to be dis-
lodged from the hope offered in the gospel which you heard.
This is the gospel which has been proclaimed in the whole
creation under heaven; and I, Paul, have become its
minister.

24  It is now my happiness to suffer for you. This is my way
of helping to complete, in my poor human flesh, the full
tale of Christ's afflictions still to be endured, for the sake
25 of his body which is the church. I became its servant by
virtue of the task assigned to me by God for your benefit:
26 to deliver his message in full; to announce the secret hidden
for long ages and through many generations, but now dis-
27 closed to God's people, to whom it was his will to make
it known—to make known how rich and glorious it is
among all nations. The secret is this: Christ in[c] you, the
hope of a glory to come.

[a] *Or* with fortitude and patience, and to give joyful thanks . . .
[b] *Or* image of the invisible God, born before . . .          [c] *Or* among.

He it is whom we proclaim. We admonish everyone with- 28
out distinction, we instruct everyone in all the ways of
wisdom, so as to present each one of you as a mature
member of Christ's body. To this end I am toiling strenu- 29
ously with all the energy and power of Christ at work in
me. For I want you to know how strenuous are my exer- 2
tions for you and the Laodiceans and all who have never
set eyes on me. I want them to continue in good heart 2
and in the unity of love, and to come to the full wealth of
conviction which understanding brings, and grasp God's
secret. That secret is Christ himself; in him lie hidden all 3
God's treasures of wisdom and knowledge. I tell you this 4
to save you from being talked[a] into error by specious arguments. For though absent in body, I am with you in spirit, 5
and rejoice to see your orderly array and the firm front
which your faith in Christ presents.

THEREFORE, SINCE JESUS was delivered to you as 6
Christ and Lord, live your lives in union with him. Be 7
rooted in him; be built in him; be consolidated in the faith
you were taught;[b] let your hearts overflow with thankful-
ness. Be on your guard; do not let your minds be captured 8
by hollow and delusive speculations, based on traditions of
man-made teaching and centred on the elemental spirits
of the universe[c] and not on Christ.

For it is in Christ that the complete being of the Godhead 9
dwells embodied,[d] and in him you have been brought to 10
completion. Every power and authority in the universe is
subject to him as Head. In him also you were circumcised, 11
not in a physical sense, but by being divested of the lower
nature; this is Christ's way of circumcision. For in bap- 12
tism[e] you were buried with him, in baptism also you were
raised to life with him through your faith in the active
power of God who raised him from the dead. And although 13
you were dead because of your sins and because you were
morally uncircumcised, he has made you alive with Christ.
For he has forgiven us all our sins; he has cancelled the 14
bond which pledged us to the decrees of the law. It stood
against us, but he has set it aside, nailing it to the cross. On 15
that cross he discarded the cosmic powers and authorities

---

[a] *Or* What I mean is this: no one must talk you . . .     [b] *Or by*
your faith, as you were taught.     [c] *Or* the elements of the natural
world, *or* elementary ideas belonging to this world.     [d] *Or* cor-
porately.     [e] *Or* . . . nature, in the very circumcision of Christ
himself; for in baptism . . .

like a garment; he made a public spectacle of them and led them[a] as captives in his triumphal procession.

16 ALLOW NO ONE therefore to take you to task about what you eat or drink, or over the observance of festival, 17 new moon, or sabbath. These are no more than a shadow 18 of what was to come; the solid reality is Christ's. You are not to be disqualified by the decision of people who go in for self-mortification and angel-worship, and try to enter into some vision of their own. Such people, bursting with 19 the futile conceit of worldly minds, lose hold upon the Head; yet it is from the Head that the whole body, with all its joints and ligaments, receives its supplies, and thus knit together grows according to God's design.

20 Did you not die with Christ and pass beyond reach of the elemental spirits of the universe[b]? Then why behave as though you were still living the life of the world? Why let 21 people dictate to you: 'Do not handle this, do not taste 22 that, do not touch the other'—all of them things that must perish as soon as they are used? That is to follow merely 23 human injunctions and teaching. True, it has an air of wisdom, with its forced piety, its self-mortification, and its severity to the body; but it is of no use at all in combating sensuality.

3 Were you not raised to life with Christ? Then aspire to the realm above, where Christ is, seated at the right hand 2 of God, and let your thoughts dwell on that higher realm, 3 not on this earthly life. I repeat, you died; and now your 4 life lies hidden with Christ in God. When Christ, who is our life, is manifested, then you too will be manifested with him in glory.

5 Then put to death those parts of you which belong to the earth—fornication, indecency, lust, foul cravings, and 6 the ruthless greed which is nothing less than idolatry. Be-7 cause of these, God's dreadful judgement is impending; and in the life you once lived these are the ways you yourselves 8 followed. But now you must yourselves lay aside all anger, passion, malice, cursing, filthy talk—have done with them! 9 Stop lying to one another, now that you have discarded the 10 old nature with its deeds and have put on the new nature,

---

[a] *Or* he stripped himself of his physical body, and thereby boldly made a spectacle of the cosmic powers and authorities, and led them . . .; *or* he despoiled the cosmic powers and authorities, and boldly made a spectacle of them, leading them . . .     [b] *Or* the elements of the natural world, *or* elementary ideas belonging to this world.

which is being constantly renewed in the image of its
Creator and brought to know God. There is no question 11
here of Greek and Jew, circumcised and uncircumcised,
barbarian, Scythian, slave and freeman; but Christ is all,
and is in all.

Then put on the garments that suit God's chosen people, 12
his own, his beloved: compassion, kindness, humility,
gentleness, patience. Be forbearing with one another, and 13
forgiving, where any of you has cause for complaint: you
must forgive as the Lord forgave you. To crown all, there 14
must be love, to bind all together and complete the whole.
Let Christ's peace be arbiter in your hearts; to this peace 15
you were called as members of a single body. And be filled
with gratitude. Let the message of Christ dwell among you 16
in all its richness. Instruct and admonish each other with
the utmost wisdom. Sing thankfully in your hearts to God,*a*
with psalms and hymns and spiritual songs. Whatever you 17
are doing, whether you speak or act, do everything in the
name of the Lord Jesus, giving thanks to God the Father
through him.

W IVES, BE SUBJECT to your husbands; that is your 18
Christian duty. Husbands, love your wives and do not be 19
harsh with them. Children, obey your parents in every- 20
thing, for that is pleasing to God and is the Christian way.
Fathers, do not exasperate your children, for fear they 21
grow disheartened. Slaves, give entire obedience to your 22
earthly masters, not merely with an outward show of service, to curry favour with men, but with single-mindedness,
out of reverence for the Lord. Whatever you are doing, 23
put your whole heart into it, as if you were doing it
for the Lord and not for men, knowing that there is a 24
Master who will give you your heritage as a reward for
your service. Christ is the Master whose slaves you must be.
Dishonesty will be requited, and he has no favourites. 25
Masters, be just and fair to your slaves, knowing that you 4
too have a Master in heaven.

Persevere in prayer, with mind awake and thankful 2
heart; and include a prayer for us, that God may give us an 3
opening for preaching, to tell the secret of Christ; that
indeed is why I am now in prison. Pray that I may make 4
the secret plain, as it is my duty to do.

Behave wisely towards those outside your own number; 5

*a Some witnesses read* the Lord.

6 use the present opportunity to the full. Let your conversation be always gracious, and never insipid; study how best to talk with each person you meet.

7 YOU WILL HEAR all about my affairs from Tychicus, our dear brother and trustworthy helper and fellow-
8 servant in the Lord's work. I am sending him to you on purpose to let you know all about us and to put fresh
9 heart into you. With him comes Onesimus, our trustworthy and dear brother, who is one of yourselves. They will tell you all the news here.

10 Aristarchus, Christ's captive like myself, sends his greetings; so does Mark, the cousin of Barnabas (you have had instructions about him; if he comes, make him wel-
11 come), and Jesus Justus. Of the Jewish Christians, these are the only ones who work with me for the kingdom of
12 God, and they have been a great comfort to me. Greetings from Epaphras, servant of Christ, who is one of yourselves. He prays hard for you all the time, that you may stand fast, ripe in conviction[a] and wholly devoted to doing God's will.
13 For I can vouch for him, that he works tirelessly for you
14 and the people at Laodicea and Hierapolis. Greetings to you from our dear friend Luke, the doctor, and from
15 Demas. Give our greetings to the brothers at Laodicea, and
16 Nympha and the congregation at her house.[b] And when this letter is read among you, see that it is also read to the congregation at Laodicea, and that you in return read
17 the one from Laodicea. This special word to Archippus: 'Attend to the duty entrusted to you in the Lord's service, and discharge it to the full.'

18 This greeting is in my own hand—PAUL. Remember I am in prison. God's grace be with you.

[a] Or *stand fast, mature and complete* . . .    [b] *Some witnesses read* Nymphas and the congregation at his house.

# THE
# FIRST LETTER OF PAUL
# TO THE
# THESSALONIANS

## HOPE AND DISCIPLINE

FROM PAUL, Silvanus, and Timothy to the con- 1
gregation of Thessalonians who belong to God the
Father and the Lord Jesus Christ.
Grace to you and peace.

We always thank God for you all, and mention you in 2
our prayers continually. We call to mind, before our God 3
and Father, how your faith has shown itself in action, your
love in labour, and your hope of our Lord Jesus Christ in
fortitude. We are certain, brothers beloved by God, that 4
he has chosen you and that[a] when we brought you the 5
Gospel, we brought it not in mere words but in the power
of the Holy Spirit, and with strong conviction, as you
know well. That is the kind of men we were. at Thessalonica, and it was for your sake.

And you, in your turn, followed the example set by us 6
and by the Lord; the welcome you gave the message meant
grave suffering for you, yet you rejoiced in the Holy
Spirit; thus you have become a model for all believers in 7
Macedonia and in Achaia. From Thessalonica the word of 8
the Lord rang out; and not in Macedonia and Achaia
alone, but everywhere your faith in God has reached men's
ears. No words of ours are needed, for they themselves 9
spread the news of our visit to you and its effect: how you
turned from idols, to be servants of the living and true
God, and to wait expectantly for the appearance from 10
heaven of his Son Jesus, whom he raised from the dead,
Jesus our deliverer from the terrors of judgement to come.

You know for yourselves, brothers, that our visit to you 2

[a] *Or . . . chosen you, because . . .*

345

2 was not fruitless. Far from it; after all the injury and outrage which to your knowledge we had suffered at Philippi, we declared the gospel of God to you frankly and fear-
3 lessly, by the help of our God. A hard struggle it was. Indeed, the appeal we make never springs from error or base
4 motive; there is no attempt to deceive; but God has approved us as fit to be entrusted with the Gospel, and on those terms we speak. We do not curry favour with men; we seek only the favour of God, who is continually testing
5 our hearts. Our words have never been flattering words, as you have cause to know; nor, as God is our witness,
6 have they ever been a cloak for greed. We have never sought honour from men, from you or from anyone else, although as Christ's own envoys we might have made our
7 weight felt; but we were as gentle with you as a nurse
8 caring fondly for her children. With such yearning love we chose to impart to you not only the gospel of God but
9 our very selves, so dear had you become to us. Remember, brothers, how we toiled and drudged. We worked for a living night and day, rather than be a burden to anyone, while we proclaimed before you the good news of God.
10 We call you to witness, yes and God himself, how devout and just and blameless was our behaviour towards you
11 who are believers. As you well know, we dealt with you one by one, as a father deals with his children, appealing to you by encouragement, as well as by solemn injunctions,
12 to live lives worthy of the God who calls you into his kingdom and glory.
13 This is why we thank God continually, because when we handed on God's message, you received it, not as the word of men, but as what it truly is, the very word of God at[a]
14 work in you who hold the faith. You have fared like the congregations in Judaea, God's people in Christ Jesus. You have been treated by your countrymen as they are treated
15 by the Jews, who killed the Lord Jesus and the prophets[b] and drove us out, the Jews who are heedless of God's will
16 and enemies of their fellow-men, hindering us from speaking to the Gentiles to lead them to salvation. All this time they have been making up the full measure of their guilt, and now retribution has overtaken them for good and all.[c]

17 MY FRIENDS, when for a short spell you were lost to us —lost to sight, not to our hearts—we were exceedingly

*[a] Or* word of God who is at . . . *[b] Some witnesses read* their own prophets. *[c] Or* now at last retribution has overtaken them.

anxious to see you again. So we did propose to come 18
to Thessalonica—I, Paul, more than once—but Satan
thwarted us. For after all, what hope or joy or crown of 19
pride is there for us, what indeed but you, when we stand
before our Lord Jesus at his coming? It is you who are 20
indeed our glory and our joy.

So when we could bear it no longer, we decided to remain 3
alone at Athens, and sent Timothy, our brother and God's 2
fellow-worker[a] in the service of the gospel of Christ, to
encourage you to stand firm for the faith and, under all 3
these hardships, not to be shaken;[b] for you know that this
is our appointed lot. When we were with you we warned 4
you that we were bound to suffer hardship; and so it has
turned out, as you know. And thus it was that when I 5
could bear it no longer, I sent to find out about your faith,
fearing that the tempter might have tempted you and my
labour might be lost.

But now Timothy has just arrived from Thessalonica, 6
bringing good news of your faith and love. He tells us that
you always think kindly of us, and are as anxious to see us
as we are to see you. And so in all our difficulties and hard- 7
ships your faith reassures us about you. It is the breath of 8
life to us that you stand firm in the Lord. What thanks can 9
we return to God for you? What thanks for all the joy you
have brought us, making us rejoice before our God while 10
we pray most earnestly night and day to be allowed to see
you again and to mend your faith where it falls short?

May our God and Father himself, and our Lord Jesus, 11
bring us direct to you; and may the Lord make your love 12
mount and overflow towards one another and towards all,
as our love does towards you. May he make your hearts 13
firm, so that you may stand before our God and Father
holy and faultless when our Lord Jesus comes with all
those who are his own.

AND NOW, MY FRIENDS, we have one thing to beg and 4
pray of you, by our fellowship with the Lord Jesus. We
passed on to you the tradition of the way we must live to
please God; you are indeed already following it, but we
beg you to do so yet more thoroughly.

For you know what orders we gave you, in the name of 2
the Lord Jesus. This is the will of God, that you should be 3
holy: you must abstain from fornication; each one of you 4

---

[a] *Or* and fellow-worker for God; *one witness has simply* and fellow-worker.     [b] *Or* beguiled away.

must learn to gain mastery over his body, to hallow and
5 honour it, not giving way to lust like the pagans who are
6 ignorant of God; and no man must do his brother wrong
in this matter,[a] or invade his rights, because, as we told
you before with all emphasis, the Lord punishes all such
7 offences. For God called us to holiness, not to impurity.
8 Anyone therefore who flouts these rules is flouting, not
man, but God who bestows upon you his Holy Spirit.

9     About love for our brotherhood you need no words of
mine, for you are yourselves taught by God to love one
10 another, and you are in fact practising this rule of love
towards all your fellow-Christians throughout Macedonia.
11 Yet we appeal to you, brothers, to do better still. Let it
be your ambition to keep calm and look after your own
business, and to work with your hands, as we ordered you,
12 so that you may command the respect of those outside
your own number, and at the same time may never be
in want.

13 WE WISH YOU not to remain in ignorance, brothers,
about those who sleep in death; you should not grieve like
14 the rest of men, who have no hope. We believe that Jesus
died and rose again; and so it will be for those who died
as Christians; God will bring them to life with Jesus.[b]
15     For this we tell you as the Lord's word: we who are left
alive until the Lord comes shall not forestall those who
16 have died; because at the word of command, at the sound
of the archangel's voice and God's trumpet-call, the Lord
himself will descend from heaven; first the Christian dead
17 will rise, then we who are left alive shall join them, caught
up in clouds to meet the Lord in the air. Thus we shall
18 always be with the Lord. Console one another, then, with
these words.

5     About dates and times, my friends, we need not write
2 to you, for you know perfectly well that the Day of the
3 Lord comes like a thief in the night. While they are talking
of peace and security, all at once calamity is upon them,
sudden as the pangs that come upon a woman with child;
4 and there will be no escape. But you, my friends, are not
in the dark, that the day should overtake you like a thief.[c]
5 You are all children of light, children of day. We do not
6 belong to night or darkness, and we must not sleep like

---

[a] Or must overreach his brother in his business (or in lawsuits).
[b] Or will bring them in company with Jesus.     [c] Some witnesses
read thieves.

the rest, but keep awake and sober. Sleepers sleep at night, 7
and drunkards are drunk at night, but we, who belong to 8
daylight, must keep sober, armed with faith and love for
coat of mail, and the hope of salvation for helmet. For God 9
has not destined us to the terrors of judgement, but to the
full attainment of salvation through our Lord Jesus Christ.
He died for us so that we, awake or asleep, might live in 10
company with him. Therefore hearten one another, fortify 11
one another—as indeed you do.

WE BEG YOU, BROTHERS, to acknowledge those who 12
are working so hard among you, and in the Lord's fellowship are your leaders and counsellors. Hold them in the 13
highest possible esteem and affection for the work they do.

You must live at peace among yourselves. And we would 14
urge you, brothers, to admonish the careless, encourage
the faint-hearted, support the weak, and to be very patient
with them all.

See to it that no one pays back wrong for wrong, but 15
always aim at doing the best you can for each other and
for all men.

Be always joyful; pray continually; give thanks what- 16 17 18
ever happens; for this is what God in Christ wills for you.

Do not stifle inspiration, and do not despise prophetic 19 20
utterances, but bring them all to the test and then keep 21
what is good in them and avoid the bad of whatever kind.[a] 22

May God himself, the God of peace, make you holy in 23
every part, and keep you sound in spirit, soul, and body,
without fault when our Lord Jesus Christ comes. He who 24
calls you is to be trusted; he will do it.

Brothers, pray for us also. 25

Greet all our brothers with the kiss of peace. 26

I adjure you by the Lord to have this letter read to the 27
whole brotherhood.

The grace of our Lord Jesus Christ be with you! 28

[a] *Or* . . . utterances. Put everything to the test; keep hold of what is
good and avoid every kind of evil.

# THE
# SECOND LETTER OF PAUL
# TO THE
# THESSALONIANS

## HOPE AND DISCIPLINE

1 FROM PAUL, Silvanus, and Timothy to the congregation of Thessalonians who belong to God our Father and the Lord Jesus Christ.

2 Grace to you and peace from God the Father and the Lord Jesus Christ.

3 Our thanks are always due to God for you, brothers. It is right that we should thank him, because your faith increases mightily, and the love you have, each for all and

4 all for each, grows ever greater. Indeed we boast about you ourselves among the congregations of God's people, because your faith remains so steadfast under all your persecutions,

5 and all the troubles you endure. See how this brings out the justice of God's judgement. It will prove you worthy of the kingdom of God, for which indeed you are suffering.

6 It is surely just that God should balance the account by

7 sending trouble to those who trouble you, and relief to you who are troubled, and to us as well, when our Lord Jesus

8 Christ is revealed from heaven with his mighty angels in blazing fire. Then he will do justice upon those who refuse to acknowledge God and upon those who will not obey[a] the

9 gospel of our Lord Jesus. They will suffer the punishment of eternal ruin, cut off from the presence of the Lord and

10 the splendour of his might, when on that great Day he comes to be glorified among his own and adored among all believers; for you did indeed believe the testimony we brought you.

11 With this in mind we pray for you always, that our God may count you worthy of his calling, and mightily bring

[a] Or justice upon those who refuse . . . and will not obey . . .

350

to fulfilment every good purpose and every act inspired by
faith, so that the name of our Lord Jesus may be glorified 12
in you, and you in him, according to the grace of our God
and the Lord Jesus Christ.

AND NOW, BROTHERS, about the coming of our Lord 2
Jesus Christ and his gathering of us to himself: I beg you,
do not suddenly lose your heads or alarm yourselves, 2
whether at some oracular utterance, or pronouncement, or
some letter purporting to come from us, alleging that the
Day of the Lord is already here. Let no one deceive you 3
in any way whatever. That day cannot come before the
final rebellion against God, when wickedness will be revealed in human form, the man doomed to perdition. He 4
is the Enemy. He rises in his pride against every god, so
called, every object of men's worship, and even takes his
seat in the temple of God claiming to be a god himself.
    You cannot but remember that I told you this while I 5
was still with you; you must now be aware of the restrain- 6
ing hand which ensures that he shall be revealed only at
the proper time. For already the secret power of wicked- 7
ness is at work, secret only for the present until the Re-
strainer disappears from the scene. And then he will be 8
revealed, that wicked man whom the Lord Jesus will
destroy with the breath of his mouth, and annihilate by the
radiance of his coming. But the coming of that wicked man 9
is the work of Satan. It will be attended by all the powerful
signs and miracles of the Lie, and all the deception that 10
sinfulness can impose on those doomed to destruction.
Destroyed they shall be, because they did not open their
minds to love of the truth, so as to find salvation. There- 11
fore God puts them under a delusion, which works upon
them to believe the lie, so that they may all be brought to 12
judgement, all who do not believe the truth but make
sinfulness their deliberate choice.

BUT WE ARE BOUND to thank God always for you, 13
brothers beloved by the Lord, because from the beginning
of time God chose you[a] to find salvation in the Spirit that
consecrates you, and in the truth that you believe. It was 14
for this that he called you through the gospel we brought,
so that you might possess for your own the splendour of
our Lord Jesus Christ.

    [a] *Some witnesses read* because God chose you as his firstfruits ...

15 Stand firm, then, brothers, and hold fast to the traditions which you have learned from us by word or by letter.
16 And may our Lord Jesus Christ himself and God our Father, who has shown us such love, and in his grace has given us such unfailing encouragement and such bright
17 hopes, still encourage and fortify you in every good deed and word!

3 And now, brothers, pray for us, that the word of the Lord may have everywhere the swift and glorious course
2 that it has had among you, and that we may be rescued from wrong-headed and wicked men; for it is not all who
3 have faith. But the Lord is to be trusted, and he will
4 fortify you and guard you from the evil one. We feel perfect confidence about you, in the Lord, that you are doing
5 and will continue to do what we order. May the Lord direct your hearts towards God's love and the steadfastness of Christ!

6 These are our orders to you, brothers, in the name of our Lord Jesus Christ: hold aloof from every Christian brother who falls into idle habits, and does not follow the
7 tradition you received from us. You know yourselves how you ought to copy our example: we were no idlers among
8 you; we did not accept board and lodging from anyone without paying for it; we toiled and drudged, we worked for a living night and day, rather than be a burden to any
9 of you—not because we have not the right to maintenance,
10 but to set an example for you to imitate. For even during our stay with you we laid down the rule: the man who will
11 not work shall not eat. We mention this because we hear that some of your number are idling their time away,
12 minding everybody's business but their own. To all such we give these orders, and we appeal to them in the name of the Lord Jesus Christ to work quietly for their living.

13 14 But you, my friends, must never tire of doing right. If anyone disobeys our instructions given by letter, mark him well, and have no dealings with him until he is ashamed of
15 himself. I do not mean treat him as an enemy, but give
16 him friendly advice, as one of the family. May the Lord of peace himself give you peace at all times and in all ways.*a* The Lord be with you all.

17 The greeting is in my own hand, signed with my name, PAUL; this authenticates all my letters; this is how I
18 write. The grace*b* of our Lord Jesus Christ be with you all.

*a Some witnesses read at all times, wherever you may be.*    *b Or...*
letters. My message is this: the grace . . .

# THE
# FIRST LETTER OF
# PAUL TO
# TIMOTHY

## CHURCH ORDER

FROM PAUL, APOSTLE of Christ Jesus by com- 1
mand of God our Saviour and Christ Jesus our hope,
to Timothy his true-born son in the faith. 2
Grace, mercy, and peace to you from God the Father
and Christ Jesus our Lord.

When I was starting for Macedonia, I urged you to stay 3
on at Ephesus. You were to command certain persons to
give up teaching erroneous doctrines and studying those 4
interminable myths and genealogies, which issue in mere
speculation and cannot make known God's plan for us,
which works through faith.[a]

The aim and object of this command is the love which 5
springs from a clean heart, from a good conscience, and
from faith that is genuine. Through falling short of these, 6
some people have gone astray into a wilderness of words.
They set out to be teachers of the moral law, without 7
understanding either the words they use or the subjects
about which they are so dogmatic.

We all know that the law is an excellent thing, provided 8
we treat it as law, recognizing that it is not aimed at good 9
citizens, but at the lawless and unruly, the impious and
sinful, the irreligious and worldly; at parricides and matri-
cides, murderers and fornicators, perverts, kidnappers, 10
liars, perjurers—in fact all whose behaviour flouts the
wholesome teaching which conforms with the gospel en- 11
trusted to me, the gospel which tells of the glory of God in
his eternal felicity.

I thank him who has made me equal to the task, Christ 12

[a] Or cannot promote the faithful discharge of God's stewardship.

Jesus our Lord; I thank him for judging me worthy of this
13 trust and appointing me to his service—although in the
past I had met him with abuse and persecution and outrage. But because I acted ignorantly in unbelief I was
14 dealt with mercifully; the grace of our Lord was lavished
upon me, with the faith and love which are ours in Christ
Jesus.

15 Here are words you may trust, words that merit full
acceptance: 'Christ Jesus came into the world to save
16 sinners'; and among them I stand first. But I was mercifully dealt with for this very purpose, that Jesus Christ
might find in me the first occasion for displaying all his
patience, and that I might be typical of all who were in
17 future to have faith in him and gain eternal life. Now to
the King of all worlds, immortal, invisible, the only God,
be honour and glory for ever and ever! Amen.

18 This charge, son Timothy, I lay upon you, following that
prophetic utterance which first pointed you out to me. So
19 fight gallantly, armed with faith and a good conscience.
It was through spurning conscience that certain persons
20 made shipwreck of their faith, among them Hymenaeus
and Alexander, whom I consigned to Satan, in the hope
that through this discipline they might learn not to be
blasphemous.

2 First of all, then, I urge that petitions, prayers,
intercessions, and thanksgivings be offered for all men;
2 for sovereigns and all in high office, that we may lead a
tranquil and quiet life in full observance of religion and
3 high standards of morality. Such prayer is right, and ap-
4 proved by God our Saviour, whose will it is that all men
5 should find salvation and come to know the truth. For
there is one God, and also one mediator between God and
6 men, Christ Jesus, himself man, who sacrificed himself to
win freedom for all mankind, so providing, at the fitting
7 time, proof of the divine purpose; of this I was appointed
herald and apostle (this is no lie, but the truth), to instruct
the nations in the true faith.

8 It is my desire, therefore, that everywhere prayers be
said by the men of the congregation, who shall lift up their
hands with a pure intention, excluding angry or quarrel-
9 some thoughts. Women again must dress in becoming
manner, modestly and soberly, not with elaborate hair-
styles, not decked out with gold or pearls, or expensive
10 clothes, but with good deeds, as befits women who claim to

be religious. A woman must be a learner, listening quietly 11
and with due submission. I do not permit a woman to be 12
a teacher, nor must woman domineer over man; she should
be quiet. For Adam was created first, and Eve afterwards; 13
and it was not Adam who was deceived; it was the woman 14
who, yielding to deception, fell into sin. Yet she will be 15
saved through motherhood[a]—if only women continue in
faith,[b] love, and holiness, with a sober mind.

There is a popular saying:[c] 'To aspire to leadership is an 3
honourable ambition.' Our leader, therefore, or bishop, 2
must be above reproach, faithful to his one wife,[d] sober,
temperate, courteous, hospitable, and a good teacher; he 3
must not be given to drink, or a brawler, but of a forbearing disposition, avoiding quarrels, and no lover of money.
He must be one who manages his own household well and 4
wins obedience from his children, and a man of the highest
principles. If a man does not know how to control his own 5
family, how can he look after a congregation of God's
people? He must not be a convert newly baptized, for fear 6
the sin of conceit should bring upon him a judgement con-
trived by the devil.[e] He must moreover have a good 7
reputation with the non-Christian public, so that he may
not be exposed to scandal and get caught in the devil's
snare.

Deacons, likewise, must be men of high principle, not 8
indulging in double talk, given neither to excessive drinking nor to money-grubbing. They must be men who com- 9
bine a clear conscience with a firm hold on the deep truths
of our faith. No less than bishops, they must first undergo 10
a scrutiny, and if there is no mark against them, they may
serve. Their wives,[f] equally, must be women of high prin- 11
ciple, who will not talk scandal, sober and trustworthy in
every way. A deacon must be faithful to his one wife,[g] and 12
good at managing his children and his own household. For 13
deacons with a good record of service may claim a high
standing and the right to speak openly on matters of the
Christian faith.

I am hoping to come to you before long, but I write this 14
in case I am delayed, to let you know how men ought to 15

[a] *Or* saved through the Birth of the Child, *or* brought safely through
childbirth.     [b] *Or* if only husband and wife continue in mutual
fidelity . . .     [c] *Some witnesses read* Here are words you may trust,
*which some interpreters attach to the end of the preceding paragraph.*
[d] *Or* married to one wife, *or* married only once.     [e] *Or* the judgement once passed on the devil.     [f] *Or* . . . serve. Deaconesses . . .
[g] *Or* married to one wife, *or* married only once.

conduct themselves in God's household, that is, the church of the living God, the pillar and bulwark of the truth.
16 And great beyond all question is the mystery of our religion:

'He who was manifested in the body,
vindicated in the spirit,
seen by angels;
who was proclaimed among the nations,
believed in throughout the world,
glorified in high heaven.'

4 THE SPIRIT SAYS expressly that in after times some will desert from the faith and give their minds to sub-
2 versive doctrines inspired by devils, through the specious falsehoods of men whose own conscience is branded with
3 the devil's sign. They forbid marriage and inculcate abstinence from certain foods, though God created them to be enjoyed with thanksgiving by believers who have
4 inward knowledge of the truth. For everything that God created is good, and nothing is to be rejected when it is
5 taken with thanksgiving, since it is hallowed by God's own word and by prayer.

6 By offering such advice as this to the brotherhood you will prove a good servant of Christ Jesus, bred in the precepts of our faith and of the sound instruction which you
7 have followed. Have nothing to do with those godless myths, fit only for old women. Keep yourself in training
8 for the practice of religion. The training of the body does bring limited benefit, but the benefits of religion are without limit, since it holds promise not only for this life but
9 for the life to come. Here are words you may trust, words
10 that merit full acceptance: 'With this before us we labour and struggle,[a] because[b] we have set our hope on the living God, who is the Saviour of all men'—the Saviour, above all, of believers.

11 12 Pass on these orders and these teachings. Let no one slight you because you are young, but make yourself an example to believers in speech and behaviour, in love,
13 fidelity, and purity. Until I arrive devote your attention to the public reading of the scriptures, [to exhortation,
14 and to teaching. Do not neglect the spiritual endowment you possess, which was given you, under the guidance of

---

[a] *Some witnesses read* suffer reproach.     [b] *Or since* 'It holds promise . . . to come.' *These are words . . .* acceptance. *For this is the aim of all our labour and struggle, since . . .*

prophecy, through the laying on of the hands of the elders as a body.[a]

Make these matters your business and your absorbing 15 interest, so that your progress may be plain to all. Per- 16 severe in them, keeping close watch on yourself and your teaching; by doing so you will further the salvation of yourself and your hearers.

Never be harsh with an elder; appeal to him as if he 5 were your father. Treat the younger men as brothers, the 2 older women as mothers, and the younger as your sisters, in all purity.

The status of widow is to be granted only to widows 3 who are such in the full sense. But if a widow has children 4 or grandchildren, then they should learn as their first duty to show loyalty to the family and to repay what they owe to their parents and grandparents; for this God approves. A widow, however, in the full sense, one who is alone in 5 the world, has all her hope set on God, and regularly attends the meetings for prayer and worship night and day. But a widow given over to self-indulgence is as good 6 as dead. Add these orders to the rest, so that the widows 7 may be above reproach. But if anyone does not make pro- 8 vision for his relations, and especially for members of his own household, he has denied the faith and is worse than an unbeliever.

A widow should not be put on the roll under sixty years 9 of age. She must have been faithful in marriage to one man, and must produce evidence of good deeds performed, 10 showing whether she has had the care of children, or given hospitality, or washed the feet of God's people, or supported those in distress—in short, whether she has taken every opportunity of doing good.

Younger widows may not be placed on the roll. For when 11 their passions draw them away from Christ, they hanker after marriage and stand condemned for breaking their 12 troth with him. Moreover, in going round from house to 13 house they learn to be idle, and worse than idle, gossips and busybodies, speaking of things better left unspoken. It is 14 my wish, therefore, that young widows shall marry again, have children, and preside over a home; then they will give no opponent occasion for slander. For there have in 15 fact been some who have taken the wrong turning and gone to the devil.

If a Christian man or woman has widows in the family, 16

[a] Or through your ordination as an elder.

he must support them himself;[a] the congregation must be relieved of the burden, so that it may be free to support those who are widows in the full sense of the term.

17 Elders who do well as leaders should be reckoned worthy of a double stipend, in particular those who labour at
18 preaching and teaching. For Scripture says, 'You shall not muzzle a threshing ox'; and besides, 'the worker earns his pay'.

19 Do not entertain a charge against an elder unless it is
20 supported by two or three witnesses. Those who commit sins you must expose publicly, to put fear into the others.
21 Before God and Christ Jesus and the angels who are his chosen, I solemnly charge you, maintain these rules, and never pre-judge the issue, but act with strict impartiality.
22 Do not be over-hasty in laying on hands in ordination,[b] or you may find yourself responsible for other people's misdeeds; keep your own hands clean.
23 Stop drinking nothing but water; take a little wine for your digestion, for your frequent ailments.
24 While there are people whose offences are so obvious that they run before them into court, there are others
25 whose offences have not yet overtaken them. Similarly, good deeds are obvious, or even if they are not, they cannot be concealed for ever.

6 All who wear the yoke of slavery must count their own masters worthy of all respect, so that the name of God and
2 the Christian teaching are not brought into disrepute. If the masters are believers, the slaves must not respect them any less for being their Christian brothers. Quite the contrary; they must be all the better servants because those who receive the benefit of their service are one with them in faith and love.

3 THIS IS WHAT you are to teach and preach. If anyone is teaching otherwise, and will not give his mind to wholesome precepts—I mean those of our Lord Jesus Christ—
4 and to good religious teaching, I call him a pompous ignoramus. He is morbidly keen on mere verbal questions and quibbles, which give rise to jealousy, quarrelling,
5 slander, base suspicions, and endless wrangles: all typical of men who have let their reasoning powers become atrophied and have lost grip of the truth. They think religion

[a] *Some witnesses read* If a Christian woman has widows in her family, she must support them herself.     [b] *Or* in restoring an offender by the laying on of hands.

should yield dividends; and of course religion does yield 6
high dividends, but only to the man whose resources are
within him. We brought nothing into the world; for that 7
matter we cannot take anything with us when we leave,
but if we have food and covering we may rest content. 8
Those who want to be rich fall into temptations and snares 9
and many foolish harmful desires which plunge men into
ruin and perdition. The love of money is the root of all evil 10
things, and there are some who in reaching for it have
wandered from the faith and spiked themselves on many
thorny griefs.

But you, man of God, must shun all this, and pursue 11
justice, piety, fidelity, love, fortitude, and gentleness. Run 12
the great race of faith and take hold of eternal life. For to
this you were called; and you confessed your faith nobly
before many witnesses. Now in the presence of God, who 13
gives life to all things, and of Jesus Christ, who himself
made the same noble confession and gave his testimony to
it before Pontius Pilate, I charge you to obey your orders 14
irreproachably and without fault until our Lord Jesus
Christ appears. That appearance God will bring to pass in 15
his own good time—God who in eternal felicity alone holds
sway. He is King of kings and Lord of lords; he alone 16
possesses immortality, dwelling in unapproachable light.
No man has ever seen or ever can see him. To him be
honour and might for ever! Amen.

Instruct those who are rich in this world's goods not to 17
be proud, and not to fix their hopes on so uncertain a thing
as money, but upon God, who endows us richly with all
things to enjoy. Tell them to do good and to grow rich in 18
noble actions, to be ready to give away and to share, and 19
so acquire a treasure which will form a good foundation
for the future. Thus they will grasp the life which is life
indeed.

Timothy, keep safe that which has been entrusted to 20
you. Turn a deaf ear to empty and worldly chatter, and the
contradictions of so-called 'knowledge', for many who lay 21
claim to it have shot far wide of the faith.

Grace be with you all!

# THE
# SECOND LETTER OF
# PAUL TO
# TIMOTHY

## CHARACTER OF A CHRISTIAN
## MINISTER

1 FROM PAUL, APOSTLE of Jesus Christ by the
will of God, whose promise of life is fulfilled in Christ
2 Jesus, to Timothy his dear son.

Grace, mercy, and peace to you from God the Father
and our Lord Jesus Christ.

3 I thank God—whom I, like my forefathers, worship
with a pure intention—when I mention you in my prayers;
4 this I do constantly night and day. And when I remember
the tears you shed, I long to see you again to make my
5 happiness complete. I am reminded of the sincerity of your
faith, a faith which was alive in Lois your grandmother
and Eunice your mother before you, and which, I am confident, lives in you also.

6 That is why I now remind you to stir into flame the gift
of God which is within you through the laying on of my
7 hands. For the spirit that God gave us is no craven spirit,
8 but one to inspire strength, love, and self-discipline. So
never be ashamed of your testimony to our Lord, nor of
me his prisoner, but take your share of suffering for the
9 sake of the Gospel, in the strength that comes from God. It
is he who brought us salvation and called us to a dedicated
life, not for any merit of ours but of his own purpose and
his own grace, which was granted to us in Christ Jesus
10 from all eternity, but has now at length been brought fully
into view by the appearance on earth of our Saviour Jesus
Christ. For he has broken the power of death and brought
life and immortality to light through the Gospel.

11 Of this Gospel I, by his appointment, am herald, apostle,
12 and teacher. That is the reason for my present plight; but

I am not ashamed of it, because I know who it is in whom[a]
I have trusted, and am confident of his power to keep safe
what he has put into my charge,[b] until the great Day.
Keep before you an outline of the sound teaching which[c] 13
you heard from me, living by the faith and love which are
ours in Christ Jesus. Guard the treasure put into our 14
charge, with the help of the Holy Spirit dwelling within us.

As you know, everyone in the province of Asia deserted 15
me, including Phygelus and Hermogenes. But may the 16
Lord's mercy rest on the house of Onesiphorus! He has
often relieved me in my troubles. He was not ashamed to
visit a prisoner, but took pains to search me out when he 17
came to Rome, and found me. I pray that the Lord may 18
grant him to find mercy from the Lord on the great Day.
The many services he rendered at Ephesus you know better
than I could tell you.

Now therefore, my son, take strength from the grace of 2
God which is ours in Christ Jesus. You heard my teaching 2
in the presence of many witnesses; put that teaching into
the charge of men you can trust, such men as will be
competent to teach others.

Take your share of hardship, like a good soldier of Christ 3
Jesus. A soldier on active service will not let himself be 4
involved in civilian affairs; he must be wholly at his commanding officer's disposal. Again, no athlete can win a 5
prize unless he has kept the rules. The farmer who gives 6
his labour has first claim on the crop. Reflect on what I 7
say, for the Lord will help you to full understanding.

Remember Jesus Christ, risen from the dead, born of 8
David's line. This is the theme of my gospel, in whose 9
service I am exposed to hardship, even to the point of
being shut up like a common criminal; but the word of
God is not shut up. And I endure it all for the sake of God's 10
chosen ones, with this end in view, that they too may
attain the glorious and eternal salvation which is in Christ
Jesus.

Here are words you may trust: 11

'If we died with him, we shall live with him;
    if we endure, we shall reign with him. 12
If we deny him, he will deny us.
If we are faithless, he keeps faith, 13
    for he cannot deny himself.'

*a Or* I know the one whom . . .         *b Or* what I have put into his
charge.         *c Or* Keep before you as a model of sound teaching that
which . . .

¹⁴ GO ON REMINDING people of this, and charge them
solemnly before God to stop disputing about mere words;
¹⁵ it does no good, and is the ruin of those who listen. Try
hard to show yourself worthy of God's approval, as a
labourer who need not be ashamed; be straightforward in
¹⁶ your proclamation of the truth. Avoid empty and worldly
chatter; those who indulge in it will stray further and
¹⁷ further into godless courses, and the infection of their
teaching will spread like a gangrene. Such are Hymenaeus
¹⁸ and Philetus; they have shot wide of the truth in saying
that our resurrection has already taken place, and are
¹⁹ upsetting people's faith. But God has laid a foundation,
and it stands firm, with this inscription: 'The Lord knows
his own', and, 'Everyone who takes the Lord's name upon
²⁰ his lips must forsake wickedness.' Now in any great house
there are not only utensils of gold and silver, but also
others of wood or earthenware; the former are valued, the
²¹ latter held cheap. To be among those which are valued and
dedicated, a thing of use to the Master of the house, a man
must cleanse himself from all those evil things;*ᵃ* then he
will be fit for any honourable purpose.

²² Turn from the wayward impulses of youth, and pursue
justice, integrity, love, and peace with all who invoke
²³ the Lord in singleness of mind. Have nothing to do with
foolish and ignorant speculations. You know they breed
²⁴ quarrels, and the servant of the Lord must not be quarrel-
some, but kindly towards all. He should be a good teacher,
²⁵ tolerant, and gentle when discipline is needed for the re-
fractory. The Lord may grant them a change of heart and
²⁶ show them the truth, and thus they may come to their
senses and escape from the devil's snare, in which they
have been caught and held at his will.*ᵇ*

3 You must face the fact: the final age of this world is to
² be a time of troubles. Men will love nothing but money and
self; they will be arrogant, boastful, and abusive; with no
³ respect for parents, no gratitude, no piety, no natural
affection; they will be implacable in their hatreds, scandal-
mongers, intemperate and fierce, strangers to all goodness,
⁴ traitors, adventurers, swollen with self-importance. They
will be men who put pleasure in the place of God,
⁵ men who preserve the outward form of religion, but
are a standing denial of its reality. Keep clear of men
⁶ like these. They are the sort that insinuate themselves into

---

*ᵃ Or must separate himself from these persons.*     *ᵇ Or escape from
the devil's snare, caught now by God and made subject to his will.*

362

private houses and there get miserable women into their clutches, women burdened with a sinful past, and led on by all kinds of desires, who are always wanting to be ⁷ taught, but are incapable of reaching a knowledge of the truth. As Jannes and Jambres defied Moses, so these men ⁸ defy the truth; they have lost the power to reason, and they cannot pass the tests of faith. But their successes ⁹ will be short-lived, for, like those opponents of Moses, they will come to be recognized by everyone for the fools they are.

But you, my son, have followed, step by step, my teach- 10 ing and my manner of life, my resolution, my faith, patience, and spirit of love, and my fortitude under perse- 11 cutions and sufferings—all that I went through at Antioch, at Iconium, at Lystra, all the persecutions I endured; and the Lord rescued me out of them all. Yes, persecution will 12 come to all who want to live a godly life as Christians, whereas wicked men and charlatans will make progress 13 from bad to worse, deceiving and deceived. But for your 14 part, stand by the truths you have learned and are assured of. Remember from whom you learned them; remember 15 that from early childhood you have been familiar with the sacred writings which have power to make you wise and lead you to salvation through faith in Christ Jesus. Every 16 inspired scripture has its use for teaching the truth and refuting error, or for reformation of manners and discipline in right living, so that the man who belongs to God may 17 be efficient and equipped for good work of every kind.

Before God, and before Christ Jesus who is to judge men 4 living and dead, I charge you solemnly by his coming appearance and his reign, proclaim the message, press 2 it home on all occasions,*ᵃ* convenient or inconvenient, use argument, reproof, and appeal, with all the patience that the work of teaching requires. For the time will come when 3 they will not stand wholesome teaching, but will follow their own fancy and gather a crowd of teachers to tickle their ears. They will stop their ears to the truth and turn 4 to mythology. But you yourself must keep calm and sane 5 at all times; face hardship, work to spread the Gospel, and do all the duties of your calling.

As for me, already my life is being poured out on the 6 altar, and the hour for my departure is upon me. I have 7 run the great race, I have finished the course, I have

*ᵃ Or be on duty at all times.*

8 kept faith. And now the prize awaits me, the garland of righteousness which the Lord, the all-just Judge, will award me on that great Day; and it is not for me alone, but for all who have set their hearts on his coming appearance.

9 10 Do your best to join me soon; for Demas has deserted me because his heart was set on this world; he has gone to Thessalonica, Crescens to Galatia,[a] Titus to Dalmatia; 11 I have no one with me but Luke. Pick up Mark and bring 12 him with you, for I find him a useful assistant. Tychicus 13 I have sent to Ephesus. When you come, bring the cloak I left with Carpus at Troas, and the books, above all my notebooks.

14 Alexander the copper-smith did me a great deal of 15 harm. Retribution will fall upon him from the Lord. You had better be on your guard against him too, for he vio- 16 lently opposed everything I said. At the first hearing of my case no one came into court to support me; they all left me in the lurch; I pray that it may not be held against 17 them. But the Lord stood by me and lent me strength, so that I might be his instrument in making the full proclama- tion of the Gospel for the whole pagan world to hear; and 18 thus I was rescued out of the lion's jaws. And the Lord will rescue me from every attempt to do me harm, and keep me safe until his heavenly reign begins.[b] Glory to him for ever and ever! Amen.

19 Greetings to Prisca and Aquila, and the household of Onesiphorus.

20 Erastus stayed behind at Corinth, and I left Trophimus 21 ill at Miletus. Do try to get here before winter.

Greetings from Eubulus, Pudens, Linus, and Claudia, and from all the brotherhood here.

22 The Lord be with your spirit. Grace be with you all!

[a] *Or* Gaul; *some witnesses read* Gallia.     [b] *Or* from all that evil can do, and bring me safely into his heavenly kingdom.

# THE
# LETTER OF PAUL TO
# TITUS

## TRAINING FOR THE CHRISTIAN LIFE

FROM PAUL, SERVANT of God and apostle of 1
Jesus Christ, marked as such by faith and knowledge
and hope—the faith of God's chosen people, knowledge of the truth as our religion has it, and the hope of 2
eternal life.[a] Yes, it is eternal life that God, who cannot lie,
promised long ages ago, and now in his own good time he 3
has openly declared himself in the proclamation which was
entrusted to me by ordinance of God our Saviour.

To Titus, my true-born son in the faith which we share, 4
grace and peace from God our Father and Christ Jesus our
Saviour.

My intention in leaving you behind in Crete was that 5
you should set in order what was left over, and in particular
should institute elders in each town. In doing so, observe
the tests I prescribed: is he a man of unimpeachable 6
character, faithful to his one wife,[b] the father of children
who are believers, who are under no imputation of loose
living, and are not out of control? For as God's steward 7
a bishop must be a man of unimpeachable character. He
must not be overbearing or short-tempered; he must be no
drinker, no brawler, no money-grubber, but hospitable, 8
right-minded, temperate, just, devout, and self-controlled.
He must adhere to the true doctrine, so that he may be 9
well able both to move his hearers with wholesome teaching and to confute objectors.

There are all too many, especially among Jewish con- 10
verts, who are out of all control; they talk wildly and lead
men's minds astray. Such men must be curbed, because 11

---

[a] Or apostle of Jesus Christ, to bring God's chosen people to faith and
to a knowledge of the truth as our religion has it, with its hope for
eternal life.    [b] See note on 1 Timothy 3. 2.

they are ruining whole families by teaching things they
12 should not, and all for sordid gain. It was a Cretan prophet,
one of their own countrymen, who said, 'Cretans were
13 always liars, vicious brutes, lazy gluttons'—and he told
the truth! All the more reason why you should pull them
14 up sharply, so that they may come to a sane belief, instead
of lending their ears to Jewish myths and commandments
of merely human origin, the work of men who turn their
backs upon the truth.

15 To the pure all things are pure; but nothing is pure to
the tainted minds of disbelievers, tainted alike in reason
16 and conscience. They profess to acknowledge God, but
deny him by their actions. Their detestable obstinacy dis-
qualifies them for any good work.

2 For your own part, what you say must be in keeping
2 with wholesome doctrine. Let the older men know that
they should be sober, high-principled, and temperate,
3 sound in faith, in love, and in endurance. The older women,
similarly, should be reverent in their bearing, not scandal-
mongers or slaves to strong drink; they must set a high
4 standard, and school the younger women to be loving
5 wives and mothers, temperate, chaste, and kind, busy at
home, respecting the authority of their own husbands.
Thus the Gospel will not be brought into disrepute.

6 7 Urge the younger men, similarly, to be temperate in all
things, and set them a good example yourself. In your
8 teaching, you must show integrity and high principle, and
use wholesome speech to which none can take exception.
This will shame any opponent, when he finds not a word
to say to our discredit.

9 Tell slaves to respect their masters' authority in everything, and to comply with their demands without answer-
10 ing back; not to pilfer, but to show themselves strictly
honest and trustworthy; for in all such ways they will add
lustre to the doctrine of God our Saviour.

11 For the grace of God has dawned upon the world with
12 healing for all mankind; and by it we are disciplined to
renounce godless ways and worldly desires, and to live a
life of temperance, honesty, and godliness in the present
13 age, looking forward to the happy fulfilment of our hope
when the splendour of our great God and Saviour[a] Christ
14 Jesus will appear. He it is who sacrificed himself for us, to
set us free from all wickedness and to make us a pure
people marked out for his own, eager to do good.

[a] *Or of the great God and our Saviour . . .*

These, then, are your themes; urge them and argue 15 them. And speak with authority: let no one slight you.

Remind them to be submissive to the government and 3 the authorities, to obey them, and to be ready for any honourable form of work;[a] to slander no one, not to pick 2 quarrels, to show forbearance and a consistently gentle disposition towards all men.

For at one time we ourselves in our folly and obstinacy 3 were all astray. We were slaves to passions and pleasures of every kind. Our days were passed in malice and envy; we were odious ourselves and we hated one another. But 4 when the kindness and generosity of God our Saviour dawned upon the world, then, not for any good deeds of 5 our own, but because he was merciful, he saved us through the water of rebirth and the renewing power of[b] the Holy Spirit. For he sent down the Spirit upon us plentifully 6 through Jesus Christ our Saviour, so that, justified by his 7 grace, we might in hope become heirs to eternal life. These 8 are words you may trust.

Such are the points I should wish you to insist on. Those who have come to believe in God should see that they engage in honourable occupations, which are not only honourable in themselves, but also useful to their fellow-men.[c] But steer clear of foolish speculations, genealogies, 9 quarrels, and controversies over the Law; they are unprofitable and pointless.

A heretic should be warned once, and once again; after 10 that, have done with him, recognizing that a man of that 11 sort has a distorted mind and stands self-condemned in his sin.

When I send Artemas to you, or Tychicus, make haste 12 to join me at Nicopolis, for that is where I have determined to spend the winter. Do your utmost to help Zenas 13 the lawyer and Apollos on their travels, and see that they are not short of anything. And our own people must be 14 taught to engage in honest employment to produce the necessities of life; they must not be unproductive.

All who are with me send you greetings. My greetings 15 to those who are our friends in truth.[d] Grace be with you all!

---

[a] *Or* ready always to do good.      [b] *Or* the water of rebirth and of renewal by . . .      [c] *Or* should make it their business to practise virtue. These precepts are good in themselves and useful to society.
[d] *Or* our friends in the faith.

# THE
# LETTER OF PAUL TO
# PHILEMON

## A RUNAWAY SLAVE

¹ FROM PAUL, a prisoner of Christ Jesus, and our
colleague Timothy, to Philemon our dear friend and
² fellow-worker, and Apphia our sister, and Archippus
our comrade-in-arms, and the congregation at your house.
³ Grace to you and peace from God our Father and the
Lord Jesus Christ.
⁴ I thank my God always when I mention you in my
⁵ prayers, for I hear of your love and faith towards the Lord
⁶ Jesus and towards all God's people. My prayer is that your
fellowship with us in our common faith may deepen the
understanding of all the blessings that our union with
⁷ Christ brings us.ᵃ For I am delighted and encouraged by
your love; through you, my brother, God's people have
been much refreshed.
⁸ Accordingly, although in Christ I might make bold to
⁹ point out your duty, yet, because of that same love, I
would rather appeal to you. Yes, I, Paul, ambassador as
¹⁰ I am of Christ Jesus—and now his prisoner—appeal to
you about my child, whose father I have become in this
prison.
¹¹ I mean Onesimus, once so little use to you, but now use-
¹² ful indeed, both to you and to me. I am sending him back
¹³ to you, and in doing so I am sending a part of myself. I
should have liked to keep him with me, to look after me
¹⁴ as you would wish, here in prison for the Gospel. But I
would rather do nothing without your consent, so that
your kindness may be a matter not of compulsion, but of
¹⁵ your own free will. For perhaps this is why you lost him
¹⁶ for a time, that you might have him back for good, no
longer as a slave, but as more than a slave—as a dear

ᵃ Or that bring us to Christ.

368

brother, very dear indeed to me and how much dearer to you, both as man and as Christian.

If, then, you count me partner in the faith, welcome him 17 as you would welcome me. And if he has done you any 18 wrong or is in your debt, put that down to my account. Here is my signature, PAUL; I undertake to repay—not 19 to mention that you owe your very self to me as well. Now 20 brother, as a Christian, be generous with me, and relieve my anxiety; we are both in Christ!

I write to you confident that you will meet my wishes; 21 I know that you will in fact do better than I ask. And one 22 thing more: have a room ready for me, for I hope that, in answer to your prayers, God will grant me to you.

Epaphras, Christ's captive like myself, sends you greet- 23 ings. So do Mark, Aristarchus, Demas, and Luke, my 24 fellow-workers.

The grace of the Lord Jesus Christ be with your spirit! 25

# A LETTER TO

# HEBREWS

## CHRIST DIVINE AND HUMAN

**1** WHEN IN FORMER TIMES God spoke to
our forefathers, he spoke in fragmentary and
**2** varied fashion through the prophets. But in this
the final age he has spoken to us in the Son whom he has
made heir to the whole universe, and through whom he
**3** created all orders of existence: the Son who is the efful-
gence of God's splendour and the stamp of God's very
being, and sustains[a] the universe by his word of power.
When he had brought about the purgation of sins, he took
**4** his seat at the right hand of Majesty on high, raised as far
above the angels, as the title he has inherited is superior
to theirs.

**5** For God never said to any angel, 'Thou art my Son;
today I have begotten thee', or again, 'I will be father to
**6** him, and he shall be my son.' Again, when he presents the
first-born to the world, he says, 'Let all the angels of God
**7** pay him homage.' Of the angels he says,

'He who makes his angels winds,
and his ministers a fiery flame';

**8** but of the Son,

'Thy throne, O God, is for ever and ever,
and the sceptre[b] of justice is the sceptre of his kingdom.
**9** Thou hast loved right and hated wrong;
therefore, O God, thy God[c] has set thee above thy fellows,
by anointing with the oil of exultation.'

**10** And again,

'By thee, Lord, were earth's foundations laid of old,
and the heavens are the work of thy hands.
**11** They shall pass away, but thou endurest;
like clothes they shall all grow old;

---

[a] *Or* bears along.
and thy sceptre . . .

[b] *Or* God is thy throne for ever and ever,

[c] *Or* therefore God who is thy God . . .

thou shalt fold them up like a cloak;      12
yes, they shall be changed like any garment.
But thou art the same, and thy years shall have no end.'

To which of the angels has he ever said, 'Sit at my right   13
hand until I make thy enemies thy footstool'? What are   14
they all but ministrant spirits, sent out to serve, for the
sake of those who are to inherit salvation?

Thus we are bound to pay all the more heed to what we   2
have been told, for fear of drifting from our course. For if   2
the word spoken through angels had such force that any
transgression or disobedience met with due retribution,
what escape can there be for us if we ignore a deliverance   3
so great? For this deliverance was first announced through
the lips of the Lord himself; those who heard him confirmed it to us, and God added his testimony by signs, by   4
miracles, by manifold works of power, and by distributing
the gifts of the Holy Spirit at his own will.

For it is not to angels that he has subjected the world   5
to come, which is our theme. But there is somewhere a   6
solemn assurance which runs:

'What is man, that thou rememberest him,
or the son of man, that thou hast regard to him?
Thou didst make him for a short while lower than the   7
    angels;
thou didst crown him with glory and honour;
thou didst put all things in subjection beneath his feet.'   8

For in subjecting all things to him, he left nothing that is
not subject. But in fact we do not yet see all things in subjection to man. In Jesus, however, we do see one who[a] for   9
a short while was made lower than the angels, crowned
now with glory and honour because he suffered death, so
that, by God's gracious will, in tasting death he should
stand[b] for us all.

It was clearly fitting that God for whom and through   10
whom all things exist should, in bringing many sons to
glory, make the leader who delivers them perfect through
sufferings. For a consecrating priest and those whom he   11
consecrates are all of one stock; and that is why the Son
does not shrink from calling men his brothers, when he   12
says, 'I will proclaim thy name to my brothers; in full
assembly I will sing thy praise'; and again, 'I will keep my   13

[a] *Or* in subjection to him. But we see Jesus, who . . .      [b] *Some*
*witnesses read* so that apart from God he should taste death . . .

trust fixed on him'; and again, 'Here am I, and the children
14 whom God has given me.' The children of a family share
the same flesh and blood; and so he too shared ours, so
that through death he might break the power of him who
15 had death at his command, that is, the devil; and might
liberate those who, through fear of death, had all their
16 lifetime been in servitude. It is not angels, mark you, that
17 he takes to himself, but the sons of Abraham. And therefore he had to be made like these brothers of his in every
way, so that he might be merciful and faithful as their
high priest before God, to expiate the sins of the people.
18 For since he himself has passed through the test of suffering, he is able to help those who are meeting their test now.

3    Therefore, brothers in the family of God, who share a
heavenly calling, think of the Apostle and High Priest of
2 the religion we profess,[a] who was faithful to God who appointed him. Moses also was faithful in God's household;
3 and Jesus, of whom I speak, has been deemed worthy of
greater honour than Moses, as the founder of a house
4 enjoys more honour than his household. For every house
5 has its founder; and the founder of all is God. Moses, then,
was faithful as a servitor in God's whole household; his
task was to bear witness to the words that God would
6 speak; but Christ is faithful as a son, set over his household. And we are that household of his, if only we are
fearless and keep our hope high.

7 'TODAY', THEREFORE, as the Holy Spirit says—

   'Today if you hear his voice,
8      do not grow stubborn as in those days of rebellion,
       at that time of testing in the desert,
9      where your forefathers tried me and tested me,
       and saw[b] the things I did for forty years.
10   And so, I was indignant with that generation
     and I said, Their hearts are for ever astray;
       they would not discern my ways;
11     as I vowed in my anger, they shall never enter my rest.'

12   See to it, brothers, that no one among you has the
wicked, faithless heart of a deserter from the living God;
13 but day by day, while that word 'Today' still sounds in your
ears, encourage one another, so that no one of you is made
14 stubborn by the wiles of sin. For we have become Christ's

   [a] Or of him whom we confess as God's Envoy and High Priest.
   [b] Or though they saw . . .

partners[a] if only we keep our original confidence firm to the end.

When Scripture says, 'Today if you hear his voice, do not 15 grow stubborn as in those days of rebellion', who, I ask, 16 were those who heard and rebelled? All those, surely, whom Moses had led out of Egypt. And with whom was 17 God indignant for forty years? With those, surely, who had sinned, whose bodies lay where they fell in the desert. And 18 to whom did he vow that they should not enter his rest, if not to those who had refused to believe? We perceive 19 that it was unbelief which prevented their entering.

Therefore we must have before us the fear that while the 4 promise of entering his rest remains open, one or another among you should be found to have missed his chance. For indeed we have heard the good news, as they did. But 2 in them the message they heard did no good, because it met with no faith in those who heard it. It is we, we who 3 have become believers, who enter the rest referred to in the words, 'As I vowed in my anger, they shall never enter my rest.' Yet God's work has been finished ever since the world was created; for does not Scripture somewhere speak 4 thus of the seventh day: 'God rested from all his work on the seventh day'?—and once again in the passage above 5 we read, 'They shall never enter my rest.' The fact remains 6 that someone must enter it, and since those who first heard the good news failed to enter through unbelief, God 7 fixes another day. Speaking through the lips of David after many long years, he uses the words already quoted: 'Today if you hear his voice, do not grow stubborn.' If 8 Joshua had given them rest, God would not thus have spoken of another day after that. Therefore, a sabbath 9 rest still awaits the people of God; for anyone who enters 10 God's rest, rests from his own work as God did from his. Let us then make every effort to enter that rest, so that no 11 one may fall by following this evil example of unbelief.

For the word of God is alive and active. It cuts more 12 keenly than any two-edged sword, piercing as far as the place where life and spirit, joints and marrow, divide. It sifts the purposes and thoughts of the heart. There is 13 nothing in creation that can hide from him; everything lies naked and exposed to the eyes of the One with whom we have to reckon.

Since therefore we have a great high priest who has 14 passed through the heavens, Jesus the Son of God, let us

[a] Or have been given a share in Christ.

373

15 hold fast to the religion we profess. For ours is not a high
priest unable to sympathize with our weaknesses, but one
who, because of his likeness to us, has been tested every
16 way,ᵃ only without sin. Let us therefore boldly approach
the throne of our gracious God, where we may receive
mercy and in his grace find timely help.


## THE SHADOW AND THE REAL

5 FOR EVERY HIGH PRIEST is taken from among
men and appointed their representative before God,
2 to offer gifts and sacrifices for sins. He is able to bear
patiently with the ignorant and erring, since he too is beset
3 by weakness; and because of this he is bound to make sin-
4 offerings for himself no less than for the people. And nobody arrogates the honour to himself: he is called by God,
5 as indeed Aaron was. So it is with Christ: he did not confer upon himself the glory of becoming high priest; it was
granted by God, who said to him, 'Thou art my Son; today
6 I have begotten thee'; as also in another place he says,
'Thou art a priest for ever, in the succession of Melchiz-
7 edek.' In the days of his earthly life he offered up prayers
and petitions, with loud cries and tears, to God who was
able to deliver him from the grave. Because of his humble
8 submission his prayer was heard: son though he was, he
9 learned obedience in the school of suffering, and, once
perfected, became the source of eternal salvation for all
10 who obey him, named by God high priest in the succession
of Melchizedek.

11    About Melchizedek we have much to say, much that is
difficult to explain, now that you have grown so dull of
12 hearing. For indeed, though by this time you ought to be
teachers, you need someone to teach you the ABC of God's
oracles over again; it has come to this, that you need milk
13 instead of solid food. Anyone who lives on milk, being an
14 infant, does not knowᵇ what is right. But grown men can
take solid food; their perceptions are trained by long use
to discriminate between good and evil.

6    Let us then stop discussing the rudiments of Christianity.
We ought not to be laying over again the foundations of
faith in God and of repentance from the deadness of our

ᵃ *Or who has been tested every way, as we are.*     ᵇ *Or is incom-*
*petent to speak of . . .*

former ways, by instruction[a] about cleansing rites and the 2
laying-on-of-hands, about the resurrection of the dead
and eternal judgement. Instead, let us advance towards
maturity; and so we shall, if God permits.                3

For when men have once been enlightened, when they 4
have had a taste of the heavenly gift and a share in the
Holy Spirit, when they have experienced the goodness of 5
God's word and the spiritual energies of the age to come,
and after all this have fallen away, it is impossible to 6
bring them again to repentance; for with their own hands
they are crucifying[b] the Son of God and making mock of
his death. When the earth drinks in the rain that falls 7
upon it from time to time, and yields a useful crop to those
for whom it is cultivated, it is receiving its share of blessing
from God; but if it bears thorns and thistles, it is worthless 8
and God's curse hangs over it; the end of that is burning.
But although we speak as we do, we are convinced that 9
you, my friends, are in the better case, and this makes for
your salvation. For God would not be so unjust as to forget 10
all that you did for love of his name, when you rendered
service to his people, as you still do. But we long for every 11
one of you to show the same eager concern, until your hope
is finally realized. We want you not to become lazy, but 12
to imitate those who, through faith and patience, are in-
heriting the promises.

When God made his promise to Abraham, he swore by 13
himself, because he had no one greater to swear by: 'I vow 14
that I will bless you abundantly and multiply your descendants.' Thus it was that Abraham, after patient wait- 15
ing, attained the promise. Men swear by a greater than 16
themselves, and the oath provides a confirmation to end
all dispute; and so God, desiring to show even more clearly 17
to the heirs of his promise how unchanging was his purpose,
guaranteed it by oath. Here, then, are two irrevocable acts 18
in which God could not possibly play us false, to give
powerful encouragement to us, who have claimed his protection by grasping[c] the hope set before us. That hope we 19
hold. It is like an anchor for our lives, an anchor safe and
sure. It enters in through the veil, where Jesus has entered 20
on our behalf as forerunner, having become a high priest
for ever in the succession of Melchizedek.

---

[a] *Or, according to some witnesses,* laying the foundations over again:
repentance from the deadness of our former ways and faith in God,
instruction . . .          [b] *Or* crucifying again.          [c] *Or* to give to us,
who have claimed his protection, a powerful incentive to grasp . . .

7 THIS MELCHIZEDEK, king of Salem, priest of God Most High, met Abraham returning from the rout of the 2 kings and blessed him; and Abraham gave him a tithe of everything as his portion. His name, in the first place, means 'king of righteousness'; next he is king of Salem, 3 that is, 'king of peace'. He has no father, no mother, no lineage; his years have no beginning, his life no end. He is like the Son of God: he remains a priest for all time.

4 Consider now how great he must be for Abraham the patriarch to give him a tithe of the finest of the spoil. 5 The descendants of Levi who take the priestly office are commanded by the Law to tithe the people, that is, their kinsmen, although they too are descendants of Abraham. 6 But Melchizedek, though he does not trace his descent from them, has tithed Abraham himself, and given his 7 blessing to the man who received the promises; and beyond all dispute the lesser is always blessed by the greater. 8 Again, in the one instance tithes are received by men who must die; but in the other, by one whom Scripture affirms 9 to be alive. It might even be said that Levi, who receives 10 tithes, has himself been tithed through Abraham; for he was still in his ancestor's loins when Melchizedek met him.

11 Now if perfection had been attainable through the Levitical priesthood (for it is on this basis that the people were given the Law), what further need would there have been to speak of another priest arising, in the succession 12 of Melchizedek, instead of the succession of Aaron? For a 13 change of priesthood must mean a change of law. And the one here spoken of belongs to a different tribe, no member 14 of which has ever had anything to do with the altar. For it is very evident that our Lord is sprung from Judah, a tribe to which Moses made no reference in speaking of priests.

15 The argument becomes still clearer, if the new priest 16 who arises is one like Melchizedek, owing his priesthood not to a system of earth-bound rules but to the power of 17 a life that cannot be destroyed. For here is the testimony: 'Thou art a priest for ever, in the succession of Melchiz-18 edek.' The earlier rules are cancelled as impotent and use-19 less, since the Law brought nothing to perfection; and a better hope is introduced, through which we draw near to God.

20 How great a difference it makes that an oath was sworn! 21 There was no oath sworn when those others were made priests; but for this priest an oath was sworn, as Scripture

says of him: 'The Lord has sworn and will not go back on his word, "Thou art a priest for ever."' How far superior 22 must the covenant also be of which Jesus is the guarantor! Those other priests are appointed in numerous succession, 23 because they are prevented by death from continuing in office; but the priesthood which Jesus holds is perpetual, 24 because he remains for ever. That is why he is also able to 25 save absolutely those who approach God through him; he is always living to plead on their behalf.

Such a high priest does indeed fit our condition—devout, 26 guileless, undefiled, separated from sinners, raised high above the heavens. He has no need to offer sacrifices daily, 27 as the high priests do, first for his own sins and then for those of the people; for this he did once and for all when he offered up himself. The high priests made by the Law are 28 men in all their frailty; but the priest appointed by the words of the oath which supersedes the Law is the Son, made perfect now for ever.

Now THIS IS my main point: just such a high priest 8 we have, and he has taken his seat at the right hand of the throne of Majesty in the heavens, a ministrant in the real 2 sanctuary, the tent pitched by the Lord and not by man. Every high priest is appointed to offer gifts and sacrifices; 3 hence, this one too must have[a] something to offer. Now if 4 he had been on earth, he would not even have been a priest, since there are already priests who offer the gifts which the Law prescribes, though they minister in a sanctuary which 5 is only a copy and shadow of the heavenly. This is implied when Moses, about to erect the tent, is instructed by God: 'See to it that you make everything according to the pattern shown you on the mountain.' But in fact the ministry 6 which has fallen to Jesus is as far superior to theirs as are the covenant he mediates and the promises upon which it is legally secured.

Had that first covenant been faultless, there would have 7 been no need to look for a second in its place. But God, 8 finding fault with them, says, 'The days are coming, says the Lord, when I will conclude a new covenant with the house of Israel and the house of Judah. It will not be like 9 the covenant I made with their forefathers when I took them by the hand to lead them out of Egypt; because they did not abide by the terms of that covenant, and I abandoned them, says the Lord. For the covenant I will 10

[a] Or *must have had.*

make with the house of Israel after those days, says the Lord, is this: I will set my laws in their understanding and write them on their hearts; and I will be their God, and
11 they shall be my people. And they shall not teach one another, saying to brother and fellow-citizen,[a] "Know the
12 Lord!" For all of them, high and low, shall know me; I will be merciful to their wicked deeds, and I will remember
13 their sins no more.' By speaking of a new covenant, he has pronounced the first one old; and anything that is growing old and ageing will shortly disappear.

9 THE FIRST COVENANT indeed had its ordinances of divine service and its sanctuary, but a material sanctuary.
2 For a tent was prepared—the first tent—in which was the lamp-stand, and the table with the bread of the Presence;
3 this is called the Holy Place. Beyond the second curtain
4 was the tent called the Most Holy Place. Here was a golden altar of incense, and the ark of the covenant plated all over with gold, in which were a golden jar containing the manna, and Aaron's staff which once budded, and the
5 tablets of the covenant; and above it the cherubim of God's glory, overshadowing the place of expiation. On these we cannot now enlarge.
6 Under this arrangement, the priests are always entering
7 the first tent in the discharge of their duties; but the second is entered only once a year, and by the high priest alone, and even then he must take with him the blood which he offers on his own behalf and for the people's sins
8 of ignorance. By this the Holy Spirit signifies that so long as the earlier tent still stands, the way into the sanctuary
9 remains unrevealed. All this is symbolic, pointing to the present time. The offerings and sacrifices there prescribed
10 cannot give the worshipper inward perfection. It is only a matter of food and drink and various rites of cleansing— outward ordinances in force until the time of reformation.
11 But now Christ has come, high priest of good things already in being.[b] The tent of his priesthood is a greater and more perfect one, not made by men's hands, that is,
12 not belonging to this created world; the blood of his sacrifice is his own blood, not the blood of goats and calves; and thus he has entered the sanctuary once and for all and
13 secured an eternal deliverance. For if the blood of goats and bulls and the sprinkled ashes of a heifer have power to

---

[a] *Some witnesses read* brother and neighbour.     [b] *Some witnesses read* good things which were (*or* are) to be.

hallow those who have been defiled and restore their external purity, how much greater is the power of the blood 14 of Christ; he offered himself without blemish to God, a spiritual and eternal sacrifice; and his blood will cleanse our conscience from the deadness of our former ways and fit us for the service of the living God.

And therefore he is the mediator of a new covenant, or 15 testament, under which, now that there has been a death to bring deliverance from sins committed under the former covenant, those whom God has called may receive the promise of the eternal inheritance. For where there is a 16 testament it is necessary for the death of the testator to be established. A testament is operative only after a death: 17 it cannot possibly have force while the testator is alive. Thus we find that the former covenant itself was not in- 18 augurated without blood. For when, as the Law directed, 19 Moses had recited all the commandments to the people, he took the blood of the calves, with water, scarlet wool, and marjoram, and sprinkled the law-book itself and all the people, saying, 'This is the blood of the covenant which God 20 has enjoined upon you.' In the same way he also sprinkled 21 the tent and all the vessels of divine service with blood. Indeed, according to the Law, it might almost be said, 22 everything is cleansed by blood and without the shedding of blood there is no forgiveness.

If, then, these sacrifices cleanse the copies of heavenly 23 things, those heavenly things themselves require better sacrifices to cleanse them. For Christ has entered, not that 24 sanctuary made by men's hands which is only a symbol of the reality, but heaven itself, to appear now before God on our behalf. Nor is he there to offer himself again and 25 again, as the high priest enters the sanctuary year by year with blood not his own. If that were so, he would have had 26 to suffer many times since the world was made. But as it is, he has appeared once and for all at the climax of history to abolish sin by the sacrifice of himself. And as it is the 27 lot of men to die once, and after death comes judgement, so Christ was offered once to bear the burden of men's 28 sins,[a] and will appear a second time, sin done away, to bring salvation to those who are watching for him.

FOR THE LAW contains but a shadow, and no true image,[b] 10 of the good things which were to come; it provides for the

[a] *Or* to remove men's sins.        [b] *One witness reads* a shadow and likeness . . .

same sacrifices year after year, and with these it can never bring the worshippers to perfection for all time.[a]

2 If it could, these sacrifices would surely have ceased to be offered, because the worshippers, cleansed once for

3 all, would no longer have any sense of sin. But instead, in these sacrifices year after year sins are brought to mind,

4 because sins can never be removed by the blood of bulls and goats.

5 That is why, at his coming into the world, he says:

'Sacrifice and offering thou didst not desire,
but thou hast prepared a body for me.

6 Whole-offerings and sin-offerings thou didst not delight in.

7 Then I said, "Here am I: as it is written of me in the scroll, I have come, O God, to do thy will."'

8 First he says, 'Sacrifices and offerings, whole-offerings and sin-offerings, thou didst not desire nor delight in'—although

9 the Law prescribes them—and then he says, 'I have come to do thy will.' He thus annuls the former to establish the

10 latter. And it is by the will of God that we have been consecrated, through the offering of the body of Jesus Christ once and for all.

11 Every priest stands performing his service daily and offering time after time the same sacrifices, which can

12 never remove sins. But Christ offered for all time one sacrifice for sins, and took his seat at the right hand of

13 God, where he waits henceforth until his enemies are made

14 his footstool. For by one offering he has perfected for all

15 time those who are thus consecrated. Here we have also

16 the testimony of the Holy Spirit: he first says, 'This is the covenant which I will make with them after those days, says the Lord: I will set my laws in their hearts and write

17 them on their understanding'; then he adds, 'and their sins

18 and wicked deeds I will remember no more at all.' And where these have been forgiven, there are offerings for sin no longer.

19 So now, my friends, the blood of Jesus makes us free

20 to enter boldly into the sanctuary by the new, living way which he has opened for us through the curtain, the way

21 of his flesh.[b] We have, moreover, a great priest set over the

22 household of God; so let us make our approach in sincerity

---

[a] *Or* bring to perfection the worshippers who come continually.
[b] *Or* through the curtain of his flesh.

of heart and full assurance of faith, our guilty hearts sprinkled clean, our bodies washed with pure water. Let 23 us be firm and unswerving in the confession of our hope, for the Giver of the promise may be trusted. We ought to 24 see how each of us may best arouse others to love and active goodness, not staying away from our meetings, as 25 some do, but rather encouraging one another, all the more because you see the Day drawing near.

For if we wilfully persist in sin after receiving the know- 26 ledge of the truth, no sacrifice for sins remains: only a 27 terrifying expectation of judgement and a fierce fire which will consume God's enemies. If a man disregards 28 the Law of Moses, he is put to death without pity on the evidence of two or three witnesses. Think how much more 29 severe a penalty that man will deserve who has trampled under foot the Son of God, profaned the blood of the covenant by which he was consecrated, and affronted God's gracious Spirit! For we know who it is that has said, 30 'Justice is mine: I will repay'; and again, 'The Lord will judge his people.' It is a terrible thing to fall into the 31 hands of the living God.

Remember the days gone by, when, newly enlightened, 32 you met the challenge of great sufferings and held firm. Some of you were abused and tormented to make a public 33 show, while others stood loyally by those who were so treated. For indeed you shared the sufferings of the 34 prisoners, and you cheerfully accepted the seizure of your possessions, knowing that you possessed something better and more lasting. Do not then throw away your confidence, 35 for it carries a great reward. You need endurance, if you 36 are to do God's will and win what he has promised. For 37 'soon, very soon' (in the words of Scripture), 'he who is to come will come; he will not delay; and by faith my right- 38 eous servant shall find life; but if a man shrinks back, I take no pleasure in him.' But we are not among those who 39 shrink back and are lost; we have the faith to make life our own.

# A CALL TO FAITH

AND WHAT IS FAITH? Faith gives substance[a] to 11 our hopes, and makes us certain of realities we do not see.

[a] *Or* assurance.

2    It is for their faith that the men of old stand on record.

3    By faith we perceive that the universe was fashioned by the word of God, so that the visible came forth from the invisible.

4    By faith Abel offered a sacrifice greater than Cain's, and through faith his goodness was attested, for his offerings had God's approval; and through faith he continued to speak after his death.

5    By faith Enoch was carried away to another life without passing through death; he was not to be found, because God had taken him. For it is the testimony of Scripture

6    that before he was taken he had pleased God, and without faith it is impossible to please him; for anyone who comes to God must believe that he exists and that he rewards those who search for him.

7    By faith Noah, divinely warned about the unseen future, took good heed and built an ark to save his household. Through his faith he put the whole world in the wrong, and made good his own claim to the righteousness which comes of faith.

8    By faith Abraham obeyed the call to go out to a land destined for himself and his heirs, and left home without

9    knowing where he was to go. By faith he settled as an alien in the land promised him, living in tents, as did Isaac

10   and Jacob, who were heirs to the same promise. For he was looking forward to the city with firm foundations, whose architect and builder is God.

11   By faith even Sarah herself received strength to conceive, though she was past the age, because she judged

12   that he who had promised would keep faith; and therefore from one man, and one as good as dead, there sprang descendants numerous as the stars or as the countless grains of sand on the sea-shore.

13   All these persons died in faith. They were not yet in possession of the things promised, but had seen them far ahead and hailed them, and confessed themselves no more

14   than strangers or passing travellers on earth. Those who use such language show plainly that they are looking for

15   a country of their own. If their hearts had been in the country they had left, they could have found oppor-

16   tunity to return. Instead, we find them longing for a better country—I mean, the heavenly one. That is why God is not ashamed to be called their God; for he has a city ready for them.

By faith Abraham, when the test came, offered up Isaac: 17
he had received the promises, and yet he was on the point
of offering his only son, of whom he had been told, 18
'Through the line of Isaac your descendants shall be
traced.'[a] For he reckoned that God had power even to 19
raise from the dead—and from the dead, he did, in a sense,
receive him back.

By faith Isaac blessed Jacob and Esau and spoke of 20
things to come. By faith Jacob, as he was dying, blessed 21
each of Joseph's sons, and worshipped God, leaning on the
top of his staff. By faith Joseph, at the end of his life, 22
spoke of the departure of Israel from Egypt, and instructed
them what to do with his bones.

By faith, when Moses was born, his parents hid him for 23
three months, because they saw what a fine child he was;
they were not afraid of the king's edict. By faith Moses, 24
when he grew up, refused to be called the son of Pharaoh's
daughter, preferring to suffer hardship with the people of 25
God rather than enjoy the transient pleasures of sin. He 26
considered the stigma that rests on God's Anointed greater
wealth than the treasures of Egypt, for his eyes were fixed
upon the coming day of recompense. By faith he left Egypt, 27
and not because he feared the king's anger; for he was
resolute, as one who saw the invisible God.

By faith he celebrated the Passover and sprinkled the 28
blood, so that the destroying angel might not touch the
first-born of Israel. By faith they crossed the Red Sea as 29
though it were dry land, whereas the Egyptians, when they
attempted the crossing, were drowned.

By faith the walls of Jericho fell down after they had 30
been encircled on seven successive days. By faith the 31
prostitute Rahab escaped the doom of the unbelievers,
because she had given the spies a kindly welcome.

Need I say more? Time is too short for me to tell the 32
stories of Gideon, Barak, Samson, and Jephthah, of David
and Samuel and the prophets. Through faith they over- 33
threw kingdoms, established justice, saw God's promises
fulfilled. They muzzled ravening lions, quenched the fury 34
of fire, escaped death by the sword. Their weakness was
turned to strength, they grew powerful in war, they put
foreign armies to rout. Women received back their dead 35
raised to life. Others were tortured to death, disdaining
release, to win a better resurrection. Others, again, had to 36
face jeers and flogging, even fetters and prison bars. They 37

[a] Or *God's call shall be for your descendants in the line of Isaac.*

were stoned,[a] they were sawn in two, they were put to the sword, they went about dressed in skins of sheep or goats, 38 in poverty, distress, and misery. They were too good for a world like this. They were refugees in deserts and on the 39 hills, hiding in caves and holes in the ground. These also, one and all, are commemorated for their faith; and yet 40 they did not enter upon the promised inheritance, because, with us in mind, God had made a better plan, that only in company with us should they reach their perfection.

12 AND WHAT OF OURSELVES? With all these witnesses to faith around us like a cloud, we must throw off every encumbrance, every sin to which we cling,[b] and run with 2 resolution the race for which we are entered, our eyes fixed on Jesus, on whom faith depends from start to finish: Jesus who, for the sake of the joy that lay ahead of him,[c] endured the cross, making light of its disgrace, and has taken his seat at the right hand of the throne of God.

3    Think of him who submitted to such opposition from sinners: that will help you not to lose heart and grow faint. 4 In your struggle against sin, you have not yet resisted to 5 the point of shedding your blood. You have forgotten the text of Scripture which addresses you as sons and appeals to you in these words:

'My son, do not think lightly of the Lord's discipline,
    nor lose heart when he corrects you;
6    for the Lord disciplines those whom he loves;
    he lays the rod on every son whom he acknowledges.'

7 You must endure it as discipline: God is treating you as sons. Can anyone be a son, who is not disciplined by his 8 father? If you escape the discipline in which all sons 9 share, you must be bastards and no true sons. Again, we paid due respect to the earthly fathers who disciplined us; should we not submit even more readily to our spiritual 10 Father, and so attain life? They disciplined us for this short life according to their lights; but he does so for our 11 true welfare, so that we may share his holiness. Discipline, no doubt, is never pleasant; at the time it seems painful, but in the end it yields for those who have been trained by 12 it the peaceful harvest of an honest life. Come, then, stiffen 13 your drooping arms and shaking knees, and keep your

---

[a] *Some witnesses insert* they were put to the question.    [b] *Or* every clinging sin; *one witness reads* the sin which all too readily distracts us.
[c] *Or* who, in place of the joy that was open to him, . . .

steps from wavering. Then the disabled limb will not be put out of joint, but regain its former powers.

Aim at peace with all men, and a holy life, for without 14 that no one will see the Lord. Look to it that there is no 15 one among you who forfeits the grace of God, no bitter, noxious weed growing up to poison the whole, no immoral 16 person, no one worldly-minded like Esau. He sold his birthright for a single meal, and you know that although 17 he wanted afterwards to claim the blessing, he was rejected; though he begged for it to the point of tears, he found no way open for second thoughts.

REMEMBER WHERE YOU STAND: not before the palp- 18 able, blazing fire of Sinai, with the darkness, gloom, and whirlwind, the trumpet-blast and the oracular voice, 19 which they heard, and begged to hear no more; for they 20 could not bear the command, 'If even an animal touches the mountain, it must be stoned.' So appalling was the 21 sight, that Moses said, 'I shudder with fear.'

No, you stand before Mount Zion and the city of the 22 living God, heavenly Jerusalem, before myriads of angels, the full concourse and assembly of the first-born citizens 23 of heaven, and God the judge of all, and the spirits of good men made perfect, and Jesus the mediator of a new cove- 24 nant, whose sprinkled blood has better things to tell than the blood of Abel. See that you do not refuse to hear the 25 voice that speaks. Those who refused to hear the oracle speaking on earth found no escape; still less shall we escape if we refuse to hear the One who speaks from heaven. Then indeed his voice shook the earth, but now he has 26 promised, 'Yet once again I will shake not earth alone, but the heavens also.' The words 'once again'—and only 27 once—imply that the shaking of these created things means their removal, and then what is not shaken will remain. The kingdom we are given is unshakable; let us 28 therefore give thanks to God, and so worship him as he would be worshipped, with reverence and awe; for our 29 God is a devouring fire.

NEVER CEASE TO LOVE your fellow-Christians.                    13
Remember to show hospitality. There are some who, by 2 so doing, have entertained angels without knowing it.

Remember those in prison as if you were there with 3 them; and those who are being maltreated, for you like them are still in the world.

4 Marriage is honourable; let us all keep it so, and the marriage-bond inviolate; for God's judgement will fall on fornicators and adulterers.

5 Do not live for money; be content with what you have; for God himself has said, 'I will never leave you or desert

6 you'; and so we can take courage and say, 'The Lord is my helper, I will not fear; what can man do to me?'

7 Remember your leaders, those who first spoke God's message to you; and reflecting upon the outcome of their life and work, follow the example of their faith.

8 Jesus Christ is the same yesterday, today, and for ever.

9 So do not be swept off your course by all sorts of outlandish teachings; it is good that our souls should gain their strength from the grace of God, and not from scruples about what we eat, which have never done any good to those who were governed by them.

10 Our altar is one from which[a] the priests of the sacred

11 tent have no right to eat. As you know, those animals whose blood is brought as a sin-offering by the high priest into the sanctuary, have their bodies burnt outside the

12 camp, and therefore Jesus also suffered outside the gate,

13 to consecrate the people by his own blood. Let us then go to him outside the camp, bearing the stigma that he bore.

14 For here we have no permanent home, but we are seekers

15 after the city which is to come. Through Jesus, then, let us continually offer up to God the sacrifice of praise, that

16 is, the tribute of lips which acknowledge his name, and never forget to show kindness and to share what you have with others; for such are the sacrifices which God approves.

17 Obey your leaders and defer to them; for they are tireless in their concern for you, as men who must render an account. Let it be a happy task for them, and not pain and grief, for that would bring you no advantage.

18 Pray for us; for we are convinced that our conscience is

19 clear; our one desire is always to do what is right. All the more earnestly I ask for your prayers, that I may be restored to you the sooner.

20 May the God of peace, who brought up from the dead our Lord Jesus, the great Shepherd of the sheep, by the

21 blood of the eternal covenant, make you perfect in all goodness so that you may do his will; and may he make of us what he would have us be through Jesus Christ, to whom be glory for ever and ever! Amen.

[a] *Or one like that from which . . .*

I beg you, brothers, bear with this exhortation; for it is 22
after all a short letter. I have news for you: our friend 23
Timothy has been released; and if he comes in time he will
be with me when I see you.

Greet all your leaders and all God's people. Greetings to 24
you from our Italian friends.

God's grace be with you all!                               25

# A LETTER OF
# JAMES

## PRACTICAL RELIGION

1 FROM JAMES, a servant of God and the Lord Jesus Christ.

Greetings to the Twelve Tribes dispersed throughout the world.

2,3,4 My brothers, whenever you have to face trials of many kinds, count yourselves supremely happy, in the knowledge that such testing of your faith breeds fortitude, and if you give fortitude full play you will go on to complete a 5 balanced character that will fall short in nothing. If any of you falls short in wisdom, he should ask God for it and it will be given him, for God is a generous giver who 6 neither refuses nor reproaches anyone. But he must ask in faith, without a doubt in his mind; for the doubter is like 7 a heaving sea ruffled by the wind. A man of that kind must 8 not expect the Lord to give him anything; he is doubleminded, and never can keep[a] a steady course.

9 The brother in humble circumstances may well be 10 proud that God lifts him up; and the wealthy brother must find his pride in being brought low. For the rich man 11 will disappear like the flower of the field; once the sun is up with its scorching heat the flower withers, its petals fall, and what was lovely to look at is lost for ever. So shall the rich man wither away as he goes about his business.

12 Happy the man who remains steadfast under trial, for having passed that test he will receive for his prize the gift 13 of life promised to those who love God. No one under trial or temptation should say, 'I am being tempted by God'; for God is untouched by evil,[b] and does not himself tempt 14 anyone. Temptation arises when a man is enticed and 15 lured away by his own lust; then lust conceives, and gives birth to sin; and sin full-grown breeds death.

[a] Or anything; a double-minded man never keeps... [b] Or God cannot be tempted by evil.

388

Make no mistake, my friends. All good giving, every per-  16 17
fect gift, comes[a] from above, from the Father of the lights
of heaven. With him there is no variation, no play of
passing shadows.[b] Of his set purpose, by declaring the  18
truth, he gave us birth to be a kind of firstfruits of his
creatures.

Of that you may be certain, my friends. But each of you  19
must be quick to listen, slow to speak, and slow to be angry.
For a man's anger cannot promote the justice of God.  20
Away then with all that is sordid, and the malice that  21
hurries to excess, and quietly accept the message planted
in your hearts, which can bring you salvation.

Only be sure that you act on the message and do not  22
merely listen; for that would be to mislead yourselves. A  23
man who listens to the message but never acts upon it is
like one who looks in a mirror at the face nature gave him.
He glances at himself and goes away, and at once forgets  24
what he looked like. But the man who looks closely into the  25
perfect law, the law that makes us free, and who lives in its
company, does not forget what he hears, but acts upon it;
and that is the man who by acting will find happiness.

A man may think he is religious, but if he has no control  26
over his tongue, he is deceiving himself; that man's religion
is futile. The kind of religion which is without stain or  27
fault in the sight of God our Father is this: to go to the
help of orphans and widows in their distress and keep one-
self untarnished by the world.

My brothers, believing as you do in our Lord Jesus  2
Christ, who reigns in glory, you must never show snobbery.
For instance, two visitors may enter your place of wor-  2
ship, one a well-dressed man with gold rings, and the other
a poor man in shabby clothes. Suppose you pay special  3
attention to the well-dressed man and say to him, 'Please
take this seat', while to the poor man you say, 'You can
stand; or you may sit here[c] on the floor by my footstool',
do you not see that you are inconsistent and judge by false  4
standards?

Listen, my friends. Has not God chosen those who are  5
poor in the eyes of the world to be rich in faith and to
inherit the kingdom he has promised to those who love

---

[a] *Or* All giving is good, and every perfect gift comes . . .        [b] *Some*
*witnesses read* no variation, or shadow caused by change.        [c] *Some*
*witnesses read* Stand where you are or sit here . . .; *others read* Stand
where you are or sit . . .

6 him? And yet you have insulted the poor man. Moreover, are not the rich your oppressors? Is it not they who drag
7 you into court and pour contempt on the honoured name by which God has claimed you?

8 If, however, you are observing the sovereign law laid down in Scripture, 'Love your neighbour as yourself', that
9 is excellent. But if you show snobbery, you are committing a sin and you stand convicted by that law as transgressors.
10 For if a man keeps the whole law apart from one single
11 point, he is guilty of breaking all of it. For the One who said, 'Thou shalt not commit adultery', said also, 'Thou shalt not commit murder.' You may not be an adulterer, but if you commit murder you are a law-breaker all the
12 same. Always speak and act as men who are to be judged
13 under a law of freedom. In that judgement there will be no mercy for the man who has shown no mercy. Mercy triumphs over judgement.

14 My BROTHERS, what use is it for a man to say he has faith when he does nothing to show it? Can that faith save
15 him? Suppose a brother or a sister is in rags with not
16 enough food for the day, and one of you says, 'Good luck to you, keep yourselves warm, and have plenty to eat', but does nothing to supply their bodily needs, what is the
17 good of that? So with faith; if it does not lead to action, it is in itself a lifeless thing.
18 But someone may object: 'Here is one who claims to have faith and another who points to his deeds.' To which I reply: 'Prove to me that this faith you speak of is real though not accompanied by deeds, and by my deeds I will
19 prove to you my faith.' You have faith enough to believe that there is one God. Excellent! The devils have faith like
20 that, and it makes them tremble. But can you not see, you
21 quibbler, that faith divorced from deeds is barren? Was it not by his action, in offering his son Isaac upon the altar,
22 that our father Abraham was justified? Surely you can see that faith was at work in his actions, and that by these
23 actions the integrity of his faith was fully proved. Here was fulfilment of the words of Scripture: 'Abraham put his faith in God, and that faith was counted to him as righteousness'; and elsewhere he is called 'God's friend'.
24 You see then that a man is justified by deeds and not by
25 faith in itself. The same is true of the prostitute Rahab also. Was not she justified by her action in welcoming the messengers into her house and sending them away by a

different route? As the body is dead when there is no breath 26
left in it, so faith divorced from deeds is lifeless as a corpse.

MY BROTHERS, not many of you should become teachers, 3
for you may be certain that we who teach shall ourselves
be judged with greater strictness. All of us often go wrong; 2
the man who never says a wrong thing is a perfect character, able to bridle his whole being. If we put bits into 3
horses' mouths to make them obey our will, we can direct
their whole body. Or think of ships: large they may be, yet 4
even when driven by strong gales they can be directed by
a tiny rudder on whatever course the helmsman chooses.
So with the tongue. It is a small member but it can make 5
huge claims.*a*

What an immense stack of timber*b* can be set ablaze by
the tiniest spark! And the tongue is in effect a fire. It 6
represents among our members the world with all its
wickedness; it pollutes our whole being; it keeps the wheel
of our existence red-hot, and its flames are fed by hell.
Beasts and birds of every kind, creatures that crawl on the 7
ground or swim in the sea, can be subdued and have been
subdued by mankind; but no man can subdue the tongue. 8
It is an intractable evil, charged with deadly venom. We 9
use it to sing the praises of our Lord and Father, and we
use it to invoke curses upon our fellow-men who are made
in God's likeness. Out of the same mouth come praises and 10
curses. My brothers, this should not be so. Does a fountain 11
gush with both fresh and brackish water from the same
opening? Can a fig-tree, my brothers, yield olives, or a 12
vine figs? No more does salt water yield fresh.

WHO AMONG YOU is wise or clever? Let his right con- 13
duct give practical proof of it, with the modesty that
comes of wisdom. But if you are harbouring bitter jealousy 14
and selfish ambition in your hearts, consider whether your
claims are not false, and a defiance of the truth. This is 15
not the wisdom that comes from above; it is earth-bound,
sensual, demonic. For with jealousy and ambition come 16
disorder and evil of every kind. But the wisdom from above 17
is in the first place pure; and then peace-loving, consider-
ate, and open to reason; it is straightforward and sincere,
rich in mercy and in the kindly deeds that are its fruit. True 18
justice is the harvest reaped by peacemakers from seeds
sown in a spirit of peace.

     *a Or* it is a great boaster.       *b Or* What a huge forest . . .

4 　What causes conflicts and quarrels among you? Do they
not spring from the aggressiveness of your bodily desires?
2 You want something which you cannot have, and so you
are bent on murder; you are envious, and cannot attain
your ambition, and so you quarrel and fight. You do not
3 get what you want, because you do not pray for it. Or, if
you do, your requests are not granted because you pray
from wrong motives, to spend what you get on your plea-
4 sures. You false, unfaithful creatures! Have you never
learned that love of the world is enmity to God? Whoever
chooses to be the world's friend makes himself God's
5 enemy. Or do you suppose that Scripture has no meaning
when it says that the spirit which God implanted in man
6 turns towards envious desires? And yet the grace he gives
is stronger. Thus Scripture says, 'God opposes the arrogant
7 and gives grace to the humble.' Be submissive then to
8 God. Stand up to the devil and he will turn and run. Come
close to God, and he will come close to you. Sinners, make
your hands clean; you who are double-minded, see that
9 your motives are pure. Be sorrowful, mourn and weep.
Turn your laughter into mourning and your gaiety into
10 gloom. Humble yourselves before God and he will lift you
high.

11 　Brothers, you must never disparage one another. He
who disparages a brother or passes judgement on his
brother disparages the law and judges the law. But if you
judge the law, you are not keeping it but sitting in judge-
12 ment upon it. There is only one lawgiver and judge, the
One who is able to save life and destroy it. So who are you
to judge your neighbour?

13 A WORD WITH YOU, you who say, 'Today or tomorrow
we will go off to such and such a town and spend a year
14 there trading and making money.' Yet you have no idea
what tomorrow will bring. Your life, what is it? You are
no more than a mist, seen for a little while and then dis-
15 persing. What you ought to say is: 'If it be the Lord's will,
16 we shall live to do this or that.' But instead, you boast and
17 brag, and all such boasting is wrong. Well then, the man
who knows the good he ought to do and does not do it is
a sinner.

5 　Next a word to you who have great possessions. Weep
2 and wail over the miserable fate descending on you. Your
3 riches have rotted; your fine clothes are moth-eaten; your
silver and gold have rusted away, and their very rust will

be evidence against you and consume your flesh like fire. You have piled up wealth in an age that is near its close. The wages you never paid to the men who mowed your 4 fields are loud against you, and the outcry of the reapers has reached the ears of the Lord of Hosts. You have lived 5 on earth in wanton luxury, fattening yourselves like cattle —and the day for slaughter has come. You have condemned 6 the innocent and murdered him; he offers no resistance.

Be patient, my brothers, until the Lord comes. The 7 farmer looking for the precious crop his land may yield can only wait in patience, until the autumn and spring rains have fallen. You too must be patient and stout-hearted, 8 for the coming of the Lord is near. My brothers, do not 9 blame your troubles on one another, or you will fall under judgement; and there stands the Judge, at the door. If you 10 want a pattern of patience under ill-treatment, take the prophets who spoke in the name of the Lord; remember: 11 'We count those happy who stood firm.' You have all heard how Job stood firm, and you have seen how the Lord treated him in the end. For the Lord is full of pity and compassion.

ABOVE ALL THINGS, my brothers, do not use oaths, 12 whether 'by heaven' or 'by earth' or by anything else. When you say yes or no, let it be plain 'Yes' or 'No', for fear that you expose yourselves to judgement.

Is anyone among you in trouble? He should turn to 13 prayer. Is anyone in good heart? He should sing praises. Is one of you ill? He should send for the elders of the con- 14 gregation to pray over him and anoint him with oil in the name of the Lord. The prayer offered in faith will save the 15 sick man, the Lord will raise him from his bed, and any sins he may have committed will be forgiven. Therefore 16 confess your sins to one another, and pray for one another, and then you will be healed. A good man's prayer is power- ful and effective. Elijah was a man with human frailties 17 like our own; and when he prayed earnestly that there should be no rain, not a drop fell on the land for three years and a half; then he prayed again, and down came 18 the rain and the land bore crops once more.

My brothers, if one of your number should stray from 19 the truth and another succeed in bringing him back, be 20 sure of this: any man who brings a sinner back from his crooked ways will be rescuing his soul from death and cancelling innumerable sins.

# THE FIRST LETTER OF

# PETER

## THE CALLING OF A CHRISTIAN

1 FROM PETER, APOSTLE of Jesus Christ, to
those of God's scattered people who lodge for a while
in Pontus, Galatia, Cappadocia, Asia, and Bithynia—
2 chosen of old in the purpose of God the Father, hallowed
to his service by the Spirit, and consecrated with the
sprinkled blood of Jesus Christ.

Grace and peace to you in fullest measure.

3 Praise be to the God and Father of our Lord Jesus Christ,
who in his great mercy gave us new birth into a living hope
4 by the resurrection of Jesus Christ from the dead! The
inheritance to which we are born is one that nothing can
5 destroy or spoil or wither. It is kept for you in heaven, and
you, because you put your faith in God, are under the protection of his power until salvation comes—the salvation
which is even now in readiness and will be revealed at the
end of time.

6 This is cause for great joy, even though now you smart
for a little while, if need be, under trials of many kinds.
7 Even gold passes through the assayer's fire, and more
precious than perishable gold is faith which has stood the
test. These trials come so that your faith may prove itself
worthy of all praise, glory, and honour when Jesus Christ
is revealed.

8 You have not seen him, yet you love him; and trusting
in him now without seeing him, you are transported with
9 a joy too great for words, while you reap the harvest of
10 your faith, that is, salvation for your souls. This salvation
was the theme which the prophets pondered and explored,
those who prophesied about the grace of God awaiting you.
11 They tried to find out what was the time,[a] and what the
circumstances, to which the spirit of Christ in them pointed,
foretelling the sufferings in store for Christ and the splen-
12 dours to follow; and it was disclosed to them that the

[a] Or who was the person . . .

394

matter they treated of was not for their time but for yours.
And now it has been openly announced to you through
preachers who brought you the Gospel in the power of the
Holy Spirit sent from heaven. These are things that angels
long to see into.

You must therefore be mentally stripped for action, 13
perfectly self-controlled. Fix your hopes on the gift of
grace which is to be yours when Jesus Christ is revealed.
As obedient children, do not let your characters be shaped 14
any longer by the desires you cherished in your days of
ignorance. The One who called you is holy; like him, be 15
holy in all your behaviour, because Scripture says, 'You 16
shall be holy, for I am holy.'

If you say 'our Father' to the One who judges every man 17
impartially on the record of his deeds, you must stand in
awe of him while you live out your time on earth. Well you 18
know that it was no perishable stuff, like gold or silver,
that bought your freedom from the empty folly of your
traditional ways. The price was paid in precious blood, as 19
it were of a lamb without mark or blemish—the blood of
Christ. Predestined before the foundation of the world, he 20
was made manifest in this last period of time for your sake.
Through him you have come to trust in God who raised 21
him from the dead and gave him glory, and so your faith
and hope are fixed on God.

Now that by obedience to the truth you have purified 22
your souls until you feel sincere affection towards your
brother Christians, love one another whole-heartedly with
all your strength. You have been born anew, not of mortal 23
parentage but of immortal, through the living and enduring word of God.<sup>a</sup> For (as Scripture says) 24

> 'All mortals are like grass;
> all their splendour like the flower of the field;
> the grass withers, the flower falls;
> but the word of the Lord endures for evermore.' 25

And this 'word' is the word of the Gospel preached to you.

Then away with all malice and deceit, away with all 2
pretence and jealousy and recrimination of every kind!
Like the new-born infants you are, you must crave for 2
pure milk (spiritual milk, I mean), so that you may thrive
upon it to your souls' health. Surely you have tasted that 3
the Lord is good.

So come to him, our living Stone—the stone rejected by 4

<sup>a</sup> *Or* through the word of the living and enduring God.

5 men but choice and precious in the sight of God. Come,
and let yourselves be built, as living stones, into a spiritual
temple; become a holy priesthood,*a* to offer spiritual sacri-
6 fices acceptable to God through Jesus Christ. For it stands
written:

'I lay in Zion a choice corner-stone of great worth.
The man who has faith in it will not be put to shame.'

7 The great worth of which it speaks is for you who have
faith. For those who have no faith, the stone which the
builders rejected has become not only the corner-stone,*b*
8 but also 'a stone to trip over, a rock to stumble against'.
They fall when they disbelieve the Word. Such was their
appointed lot!

9 But you are a chosen race, a royal priesthood, a dedicated nation, and a people claimed by God for his own, to
proclaim the triumphs of him who has called you out of
10 darkness into his marvellous light. You are now the people
of God, who once were not his people; outside his mercy
once, you have now received his mercy.

11 DEAR FRIENDS, I beg you, as aliens in a foreign land,
to abstain from the lusts of the flesh which are at war with
12 the soul. Let all your behaviour be such as even pagans can
recognize as good, and then, whereas they malign you as
criminals now, they will come to see for themselves that
you live good lives, and will give glory to God on the day
when he comes to hold assize.

13 Submit yourselves to every human institution for the
sake of the Lord, whether to the sovereign as supreme,
14 or to the governor as his deputy for the punishment of
criminals and the commendation of those who do right.
15 For it is the will of God that by your good conduct you
should put ignorance and stupidity to silence.

16 Live as free men; not however as though your freedom
were there to provide a screen for wrongdoing, but as slaves
17 in God's service. Give due honour to everyone: love to the
brotherhood, reverence to God, honour to the sovereign.

18 Servants, accept the authority of your masters with all
due submission, not only when they are kind and con-
19 siderate, but even when they are perverse. For it is a fine*c*
thing if a man endure the pain of undeserved suffering
20 because God is in his thoughts. What credit is there in

*a* Or a spiritual temple for the holy work of priesthood.        *b* Or the
apex of the building.        *c* Or creditable.

fortitude when you have done wrong and are beaten for it? But when you have behaved well and suffer for it, your fortitude is a fine thing[a] in the sight of God. To that you were called, because Christ suffered[b] on your behalf, and thereby left you an example; it is for you to follow in his steps. He committed no sin, he was convicted of no falsehood; when he was abused he did not retort with abuse, when he suffered he uttered no threats, but committed his cause to the One who judges justly. In his own person he carried our sins to[c] the gibbet, so that we might cease to live for sin and begin to live for righteousness. By his wounds you have been healed. You were straying like sheep, but now you have turned towards the Shepherd and Guardian of your souls.

In the same way you women must accept the authority of your husbands, so that if there are any of them who disbelieve the Gospel they may be won over, without a word being said, by observing the chaste and reverent behaviour of their wives. Your beauty should reside, not in outward adornment—the braiding of the hair, or jewellery, or dress —but in the inmost centre of your being, with its imperishable ornament, a gentle, quiet spirit, which is of high value in the sight of God. Thus it was among God's people in days of old: the women who fixed their hopes on him adorned themselves by submission to their husbands. Such was Sarah, who obeyed Abraham and called him 'my master'. Her children you have now become, if you do good and show no fear.

In the same way, you husbands must conduct your married life with understanding: pay honour to the woman's body, not only because it is weaker, but also because you share together in the grace of God which gives you life. Then your prayers will not be hindered.

To sum up: be one in thought and feeling, all of you; be full of brotherly affection, kindly and humble-minded. Do not repay wrong with wrong, or abuse with abuse; on the contrary, retaliate with blessing, for a blessing is the inheritance to which you yourselves have been called.

> 'Whoever loves life and would see good days
> must restrain his tongue from evil
> and his lips from deceit;
> must turn from wrong and do good,
> seek peace and pursue it.

---

[a] *Or* is creditable.       [b] *Some witnesses read* died.       [c] *Or* on.

12  For the Lord's eyes are turned towards the righteous,
    his ears are open to their prayers;
    but the Lord's face is set against wrong-doers.'

13  WHO IS GOING to do you wrong if you are devoted to
14  what is good? And yet if you should suffer for your virtues,
    you may count yourselves happy. Have no fear of them:[a]
15  do not be perturbed, but hold the Lord Christ in reverence
    in your hearts.[b] Be always ready with your defence when-
    ever you are called to account for the hope that is in you,
16  but make that defence with modesty and respect. Keep
    your conscience clear, so that when you are abused, those
    who malign your Christian conduct may be put to shame.
17  It is better to suffer for well-doing, if such should be the
18  will of God, than for doing wrong. For Christ also died[c] for
    our sins[d] once and for all. He, the just, suffered for the
    unjust, to bring us to God.

    In the body he was put to death; in the spirit he was
19  brought to life. And in the spirit he went and made his
20  proclamation to the imprisoned spirits. They had refused
    obedience long ago, while God waited patiently in the days
    of Noah and the building of the ark, and in the ark a few
    persons, eight in all, were brought to safety through the
21  water. This water prefigured the water of baptism through
    which you are now brought to safety. Baptism is not the
    washing away of bodily pollution, but the appeal made to
    God by a good conscience; and it brings salvation through
22  the resurrection of Jesus Christ, who entered heaven after
    receiving the submission of angelic authorities and powers,
    and is now at the right hand of God.

4   Remembering that Christ endured bodily suffering, you
    must arm yourselves with a temper of mind like his. When
    a man has thus endured bodily suffering he has finished
2   with sin, and for the rest of his days on earth he may live,
    not for the things that men desire, but for what God wills.
3   You had time enough in the past to do all the things that
    men want to do in the pagan world. Then you lived in
    licence and debauchery, drunkenness, revelry, and tippling,
4   and the forbidden worship of idols. Now, when you no
    longer plunge with them into all this reckless dissipation,
    they cannot understand it, and they vilify you accordingly;
5   but they shall answer for it to him who stands ready to

---

[a] *Or Do not fear what they fear.*    [b] *Or hold Christ in reverence in your hearts, as Lord.*    [c] *Some witnesses read suffered.*
[d] *Some witnesses read for sins; others read for sins on our behalf.*

pass judgement on the living and the dead. Why was the 6
Gospel preached to those who are dead? In order that,
although in the body they received the sentence common
to men, they might in the spirit be alive with the life of
God.

The end of all things is upon us, so you must lead an 7
ordered and sober life, given to prayer. Above all, keep 8
your love for one another at full strength, because love
cancels innumerable sins. Be hospitable to one another 9
without complaining. Whatever gift each of you may have 10
received, use it in service to one another, like good
stewards dispensing the grace of God in its varied forms.
Are you a speaker? Speak as if you uttered oracles of God. 11
Do you give service? Give it as in the strength which God
supplies. In all things so act that the glory may be God's
through Jesus Christ; to him belong glory and power for
ever and ever. Amen.

My DEAR FRIENDS, do not be bewildered by the fiery 12
ordeal that is upon you, as though it were something extraordinary. It gives you a share in Christ's sufferings, and 13
that is cause for joy; and when his glory is revealed, your
joy will be triumphant. If Christ's name is flung in your 14
teeth as an insult, count yourselves happy, because then
that glorious Spirit which is the Spirit of God is resting
upon you. If you suffer, it must not be for murder, theft, 15
or sorcery,[a] nor for infringing the rights of others. But if 16
anyone suffers as a Christian, he should feel it no disgrace,
but confess that name to the honour of God.

The time has come for the judgement to begin; it is be- 17
ginning with God's own household. And if it is starting
with you, how will it end for those who refuse to obey the
gospel of God? It is hard enough for the righteous to be 18
saved; what then will become of the impious and sinful?
So even those who suffer, if it be according to God's will, 19
should commit their souls to him—by doing good; their
Maker will not fail them.

And now I appeal to the elders of your community, as 5
a fellow-elder and a witness of Christ's sufferings, and also
a partaker in the splendour that is to be revealed. Tend 2
that flock of God whose shepherds you are, and do it, not
under compulsion, but of your own free will, as God would
have it; not for gain but out of sheer devotion; not 3
tyrannizing over those who are allotted to your care, but

[a] Or other crime.

4 setting an example to the flock. And then, when the Head Shepherd appears, you will receive for your own the unfading garland of glory.

5 In the same way you younger men must be subordinate to your elders. Indeed, all of you should wrap yourselves in the garment of humility towards each other, because God sets his face against the arrogant but favours the

6 humble. Humble yourselves then under God's mighty hand,

7 and he will lift you up in due time. Cast all your cares on him, for you are his charge.

8 Awake! be on the alert! Your enemy the devil, like a roaring lion, prowls round looking for someone to devour.

9 Stand up to him, firm in faith, and remember that your brother Christians are going through the same kinds of

10 suffering while they are in the world. And the God of all grace, who called you into his eternal glory in Christ, will himself, after your brief suffering, restore, establish, and

11 strengthen you on a firm foundation. He holds dominion for ever and ever. Amen.

12 I write you this brief appeal through Silvanus, our trusty brother as I hold him, adding my testimony that this is the true grace of God. In this stand fast.

13 Greetings from her who dwells in Babylon, chosen by

14 God like you, and from my son Mark. Greet one another with the kiss of love.

Peace to you all who belong to Christ!

# THE SECOND LETTER OF
# PETER

## THE REMEDY FOR DOUBT

**F**ROM SIMEON PETER, servant and apostle of 1
Jesus Christ, to those who through the justice of our
God and Saviour Jesus Christ share our faith and
enjoy equal privilege with ourselves.

Grace and peace be yours in fullest measure, through the 2
knowledge of God and Jesus our Lord.

His divine power has bestowed on us everything that 3
makes for life and true religion, enabling us to know the
One who called us by his own splendour and might.
Through this might and splendour he has given us his 4
promises, great beyond all price, and through them you
may escape the corruption with which lust has infected
the world, and come to share in the very being of God.

With all this in view, you should try your hardest to 5
supplement your faith with virtue, virtue with knowledge,
knowledge with self-control, self-control with fortitude, 6
fortitude with piety, piety with brotherly kindness, and 7
brotherly kindness with love.

These are gifts which, if you possess and foster them, 8
will keep you from being either useless or barren in the
knowledge of our Lord Jesus Christ. The man who lacks 9
them is short-sighted and blind; he has forgotten how he
was cleansed from his former sins. All the more then, my 10
friends, exert yourselves to clinch God's choice and calling
of you. If you behave so, you will never come to grief. Thus 11
you will be afforded full and free admission into the eternal
kingdom of our Lord and Saviour Jesus Christ.

And so I will not hesitate to remind you of this again 12
and again, although you know it and are well grounded in
the truth that has already reached you. Yet I think it 13
right to keep refreshing your memory so long as I still
lodge in this body. I know that very soon I must leave it; 14
indeed our Lord Jesus Christ has told me so.[a] But I will 15

---

[a] *Or* I must leave it, as our Lord Jesus Christ told me.

see to it that after I am gone you will have means of remembering these things at all times.

16 It was not on tales artfully spun that we relied when we
told you of the power of our Lord Jesus Christ and his
17 coming; we saw him with our own eyes in majesty, when
at the hands of God the Father he was invested with
honour and glory, and there came to him from the sublime
Presence a voice which said: 'This is my Son, my Beloved,ᵃ
18 on whom my favour rests.' This voice from heaven we
ourselves heard; when it came, we were with him on the
sacred mountain.

19 All this only confirms for us the message of the prophets,ᵇ
to which you will do well to attend, because it is like a
lamp shining in a murky place, until the day breaks and
the morning star rises to illuminate your minds.

20 BUT FIRST NOTE THIS: no one can interpret any pro-
21 phecy of Scripture by himself. For it was not through any
human whim that men prophesied of old; men they were, but,
impelled by the Holy Spirit, they spoke the words of God.

2 But Israel had false prophets as well as true; and you
likewise will have false teachers among you. They will
import disastrous heresies, disowning the very Master who
bought them, and bringing swift disaster on their own
2 heads. They will gain many adherents to their dissolute
practices, through whom the true way will be brought into
3 disrepute. In their greed for money they will trade on your
credulity with sheer fabrications.

But the judgement long decreed for them has not been
4 idle; perdition waits for them with unsleeping eyes. God
did not spare the angels who sinned, but consigned them
to the dark pits of hell,ᶜ where they are reserved for judge-
5 ment. He did not spare the world of old (except for Noah,
preacher of righteousness, whom he preserved with seven
others), but brought the deluge upon that world of godless
6 men. The cities of Sodom and Gomorrah God burned to
ashes, and condemned them to total destruction, making
them an object-lesson for godless men in future days.
7 But he rescued Lot, who was a good man, shocked by the
8 dissolute habits of the lawless society in which he lived;
day after day every sight, every sound, of their evil courses
9 tortured that good man's heart. Thus the Lord is well able

---

ᵃ *Or* This is my only Son.     ᵇ *Or* And in the message of the
prophets we have something still more certain.     ᶜ *Some witnesses
read* consigned them to darkness and chains in hell.

to rescue the godly out of trials, and to reserve the wicked
under punishment until the day of judgement.

Above all he will punish those who follow their abomin-  10
able lusts. They flout authority; reckless and headstrong,
they are not afraid to insult celestial beings, whereas angels,  11
for all their superior strength and might, employ no insults
in seeking judgement against them before the Lord.

These men are like brute beasts, born in the course of  12
nature to be caught and killed. They pour abuse upon things
they do not understand; like the beasts they will perish,
suffering hurt for the hurt they have inflicted. To carouse  13
in broad daylight is their idea of pleasure; while they sit
with you at table they are an ugly blot on your company,
because they revel in their own deceptions.[a]

They have eyes for nothing but women, eyes never at  14
rest from sin. They lure the unstable to their ruin; past
masters in mercenary greed, God's curse is on them! They  15
have abandoned the straight road and lost their way.
They have followed in the steps of Balaam son of Beor,
who consented to take pay for doing wrong, but had his  16
offence brought home to him when the dumb beast spoke
with a human voice and put a stop to the prophet's madness.

These men are springs that give no water, mists driven by  17
a storm; the place reserved for them is blackest darkness.
They utter big, empty words, and make of sensual lusts  18
and debauchery a bait to catch those who have barely
begun to escape from their heathen environment. They  19
promise them freedom, but are themselves slaves of corruption; for a man is the slave of whatever has mastered
him. They had once escaped the world's defilements through  20
the knowledge of our Lord and Saviour Jesus Christ; yet
if they have entangled themselves in these all over again,
and are mastered by them, their plight in the end is worse
than before. How much better never to have known the  21
right way, than, having known it, to turn back and abandon the sacred commandments delivered to them! For them  22
the proverb has proved true: 'The dog returns to its own
vomit', and, 'The sow after a wash rolls in the mud again.'

THIS IS NOW my second letter to you, my friends. In  3
both of them I have been recalling to you what you already
know, to rouse you to honest thought. Remember the pre-  2
dictions made by God's own prophets, and the commands
given by the Lord and Saviour through your apostles.

          [a] *Some witnesses read* in their love-feasts.

3 Note this first: in the last days there will come men who
4 scoff at religion and live self-indulgent lives, and they will
say: 'Where now is the promise of his coming? Our fathers
have been laid to their rest, but still everything continues
exactly as it has always been since the world began.'
5 In taking this view they lose sight of the fact[a] that there
were heavens and earth long ago, created by God's word
6 out of water and with water; and by water that first world
7 was destroyed, the water of the deluge. And the present
heavens and earth, again by God's word, have been kept
in store for burning; they are being reserved until the day
of judgement when the godless will be destroyed.
8 And here is one point, my friends, which you must not
lose sight of: with the Lord one day is like a thousand years
9 and a thousand years like one day. It is not that the Lord
is slow in fulfilling his promise, as some suppose, but that
he is very patient with you, because it is not his will for
any to be lost, but for all to come to repentance.
10 But the Day of the Lord will come; it will come, un-
expected as a thief. On that day the heavens will disappear
with a great rushing sound, the elements will disintegrate in
flames, and the earth with all that is in it will be laid bare.[b]
11 Since the whole universe is to break up in this way,
think what sort of people you ought to be, what devout and
12 dedicated lives you should live! Look eagerly for the coming
of the Day of God and work to hasten it on; that day will
set the heavens ablaze until they fall apart, and will melt the
13 elements in flames. But we have his promise, and look forward to new heavens and a new earth, the home of justice.
14 With this to look forward to, do your utmost to be found
at peace with him, unblemished and above reproach in his
15 sight. Bear in mind that our Lord's patience with us is our salvation, as Paul, our friend and brother, said when he wrote to
16 you with his inspired wisdom. And so he does in all his other
letters, wherever he speaks of this subject, though they contain
some obscure passages, which the ignorant and unstable mis-
interpret to their own ruin, as they do the other scriptures.[c]
17 But you, my friends, are forewarned. Take care, then,
not to let these unprincipled men seduce you with their
18 errors; do not lose your own safe foothold. But grow in the
grace and in the knowledge of our Lord and Saviour Jesus
Christ.[d] To him be glory now and for all eternity!

[a] *Or* They choose to overlook the fact . . .    [b] *Some witnesses read*
will be burnt up.    [c] *Or* his other writings.    [d] *Or* But grow up,
by the grace of our Lord and Saviour Jesus Christ, and by knowing him.

# THE FIRST LETTER OF
# JOHN

## RECALL TO FUNDAMENTALS

IT WAS THERE from the beginning; we have heard 1
it; we have seen it with our own eyes; we looked upon
it, and felt it with our own hands; and it is of this we
tell. Our theme is the word of life. This life was made 2
visible; we have seen it and bear our testimony; we here
declare to you the eternal life which dwelt with the Father
and was made visible to us. What we have seen and heard 3
we declare to you, so that you and we together may share
in a common life, that life which we share with the Father
and his Son Jesus Christ. And we write this in order that 4
the joy of us all may be complete.

Here is the message we heard from him and pass on to 5
you: that God is light, and in him there is no darkness at
all. If we claim to be sharing in his life while we walk in the 6
dark, our words and our lives are a lie; but if we walk in 7
the light as he himself is in the light, then we share together a common life, and we are being cleansed from every
sin by the blood of Jesus his Son.

If we claim to be sinless, we are self-deceived and 8
strangers to the truth. If we confess our sins, he is just, 9
and may be trusted to forgive our sins and cleanse us from
every kind of wrong; but if we say we have committed no 10
sin, we make him out to be a liar, and then his word has
no place in us.

My children, in writing thus to you my purpose is that 2
you should not commit sin. But should anyone commit a
sin, we have one to plead our cause[a] with the Father, Jesus
Christ, and he is just. He is himself the remedy for the 2
defilement of our sins, not our sins only but the sins of all
the world.

Here is the test by which we can make sure that we know 3
him: do we keep his commands? The man who says, 'I 4
know him', while he disobeys his commands, is a liar and

---

[a] *Literally* we have an advocate . . .

⁵ a stranger to the truth; but in the man who is obedient to his word, the divine love has indeed come to its perfection.

Here is the test by which we can make sure that we are
⁶ in him: whoever claims to be dwelling in him, binds him-
⁷ self to live as Christ himself lived. Dear friends, I give you no new command. It is the old command which you always had before you; the old command is the message which you
⁸ heard at the beginning. And yet again it is a new command that I am giving you—new in the sense that the darkness is passing and the real light already shines. Christ has made this true, and it is true in your own experience.
⁹ A man may say, 'I am in the light'; but if he hates his
¹⁰ brother, he is still in the dark. Only the man who loves his brother dwells in light: there is nothing to make him
¹¹ stumble. But one who hates his brother is in darkness; he walks in the dark and has no idea where he is going, because the darkness has made him blind.

¹²       I write to you, my children, because your sins have been forgiven for his sake.ᵃ

¹³       I write to you, fathers, because you know him who is and has been from the beginning.ᵇ

       I write to you, young men, because you have mastered the evil one.

       To you, children, I have written because you know the Father.

¹⁴       To you, fathers, I have written because you know him who is and has been from the beginning.ᵇ

       To you, young men, I have written because you are strong; God's word remains in you, and you have mastered the evil one.

¹⁵     Do not set your hearts on the godless world or anything in it. Anyone who loves the world is a stranger to the
¹⁶ Father's love. Everything the world affords, all that panders to the appetites or entices the eyes, all the glamour of its life, springs not from the Father but from the godless
¹⁷ world. And that world is passing away with all its allurements, but he who does God's will stands for evermore.

¹⁸ MY CHILDREN, this is the last hour! You were told that Antichrist was to come, and now many antichrists have appeared; which proves to us that this is indeed the last
¹⁹ hour. They went out from our company, but never really

---

ᵃ *Or* forgiven, since you bear his name.    ᵇ *Or* him whom we have known from the beginning.

belonged to us; if they had, they would have stayed with us. They went out, so that it might be clear that not all in our company truly belong to it.[a]

You, no less than they, are among the initiated;[b] this is 20 the gift of the Holy One, and by it you all have knowledge.[c] It is not because you are ignorant of the truth that I have 21 written to you, but because you know it, and because lies, one and all, are alien to the truth.

Who is the liar? Who but he that denies that Jesus is 22 the Christ? He is Antichrist, for he denies both the Father and the Son: to deny the Son is to be without the Father; 23 to acknowledge the Son is to have the Father too. You 24 therefore must keep in your hearts that which you heard at the beginning; if what you heard then still dwells in you, you will yourselves dwell in the Son and also in the Father. And this is the promise that he himself gave us, 25 the promise of eternal life.

So much for those who would mislead you. But as for 26 27 you, the initiation[d] which you received from him stays with you; you need no other teacher, but learn all you need to know from his initiation, which is real and no illusion. As he taught you, then, dwell in him.

Even now, my children, dwell in him, so that when he 28 appears we may be confident and unashamed before him at his coming. If you know that he is righteous, you must 29 recognize that every man who does right is his child. How 3 great is the love that the Father has shown to us! We were called God's children, and such we are;[e] and the reason why the godless world does not recognize us is that it has not known him. Here and now, dear friends, we are God's 2 children; what we shall be has not yet been disclosed, but we know that when it is disclosed[f] we shall be like him,[g] because we shall see him as he is. Everyone who has this 3 hope before him purifies himself, as Christ is pure.

To commit sin is to break God's law: sin, in fact, is law- 4 lessness. Christ appeared, as you know, to do away with 5 sins, and there is no sin in him. No man therefore who 6 dwells in him is a sinner; the sinner has not seen him and does not know him.

[a] *Or* that none of them truly belong to us.     [b] *Literally* have an anointing (*Greek* chrism).     [c] *Some witnesses read* you have all knowledge.     [d] *Literally* the anointing.     [e] *Or* We are called children of God! Not only called, we really are his children.     [f] *Or* when he appears.     [g] *Or* we are God's children, though he has not yet appeared; what we shall be we know, for when he does appear we shall be like him.

7 My children, do not be misled: it is the man who does
8 right who is righteous, as God is righteous; the man who
sins is a child of the devil, for the devil has been a sinner
from the first; and the Son of God appeared for the very
purpose of undoing the devil's work.

9 A child of God does not commit sin, because the divine
seed remains in him; he cannot be a sinner, because he is
10 God's child. That is the distinction between the children
of God and the children of the devil: no one who does not
do right is God's child, nor is anyone who does not love his
11 brother. For the message you have heard from the beginning
12 is this: that we should love one another; unlike Cain, who
was a child of the evil one and murdered his brother. And
why did he murder him? Because his own actions were
wrong, and his brother's were right.

13 My brothers, do not be surprised if the world hates you.
14 We for our part have crossed over from death to life; this
we know, because we love our brothers. The man who does
15 not love is still in the realm of death, for everyone who
hates his brother is a murderer, and no murderer, as you
16 know, has eternal life dwelling within him. It is by this
that we know what love is: that Christ laid down his life
for us. And we in our turn are bound to lay down our lives
17 for our brothers. But if a man has enough to live on, and yet
when he sees his brother in need shuts up his heart against
him, how can it be said that the divine love[a] dwells in him?

18 My children, love must not be a matter of words or talk;
19 it must be genuine, and show itself in action. This is how
we may know that we belong to the realm of truth, and
20 convince ourselves in his sight that even if our conscience
condemns us, God is greater than our conscience[b] and
knows all.

21 Dear friends, if our conscience does not condemn us,
22 then we can approach God with confidence, and obtain
from him whatever we ask, because we are keeping his
23 commands and doing what he approves. This is his command: to give our allegiance to his Son Jesus Christ and
24 love one another as he commanded. When we keep his
commands we dwell in him and he dwells in us. And this is
how we can make sure that he dwells within us: we know
it from the Spirit he has given us.

[a] Or *that love for God* . . .      [b] *Or* and reassure ourselves in his
sight in matters where our conscience condemns us, because God is
greater than our conscience . . .; *or* and yet we shall do well to convince ourselves that if even our own conscience condemns us, still more
will God who is greater than conscience . . .

But do not trust any and every spirit, my friends; 4
test the spirits, to see whether they are from God, for
among those who have gone out into the world there are
many prophets falsely inspired. This is how we may recog- 2
nize the Spirit of God: every spirit which acknowledges
that Jesus Christ has come in the flesh is from God, and 3
every spirit which does not thus acknowledge Jesus is not
from God. This is what is meant by 'Antichrist';[a] you have
been told that he was to come, and here he is, in the world
already!

But you, my children, are of God's family, and you have 4
the mastery over these false prophets, because he who
inspires you is greater than he who inspires the godless
world. They are of that world, and so therefore is their 5
teaching; that is why the world listens to them. But we 6
belong to God, and a man who knows God listens to us,
while he who does not belong to God refuses us a hearing.
That is how we distinguish the spirit of truth from the
spirit of error.

Dear friends, let us love one another, because love is 7
from God. Everyone who loves is a child of God and knows
God, but the unloving know nothing of God. For God is 8
love; and his love was disclosed to us in this, that he sent 9
his only Son into the world to bring us life. The love I speak 10
of is not our love for God, but the love he showed to us in
sending his Son as the remedy for the defilement of our
sins. If God thus loved us, dear friends, we in turn are 11
bound to love one another. Though God has never been 12
seen by any man, God himself dwells in us if we love one
another; his love is brought to perfection within us.

Here is the proof that we dwell in him and he dwells in 13
us: he has imparted his Spirit to us. Moreover, we have 14
seen for ourselves, and we attest, that the Father sent the
Son to be the saviour of the world, and if a man acknow- 15
ledges that Jesus is the Son of God, God dwells in him and
he dwells in God. Thus we have come to know and believe 16
the love which God has for us.

God is love; he who dwells in love is dwelling in God, and
God in him. This is for us the perfection of love, to have 17
confidence on the day of judgement, and this we can have,
because even in this world we are as he is. There is no room 18
for fear in love; perfect love banishes fear. For fear brings
with it the pains of judgement, and anyone who is afraid
has not attained to love in its perfection. We love because 19

[a] Or This is the spirit of Antichrist.

20 he loved us first. But if a man says, 'I love God', while hating his brother, he is a liar. If he does not love the brother whom he has seen, it cannot be that he loves God 21 whom he has not seen. And indeed this command comes to us from Christ himself: that he who loves God must also love his brother.

5 Everyone who believes that Jesus is the Christ is a child of God, and to love the parent means to love his child; 2 it follows that when we love God and obey his commands 3 we love his children too. For to love God is to keep his 4 commands; and they are not burdensome, because every child of God is victor over the godless world. The victory 5 that defeats the world is our faith, for who is victor over the world but he who believes that Jesus is the Son of God?

6 This is he who came with water and blood: Jesus Christ. He came, not by water alone, but by water and blood; and there is the Spirit to bear witness, because the Spirit is 7 8 truth. For there are three witnesses, the Spirit, the water, 9 and the blood, and these three are in agreement. We accept human testimony, but surely divine testimony is stronger, and this threefold testimony is indeed that of God himself, 10 the witness he has borne to his Son. He who believes in the Son of God has this testimony in his own heart, but he who disbelieves God, makes him out to be a liar, by refusing to 11 accept God's own witness to his Son. The witness is this: that God has given us eternal life, and that this life is 12 found in his Son. He who possesses the Son has life indeed; he who does not possess the Son of God has not that life.

13 THIS LETTER is to assure you that you have eternal life. It is addressed to those who give their allegiance to the Son of God.

14 We can approach God with confidence for this reason: if we make requests which accord with his will he listens 15 to us; and if we know that our requests are heard, we know also that the things we ask for are ours.

16 If a man sees his brother committing a sin which is not a deadly sin, he should pray to God for him, and he will grant him life—that is, when men are not guilty of deadly sin. There is such a thing as deadly sin, and I do not sug- 17 gest that he should pray about that; but although all wrongdoing is sin, not all sin is deadly sin.

18 We know that no child of God is a sinner; it is the Son of God who keeps him safe, and the evil one cannot touch him.

We know that we are of God's family, while the whole [19] godless world lies in the power of the evil one.

We know that the Son of God has come and given us [20] understanding to know him who is real; indeed we are in him who is real, since we are in his Son Jesus Christ. This is the true God, this is eternal life. My children, be on the [21] watch against false gods.

# THE SECOND LETTER OF

# JOHN

## TRUTH AND LOVE

1 THE ELDER to the Lady chosen by God, and her children, whom I love in truth—and not I alone but 2 all who know the truth—for the sake of the truth that dwells among us and will be with us for ever.

3 Grace, mercy, and peace shall be with us from God the Father and from Jesus Christ the Son of the Father, in truth and love.

4 I was delighted to find that some of your children are living by the truth, as we were commanded by the Father. 5 And now I have a request to make of you. Do not think I am giving a new command; I am recalling the one we have had before us from the beginning: let us love one another. 6 And love means following the commands of God. This is the command which was given you from the beginning, to be your rule of life.

7 Many deceivers have gone out into the world, who do not acknowledge Jesus Christ as coming in the flesh. These are the persons described as the Antichrist, the arch-8 deceiver. Beware of them, so that you may not lose all that we worked for, but receive your reward in full. 9 Anyone who runs ahead too far, and does not stand by the doctrine of the Christ, is without God; he who stands by that doctrine possesses both the Father and the Son. 10 If anyone comes to you who does not bring this doctrine, do not welcome him into your house or give him a greeting; 11 for anyone who gives him a greeting is an accomplice in his wicked deeds.

12 I have much to write to you, but I do not care to put it down in black and white. But I hope to visit you and talk 13 with you face to face, so that our joy may be complete. The children of your Sister, chosen by God, send their greetings.

# THE THIRD LETTER OF

# JOHN

## TROUBLE IN THE CHURCH

THE ELDER to dear Gaius, whom I love in truth. 1
My dear Gaius, I pray that you may enjoy good 2
health, and that all may go well with you, as I know
it goes well with your soul. I was delighted when friends 3
came and told me how true you have been; indeed you are
true in your whole life. Nothing gives me greater joy than 4
to hear that my children are living by the truth.

My dear friend, you show a fine loyalty in everything 5
that you do for these our fellow-Christians, strangers
though they are to you. They have spoken of your kind- 6
ness before the congregation here. Please help them on their
journey in a manner worthy of the God we serve. It was on 7
Christ's work that they went out; and they would accept
nothing from pagans. We are bound to support such men, 8
and so play our part in spreading the truth.

I sent a letter to the congregation, but Diotrephes, their 9
would-be leader,[a] will have nothing to do with us. If I 10
come, I will bring up the things he is doing. He lays base-
less and spiteful charges against us; not satisfied with that,
he refuses to receive our friends, and he interferes with
those who would do so, and tries to expel them from the
congregation.

My dear friend, do not imitate bad examples, but good 11
ones. The well-doer is a child of God; the evil-doer has
never seen God.

Demetrius gets a good testimonial from everybody— 12
yes, and from the truth itself. I add my testimony, and you
know that my testimony is true.

I have much to write to you, but I do not care to set it 13
down with pen and ink. I hope to see you very soon, and 14
we will talk face to face. Peace be with you. Our friends
send their greetings. Greet our friends one by one.

[a] Or who enjoys being their leader.

413

# A LETTER OF

# JUDE

## THE DANGER OF FALSE BELIEF

1 FROM JUDE, servant of Jesus Christ and brother of James, to those whom God has called, who live in the love of God the Father and in the safe keeping of Jesus Christ.

2 Mercy, peace, and love be yours in fullest measure.

3 My friends, I was fully engaged in writing to you about our salvation—which is yours no less than ours—when it became urgently necessary to write at once and appeal to you to join the struggle in defence of the faith, the faith 4 which God entrusted to his people once and for all. It is in danger from certain persons who have wormed their way in, the very men whom Scripture long ago marked down for the doom they have incurred. They are the enemies of religion; they pervert the free favour of our God into licentiousness, disowning Jesus Christ, our only Master and Lord.[a]

5 You already know it all, but let me remind you how the Lord,[b] having once delivered the people of Israel out of Egypt, next time destroyed those who were guilty of un-6 belief. Remember too the angels, how some of them were not content to keep the dominion given to them but abandoned their proper home; and God has reserved them for judgement on the great Day, bound beneath the dark-7 ness in everlasting chains. Remember Sodom and Gomorrah and the neighbouring towns; like the angels, they committed fornication and followed unnatural lusts; and they paid the penalty in eternal fire, an example for all to see.

8 So too with these men today. Their dreams lead them to defile the body, to flout authority, and to insult celestial 9 beings. In contrast, when the archangel Michael was in debate with the devil, disputing the possession of Moses's

[a] Or disowning our one and only Master, and Jesus Christ our Lord.
[b] Some witnesses read Jesus (which might be understood as Joshua).

414

body, he did not presume to condemn him in insulting words,[a] but said, 'May the Lord rebuke you!'

But these men pour abuse upon things they do not 10 understand; the things they do understand, by instinct like brute beasts, prove their undoing. Alas for them! They 11 have gone the way of Cain; they have plunged into Balaam's error for pay; they have rebelled like Korah, and they share his doom.

These men are a blot on your love-feasts, where they eat 12 and drink without reverence. They are shepherds who take care only of themselves. They are clouds carried away by the wind without giving rain, trees that in season bear no fruit, dead twice over and pulled up by the roots. They are 13 fierce waves of the sea, foaming shameful deeds; they are stars that have wandered from their course, and the place for ever reserved for them is blackest darkness.

It was to them that Enoch, the seventh in descent from 14 Adam, directed his prophecy when he said: 'I saw the Lord come with his myriads of angels, to bring all men to 15 judgement and to convict all the godless of all the godless deeds they had committed, and of all the defiant words which godless sinners had spoken against him.'

They are a set of grumblers and malcontents. They 16 follow their lusts. Big words come rolling from their lips, and they court favour to gain their ends. But you, my 17 friends, should remember the predictions made by the apostles of our Lord Jesus Christ. This was the warning 18 they gave you: 'In the final age there will be men who pour scorn on religion, and follow their own godless lusts.'

These men draw a line between spiritual and unspiritual 19 persons, although they are themselves[b] wholly unspiritual. But you, my friends, must fortify yourselves in your most 20 sacred faith. Continue to pray in the power of the Holy Spirit. Keep yourselves in the love of God, and look for- 21 ward to the day when our Lord Jesus Christ in his mercy will give eternal life.

There are some doubting souls who need your pity;[c] 22 snatch them from the flames and save them.[d] There are 23 others for whom your pity must be mixed with fear; hate the very clothing that is contaminated with sensuality.

---

[a] *Or* to charge him with blasphemy.          [b] *Or* These men create divisions; they are . . .          [c] *Some witnesses read* There are some who raise disputes; these you should refute.          [d] *So one witness;* the rest read some you should snatch from the flames and save.

24  Now to the One who can keep you from falling and set
    you in the presence of his glory, jubilant and above re-
25  proach, to the only God our Saviour, be glory and majesty,
    might and authority, through Jesus Christ our Lord, before
    all time, now, and for evermore. Amen.

# THE REVELATION
## OF JOHN

# THE REVELATION
# OF JOHN

THIS IS THE REVELATION given by God to **1**
Jesus Christ. It was given to him so that he might
show his servants what must shortly happen. He
made it known by sending his angel to his servant John,
who, in telling all that he saw, has borne witness to the **2**
word of God and to the testimony of Jesus Christ.[a]

Happy is the man who reads, and happy those who **3**
listen to the words of this prophecy and heed what is
written in it. For the hour of fulfilment is near.

## A MESSAGE FROM CHRIST
## TO THE CHURCHES

JOHN TO THE SEVEN CHURCHES in the pro- **4**
vince of Asia.

Grace be to you and peace, from him who is and who
was and who is to come, from the seven spirits before his
throne, and from Jesus Christ, the faithful witness, the **5**
first-born from the dead and ruler of the kings of the
earth.

To him who loves us and freed us from our sins with
his life's blood, who made of us a royal house, to serve as **6**
the priests of his God and Father—to him be glory and
dominion for ever and ever! Amen.

Behold, he is coming with the clouds! Every eye shall **7**
see him, and among them those who pierced him; and all
the peoples of the world shall lament in remorse. So it shall
be. Amen.

'I am the Alpha and the Omega', says the Lord God, **8**
who is and who was and who is to come, the sovereign
Lord of all.

I, John, your brother, who share with you in the suffer- **9**
ing and the sovereignty and the endurance which is ours

[a] *Or has borne his testimony to the word of God and to Jesus Christ.*

in Jesus—I was on the island called Patmos because I had
10 preached God's word and borne my testimony to Jesus. It
was on the Lord's day, and I was caught up by the Spirit;
and behind me I heard a loud voice, like the sound of a
11 trumpet, which said to me, 'Write down what you see on
a scroll and send it to the seven churches: to Ephesus,
Smyrna, Pergamum, Thyatira, Sardis, Philadelphia, and
12 Laodicea.' I turned to see whose voice it was that spoke
to me; and when I turned I saw seven standing lamps of
13 gold, and among the lamps one like a son of man, robed
14 down to his feet, with a golden girdle round his breast. The
hair of his head was white as snow-white wool, and his
15 eyes flamed like fire; his feet gleamed like burnished brass
refined in a furnace, and his voice was like the sound of
16 rushing waters. In his right hand he held seven stars, and
out of his mouth came a sharp two-edged sword; and his
face shone like the sun in full strength.

17      When I saw him, I fell at his feet as though dead. But he
laid his right hand upon me and said, 'Do not be afraid.
18 I am the first and the last, and I am the living one; for I
was dead and now I am alive for evermore, and I hold the
19 keys of Death and Death's domain. Write down therefore
what you have seen, what is now, and what will be hereafter.

20      'Here is the secret meaning of the seven stars which you
saw in my right hand, and of the seven lamps of gold: the
seven stars are the angels of the seven churches, and the
seven lamps are the seven churches.

2   'TO THE ANGEL of the church at Ephesus write:
   '"These are the words of the One who holds the seven
stars in his right hand and walks among the seven lamps of
2 gold: I know all your ways, your toil and your fortitude.
I know you cannot endure evil men; you have put to the
proof those who claim to be apostles but are not, and have
3 found them false. Fortitude you have; you have borne up
4 in my cause and never flagged. But I have this against you:
5 you have lost your early love. Think from what a height you
have fallen; repent, and do as you once did. Otherwise, if
you do not repent, I shall come to you and remove your
6 lamp from its place. Yet you have this in your favour: you
7 hate the practices of the Nicolaitans, as I do. Hear, you
who have ears to hear, what the Spirit says to the churches!
To him who is victorious I will give the right to eat from
the tree of life that stands in the Garden of God."

'To the angel of the church at Smyrna write:  8

'"These are the words of the First and the Last, who was dead and came to life again: I know how hard pressed you  9 are, and poor—and yet you are rich; I know how you are slandered by those who claim to be Jews but are not—they are Satan's synagogue. Do not be afraid of the suffering  10 to come. The Devil will throw some of you into prison, to put you to the test; and for ten days you will suffer cruelly. Only be faithful till death, and I will give you the crown of life. Hear, you who have ears to hear, what the Spirit  11 says to the churches! He who is victorious cannot be harmed by the second death."

'To the angel of the church at Pergamum write:  12

'"These are the words of the One who has the sharp two-edged sword: I know where you live; it is the place where  13 Satan has his throne. And yet you are holding fast to my cause. You did not deny your faith in me even at the time when Antipas, my faithful witness, was killed in your city, the home of Satan. But I have a few matters to bring  14 against you: you have in Pergamum some that hold to the teaching of Balaam, who taught Balak to put temptation in the way of the Israelites. He encouraged them to eat food sacrificed to idols and to commit fornication, and in the  15 same way you also have some who hold the doctrine of the Nicolaitans. So repent! If you do not, I shall come to you  16 soon and make war upon them with the sword that comes out of my mouth. Hear, you who have ears to hear, what  17 the Spirit says to the churches! To him who is victorious I will give some of the hidden manna; I will give him also a white stone, and on the stone will be written a new name, known to none but him that receives it."

'To the angel of the church at Thyatira write:  18

'"These are the words of the Son of God, whose eyes flame like fire and whose feet gleam like burnished brass: I know all your ways, your love and faithfulness, your  19 good service and your fortitude; and of late you have done even better than at first. Yet I have this against you:  20 you tolerate that Jezebel, the woman who claims to be a prophetess, who by her teaching lures my servants into fornication and into eating food sacrificed to idols. I have  21 given her time to repent, but she refuses to repent of her fornication. So I will throw her on to a bed of pain,*a* and  22 plunge her lovers into terrible suffering, unless they forswear what she is doing; and her children I will strike dead.  23

*a One witness reads into a furnace.*

421

This will teach all the churches that I am the searcher of men's hearts and thoughts, and that I will reward each one 24 of you according to his deeds. And now I speak to you others in Thyatira, who do not accept this teaching and have had no experience of what they like to call the deep secrets of Satan; on you I will impose no further burden. 25 26 Only hold fast to what you have, until I come. To him who is victorious, to him who perseveres in doing my will to the 27 end, I will give authority over the nations—that same authority which I received from my Father—and he shall rule them with an iron rod, smashing them to bits like 28 earthenware; and I will give him also the star of dawn. 29 Hear, you who have ears to hear, what the Spirit says to the churches!"

3    'To the angel of the church at Sardis write:

'"These are the words of the One who holds the seven spirits of God, the seven stars: I know all your ways; that though you have a name for being alive, you are dead. 2 Wake up, and put some strength into what is left, which must otherwise die! For I have not found any work of 3 yours completed in the eyes of my God. So remember the teaching you received; observe it, and repent. If you do not wake up, I shall come upon you like a thief, and you 4 will not know the moment of my coming. Yet you have a few persons in Sardis who have not polluted their clothing. They shall walk with me in white, for so they deserve. 5 He who is victorious shall thus be robed all in white; his name I will never strike off the roll of the living, for in the presence of my Father and his angels I will acknowledge 6 him as mine. Hear, you who have ears to hear, what the Spirit says to the churches!"

7    'To the angel of the church at Philadelphia write:

'"These are the words of the holy one, the true one, who holds the key of David; when he opens none may shut, 8 when he shuts none may open: I know all your ways; and look, I have set before you an open door, which no one can shut. Your strength, I know, is small, yet you have ob- 9 served my commands and have not disowned my name. So this is what I will do: I will make those of Satan's syna- gogue, who claim to be Jews but are lying frauds, come and fall down at your feet; and they shall know that you 10 are my beloved people. Because you have kept my com- mand and stood fast, I will also keep you from the ordeal that is to fall upon the whole world and test its inhabitants. 11 I am coming soon; hold fast what you have, and let no one

rob you of your crown. He who is victorious—I will make   12
him a pillar in the temple of my God; he shall never leave
it. And I will write the name of my God upon him, and the
name of the city of my God, that new Jerusalem which is
coming down out of heaven from my God, and my own
new name. Hear, you who have ears to hear, what the   13
Spirit says to the churches!"

'To the angel of the church at Laodicea write:   14

'"These are the words of the Amen, the faithful and true
witness, the prime source of all God's creation: I know all   15
your ways; you are neither hot nor cold. How I wish you
were either hot or cold! But because you are lukewarm,   16
neither hot nor cold, I will spit you out of my mouth.
You say, 'How rich I am! And how well I have done! I   17
have everything I want.' In fact, though you do not know
it, you are the most pitiful wretch, poor, blind, and naked.
So I advise you to buy from me gold refined in the fire, to   18
make you truly rich, and white clothes to put on to hide
the shame of your nakedness, and ointment for your eyes
so that you may see. All whom I love I reprove and disci-   19
pline. Be on your mettle therefore and repent. Here I stand   20
knocking at the door; if anyone hears my voice and
opens the door, I will come in and sit down to supper
with him and he with me. To him who is victorious I will   21
grant a place on my throne, as I myself was victorious
and sat down with my Father on his throne. Hear,   22
you who have ears to hear, what the Spirit says to the
churches!"'

# THE OPENING OF THE SEALED BOOK

AFTER THIS I LOOKED, and there before my   4
eyes was a door opened in heaven; and the voice that
I had first heard speaking to me like a trumpet said, 'Come
up here, and I will show you what must happen hereafter.'
At once I was caught up by the Spirit. There in heaven   2
stood a throne, and on the throne sat one whose appear-   3
ance was like the gleam of jasper and cornelian; and round
the throne was a rainbow, bright as an emerald. In a circle   4
about this throne were twenty-four other thrones, and on
them sat twenty-four elders, robed in white and wearing
crowns of gold. From the throne went out flashes of   5
lightning and peals of thunder. Burning before the throne
were seven flaming torches, the seven spirits of God, and in   6

front of it stretched what seemed a sea of glass, like a sheet
of ice.

7   In the centre, round the throne itself, were four living
creatures, covered with eyes, in front and behind. The first
creature was like a lion, the second like an ox, the third
8   had a human face, the fourth was like an eagle in flight. The
four living creatures, each of them with six wings, had eyes
all over, inside and out; and by day and by night without
a pause they sang:

> 'Holy, holy, holy is God the sovereign Lord of all, who
> was, and is, and is to come!'

9   As often as the living creatures give glory and honour
and thanks to the One who sits on the throne, who lives
10  for ever and ever, the twenty-four elders fall down before
the One who sits on the throne and worship him who lives
for ever and ever; and as they lay their crowns before the
throne they cry:

11  > 'Thou art worthy, O Lord our God, to receive glory
> and honour and power, because thou didst create all
> things; by thy will they were created, and have their
> being!'

5   Then I saw in the right hand of the One who sat on the
throne a scroll, with writing inside and out, and it was
2   sealed up with seven seals. And I saw a mighty angel proclaiming in a loud voice, 'Who is worthy to open the scroll
3   and to break its seals?' There was no one in heaven or on
earth or under the earth able to open the scroll or to look
4   inside it. I was in tears because no one was found who was
5   worthy to open the scroll or to look inside it. But one of the
elders said to me: 'Do not weep; for the Lion from the
tribe of Judah, the Scion of David, has won the right to
open the scroll and break its seven seals.'

6   Then I saw standing in the very middle of the throne,
inside the circle of living creatures and the circle of elders,[a]
a Lamb with the marks of slaughter upon him. He had
seven horns and seven eyes, the eyes which are the seven
7   spirits of God sent out over all the world. And the Lamb
went up and took the scroll from the right hand of the One
8   who sat on the throne. When he took it, the four living
creatures and the twenty-four elders fell down before the
Lamb. Each of the elders had a harp, and they held golden

[a] Or standing between the throne, with the four living creatures, and
the elders . . .

bowls full of incense, the prayers of God's people, and they 9
were singing a new song:

> 'Thou art worthy to take the scroll and to break its
> seals, for thou wast slain and by thy blood didst pur-
> chase for God men of every tribe and language, people
> and nation; thou hast made of them a royal house, to 10
> serve our God as priests; and they shall reign upon
> earth.'

Then as I looked I heard the voices of countless angels. 11
These were all round the throne and the living creatures
and the elders. Myriads upon myriads there were, thousands upon thousands, and they cried aloud: 12

> 'Worthy is the Lamb, the Lamb that was slain, to
> receive all power and wealth, wisdom and might,
> honour and glory and praise!'

Then I heard every created thing in heaven and on earth 13
and under the earth and in the sea, all that is in them,
crying:

> 'Praise and honour, glory and might, to him who sits
> on the throne and to the Lamb for ever and ever!'

And the four living creatures said, 'Amen', and the elders 14
fell down and worshipped.

THEN I WATCHED as the Lamb broke the first of the 6
seven seals; and I heard one of the four living creatures
say in a voice like thunder, 'Come!' And there before my 2
eyes was a white horse, and its rider held a bow. He was
given a crown, and he rode forth, conquering and to conquer.

When the Lamb broke the second seal, I heard the 3
second creature say, 'Come!' And out came another horse, 4
all red. To its rider was given power to take peace from
the earth and make men slaughter one another; and he
was given a great sword.

When he broke the third seal, I heard the third creature 5
say, 'Come!' And there, as I looked, was a black horse; and
its rider held in his hand a pair of scales. And I heard what 6
sounded like a voice from the midst of the living creatures,
which said, 'A whole day's wage for a quart of flour, a
whole day's wage for three quarts of barley-meal! But
spare the olive and the vine.'

7 When he broke the fourth seal, I heard the voice of the
8 fourth creature say, 'Come!' And there, as I looked, was
another horse, sickly pale; and its rider's name was Death,
and Hades came close behind. To him was given power
over a quarter of the earth, with the right to kill by sword
and by famine, by pestilence and wild beasts.

9 When he broke the fifth seal, I saw underneath[a] the
altar the souls of those who had been slaughtered for God's
10 word and for the testimony they bore. They gave a great
cry: 'How long, sovereign Lord, holy and true, must it be
before thou wilt vindicate us and avenge our blood on the
11 inhabitants of the earth?' Each of them was given a white
robe; and they were told to rest a little while longer, until
the tally should be complete of all their brothers in Christ's
service who were to be killed as they had been.

12 Then I watched as he broke the sixth seal. And there
was a violent earthquake; the sun turned black as a
13 funeral pall and the moon all red as blood; the stars in the
14 sky fell to the earth, like figs shaken down by a gale; the
sky vanished, as a scroll is rolled up, and every mountain
15 and island was moved from its place. Then the kings of the
earth, magnates and marshals, the rich and the powerful,
and all men, slave or free, hid themselves in caves and
16 mountain crags; and they called out to the mountains and
the crags, 'Fall on us and hide us from the face of the One
who sits on the throne and from the vengeance of the
17 Lamb.' For the great day of their vengeance has come, and
who will be able to stand?

7 After this I saw four angels stationed at the four corners
of the earth, holding back the four winds so that no wind
2 should blow on sea or land or on any tree. Then I saw
another angel rising out of the east, carrying the seal of
the living God; and he called aloud to the four angels who
3 had been given the power to ravage land and sea: 'Do no
damage to sea or land or trees until we have set the seal
4 of our God upon the foreheads of his servants.' And I
heard the number of those who had received the seal. From
all the tribes of Israel there were a hundred and forty-four
5 thousand: twelve thousand from the tribe of Judah, twelve
thousand from the tribe of Reuben, twelve thousand from
6 the tribe of Gad, twelve thousand from the tribe of Asher,
twelve thousand from the tribe of Naphtali, twelve thou-
7 sand from the tribe of Manasseh, twelve thousand from the
tribe of Simeon, twelve thousand from the tribe of Levi,

[a] *Or at the foot of . . .*

twelve thousand from the tribe of Issachar, twelve thousand 8 from the tribe of Zebulun, twelve thousand from the tribe of Joseph, and twelve thousand from the tribe of Benjamin.

After this I looked and saw a vast throng, which no one 9 could count, from every nation, of all tribes, peoples, and languages, standing in front of the throne and before the Lamb. They were robed in white and had palms in their hands, and they shouted together: 10

> 'Victory to our God who sits on the throne, and to the Lamb!'

And all the angels stood round the throne and the elders 11 and the four living creatures, and they fell on their faces before the throne and worshipped God, crying: 12

> 'Amen! Praise and glory and wisdom, thanksgiving and honour, power and might, be to our God for ever and ever! Amen.'

Then one of the elders turned to me and said, 'These 13 men that are robed in white—who are they and from where do they come?' But I answered, 'My lord, you know, 14 not I.' Then he said to me, 'These are the men who have passed through the great ordeal; they have washed their robes and made them white in the blood of the Lamb. That is why they stand before the throne of God and 15 minister to him day and night in his temple; and he who sits on the throne will dwell with them. They shall never 16 again feel hunger or thirst, the sun shall not beat on them nor any scorching heat, because the Lamb who is at the 17 heart of the throne will be their shepherd and will guide them to the springs of the water of life; and God will wipe all tears from their eyes.'

Now when the Lamb broke the seventh seal, there was 8 silence in heaven for what seemed half an hour. Then I 2 looked, and the seven angels that stand in the presence of God were given seven trumpets.

Then another angel came and stood at the altar, holding 3 a golden censer; and he was given a great quantity of incense to offer with the prayers of all God's people upon the golden altar in front of the throne. And from the 4 angel's hand the smoke of the incense went up before God with the prayers of his people. Then the angel took the 5 censer, filled it from the altar fire, and threw it down upon the earth; and there were peals of thunder, lightning, and an earthquake.

## THE POWERS OF DARKNESS
## CONQUERED

6 THEN THE SEVEN ANGELS that held the seven trumpets prepared to blow them.

7 The first blew his trumpet; and there came hail and fire mingled with blood, and this was hurled upon the earth. A third of the earth was burnt, a third of the trees were burnt, all the green grass was burnt.

8 The second angel blew his trumpet; and what looked like a great blazing mountain was hurled into the sea. A third 9 of the sea was turned to blood, a third of the living creatures in it died, and a third of the ships on it foundered.

10 The third angel blew his trumpet; and a great star shot from the sky, flaming like a torch; and it fell on a third of 11 the rivers and springs. The name of the star was Wormwood; and a third of the water turned to wormwood, and men in great numbers died of the water because it had been poisoned.

12 The fourth angel blew his trumpet; and a third part of the sun was struck, a third of the moon, and a third of the stars, so that the third part went dark and a third of the light of the day failed, and of the night.

13 Then I looked, and I heard an eagle calling with a loud cry as it flew in mid-heaven: 'Woe, woe, woe to the inhabitants of the earth when the trumpets sound which the three last angels must now blow!'

9 Then the fifth angel blew his trumpet; and I saw a star that had fallen from heaven to earth, and the star was 2 given the key of the shaft of the abyss. With this he opened the shaft of the abyss; and from the shaft smoke rose like smoke from a great furnace, and the sun and the air were 3 darkened by the smoke from the shaft. Then over the earth, out of the smoke, came locusts, and they were given 4 the powers that earthly scorpions have. They were told to do no injury to the grass or to any plant or tree, but only to those men who had not received the seal of God on 5 their foreheads. These they were allowed to torment for five months, with torment like a scorpion's sting; but they 6 were not to kill them. During that time these men will seek death, but they will not find it; they will long to die, but death will elude them.

7 In appearance the locusts were like horses equipped for battle. On their heads were what looked like golden crowns;

428

their faces were like human faces and their hair like 8
women's hair; they had teeth like lions' teeth, and wore 9
breastplates like iron; the sound of their wings was like
the noise of horses and chariots rushing to battle; they had 10
tails like scorpions, with stings in them, and in their tails
lay their power to plague mankind for five months. They 11
had for their king the angel of the abyss, whose name,
in Hebrew, is Abaddon, and in Greek, Apollyon, or the
Destroyer.

The first woe has now passed. But there are still two 12
more to come.

The sixth angel then blew his trumpet; and I heard a 13
voice coming from between the horns of the golden altar
that stood in the presence of God. It said to the sixth 14
angel, who held the trumpet: 'Release the four angels held
bound at the great river Euphrates!' So the four angels 15
were let loose, to kill a third of mankind. They had been
held ready for this moment, for this very year and month,
day and hour. And their squadrons of cavalry, whose 16
count I heard, numbered two hundred million.

This was how I saw the horses and their riders in my 17
vision: They wore breastplates, fiery red, blue, and sulphur-
yellow; the horses had heads like lions' heads, and out of
their mouths came fire, smoke, and sulphur. By these 18
three plagues, that is, by the fire, the smoke, and the sulphur that came from their mouths, a third of mankind was
killed. The power of the horses lay in their mouths, and in 19
their tails also; for their tails were like snakes, with heads,
and with them too they dealt injuries.

The rest of mankind who survived these plagues still did 20
not abjure the gods their hands had fashioned, nor cease
their worship of devils and of idols made from gold, silver,
bronze, stone, and wood, which cannot see or hear or walk.
Nor did they repent of their murders, their sorcery, their 21
fornication, or their robberies.

THEN I SAW another mighty angel coming down from 10
heaven. He was wrapped in cloud, with the rainbow round
his head; his face shone like the sun and his legs were like
pillars of fire. In his hand he held a little scroll unrolled. 2
His right foot he planted on the sea, and his left on the land.
Then he gave a great shout, like the roar of a lion; and when 3
he shouted, the seven thunders spoke. I was about to 4
write down what the seven thunders had said; but I heard
a voice from heaven saying, 'Seal up what the seven

5 thunders have said; do not write it down.' Then the angel
that I saw standing on the sea and the land raised his right
6 hand to heaven and swore by him who lives for ever and
ever, who created heaven and earth and the sea and every-
7 thing in them: 'There shall be no more delay; but when
the time comes for the seventh angel to sound his trumpet,
the hidden purpose of God will have been fulfilled, as he
promised to his servants the prophets.'

8 Then the voice which I heard from heaven was speaking
to me again, and it said, 'Go and take the open scroll in the
9 hand of the angel that stands on the sea and the land.' So
I went to the angel and asked him to give me the little
scroll. He said to me, 'Take it, and eat it. It will turn your
stomach sour, although in your mouth it will taste sweet as
10 honey.' So I took the little scroll from the angel's hand and
ate it, and in my mouth it did taste sweet as honey; but
when I swallowed it my stomach turned sour.

11 Then they said to me, 'Once again you must utter
prophecies over peoples and nations and languages and
many kings.'

11 I was given a long cane, a kind of measuring-rod, and
told: 'Now go and measure the temple of God, the altar,
2 and the number of the worshippers. But have nothing to
do with the outer court of the temple; do not measure
that; for it has been given over to the Gentiles, and they
will trample the Holy City underfoot for forty-two months.
3 And I have two witnesses, whom I will appoint to prophesy, dressed in sackcloth, all through those twelve
4 hundred and sixty days.' These are the two olive-trees and
the two lamps that stand in the presence of the Lord of the
5 earth. If anyone seeks to do them harm, fire pours from
their mouths and consumes their enemies; and thus shall
6 the man die who seeks to do them harm. These two have
the power to shut up the sky, so that no rain may fall
during the time of their prophesying; and they have the
power to turn water to blood and to strike the earth at will
7 with every kind of plague. But when they have completed
their testimony, the beast that comes up from the abyss
will wage war upon them and will defeat and kill them.
8 Their corpses will lie in the street of the great city, whose
name in allegory is Sodom, or Egypt, where also their
9 Lord was crucified. For three days and a half men from
every people and tribe, of every language and nation,
10 gaze upon their corpses and refuse them burial. All men
on earth gloat over them, make merry, and exchange

presents; for these two prophets were a torment to the whole earth. But at the end of the three days and a half 11 the breath of life from God came into them; and they stood up on their feet to the terror of all who saw it. Then a loud 12 voice was heard speaking to them from heaven, which said, 'Come up here!' And they went up to heaven in a cloud, in full view of their enemies. At that same moment there 13 was a violent earthquake, and a tenth of the city fell. Seven thousand people were killed in the earthquake; the rest in terror did homage to the God of heaven.

The second woe has now passed. But the third is soon 14 to come.

Then the seventh angel blew his trumpet; and voices 15 were heard in heaven shouting:

'The sovereignty of the world has passed to our Lord and his Christ, and he shall reign for ever and ever!'

And the twenty-four elders, seated on their thrones before 16 God, fell on their faces and worshipped God, saying: 17

'We give thee thanks, O Lord God, sovereign over all, who art and who wast, because thou hast taken thy great power into thy hands and entered upon thy reign. The nations raged, but thy day of retribution 18 has come. Now is the time for the dead to be judged; now is the time for recompense to thy servants the prophets, to thy dedicated people, and all who honour thy name, both great and small, the time to destroy those who destroy the earth.'

Then God's temple in heaven was laid open, and within 19 the temple was seen the ark of his covenant. There came flashes of lightning and peals of thunder, an earthquake, and a storm of hail.

NEXT APPEARED a great portent in heaven, a woman 12 robed with the sun, beneath her feet the moon, and on her head a crown of twelve stars. She was pregnant, and in the 2 anguish of her labour she cried out to be delivered. Then 3 a second portent appeared in heaven: a great red dragon with seven heads and ten horns; on his heads were seven diadems, and with his tail he swept down a third of the 4 stars in the sky and flung them to the earth. The dragon stood in front of the woman who was about to give birth, so that when her child was born he might devour it. She 5 gave birth to a male child, who is destined to rule all nations with an iron rod. But her child was snatched up to

6 God and his throne; and the woman herself fled into the wilds, where she had a place prepared for her by God, there to be sustained for twelve hundred and sixty days.

7 Then war broke out in heaven. Michael and his angels waged war upon the dragon. The dragon and his angels

8 fought, but they had not the strength to win, and no foot-

9 hold was left them in heaven. So the great dragon was thrown down, that serpent of old that led the whole world astray, whose name is Satan, or the Devil—thrown down to the earth, and his angels with him.

10 Then I heard a voice in heaven proclaiming aloud: 'This is the hour of victory for our God, the hour of his sovereignty and power, when his Christ comes to his rightful rule! For the accuser of our brothers is overthrown, who

11 day and night accused them before our God. By the sacrifice of the Lamb they have conquered him, and by the testimony which they uttered;[a] for they did not hold their

12 lives too dear to lay them down. Rejoice then, you heavens and you that dwell in them! But woe to you, earth and sea, for the Devil has come down to you in great fury, knowing that his time is short!'

13 When the dragon found that he had been thrown down to the earth, he went in pursuit of the woman who had

14 given birth to the male child. But the woman was given two great eagle's wings, to fly to the place in the wilds where for three years and a half she was to be sustained,

15 out of reach of the serpent. From his mouth the serpent spewed a flood of water after the woman to sweep her away

16 with its spate. But the earth came to her rescue and opened its mouth and swallowed the river which the dragon

17 spewed from his mouth. At this the dragon grew furious with the woman, and went off to wage war on the rest of her offspring, that is, on those who keep God's command-

13 ments and maintain their testimony to Jesus. He took his stand on the sea-shore.

Then[b] out of the sea I saw a beast rising. It had ten horns and seven heads. On its horns were ten diadems, and on

2 each head a blasphemous name. The beast I saw was like a leopard, but its feet were like a bear's and its mouth like a lion's mouth. The dragon conferred upon it his power

3 and rule, and great authority. One of its heads appeared to have received a death-blow; but the mortal wound was

---

[a] *Or* the word of God to which they bore witness.     [b] *Some witnesses read* . . . testimony to Jesus. Then I stood by the sea-shore and . . .

healed. The whole world went after the beast in wondering admiration. Men worshipped the dragon because he had 4 conferred his authority upon the beast; they worshipped the beast also, and chanted, 'Who is like the Beast? Who can fight against it?'

The beast was allowed to mouth bombast and blasphemy, 5 and was given the right to reign for forty-two months. It 6 opened its mouth in blasphemy against God, reviling his name and his heavenly dwelling.*a* It was also allowed to 7 wage war on God's people and to defeat them, and was granted*b* authority over every tribe and people, language and nation. All on earth will worship it, except those whose 8 names the Lamb that was slain keeps in his roll of the living, written there since the world was made.

Hear, you who have ears to hear! Whoever is to be made 9 10 prisoner, a prisoner he shall be. Whoever takes the sword to kill, by the sword he is bound to be killed. This is where the fortitude and faithfulness of God's people have their place.

Then I saw another beast, which came up out of the 11 earth; it had two horns like a lamb's, but spoke like a dragon. It wielded all the authority of the first beast in its 12 presence, and made the earth and its inhabitants worship this first beast, whose mortal wound had been healed. It 13 worked great miracles, even making fire come down from heaven to earth before men's eyes. By the miracles it was 14 allowed to perform in the presence of the beast it deluded the inhabitants of the earth, and made them erect an image in honour of the beast that had been wounded by the sword and yet lived. It was allowed to give breath to 15 the image of the beast, so that it could speak, and could cause all who would not worship the image to be put to death. Moreover, it caused everyone, great and small, rich 16 and poor, slave and free, to be branded with a mark on his right hand or forehead, and no one was allowed to buy or 17 sell unless he bore this beast's mark, either name or number. (Here is the key; and anyone who has intelligence may 18 work out the number of the beast. The number represents a man's name, and the numerical value of its letters is six hundred and sixty-six.)

---

*a  Some witnesses read* reviling his name and his dwelling-place, that is, those that live in heaven.     *b  Some witnesses read* It was granted ... *(omitting the words* was also ... them, and).

## VISIONS OF THE END

14 THEN I LOOKED, and on Mount Zion stood the Lamb, and with him were a hundred and forty-four thousand who had his name and the name of his Father 2 written on their foreheads. I heard a sound from heaven like the noise of rushing water and the deep roar of thunder; 3 it was the sound of harpers playing on their harps. There before the throne, and the four living creatures and the elders, they were singing a new song. That song no one could learn except the hundred and forty-four thousand, 4 who alone from the whole world had been ransomed. These are men who did not defile themselves with women, for they have kept themselves chaste, and they follow the Lamb wherever he goes. They have been ransomed as the 5 firstfruits of humanity for God and the Lamb. No lie was found in their lips; they are faultless.

6 Then I saw an angel flying in mid-heaven, with an eternal gospel to proclaim to those on earth, to every 7 nation and tribe, language and people. He cried in a loud voice, 'Fear God and pay him homage; for the hour of his judgement has come! Worship him who made heaven and earth, the sea and the water-springs!'

8 Then another angel, a second, followed, and he cried, 'Fallen, fallen is Babylon the great, she who has made all nations drink the fierce wine of[a] her fornication!'

9 Yet a third angel followed, crying out loud, 'Whoever worships the beast and its image and receives its mark on 10 his forehead or hand, he shall drink the wine of God's wrath, poured undiluted into the cup of his vengeance. He shall be tormented in sulphurous flames before the 11 holy angels and before the Lamb. The smoke of their torment will rise for ever and ever, and there will be no respite day or night for those who worship the beast and its image 12 or receive the mark of its name.' This is where the fortitude of God's people has its place—in keeping God's commands and remaining loyal to Jesus.

13 Moreover, I heard a voice from heaven, saying, 'Write this: "Happy are the dead who die in the faith of Christ! Henceforth",[b] says the Spirit,[c] "they may rest from their labours; for they take with them the record of their deeds."'

[a] Or drink the wine of God's wrath upon . . .      [b] Or Assuredly.
[c] Some witnesses read ". . . the dead who henceforth die in the faith of Christ!" "Yes," says the Spirit . . .

Then as I looked there appeared a white cloud, and on 14
the cloud sat one like a son of man. He had on his head
a crown of gold and in his hand a sharp sickle. Another 15
angel came out of the temple and called in a loud voice to
him who sat on the cloud: 'Stretch out your sickle and
reap; for harvest-time has come, and earth's crop is over-
ripe.' So he who sat on the cloud put his sickle to the earth 16
and its harvest was reaped.

Then another angel came out of the heavenly temple, and 17
he also had a sharp sickle. Then from the altar came yet 18
another, the angel who has authority over fire, and he
shouted to the one with the sharp sickle: 'Stretch out your
sickle, and gather in earth's grape-harvest, for its clusters
are ripe.' So the angel put his sickle to the earth and 19
gathered in its grapes, and threw them into the great winepress of God's wrath. The winepress was trodden outside 20
the city, and for two hundred miles around blood flowed
from the press to the height of the horses' bridles.

Then I saw another great and astonishing portent in 15
heaven: seven angels with seven plagues, the last plagues
of all, for with them the wrath of God is consummated.

I saw what seemed a sea of glass shot with fire, and 2
beside the sea of glass, holding the harps which God had
given them, were those who had won the victory over the
beast and its image and the number of its name.

They were singing the song of Moses, the servant of God, 3
and the song of the Lamb, as they chanted:

'Great and marvellous are thy deeds, O Lord God,
sovereign over all; just and true are thy ways, thou
king of the ages.[a] Who shall not revere thee, Lord, 4
and do homage to thy name? For thou alone art holy.
All nations shall come and worship in thy presence,
for thy just dealings stand revealed.'

After this, as I looked, the sanctuary of the heavenly 5
Tent of Testimony was thrown open, and out of it came 6
the seven angels with the seven plagues. They were robed
in fine linen, clean and shining, and had golden girdles
round their breasts. Then one of the four living creatures 7
gave the seven angels seven golden bowls full of the wrath
of God who lives for ever and ever; and the sanctuary was 8
filled with smoke from the glory of God and his power, so
that no one could enter it until the seven plagues of the
seven angels were completed.

[a] *Some witnesses read* king of the nations.

**16**  Then from the sanctuary I heard a loud voice, and it said to the seven angels, 'Go and pour out the seven bowls of God's wrath on the earth.'

2  So the first angel went and poured his bowl on the earth; and foul malignant sores appeared on those men that wore the mark of the beast and worshipped its image.

3  The second angel poured his bowl on the sea, and it turned to blood like the blood from a corpse; and every living thing in the sea died.

4  The third angel poured his bowl on the rivers and springs, and they turned to blood.

5  Then I heard the angel of the waters say, 'Just art thou in these thy judgements, thou Holy One who art and wast; 6 for they shed the blood of thy people and of thy prophets, and thou hast given them blood to drink. They have their 7 deserts!' And I heard the altar cry, 'Yes, Lord God, sovereign over all, true and just are thy judgements!'

8  The fourth angel poured his bowl on the sun; and it was 9 allowed to burn men with its flames. They were fearfully burned; but they only cursed the name of God who had the power to inflict such plagues, and they refused to repent or do him homage.

10  The fifth angel poured his bowl on the throne of the beast; and its kingdom was plunged in darkness. Men 11 gnawed their tongues in agony, but they only cursed the God of heaven for their sores and pains, and would not repent of what they had done.

12  The sixth angel poured his bowl on the great river Euphrates; and its water was dried up, to prepare the way for the kings from the east.

13  Then I saw coming from the mouth of the dragon, the mouth of the beast, and the mouth of the false prophet, 14 three foul spirits like frogs. These spirits were devils, with power to work miracles. They were sent out to muster all the kings of the world for the great day of battle of God 15 the sovereign Lord. ('That is the day when I come like a thief! Happy the man who stays awake and keeps on his clothes, so that he will not have to go naked and ashamed 16 for all to see!') So they assembled the kings at the place called in Hebrew Armageddon.

17  Then the seventh angel poured his bowl on the air; and out of the sanctuary came a loud voice from the throne, 18 which said, 'It is over!' And there followed flashes of lightning and peals of thunder, and a violent earthquake, like none before it in human history, so violent it was.

The great city was split in three; the cities of the world   19
fell in ruin; and God did not forget Babylon the great, but
made her drink the cup which was filled with the fierce
wine of his vengeance. Every island vanished; there was   20
not a mountain to be seen. Huge hailstones, weighing   21
perhaps a hundredweight, fell on men from the sky; and
they cursed God for the plague of hail, because that plague
was so severe.

THEN ONE OF THE SEVEN ANGELS that held the   17
seven bowls came and spoke to me and said, 'Come,
and I will show you the judgement on the great whore,
enthroned above the ocean. The kings of the earth have   2
committed fornication with her, and on the wine of her
fornication men all over the world have made themselves
drunk.' In the Spirit he carried me away into the wilds,   3
and there I saw a woman mounted on a scarlet beast which
was covered with blasphemous names and had seven heads
and ten horns. The woman was clothed in purple and   4
scarlet and bedizened with gold and jewels and pearls. In
her hand she held a gold cup, full of obscenities and the
foulness of her fornication; and written on her forehead   5
was a name with a secret meaning: 'Babylon the great, the
mother of whores and of every obscenity on earth.' The   6
woman, I saw, was drunk with the blood of God's people
and with the blood of those who had borne their testimony
to Jesus.

As I looked at her I was greatly astonished. But the   7
angel said to me, 'Why are you so astonished? I will tell
you the secret of the woman and of the beast she rides,
with the seven heads and the ten horns. The beast you   8
have seen is he who once was alive, and is alive no longer,
but has yet to ascend out of the abyss before going to
perdition. Those on earth whose names have not been
inscribed in the roll of the living ever since the world
was made will all be astonished to see the beast; for he
once was alive, and is alive no longer, and has still to
appear.

'But here is the clue for those who can interpret it. The   9
seven heads are seven hills on which the woman sits. They   10
represent also seven kings,ᵃ of whom five have already
fallen, one is now reigning, and the other has yet to come;
and when he does come he is only to last for a little while.
As for the beast that once was alive and is alive no longer, he   11

———
ᵃ Or emperors.

is an eighth—and yet he is one of the seven, and he is going
12 to perdition. The ten horns you saw are ten kings who have
not yet begun to reign, but who for one hour are to share
13 with the beast the exercise of royal authority; for they
have but a single purpose among them and will confer
14 their power and authority upon the beast. They will wage
war upon the Lamb, but the Lamb will defeat them, for
he is Lord of lords and King of kings, and his victory will be
shared by his followers, called and chosen and faithful.'[a]

15    Then he said to me, 'The ocean you saw, where the great
whore sat, is an ocean of peoples and populations, nations
16 and languages. As for the ten horns you saw, they together
with the beast will come to hate the whore; they will strip
her naked and leave her desolate, they will batten on her
17 flesh and burn her to ashes. For God has put it into their
heads to carry out his purpose, by making common cause
and conferring their sovereignty upon the beast until all
18 that God has spoken is fulfilled. The woman you saw is the
great city that holds sway over the kings of the earth.'

18    After this I saw another angel coming down from heaven;
he came with great authority and the earth was lit up with
2 his splendour. Then in a mighty voice he proclaimed,
'Fallen, fallen is Babylon the great! She has become a
dwelling for demons, a haunt for every unclean spirit, for
3 every vile and loathsome bird. For all nations have drunk
deep of[b] the fierce wine of her fornication; the kings of the
earth have committed fornication with her, and merchants
the world over have grown rich on her bloated wealth.'

4    Then I heard another voice from heaven that said:
'Come out of her, my people, lest you take part in her sins
5 and share in her plagues. For her sins are piled high as
6 heaven, and God has not forgotten her crimes. Pay her
back in her own coin, repay her twice over for her deeds!
7 Double for her the strength of the potion she mixed! Mete
out grief and torment to match her voluptuous pomp! She
says in her heart, "I am a queen on my throne! No mourn-
8 ing for me, no widow's weeds!" Because of this her plagues
shall strike her in a single day—pestilence, bereavement,
famine, and burning—for mighty is the Lord God who has
pronounced her doom!'

9    The kings of the earth who committed fornication with
her and wallowed in her luxury will weep and wail over
10 her, as they see the smoke of her conflagration. They will

---

[a] *Or . . .* kings, and his followers are faithful men, called and selected
for service.    [b] *Other witnesses read* have been ruined by . . .

stand at a distance, for horror at her torment, and will say, 'Alas, alas for the great city, the mighty city of Babylon! In a single hour your doom has struck!'

The merchants of the earth also will weep and mourn for [11] her, because no one any longer buys their cargoes, cargoes [12] of gold and silver, jewels and pearls, cloths of purple and scarlet, silks and fine linens; all kinds of scented woods, ivories, and every sort of thing made of costly woods, bronze, iron, or marble; cinnamon and spice, incense, per- [13] fumes and frankincense; wine, oil, flour and wheat, sheep and cattle, horses, chariots, slaves, and the lives of men. 'The fruit you longed for', they will say, 'is gone from you; [14] all the glitter and the glamour are lost, never to be yours again!' The traders in all these wares, who gained their [15] wealth from her, will stand at a distance for horror at her torment, weeping and mourning and saying, 'Alas, alas for [16] the great city, that was clothed in fine linen and purple and scarlet, bedizened with gold and jewels and pearls! Alas that in one hour so much wealth should be laid [17] waste!'

Then all the sea-captains and voyagers, the sailors and those who traded by sea, stood at a distance and cried out [18] as they saw the smoke of her conflagration: 'Was there ever a city like the great city?' They threw dust on their [19] heads, weeping and mourning and saying, 'Alas, alas for the great city, where all who had ships at sea grew rich on her wealth! Alas that in a single hour she should be laid waste!'

But let heaven exult over her; exult, apostles and pro- [20] phets and people of God; for in the judgement against her he has vindicated your cause!

Then a mighty angel took up a stone like a great mill- [21] stone and hurled it into the sea and said, 'Thus shall Babylon, the great city, be sent hurtling down, never to be seen again! No more shall the sound of harpers and min- [22] strels, of flute-players and trumpeters, be heard in you; no more shall craftsmen of any trade be found in you; no more shall the sound of the mill be heard in you; no more shall [23] the light of the lamp be seen in you; no more shall the voice of the bride and bridegroom be heard in you! Your traders were once the merchant princes of the world, and with your sorcery you deceived all the nations.'

For the blood of the prophets and of God's people was [24] found in her, the blood of all who had been done to death on earth.

19 After this I heard what sounded like the roar of a vast throng in heaven; and they were shouting:

2 'Alleluia! Victory and glory and power belong to our God, for true and just are his judgements! He has condemned the great whore who corrupted the earth with her fornication, and has avenged upon her the blood of his servants.'

3 Then once more they shouted:

'Alleluia! The smoke goes up from her for ever and ever!'

4 And the twenty-four elders and the four living creatures fell down and worshipped God as he sat on the throne, and they too cried:

'Amen! Alleluia!'

5 Then a voice came from the throne which said: 'Praise our God, all you his servants, you that fear him, both great and small!'

6 Again I heard what sounded like a vast crowd, like the noise of rushing water and deep roars of thunder, and they cried:

7 'Alleluia! The Lord our God, sovereign over all, has entered on his reign! Exult and shout for joy and do him homage, for the wedding-day of the Lamb has 8 come! His bride has made herself ready, and for her dress she has been given fine linen, clean and shining.'

(Now the fine linen signifies the righteous deeds of God's people.)

9 Then the angel said to me, 'Write this: "Happy are those who are invited to the wedding-supper of the Lamb!"' 10 And he added, 'These are the very words of God.' At this I fell at his feet to worship him. But he said to me, 'No, not that! I am but a fellow-servant with you and your brothers who bear their testimony to Jesus. It is God you must worship. Those who bear testimony to Jesus are inspired like the prophets.'[a]

11 THEN I SAW heaven wide open, and there before me was a white horse; and its rider's name was Faithful and 12 True, for he is just in judgement and just in war. His

[a] Or . . . worship. For testimony to Jesus is the spirit that inspires prophets.

eyes flamed like fire, and on his head were many diadems. Written upon him was a name known to none but himself, and he was robed in a garment drenched in blood.ª He was 13 called the Word of God, and the armies of heaven followed 14 him on white horses, clothed in fine linen, clean and shining. From his mouth there went a sharp sword with which to 15 smite the nations; for he it is who shall rule them with an iron rod, and tread the winepress of the wrath and retribution of God the sovereign Lord. And on his robe and on his 16 thigh there was written the name: 'King of kings and Lord of lords.'

Then I saw an angel standing in the sun, and he cried 17 aloud to all the birds flying in mid-heaven: 'Come and gather for God's great supper, to eat the flesh of kings and 18 commanders and fighting men, the flesh of horses and their riders, the flesh of all men, slave and free, great and small!' Then I saw the beast and the kings of the earth and their 19 armies mustered to do battle with the Rider and his army. The beast was taken prisoner, and so was the false prophet 20 who had worked miracles in its presence and deluded those that had received the mark of the beast and worshipped its image. The two of them were thrown alive into the lake of fire with it sulphurous flames. The rest were killed by 21 the sword which went out of the Rider's mouth; and all the birds gorged themselves on their flesh.

Then I saw an angel coming down from heaven with the 20 key of the abyss and a great chain in his hands. He seized 2 the dragon, that serpent of old, the Devil or Satan, and chained him up for a thousand years; he threw him into 3 the abyss, shutting and sealing it over him, so that he might seduce the nations no more till the thousand years were over. After that he must be let loose for a short while.

Then I saw thrones, and upon them sat those to whom 4 judgement was committed. I could see the souls of those who had been beheaded for the sake of God's word and their testimony to Jesus, those who had not worshipped the beast and its image or received its mark on forehead or hand. These came to life again and reigned with Christ for a thousand years, though the rest of the dead did not 5 come to life until the thousand years were over. This is the first resurrection. Happy indeed, and one of God's own 6 people, is the man who shares in this first resurrection! Upon such the second death has no claim; but they shall be

ª *Some witnesses read* spattered with blood.

priests of God and of Christ, and shall reign with him for the thousand years.

7 When the thousand years are over, Satan will be let
8 loose from his dungeon; and he will come out to seduce the nations in the four quarters of the earth and to muster them for battle, yes, the hosts of Gog and Magog, countless
9 as the sands of the sea. So they marched over the breadth of the land and laid siege to the camp of God's people and the city that he loves. But fire came down on them from
10 heaven and consumed them; and the Devil, their seducer, was flung into the lake of fire and sulphur, where the beast and the false prophet had been flung, there to be tormented day and night for ever.

11 Then I saw a great white throne, and the One who sat upon it; from his presence earth and heaven vanished
12 away, and no place was left for them. I could see the dead, great and small, standing before the throne; and books were opened. Then another book was opened, the roll of the living. From what was written in these books the dead
13 were judged upon the record of their deeds. The sea gave up its dead, and Death and Hades gave up the dead in their keeping; they were judged, each man on the record
14 of his deeds. Then Death and Hades were flung into the
15 lake of fire. This lake of fire is the second death; and into it were flung any whose names were not to be found in the roll of the living.

21 Then I saw a new heaven and a new earth, for the first heaven and the first earth had vanished, and there was no
2 longer any sea. I saw the holy city, new Jerusalem, coming down out of heaven from God, made ready like a bride
3 adorned for her husband. I heard a loud voice proclaiming from the throne: 'Now at last God has his dwelling among men! He will dwell among them and they shall be his
4 people, and God himself will be with them.ᵃ He will wipe every tear from their eyes; there shall be an end to death, and to mourning and crying and pain; for the old order has passed away!'

5 Then he who sat on the throne said, 'Behold! I am making all things new!' (And he said to me, 'Write this down;
6 for these words are trustworthy and true. Indeed they are already fulfilled.') 'I am the Alpha and the Omega, the beginning and the end. A draught from the water-springs

ᵃ *Some witnesses read* God-with-them shall himself be their God (*see Isaiah 7. 14; 8. 8*).

of life will be my free gift to the thirsty. All this is the 7
victor's heritage; and I will be his God and he shall be my
son. But as for the cowardly, the faithless, and the vile, 8
murderers, fornicators, sorcerers, idolaters, and liars of
every kind, their lot will be the second death, in the lake
that burns with sulphurous flames.'

Then one of the seven angels that held the seven bowls 9
full of the seven last plagues came and spoke to me and
said, 'Come, and I will show you the bride, the wife of the
Lamb.' So in the Spirit he carried me away to a great high 10
mountain, and showed me the holy city of Jerusalem
coming down out of heaven from God. It shone with the 11
glory of God; it had the radiance of some priceless jewel,
like a jasper, clear as crystal. It had a great high wall, 12
with twelve gates, at which were twelve angels; and on
the gates were inscribed the names of the twelve tribes
of Israel. There were three gates to the east, three to the 13
north, three to the south, and three to the west. The city 14
wall had twelve foundation-stones, and on them were the
names of the twelve apostles of the Lamb.

The angel who spoke with me carried a gold measuring- 15
rod, to measure the city, its walls, and its gates. The city 16
was built as a square, and was as wide as it was long. It
measured by his rod twelve thousand furlongs, its length
and breadth and height being equal. Its wall was one 17
hundred and forty-four cubits high, that is, by human
measurements, which the angel was using. The wall was 18
built of jasper, while the city itself was of pure gold, bright
as clear glass. The foundations of the city wall were a- 19
dorned with jewels of every kind, the first of the foundation-
stones being jasper, the second lapis lazuli, the third
chalcedony, the fourth emerald, the fifth sardonyx, the 20
sixth cornelian, the seventh chrysolite, the eighth beryl,
the ninth topaz, the tenth chrysoprase, the eleventh tur-
quoise, and the twelfth amethyst. The twelve gates were 21
twelve pearls, each gate being made from a single pearl.
The streets of the city were of pure gold, like translucent
glass.

I saw no temple in the city; for its temple was the sove- 22
reign Lord God and the Lamb. And the city had no need 23
of sun or moon to shine upon it; for the glory of God gave
it light, and its lamp was the Lamb. By its light shall the 24
nations walk, and the kings of the earth shall bring into it
all their splendour. The gates of the city shall never be 25
shut by day—and there will be no night. The wealth and 26

27 splendour of the nations shall be brought into it; but nothing unclean shall enter, nor anyone whose ways are false or foul, but only those who are inscribed in the Lamb's roll of the living.

22 Then he showed me the river of the water of life, sparkling like crystal, flowing from the throne of God and 2 of the Lamb down the middle of the city's street. On either side of the river stood a tree of life, which yields twelve crops of fruit, one for each month of the year; the leaves 3 of the trees serve for the healing of the nations. Every accursed thing shall disappear. The throne of God and of the Lamb will be there, and his servants shall worship 4 him; they shall see him face to face, and bear his name on 5 their foreheads. There shall be no more night, nor will they need the light of lamp or sun, for the Lord God will give them light; and they shall reign for evermore.

6 THEN HE SAID to me, 'These words are trustworthy and true. The Lord God who inspires the prophets has sent his 7 angel to show his servants what must shortly happen. And, remember, I am coming soon!'
Happy is the man who heeds the words of prophecy 8 contained in this book! It is I, John, who heard and saw these things. And when I had heard and seen them, I fell in worship at the feet of the angel who had shown them to 9 me. But he said to me, 'No, not that! I am but a fellow-servant with you and your brothers the prophets and those who heed the words of this book. It is God you must 10 worship.' Then he told me, 'Do not seal up the words of prophecy in this book, for the hour of fulfilment is near. 11 Meanwhile, let the evil-doer go on doing evil and the filthy-minded wallow in his filth, but let the good man persevere in his goodness and the dedicated man be true to his dedication.'

12 'Yes, I am coming soon, and bringing my recompense 13 with me, to requite everyone according to his deeds! I am the Alpha and the Omega, the first and the last, the beginning and the end.'

14 Happy are those who wash their robes clean! They will have the right to the tree of life and will enter by the gates 15 of the city. Outside are dogs, sorcerers and fornicators, murderers and idolaters, and all who love and practise deceit.

16 'I, Jesus, have sent my angel to you with this testimony for the churches. I am the scion and offspring of David, the bright star of dawn.'

444

'Come!' say the Spirit and the bride.                17
'Come!' let each hearer reply.
Come forward, you who are thirsty; accept the water of life, a free gift to all who desire it.

For my part, I give this warning to everyone who is   18
listening to the words of prophecy in this book: should anyone add to them, God will add to him the plagues described in this book; should anyone take away from the   19
words in this book of prophecy, God will take away from him his share in the tree of life and the Holy City, described in this book.

He who gives this testimony speaks: 'Yes, I am coming   20
soon!'

Amen. Come, Lord Jesus!
The grace of the Lord Jesus be with you all.[a]      21

---

[a] *Some witnesses read* with all; *others read* with all God's people; *others read* with God's people; *some add* Amen.